ROMAN MEDALLIONS

BY

JOCELYN M. C. TOYNBEE
M. A. (CANTAB.), D. PHIL. (OXON.), F. S. A.

NUMISMATIC STUDIES
No. 5

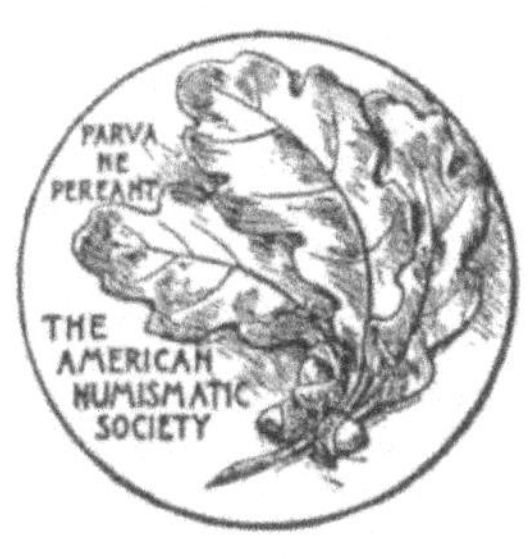

THE AMERICAN NUMISMATIC SOCIETY
NEW YORK
1944

PRESS OF
INTELLIGENCER PRINTING CO.
LANCASTER, PA.

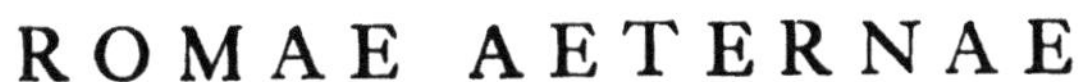
ROMAE AETERNAE

PREFACE

As the title of this Series implies, Roman medallions are essentially a branch of numismatic studies. Yet as special pieces, struck primarily, not for circulation as cash, but for presentation as gifts, they stand quite distinctly apart from the regular coinage and deserve separate treatment on their own merits. If their closest kinship is with the art of the die-cutter, they are also nearly related to the arts of the gem-engraver, the sculptor and the painter; and if their interest is mainly numismatic, there are few other fields of classical archaeology for which they are not significant. Moreover, Roman medallions constituted in themselves a new department of art and a new category of historical documents, offering in their large flans possibilities, both in style and in content, beyond the range of the current coins of the state. They claim the attention, not only of numismatists and archaeological specialists, but of all students of the life, thought and history of imperial Rome.

I was first attracted to the study of Roman medallions some twenty years ago, when starting work on the general problems of Hadrianic art; for it was in Hadrian's principate that the great continuous series of bronze medallions proper was really inaugurated. The time now seems to be ripe for a new investigation of the subject. While long and important contributions to periodic literature and encyclopaedias abound and catalogues of part, at least, of some of the great public and private collections have appeared, books specially devoted to medallions have been few. W. Froehner's *Les médaillons de l'empire romain* (Paris, 1878) has, needless to say, long been out of date. F. Gnecchi's monumental work, *I medaglioni romani* (Milan, 1912), to which all students in this field owe a debt of the deepest gratitude, is, in the main, a *corpus*, splendidly illustrated, of the material available to him at that time. His introduction is somewhat slight and unsatisfactory; and he leaves the primary problem, that of defining what a Roman medallion is, unsolved. Much of the matter which he includes in his first and third volumes does not, in the light of further researches, fall within the scope of the subject at all. Again, since Gnecchi's day a whole mass of new material has come to light and it has been possible to obtain reproductions of many medallions which he listed but did not illustrate. Plates I–XXXIX of this present work represent an attempt at a photographic record of the great bulk of medallion types and variants, so far accessible to me, which were unknown to, or not reproduced by, Gnecchi. I am well aware that many of my reproductions are poor or imperfect, largely as a result of the outbreak of the war before my studies had reached their close. But in these times, when so many archaeological monuments have been lost or destroyed, the interests of scholarship seem to demand the subordination of aesthetic considerations to completeness of record. For the obvious, but unavoidable, gaps in my study of the collections, I refer the reader to the list at the end of the book. Plates XL–XLIX contain pieces already illustrated in Gnecchi's plates. They are supplementary to the rest, being intended to provide a chronological visual survey of the iconographic and artistic development of Roman medallions; and it is hoped that they may make the book of greater service to the general student. References to the plates are generally made in the footnotes and such references have been emphasized, for convenience, through the use of bold face type.

In writing this book I have tried to examine afresh the outstanding problems of Roman medallions—their definition, their relation to the normal coinage, their mints and provenances, the occasions for which they were issued and the nature of their recipients. I have also attempted a discussion of the varying characteristics of medallions during the three main phases of their history and a survey of all reverse types and variants known to me up to the present, classified according to the subjects represented. Finally, I have added some suggestions as to the role played by medallions in the political, religious and artistic life of the Roman Empire. My work claims to be of a general and preliminary character only. It was obviously impossible in a book of this size to work out the exact date, and elucidate the exact significance, of each individual type. The reverse types of the fourth century in particular require more detailed discussion and classification than space has permitted here. Again, I have not attacked the fascinating task of attempting to identify the hands of particular artists and to classify medallion types on those lines. Such work must be reserved for the next undertaking which I already have in hand, and to which this book is, in part, meant to be introductory, namely the compilation of a new chronological *corpus* of all known medallion types and their variants.

The debts which I owe for help and encouragement in producing this book are too numerous to be acknowledged in full detail. But I should like to express my special gratitude to the following:—to the late Professor Percy Gardner of Oxford, in whose company I first perused the pages of Gnecchi; to Mr. Harold Mattingly, Assistant Keeper in the Department of Coins and Medals, British Museum, who read the book in typescript and made many important suggestions; to the late Mrs. Arthur Strong,* for her great kindness and invaluable assistance to me while I was working in Rome; and to the keepers and owners of the public and private collections for giving me facilities for study and for furnishing casts, in particular to Mr. John Allan, Keeper of Coins and Medals, British Museum, M. Jean Babelon of the Cabinet des Médailles, Bibliothèque Nationale, Paris, Dr. Liegle of the Kaiser-Friedrich Museum, Berlin, Dr. K. Pink of the Kunsthistorisches Museum, Vienna, Marchese Camillo Serafini of the Gabinetto Numismatico, Biblioteca Apostolica Vaticana and Signorina S. L. Cesano of the Museo Nazionale Romano delle Terme, both of whom gave me special personal facilities for studying the two great collec-

* Mrs. Strong died in Rome on September 16, 1943 while this Preface was being written. I should like to add my personal testimony to the unique service which her inspiration, learning and devotion have rendered to Roman archaeology.

tions under their respective care, Mr. S. P. Noe of the Museum of the American Numismatic Society, New York, who supplied me with details, photographs and casts of material available in the United States, Miss Anne S. Robertson of the Hunterian Museum, Glasgow University, Mr. H. P. Hall, of Pentreheylin Hall, Llanymynech, Wales, M. R. Jameson of Paris and Signor G. Mazzini of Turin. My warm thanks are also due to the University of Cambridge and to Newnham College, Cambridge, for granting me leave of absence from my duties during the academic year 1937–1938, thus enabling me to travel and study on the Continent and to enjoy that spirit of international friendship and co-operation in the world of scholarship which war may interrupt, but cannot destroy; to Lady Margaret Hall, Oxford, for electing me to the Susette Taylor Travelling Fellowship for 1937–1938; to the Trustees of the Leverhulme Research Fellowships for awarding me a research grant during the same period; to Newnham College for electing me Mary Bateson Research Fellow for 1938–1941; to Mr. Raleigh Radford, Director of the British School at Rome; to Professor Alföldi of Budapest; and to Miss Grace Briggs of Newnham College, Cambridge, and University College, London, for valuable assistance in compiling the Bibliography.

Of my proximate debts the greatest of all is to the American Numismatic Society of New York, for its kindness and generosity in undertaking, in these troubled times, the publication of this book, which, owing to war conditions in this country, might otherwise have had long to wait before it could see the light of day. I count it an honor indeed that I should have shared in forging one small link in the chain of scholarship which binds the Old World to the New.

This book is dedicated, in all humility and with deep affection, to the birthplace of Roman medallions—the City of Rome.

JOCELYN M. C. TOYNBEE

Newnham College
Cambridge, England
September 1943

TABLE OF CONTENTS

PART V. MEDALLIONS AND IMPERIAL LIFE

LIST OF ABBREVIATIONS

AA.........*Archäologischer Anzeiger.*
AJ.........*Archaeological Journal.*
AM........*Mitteilungen des deutschen archäologischen Instituts: Athenische Abteilung.*
BC.........*Bullettino della commissione archeologica comunale di Roma.*
BM........*Berliner Münzblätter.*
BMCCRE...*British Museum Catalogue of Coins of the Roman Empire.*
BMCGC.....*British Museum Catalogue of Greek Coins.*
BMF.......*Blätter für Münzfreunde.*
BMQ.......*British Museum Quarterly.*
C^2..........Cohen, *Description historique des monnaies frappées sous l'empire romain*, ed. 2.
CAH.......*Cambridge Ancient History.*
CIL........*Corpus Inscriptionum Latinarum.*
CR.........*Classical Review.*
FM.........*Frankfurter Münzzeitung.*
G..........F. Gnecchi, *I medaglioni romani* (1912).
Grueber.....*Roman Medallions in the British Museum* (1874).
ILS........Dessau, *Inscriptiones Latinae Selectae.*
JDAI.......*Jahrbuch des deutschen archäologischen Instituts.*
JHS........*Journal of Hellenic Studies.*
JIAN.......*Journal international d'archéologie numismatique.*
JPEK......*Jahrbuch für praehistorische und ethnographische Kunst.*
JRS........*Journal of Roman Studies.*
Kubitschek..*Ausgewählte römische Medaillons der kaiserlichen Münzsammlung in Wien* (1909).
Maurice.....*Numismatique constantinienne*, I (1908), II (1911), III (1912).
NC.........*Numismatic Chronicle.*
NK.........*Numismatikai Közlöny.*
NNM.......*Numismatic Notes and Monographs.*
NZ.........*Numismatische Zeitschrift.*
PBSR......*Papers of the British School at Rome.*
P-W[2].......Pauly-Wissowa, *Real-Encyclopädie der classischen Altertumswissenschaft* (Neue Bearbeitung).
RA.........*Revue archéologique.*
RIC........Mattingly and Sydenham, *The Roman Imperial Coinage.*
RIN........*Rivista italiana di numismatica.*
RM.........*Mitteilungen des deutschen archäologischen Instituts: Römische Abteilung.*
RN.........*Revue de numismatique.*
Strack......P. L. Strack, *Untersuchungen zur römischen Reichsprägung des zweiten Jahrhunderts*, I: *Reichsprägung zur Zeit des Traian*, II: *Reichsprägung zur Zeit des Hadrian*, III: *Reichsprägung zur Zeit des Antoninus Pius* (1931, 1933, 1938).
Vjestnik.....*Vjestnik Hrvatskoga arheološkog društva u Zagrebu.*
ZN.........*Zeitschrift für Numismatik.*

PART I

MEDALLIONS AND COINS

CHAPTER I

THE DEFINITION OF THE TERM "ROMAN MEDALLION"

The numismatic vocabulary of ancient Rome contained no separate words corresponding to our modern terms "medal" and its augmentative "medallion." As stated at the very opening of a book on Roman medallions, this fact might appear, at first sight, disconcerting. But it can be readily explained. In so far as our term "medal" connotes a memorial piece, struck to commemorate an event or idea, the whole of the Roman imperial coinage may be described as essentially medallic in character. To the vast bulk of modern coin types, conspicuous for their lack of variety both in design and execution, devoid of vital topical interest and repeated with wearisome monotony over long consecutive periods of time, the coin types of the Roman Empire present a contrast which is no less striking for being obvious and, by now, thoroughly familiar. From the middle of the first century onwards the imperial government had appreciated, as few governments have done before or since, not only the function of coinage as a mirror of contemporary life, of the political, social, spiritual and artistic aspirations of the age, but also its immense and unique possibilities as a far-reaching instrument of propaganda. Modern methods of disseminating news and modern vehicles of propaganda, from postage-stamps to broadcasting and the press, have their counterpart in the imperial coinage, where yearly, monthly, we might almost say daily novelties and variations in types record the sequence of public events and reflect the aims and ideologies of those who controlled the state. Thus there are few Roman imperial coins which could not, in this sense of the term, be described as "medals"; and from the purely commemorative point of view the distinction between coin and medal would be one of degree rather than of kind. A medal is, of course, not merely commemorative. It is also donative, intended to reach a special section only of the community and hence deliberately limited in the scope of its appeal. In other words, for all its superficial resemblance to a coin, the primary purpose of a medal is not circulation as currency but distribution as a gift. But here again, in the case of Rome, there is the influence of donative coins to be reckoned with; there are the congiaria and liberalitates, distributions of coins by the Emperors at all periods to the poor of Rome, and the military issues which, from the middle of the third century onwards, played a role so important as to imprint their character upon the general currency of the Roman state.[1] Such issues may well have tended to emphasize the medallic functions of the Roman coinage as a whole and hence to obscure the need for some separate term by which to differentiate pieces designed specifically as individual gifts from donative coins issued *en masse* as currency for civilians and troops alike. The more medallic the coinage, the less sharply defined the specialized functions of the medal. In the third place, a modern medal is immediately distinguishable from a coin by its external characteristics.

[1] Alföldi, *L'antiquité classique*, May 1938, pp. 15 f.; *CAH* xii, pp. 221 f.

The right of issue and of portraiture does not belong exclusively to the state: following closely upon this, the subjects and ideas commemorated are not confined to those which are of public or official interest; and so far as concerns the choice of metals and the standards of weight and size, there is no necessary connection or correlation between medals and the current coinage. But throughout the whole range of Roman imperial issues such complete independence of the ordinary official and legal monetary systems is a phenomenon quite unknown. The Roman world was, in fact, unacquainted with the medal or medallion in the strict modern sense of those terms. In what sense, then, are we justified in using the term "Roman medallion"?

It should now be clear that the Roman medal, unlike its modern counterpart, admits of no ready-made, hard-and-fast single definition. The frontier between coin and medallion can never be drawn with absolute precision; and there will always remain a certain number of border-line pieces which can, with almost equal justice, be claimed by either side. But there are, among the varied products of the Roman imperial mints, numerous pieces, falling into certain well-defined categories, which, while they conform externally to many of the general rules governing the ordinary coinage, undoubtedly stand above and apart from the regular currencies, pieces which cannot be in any way adequately covered by the term "coin" and which, in spite of their obvious divergencies from modern medals, filled a quite special and unmistakably medallic role. To these Roman approximations to the modern medal we may apply the following general definition: they are "monetiform" (or "coin-like") pieces which never correspond completely to any of the coin denominations in regular use and which the evidence, external and internal, proves to have been struck by the Emperor for special or solemn commemoration and to have been primarily and specifically intended for presentation or distribution as individual, personal gifts, any idea of their circulation as currency being either wholly absent or, at the most, quite secondary and subordinate. A satisfactory "label" for such pieces is not easy to come by. "Medal" is best avoided as conveying a false impression of identity with the modern counterpart. The traditional term "medallion" is likewise open to criticism as being itself suggestive of the modern medal, while as an augmentative by derivation it fails, in strict logic, to do justice to those smaller pieces the medallic character of which does not depend on size. But there are obvious practical objections to uprooting a term which has been consecrated by long service in the numismatic world: a single word which could be used as a convenient and suitable substitute is still to seek; and while we frankly admit it to be, in some senses, conventional, we can at least justify the retention of the term "medallion" as directly applicable to the very large pieces, whether of gold, silver or bronze, medallic pieces *par excellence*, in which differentiation from the current coinage was most patently and consciously stressed.[2]

[2] Compare the view of Roman medallions outlined by B. Laum in his *Über das Wesen des Münzgeldes* (1930), SS. 11–21. According to Laum "medallion" was included in "moneta." But the term "moneta" did not in ancient times necessarily imply suitability for circulation; and it is unsuitability for circulation which distinguishes medallions from coins.

CHAPTER II

THE CLASSIFICATION OF ROMAN MEDALLIONS

Having found a general definition and a common name to cover our various medallic series, we can now proceed to their classification. Roman medallions, as we have defined them, fall into three main categories:—I. Medallions proper; II. Money medallions; III. Pseudo medallions.

I. Medallions Proper.

Medallions in the strictest sense of the term are those bronze pieces which are clearly differentiated from the regular currency by certain well-defined features of structure, style and content. Most important and characteristic are the large bronze medallions easily recognizable as exceeding the ordinary bronze coins of largest denomination—the sestertii, down to Gallienus—in size of diameter, thickness of flan and weight. Occasionally the specifically medallic character of such a piece is made immediately apparent to the eye by the addition of a broad rim or circle framing the central design. Such rims are decorated with concentric grooves and bevels or with ornamental borders of varying degrees of elaboration. In some cases rim and centre form one single flan; in others the rim was added to the central flan in ancient times. "Framed" medallions first occur under Hadrian, become specially numerous under Antoninus Pius and continue under the Antonine and Severan dynasties down to the reign of Alexander Severus.[1] Some pieces, again, are set in narrow grooved or bevelled rims.[2] In the case of other pieces, struck on particularly large flans exceeding in area the space required for the actual types, a plain, "natural" rim is formed round the designs on either side.[3] From Antoninus Pius down to Diocletian and Maximian another favourite device for stressing, externally, medallic character was that of striking a piece on a disc composed of two

[1] The following is an analysis of "framed" medallions known to the present writer (including a few doubtful pieces):—Trajan: 1, Hadrian: 20, Sabina: 1, Aelius Verus: 1, Antoninus Pius: 26, Faustina I: 3, Marcus Aurelius: 11, Marcus Aurelius and Lucius Verus: 1, Faustina II: 2, Lucius Verus: 6, Lucilla: 1 (very doubtful, probably false), Commodus: 7, Albinus: 1, Septimius Severus: 2, Julia Domna: 1, Geta: 3, Elagabalus: 1, Elagabalus and Aquilia Severa: 1, Alexander Severus and Julia Mamaea: 1. A few later and mostly quite abnormal pieces may be noted:—Gordian III: 2 (1 = PROFECTIO AVG: obverse and reverse are formed of thin plates of silver applied to the central bronze flan. 2 = VICTORIA AVG and round temple: the obverse is made of a thin silver plate and applied to the central bronze flan), Philip I, Otacilia and Philip II: 1 (= EX ORACVLO APOLLINIS and round temple: obverse and reverse are formed of thin silver plates applied to the central bronze flan, the obverse plate having now gone), Trebonianus Gallus and Volusianus: 1 (= six-horse chariot: obverse and reverse are formed of thin silver plates applied to the central bronze flan, the obverse plate having now gone), Valerian and Gallienus: 1 (= ADVENTVS AVGG: normal piece).

[2] E. g. G II, tavv. 39, no. 8; 42, no. 8; III, tavv. 146, nos. 3, 8; 147, no. 7; 149, no. 7.

[3] E. g. G II, tavv. 39, nos. 7, 9; 40, no. 3; 52, no. 4; 57, no. 4; 61, no. 4; 65, no. 6; 67, no. 2; 71, no. 1; 72, no. 3.

metals, with a central portion of one metal and an outer rim of another.[4] The two metals thus employed were either two qualities of bronze or copper and bronze, the inner part being of the softer metal, the better to receive the impression of the types, the outer part being harder and more resisting. Often the line of division between the two metals runs through the letters of the circumference legends, showing that the two were put together to form a single flan before the piece was struck. Not infrequently fine pictorial and colouristic effects are produced by the juxtaposition of red centre and yellow rim. The bi-metallic process was clearly intended to attract the eye; just as, in the third century, bronze pieces were plated and silver pieces gilded, as a simple, if somewhat crude and superficial, method of enhancing their medallic aspect.[5]

But such obvious devices were, after all, the exception rather than the rule. The great majority of large bronze medallions remain sufficiently stamped as such by size of diameter and thickness of flan; while, from the practical point of view, their intrinsic unsuitability for circulation as currency is only relatively less patent than that of "framed" and bi-metallic pieces. Weight, on the other hand, has long been the rallying-point of those who would deny us the use of the word "medallion" in any real sense of the term. According to Kenner[6] and to the earlier theory of Gnecchi[7] the large bronze medallions down to Gallienus are nothing more than multiples of asses and sestertii. Gnecchi, again, in his later work, while rejecting his former equation of bronze medallion with multiple coin, takes 1318 bronze pieces dating from the time of Hadrian to that of Gallienus, works out their average weight as being *c.* 50.07 grammes and from this concludes that the value of a medallion was normally fixed at that of a double sestertius.[8] But the appeal to averages can often be very misleading and produce, as in the present case, a totally false impression. Discounting the exceptional "framed" and bi-metallic pieces, weights of large bronze medallions of this period can be registered for almost every point on the scale from *c.* 30 to *c.* 83 grammes. *C.* 50 grammes may represent the commonest weight, but

[4] The following is an analysis of bi-metallic medallions known to the present writer (including a few doubtful pieces):—Antoninus Pius: 1, Marcus Aurelius: 3, Lucius Verus: 1, Lucilla: 1, Commodus: 142, Albinus: 1, Julia Domna: 6, Caracalla: 1, Geta: 1, Macrinus: 1, Diadumenianus: 1, Elagabalus: 5, Alexander Severus: 24, Alexander Severus and Julia Mamaea: 16, Julia Mamaea: 7, Maximinus: 7, Maximinus and Maximus: 4, Pupienus: 1, Gordian III: 79, Philip I: 11, Philip I and Philip II: 3, Philip I, Otacilia and Philip II: 21, Philip II: 9, Philip II and Otacilia: 1, Trajan Decius and Etruscilla: 1, Etruscilla: 3, Hostilianus: 2, Trebonianus Gallus: 8, Trebonianus Gallus and Volusianus: 6, Volusianus: 4, Valerian: 5, Valerian and Gallienus: 5, Gallienus: 9, Gallienus and Salonina: 1, Gallienus and Saloninus: 3, Salonina: 4, Saloninus: 1, Postumus: 5, Claudius Gothicus: 1, Tacitus: 3, Probus: 11, Carus and Carinus: 1, Numerianus: 3, Magnia Urbica: 4, Diocletian: 6, Diocletian and Maximian: 2, Maximian: 3. One medallion of Commodus (in Berlin: G II, tav. 77, no. 3) shows the unusual phenomenon of a bi-metallic piece set in a frame.

[5] E. g. silver and bronze Tres Monetae medallions from Caracalla to the Diocletianic Tetrarchy. In the Evans Collection, now dispersed, there was a piece of Annia Faustina said to be composed of a silver disc set in a bronze rim (*Evans Collection Sale Catalogue* 1934, p. 107, no. 1614, pl. 50). The type, however, is that of an ordinary sestertius; the inner disc may thus be only silvered bronze and the piece an example of a bi-metallic pseudo medallion (*vide infra* p. 26).

[6] "Der römische Medaillon" (*NZ* 1887, SS. 1–173).

[7] E. g. *Roman Coins*, ed. 2, 1903, pp. 130–139.

[8] G I, p. xxx.

it does not necessarily imply a consciously fixed standard: were this so, we should hardly expect to find so many pieces, at both ends of the scale, failing thus conspicuously to conform to it. Kenner's system of multiples is too elaborate, and Gnecchi's double sestertius theory is too simple, to fit the facts of the actual weights, which suggest, on the contrary, a complete absence of any fixed scheme or standard. For the post-Gallienic period, with the increasing disparity, not in structure only but also in style and content, between the large bronze medallions and the largest bronze coins, the multiple theory is obviously even less tenable.

Thus the main structural features of the large bronze medallions proper—size and thickness of flan and extreme variability of weight in the case of all pieces and the use of "frames" and bi-metallic striking in special cases—combine to establish the conclusion that they were never originally intended to circulate as coin of the realm. Some large medallions may, of course, have circulated later as currency accidentally, as it were; and this might account for the poor condition in which certain pieces have come down to us. But causes other than circulation can obviously be assigned to wear: even "framed" medallions, where circulation was clearly out of the question, are not wholly exempt from it.

When we turn from the structure to the style of our large bronze pieces we find again that they exhibit essentially medallic characteristics. The obverse dies, with their high relief and exquisite finish, provide a unique series of imperial portraits unsurpassed in the history of Roman iconography; while the reverse designs display a standard of skill and beauty which is normally quite unparalleled on the regular coinage. Bronze medallions are, before anything else, works of art; and here the distinction between coin and medallion is patently not one of degree only, but of kind. Closely allied to the artistic aspect of medallions is the question of their rarity and variety. Such outstanding and often superb products of the medallist's art were not turned out in the mass. Bronze medallions are comparatively rare as a class and, with a few exceptions, rare individually. It is quite usual for a type to be represented by one example, or, at the most, by a very few examples; and subsequent discoveries have confirmed the opinion expressed by Gnecchi in 1912, that at every new medallion find the odds are in favour of new types, or at any rate new variants or combinations of types, being brought to light.[9] When confronted with two or more pieces displaying identical obverse or reverse types, it is fairly normal, in the early period, to find that they were struck from identical dies. On the other hand, general identity of type is often accompanied by small die variations between one piece and its fellows; and indeed, in view of the hard blows required for striking dies in such high relief, the number of specimens obtainable from a single die can never have been great. Again, the same reverse die is often combined with two or more different obverses, and vice versa; nor is it rare to find the same reverse die combined with obverses of two or more Emperors or Empresses. But it is exceptional to discover two or more pieces struck from identical dies both on obverse and reverse simultaneously. Finally, the content of the large bronze

[9] G I, p. li.

medallions proper reveals no less strikingly than do their structure and style a genuine independence of the regular currencies. Taken as a whole, the vast majority of medallion types either do not appear at all on ordinary coins or are only found there in less rich and complex versions. Some medallion types may seem to be mere elaborations of coin types. But a large proportion of the subjects depicted are derived, not from coins, but from major works of art; and thus the work of the medallist is linked less closely, in a sense, with that of the coin-designer than with that of the sculptor or of the painter. In their wealth and variety of interest the types unmistakably affirm the primary role of medallions as gift pieces presented to special persons on special occasions.

There remains a small and mysterious group of large bronze pieces to be considered, the unilateral medallions, so called from their blank reverses, but corresponding to the large medallions proper in size of diameter and thickness of flan, in the scale of their weights and in the style and technique of their obverse portraiture.[10] Some of these, although recorded as unilateral, were obviously not so originally: sometimes the obverse has been cut from the reverse, while in other cases the reverse design has been scraped off or has virtually disappeared through wear. But others are genuinely unilateral. They have smooth, polished backs, sometimes slightly concave or ornamented with a central boss: they show no sign of having ever received a reverse type. Of the various explanations offered to account for these unilateral pieces—that they were "proofs" or experiments for obverse dies, samples of their work submitted by medallists competing for posts at the mint or specimens of imperial iconography destined to serve as models for provincial issues—none are really conclusive or wholly satisfactory. They remain a problem as yet unsolved. Meanwhile they must be included in our series on the grounds of their structure and style; nor is there anything to exclude the possibility that they were issued as presentation pieces of an experimental and quite exceptional type.

Our account of the large bronze pieces would be incomplete without at least a statement at this point of the well-known fact that the letters S C, which down to Gallienus appear normally, though not invariably, on the ordinary bronze coinage, are, with a few exceptions, omitted on the bronze medallions proper. To the problem of the real significance of these letters we shall afterwards return.[11] For the moment it is enough to insist that their presence or absence cannot rightly be used as a criterion in itself for distinguishing between coin and medallion, although their absence on the vast majority of medallions is a matter of obvious importance.

So far we have applied to bronze medallions proper the three criteria of structure, style and content. In the case of the large pieces, all three factors may be taken together as equally decisive. We now come to a series of smaller bronze pieces which are less clearly differentiated by their structure from the current coinage, but where style and content become the really decisive factors in vindicating

[10] The following examples have been personally examined by the present writer:—Hadrian: 5, Antoninus Pius: 2, Faustina I: 2, Marcus Aurelius: 7, Lucius Verus: 1 (a doubtful piece), Lucilla: 1, Commodus: 4, Carinus and Numerianus: 1.

[11] *Vide infra* pp. 45 ff.

their claim to be classed as true medallions. In size of diameter, in thickness of flan and in weight such pieces are often indistinguishable from coins of the regular denominations. Weights, it is true, are, on the whole, more variable than in the ordinary currencies; and there are pieces of regular coin dimensions the weight of which is distinctly higher than the normal weight of the corresponding coins.[12] In the third century we even find small bi-metallic pieces, the medallic character of which is thus placed beyond doubt on structural grounds.[13] But for the most part, in detecting the small medallions, we must take as our true criteria high relief, special finish and fineness of touch, rarity and the use of reverse types unusual in themselves or tallying with those of the large medallions. It is here, above all, that the boundary between coin and medallion often becomes so difficult to draw. Gnecchi's adherence to the S C criterion for these smaller pieces led, as we shall see later, to somewhat strange results.[14] There is, in fact, no royal road that we can follow. Each piece must be considered on its own merits and tested by its style and content. If the results are such as to establish its character as a special commemorative piece, suitable for solemn presentation within a restricted field, then we may safely include it in our class of medallions proper. It must, however, be borne in mind that the circulation of these smaller medallions as currency, if not originally intended, was rendered far more likely than in the case of the larger pieces, owing to their structural similarity to regular coins. The great majority of smaller bronze medallions proper were struck by Hadrian, Trajan and the Antonine Emperors down to Commodus. Pieces of sestertius size are most frequent under Trajan and Hadrian, after whose time they grow gradually rarer. Pieces of dupondius and as dimensions are also fairly frequent under Hadrian, while of the period from Pius to Commodus they are a regular and characteristic feature. In the second quarter of the third century these miniature bronze medallions were again much in vogue. A specially fine series was issued under Alexander Severus, some pieces bearing the formula S C on the reverse, but inseparable, on grounds of style and content, from those without it; the exclusion of these S C pieces by Gnecchi from the medallion category is an instance of the fallaciousness of his criterion. Again, for the period from Gordian III to Gallienus we have a certain number of small bronze pieces of undoubtedly medallic character. From Gallienus onwards it becomes increasingly hard to differentiate small true medallions from ordinary coins on stylistic grounds: content is often the only guide. With Constantine I the history of small bronze medallions virtually comes to an end.

[12] E. g. a small bronze medallion of Hadrian in the British Museum, with the reverse type of the infant Juppiter suckled by the she-goat Amalthea, weighing 14.89 grammes (*BMCCRE* III, p. 442, no. 1362 A; Strack II, Taf. 16, Nr. 444). Pl. I, 1.

[13] E. g. small medallions of Alexander Severus and Julia Mamaea (ROMAE AETERNAE: Paris, no. 7469 = G III, tav. 153, no. 8) and of Julia Mamaea (TEMPORVM FELICITAS: Vienna, no. 105747). Two other small medallions of Alexander Severus and Julia Mamaea, showing the "liberalitas" type (Royal Collection, Turin; National Museum (Gnecchi), Rome), are composed of silver centres set in bronze 'rims' (G III, p. 45, no. 9, tav. di suppl., no. 3).

[14] *Vide infra* pp. 28 ff.

II. MONEY MEDALLIONS.

Money medallions are gold and silver pieces which exceed in size and weight the standard unit of contemporary currency. They were struck on a fixed system as true multiples of gold and silver coins and could therefore, legally, be used as money. They passed through the same periods of decline and revival in quality of metal as did the coinage. From the reign of Gallienus, when the silver coinage, which had been steadily declining, was replaced by silver-washed copper (billon), until well on into the reign of Constantine, when the silver currency was again revived,[15] there were practically no real silver medallions; and the weights of both gold and silver multiples, at all periods, vary and rise and fall with the weights of the ordinary coins. But money medallions are not mere multiple coins. Unlike the so-called "cistophoric medallions," struck in Asia and equivalent to three denarii, they did not form part of the regular currency. The first proof of this is their rarity as a class in general and as individual examples in particular. Nor do they occur numerically in the same proportions as the gold and silver coins in successive periods of imperial history. In the first and second centuries both gold and silver medallions are extremely rare, especially the gold. In the third century down to Gallienus silver medallions are more plentiful; whereas gold medallions of the early third century, before the accession of Gallienus, are still scarce, though, according to Lampridius, numbers of gold multiples, ranging in value from that of 2 to that of 100 aurei, were struck by Elagabalus and demonetized by Alexander Severus.[16] It is not until the late third and fourth centuries that multiples as a class become in any degree common. In the fourth century, after Constantine's revival of the silver coinage, we have a fairly continuous series, from Constantius II to Arcadius, of large multiples of the silver miliarensia. But the really characteristic money medallions of the later Empire from Diocletian onwards are the gold pieces, multiples first of aurei tariffed at one-sixtieth of a pound and then, after *c.* 310, normally of solidi tariffed at one seventy-second of a pound, ranging in size and weight from the 1½-solidi pieces first issued by Constantine I to the 72-solidi piece of Valens from Szilágy Sómlyó.[17] Here again the individual rarity of these gold pieces excludes the mere multiple coin theory of their origin. It is true that in the case of the smaller multiples—the 1½-solidi and the 2-solidi pieces—the number of known examples of a single type, or of variants of a single type, can be as many as sixteen;[18] and the actual circulation of such pieces as money is certainly well within the bounds of possibility. But for the larger multiples one example, or at the most two or three known examples, of any given type is the general rule: and it is hard to imagine that such highly individualized pieces can ever have actually served as legal tender. In the second place, even the lesser multiples stand distinctly apart from the regular

[15] Although Diocletian issued a restored denarius, the argenteus, at the time of his reform, scarcely any silver coins were struck between *c.* 307 and 330 (Mattingly, *Roman Coins*, p. 223, n. 4).

[16] *Vide infra* p. 23.

[17] In Vienna. G I, tav. 17, no. 1.

[18] E. g. EQVIS ROMANVS 1½-solidi pieces of Constantine I. G I, tav. 6, no. 12.

aurei and solidi in their style and content and the fine state of preservation in which they have come down to us. As for the larger multiples, their size and high intrinsic value, their fine style and technique and the varied and individual character of both obverse portraits and reverse designs mark them out as rare and special presentation pieces, potentially money but actually preserved and treasured by their recipients as tokens of honor or pledges of imperial favor.

Thus in the primary purpose of their issue money medallions are no less true medallions than the bronze medallions proper. Both alike were intended, not for circulation, but for special or solemn distribution as gifts. The difference lies in the essence of the gifts. The point of a bronze medallion was its structural and stylistic beauty and the interest of its type; it was as a work of art or as a commemorative record, not as an object of material value, that the gift was both offered and received. Money medallions are also, normally, works of outstanding artistic merit, particularly from the iconographical point of view; while in content their types can rival those of the bronze as historical and political documents of the highest significance. But struck as they were in the precious metals and on carefully fixed standards, it was inevitable that their intrinsic monetary worth should assume an importance at least equal to that of all their other assets; and their prevalence under the later Empire reflects the spirit of an age in which, under the pressure of economic and other causes, cultural values were beginning to yield place to those of a more materialistic order. Emphasis is, indeed, laid upon the monetary value of multiples as gifts in two literary texts, the well-known passages from Lampridius' *Vita Alexandri Severi* (ch. 38) and from Gregory of Tours' *Historia Ecclesiastica Francorum* (vi, 2). The passage of Lampridius runs as follows:—"formas binarias ternarias et quaternarias et denarias etiam atque amplius usque ad liberales[19] quoque et centenarias, quas Heliogabalus invenerat, resolvi praecepit neque in usu cuiusquam versari; atque ex eo his materiae nomen inditum est, cum diceret plus largiendi hanc esse imperatori causam, si, cum multos solidos minores dare posset, dans decem vel amplius una forma triginta et quinquaginta et centum dare cogeretur." We notice here, first, that the terms "formae binariae," "ternariae" etc., imply a graduated scale of multiples struck on fixed monetary standards, while all the stress is laid upon weight and intrinsic value, to the exclusion of content and style; secondly, that these multiples are regarded as forming part of the same system of largess as that under which ordinary coins were distributed; and, thirdly, that the issue of large gift pieces, the equivalent "una forma" of several, or many, gold units, was an arbitrary matter, superadded as an "extra" to the ordinary coinage and dependent upon the Emperor's personal will. The phrase "in usu cuiusquam versari" does not necessarily imply actual circulation, though it does suggest the possibility of putting such pieces to some kind of commercial use. It is another question whether multiples of so large a size would really have been struck as early as the first half of the

[19] Kenner's emendation of the meaningless MSS readings "libribres" and "bilibres" (= 100 aurei = *centenariae*, since one aureus = 1/50th of a Roman pound at the time of Alexander Severus) has been adopted here.

third century or whether the writer's statement has been colored by his knowledge of the great gold medallions of the later Empire. At any rate it would appear that Alexander's demonetization order was very thoroughly carried out: only one gold multiple of Elagabalus, the binio in Berlin,[20] has, so far as we know at present, come down to us. On the other hand, a few gold pieces issued by Alexander himself are known to us—a binio in Paris,[21] a binio in Munich,[22] the famous 8-aurei piece in Paris, found at Tarsus in 1867,[23] and the lost Paris 4 (?)-aurei piece of Alexander Severus and Julia Mamaea.[24] Our second text describes a presentation of large gold medallions by the Emperor Tiberius II Constantinus (578–582) to King Chilperic:—"aureos etiam singularum librarum pondere, quos imperator misit, ostendit, habentes ab una parte iconem imperatoris pictam, et scriptum in circulo, TIBERII CONSTANTINI PERPETVI AVGVSTI: ab alia vero parte habentes quadrigam et ascensorem, continentesque scriptum, GLORIA ROMANORVM." The importance of this passage as throwing light upon the purpose of medallion issues will be discussed later.[25] Its immediate interest for us lies in the use of the term "aurei" for such pieces, indicating the fundamentally monetary character of gold multiples even of the largest size.[26] Again, the decree issued "de expensis ludorum" by Valentinian II, Theodosius I and Arcadius in 384, forbidding privati to distribute as gifts heavier silver coins (nummi) than those weighing one-sixtieth of a pound, links the silver multiples to the coin system.[27] At the same time, the decree implies a real distinction between multiples and ordinary coins. One-sixtieth of a pound represents the weight of the heaviest miliarensia of the period. These, being part of the regular currency, might be distributed by private individuals, while the right of distributing multiples was reserved for the Emperor, a further proof that they were regarded as special gift pieces of a rare and exceptional character.

III. PSEUDO MEDALLIONS.

We have defined medallions as pieces clearly distinguished in one way or another from regular coins and intended, not for circulation, but for special or solemn presentation as commemorative gifts. This definition must, as we have seen, include a series of bronze pieces the differentiation of which from coins lies less in structure than in style and content; and inasmuch as style and content are, in the

[20] G I, tav. 1, no. 7.

[21] G I, tav. 1, no. 10.

[22] PAX AETERNA AVG: Pax standing to left (**Pl. XXIX, 1**).

[23] G I, tav. 1, no. 9 (**Pl. XLIV, 5**).

[24] G I, p. 5, no. 1: FELICITAS TEMPORVM (**Pl. XXVII, 2**). A rubbing of another, probably 4-aurei, piece of Alexander Severus was seen by the present writer at the British Museum in Sept., 1938:—obv. = IMP CAES M AVR SEV ALEXANDER AVG; bust of Alexander Severus, laureate, to right, seen three-quarters to front, with paludamentum and cuirass: rev. = P M TR P COS P P; Alexander Severus in slow quadriga to right, holding eagle-topped sceptre in left hand and reins and olive-branch in right hand: diameter = 29 mm. The present owner of this medallion is unknown.

[25] *Vide infra* pp. 117 f.

[26] Chilperic's medallions were each worth 72 solidi and weighed 327 grammes apiece.

[27] *Cod. Theod.* 15, 9, 1:—"cum publica celebrantur officia, sit sportulis nummus argenteus, alia materia diptychis: nec maiorem argenteum nummum fas sit expendere quam qui formari solet cum argenti libra una in argenteos sexaginta dividitur." This passage is in agreement with the general imperial policy of forbidding private largitiones on a lavish scale.

case of the bronze, a more searching test of medallic character than outward structure, we have classed this series among medallions proper. Pseudo medallions, on the other hand, are bronze pieces differentiated from coins solely by structural, external and, in a sense, superficial features. Struck, in most cases, from actual coin dies, they show specifically medallic traits neither in style nor in types.[28] Yet at the time of their coining deliberate steps were taken to exclude them from circulation as regular currency, to lift them, in fact, out of the category of coins into that of "medals." Such steps include the striking of dupondius and as types on sestertius flans and of sestertius types on medallion flans; the striking (very rarely) of sestertii in two metals; the mounting of sestertii in narrow rims; and the striking of sestertius types on large discs, so that the designs are framed by more or less elaborate bevelled or grooved rims, corresponding to those of the great "framed" bronze medallions proper. According to Blanchet[29] and Mowat[30] these "mounted" coins were experimental or trial pieces, "proofs" from dies to be submitted to the Emperor before large numbers were struck off, the object of the large flans being to avoid confusion between them and current money. Had this been their purpose we should expect to find such pieces spread fairly evenly over the whole imperial period down to the second half of the third century. But while most reigns down to that of Gallienus are represented by at least one example of sestertii struck on normal-sized medallion flans, they are far commoner in the first and early second centuries than in later times. As for the "framed" pieces, they are fairly abundant in the first century and under Trajan and Hadrian, but grow rarer from the time of the Antonines onwards: incidentally, the variety and careful workmanship which characterize these "frames" suggest that they served a more positive and aesthetic purpose than the mere avoidance of confusion with ordinary coins. Pseudo medallions, or "medallised" coins, are, in fact, essentially a feature of the early imperial period; and although they are still to be found under later Emperors, their chief part was played before the history of bronze medallions proper seriously begins. We may see in them the precursors of the true medallion, the first stage in the evolution of special commemorative and donative pieces standing apart from the regular currency; and, as such, they cannot logically be excluded from the study of Roman medallions.

A brief review of representative pseudo medallions of the first century may serve to illustrate this phase of development. Under Augustus a number of pieces show dupondius and as types struck on sestertius or medallion flans. For example, the common as reverse type of Agrippa, Neptune standing with trident and dolphin,[31] appears on a piece, formerly in the Evans Collection, measuring 38 mm. in diameter and weighing 58.77 grammes.[32] As and dupondius types of the Tresviri Monetales

[28] The large majority of Gnecchi's so-called "senatorial medallions," figured in Vol. III, tavv. 159, 160, are really pseudo medallions, coin types struck on medallion flans. The obverses of two pieces of Antoninus Pius (G III, tav. 160, nos. 2, 5) appear, however, to have been struck from medallion dies (= G II, tavv. 43, no. 3; 48, no. 3). One piece of Antoninus Pius with S C (G III, tav. 160, no. 3) must, on grounds both of style and type, be classed as a true medallion proper.

[29] *RN* 1896, pp. 235 ff.

[30] *RIN* 1911, pp. 165 ff.

[31] *RIC* I, p. 108, no. 32.

[32] *Evans Collection Sale Catalogue* 1934, p. 71, no. 1220, pl. 33. This piece would appear, however, to be of doubtful antiquity.

are struck on sestertius and medallion flans measuring from 35 to 39 mm. in diameter and sestertius types of the moneyers occur on medallion flans: of the latter there is a striking example with a diameter of 43 mm.[33] Noteworthy among pseudo medallions of Divus Augustus are a specially heavy medallion flan in the British Museum, weighing 72.16 grammes, with the as type of S C and thunderbolt,[34] and a restoration of Nerva formerly in the Vierordt Collection, a large "framed" piece measuring 52 mm. in all and weighing 91.3 grammes.[35] For the reign of Gaius we may mention a piece at Gotha with the well-known sestertius type of the three princesses[36] set in a narrow rim, the whole measuring 40 mm.; and a heavily rimmed piece of Agrippina I in the British Museum with the carpentum type,[37] 48 mm. in total diameter and 107.27 grammes in weight. Claudius is represented by a few pieces. For Nero eleven examples are known to the present writer, all stamped with familiar sestertius and dupondius types.[38] Eight of these have "frames" or rims of varying size and elaboration, grooved or bevelled, and they range in diameter from 45 to 56 mm. and in weight from 51.37 to 88.45 grammes. Thus, in the case of Neronian pseudo medallions, those of the "framed" type, in which the medallic character is most conspicuously stressed, form the great majority of extant pieces and they may be regarded as forerunners of the large "framed" medallions proper of the Hadrianic and Antonine periods. A pseudo medallion of Galba at Naples, with a regular sestertius and dupondius type struck on a medallion flan,[39] appears to be our first example of a genuinely bi-metallic piece: on the obverse the line of division between the two metals can be clearly seen cutting through the letters of the circumference legend. Under the Flavians pseudo medallions were rarer: we may note in passing that the Vespasianic piece in Paris, described by Gnecchi as "the first senatorial medallion," is simply a regular sestertius struck on a medallion flan.[40] In the case of the vast majority of first-century pseudo medallions the relative positions of obverse and reverse dies are ↑↓.[41]

With the advent of the bronze medallion proper under Trajan and Hadrian pseudo medallions no longer possess the same significance as representing Rome's earliest excursions into the medallic field. Henceforth they appear as exceptional pieces, merely supplementing the true medallion issues, and a brief illustrative summary of their post-first-century history will serve our purpose here. At first, indeed, they remain fairly numerous. No less than twelve pieces of Hadrian have

[33] *Vierordt Collection Sale Catalogue* 1923, p. 35, no. 630, pl. 7: weight = 31.6 grammes (now in the Hall Collection at Llanymynech).

[34] *RIC* I, p. 95, no. 1.

[35] *Vierordt Collection Sale Catalogue* 1923, p. 37, no. 654, pl. 8.

[36] *RIC* I, p. 117, no. 26, pl. 7, no. 115.

[37] *RIC* I, p. 118, no. 42, pl. 8, no. 123.

[38] E. g. Annona and Ceres, Victory advancing to left or right, Temple of Janus, Triumphal Arch, Roma, Securitas, Temple of Concordia, Harbour of Ostia. A remarkable piece with the Ostia type, formerly in the Walters Collection, is practically equivalent to four sestertii (*NC* 1915, p. 329, pl. 16, no. 4): it is, however, possibly false.

[39] Diameter = 40 mm., weight = 47.1 grammes. *Cf. RIC* I, pp. 204, 206, nos. 50, 69.

[40] Diameter = 40 mm., weight = 40.3 grammes. G III, p. 89, no. 27, tav. 159, no. 1.

[41] *Vide infra* p. 130 ff.

been personally examined by the present writer and of these eight are "framed." For Antoninus Pius several fine specimens have been published by Gnecchi.[42] But under the later Antonine Emperors the output gradually declines, Commodus, the most prolific striker of bronze medallions proper, being represented by only one pseudo medallic piece, so far as the present writer is aware.[43] With the Severan dynasty pseudo medallions become somewhat commoner again. Noteworthy are two specially fine specimens of Julia Domna at Milan with the sacrifice-to-Vesta sestertius types, both struck on bi-metallic flans;[44] a bi-metallic piece of Caracalla in Paris, with the Aesculapius sestertius type;[45] and a piece of Geta in the British Museum of quite outstanding beauty, with the sestertius type of Bacchus and Hercules (DI PATRII) set in a broad rim adorned with two borders of dots.[46] Alexander Severus is represented by five pseudo medallions, Julia Mamaea by one piece. For Gordian III we have two fine specimens, both with an adlocutio scene on the reverse and probably struck from the same dies.[47] Philip I, Otacilia, Hostilianus, Trebonianus Gallus,[48] Volusianus and Valerian are all represented by one or more pieces. For Salonina we have a heavy piece in Paris[49] and a lighter piece at Oxford. Finally, our series closes with a piece in Paris issued by Claudius Gothicus, showing an as type struck on a medallion flan.[50]

The interest and importance of pseudo medallions lies, then, first in their historical role as forerunners of the true medallion and secondly in their own specifically medallic character regarded from the purely structural point of view. But in style and content their kinship is with the regular coinage, and it is, obviously, to histories of the latter that we must turn for their classification and for the interpretation of their types. They add little to our knowledge of the special contribution made by medallions as such to the history of politics, religion and art in imperial times. We have now sketched out and illustrated the story of their development, and in the chapters which follow they will receive only incidental attention.

[42] G III, tav. 160, nos. 1, 2, 4, 5, 7, 8. For the Tiberis type (no. 2) *cf. Levis Collection Sale Catalogue* 1925, pl. 24, no. 579.

[43] Sestertius type on medallion flan (38 mm.) at Milan.

[44] *RIN* 1892, p. 306, no. 33, tav. 7, no. 3: diameter = 36 mm., weight = 43.3 grammes; G III, tav. 160, no. 9. *Cf. RIC* IV, i, pp. 311, 313, nos. 594, 607.

[45] *Cf. RIC* IV, i, p. 301, no. 538.

[46] *Cf. RIC* IV, i, p. 330, no. 112, pl. 16, no. 7. **Pl. I, 2.**

[47] Milan (37 mm., 41.5 grammes) and Messrs. Seaby, Oct. 1938 (39 mm., 46.6 grammes).

[48] E. g. small bi-metallic piece in Berlin with type of Salus. **Pl. I, 3.** *Cf.* C^2 V, p. 251, no. 120.

[49] Weight = 57.15 grammes. *Cf. RIC* V, i, p. 112, no. 46, pl. 4, no. 62.

[50] *Cf. RIC* V, i, p. 234, no. 267a, pl. 6, no. 90.

CHAPTER III

COINS INCORRECTLY CLASSED AS MEDALLIONS. MEDALLIC COINS. BORDER-LINE PIECES

I. Coins Incorrectly Classed as Medallions.

In the foregoing chapters we have attempted to show that all pieces to which we have applied the term "medallion," whether they be medallions proper, money medallions or pseudo medallions, have certain features in common: they were deliberately set apart by structure, style or content—or by two, or by all three, elements combined—from the ordinary current coinage of the Roman state, and they were struck as exceptional issues and intended for special or solemn presentation on important occasions. The application of these criteria will necessarily exclude from the category of medallions much of the material amassed by Gnecchi in the first and third volumes of his corpus. Coins incorrectly classed by Gnecchi as medallions may be grouped under four headings:—(i) ordinary aes coins of the first three centuries which do not bear the letters S C on their reverses; (ii) the double sestertii of Trajan Decius and Etruscilla; (iii) third-century aurei the weight of which is slightly higher than the normal; (iv) gift and festival coins, such as the bronze, or silvered bronze, quinarii issued from the time of Valerian to that of Diocletian, and the silver miliarensia struck from the time of Constantine onwards.

(i) At the end of his third volume Gnecchi has collected a small group of so-called "senatorial medallions," heavy bronze pieces with S C on the reverse, the large majority of which are, in reality, pseudo medallions, coin types struck on medallion flans.[1] These pieces excepted, the presence of the letters S C on a given piece invariably spells for Gnecchi "coin," their absence "medallion," with the result that he has forced into the medallion category whole groups of quite common aes coins, on which specifically medallic features, whether of structure, style or content, are all to seek. The appearance, as a general rule, of S C on the regular aes coinage is a question which we shall have to reconsider later in connection with mints.[2] But whatever degree of senatorial authority, real or fictitious, over the aes coinage these letters may imply, the evidence of the coins themselves suggests, of course, that the Emperors exercised a direct and continuous influence upon the occasions of aes issues and the choice of aes types. Thus the absence of S C on the common adlocutio coins of Gaius[3] probably means no more than a specially personal interest in cash issued in the first instance, it may be, as pay for the imperial Guards.[4] In style and weight these pieces are normal sestertii: they are not medallions.

[1] *Vide supra* p. 25, note 28. [2] *Vide infra* pp. 45 ff. [3] G III, tav. 141, no. 1.

[4] Dio (59, 2, 1) says that Gaius on his accession not only distributed to the praetorians the sum bequeathed to them by his predecessor, but established another precedent by adding as much more on his own account:—καὶ ἑτέρας τοσαύτας (sc. δραχμάς) προσεπέδωκε. Were his non-S C sestertii struck for this purpose?

Similarly, specially personal connections with the Emperor would account for the absence of the ordinary formula on the memorial sestertii of Agrippina, with the carpentum and legend S P Q R MEMORIAE AGRIPPINAE on their reverses,[5] and on the common sestertii depicting the oak-wreath offered to the Emperor by the Senate and People of Rome, combined with the legends S P Q R P P, or EX S C, OB CIVES SERVATOS, issued under Gaius, Claudius, Galba, Vitellius, Vespasian and Titus,[6] and with the legend S P Q R ADSERTORI LIBERTATIS PVBLICAE, issued under Vespasian.[7] But the clearest proof of the close association of Emperor and Senate in the matter of the coinage, and of the absence of any fixed principle delimiting their respective spheres, is afforded by Nero's principate. From 54 to 64 the aurei and denarii struck at Rome consistently bear in the field of their reverses the more indirect senatorial formula EX S C;[8] and when, *c.* 64,[9] the aes coinage was revived at the mints of Rome and Lugdunum, after having been in abeyance since the last years of Claudius, a considerable proportion of the reverse types were struck either with the letters S C or without them.[10] There would seem, then, to be no reason for regarding the Neronian bronze pieces figured on Gnecchi's plates 141 and 142 as anything but normal coins, although they may, as Sydenham suggests, have been issued in the first instance at the Emperor's personal instigation and some of the copper asses without S C show a style of portraiture which is particularly close to that of the aurei and denarii of 60 to 64, as distinct from the style of Nero's later portraits.[11] On the worn adlocutio coin of Galba, illustrated by Gnecchi as being without S C,[12] these letters may well have been obliterated; and wear, or imperfect striking, would seem to account for their absence on the VICTORIA NAVALIS dupondius of Vespasian.[13] The specially personal character of the T ET DOM C sestertii of Vespasian might explain the substitution there of the less direct EX S C for the ordinary senatorial formula.[14] The pieces of Vespasian and Titus with caduceus between crossed cornuacopiae and no S C on their reverses are all of eastern mintage.[15] The Vespasianic piece, figured by Gnecchi, with heads of Titus and Domitian on the reverse is now unverifiable.[16] And it may be said here, once and for all, that none of the bronze pieces, quoted or illustrated by Gnecchi, which have on their reverses either the head or bust of the reigning Emperor, or of his Empress, or of any other member, or members, of the imperial family, can be classed as medallions merely on the ground that they have no S C, when they are of normal coin weight and are executed in ordinary coin style. On many such pieces with double portraits the S C formula actually occurs: for its absence on others the strictly personal interest of the reverse type offers

[5] G III, tav. 141, no. 3.
[6] G III, tavv. 141, nos. 2, 4; 142, nos. 6, 7, 8, 10, 11, 13.
[7] G III, tav. 142, no. 12. *Cf.* the sestertius commemorating the gift of a ceremonial shield by the ordo equester to the young Nero (G III, tav. 141, no. 9).
[8] *BMCCRE* I, pp. 200–207.
[9] *BMCCRE* I, pp. clxviii–clxx.
[10] E. g. adlocutio, Annona and Ceres, decursio, Market (MAC AVG), Victory advancing to left, imperial Genius (GENIO AVGVSTI), Nero as Apollo, agonistic table, etc. (CERTAMEN QVINQ ROMAE CON), emblems of Minerva. The Neronian pieces without S C are, however, rare as compared with those with S C.
[11] E. A. Sydenham, *The Coinage of Nero*, pp. 38, 76, 103.
[12] G III, tav. 142, no. 5.
[13] G III, tav. 143, no. 2.
[14] G III, tav. 142, no. 14.
[15] G III, tav. 143, nos. 1, 3. *Cf. RIC* II, pp. 109–112.
[16] G III, tav. 143, no. 5.

adequate explanation. The ANNONA AVG pieces of Titus, showing Annona standing to left as reverse type, are simply sestertii without S C:[17] the coin is a common one and the style shows no specifically medallic traits. Titus, the "darling of mankind," may well have shown a specially personal concern for his people's corn-supply. The *reductio ad absurdum* of Gnecchi's S C criterion is seen in his inclusion among medallions of coins of the mines struck under Trajan and Hadrian[18] and of common quadrantes without S C of Trajan, Hadrian and Antoninus Pius, whether of Roman or eastern mintage.[19] The Hadrianic piece showing on the reverse a decastyle temple with the legends S P Q R around and EX S C in the exergue is an ordinary sestertius,[20] a variant of the sestertius with the legends S C in the field and S P Q R in the exergue.[21] Similarly, we must regard as ordinary sestertii the pieces of Faustina I with the legend EX S C and the types of carpentum drawn by two mules and biga drawn by two elephants on their reverses.[22] Finally, the absence of S C on a number of sestertii and asses, figured by Gnecchi, of Trajan,[23] Hadrian,[24] Antoninus Pius,[25] Commodus[26] and Caracalla[27] can be easily explained by the simple fact of obliteration due to working over or to wear. From the middle of the third century onwards the letters S C are no longer so normally the accompaniment of the reverse type on ordinary asses, while from Gallienus onwards the same is true of ordinary sestertii. We can therefore exclude from the category of medallions a number of pieces illustrated on Gnecchi's plates 154 to 158 (Hostilianus to Maximian) the style and content of which are alike devoid of medallic characteristics.[28]

(ii) The double sestertii introduced by Trajan Decius, with the legends FELICITAS SAECVLI, LIBERALITAS AVG and VICTORIA AVG corresponding to his own portrait on the obverse and with PVDICITIA AVG corresponding to the obverse portrait of Etruscilla, all have the formula S C and are classed by Gnecchi among his "senatorial medallions."[29] Often quasi-medallic in style and always struck upon thick, heavy flans, these pieces undoubtedly bear an outward and superficial resemblance to true medallions. They are, however, in actual fact mere multiples of ordinary coins, an experiment in the minting of 2-sestertii pieces. Relatively common and confined to a limited repertory of fixed types, they are neither rare and exceptional in content, as are the gold and silver money medallions, nor are they differentiated from ordinary coins by variability in weight or by variety in subject-matter, as are the bronze medallions proper. So far from being set apart in any way from the regular currency of the reign, they form an essential element in it, and are thus automatically excluded from the medallion category under our definition of the term.

[17] G III, tav. 143, no. 6.

[18] G III, tavv. 144, nos. 1, 2, 3; 148, nos. 6, 7, 8.

[19] G III, tavv. 148, nos. 1–5; 149, no. 9.

[20] G III, tav. 145, no. 11. *Cf. BMCCRE* III, p. 476, note to no. 1554.

[21] *RIC* II, pl. 15, no. 318.

[22] G III, tav. 149, nos. 14, 15.

[23] G III, tav. 143, nos. 9, 13.

[24] G III, tavv. 144, nos. 4, 5, 13; 147, no. 5.

[25] G III, tav. 148, no. 11.

[26] G III, tavv. 151, nos. 11, 12, 13; 152, no. 1.

[27] G III, tav. 152, no. 9.

[28] G III, tav. 154, nos. 4, 6, 7, 11, 20; 155, nos. 13, 14, 15, 16, 18; 156, nos. 1, 7–11, 12, 13, 16; 157, nos. 7, 10, 12, 13; 158, nos. 1, 2, 3, 7, 9, 10, 21, 22, 23. The sestertii of Postumus, although somewhat medallic in character, cannot be regarded as other than current coins.

[29] G III, tav. 161, nos. 1–5.

(iii) Apart from two barbaric aurei inexplicably included among the gold medallions,[30] Gnecchi classes as medallions a number of third-century aurei the weight of which is slightly higher than the normal, and which, since they show no specifically medallic traits and are not multiples of the unitary standard, should be more accurately described as heavy coins. Such are the gold pieces of Elagabalus weighing under eight grammes,[31] that of Valerian weighing only 5.3 grammes,[32] those of Saloninus,[33] Severina[34] and Tacitus[35] weighing under seven grammes and those of Diocletian weighing less than six grammes.[36]

(iv) In his first and third volumes Gnecchi includes as medallions a number of gift or festival coins, which are, like the double sestertii of Trajan Decius, only outwardly and superficially medallic in character. The bronze, or silvered bronze, quinarii, described by Gnecchi as "modulo minimo" and ranging from the reign of Valerian to that of Diocletian,[37] are, indeed, often distinctively medallic both in content and execution. In the case of the silver miliarensia, first issued by Constantine the Great,[38] the types are either identical, or closely connected, with those of their comparatively rare silver multiples, or money medallions, where such corresponding multiples exist; and while there are many miliarensia for which no corresponding multiples are known and a certain number of multiples for which we have no corresponding miliarensia, such combinations as we do possess definitely suggest that the miliarensia formed part of the same series as the multiples and were issued for the same occasions. But the fact that both quinarii and miliarensia were issued in large quantities as normal denominations indicates that they were distributed *en masse* as actual money gifts, not specially or solemnly presented, after the manner of medallions, as souvenirs to a restricted circle of persons of high status. Thus both have their place inside the ordinary currency. Under the later Empire the distribution of large quantities of cash at festivals and on special occasions, whether as pay for the troops or as doles for the people, came to be one of the normal processes of putting new coinage into circulation; and the true kinship of the quinarii and miliarensia is, not with medallions, but with such series as the Isis-festival coins issued for the imperial vota publica on January 3. These series have been fully discussed elsewhere.[39] Here it is sufficient to note that all such Isis coins are, in a sense, medallic in content, in so far as their types contain references of a highly specialized and restricted kind; while on some individual specimens medallic content is balanced by at least quasi-medallic style.[40]

[30] G I, tav. 2, nos. 1, 5.
[31] G I, tav. 1, no. 8.
[32] G I, p. 6, no. 1. The weight given by Gnecchi (5.6 grammes) is inexact.
[33] G I, p. 8, no. 1.
[34] G I, p. 9, no. 1.
[35] G I, p. 9, no. 1.
[36] G I, tav. 4, no. 11.
[37] G III, pp. 51–86 (*passim*), tavv. 155–158 (*passim*).
[38] G I, pp. 57–84 (*passim*), tavv. 28–37 (*passim*).
[39] A. Alföldi, *A Festival of Isis in Rome under the Christian Emperors of the Fourth Century.*
[40] E. g. *ibid*, pls. 2, nos. 16–21; 19, no. 29.

II. MEDALLIC COINS.

Medallic coins are here defined as coins of normal, or slightly supra-normal, weight and size, showing normal reverse types, but with obverse portraits which are either distinctively medallic in style or struck from definite medallion dies. Such pieces cannot be classed as medallions. They are not, with a very few exceptions, set apart structurally from the regular currency, as are the pseudo medallions, nor are they differentiated from ordinary coins, as are the bronze medallions proper, by medallic style in both obverse and reverse types and by the content of the reverse design. Moreover, such combinations of medallion obverse with coin reverse are extremely spasmodic and rare. In fact, in these isolated instances of medallion obverse dies applied to common coins we seem to encounter genuine "freaks" or, at the most, experiments in imparting to normal pieces a medallic aspect without lifting them out of the category of current coinage of the realm; and the same idea would appear to lie behind coins the obverses of which are executed in true medallion style, but for which specific known medallion dies have not been employed.[41] Two fine examples of Hadrianic medallic coins, one in the Ryan Collection,[42] the other formerly in the Trau Collection,[43] have the regular PAX AVG S C sestertius reverse, while the obverse is struck from a large bronze medallion die.[44] A sestertius of Antoninus Pius in Berlin has the normal Annona reverse of 139,[45] but the obverse is struck from a medallion die used for several large bronze medallions issued during the first year of his principate.[46] A sestertius of Lucius Verus, formerly in the Vierordt Collection, has a fine medallic obverse portrait and a reverse type (CONCORD AVGVSTOR) shared by medallions and coins.[47] Berlin also possesses two small bronze pieces of Gordian III (measuring 28 mm. in diameter and weighing 10.81 and 10.55 grammes respectively) with ordinary reverse types, Apollo seated, with branch and lyre, and Fortuna seated, with legend FORTVNA REDVX S C; on both the obverse portrait, executed in high relief and in medallic style, is struck from a small bronze medallion die of the Emperor.[48] In the Lawrence Collection there is a bi-metallic as of Philip I with obverse struck from a small medallion die[49] and a coin reverse type—Liberalitas standing, with legend LIBERALITAS AVG II S C; the use of two metals shows that this piece was structurally differentiated from a coin and was not struck for ordinary circulation. A series of asses of Aurelian, struck at Milan (?), affords an interesting example of medallic coins with ordinary coin reverse types and obverses which, without being struck from known medallion dies, are quite distinctively medallic in character. These all bear on the obverse a portrait,

[41] E. g. (1) sestertius of Trajan with reverse type of Spes and on the obverse a remarkable deep bust of Trajan in high relief, with upper arm bare and aegis (Strack I, Taf. 7, Nr. 403) (**Pl. XX. 10**); (2) as of Alexander Severus in the Hall Collection, Llanymynech, with reverse legend AEQVITAS and obverse portrait in very high relief.

[42] Diameter = 35 mm., weight = 28.18 grammes.

[43] *Trau Collection Sale Catalogue* 1935, Taf. 17, Nr. 1267. Diameter = 33 mm. (weight not given). **Pl. I, 4.**

[44] G II, tav. 42, nos. 3, 4.

[45] Strack III, Taf. 8, Nr. 751. **Pl. I, 5.**

[46] G II, tavv. 46, no. 8; 48, no. 5; 55, no. 1.

[47] *Vierordt Collection Sale Catalogue* 1923, pl. 38, no. 1675. **Pl. I, 6.**

[48] G III, tav. 153, nos. 13, 15.

[49] G III, tav. 153, no. 16.

not of Aurelian, but of Sol (or Sol-Aurelian?) with the legend SOL DOMINVS IMPERI ROMANI and showing his bust either bare-headed to right[50] or radiate to right, with four horses to right below,[51] or radiate to front, with four horses below, two to right and two to left.[52] The reverses are executed in common coin style: they bear the legend AVRELIANVS AVG CONS (ecravit?) and show the Emperor sacrificing at a tripod, either laureate, wearing military dress and holding a long transverse spear, or veiled and togate and holding either a short sceptre or a scroll. But the high relief of the obverse portrait, and the substitution of the bust and legend of the god for the portrait of the Emperor and the imperial titles, serve to distinguish these pieces from ordinary coins. It is, indeed, hard to decide in the case of this Aurelianic series whether we are dealing with medallic coins or with small bronze medallions proper, commemorating, it would appear, no less momentous an event than the institution of the worship of Sol Invictus as an official cult of the Roman state. The plain coin style of the reverses inclines us, on the whole, to assign them to the former category.[53]

III. BORDER-LINE PIECES.

Since the Roman imperial coinage does not, of its very nature, admit of a precise delimitation of frontier between coin and medallion, we have to reckon with a number of border-line cases, pieces the majority of which, in the present writer's opinion, approach more nearly to medallions than to coins and can with justice be claimed as belonging to the former category, while they remain classifiable as coins from certain points of view. For instance, some Hadrianic and Antonine bronze pieces without S C, classed here as small medallions proper in virtue of the special character of their content and their rarity, combined with a decidedly more, rather than less, medallic style, have been included, on structural grounds, as ordinary sestertii in *The Roman Imperial Coinage* and in the *Catalogue of Coins of the Roman Empire in the British Museum.* The following examples may be cited. The ROMVLO CONDITORI pieces of Hadrian, struck between 134 and 138, are of sestertius weight and display a fairly common aureus and denarius type of that time; but they are known from only two examples, each with a different obverse, are medallic in style on both sides and suggest the application of a regular gold and silver coin type to bronze for the purpose of special presentation.[54] The IOVI/OPTIMO/MAXIMO/S P Q R in the oak-wreath pieces of Hadrian are sestertii as regards diameter and weight; but these again are known from only two specimens, each again with different obverse portraits, and both on obverse and reverse they are quite decisively medallic in style.[55] The S P Q R / AN F F / HADRIANO / AVG P P in an oak-wreath piece in Paris[56]

[50] G III, tav. 156, nos. 3, 4. [51] *RIC* V, i. p. 301, no. 320. **Pl. I, 7.** [52] G III, tav. 156, nos. 5, 6.

[53] The term "medallic coin" is not used here to include that very considerable number of coins the obverse portraits of which, although struck from ordinary coin dies, show specially fine and careful style.

[54] Rome (Gnecchi), Vienna. G III, tav. 145, no. 7. RIC II, p. 439, no. 776 gives a sestertius with this type and S C; but no such sestertius is mentioned by Strack or in *BMCCRE:* the bronze piece mentioned in *BMCCRE* III, p. 442, no. † as being in the Ashmolean Collection is the core of a plated denarius.

[55] Paris, Rome (Gnecchi Collection). G III, tav. 145, nos. 4, 5; *BMCCRE* III, pl. 84, no. 1.

[56] *BMCCRE* III, pl. 84, no. 2. **Pl. I, 8.**

has the weight and diameter of a small sestertius and repeats a type combined with S C on a sestertius in the Ryan Collection;[57] but the Ryan piece has a quite different obverse legend and portrait and is executed in common coin style, whereas the Paris piece is in medallic style and is obviously a smaller edition of the large bronze medallion proper with this type in the Gnecchi Collection in Rome.[58] The Antonine piece, formerly in the Evans, now in the Ryan, Collection with S P Q R / AN F F / OPTIMO / PRINCIPI / PIO in an oak-wreath[59] is again a smaller edition, of sestertius weight and size, of two large medallions proper in Paris (same obverse portrait) and Florence (different obverse portrait) respectively.[60] Finally, the S P Q R / AMPLIA / TORI / CIVIVM in an oak-wreath type of Antoninus Pius is stated to have been "struck certainly as an ordinary sestertius" on the strength of a British Museum cast;[61] but the two other known specimens of this reverse type are large bronze medallions proper.[62]

After Antoninus Pius sestertius-size medallions are rare; while the still smaller bronze medallions are, down to Gallienus, easily distinguishable on the whole from ordinary coins and afford few examples of border-line pieces. But from Gallienus down to the Diocletianic Tetrarchy we are confronted with a number of bronze pieces classifiable, roughly, as asses in size and weight, but of a style and content which suggest that they are "strikes" from small gold and silver medallion dies, issued either as "proofs," or trial pieces, or as presentation pieces for individuals of lower standing than the recipients of the precious metals. A large proportion of these bronze "strikes" belong to the reign of Gallienus himself. The legend VOTIS / DECENNA / LIBVS in a laurel-wreath occurs on the reverse of ordinary asses of the reign; but the type also appears on two medallic bronze pieces, with a different obverse legend from that of the coins, in Rome (Gnecchi Collection) and the British Museum respectively, both of which may well be replicas of a gold original.[63] Two bronze pieces, one in Berlin, the other in the Vatican, struck in honor of the consular procession of January, 264, show a decidedly medallic obverse, a deep bust of the Emperor to left, wearing consular dress, with the legend GALLIENVM AVG SENATVS, while the reverse depicts Gallienus in a slow quadriga to left, holding an eagle-topped sceptre.[64] Paris possesses a bronze "strike" from the small gold medallion, in the same collection, with reverse legend P M TR P II COS III [*sic*] P P and a scene of imperial sacrifice as reverse type.[65] The collections at Vienna and Bologna each possess a bronze "strike" from the dies of a well-known gold medallion with reverse legend VIRT GALLIENI AVG and the type of Hercules standing to front with club, lion's-skin and branch;[66] and there exist a number of similar bronze pieces, distributed over several

[57] *BMCCRE* III, pl. 89, no. 3.

[58] G II, tav. 40, no. 4.

[59] *Evans Collection Sale Catalogue* 1934, pl. 43, no. 1449. **Pl. I, 9.**

[60] G II, tav. 48, no. 4 (Florence medallion quoted (p. 14, no. 44) with wrong obverse).

[61] *RIC* III, p. 119, no. 721.

[62] Paris, Florence. G II, tav. 48, no. 3.

[63] G III, tav. 155, no. 3; *RIC* V, i, pl. 11, no. 168.

[64] G III, p. 55, no. 67; *ZN* 1930, Taf. I, nos. 4, 5 (**Pl. XIV, 5, 6**).

[65] G I, tav. 3, no. 1; R. Mowat, "Contributions à la numismatique de Gallien" (*Recueil de Mémoires publiés par la Société Nationale des Antiquaires de France à l'occasion de son centenaire* 1804–1904, p. 318, pl. 17, nos. 4, 5).

[66] G I, tav. 3, nos. 3, 4.

collections, with the reverse type and legend of FIDES MILITVM,[67] which may possibly be "strikes" from other variants of the known gold medallions with this legend and device.[68] Gnecchi rightly identifies as a bronze "prova" of a lost gold medallion an interesting piece in Rome (Gnecchi Collection) with the obverse legend CONSERVATORI ORBIS and the head of Gallienus, crowned with reeds, to left and on the reverse VBIQVE PAX, with Victory in a swift biga to right.[69] R. Mowat also sees a "strike" from gold dies in the small bronze piece in Vienna with reverse ALACRITATI and Pegasus springing to right and with obverse portrait identical with that on the small gold Hercules medallions, mentioned above.[70] In Vienna, again, we find a bronze copy[71] of the billon medallion OB REDDIT LIBERT;[72] and Berlin possesses a small bronze piece with GERMANICVS MAXIMVS and a trophy between two seated captives on the reverse:[73] this legend and type do not occur elsewhere on the aes of the reign, but are found on antoniniani, and our piece may be a "strike" from the dies of a small billon medallion. Passing on to the Gallic Empire, there is an interesting piece of Tetricus I in Paris,[74] described by A. Blanchet as a copy of a lost gold medallion:[75] the obverse shows a radiate bust of Tetricus to left, holding a richly decorated round shield, while the reverse depicts the Emperor standing to left in pontifical dress, sceptre in hand, and sacrificing over a tripod. Under Probus the FIDES MILITVM type and legend appear again on a number of bronze pieces[76] possibly representing two variants of the extant gold medallion.[77] A fine piece of Probus in Rome (Gnecchi Collection) shows a trophy between two captives on the reverse and on the obverse an indubitably medallic portrait, suggesting a gold medallion as original—a deep radiate bust of the Emperor to left, leading a horse by the bridle and holding a spear and a round, decorated shield.[78]

Under the Diocletianic Tetrarchy our series of bronze "strikes" or copies continues. Diocletian is represented by a piece in the Laffranchi Collection in Milan, well preserved and with a reverse executed in so uncommonly fine a style that it might well be mistaken in reproduction for a gold piece; the reverse bears the legend IOVI CONSERVAT and a complex design—on the right Juppiter standing to left, naked and holding sceptre and thunderbolt, on the left the Emperor standing to right in military dress, sacrificing over a tripod and holding a long sceptre, while Victory stands behind him and places a wreath upon his head.[79] A worn as-size piece of Maximian in Berlin, with a large medallic head of the Emperor, wearing a lion's-skin, on the obverse and on the reverse HERCVLI VICTORI and Hercules seated to front with club, lion's-skin, quiver and bow,[80] may possibly be a "strike" from

[67] G III, tav. 154, no. 18.

[68] G I, tav. 2, nos. 8, 10, 11.

[69] G I, tav. 3, no. 2.

[70] R. Mowat, *op. cit.*, pp. 317, 318, pl. 17, no. 3. **Pl. II, 1.**

[71] Nr. 19981. *ZN* 1930, Taf. 1, Nr. 2 (wrongly described as billon on S. 2, Nr. 4).

[72] G I, tav. 27, no. 5.

[73] Unpublished. **Pl. II, 2.**

[74] No. 78616. **Pl. II, 3.**

[75] *Revue française de numismatique* 1896, p. 231.

[76] G III, tav. 157, nos. 8, 9. An example of this type set in a contemporary frame was seen in trade by the present writer in June, 1939.

[77] G I, tav. 3, no. 17.

[78] G III, tav. 157, no. 11. It is almost impossible to decide whether the pieces figured on tav. 157, nos. 10, 12, 13 are to be regarded as "fine style" asses or as "strikes" from lost gold medallion dies.

[79] G III, tav. 158, no. 8.

[80] G III, tav. 158, no. 20.

gold dies, or, more probably, a small edition of a large bronze medallion proper.[81] Finally, we have a series of five vota publica pieces issued in the names of all four Emperors, each unique and, as a group, outstanding among the common Isis-festival coins to which in content they belong, copies, it may be, of gold pieces struck on the same occasion but for presentation to specially favored persons. The reverses bear the legend VOTA PVBLICA and the type either of Neptune and Isis standing confronted or of Isis and Serapis on board ship; the obverses show deep busts of the Emperors, either radiate, with paludamentum and sceptre or with cuirass, aegis, spear, two javelins and shield, or laureate, with consular dress, branch and scroll.[82]

One of our most difficult border-line problems is presented by a series of bronze pieces of Gallienus, bearing on the obverse the legend GENIVS P R and the radiate head of Gallienus, crowned by a modius, or turret, to right and on the reverse either a large S C in a laurel-wreath[83] or INT / S C / VRB in a laurel-wreath.[84] It has been suggested that these pieces were issued towards the end of Gallienus' reign on his return to Rome from the East, when he was saluted as "Genius Populi Romani," INT VRB standing for "intrat (or "intravit") urbem."[85] The large quantities in which these pieces—especially those with the INT VRB reverse legend—were issued seem to indicate that they were gift sestertii and dupondii, having their place in the regular currency and comparable with the bronze, or silvered bronze, quinarii, the silver miliarensia and the Isis-festival coins. On the other hand, whereas these issues played their part in the state coinage over a period extending for many years, the GENIVS P R pieces were clearly a very special issue struck for one single occasion and commemorating a single event. Moreover, the very peculiar type of obverse, showing the Emperor under the guise of the Genius and without mention of the imperial name and titles, would appear to exclude these pieces from the category of current coins of the realm. Medallic, too, are the high relief of the majority of the obverse portraits and the careful, finished style. All things considered, one might regard the pieces of this series as medallions, issued in unusually large numbers for presentation to a wide range of individuals, perhaps to all court officials, senators and knights, as a personal acknowledgment by the Emperor of the welcome accorded to him on his entry into Rome.

[81] *Cf.* two large bronze medallions with similar reverse type in Rome and Munich respectively (G II, tav. 126, no. 4).

[82] G III, tav. 158, nos. 11 (Diocletian), 24 (wrongly ascribed to Maximian, instead of to Galerius), 30 (Constantius Chlorus); A. Alföldi, *op. cit.*, pl. 1, nos. 1 (Diocletian), 2 (Maximian). *Vide infra* p. 78.

[83] G III, tav. 161, no. 6.

[84] *RIC* V, i. pl. 9, no. 139. **Pl. II, 4.**

[85] *CAH* xii, p. 189; *RM* 1934, S. 90 f. This interpretation of the reverse legend would seem to weight the balance in favor of identifying the object worn on the obverse head as a turret, rather than as a modius. Gallienus enters the city as her protector and is thus symbolically turreted. The object is certainly worn in the position occupied by a modius when affected as head-gear; and it is not the usual mural crown, which encircles the head. On the other hand its details most definitely suggest masonry walls and towers. The only earlier representation of the turreted Genius Populi Romani known to the present writer is that on the Severan Porta Argentariorum at Rome (*PBSR*, Suppl. Paper, 1939, p. 34, fig. 19). The mural crown next appears as an attribute of the Genius Populi Romani on the GENIO POP ROM Gallic coins of Maximian (Maurice I, pl. 2, no. 12).

The large bronze pieces issued under emperors of the fourth century, from Julian onwards, with mint-marks in the exergue, form our last series of bronze border-line cases. The presence of the mint-marks and the style, generally speaking, of many of the reverse designs would justify the classification of such pieces as large coins. On the other hand, the relatively small number of known examples of any given type and the fact that certain of the types themselves, e. g. the Tres Monetae, are regular medallion types, make it also possible to regard them as medallions. Examples of these indeterminate pieces are those with the legends VIRTVS CAESARIS[86] and MONETA AVG[87] of Julian, VICTORIA ROMANORVM,[88] MONETA AVG[89] and VICTORIA AVGVSTI N[90] of Jovian, REPARATIO FEL TEMP of Procopius,[91] RESTITVTOR REIPVBLICAE[92] and MONETA AVGGG[93] of Valentinian I, RESTITVTOR REIPVBLICAE,[94] MONETA AVGG or AVGGG,[95] VRBS ROMA[96] and VICTORIA AVGGG[97] of Valens, and RESTITVTOR REIPVBLICAE,[98] VRBS ROMA[99] and VICTORIA AVGVSTORVM[100] of Gratian. Some of these mint-marked pieces, such as the REPARATIO FEL TEMP / S M K A piece of Procopius at Milan, and the bronze pieces of Julian, Jovian, Valentinian I, Valens and Gratian with the Roman mint-mark, are decidedly more medallic than others; and in view of the close correspondence which we often find in style, content and structure between the pieces which bear mint-marks and others which do not, any kind of hard-and-fast distinction between the former as coins and the latter as medallions would certainly be exposed to criticism as being a conventional and arbitrary one. On the whole it is best to admit that we cannot really decide whether we are dealing here with presentation pieces or with rare and outstanding coins.

As regards the precious metals, there are a number of pieces, both in gold and silver, medallic in style and type and structurally slightly heavier than the contemporary normal coin denominations, which lie on the border-line between coins and medallions. Three silver pieces of Trajan Decius, one weighing 3.9 grammes, with heads of Herennius and Hostilianus on the reverse,[101] the other two weighing 5.2 and 4.5 grammes, with busts of Etruscilla, Herennius and Hostilianus on the reverse,[102] and one piece of Herennius weighing 4 grammes, with a tetrastyle temple as reverse type,[103] all show medallic style; their weight, however, is no criterion, since Decius' antoniniani range from 2.36 to 7.9 grammes.[104] During the latter

[86] G II, tav. 139, no. 10.

[87] G II, tav. 139, no. 7.

[88] Jovian standing to left in military dress, with labarum and Victory (known examples are fairly numerous: e. g. piece in Budapest). **Pl. II, 5.**

[89] G II, tav. 139, nos. 11, 12.

[90] G II, p. 157, no. 4.

[91] G II, tav. 140, no. 6.

[92] *Weber Collection Sale Catalogue* 1909, Taf. 51, Nr. 2723.

[93] Vienna: Nr. 46694.

[94] Valens standing to front in military dress with vexillum and Victory (known examples are fairly numerous).

[95] G II, tav. 140, no. 4.

[96] In Dresden (**Pl. XXXV, 9**).

[97] Victory advancing to left, holding wreath and palm (Padua, Bansa Collection).

[98] G II, p. 158, no. 1 (**Pl. XXXII, 6**).

[99] G II, tav. 140, nos. 7, 8.

[100] G II, tav. 140, no. 9.

[101] G I, tav. 24, no. 10: Rome (Gnecchi).

[102] G I, tav. 24, no. 11: Berlin, Paris.

[103] G I, tav. 24, no. 12: Paris.

[104] *NC* 1939, p. 40 (Dorchester Hoard). Contrast the silver piece of Julia Mamaea with busts of Alexander Severus and Orbiana on the reverse, weighing 5.4 grammes, which seems to be a genuine example of a double denarius or money medallion (G I, tav. 23, no. 5; *vide infra* p. 148).

half of the third century we meet with gold pieces weighing from 7 + to 9 + grammes, that is to say intermediate in weight between a single normal aureus and two aurei, which might be described either as abnormally heavy coins or as small medallions. Such are four pieces of Aurelian with the legends ADVENTVS AVG,[105] VIRTVS AVG[106] and CONCORDIA AVG[107] and fourteen pieces of Probus with the following legends:— ADLOCVTIO AVG,[108] ADVENTVS AVG,[109] HERCVLI HERIMANTHIO,[110] SOLI INVICTO COMITI AVG,[111] FIDES MILITVM,[112] TEMP FELICITAS,[113] ROMAE AETERNAE,[114] SECVRITAS SAECVLI[115] and VICTORIAE AVGVSTI.[116] Of these pieces seven examples (one unverifiable) of the adventus type of Aurelian,[117] two of the adlocutio type of Probus and three of the TEMP FELICITAS type of Probus are recorded by Gnecchi; a fourth example of the last piece is in Copenhagen[118] and four examples of the Sol type of Probus are known to the present writer. But the other eight pieces are each known from only one (now verifiable) specimen. Such rarity, combined with the notably high relief and exquisite technique of the majority of extant specimens, would seem to substantiate quite decisively their claim to be money medallions, struck more or less to the standard of one aureus and a half and precursors of the fourth century series of 1½-solidi medallions inaugurated by Constantine I.

Less certain is the status of a few silver pieces issued in the names of Licinius I, Constantine I, Crispus and Constantine II. These pieces might be reckoned as heavy miliarensia, which we have, as a class, already relegated to the category of current coins. But their outstandingly medallic style, the unusual interest of their content and, in several cases, size and weight somewhat exceeding that of the average heavy miliarensia, all produce the impression that they were special issues, struck, perhaps, as multiples of siliquae, set apart from the common coinage for some special purpose.[119] One reverse type, common to all four imperial persons, was struck in commemoration of the vicennalia of Constantine I, celebrated from 325 to 326. It bears the circumference legend VOTA ORBIS ET VRBIS SEN ET P R and shows a circular cippus (or milestone?) set on a square basis. The pieces of Constantine I[120] and Constantine II[121] have XX / XXX / AVG inscribed on the cippus and a star in the field on either side of it; those of Licinius I[122] and Crispus[123] have XX / XXX / MVL / FEL inscribed on the cippus and an L in the field to the left of it, while a kind of fire, or flaming brazier, rests on the top of the cippus. The obverse portraits

[105] G I, tav. 3, nos. 9, 10, 11.
[106] G I, tav. 3, no. 13.
[107] G I, tav. 3, no. 12.
[108] G I, tav. 3, no. 16.
[109] Gotha: Probus on horseback to left. Pl. II, 6.
[110] G I, tav. 4, no. 1.
[111] Variant (1) in Berlin, B. M. and formerly in the Weber Collection (*Weber Collection Sale Catalogue* 1909, Taf. 40, Nr. 2414). (2) Variant in Jameson Collection, Paris (*Jameson Collection Catalogue* III, pl. 22, no. 467). Pl. II, 7, 8.
[112] G I, tav. 3, no. 17.
[113] G I, tav. 4, no. 2; p. 10, no. 7 (formerly in Paris). Pl. II, 9.
[114] Vienna. Pl. II, 10.
[115] G I, p. 10, no. 5.
[116] G I, tav. 4, no. 3.
[117] Pl. XLVII, 2.
[118] Ramus Cat. No. 282A. Pl. II, 11.
[119] These pieces were, moreover, with one possible exception, all struck before the regular issue of heavy miliarensia began *c.* 330 (*vide infra* p. 168).
[120] G I, tav. 29, no. 5.
[121] Ulrich-Bansa, *Note sulla zeccha di Aquileia romana*, tav. 2, no. 11. Pl. II, 12.
[122] G I, tav. 28, no. 8.
[123] Ulrich-Bansa, *op. cit.*, tav. 2, no. 10. Pl. II, 13.

are all distinctive. Those of Licinius I and Constantine I show the bust of the Emperor to left, wearing an elaborate crested helmet and cuirass and holding a spear and round shield; but there is also a variant of Constantine I with obverse bust radiate to left, wearing a cuirass and holding a spear.[124] The busts of Crispus and Constantine II are shown radiate to left, wearing paludamentum and cuirass, with a globe held in the left hand and the right hand raised. All specimens so far known bear the mint-mark of Aquileia, with the exception of a variant of Crispus which was struck at Siscia and shows two stars, instead of an L, in the field of the reverse.[125] Each type or variant is known from one example only. The pieces vary in diameter from 25 mm. to 27 mm. and in weight from 4.95 grammes to 6.32 grammes, but were originally heavier, as all are pierced by a hole. Another remarkable silver piece of Constantine I, known from two examples in Vienna (24 mm., 5.56 grammes, pierced by a hole) and Leningrad (24 mm., 6.65 grammes) respectively,[126] shows on the obverse the bust of the Emperor seen almost full-face, wearing a crested helmet, holding a horse by the bridle and carrying sceptre and round shield.[127] The reveıse contains a complicated design—the Emperor, accompanied by his Praetorian Prefect, standing on a platform between two signa and addressing a crowd of soldiers, accompanied by horses, below. A fine piece of Crispus in Berlin, found at Cologne, has on the obverse an exceptionally deep bust of the prince, wearing paludamentum and cuirass and holding a spear and a globe surmounted by a Victory; the reverse bears the legend MONETA AVGG ET CAESS NN and the type of the Tres Monetae.[128] The piece was struck at Aquileia and may have been presented to Crispus on the occasion of a visit to the local mint (in 321?).[128a] It measures 25 mm. in diameter, weighs 6.54 grammes and is pierced by a hole. The obverse shows a remarkably close resemblance to that of a large gold medallion of Licinius II in Paris, also struck at Aquileia.[129] Lastly, there is a piece of Constantine II in Vienna, struck in Rome, with an ordinary obverse portrait and a reverse type—three signa—which appears not infrequently upon normal miliarensia of the later Emperors.[130] But the execution is particularly careful, the diameter measures 26 mm. and the weight, 6.04 grammes, is, in view of the fact that the flan is pierced by a hole, exceptionally high. After Constantine II these outstanding pieces no longer occur; and we may regard them as experiments made in the early days after the new denominations were introduced.[131]

[124] *Ibid.*, tav. 2, no. 8. **Pl. II, 14.**

[125] Found at Aquileia and now in the local museum.

[126] G I, tav. 29, no. 3; *ZN* 1930, Taf. 3, Nr. 18.

[127] *Vide infra* pp. 177, 211. Alföldi (*Pisciculi Franz Joseph Dölger dargeboten*, 1939, S. 4 ff.) dates this piece to *c*. 315.

[128] G I, tav. 29, no. 11.

[128a] *Cf*. Ulrich-Bansa, *op. cit.*, p. 21.

[129] G I, tav. 6, no. 6 (**Pl. XLVIII, 5**). Also struck in 321, for Licinius II's quinquennalia? *Cf*. Ulrich-Bansa, *op. cit.*, pp. 19 f.

[130] G I, tav. 29, no. 15. An allusion to the Sarmatian victories of 332?

[131] It is possible that we should also include in this series a piece of Constantine I in Rome (Gnecchi) with VOTIS / XXX in a laurel-wreath as reverse type (G I, tav. 29, no. 7). It is 23 mm. in diameter and weighs 5.8 grammes, but the original weight must have been over 6 grammes as a portion of the flan has been broken away. Both obverse and reverse types are identical with those of a "Fest-aureus" of Constantine I (*vide infra* p. 40) note 139.

Our final group of border-line cases consists of a series of gold pieces ranging in date from the time of Constantine I to that of Arcadius, weighing 5+ grammes, that is to say, struck, not on the standard of the contemporary solidus of one seventy-second of a pound, but on the basis of the old Diocletianic aureus of one sixtieth of a pound. Being only slightly larger and heavier than the normal solidi these pieces obviously could, and no doubt did, pass into use as current money. But this revival of an obsolete coin standard can only mean that, at the time of their issue, they were deliberately differentiated from the ordinary currency to serve a particular end. Content, style and rarity all point to the same conclusion. Of the forty specimens known to the present writer, thirty-one display reverse designs of a type which proves beyond question that they were intended for "Fest-aurei," commemorative pieces distributed as presents on special occasions. Fifteen of these pieces—six of Constantine I,[132] four of Constantius II,[133] one of Constans,[134] one of Valentinian I,[135] two of Valentinian II[136] and one of Eugenius[137]—show the Emperor standing in a frontal chariot holding in his left hand a sceptre (or, in one case, that of Valentinian I, a globe surmounted by a Victory) and with his right hand either raised in greeting (as on three of the six specimens of Constantine I) or scattering a shower of coins. The occasion must, in this case, have been an imperial largitio and the "Fest-aurei" presents for certain favored individuals in memory of the event. Again, sixteen pieces allude in various ways to imperial vota, occasions which were, as we shall see later, prolific in the issue both of gold and silver money medallions and, to a lesser extent, of bronze medallions proper.[138] Nine specimens show vota inscriptions in a wreath;[139] four show one Victory,[140] two show two Victories,[141] holding up a wreath encircling a vota inscription; while one shows three Emperors enthroned to front with VOT V inscribed upon the central Emperor's footstool.[142] The other nine pieces have less distinctively "occasional" types. Three of Constantius II show the Emperor walking to the right and holding a spear and a trophy, while a captive is seated on either side of him.[143] Two pieces,

[132] Rome: 1, Copenhagen: 1, Turin, Mazzini Collection: 1, Vienna: 3. The Copenhagen piece weighs only 4.93 grammes, but this must be due to wear. G I, tav. 8, nos. 7, 9; Kubitschek Taf. 14, Nrr. 251, 252 (mint-mark CONS). **Pl. II, 15, 16.**

[133] Paris (no. 43): 1, Paris, Jameson Collection: 1, B. M. (mint-mark SMANT): 1, Leningrad (mint-mark SMANT): 1. *Jameson Collection Catalogue* IV, pl. 26, no. 534. **Pl. II, 17.**

[134] Paris no. 1574. Maurice I, pl. 15, no. 4. **Pl. III, 1.**

[135] B. M. **Pl. III, 2.**

[136] Formerly Paris: 1, formerly Trau Collection: 1. *Trau Collection Sale Catalogue* 1935, Taf. 52, Nr. 4572. **Pl. III, 3.**

[137] *NZ* 1936, S. 36. Seen at a Yugoslav dealer's in 1936.

[138] *Vide infra* pp. 79 ff.

[139] Constantine I: 7 (VOTIS / XXX in wreath: G III, tav. di. suppl. no. 11; *Trau Collection Sale Catalogue* 1935, Taf. 44, Nr. 3889. **Pl. III, 4.**); Constantine II: 1 (VOTIS / X in wreath: Vienna; Kubitschek Taf. 15, Nr. 273. **Pl. III, 5.**); Magnentius: 1 (VOT / V / MVLT / X in wreath: Vienna: G I, tav. 14, no. 3).

[140] Constantine I: 3 (B. M. Vienna, formerly in Trau Collection: G I, tav. 8, no. 5); Constans: 1 (Paris, Beistegui Collection: J. Babelon, *La collection de monnaies et médailles de M. Carlos de Beistegui*, pl. 13, no. 236. **Pl. III, 6.**).

[141] Constantius II: 1 (B. M.: G I, p. 32, no. 42); Constans: 1 (Paris: G I, tav. 10, no. 1).

[142] Constans (Paris, Jameson Collection: *Jameson Collection Catalogue* III, pl. 23, no. 482. **Pl. III, 7.**).

[143] One in Vienna and two formerly in Paris: G I, p. 33, nos. 49, 50 (*RN* 1906, pl. 9, no. 16).

one of Gratian[144] and the other of Arcadius,[145] show a Victory advancing towards the left and holding a wreath and a palm. The remaining four are unique specimens—Sol standing to left,[146] Sol crowning the Emperor,[147] Victoria and Libertas[148] and the Emperor standing, holding a labarum and a globe surmounted by Victory and spurning a captive with his foot.[149] Thus content, style and, in some cases, rarity combine with abnormal weight to push this group of "Fest-aurei" more than half over the border-line onto the side of medallions.

[144] Vienna. **Pl. III, 8.**

[145] Tolstoi, *Monnaies byzantines*, pl. 1, no. 2. **Pl. III, 9.**

[146] Constantine I (Vienna: G I, tav. 8, no. 2).

[147] Constantine II (Paris: G I, tav. 9, no. 5. The diameter of this piece (22 mm.) is that of a "Fest-aureus" and the weight (7.63 grammes), were the ring subtracted, would be 5 + grammes).

[148] Magnentius (*Münzhandlung Basel Sale Catalogue* March 18, 1936, Taf. 26, Nr. 2041 (**Pl. VI, 7**)).

[149] Valens (Gotha). **Pl. III, 10.**

PART II

MINTS AND PROVENANCES

CHAPTER I

MINTS

Roman medallions, being public and official issues controlled by the state, have, as we should expect, the same mint history, generally speaking, as the regular coinage. After the death of Commodus Rome lost that undisputed monopoly of the strictly imperial currency which had been hers since Flavian times; and during the first half of the third century provincial mints were striking, almost exclusively in the precious metals, at Lugdunum, Antioch, Alexandria, Laodicea ad Mare, Emesa (?), Nicomedia and Viminacium (?).[1] But emergency, or at least political convenience, were still regarded as the *raison d'être* of such provincial mintings; Rome still remained the mint *par excellence* for imperial aes; and from Domitian down to Gallienus medallions, in their capacity as presentation pieces for special or solemn occasions, whether bronze medallions proper, large or small, or money medallions,[2] were normally issued from the centre of the Empire, at the Roman mint. Thus for the first two and a half centuries of imperial history Rome is the only mint-city with which the student of medallions is concerned. How was the Roman mint organized and by what authorities was it controlled? Such questions have, obviously, an immediate bearing upon our subject, particularly upon that well-known characteristic of the vast majority of bronze medallions proper, to which we have already referred,[3] namely the absence of the letters S C from their reverses. We have now to consider what the presence of these letters, and, conversely, their absence, really signify. According to the most familiar, and hitherto most widely accepted, view,[4] the imperial coinage was, until the time of Gallienus, controlled by a "dyarchy" of Senate and Emperor, the former having authority over the main bulk of the aes, while the latter had, after 12 B. C., the exclusive right of coining in the precious metals: this duality of control implied a duality of mints : the senatorial mint continued, until the middle of the third century, to function in the temple of Juno Moneta on the Capitol, as under the Republic, now issuing only aes stamped with S C as the mark of the Senate's authority; and Gaius, when he transferred the minting of imperial gold and silver from Lugdunum to Rome, set up in some other quarter of the city an imperial mint, directed from Trajan's time, at least, by a procurator monetae,[5] which issued, in addition to gold and silver, imperial aes without the letters S C. On this view the presence or absence of S C on a bronze piece is equivalent to a mint-mark, denoting senatorial mint in the one

[1] *RIC* I, pp. 7 f.; IV, i, p. 64; K. Pink, "The Mints of the Roman Empire" (*Trans. Internat. Num. Congr.* 1936, pp. 241 f.).

[2] The two gold money medallions of Augustus—the 4-aurei piece from Pompeii at Naples (G I, tav. 1, no. 1) and the much disputed 4-aurei piece at Este, said to have been found at Este in 1925 (S. L. Cesano, *Numismatica augustea*, 1937, pp. 32 ff., tav. 5, nos. 1, 2)—were presumably struck at Lugdunum.

[3] *Vide supra* p. 20. [4] *RIC* I, p. 16; Mattingly, *op. cit.*, pp. 131 f. [5] *ILS*, I, 1352.

case, imperial mint in the other. P. L. Strack, while maintaining the theory of dual control as reflected, so he believes, in the Senate's "Selbständigkeit" in the choice of types,[6] inclines to deny the duality of mints, not only for Trajan's day, but also for earlier imperial times: until *c.* A. D. 80 both the senatorial and imperial officinae were housed on the Capitol, after that date in the Moneta Caesaris situated in the third region on the Via Labicana.[7] On Strack's view the presence or absence of S C denotes, not mints, but officinae, senatorial on the one hand as opposed to imperial on the other. If the above views be accepted, it follows that the bronze medallions proper were, with the exception of the few pieces marked S C, issued by an imperial minting authority quite distinct from the senatorial minting authority which controlled the regular aes coinage, the two authorities being at all events mutually independent and perhaps working through organizations housed under different roofs. Such theories of two separate mints and of dual control can, obviously, tend to an indiscriminate grouping together of all non- S C pieces, either as medallions, with Gnecchi, or, with Strack as "kaiserliche Bronze." The problem of the Roman mint is thus not without importance for the general question of defining the relation of medallions to the other aes issues.

On the other hand, the results of recent research are all in favor of the probability that from the earliest days of the Principate the city of Rome knew but one mint and one single minting authority, that of the Princeps himself.[8] It will be generally admitted that Augustus' express anxiety to preserve republican forms was, in fact, exactly proportionate to his actual possession, and exercise, of an all-embracing personal authority superior to that of all others, described by himself as "auctoritas."[9] The notion that he could, in any real sense, have "renounced" or "resigned" to the Senate an aes currency which, with the exception of the smallest denomination, the quadrans, bore his image and superscription or, at the least, some definite reference to his personal achievements, harmonizes ill with what we know of his position and of his sense of the propaganda value of the coinage. We can gauge the conventional nature of the appearance of moneyers' names (III VIRI A A A F F) on the early Roman gold and silver coinage issued between 19 and 12 B. C., and on the Roman aes issued between 23 and 4 B. C., from the fact that these issues were suspended during Augustus' absences from Rome in 20 to 19 and 15 to 14[10] and that after 4 (or 7?) B. C.[11] these names quietly disappear forever from the coinage of the Roman state, although it is known from inscriptions that the officials themselves existed until as late as the third century. But we have no evidence

[6] Strack I, S. 5. This view is still maintained (unconvincingly, in the present writer's opinion) in Strack's third volume, SS. 25 ff., 40 ff.

[7] Strack I, S. 7, Anm. 16; Platner & Ashby, *A Topographical Dictionary of Ancient Rome*, pp. 345 f.; G. Lugli, *I monumenti antichi di Roma e suburbio* III: *a traverso le regioni*, p. 389. It is certainly improbable that Gaius, when he closed the imperial mint at Lugdunum, so scrupulously respected republican susceptibilities as to open a new establishment in another part of Rome if the officinae for gold and silver coinage could be conveniently housed in the existing mint on the Capitol.

[8] *Cf.* K. Pink, *Klio* 1936, S. 223 and in a personal letter to the present writer "ich bin überzeugt. dass es nur ein Münzamt gab, dass es ganz unter Kaiserlichen Einfluss stand."

[9] *Res Gestae* 34. [10] *BMCCRE* I, p. xcvi. [11] *Ibid.* I, p. xcviii.

that their duties were more than nominal or, at the most, trivial or implied in any way the existence throughout this period of a separate senatorial mint. Certainly in Trajan's time, possibly earlier, the task of providing a due supply of suitable metals, of aes as well as of silver and gold, was assigned to an imperial freedman—optio et exactor auri argenti aeris.[12] As for the senatorial formula S C upon the aes, impressive as it may seem at first sight, it constitutes no conclusive argument for an independent senatorial mint in Rome or for an independent senatorial mint control. That it had, indeed, no essential or exclusive connection with the Roman mint has been proved by a recent study of the official Augustan coinage of the East.[13] There S C occurs on several varieties of official currency struck at various mints in Syria, in Cyprus and possibly in Asia; it is shown to be parallel to the formula C A, interpreted as "Caesaris auctoritate," which appears on official currencies of Asian, Cypriot and Syrian mintage; and the conclusion is drawn that S C stands for the senatusconsulta, valid all over the Empire, which immediately sanctioned the coinage but which were passed in the first instance on Augustus' motion (Caesaris auctoritate), his authority to make such motions being the ius senatus consulendi inherent in his tribunicia potestas and the ius relationis specially conferred. Thus S C is no senatorial mint-mark; nor does it denote independent senatorial management of the aes coinage either in Rome or in the provinces. There was no dyarchy; the aes, no less than the gold and silver, was under the ultimate control of the Princeps' auctoritas. But in so far as the senatusconsultum was part of the machinery employed for the production of aes the formula expresses a real cooperation in this department of Senate with Princeps:[14] and in the Augustan period, at any rate, it can hardly be described as "a mere sign without legal importance"[15] or as a fiction of Augustan ideology.[16] Passing on into post-Augustan times, the absence of S C on the adlocutio coins of Gaius, the issue, that is to say, of these pieces without the intervention of a senatusconsultum, can, as we saw,[17] be readily explained. The presence of the indirect formula EX S C on the early gold and silver of Nero's reign suggests a desire to preserve the tradition of senatorial collaboration in the coinage at a time when no aes was issuing from the Roman mint. But as regards Nero's parallel issues of S C and non- S C aes, it is less easy to see why a formal senatusconsultum should have been passed in the one case and not in the other; while the S C on the African coinage of Clodius Macer, "nominally a friend of the constitution, in fact a brigand and pirate,"[18] has, of course, a purely fictitious and unblushingly propagandist significance. It is interesting to speculate how far S C on the aes from the Flavian period onwards really denoted the actual

[12] *ILS* I, 1634, 1635. [13] In a forthcoming work by M. Grant of Trinity College, Cambridge.

[14] Cf. Regling *s. v.* S C in Schrötter's *Wörterbuch der Münzkunde*:—"Von einer förmlichen Dyarchie von Kaiser und Senat im M.-Wesen. . . keine Rede ist . . . Es handelt sich vielmehr nur um eine Mitwirkung des Senates, deren Art sehr mannigfaltig gewesen sein kann." The Senate *arranged for* the striking of the aes.

[15] K. Pink, *Trans. Internat. Num. Congr.* 1936, p. 240.

[16] K. Pink, *Klio* 1936, S. 226 f.:—"Der Sinn dieser Formel, die für die ideologie des Augustus typisch ist, ist m. E. nur fiktiv, eine Art Idealprägerecht des Senats, praktisch gleich Null, wenn ein starker Herrscher regierte." [17] *Vide supra* p. 28. [18] *RIC* I, p. 193.

passing of a senatusconsultum for every issue or whether it had become merely polite and conventional. Medallions may throw some light upon this problem. It is perfectly obvious why S C should be normally absent from presentation pieces, standing outside the regular currencies and endowed with a special character as personal gifts from the Emperor to individuals. A senatusconsultum was clearly out of the question there; and it is difficult to believe that a senatusconsultum should have been specially invoked for striking the rare, but true, medallions with S C on their reverses, in particular, the small S C pieces of the third century, indistinguishable in style and content from the parallel pieces without that formula. If, however, by the second and third centuries the letters survived on the ordinary aes currency as a tradition, no longer necessarily implying an actual legal enactment, we can understand how they could occasionally appear on gift pieces not originally intended for regular circulation. Similarly, the continuance into the second and third centuries of pseudo medallions, issued as occasional presentation pieces along with the great series of medallions proper, is more easily explicable if the senatorial formula on their reverses had by then largely lost its original connotation and become, to some extent, at any rate, a symbol.

We may conclude that until the middle of the third century true bronze medallions, money medallions and pseudo medallions were all alike the product of a single Roman mint under imperial control; that the medallions proper almost undoubtedly, the gold and silver multiples very probably, were struck in special officinae of their own, but beneath the same roof as the regular coinage, with obverse portraits and reverse designs deliberately planned in association with the ordinary coin types so as not to overlap, as a general rule, with the latter, but to display a distinctive style and content consonant with their distinctive role; and that the structural continuity of true medallions with first-century pseudo medallions implies an unbroken medallic tradition in the Roman imperial mint from its earliest years.[19]

With the reign of Gallienus we reach a turning-point in the mint history of Roman medallions, which were issued henceforth not only in Rome but at the new imperial mints now officially established in Italy and in the provinces. For medallions and coins alike specimen portraits of the Emperors, and even models or sketches of reverse types, may well have been supplied to the provincial mints from Rome. But the marked variations in style and in details, particularly clear in the case of medallions, leave little room for doubt that the actual dies were cut locally and reflect the taste and mannerisms of local schools. Gold money medallions are generally mint-marked from the time of Diocletian, occasionally earlier, and from Constantine I onwards the silver is mint-marked as well. Very rarely we encounter mint-marks on aes. But the gold and silver medallions of Gallienus, most of the gold medallions of his successors down to Diocletian and the vast bulk of the bronze medallions from those of Gallienus to the end of the series must be assigned to their mints on grounds of style and content alone. Such attributions are always difficult to make and are often admittedly uncertain. Each unmarked type must be

[19] *Cf. BMCCRE* IV, pp. xvii f.

treated individually and attributed by means of a careful study of established coin mint styles. Here we must be content with some illustrations of the methods employed in attributing unmarked medallions and with a brief survey of medallion mints as the mint-marks have revealed them to us.

None of the medallions of Gallienus bear mint-marks. Many of his bronze pieces would appear to have been issued at the Roman mint; but a fair proportion of the gold and silver and a few of the aes medallions can be attributed, on the grounds of their portrait style, to the two other central mints of the Empire—Milan and Siscia. We may illustrate this process by a few examples. The bare bust, cut in a slight curve at the base and coming down to a sharp point in front, which is characteristic of Gallienus' Milanese portraits,[20] appears on his gold medallions with Hercules standing to left (VIRT GALLIENI AVG)[21] and on small bronze pieces with the same reverse type, on his two gold pieces with a scene of imperial sacrifice on their reverses (P M TR P II COS/III [*sic*] P P[22] and P M TR P VIII COS IIII P P)[23] and on the Beistegui gold medallion with the reverse type GALLIE/NVS AVG OB/FIDEM RE/SERVATAM in a laurel-wreath.[24] This portrait type shows a square jaw, a slightly upward glance and upward tilt of the head, a thick, somewhat protruding "thatch" of curling locks above the brow, short, neat curling locks on the nape of the neck and a light beard, forming a roughly diagonal line from ear to chin and spreading a short way down the neck under the chin. Thus, on the strength of its portrait, with its square jaw, upward glance and upward tilt of the head and its similarly treated hair and beard, we may assign to the Milanese mint the fine silver medallion at Milan with adlocutio reverse type and the Emperor wearing taenia only on the obverse.[25] So, too, we may ascribe to the mint of Milan, in view of their portraits with square jaw and similar hair and beard, two small bronze medallions, one with reverse type of Diana running to the right (DIANA FELIX),[26] the other with reverse type of Victory, with wings outspread, seen from the front and holding a garland in both hands (VICTORIA AVGG/ƧƆ):[27] both of these pieces have identical obverse busts. Again, as regards Siscia, we can with some confidence attribute to her mint, on grounds of subject-matter, a large silver medallion in Paris showing on its reverse (FIDES EXERCITVS) the Emperor standing with Victory and Virtus (?) between two river-deities who, in this Gallienic context, can be none other than the two Pannonian rivers, the Save and the Drave, or, perhaps, the Save and the Colapis, at the junction of which Siscia stood.[28] From this piece, and from a better-preserved bronze medallion in Berlin with identical obverse and of unmistakably identical mintage, but combined with a different reverse (XX COS . . . MARINIANO),[29] we can

[20] This is proved by the billon coinage with this type of bust and the mint-marks MP, MS, MT.

[21] G I, tav. 3, nos. 3, 4.

[22] G I, tav. 3, no. 1.

[23] R. Mowat, *op. cit.*, pl. 17, no. 2. **Pl. III, 11.**

[24] J. Babelon, *op. cit.*, pl. 12, no. 229. **Pl. III, 12.**

[25] G I, tav. 26, no. 7 (**Pl. XLVI, 4**).

[26] G III, tav. 154, no. 14.

[27] *Trans. Internat. Num. Congr.* 1936, pl. 16, no. 10. **Pl. III, 13.**

[28] G I, tav. 26, no. 8; Alföldi, *NK* 1927–28, p. 47, no. 2, pl. 5, nos. 27, 28; but see Alföldi *ZN* 1927, S. 202, Anm. 1.

[29] G II, tav. 113, no. 10; but see Alföldi, *op. cit.*, S. 202, where this piece is ascribed to Milan.

establish the well-marked characteristics of a medallion portrait style of Gallienus ascribable, at least, to Siscia. These characteristics—a laurel-wreath with particularly long, spiky leaves, long, straight parallel locks of hair above the brow, long, heavy locks on the nape of the neck and a heavy, square-shaped beard covering a large part of the cheek and the side of the neck[30]—likewise occur on silver medallions with Pax seated to left (PAX AVG), one piece with cuirassed bust,[31] three with bare bust cut at the base in a scalloped line with two indentations, one of them deep, and with one taenia-end straying across it.[32] This last type of bust would appear to be a regular Siscian (?) feature, for we also find it on several pieces combined with the other characteristics attributable to that mint, for example, on the silver VBERITAS AVG medallion in Paris,[33] on the gold "Tres Monetae" medallion in the British Museum[34] and on a small gold piece, also in the British Museum, with FIDES/MILI/TVM in a laurel-wreath.[35]

The medallions of the Gallic Emperors—Postumus, Victorinus, Tetricus I and Tetricus II—were, obviously, issued at the Gallic mints of Lugdunum and Cologne. No mint-marked medallions occur for Claudius Gothicus, Aurelian, Tacitus and Florian. Most of the bronze medallions of Claudius, Tacitus and Florian appear to have been struck in Rome. Of the small gold medallions of Aurelian some, with obverse portrait showing a large head and radiate crown and reverse ADVENTVS AVG,[36] may be attributed to the Roman mint. The piece showing Mars (VIRTVS AVG)[37] may have been struck at Lugdunum;[38] and with this piece, in view of its portrait style, goes the large bronze medallion with Sol in quadriga (SOLI INVICTO), which has, indeed, the appearance of being a bronze "strike" from the dies of a lost gold piece.[39] The small gold piece with Concordia seated (CONCORDIA AVG)[40] suggests Siscian mintage.[41]

It is with Probus that we first encounter mint-marks on medallions, on seven gold and three bronze pieces, all of Siscia. The interesting antoninianus reverse type with the legend SISCIA PROBI AVG and Siscia seated between two river-deities, the Save and the Colapis,[42] seems to indicate a special tie between the Pannonian mint-city and the Pannonian Emperor, native of Sirmium; and in view of the fact that Siscia is the only mint mentioned on medallions dating from Probus to the accession of Diocletian, it has been suggested that there was a special medallion *atelier* at Siscia during this period.[43] As for unmarked small gold pieces, three may

[30] Alföldi, however, attributes the portraits with these characteristics to the mint of Cologne (*JRS* 30, 1940, pp. 1 ff.).
[31] G II, tav. 114, no. 6.
[32] G II, tav. 114, nos. 7, 8.
[33] G I, tav. 27, no. 6.
[34] G I, tav. 2, no. 12. *Cf.* bronze examples of the same medallion (G II, tav. 114, no. 2).
[35] G I, p. 7, no. 8 (**Pl. XIX, 2**).
[36] G I, tav. 3, nos. 9, 10, 11.
[37] G I, tav. 3, no. 13.
[38] *Cf.* portrait of *RIC* V, i, pl. 8, no. 133, attributed on p. 265, no. 1 to Lugdunum.
[39] G II, tav. 117, nos. 9, 10.
[40] G I, tav. 3, no. 12.
[41] *Cf.* portrait of *RIC* V, i, pl. 7, no. 98, attributed on p. 288, no. 216 to Siscia.
[42] *RIC* V, ii, pl. 3, no. 7.
[43] B. Horvat, *Numismatika* 1933, p. 22. Examples of mint-marked gold pieces of Probus are:—G I, tav. 4, nos. 2, 3; *RIC* V, ii, p. 80, no. 594, *cf.* pl. 3, no. 11; Rome seated (ROMAE AETERNAE) in Vienna (not in Cohen or Gnecchi) (**Pl. II, 10**). Bronze pieces are:—G II, tav. 121, no. 10; III, tavv. 156, no. 19; 157, no. 3.

be ascribed on the ground of their portrait style to the Siscian mint;[44] two show the same style as coins ascribed to the mint of Serdica;[45] and one shows the style and short form of obverse legend (IMP PROBVS AVG) usually associated with Probus' Roman mintage.[46] Of his large bronze medallions many were doubtless struck in Rome, while the style of some suggests Siscia. For Carus and his family we have only one mint-marked medallion, a large gold piece of Carus and Carinus struck at Siscia.[47] Some of the unmarked gold medallions of their time may be of Siscian mintage: many of the large bronze pieces were probably issued in Rome.[47a]

With the accession of Diocletian the mint-marking of gold medallions becomes for the first time not the exception but the general rule. Of the ten gold medallions of Diocletian known to the present writer eight bear mint-marks—one of Alexandria (ALE •), one of Antioch (SMA), one of Nicomedia (SMN),[48] one of Rome (PR), two of Ticinum (SMT) and two of Trier (PTR). The two remaining pieces[49] may be assigned on grounds of portrait style to the mints of Rome[50] and Cyzicus[51] respectively. Of Diocletian's bronze medallions three are mint-marked; they were respectively struck at Siscia (SIS),[52] Cyzicus (SC)[53] and, probably, in Rome (P]ROM).[54] From the general similarity of their portraits to that of the gold medallion with the mint-mark of Rome,[55] we should ascribe the great majority of his unmarked bronze medallions to Roman mintage, including those with the remarkable large bare head of the Emperor,[56] similar in type to, but different in style from, that on the large gold medallions of Alexandrian[57] and Nicomedian[58] mintage and on the smaller gold medallion of Ticinum.[59]

Of the four extant gold medallions of Diocletian and Maximian two are mint-marked. These have laureate and draped busts of the two Emperors on their obverse and on their reverse the legend IOVIO ET HERCVLIO and the two Emperors sacrificing over a tripod, above which, in the background, are small figures of Juppiter and Hercules, standing side by side upon a platform. One bears the mint-mark SMVR (Rome),[60] the other the mint-mark SMT (Ticinum).[61] The two famous pieces in Florence and Berlin respectively, with Diocletian and Maximian in an

[44] G I, tavv. 3, no. 16; 4, no. 1; ADVENTVS AVG in Gotha (not in Cohen or Gnecchi) (**Pl. II, 6**).

[45] *Jameson Collection Catalogue* III, pl. 22, no. 467 (**Pl. II, 7**); G I, tav. 3, no. 17.

[46] E.g. B.M. piece (**Pl. II, 8**)

[47] G I, tav. 4, no. 8 (**Pl. XLVII, 7**).

[48] **Pl. XLVIII, 1.**

[47a] The letters SC in the exergue of the bronze consular medallions of Numerianus and Carinus (G III, tav. 161, nos. 9, 10) may be the mint-mark of Cyzicus (*vide infra* line 16 and p. 87).

[49] *Aréthuse*, Jan. 1924, pl. 8, no. 3 (Arras) (**Pl. VIII, 1**); G I, tav. 4, no. 15.

[50] *Cf.* G I, tav. 4, no. 14 (PERPETVA FELICITAS AVGG / PR).

[51] *Cf.* aureus of Cyzicus with legend FATIS VICTRICIBVS / SC (*RIC* V, ii, pl. 12, no. 7).

[52] G II, tav. 125, no. 10.

[53] *Evans Collection Sale Catalogue* 1934, pl. 58, no. 1825. **Pl. III, 14.**

[54] G II, tav. 124, no. 1. This reading, which is Cohen's, seems much more probable than Gnecchi's AQS (= Aquileia). The letters of the mint-mark in the exergue of this piece are partly obliterated.

[55] *Vide supra* n. 50.

[56] G II, tav. 124, nos. 2, 6.

[57] G I, tav. 4, no. 12.

[58] G I, tav. 4, no. 13 (**Pl. XLVIII, 1**).

[59] G I, tav. 4, no. 10.

[60] Examples at Trier (*NZ* 1931, Taf. 1, Nr. 2) and formerly in Paris (cast in Berlin). **Pl. III, 15, 16.**

[61] Example formerly in Paris (cast in Berlin). **Pl. IV, 1.** In the possession of the Rev. E. S. Rogers there is a bronze piece with this type, but on a slightly larger scale, probably a "strike" from the dies of a gold medallion. In the exergue on its reverse there is a mint-mark, which may be SMT, but the letters are very uncertain. **Pl. IV, 2.**

elephant-quadriga to front, bear no mint-marks.[62] But they can be attributed with confidence to the mint of Rome on the score of the elephants, which are accurately and naturalistically rendered by an artist who must have been in a position to observe the animals at first hand in the Roman circus; they present a marked contrast to the comical, man-faced creatures on the Stockholm 4½-solidi piece of Constantine I and on the two 2-solidi pieces of Constantius II as Caesar, all struck at Trier in 326 and obviously designed by an artist to whom fate had denied opportunities for the study of elephants.[63] The MONETA AVGG and MONETA IOVI ET HERCVLI AVGG bronze medallions of the two Emperors were probably struck in Rome. But we may, with Horvat, assign to Siscian mintage a large bronze piece found at Siscia in the river Colapis, with reverse VICTORIAE AVGVSTORVM / VOT X and Diocletian, crowned by Victory, handing a globe to Maximian, whom another Victory also crowns:[64] for the arrangement of the imperial mantle on Maximian's left shoulder, on the obverse, we have an exact parallel in the obverse portrait of Diocletian on his Siscian bronze medallion. The 10-aureus piece, found at Arras, with busts of the four Emperors, Diocletian and Galerius on the obverse, Maximian and Constantius Chlorus on the reverse, has been assigned on stylistic grounds to a Gallic mint:[65] the style of the beards and the leaf-decoration on the shoulder of the imperial mantles certainly recall a Diocletianic antoninianus of Lugdunum mintage.[66]

Maximian's gold medallions are, with two exceptions, all mint-marked. Two bear the mint-mark of Rome (PR), two that of Ticinum (SMT)[67] and three that of Trier (PTR). Of the two unmarked gold pieces, one, a 1½-aureus at Stuttgart (IOVI CONSERVAT AVGG),[68] has the somewhat pronounced bulge at the end of the nose which seems to be characteristic of the Roman medallions. The second piece, a "framed" piece in Vienna, is too much worn to be assigned to a mint on grounds of style with any degree of certainty.[69] Three bronze medallions are mint-marked, one with SC[70] and two with SIS.[71] Since the two gold medallions of Ticinum[72] differ rather markedly from one another in style, while the portrait style of one of them[73] resembles fairly closely that of the two gold pieces with the Roman mint-mark,[74] we have no sure means of deciding to which of these two mints Maximian's unmarked bronze medallions should be assigned. Some of his bronze pieces,[75] however, may be tentatively ascribed to Trier, in view of their likeness to the gold medallion from the Arras hoard minted in that city, with obverse portrait characterized by specially coarse features and retroussé nose.[76]

[62] G I, tav. 5, nos. 1, 2.

[63] *ZN* 1928, Taf. 3, Nr. 3. **Pl. IV, 3.** G I, tav. 10, nos. 6, 7.

[64] *Numismatika* 1933, pp. 19–22, pl. 1, no. 3. **Pl. IV, 4.**

[65] A. Baldwin, "Four Medallions from the Arras Hoard" (*NNM* 28, 1926), no. 4, pp. 28ff., pl. 4 (**Pl. VIII, 2**).

[66] *RIC* V, ii, pl. 11, no. 3.

[67] **Pl. XLVIII, 2.**

[68] *Cf.* G I, p. 12, no. 3; *NZ* 1931, Taf. 1, Nr. 7 (example formerly in Paris). **Pl. IV, 5, 6.**

[69] G I, tav. 5, no. 4. K. Pink assigns this piece to the mint of Trier (*NZ* 1931, S. 30).

[70] British Museum. G III, p. 94, no. 62. **Pl. IV, 7.**

[71] *NZ* 1920, Taf. 11 (first piece on left in fourth row). **Pl. IV, 8.** G II, tav. 126, no. 5. Strikes from gold medallion dies?

[72] G I, tav. 5, nos. 3, 8.

[73] G I, tav. 5, no. 8.

[74] G I, tav. 5, nos. 5, 7.

[75] E. g. G II, tavv. 126, no. 10; 127, no. 8.

[76] *Aréthuse*, Jan., 1924, pl. 8, no. 4 (**Pl. VIII, 3**).

The gold medallions of Constantius Chlorus all have their mint-marks—one that of Rome (PROM), one that of Siscia (SIS), one that of Antioch (SMA), one that of Ticinum (PT) and eight that of Trier (seven with PTR, one with TR). One bronze piece, which shows the four Emperors sacrificing in front of a temple (ROMAE AETERNAE), has the Siscian mint-mark (SIS) and may well be a "strike" from gold medallion dies.[77] The unmarked Tres Monetae pieces can be ascribed from their portrait style, some to Rome,[78] some to Ticinum[79] and some, possibly, to Siscia.[80] The very pronouncedly sharp, hooked nose, characteristic of the gold Trier portraits, does not appear on the bronze. The 10-aureus medallion from Arras of Constantius Chlorus and Galerius bears the mint-mark of Rome (PROM).[81] With one exception, all of Galerius' gold medallions are mint-marked, one being struck at Trier (PTR), two at Serdica (SMSD and SMS) and one at Alexandria (ALE). Two of his bronze pieces bear the mint-marks of Siscia (SIS)[82] and Cyzicus (SC)[83] respectively; the rest all show a certain family likeness and are probably of Roman mintage. The solitary medallion of Galeria Valeria, a gold piece (VENERI VICTRICI), is of Alexandria (ALE).[84] Of Severus II we have one gold medallion, of Trier (TR);[85] of Maximinus Daza two gold pieces, of Antioch (SMAN)[86] and Alexandria (ALE)[87] respectively, and a much worked-over Tres Monetae bronze piece of Cyzicus (A [*sic*] C);[88] of Maxentius only unmarked Tres Monetae bronze pieces, probably of Rome;[89] and of Romulus one gold piece, the first medallion to be struck at Ostia (POST).[90]

The period extending from Gallienus to Constantine I, after Rome had ceased to be the sole mint for medallions and before the mint-marking of the gold and silver pieces was established as a universal rule, is, from the mintage point of view, the most interesting period in the history of our subject. It is the period in which the study of portrait styles plays an all-important part in determining the mintage of individual pieces; and, as such, it deserves the somewhat detailed consideration which it has received here. From Constantine I onwards all gold and silver medallions, with the exception of two "Fest-aurei" types and two small silver types of Constantine I and of a PRINCIPIA IVVENTVTIS/SARMATIA type of Constantine II as Caesar,[91] are mint-marked. Such mintage problems as now confront us are all concerned with the bronze. We will first briefly consider the bronze pieces and then conclude with an analysis of the mints from which medallions were issued in the precious metals.

[77] Vienna. *Trau Collection Sale Catalogue* 1935, Taf. 42, Nr. 3563. **Pl. IV, 9.**

[78] E. g. G II, tav. 128, no. 4; *cf.* G I, tav. 5, no. 11.

[79] E. g. G II, tav. 128, nos. 3, 7, 8; *cf. Aréthuse*, Jan., 1924, pl. 8, no. 8.

[80] E. g. G II, tav. 128, nos. 5, 6; *cf.* G I, tav. 5, no. 9.

[81] A. Baldwin, *op. cit.*, no. 1, pp. 12 ff., pl. 1 (**Pl. IX, 4**).

[82] G II, tav. 129, no. 4.

[83] Vienna. A scene of sacrifice before a temple (ROME [*sic*] AETERNAE). Not in Cohen or Gnecchi.

[84] G I, tav. 6, no. 3.

[85] G I, tav. 6, no. 4.

[86] G I, tav. 6, no. 5.

[87] Beistegui Collection. J. Babelon, *op. cit.*, pl. 12, no. 231. **Pl. IV, 10.**

[88] G II, tav. 129, no. 5.

[89] G II, tav. 129, nos. 7, 8.

[90] Formerly in Paris (cast in Berlin). **Pl. IV, 11.**

[91] This type was almost certainly struck at Trier, since the other types with the same legend and design bear the mint-mark TR.

Of the bronze medallions of the Constantinian age, from Constantine I to Constantius Gallus, a few bear mint-marks—of Trier (PTR), Constantinople (CONS and CONST), Nicomedia (SMN) and Rome (PR and R). Several of these marked pieces may well be bronze "strikes" from gold medallion dies.[92] But the vast majority of pieces of this period are unmarked. We may, with some confidence, attribute most of the unmarked pieces of Constantine I, Crispus and Constantius II to Rome, in view of their close stylistic correspondence with the bronze medallions, issued in their names, which bear the Roman mint-mark.[93] Constans has one piece with the Constantinopolitan mint-mark.[94] But his unmarked pieces, and those of Constantine II, Magnentius, Decentius and Constantius Gallus are all decidedly uniform in style; and we might, on general grounds, assign them, tentatively, also to Rome. The later bronze pieces, from Julian onwards, which lie on the border-line between medallions and coins,[95] display the marks of quite a variety of mints—Antioch, Constantinople, Nicomedia, Heraclea, Thessalonica, Sirmium, Aquileia and Rome. As we have seen,[96] many of the more medallic of these bear the mint-mark of Rome; unmarked pieces which resemble the Roman pieces closely we might, not unreasonably, attribute to the Roman mint.[97]

Turning to the study of mint-marks on the precious metals, we find that during the Constantinian period, down to Constantius Gallus, Trier was by far the most prolific of the imperial mints in the issue of money medallions. Twenty-two different medallions,[98] all in gold, were struck there for Constantine I, two in gold for Fausta, two in gold for Crispus, six in gold for Constantine II, eight in gold and one in silver for Constantius II, four in gold and one in silver for Constans, two in gold and one in silver for Magnentius and three in gold for Decentius, making a total of fifty-two.[99] Thessalonica comes next with seven gold medallions for Constantine I, six gold and one silver for Constantine II, six gold and three silver for Constantius II, five gold and two silver for Constans and one in gold for Constantius Gallus, making a total of thirty-one.[100] Third on the list is Nicomedia, with fifteen medallions of Constantine I, one of Fausta, one of Licinius I and Licinius II, one of Crispus, seven of Constantine II and four of Constantius II, twenty-nine in all and all in gold.[101] Constantinople follows close upon Nicomedia with a total of twenty-eight: eight gold and four silver medallions were struck for Constantine I, three gold

[92] E. g. Constantine I, mint-mark = PTR, location = Trier (*Acta Archaeologica* 1934, p. 100, fig. 1. **Pl. V, 1.**); (Crispus and Constantine II on reverse) mint-mark = CONS, location = Rome (G I, tav. 29, no. 10: wrongly quoted as silver); (Crispus and Constantine II on reverse) mint-mark = PTR (?), location = Vienna (*Trau Collection Sale Catalogue* 1935, Taf. 46, Nr. 3969. **Pl. V, 2.**); Constantius II (Crispus and Constantius II on reverse) mint-mark = SMN, location unknown: it is not in the British Museum, as Delbrück states (Delbrück, *Spätantike Kaiserporträts*, S. 80, Taf. 7, Nr. 2).

[93] We must except the PIETAS AVGVSTE[S] pieces of Helena (G II, tav. 128, no. 9) and Fausta (G II, tav. 133, no. 1), which are probably of eastern mintage.

[94] Paris no. 716 (G II, p. 144, no. 20).

[95] *Vide supra* p. 37.

[96] *Vide supra* p. 37.

[97] E. g. G II, tavv. 139, nos. 8, 9 (Julian); 140, no. 1 (Jovian).

[98] The statistics which follow are based on medallions which the present writer has either personally examined or found recorded in reliable sources.

[99] Mint-marks are:—PTR, PTRE, TR.

[100] Mint-marks are:—SMTS, THES, TSЄ, TES.

[101] Mint-marks are:—SMN, SMNP, SMNT, MNM, MNB, MNΓ.

and one silver for Constantine II, nine gold for Constantius II, two gold for Constans and one in silver for Constantius Gallus.[102] At Siscia twenty-seven medallions were issued, seven in gold for Constantine I, one in silver for Crispus, one in gold and one in silver for Constantine II, five in gold and three in silver for Constantius II, four in gold and four in silver for Constans and one in silver for Constantius Gallus.[103] Aquileia occupies the next place: there one gold and two silver medallions were struck for Constantine I, one silver for Licinius I, one gold for Licinius II, two silver for Crispus, one silver for Constantine II, one gold and one silver for Constantius II, six gold and two silver for Constans, four gold for Magnentius and one silver for Constantius Gallus, making a total of twenty-three.[104] From Antioch we have sixteen, all in gold: two for Constantine I, twelve for Constantius II, and two for Constans.[105] Next on the list is Sirmium with a total of ten, again all in gold; four of Constantine I, two of Crispus, one of Crispus and Constantine II, two of Constantine II and one of Constantius II.[106] From Ticinum we have seven medallions, also all gold, three of Constantine I, one of Helena, one of Fausta, one of Licinius II, and one of Constantine II.[107] In Rome four medallions were issued, one in gold for Constantine I, one in silver for Constantine II and two in gold for Constantius II.[108] Finally, there are four mints each with one medallion apiece—Milan, with one in gold of Constantius II (SMNED), Heraclea, with one in gold of Constantine I (SMHER), Lugdunum, with one in silver of Constantius Gallus (LVG) and Ostia, with one in gold of Constantine I (POST).

When we pass to the later period, from Julian onwards, we find Trier again heading the list with a total of twenty-six money medallions; five in gold of Valentinian I, six in gold and one in silver of Valens, seven in gold (including a silver copy, in Paris, of a lost gold original) of Gratian, five in gold of Valentinian II and two in gold of Eugenius.[109] From Constantinople, second on the list, we have two gold medallions of Julian, one of Jovian, one of Valentinian I, one of Gratian, one of Valentinian II, one of Theodosius I, four of Arcadius, one in silver (probably a copy of a lost gold original) of Honorius, one in silver of Theodosius II and one in gold of Marcianus, making a total of fourteen.[110] The Roman mint issued eleven medallions; three in gold for Valens, one in silver for Valentinian II, one in silver for Theodosius I, two in silver for Arcadius, one in gold and one in silver for Honorius and two in silver for Attalus.[111] From Thessalonica we have seven medallions; two in gold and one in silver of Valentinian I, three in gold of Valens and one in silver of Theodosius I.[112] Next comes Antioch, with six gold medallions; two of

[102] Mint-marks are:—CONS, CONST, M CONS, M CONSB, M CONSΔ, M CONSZ, M CONSS, KONS$\bar{N}$.

[103] Mint-mark always SIS, either alone or accompanied by a symbol.

[104] Mint-marks are:—AQ, AQS, MAQ, SMAQ.

[105] Mint-marks are:—AN, SMAN, SMANB, SMANH, SMANT, SMAN$\bar{T}$.

[106] Mint-mark always SIRM.

[107] Mint-mark always SMT. The small silver medallion of Constantine I with adlocutio scene (*Vide supra* p. 39) bears no mint-mark, but has been attributed on stylistic grounds to Ticinum.

[108] Mint-marks are:—R, PR, RM, SMR.

[109] Mint-marks are:—TR, SMTR, TROB, TROBC, TROBS, TROBT, TRPS.

[110] Mint-marks are:—CONS, CONSP, KONS$\bar{N}$, CONOB.

[111] Mint-marks are:—RE, RM, RP, RT, RMPS, ROMA.

[112] Mint-marks are:—TES, SMTES, TESOB.

Valentinian I, one of Valentinian I and Valens and three of Valens.[113] The five medallions struck at Aquileia are also in gold—one apiece for Valentinian I, Valens, Gratian, Valentinian II and Theodosius I.[114] Milan, too, has four medallions—one in gold of Valentinian I, one in gold of Theodosius I and one in gold and one in silver of Honorius.[115] Three medallions are known from the mint of Ravenna—one in gold and one in silver of Honorius and two of Galla Placidia in gold.[116] Lastly, the three mints of Ticinum, Siscia and Lugdunum each issued one medallion apiece—Ticinum one in gold for Attalus (PST), Siscia one in silver for Valentinian I (SISCP) and Lugdunum one in gold for Valentinian II (LD).

[113] Mint-marks are:—AN, ANT, ANTOB, ANOBS. The Germanic imitations from Szilágy Sómlyó (Valens) and the Russo-Polish frontier (Valentinian I and Valens) are included in this list as they doubtless represent lost originals (*vide infra* pp. 66, 68).

[114] Mint-marks are:—SMAQ, AQOB.

[115] Mint-marks are:—MD, MDPS, MED.

[116] Mint-marks are:—RV, RVPS.

CHAPTER II

PROVENANCES

It is much to be regretted that so few medallions, comparatively speaking, have come down to us accompanied by reliable records of the exact place and circumstances of their discovery.[1] Precise knowledge of these facts, determining the authenticity of pieces the technique or content of which might otherwise arouse suspicion, will obviously increase the credibility of parallel pieces of unknown provenance. Again, in at least one notable instance the antiquity, not only of the pieces themselves, but of their working-over, has been established in this way. The Capitoline Museum possesses four "framed" bronze pieces, of Hadrian,[2] Faustina II,[3] Lucius Verus[4] and Elagabalus[5] respectively, which have been so much retouched—Elagabalus' medallion has been very largely remade—that their authenticity would be gravely in doubt, were it not known foı certain that they were dug up in 1876 on the Monte della Giustizia, not far from the present site of the Stazione di Termini, and passed straight from the earth to the Museum.[6] The medallions must, then, have been tampered with, not by modern, but by ancient, hands. But knowledge of provenances is chiefly valuable for the light which they may throw upon the types of persons to whom medallions were presented and on the uses to which they were put by their recipients. Naturally, to connoisseurs of Renaissance and subsequent times, whose private acquisitions have now gone to form what is still the bulk of material in the great public collections of Europe to-day, medallions, like coins, were first and foremost objects of artistic beauty or antiquarian interest. It is only in comparatively recent times that we have come to appreciate fully their historical and archaeological implications. Hence the scarcity of provenance records. Still, the records which we have are quite sufficient to merit careful study, and one result of an analysis of find-spots will be immediately obvious: we shall have to modify very considerably the statement made by Gnecchi in 1912 to the effect that bronze medallions "meno qualche rara eccezione, vengono ritrovati a Roma e nei dintorni."[7]

Many of the bronze medallions of which the provenances are recorded by Gnecchi are, indeed, pieces in his own collection discovered (in cases where dates are

[1] Neither Grueber's Catalogue of British Museum medallions nor Macdonald's list of the Hunterian medallions at Glasgow (*NC* 1906) describe a single medallion with find-spot recorded.

[2] G III, p. 19, no. 92.

[3] G II, tav. 70, no. 1.

[4] G II, tav. 73, no. 1.

[5] G II, tav. 97, no. 1.

[6] The present writer has this on no less an authority than that of Marchese Camillo Serafini, Governor of the Vatican City and Keeper of the Papal Medagliere, who has recently rearranged the Capitoline coin-collection. *Cf.* P. E. Visconti, *BC* 1877, pp. 76–80, tavv. 6, 7.

[7] G I, p. liii. The statistics which follow are based on the corpus of Roman medallions which the present writer is in process of compiling. She has been at pains to note the find-spot in every case in which a record of it, precise or otherwise, can be traced. While not claiming as yet to have surveyed *all* existing material, she ventures to hope that the facts here collected will present a reasonably true picture of how medallion provenances are distributed.

given) between 1889 and 1912 during excavations conducted in Rome. Of these twenty-two are of the second century and six of the third, which, together with two of Maximian and one of Constantius II, make up a total of thirty-one. Gnecchi also mentions the discovery in Rome in 1909 of a fine bronze piece of Gordian III, but does not know what became of it.[8] Three of Gnecchi's bronze medallions are of provincial provenance—one found in Egypt in 1907, the second in Asia Minor and the third in Hungary in 1908; and he further records the provincial provenance of twelve other bronze pieces belonging to collections other than his own—four found in France (Reims, Autun, Baalon (Meuse) and Andacelle (Isère)), one in Germany (Cologne), three in Austria (Pettau = Poetovio, Vienna, Deutsch-Altenburg = Carnuntum), two in Hungary (one of them at Ó-Szöny = Brigetio), one in Asia Minor and one in Syria. Thus, on Gnecchi's own showing, fifteen out of the forty-seven bronze medallions the find-spots of which he mentions—that is to say, nearly a third—were discovered elsewhere than in Rome. To his list of pieces of Roman provenance Gnecchi could have added seven more—the four "framed" medallions in the Capitoline Museum, the discovery of which on the Monte della Giustizia was described as early as 1877,[9] and three pieces in the Vatican Collection, which he quotes without mention of the fact that they are noted there as having come to light in the Catacombs, one in 1906 and two in 1908. The first of these three pieces[10] is presumably one of the nine, unspecified, Vatican medallions which were discovered in the Catacombs between the middle of the nineteenth century and 1907:[11] but as no medallions other than the 1906 piece in the Vatican Collection have find-dates falling within this period affixed to them, none of the remaining eight medallions in this group can be identified with definite pieces in Gnecchi's list. Similarly, it is only by process of elimination that we are able to identify three out of another group of eight Vatican medallions which were found, apparently between 1803 and 1807, in various Catacombs and passed into the Vatican Collection in 1811—three of Commodus, one of Gordian III, one of Philip I, one of Gallienus, one of Probus and one of Valentinian I.[12] The identified pieces are those of Philip I (a pseudo medallion), Probus and Valentinian I: the last two are quoted by Gnecchi. Nine other medallions cited in Gnecchi's corpus without mention of their find-spots, though these were certainly recorded, are of non-Roman provenance—three from Northern Italy (neighborhood of Padua), one from France (Autun),

[8] G II, p. 90, no. 27. [9] *Vide supra* p. 57. [10] Valerian and Gallienus: ADVENTVS AVGG.

[11] C. Serafini, "Saggio intorno alle monete e medaglioni antichi ritrovati nelle Catacombe di Panfilo sulla Via Salaria Vetus in Roma," p. 442 (*Scritti in onore di Bartolomeo Nogara raccolti in occasione del suo lxx anno*, 1937).

[12] *Ibid.*, p. 440. *Cf.* Le Grelle, "Saggio storico delle collezioni numismatiche vaticane" in Serafini, *Le monete e le bolle plumbee pontificie del medagliere vaticano*, vol. I, 1910, pp. lii–liii, nota 2. Excluding the double sestertius of Trajan Decius, listed by Serafini with the rest, the medallions were found as follows:—Commodus (1) in Catacombs of Priscilla, 1803; Commodus (2) in Catacombs of Priscilla; Commodus (3) in unspecified Catacombs, Oct. 24, 1806; Gordian III in unspecified Catacombs; Philip I in Catacombs of Priscilla, Mar. 20, 1804; Gallienus in Catacombs of Priscilla, April, 1804; Probus in Catacombs of Calepodio, Feb., 1806; Valentinian I in unspecified Catacombs, June, 1804. It is hoped that it may be possible to identify eventually the remaining five pieces of this group, and the eight other pieces of the first group, by reference to the archives of the Vatican Library.

two from Austria (Vienna), one (most probably) from Hungary, one from Yugoslavia (Sisak = Siscia) and one from Asia Minor (Ephesus). We have, then, records of the find-spots of sixty-five (possibly seventy-eight, if we included the thirteen unidentified pieces from the Catacombs) of the bronze medallions known to Gnecchi; and of these the pieces of non-Roman provenance, so far from being "rare exceptions," amount to twenty-four, roughly a third of the whole.[13]

We are confronted by a far greater proportion of non-Roman to Roman bronze medallion provenances when we push our investigations beyond the range of Gnecchi's corpus, forty-nine pieces from provenances in the provinces and in Italy as against sixteen from Rome and her neighborhood being known to the present writer. A number of the smaller public and private collections outside Italy, the contents of which Gnecchi did not explore, contain pieces of local provenance. We also have records in sources untapped by Gnecchi of the find-spots of other pieces, themselves no longer traceable, discovered in the provinces prior to 1912. But the main bulk of our "non-Gnecchi" material is of course derived from new discoveries made subsequent to 1912, very largely as a result of the rapid development during recent years of systematic excavation on provincial sites. The Roman finds, although few in number, include some of considerable importance. One fine piece was discovered at Ostia in 1917 and is now preserved in the Museo Nazionale Romano. The remaining fifteen are in the Vatican cabinet; and with the exception of one piece of Gallienus found on the Quirinal in 1911, all were discovered in the Catacombs. In the case of one piece neither the name of the Catacombs nor the date of the discovery is recorded in the Vatican cabinet: four were found in unspecified Catacombs as early as 1908, yet somehow escaped the notice of Gnecchi; six came to light in the Panfilo Catacombs (second storey) in 1920[14] and three in the Verano Catacombs, two in 1929 and one in 1937.[15] These recent finds from the Panfilo and Verano Catacombs are of the greatest interest. The medallions were found affixed to the walls of the galleries, set round the slabs which sealed the loculi or resting-places of the dead. Their presence in these positions throws new light upon the uses to which medallions could be put and upon the attitude of their owners towards them, subjects to which we shall return in a later chapter.[16] But their discovery has also an immediate bearing upon the whole question of medallion find-spots in Rome. After the tenth century, when the bones of the most venerated of the Martyrs had been translated to the Roman churches,

[13] In this connection it is interesting to note the numbers of the bronze medallions which passed to the Vienna cabinet from the collection of the Carthusians in Rome and from the Tiepolo Collection respectively. It seems likely that many of the pieces in the first collection were found in Rome or in the immediate neighborhood; and of these eighty-seven are listed by Kenner in the Vienna Catalogue (*Jahrbuch der kunsthistorischen Sammlungen des allerhöchsten Kaiserhauses* Bd. I (1883), S. 61 ff.; Bd. II (1884), S. 54 ff.; Bd. III (1885), S. 11 ff.; Bd. V (1887), S. 12 ff.; Bd. IX (1889), S. 139 ff; Bd. XI (1890), S. 53 ff.). From the Tiepolo Collection Kenner lists fifty-nine medallions; and there is evidence to suggest that a high percentage of the pieces of which that collection was composed were found in the Eastern provinces of the Empire, not, at any rate, in Rome or Italy (*ibid.* Bd. I, S. 63).

[14] Serafini, "Saggio intorno alle monete e medaglioni antichi etc." pp. 421 ff.

[15] *Ibid.*, p. 435, nota 1.

[16] *Vide infra* pp. 120 f.

the Catacombs were gradually deserted and their memory practically lost until Bosio's preliminary archaeological researches in the middle of the sixteenth century aroused a new and lasting interest in these priceless monuments of primitive Christianity.[17] From that time onwards, during the seventeenth and eighteenth centuries and during the first half of the nineteenth century, until they were finally taken into official charge, the Catacombs were exposed to the depredations of visitors of every description, who could (and did) help themselves freely to the rich stores of antiquities there revealed.[18] That these treasures included considerable quantities of bronze medallions can be inferred from the analogy of the new discoveries; and the inference is supported by numerous accounts of finds made during these centuries and also by the remarkably large number of medallions figuring in collections formed at this period, as contrasted with their scarcity in earlier collections.[19] To the zeal with which this harvest was garnered the comparative rarity of medallion-finds in the Catacombs during the past hundred years bears striking testimony: it is only when quite new galleries are opened up, as, for instance, in the case of the second storey of the Panfilo Catacombs, that they appear in any number. Again, as Serafini points out, the areas available for digging or searching for antiquities in the soil of Rome and her suburbs, apart from the Catacombs, were extremely restricted until the middle of the nineteenth century, before excavation for the foundations of new buildings on an extensive scale began.[20] All our evidence, in fact, points to the conclusion that the Catacombs were the provenance of the vast majority of the medallions which came to light in Rome between *c.* 1600 and 1850 and are now scattered throughout the museums and private collections of the world: and to this evidence the new finds in the Panfilo and Verano Catacombs make a contribution of the first importance.

After *c.* 1850, indeed, other sites in the city began to yield medallions. We have already mentioned the discovery in 1876 on the Monte della Giustizia.[21] It was on this site, during excavations for the construction of the Stazione di Termini (1872), that there came to light the medallions which formed the nucleus of the Tyskiewicz Collection. Tyskiewicz himself describes how he secured from the agent Jandola the lion's share of the "nombre incroyable de médaillons romains" which the workmen had turned up.[22] Furthermore, he adduces the proximity of the Castra Praetoria as explaining the phenomenal fertility of this particular region—a point to which we shall return later on.[23]

We must then, it seems, allow for a very high percentage of Roman find-spots among the mass of extant bronze medallions of unrecorded provenance. But this does not affect the inaccuracy of Gnecchi's statement as to the exceptional character of bronze medallion finds outside Rome. Our records of provincial provenances unknown to Gnecchi cover a remarkably wide range of countries once within the

[17] Serafini, *op. cit.*, p. 437.
[18] *Ibid.*, pp. 439 f.
[19] *Ibid.*, pp. 441 f.
[20] *Ibid.*, p. 442.
[21] *Vide supra* p. 57.
[22] "Notes et souvenirs d'un vieux collectionneur" (*RA* 1897, pp. 368, 369).
[23] *Vide infra* p. 117.

confines of the Roman Empire.[24] Starting with Northern Italy, we have two from Aquileia (1912 and 1930) and one from Rovigo. France supplies one, Avallon (= Aballo). From Great Britain we have records of three medallions found in the Thames near old London Bridge between 1834 and 1841[25] and of one found at York;[26] while a unique medallion of Carausius (possibly a "strike" from gold medallion dies) has recently turned up in an old collection in the north of England and is believed to have been found locally. The German provenances are Trier and Cologne. Two pieces were found at Trier in 1891 and 1921 respectively, while eight pieces have come to light in Cologne, one *c.* 1890, one in 1925, one in 1929 and five at unspecified dates. From Austria are recorded one medallion from Vienna and one, possibly two, from Carnuntum. Hungary contributes four pieces, one found at Dunapentele (= Intercisa) in 1926, one (a bronze "strike" from gold dies) at Ó-Szöny (= Brigetio), one near Budapest and the fourth from an unspecified Hungarian site. Outstanding for her yield of new bronze medallion finds is Yugoslavia. Ten pieces from Sisak (= Siscia) are distributed between public and private collections in Zagreb, two of them discovered in the years 1924 and 1934 respectively: one piece, also in Zagreb, comes from Ogulin (in Liburnia), while a fine "framed" piece from Benkovac (= Asseria) is preserved in the Croatian Museum at Knin. The National Museum at Sofia contains two bronze medallions from unknown sites in Bulgaria. From Rumania we have a piece found at Adamklissi and now in the Ružička Collection in Vienna, while five medallions discovered on various sites in the Dobruja are "in deposit" in the Museum of Antiquities at Bucarest.[27] Of special interest is a recent find from Syria, a medallion of Marcus Aurelius and Lucius Verus which came to light in a private house in Dura-Europos in 1933.[28] Three medallions are recorded from Egypt, one from an unknown site and one from the Faiyum, while the third, acquired by its present owner in 1925, is said, on somewhat flimsy grounds, to have been found at Ptolemais. Our survey of bronze medallion provenances concludes with a piece from North Africa, found in 1912 at Khamissa in Algiers. Reviewing the bronze material as a whole, we may note at this point the prevalence among recorded provenances of great provincial centres of military and official life—Aquileia, Eboracum, Londinium, Augustodunum, Colonia Agrippinensis, Augusta Treverorum, Vindobona, Carnuntum, Brigetio, Poetovio, Intercisa, Siscia, Ephesus, Dura-Europos and (just possibly) Ptolemais—reserving comment upon the implications of this fact until a later stage.[29]

[24] The absence of Spain from our list is due to the fact that Gnecchi's corpus, in which no Spanish provenances are recorded, is the sole source of information regarding the Madrid medallions so far available to the present writer. It seems probable that we should discover some records at least of local medallion finds when the collections in Madrid and other Spanish cities are once more accessible.

[25] *NC* 1841, p. 158. The present location of these pieces is unknown.

[26] *Walters and Webb Collections Sale Catalogue* 1932, Nr. 1047, Taf. 11 (Walters).

[27] L. Ružička, "Römische Medaillons im Bukarester Museum" (*BMF* 1914, Nr. 4). The "deposit" is believed to be actually Moscow!

[28] Now at Yale University, New Haven, U. S. A. It seems peculiarly appropriate that a piece bearing the head of Lucius Verus should have appeared at Dura, since it was his campaigns which marked the end of the Parthian overlordship and the beginning of Roman domination in that city.

[29] *Vide infra* pp. 117 f.

No one would join issue with Gnecchi when he states that money medallions struck in the precious metals have been found "sparsi per mondo."[30] At the same time we must not run away with the impression, which he tends to convey, that the provenances of gold and silver are evenly distributed throughout the ancient world.[31] Discoveries made since his day have, as we shall see, undoubtedly tended to mark out certain regions as more fertile than others, at least as far as gold medallions are concerned.[32] Again, just as the recent finds, described above, in the Panfilo and Verano Catacombs have disproved for the bronze his contention that medallions are always found in isolation,[33] so, too, in the case of the gold, the famous Arras find of 1922 is sufficient in itself to show that the discovery of quite large groups of medallions in finds is likely to prove far less rare a phenomenon than he supposed.[34] It is, indeed, somewhat strange that Gnecchi should have emphasized quite so strongly the rarity of such discoveries when he himself cites no less than four hoards containing gold medallions—those of Velp in Holland, 1715 (six ? pieces),[35] of Helleville, near Cherbourg, Manche, 1780 (nine pieces),[36] of Szilágy-Sómlyó in Rumania, 1797 (thirteen pieces)[37] and of Ó-Szöny in Hungary, 1885 (four pieces).[38] The

[30] G I, p. liii.

[31] *Loc. cit.*, "non si saprebbe a qual regione assegnare una preferenza."

[32] The analysis which follows must remain, up to a point, tentative, pending further investigation of material in museums in Spain and North Africa.

[33] *Loc. cit.*, "i medaglioni vengono in luce sempre isolamente."

[34] *Loc. cit.*, "solo si possono citare rare eccezioni per la riunione di alcuni d'oro, come fu ad esempio nel repostiglio di Helleville."

[35] See A. Chabouillet, "Observations sur deux médaillons d'or de Honorius et de Placide" (*RN* 1883, pp. 70 ff.) and A. O. van Kerkwijk, "Les médaillons romains en or et la trouvaille de Velp en 1715" (*Mémoires du Congrès international de Numismatique*, Bruxelles, 1910, pp. 29 ff.). The number of medallions originally contained in this hoard is very uncertain. All the recorded pieces are of Honorius (reverse type = Roma enthroned to front) and Placidia (reverse type = Placidia enthroned to front); and it seems extremely probable that all the examples with these types which passed into the Paris and Hague Cabinets came from Velp. Paris now has two pieces, one of Honorius (mint of Ravenna) and one of Placidia (mint of Ravenna). But it seems that originally Paris had secured two other pieces of Honorius as well, one struck at Ravenna, the other at Milan, both of which were lost in the theft of 1831. Van Kerkwijk reproduces (*op. cit.*, pl. 4, no. 3) the drawing of a lost Paris piece showing the mint-mark MD; Berlin possesses the cast of a lost Paris piece with the mint-mark RV (*cf.* G I, tav. 20, no. 1). **Pl. V, 3.** The Hague now has two medallions, one of Honorius (mint of Ravenna) and one of Placidia (mint of Ravenna). The second piece of Placidia, which, according to Chabouillet, The Hague once possessed, was, according to van Kerkwijk, exchanged in 1870 by the director of the cabinet for coins of the Netherlands. It came from the collection of William V, Prince of Orange, and it is not known what became of it after the exchange: van Kerkwijk suggests that it may be the Paris piece. One account of the Velp discovery describes a "collier" (now vanished) to which five large gold medallions were attached (van Kerkwijk, *op. cit.*, pp. 31, 32). Are these five to be identified with five of our recorded pieces or do they represent five other lost medallions? The British Museum medallion of Honorius with the same type as the Velp pieces has the mint-mark RM (G I, tav. 19, no. 11).

[36] E. Babelon, "La trouvaille de Helleville (Manche) en 1780" (*RN* 1906, pp. 160 ff.). Babelon publishes nine pieces, but it is possible that two medallions of Constantine I, now at The Hague, also came from Helleville: see A. O. van Kerkwijk and E. Babelon, "La trouvaille de Helleville (Manche). Note additionnelle" (*RN* 1906, pp. 490 ff.). **Pl. V, 4–7; Pl. VI, 1–4.**

[37] This is the number of gold medallions from Szilágy-Sómlyó now in the Vienna cabinet. Kenner (*op. cit.*, Bd. IX, S. 140) says that they number fourteen: but this is, apparently, because he has reckoned in (*op. cit.*, Bd. XI, S. 89, Anm. 1) with the pieces from the treasure a gold medallion of Valens (*ibid.*, S. 79, Nr. 356) found, not at Szilágy-Sómlyó, but, as Kenner himself states, at Eisernes Tor. Steinbüchel, *Notice sur les médaillons romains en or du musée impérial et royal de Vienne* (1826), also lists fourteen pieces, as the result of counting as a medallion a simple aureus of Maximian with ring attached (*op. cit.*, p. 20, no. 1, pl. 1, no. 1). Kenner (*op.

find containing fifteen medallions discovered at Borča in Yugoslavia in 1879 Gnecchi does not mention, although he quotes three pieces which came from it. It still remains true, however, that a number of the gold, and nearly all the silver, extant pieces of known provenance were discovered in isolation. We will consider these before returning to the group-finds.

In view of the relatively modest numbers of extant silver medallions, taken in all, in comparison with the gold and bronze, and of the fact that we have no records, so far, of groups of them occurring in hoards, the scarcity of silver pieces of which the provenance is known to us is not surprising, Only eight are known to the present writer. Four of these were found in Rome, in the Catacombs, one in unspecified Catacombs in 1912 and three during the more recent excavations in the Panfilo (1920) and Verano (1929 and 1932) Catacombs. One comes from Northern Italy (Aquileia) and the remaining three from the provinces—from Germany (Cologne), Greece (neighborhood of Salonika) and Sardinia[39] respectively. The first thing which strikes us when we turn to gold medallion provenances is the remarkable scarcity of pieces recorded as having come to light in Rome and her neighborhood. In fact, we know of only one piece from the city herself, a small medallion of Carinus with the bust of Magnia Urbica on the reverse, found on the Capitol in 1902 and now in the Museo Nazionale Romano. It is possible, though by no means certain, that the two unique pieces of Theodosius I and Libius Severus respectively in the Mazzini Collection at Turin belonged to a hoard of treasure found at Albano between 1900 and 1910.[40] Apart from these we have only three other records of gold provenances for the whole of the Italian peninsula, namely those of the famous Augustan medallion from Pompeii (1759: Museo Nazionale, Naples), of the much disputed Augustan piece from Este (1925: Museo Nazionale Atestino) and of the medallion of Theoderic from Senigallia (1894: Museo Nazionale Romano, Gnecchi Collection). The rarity of find-spots throughout the whole area of the southern and eastern Greek-speaking provinces of the Empire is equally noteworthy. From Greece we have one (medallion of Fausta found near Athens in 1872: Vienna cabinet), from Albania one (medallion of Gallienus: Paris, Beistegui Collection), from Palestine one (medallion of Gordian III: Paris, Jameson Collection), from Cilicia one (medallion of Alexander Severus, found at Tarsus with the three famous Greek medallions in 1867: Paris, Bibliothèque Nationale) and from Cappadocia one (the great medallion of Justinian found at Caesarea in 1751 and lost from Paris in 1831). From Egypt alone of these provinces are several reported, one from Abukir (medallion of Diocletian and Maximian: Berlin) and three others (medallions of Constantius II, ex-Levis Collection, of Theodosius I, Freer Collec-

cit., Bd. IX, S. 140) also mentions "andere 10 Medaillons von Valens" found in the treasure along with the Vienna gold medallions: but he does not specify the metal of these ten pieces or give any indication of what became of them. He further states that three more gold medallions of Valens, each weighing 209.4 grammes, were reported as belonging to the find, but could not be verified.

[38] Gnecchi cites only three medallions but the hoard contained at least one other (*vide infra* p. 66 note 67).

[39] In trade, Oct., 1938, Münzhandlung Basel.

[40] *NC* 1940, p. 9.

tion, Washington, and of Honorius, Berlin,[41] respectively) from various sites unparticularized. Again, in the western provinces, find-spots set well back within the frontiers of the Empire are extremely rare. We know of one in the south of France, La Condamine, near Monaco, where a small medallion of Gallienus came to light in 1880 (Monaco).[42] Another is recorded from Great Britain, Sully, near Cardiff, where a single medallion of Diocletian appeared in a coin-hoard unearthed in 1899 (British Museum). But provenance records become in proportion more plentiful when we turn to the imperial frontiers, to the lines of Rhine and Danube, to the German limes and to the provinces of Pannonia and Moesia stretching eastwards from the Adriatic. From the Lower Rhine we know of one provenance, a site near Kessel in the Cleeves district, where a small gold piece of Constantius II was found in 1935 (Bonn);[43] while from the Upper Rhine frontier we have one provenance, the canal at Saasenheim in Alsace, a site lying between the Roman cities of Argentoratum (Strassburg) and Argentovaria (Horburg), where a medallion of Valens came to light in 1875 (Paris, Jameson Collection).[44] A 2-solidi piece of Constans (Berlin) appeared in the mud in the bed of the Mosel at Reil, near Zell.[45] The Main at Würzburg (= Segodunum?), just beyond the limes Germanicus, is the provenance of a small medallion of Gallienus found in 1886 (location unknown).[46] From the Pannonian countries records of five find-spots have come to hand—one in Austria, Pettau (= Poetovio, medallion of Constantius II, found in 1870),[47] two in Hungary, Szar-Fehér (medallion of Maximian, found in 1905) and the Danube, near Eisernes Tor (medallion of Valens, found before 1763),[48] two in Yugoslavia, Petrijanec, situated to the east of Pettau, just south of the Drave (medallion of Carus and Carinus, the only medallion in a coin-hoard discovered in 1805)[49] and an uncertain site, either Mitrovic or some point on the Lower Danube (medallion of Crispus).[50] Bulgaria, too, has yielded a respectable quota—three pieces (of Constantine I, found in 1861,[51] Constans and Valens respectively) all from unspecified sites. Lastly we come to a series of isolated medallions, all of the later Empire, discovered right outside the imperial boundaries, five in Rumania (the Roman province of Dacia was abandoned in 271), one in East Prussia and three in Denmark. Four of the Rumanian pieces are of Constantine I, one found at Starčova (Temesvar), two on unspecified sites in Transylvania[52] and one in the Dobruja at Celeiu (= Sucid-

[41] R. Zahn, *Amt. Berichte aus den preussischen Kunstsammlungen*, Oct. 1916, SS. 10 ff., Abb. 3, 4, 5; Delbrück, *op. cit.*, Taf. 19, Nr. 4. **Pl. VII.**

[42] Cited by Gnecchi without mention of provenance, for which see R. Mowat, *op. cit.*, pp. 315, 317.

[43] *NC* 1939, pp. 143 ff. **(Pl. XXXII, 2.)**

[44] The Agri Decumates were lost to the Empire *c.* 256 to 257.

[45] Cited by Gnecchi without mention of provenance, for which see *ZN* 1885, S. 8, Taf. 1, Nr. 5.

[46] R. Mowat, *op. cit.*, pp. 315 f.

[47] Cited by Gnecchi without mention of provenance, for which see *Trau Collection Sale Catalogue* 1935, S. 113, Nr. 4143.

[48] Cited by Gnecchi without mention of provenance, for which see Kenner, *op. cit.*, Bd. XI, S. 79, Nr. 356.

[49] Cited by Gnecchi without mention of provenance, for which see Kenner, *op. cit.*, Bd. V, S. 42, Nr. 195.

[50] Cited by Gnecchi without mention of provenance, for which see Kenner, *op. cit.*, Bd. IX, S. 173, Nr. 271.

[51] Cited by Gnecchi without mention of provenance, for which see Kenner, *op. cit.*, Bd. IX, S. 149, Nr. 237.

[52] One of these Transylvanian pieces is the great FELIX ADVENTVS AVGG NN medallion in the Beistegui Collection in Paris, cited by Gnecchi without mention of provenance, for which see Maurice II, pp. 238 ff. and E. Babelon, "Un nouveau médallion en or de Constantin le Grand" (*Mélanges Boissier*, 1903, pp. 49 f.) **(Pl. XVII, 11.)**

ava, 1910);[53] the fifth piece, a medallion of Gratian, was found near Arad in 1865. The East Prussian piece, a large and unique medallion of Constantius II, was discovered near the village of Hammersdorf in 1917 and is in the Königsberg museum.[54] The three Danish pieces are all in the National Museum at Copenhagen: two are of Constantius II and came to light at Tründerüp in Funen (1893)[55] and at Allesö in Funen (1908);[56] the third, a medallion of Valentinian I, was found at Faxe in Zealand (1768).[57]

We must now return to the hoards or treasure-finds which have produced, not isolated pieces, but groups, large or small, of gold medallions. Only four of these, the French hoards of Helleville (Manche), an unspecified place in Poitou (1865),[58] Planche (Ain) (1889)[59] and Arras (Pas de Calais) were found well within the boundaries of the Empire. Velp, near Arnhem (= Arenacum?), the provenance of the Dutch find, lies on the very confines of the Roman world, as does also Morenhoven, near Bonn, where two gold medallions of Magnentius turned up *c.* 1880 in a hoard containing twenty-two solidi ranging from the time of Constantine I to that of Magnentius;[60] while the Hungarian and Yugoslav hoards of Ó-Szöny (= Brigetio) and Borča (near Belgrade = Singidunum) came to light right on the Danube frontier line. Szilágy-Sómlyó, the site of the Rumanian hoard, lies far to the north of the Danube, in the one-time province of Dacia abandoned to the barbarians many years before the earliest medallion in the treasure was stiuck; and three more recent medallion group-finds were discovered even further afield—one on the borders of Poland and Russia towards the end of 1927, one at Nedzierzewo, near Kalisch, in west Poland in 1927 or 1928 and the third in southeast Poland, at Boroczzce, between Lwów and Luck, in the district of Horochów, Volhynia, in 1928. Meanwhile vast tracts of the ancient world remain unrepresented; and thus the hoards, no less than the isolated discoveries, disprove the idea that all regions have been equally fertile in gold medallion find-spots. These hoards may now be briefly reviewed in the order of their discovery.

The six pieces, all of which probably came from Velp (1715), have already been sufficiently described.[61] Six of the nine medallions from Helleville (1780) are of Constantine I; while the remaining three were struck by their father for Constantine

[53] Cited by Gnecchi without mention of provenance, for which see note in Vienna cabinet.

[54] *BMF* 1923, S. 429, Taf. 264, Nr. 13. **Pl. VI, 5.**

[55] Cited by Gnecchi without mention of provenance, for which see C. Jörgensen, *Mémoires de la Soc. Roy. des Ant. du Nord* 1900, p. 319.

[56] Not cited by Gnecchi. For provenance see A. W. Brögger, *Kria* 1921, p. 47.

[57] Cited by Gnecchi without mention of provenance, for which see C. Jörgensen, *Mémoires de la Soc. Roy. des Ant. du Nord*, 1900, p. 323 and *Nordisk Numismatisk Arsskrift* 1937, p. 76.

[58] Two 2-solidi pieces of Valentinian I and Valens respectively (*RN* 1866, pp. 113–115), found with twenty-eight solidi.

[59] Two small gold ADVENTVS AVG medallions of Aurelian (*RN* 1889, pp. 527–528, pl. 10, nos. 7, 8), found with seven aurei and some jewellery.

[60] L. Strauss, *FM* 1932, S. 384, Nr. 14, Taf. 6, Nr. 8; *Münzhandlung Basel Sale Catalogue* March 18, 1936, SS. 94, 95, Nrr. 2040, 2041, Taff. 25, 26. **Pl. VI, 6, 7.**

[61] *Vide supra* p. 62 and note 35. According to A. Chabouillet (*op. cit.*, p. 82) the medallions in this find far outnumbered the aurei.

II (one) and Constantius II (two).[62] All but one disappeared from the Bibliothèque Nationale in the great theft of 1831, but fortunately not before copies of them had been made, and all nine pieces are reproduced in E. Babelon's article on the find.[63] The majority of the Helleville medallions were large pieces, ranging from 34 mm. to 48 mm. in diameter. The Szilágy-Sómlyó (1797) medallions are, of course, very well known. All are preserved in the Vienna cabinet and have long been familiar to students from the works of von Steinbüchel, Kenner, Kubitschek and Gnecchi. They include one piece of Maximian, one of Constantine I, two of Constantius II, one of Valentinian I, seven of Valens and one of Gratian: two of Valens' medallions, with reverse legend GAVDIVM ROMANORVM/AN and the type of Valens riding to the right towards Antioch (?), standing to left, are cast, not struck, and are clearly Germanic imitations of Roman work.[64] To every piece a heavy ring is attached, while seven pieces are also set in elaborate and richly ornamented frames of Germanic workmanship. Their weights, including rings and frames, range from 9.21 to 412.72 grammes: five pieces weigh between 40 and 70, and three between 200 and 300, grammes. These facts tell a plain tale, which we must reserve until later.[65]

Of the fifteen medallions found in the spring of 1879 at the village of Borča, between Semlin and Pancevo, in the neighborhood of Belgrade, thirteen are of Constantine I, while the other two, of Constantine II and Constantius II respectively, were both struck during Constantine I's lifetime, in 325.[66] Thus of the three large medallion group-finds that have come to light so far—Szilágy-Somlyó, Borča and Arras—that of Borča is chronologically the most homogeneous; and the hoard as a whole, in its proponderance of medallions over coins—fifteen to three—bids fair to rival the hoard of Szilágy-Sómlyó with its proportion of thirteen medallions to one coin. Half of the Borča find consists of small medallions, eight 1½-solidi pieces of Constantine I. The remainder is made up of three 2-solidi pieces of Constantine I, one 3-solidi piece of Constantius II, and three 4½-solidi pieces, two of Constantine I and one of Constantine II. Of the four medallions found together at Ó-Szöny in 1885 three are of Maximian, two now in Budapest and one formerly in the Trau Collection: the fourth piece, of Diocletian, with Juppiter Victor on the reverse, is in an unlocated private collection and is known only from verbal reports.[67]

The discovery of a great hoard of gold on September 21, 1922, by laborers

[62] The two Hague pieces, if really from Helleville (*vide supra* p. 62, note 36), would add another couple to Constantine's quota.

[63] The find also included a number of aurei, eight of which are published by Babelon (*op. cit.*).

[64] A. Alföldi, "Nachahmungen römischer Goldmedaillons als germanischer Halsschmuck" (*NK* 1929–1930, SS. 10 ff.).

[65] *Vide infra* p. 118.

[66] G. Elmer, "Ein Fund römischer Goldmünzen aus Borča" (*NZ* 1930, S. 39 ff.). The treasure was found in a field after the winter floods had subsided. Elmer suggests that it represents the contents of a purse which fell into the water during a flood in Roman times.

[67] *NZ* 1891, S. 87, Taf. 4, Nrr. 3, 4; S. 89, Taf. 8, Nr. 1; S. 90. Yet another piece is attributed to the Ó-Szöny hoard by Sir Arthur Evans (*NC* 1930, p. 242). It is a medallion of Maximian and is said to show the same reverse type as the Diocletianic piece. It cannot, however, be verified from any other source. A number of aurei and denarii were found with the medallions.

working in a brickfield at Beaurains near Arras in northern France is one of the most sensational numismatic events of modern times.[68] Its importance to students of Roman medallions in particular would be hard to overestimate. Not only has it added to our material at least twenty-one extant pieces, twenty of which are unique in that they show either entirely new types or new variants of types previously known; but the descriptions of other pieces, alas! no longer extant, reported as belonging to the hoard—vague and tantalizing as they are—at least suggest the existence of heretofore little suspected features in the medallic history of the Diocletianic and early Constantinian age. Verbal reports of workmen must obviously be treated with extreme caution, but the accounts of the Beaurains laborers, among whom the treasure was at once divided, would seem to indicate that the hoard originally contained about fifty gold medallions; and if there were any truth in their statement that some were "as big as a saucer," we must reckon with the possibility that gold medallions comparable in size and weight to the largest pieces of Valens from Szilágy-Sómlyó were struck at least as early as the first decades of the fourth century. Moreover, a Ghent dealer, to whom the bulk of the treasure was taken soon after its discovery, estimated that the two largest of the medallions would together turn the scale at well over a kilogramme. They may, in fact, have each been equivalent to 100 aurei, weighing *c.* 530 grammes apiece. According to the dealer, one of these giant medallions bore on its reverse a chariot, the other a "battle scene." Such types are by no means improbable: to the first our nearest medallic parallels are the 9-solidi pieces of Constantius II, showing an imperial chariot to front drawn by six horses,[69] to the second, the 5-aurei piece of Numerianus, showing Carus and Numerianus in the act of charging barbarian foes.[70] Again, the great lead plaque in Paris, measuring 90 by 85 mm. and found in the Saône near Lyons in 1862, has been shown to date from the time of the Diocletianic Tetrarchy:[71] it can hardly be other than the "proof" of the reverse of a large gold medallion, thus furnishing independent testimony to the existence of such pieces dating from the period of the Arras hoard. But most unfortunately the curator of a local museum, convinced that such staggering objects were too good to be true, persuaded, or threatened, the dealer of Ghent into melting them down. It is heartrending to reflect how many other pieces must have met with an untimely end in the melting pot. Indeed, the famous London medallion[72] was only saved from a like fate

[68] *Aréthuse*, Jan., 1924, pp. 45 ff., pls. 7, 8; *NNM* 28, 1926; *NC* 1930, pp. 221 ff.; *ibid.*, 1933, pp. 268 ff. It would be irrelevant to our present purpose to attempt here any account of the aurei (originally numbering at least four hundred), silver plate and jewellery found with the medallions or any discussion of the vexed question of the date at which the hoard was deposited (not later than 306, according to Sir Arthur Evans, just before 314, according to A. Baldwin). **Pl. VI, 8; Pl. VIII, 1–8; Pl. IX, 1–6.**

[69] G I, tavv. 10, no. 8; 11, no. 1. *NC* 1930, pl. 17, no. 8 shows an aureus of Maximian from the hoard itself with the Emperor in a frontal quadriga on the reverse.

[70] G I, tav. 4, no. 7.

[71] E. Babelon, *Traité des monnaies grecques et romaines*, part i, pp. 947, 948, fig. 34; A. Alföldi, *ZN* 1926, SS. 167 ff., Taf. 11, Nr. 4; A. Evans, *NC* 1930, pp. 236, 237, fig. 2. **Pl. IX, 7.**

[72] *Aréthuse*, Jan., 1924, pl. 7. This piece is now scheduled as a national monument of France and is preserved in the Arras Museum. A few others are said to be also at Arras, but this the present writer was unable to verify, as the Arras cabinet was inaccessible to students in 1937–8. Two pieces are in the British Museum nd the rest are scattered about in private collections in Europe and the U. S. A.

because the workman to whose share it fell, having scruples as to whether he ought to keep it, consulted his confessor, who bade him return it to his employer. Of the twenty-one extant medallions from the hoard known to the present writer, three are of Diocletian, one is of Diocletian and Galerius, three are of Maximian, ten of Constantius Chlorus,[73] one is of Galerius and three are of Constantine I. Four are equivalent to 10 aurei (53+ to 54+ grammes), two to 8 aurei (*c.* 42 grammes), ten to 5 aurei (25+ to 26+ grammes) and two to 4 aurei (20+ to 21+ grammes), while the three Constantinian pieces are equivalent to 9 solidi (40.25 grammes), 2 solidi (8.78 grammes) and 1½ solidi (6.65 grammes) respectively. As we should expect, it is mainly the smaller fry which Fortune has spared to us.

Less imposing than the Arras hoard as regards the number of known medallions which they have yielded, but equally tantalizing, and certainly even more interesting from the point of view of provenance, are the three recent finds on Polish soil. The first of these came to light on the borders of Poland and Russia towards the end of 1927. According to accounts of the discovery the find contained an unspecified number of late Roman gold medallions, a number of fourth-century solidi, a few second- and third-century denarii and other treasure. Of the medallions only one is so far traceable and is now in the Berlin cabinet. This piece is cast, not struck, is furnished with a heavy ring and bears on the obverse busts of Valentinian I and Valens and on the reverse a design identical with those of the two Germanic pieces from Szilágy-Sómlyó: it is obviously itself also a Germanic piece and must have been produced in the same region as Valens' medallions, passing thence northward into Poland.[74] Accounts of the second hoard, found at Boroczzce in the district of Horochów, Volhynia in 1928,[75] describe a silver vessel and an earthenware vessel, both filled with Roman denarii, a "gold tablet," which completely disappeared, and one gold medallion, a piece of Jovian, set in a rich and highly ornamental frame of Germanic workmanship, with a ring attached, and now in the Archaeological Museum of Warsaw.[76] Apart from the vanished "gold tablet," which might, just

[73] A. Baldwin (*NNM* 28, 1926, p. 24) claims that her pl. 3 represents a second specimen from Arras of the medallion of Constantius Chlorus (TEMPORVM FELICITAS/PTR) published in *Aréthuse*, Jan., 1924, pl. 8, no. 7. The piece in *Aréthuse*, which she believes to be at Arras, is, she maintains, struck from dies different from those of the specimen which she figures. But the present writer, after the most minute examination, can trace no difference of dies between Baldwin, pl. 3 and *Aréthuse*, pl. 8, no. 7. It is true that the details of the obverse come out less sharply in the former than in the latter reproduction, but this could be due to a photographic defect. It would seem that only one piece is in question and that Baldwin, pl. 3 = *Aréthuse*, pl. 8, no. 7 = *Levis Collection Sale Catalogue* 1925, pl. 38, no. 977 = *NC* 1930, pl. 16, no. 6 = *Jameson Collection Catalogue* IV, pl. 26, no. 528.

[74] K. Regling, "Ein Goldmedaillon von 48 solidi" (*Amtl. Berichte aus den preussischen Kunstsammlungen* 1928, S. 67 ff.); A. Alföldi, *NK* 1929–1930, S. 14 ff., Taf. 2, Nr. 1. Alföldi suggests the possibility that this was not a separate hoard and that the medallion came from one of the other Polish finds, at Boroczzce or Kalisch. Pl. X.

[75] St. J. Gasiorowski, "Un trésor de l'époque de la migration des peuples decouvert en Volhynie" (*Bulletin international de l' Académie Polonaise des Sciences et Lettres*, 1929, nos. 1–3, pp. 27–31). The treasure was found during the construction of a railway between Lwów and Luck: the remains of what appeared to be a Roman castellum were discovered near by. *Cf.* E. Petersen, *JPEK*, 1930, SS. 67–68.

[76] Gasiorowski, *op. cit.;* Delbrück, *op. cit.*, SS. 89, 90, Abb. 27; W. Antoniewicz, "Der Fund von Boroczzce" (*NK* 1929–1930, SS. 26–28, Taf. 1). Pl. XI. Another specimen of this medallion was in Paris before the theft of 1831 (G I, p. 34, no. 1).

conceivably, have been a large gold medallion, there is no suggestion that other medallions came to light at Boroczzce; and according to one of the workmen who discovered the find, so Antoniewicz states, the medallion of Jovian was found at some distance from the two vessels. It is possible, then, that we ought to rank this piece, with the medallions of East Prussian and Danish provenance, as an isolated discovery, not as the sole survivor of a group-find. But in view of what we know about the immediate and mysterious disappearance of large gold pieces from the Arras hoard and elsewhere, we may provisionally leave it in its present context. The third Polish find, made near Kalisch in western Poland in 1927 (according to Alföldi, *op. cit.*, S. 12) or 1928 (according to Antoniewicz, *op. cit.*, S. 26), may be the provenance of a gold medallion of Valentinian I, set in a narrow frame and furnished with a ring, which has now found its way to America (Newell Collection, New York). The Kalisch hoard is said to have also contained a large gold medallion of the fourth century weighing *c.* 750 grammes, which we may safely conclude to have ended its days in the melting-pot.[77]

To sum up, we may take it that this series of important hoards sufficiently refutes Gnecchi's notion of the extreme rarity of medallion group-finds. They encourage us, indeed, to look for more. Meanwhile we may hope that some, at least, of the errant pieces from these finds may eventually come to safe harborage in accessible public or private collections.[78]

[77] *NK* 1929–1930, SS. 12, 26; E. Petersen, *op. cit.*, S. 58, Nr. 5:—"Ein Goldmedaillon von angeblich 750 gr. Gewicht. Es soll auf der einen Seite das Bild eines Reiters getragen haben; näheres konnte nicht mehr festgestellt werden. Angeblich ist das Stück nicht mehr vorhanden."

[78] According to Alföldi (*op. cit.*, S. 12) Dr. R. Gaettens—Halle, who first acquired the medallion of Valentinian now in the Newell Collection, also acquired at the same time, and possibly from the same source, a small medallion of Constantine II (26 mm., 8.97 grammes), which has since disappeared into trade.

PART III

THE PURPOSE OF ROMAN MEDALLIONS

CHAPTER I

THE OCCASIONS OF MEDALLION ISSUES (1)

In our initial definition of a Roman medallion as a piece struck for special or solemn commemoration and intended for presentation as a personal gift we have already stated the general purpose of medallion issues. But this general statement obviously involves a number of particular questions concerning the times and seasons at which presentation took place, the events, movements or ideas which the types commemorate or anticipate, the character and status of individual recipients and, finally, the uses to which recipients put their gifts. The more strictly commemorative function of medallions can be best studied on chronological lines; for there we are concerned with pieces of which the types and legends do not immediately proclaim either the moment of their issue or the character of the persons who received them, but in which the choice of types reflects, in a wider and more general way, the thought, interests and history of their age. That aspect of the subject will, therefore, be most conveniently treated as part of our study of the historical development of medallions. For the present we shall concentrate upon the study of occasions and recipients.

I. The New Year.

The familiar Roman custom of making New Year presents (strenae) would in itself have suggested to us one important and obvious occasion of medallion issues. Again, many medallion designs are, as we shall see later, exactly suited in themselves to such a context. But we are able, fortunately, to go beyond plausible conjecture and the subjective evidence afforded by the content of types and to show conclusively, on the objective evidence of legends, that some groups of medallions at least were designed as gifts offered by the Emperor on New Year's Day, whether this was reckoned according to the calendar, or according to the regnal, year.[1] We may take as our first and, in a sense, most striking example of these groups a series of New Year medallions of the late second century.

[1] Regnal New Year's Days include the dies imperii (accession day), the day of the Emperor's first reception of the tribunicia potestas, and December 10, the day from which the renewal of the tribunicia potestas was commonly reckoned. The *Feriale Duranum* (*Yale Classical Studies* vii) suggests various other "New Years" as possible occasions for medallion issues—the birthdays of the reigning Emperor and of members of his family; the birthdays of certain deified Emperors and Empresses and of deceased imperial princes (e. g. Germanicus); the dies imperii of certain deified Emperors; the anniversaries of the reigning Emperor's first imperial salutation, of his becoming pater patriae and pontifex maximus, of his becoming Caesar, of his designation as consul for the first time, and of his assumption of the toga virilis. *Cf.* Scriptores Historiae Augustae, *Vita Taciti* 9:—"divorum templum fieri iussit in quo essent statuae principum bonorum, ita ut iisdem natalibus suis et Parilibus et Kalendis Ianuariis et votis libamina ponerentur." For Augustus' custom of giving out-of-the-way coins as presents at the Saturnalia and on other occasions see Suetonius, *Div. Aug.* 75:—"Saturnalibus et si quando alias libuisset, modo munera, vestem et aurum et argentum, modo nummos omnis notae, etiam veteres regios et peregrinos."

When Commodus perished at the hands of an assassin on December 31, 192, he had just entered, on the 10th of the same month, on his eighteenth tribunician year.[2] Apart from one rare denarius[3] and a single sestertius,[4] no extant coin of Commodus bears that regnal date. This clearly shows that the main issues of new currency for 193 were not yet ready by the end of 192: they would, presumably, have appeared later on in 193, had Commodus survived. But when we turn to his medallions we are confronted with a homogeneous group of large bronze pieces of six different types, covering between them thirty-nine extant examples known to the present writer, all bearing on the reverse the date TR P XVIII. All allude to the Hercules-Commodus cult and have thus a specially intimate and personal connection with the Emperor: the obverses invariably show the head of Commodus, to right or left, hooded with the Herculean lion-skin and on well-preserved specimens it is quite clear that the Herculean figure on the reverses has the features of Commodus himself. One of these types, that of Hercules-Commodus marking out the sulcus primigenius with a plough drawn by two oxen (HERC ROM CONDITORI), is a translation onto heavy medallion flans—weighing from 49+ to 96+ grammes and in many cases struck in two metals—of a very rare coin type issued earlier in 192[5] and again on the single sestertius dated TR P XVIII. But the five other types are quite new and unknown to the regular coinage—Hercules-Commodus standing to front with club and Nemean lion held by the hind legs (HERCVLI ROMANO AVG),[6] Hercules-Commodus standing to right, leaning on his club (HERCVLI ROMANO AVG),[7] Hercules-Commodus standing to left, leaning on his club (HERCVLI ROMANO AVG),[8] Hercules-Commodus standing and seen from behind (HERCVLI ROMANO AVG)[9] and Hercules-Commodus seated to right upon a rock (HERCVLI ROMANO AVG).[10] The significance of this medallion group is obvious. It demonstrates beyond doubt that medallions of Commodus' eighteenth tribunician year, as distinct from coins, were ready for presentation as New Year gifts either on the eighteenth anniversary of his reception of the tribunician power, December 10, 192, or on January 1, 193, and were actually distributed to the persons destined to receive them, although, if the calendar year is in question, the Emperor himself did not live to see the New Year in.[11] We may, indeed, in the latter case legitimately picture the simultaneous

[2] *RIC* III, p. 356.

[3] *Ibid.*, p. 394, no. 244: reverse legend = P M TR P XVIII IMP VIII COS VII P P.

[4] *BMCCRE* IV, p. 845, no. || and note, where the reading given in *RIC* III, p. 436, no. 616—TR P XVII—is said to lack authority.

[5] The type occurs on a rare dupondius with radiate head of Commodus with lion-skin and club on the obverse (*RIC* III, p. 437, no. 629) and on a rare aureus with head of Commodus in lion-skin hood on the obverse (*ibid.*, p. 394, no. 247). It is interesting to contrast this type, in which the Emperor is definitely identified with Hercules (the reverse legends read HERC ROM COND or CONDITORI), with that on sestertii and asses of 190, which show Commodus ploughing, veiled as a priest (*ibid.*, pp. 430, 431, nos. 560, 570).

[6] G II, tav. 80, no. 4. A small bronze medallion with this reverse type and laureate head of Commodus on the obverse is said by Gnecchi (III, p. 37, no. 194) to be in the Museo Civico at Venice: but it could not be traced there by the present writer in June, 1938.

[7] G II, tav. 80, nos. 2, 3.

[8] G II, p. 55, no. 31.

[9] G II, tav. 80, nos. 5, 6 (Pl. XLIII, 3).

[10] G II, tav. 80, no. 7.

[11] *Cf. BMCCRE* IV, pp. xciv and note 2, clxxxii f. On p. cliii, note 3, it is pointed out that the appearance of COS VII for 192 instead of COS VIII for 193 in the legends of these New Year pieces can be explained by the fact

arrival, in some instances, of the gift and of the news of the death of the giver. Thus New Year's Day, whether December 10, 192, or January 1, 193, was to be the occasion for an intensive boosting of the Hercules-Commodus aspect of the imperial cult, marking the final stage in the identification of Commodus with his "patron saint" as the "Roman Hercules" *par excellence*. Neither the title HERCVLES ROMANVS nor the head of Commodus in lion-skin hood occurs on coins earlier than 192. On the reverses of earlier Hercules medallions[12] Commodus and his patron, Hercules Commodianus, are still distinct and on the obverses Commodus has not yet drawn the lion-skin hood over his head, though on one medallion of the seventeenth tribunician year he wears it tied round his neck.[13]

With these six TR P XVIII medallions we must group three others, of which the obverse portraits (head of Commodus wearing lion-skin hood), reverse legends (HERCVLI ROMANO AVGV or AVGVST) and general style and structure show them to be contemporary with the TR P XVIII pieces, though they are not actually marked with the regnal year. Their reverse designs consist of Herculean attributes—quiver, club, bow (left to right),[14] bow, club, quiver (left to right)[15] and club in the centre of the field.[16] Perhaps the six dated medallions were presented on the regnal New Year's Day (December 10), the six undated pieces on that of the calendar (January 1).

The special interest of this group of TR P XVIII of Commodus medallions is twofold. In the first place it affords, as we have seen, a clear instance in which medallions were, and coins were not, prepared for release on New Year's Day. In the second place the evidence of the legends, though absolutely conclusive, is, in a sense, indirect. The proof that the New Year, whether of the calendar or of the Emperor, was the occasion of their issue rests solely upon the tribunician date: the legends in themselves do not even suggest it in so many words. In the legends of other groups, however, New Year allusions are more obvious. Of these the most direct are the New Year greetings formulae inscribed within wreaths which are found among medallion reverse types of the second and third centuries. The earliest is a Hadrianic type—S P Q R / AN F F / HADRIANO / AVG P P within an oak (?)-wreath; it occurs on a large bronze medallion in Rome (Gnecchi Collection) and also on a small bronze piece in Paris, indistinguishable from a sestertius in size and weight, but executed in a distinctively medallic style which is clearly differentiated from the

that the consuls for 193 were already designate in December 192, while Commodus' plot to put them to death and assume the consulship himself was still a secret (Dio, 72, 22).

[12] TR P X = 185, Hercules crowning himself, between an apple tree and an altar (G II, tav. 83, nos. 5, 6); COS V = 186 to 189, Hercules leaning on club (*FM* 1931, Taf. 5, Nr. 4. Pl. XII, 1. *Cf.* coins of 183 to 184, *RIC* III, pp. 413, 414, nos. 399a, 424); TR P XVI = 191, Hercules sacrificing (G II, tav. 79, nos. 5, 6: *cf.* coins of 190 to 191, *RIC* III, pl. 15, no. 304); TR P XVII = 192, Commodus, veiled as a priest, sacrificing to Hercules (G II, tav. 85, nos. 8, 9).

[13] G II, p. 64, no. 114 (reverse type = Commodus sacrificing to Hercules). *Cf.* G II, tav. 87, no. 3 (reverse type = Four Seasons).

[14] G II, tav. 80, no. 1.

[15] G II, tavv. 77, no. 2; 79, no. 9. *Cf.* coins (all undated), e. g. *RIC* III, pl. 15, no. 310.

[16] G II, tav. 79, no. 10. *Cf.* coins (all undated), e. g. *RIC* III, pl. 16, no. 336. *Cf.* also a small medallion in Paris:—obv. = L AEL AVREL COMM AVG P FEL, bust of Commodus wearing lion-skin; rev. = P D, bow, quiver, lion-skin on club and trident (G III, p. 37, no. 200). Pl. XII, 2.

common coin style of sestertii with the same type + S C.[17] Here we have, of course, depicted the Senate's New Year gift of a wreath to the Emperor and the formula of New Year greeting—"annum faustum felicem"—which accompanied it. The compliment is recorded on the ordinary coinage issued, presumably, at, or soon after, the New Year. But in addition to this the Emperor "returned the compliment," as it were, by striking the type without S C upon medallions, which show a more elaborate obverse portrait and a fine medallic style, as New Year presents from himself for members of the Senate, so we should imagine, in token of his appreciation of their gift. A similar reverse type, combined with two varieties of obverse portrait, was issued in the name of Antoninus Pius, with S P Q R / AN F F / PRINCIPI / PIO within a laurel-wreath.[18] The close resemblance of this type to that of Hadrian's medallion has suggested the possibility that both pieces were contemporary, struck to commemorate the inauguration of the Emperors' joint reign on the day of Antoninus' adoption by Hadrian on February 25, 138, the New Year's Day of Antoninus' first, and of Hadrian's last, regnal year.[19] Unfortunately there are serious difficulties in the way of our accepting this attractive theory. As its author himself points out, it involves the anticipation by Hadrian of the anniversary of his own accession (August, 117) by more than five months, as well as the assumption by Antoninus of the title "Augustus" during Hadrian's lifetime. Nor did Antoninus bear the title "Pius" at so early a date. Moreover, the correspondence of one of Antoninus' obverse variants with the obverse portrait of a COS II medallion[20] clearly suggests that his New Year pieces were struck in 139, either on the calendar (January 1), or on the regnal (February 25), New Year's Day.[21] As for Hadrian's piece, it is possible that we should connect it with the vicennalia celebrations of August, 137, the occasion of a very special regnal New Year's Day, marked, we may assume, by the conveyance of very special greetings from Senate to Emperor. The vota vicennalia are, indeed, recorded on a small bronze medallion, the reverse of which shows VOTA / SVSCE / PTA in an oak-wreath.[22] The type does not occur at all on the aes coinage, but is found on aurei of the period,[23] while scenes of sacrifice, accompanied by the legend VOTA PVBLICA, appear on contemporary aurei, denarii and sestertii.[24] One aureus shows the Genius Senatus and the Genius Populi Romani sacrificing at an altar;[25] and our little medallion may well be an acknowledgment both of the gift and of the sacrifice offered on the Emperor's behalf. A second reverse type of Antoninus Pius, combined with two varieties of obverse and struck between 140 and 144, seems to reflect another New Year greeting from Senate to Emperor under the auspicious title of "enricher of citizens"—S P Q R / AMPLIA / TORI

[17] G II, tav. 40, no. 4; *BMCCRE* III, pls. 84, no. 2; 89, no. 3.

[18] G II, tav. 48, no. 4. *RIC* III, p. 97, no. 527A gives the legend without PIO, but this is not verified by any specimen known to the present writer. *BMCCRE* IV, p. 171, no. * gives the legend with PIO.

[19] *RIC* III, p. 6, note 1.

[20] G II, tav. 46, no. 9. See Strack III, S. 35, Anm. 83.

[21] Strack, *loc. cit.*, prefers January 1 to February 25 on the ground that Antoninus must have already been Pater Patriae by February 25, 139.

[22] Strack II, Taf. 11, Nr. 469. Pl. XII, 3.

[23] *Ibid.*, Taf. 6, Nr. 289.

[24] *Ibid.*, Taff. 4, Nr. 288; 6, Nr. 287.

[25] *Ibid.*, Taf. 6, Nr. 286.

/ CIVIVM with in alaurel-wreath.[25] A third Antonine reverse type, on a unique medallion at Gotha, unknown to Gnecchi, shows the inscription S C / PRIMI / DECEN / NALES within an oak-wreath,[26] a return-gift for the New Year from Emperor to Senate, commemorating the latter's vote of congratulation to the former on the tenth anniversary of his accession, on February 25, 148. Here again, as in the case of the Hadrianic type, Antoninus' medallion pays back, as it were, a compliment also recorded on the regular coinage, for the legend PRIMI DECENNALES COS III S C occurs on gold, silver and bronze dated TR P XI and TR P XII.[27] Inscriptions in wreaths which refer to New Year celebrations introducing new regnal periods reappear on medallions of Gallienus, who, in addition to ordinary coins with such allusions, issued medallic pieces, executed in medallic style and with medallic portraits, showing on the reverse VOTIS / DECENNA / LIBVS / S C or VOTIS / DECENNA / LIBVS framed in a laurel-wreath;[28] while border-line pieces with S P Q R / OPTIMO / PRINCIPI in a laurel-wreath[29] as their reverse design recall Antoninus' S P Q R / AN F F / OPTIMO / PRINCIPI / PIO medallion. New Year wishes of a somewhat less formal type are acknowledged in the legend of one more piece in this series of inscription-types, a small, unique bronze medallion of Faustina II in Vienna, poorly preserved, but displaying a distinctively medallic obverse portrait in high relief.[30] The reverse bears the inscription DOMVI / AVG / FELICITER within a laurel- (or oak ?) wreath. "Feliciter," the Senate's or people's cry of greeting to the imperial House, thus recorded on the medallion of an Empress, suggests New Year wishes of some special significance, perhaps for the imminent arrival of a new inmate of the imperial nursery.[31]

This more informal type of New Year greeting would again appear to be reflected in the reverse legend of a medallion of Commodus' fifteenth tribunician year—PIO IMP OMNIA FELICIA P M TR P XV IMP VIII / COS VI P P. The type accompanying this legend shows Commodus, veiled as a priest, sacrificing to Neptune.[32] Felicitas is, indeed, the dominant note struck by three of the four extant medallions issued by Commodus in 189 to 190. Another medallion, with obverse identical with that of one of the sacrifice-to-Neptune variants, bears the reverse legend TEMPOR FELICIT P M TR P XV IMP VIII COS VI P P surrounding a winged caduceus between two crossed cornuacopiae—the very attributes of the personification Felicitas and of Mercury as god of luck in commerce.[33] The third medallion of our group bears no tribunician date, but the obverse of one of its variants[34] is struck from the

[25] G II, tav. 48, no. 3. *Cf.* LOCVPLETATORI ORBIS TERRARVM sestertius of Hadrian (*RIC* II, p. 415, no. 585).

[26] *RIC* III, p. xvi. Pl. XII, 4.

[27] *RIC* III, pp. 47, 48, 132, 133, nos. 171–173, 184, 846, 853.

[28] G III, tavv. 161, nos. 7, 8; 155, no. 3.

[29] *RIC* V, i, p. 165, no. 393.

[30] Kenner, *NZ* 1879, SS. 227 f., Taf. 3, Nr. 2. Pl. XII, 5.

[31] *Cf.* Strack III, S. 116 and Nr. 716. Strack assigns the piece to 149 to 152. For the greeting "feliciter" *cf.* the Senate's acclamation of Pertinax after the death of Commodus:—"fidei praetorianorum feliciter. praetoriis cohortibus feliciter. exercitibus Romanis feliciter. pietati senatus feliciter . . . victoriae populi R. feliciter." (*Vita Commodi* 18) and the acclamation of Caracalla by the Fratres Arvales in 213:—"Auguste, Augusta! Iuliae Augustae, matri Augusti feliciter" (*ILS*, I, 451).

[32] G II, tav. 82, no. 4.

[33] G II, tav. 77, no. 3. *Cf.* coins with this type and legends TEMP FELIC and SAECVLI FELIC (*RIC* III, pp. 389, 430, 431).

[34] G II, tav. 89, no. 7.

same die as that of one of the variants of the TR P XV medallion with the processus consularis as reverse type[35] and is therefore most likely to be contemporary with it. The reverse of this third medallion shows the legend VOTIS FELICIBVS and a complicated harbor scene, with Commodus sacrificing to Serapis, who is seen on board ship in the harbor.[36] It is clear that the felicitas desired for the pious Emperor concerns the sea. As Alföldi has already pointed out,[37] the sacrifice to Neptune and the offering at the harbor to Serapis, co-protector with Isis of navigators obviously suggests some reference to the ceremonies of the Ploiaphesia or navigium Isidis, when the sacred ship was launched and prayers were offered at the opening of the sailing season on March 5. At first sight, indeed, it would seem that our felicitas medallions, if they were New Year gifts, as the legend of one of them at least implies, were presented on March 5, the sea-farers' New Year's Day. On the other hand the close connection already noted between the vota felicia and processus consularis medallions, of which the latter were presented on January 1,[38] distinctly suggests that all four were struck for presentation at the calendar New Year. Moreover, the rites depicted on the medallions of Commodus are not those described by Apuleius as offered on March 5 by the heterogeneous devotees of Isis. They are public vows, offered by the Emperor himself; and this at once suggests an official, state connection between the cult of Isis as patroness of shipping and the imperial vows or vota publica of January 3.[39] The January dating is further suggested by a series of medallions struck a century later, on which these ceremonies reappear. A large bronze piece of Diocletian, minted at Siscia, bears the same legend VOTIS FELICIBVS as does the medallion of Commodus and a similar scene of an imperial sacrifice at a harbor.[40] On the obverse the Emperor wears consular dress, pointing to the processus consularis and the calendar New Year.[41] Again, five small bronze medallions of the period show on their reverses Isis and Serapis, accompanied by the legend VOTA PVBLICA. Diocletian and Maximian each have a piece with the reverse type of Isis and Serapis in a ship and the obverse legends D N DIOCLETIANO FELICISSIMO SEN AVG and D N MAXIMIANO FELICISSIMO SEN AVG respectively,[42] the title "felicissimus" forming a link with the vota felicia of Diocletian's harbor-scene medallion and the felicitas allusions of Commodus types. For Diocletian we have also a piece with the type of Isis and Neptune standing confronted and the obverse legend IOVI DIOCLETIANO AVG;[43] and we may tentatively postulate the existence of a lost piece of Maximian with the same reverse type and the corresponding legend HERCVLI MAXIMIANO AVG. The two remaining medallions are of Constantius Chlorus and Galerius respectively, as Augusti, both with the Isis-and-Neptune reverse type.[44] These small medallions are in their turn closely associated with the fourth-century coins of the vota publica (the main theme of Alföldi's study) struck for the official Roman Isis-festival on

[35] G II, tav. 85, no. 3.
[36] G II, tav. 89, nos. 6–8.
[37] *A Festival of Isis in Rome*, p. 48.
[38] *Vide infra* pp. 83 ff.
[39] See Alföldi, *op. cit.*, pp. 49 f.
[40] G II, tav. 125, no. 10.
[41] Alföldi, *op. cit.*, p. 50 and *RM* 1935, SS. 32 ff.
[42] Alföldi, *A Festival of Isis* etc., pl. 1, nos. 1, 2. **Pl. XII, 6, 7.**
[43] G III, tav. 158, no. 11 (*vide infra* p. 211).
[44] G III, tav. 158, nos. 24, 30.

January 3. And so we may assign Commodus' TR P XV New Year medallions, with the echoes of New Year greetings in their legends, to January 190. All good luck (omnia felicia) to the pious Emperor, for with his luck (felicitas) and his "lucky" vows (vota felicia), offered for fair sailing to the seamen's patrons, are linked the fortunes of sea-borne trade in the Roman world—trade, symbolized on the second medallion of Commodus by the caduceus of Mercury, patron of commerce, while the cornuacopiae stand for the rich (felix) fruits of the seasons (tempora) brought safely to port.[45] All our extant medallions of Commodus with the TR P XV date were, then, issued for the calendar New Year, a fact which decidedly weights the balance in favor of the calendar, rather than the regnal, New Year as the occasion for which the TR P XVIII series was issued.

Until the beginning of the fourth century direct allusions on medallions to the imperial New Year vota (apart from the vota-inscriptions in wreaths and the Isis-festival group described above) are comparatively scarce. With a few exceptions, all the extant vota publica medallions appear to be connected, not with calendar, but with regnal, New Year's Days; while the majority of vota types offer a more or less objective representation of the actual scene of imperial sacrifice. The series begins with Antoninus Pius. A small and sadly worn medallion in Paris[46] bears the date TR P XII (December, 148 to December, 149)[47] on the obverse and on the reverse Pius and Marcus Aurelius sacrificing before a temple, with VOTA in the exergue. We might ascribe the issue of this piece to December 10, 148, the New Year's Day according to the new tribunician reckoning which followed the celebration of the decennalia on February 25, 148. Next comes a large medallion with VOTA in the exergue, S C in the field and Pius offering sacrifice.[48] The piece is undated, but as Strack has observed,[49] it shares an obverse type with two medallions marked TR POT XXI[50] and can therefore be assigned to the year December, 157 to December, 158. The occasion of the issue was, presumably, Pius' vicennalia, solemnized with special pomp, as the abundance of vicennalia coin types testifies, on the twentieth anniversary of his accession, February 25, 158. Two more vota types of Pius were struck in honor of the same occasion. Both are marked TR P XXII, which suggests the tribunician New Year's Day, December 10, 158, as the date of their issue, reiterating, as it were, nine months later the message of the S C vota medallion, just as the small vota piece had reiterated that of the S C PRIMI DECENNALES medallion ten years before. Each piece bears on the reverse an almost identical scene of sacrifice, one with the legend VOT SOLVTA DEC II / COS IIII[51]—marking the completion of the second of the Emperor's periods of ten regnal years, the other with the legend

[45] Note also, with Alföldi (*op. cit.*, p. 49), the recurrence of the epithets PIVS FELIX in the obverse legends of the TR P XV medallions.

[46] Strack III, Taf. 4, Nr. 602. Pl. XII, 8.

[47] For the transference of Pius' tribunician reckoning from February 25 to December 10, in 147, and the consequent dual system of dating during his reign, see *RIC* III, pp. 1 f.; Strack III, S. 1; *BMCCRE* IV, p. xxxix.

[48] G III, tav. 160, no. 6.

[49] III, S. 156, Anm. 471.

[50] G II, tavv. 48, no. 9; 50, no. 1.

[51] G II, tav. 50, no. 2.

VOT SVSCEPTA DEC III / COS IIII[52]—marking the inauguration on the same, or on the succeeding, day of his third decennium. With these two last New Year scenes of sacrifice we must group the LVD DEC / COS IIII medallions of Pius, also dated TR P XXII, the reverse type of which shows the Emperor distributing prizes, displayed on an agonistic table, for the decennial games.[53]

Several medallions with the vota-sacrifice reverse type were issued by Marcus Aurelius. These fall into two groups. Unfortunately the extant specimens of the first group, which bear the legend VOTA PVBLICA and show Marcus sacrificing in front of a temple, are all in such poor condition that the exact dates of some are hard to determine, owing to the illegibility of their reverse legends.[54] But by comparing the obverse types of the four variants in the group with those of other medallions clearly marked TR P XXII, we may safely assign them all to that date, that is to say to December 10, 167. This date is, of course, too late to coincide with the twentieth anniversary of Marcus' reception of the tribunician power, the second anniversary of which was reckoned as falling on December 10, 147.[55] Why, then, did Marcus choose this particular year, 167, for issuing medallions on the occasion of his December New Year vows? Probably because a northern campaign, the expeditio Germanica prima, was in the offing, and in anticipation of this the regnal New Year's Day of 167 may well have been celebrated with a "special intention." Marcus and his imperial colleague actually left for the northern front about the end of the year. Earlier in the year this campaign had been heralded by vota coins dated TR P XXI.[56] Marcus' second vota medallion group appeared exactly ten years later. One medallion, struck in Marcus' own name, is dated TR P XXXII (December, 177 to December, 178) and shows the legend VOTA PVBLICA accompanying an elaborate sacrificial scene with a temple in the background.[57] The second medallion, struck for the young Commodus in two variants, shows the same legend and an almost identical type and is dated TR P III (December, 177 to December, 178).[58] Again, December 10, 177, is too late a date to coincide with Marcus' thirtieth regnal anniversary; but again the choice of these particular vows as an occasion for medallion issues can be explained by the fact that he was already planning a second campaign in the north, the expeditio Germanica secunda, for the summer of 178. Four sets of vota coins issued during the years 177 and 178 attest the serious character of this northern war.[59] The last second-century vota medallion type was struck by Commodus, with reverse legend VOTA PVBLICA and the usual sacrificial scene. It is dated TR P X and we may assign it to December 10, 184, the regnal New Year's Day on which Commodus entered upon his tenth tribunician year.[60]

For the century which elapsed between Commodus and Diocletian we have eight medallions with types directly alluding to imperial vota and two others on

[52] G II, tav. 50, no. 3. The presence of victimarius and victim in a vota suscepta scene is, of course, unusual; it should be noted that this piece has been worked over.

[53] G II, tav. 46, nos. 1, 2.

[54] G II, tavv. 61, no. 3; 63, no. 2.

[55] *BMCCRE* IV, pp. lxvi, lxxxvii.

[56] *RIC* III, p. 289, no. 951.

[57] G II, tav. 63, no. 9.

[58] G II, tav. 89, nos. 2, 3.

[59] *RIC* III, pp. 310, 311, 340, 341, nos. 1226, 1235, 1236, 1584, 1594, 1598.

[60] G II, tav. 89, nos. 4, 5.

which such reference is possible. The earliest of these is a bronze piece of Caracalla, issued in 207, which depicts Victory standing, surrounded by nine Cupids, and inscribing VOTA XX on a shield.[61] Medallions of gold and bronze struck in 230 for Alexander Severus and for Alexander Severus and Julia Mamaea show the Emperor seated, crowned by Victory and accompanied by Virtus (?), who holds a shield inscribed VOT / X.[62] A bronze piece of Philip I, Otacilia and Philip II bears the legend VICTORIAE AVGVSTORVM and the type of two Victories holding up a shield inscribed VOTIS or VOTIS / X.[63] These Victory types of Caracalla and Philip represent the first appearance on medallions of what was to become the most popular *motif* for vota coins and medallions in the fourth century—that of Victory, or two Victories, holding the vota shield or wreath. Two small gold pieces of Gallienus show scenes of imperial sacrifice which may allude to vota. One is dated TR P II, suggesting the first anniversary of the Emperor's accession as its occasion.[64] Owing to some blunder, the dates of obverse and reverse on the second piece conflict, but the obverse date, 263, suggests Gallienus' decennalia.[65] A small bronze medallion of Tacitus, with reverse legend VOTIS X ET XX, shows the Emperor standing, grouped with Virtus (?) and Victory, whose shield is inscribed VOT / IS / XX.[66] As Tacitus' reign lasted only six months he was previous with his accession prayers for twenty years of rule. Florian issued a large bronze medallion on which he is portrayed with Mars (?), Roma (?) and two turreted women and the auspicious legend RESTITVTOR SAECVLI / VOT X.[67] The Victory-and-shield *motif* reappears upon the three remaining pre-Diocletianic vota medallions, on a bronze piece of Probus, with two Victories holding a shield inscribed VOTIS / X,[68] on a gold piece of Probus, with two Victories suspending a shield inscribed VOT / X upon a palm-tree[69] and on a gold piece of Carus and Carinus, with two Victories holding a shield inscribed VOTIS / X.[70]

Vota celebrations of the period of the Tetrarchies are recorded on a splendid series of gold medallions with elaborate and realistic scenes. The earliest, struck for Maximian, shows him sacrificing with his colleague Diocletian: the legend, CONCORDIA AVGG ET CAESS, suggests that it was issued for the regnal New Year's Day in 293 on which Constantius Chlorus and Galerius were appointed Caesars and the first Tetrarchy thereby formed.[71] A medallion of Diocletian from the Arras hoard bears the legend FELICITAS TEMPORVM and the two Augusti, accompanied by Felicitas, sacrificing—an obvious allusion to the vicennalia of Diocletian in 303.[72]

[61] G II, tav. 95, no. 4. [62] G I, tav. 1, no. 9 (Pl. XLIV, 5); II, tav. 99, no. 5; III, p. 45, no. 20. Pl. XII, 9.

[63] G II, tav. 109, no. 7. [64] G I, tav. 3, no. 1.

[65] R. Mowat, *op. cit.*, pl. 17, no. 2 (Pl. III, 11). [66] G III, tav. 156, no. 15.

[67] G II, tav. 118, no. 11.

[68] G III, tav. 157, no. 3. A small bronze medallion of Probus in the Gnecchi Collection in Rome (G III, tav. 157, no. 4) shows a seated Victory with a shield, the design on which, now practically obliterated, may have been vota numbers in a wreath.

[69] G I, tav. 4, no. 3. [70] G I, tav. 4, no. 8 (Pl. XLVII, 7).

[71] G I, tav. 5, no. 3 (Pl. XLVIII, 2). *Cf.* (1) bronze medallion of Diocletian and Maximian at Zagreb, struck in 293, with the legend VICTORIAE AVGVSTORVM/VOTA X and the two Augusti, each crowned by a Victory, standing confronted (*Numismatika* 1933, pl. 1, no. 3) (Pl. IV, 4); (2) bronze medallion of Maximian at Padua, struck in 295, with the legend HERCVLI VICTORI/VOT X and Hercules standing in a temple (*Boll. del Museo Civico di Padova*, 1910–1911, tav. 9, no. 2). Pl. XII, 10. [72] *Aréthuse*, Jan. 1924, Pl. 8, no. 2 (Pl. VI, 8).

Four medallions of Constantius Chlorus, one as Caesar and three as Augustus, complete the series. The first of these, known from two variants, both from Arras, has the legend TEMPORVM FELICITAS / CAESS XIII COSS V and a scene in which the two Augusti, nimbate and surrounded by the usual *entourage*, offer sacrifice in front of a temple. The year of issue is 305, in the May of which Constantius and Galerius were appointed Augusti: the vota depicted must, then, be those of January, 305, when the two Caesars entered upon their fifth consulship.[73] May 1, Constantius' first New Year's Day as Augustus, is commemorated by a vivid scene on a second medallion. The reverse bears the legend CONCORDIA AVGG ET CAESS and portrays the actual abdication of Maximian in Constantius' favor: Maximian (right) hands the globe of sovereignty to Constantius (left); and the XX in a wreath between the two figures shows that the abdication took place at the very moment when Maximian was due to celebrate his vicennalia.[74] The two other pieces of Constantius, both from Arras, portray other ceremonies of the same New Year's Day. On both we find the legend TEMPORVM FELICITAS and a scene of imperial sacrifice before a temple. One shows the two new Augusti sacrificing amid a crowd of attendants,[75] while on the other the two new Augusti and the two new Caesars co-celebrate unaccompanied.[75a]

With the early years of the fourth century, however, these vivid pictures of actual New Year ceremonies vanish completely. Interest is now concentrated almost entirely upon the vota numbers themselves, human figures being, in most cases, merely subsidiary. These figures, moreover, are no longer imperial personages actively engaged upon the celebrations but allegorical figures, for the most part, of a symbolic and subjective character—Victories, Genii, personifications of cities and the like. A few vota medallion types of the period are, indeed, unusual and distinctly picturesque. One shows three Emperors enthroned to the front with VOT V inscribed either on the footstool of the central figure or in the exergue (Constans). Others show two graceful winged Genii (symbols of fertility and prosperity ?) holding a long garland and accompanied by the legend VOTIS DECENN etc. (Constantine II as Caesar)[76] or supporting between them a wreath framing vota numbers (Constantius II), in one case with circumference legend FELICIA DECENNALIA (Constans).[77] Sometimes Roma and Constantinopolis are seated with the vota shield between them (Constantius II) or Roma sits alone with a vota shield resting on a cippus (Constantius II). But far more commonly the shield inscribed with, or the wreath framing, the vota numbers is in the charge of Victories—of two Victories, standing,[78] or of a single Victory, seated[79] or standing,[80] sometimes

[73] *NC* 1930, pl. 16, no. 5 (**Pl. VIII, 7**).

[74] G I, tav. 5, no. 9; *ZN* 1885, SS. 125 ff.

[75] *Aréthuse*, Jan., 1924, pl. 8, no. 7 (**Pl. VIII, 8**).

[75a] J. Babelon, *op. cit.*, pl. 12, no. 230 (**Pl. IX, 1**). The idea that the felicitas of the Empire is bound up with the welfare of the Augusti and Caesars is expressed in the reverse legend of a bronze medallion of Maximian: it reads SALVIS AVGG ET CAESS FEL ORBIS TERR and accompanies a type showing Moneta in the centre flanked by Roma (?) or Virtus (?) and Felicitas (?) or Abundantia (?) (G II, tav. 127, no. 10).

[76] **Pl. XLVIII, 6.**

[77] Formerly in Paris: cast in Berlin. **Pl. XII, 11.**

[78] N. B. variants, not figured by Gnecchi, of Constantius II and Constans:—G I, p. 32, no. 44 (formerly in Trau Collection: *Trau Collection Sale Catalogue* 1935, Taf. 49, Nr. 4253); p. 32, no. 42 (B. M.); p. 28, no. 18 (Milan and Vienna); p. 28, no. 16 (Gotha and B. M.). **Pl. XIII, 1–4.**

accompanied by a genius, who supports the shield. In one case Victory drives in a quadriga with the vota legend around (Constantine I). The Constantinian group of four silver pieces with the vota formula in full (VOTA ORBIS ET VRBIS SEN ET P R, with XX/XXX/AVG or XX/XXX/MVL/FEL) has already been described.[81] The remaining types consist of vota numbers inscribed within a wreath[82] or written across the field or of the formulae SIC X SIC XX etc. framed in wreaths.[83] It seems a far cry from these formal and conventional vota types, many of them shared with the regular coinage, to the vivid New Year greetings of the second century and to the realistic scenes of New Year ceremonies issued under the Tetrarchies.

Another group of New Year medallions consists of pieces of which the legends and types show them to have been struck for presentation on January 1 of those years in which the Emperor, or Caesar, himself assumed the consulship. The majority of such medallions show a reverse type directly alluding to the consulship, combined with the presence, on obverse or reverse, of the tribunician number of a year of which one consul is known to have been that Emperor, or Caesar, whose portrait the obverse bears. In other cases, where the tribunician date is not given, the nature of the type, together with the prominence assigned to the consular date, make it, at the least, extremely probable that the year of issue was that in which the consulship in question was first assumed. In other cases again, where the type itself is not directly consular in character, the emphatic position on the reverse of the consular date leaves little room for doubt that the imperial entry upon this office was the occasion for which the piece was struck. And there are also a few medallions of which the legends show that the consular allusions in their reverse types were inspired, not by the issuing Emperor's assumption of office, but by that of his heir or colleague in imperial power.

[79] N. B. AV type of Constantine I with legend GLORIA PERPETVA AVG N / ·SMTS· and MVL / XX on shield. (*Trau Collection Sale Catalogue* 1935, Taf. 45, Nr. 3912). **Pl. XIII, 5.**

[80] N. B. A type of Constantine I with legend VICTORIBVS AVGG NN VOTIS / PTR and frontal Victory holding shield inscribed X / XX (G I, tav. 8, no. 5 and *Trau Collection Sale Catalogue* 1935, Taf. 45, Nr. 3941 = Oxford piece from A. Evans bequest). **Pl. XIII, 6.**

[81] *Vide supra* pp. 38 f. It is unlikely that pieces alluding in so peculiarly explicit a manner to the actual vota celebrations held from 325 to 326 were issued in anticipation of them in 324. It does, indeed, appear that the mint of Aquileia, where four out of the five known examples were struck, was closed from 324 to 333, as far as concerns the regular currency (see Maurice I, p. 330). But this would not prevent it being specially opened for the issue of these special pieces early in 326, when Constantine passed through the city on his way back to Rome from the East. If this date be accepted we must, of course, assume that Licinius I, pardoned and honorably "retired" by Constantine after his defeat at Chrysopolis in September, 324, was still nominally "Augustus" in the early spring of 326 and that his revolt and death took place, not in 325 (see P-W *s. v.* Licinius), but subsequently to the issue of our series, in the late spring or early summer of 326 (see Ulrich-Bansa, *op. cit.*, pp. 27 ff.).

[82] N. B. two variants, not illustrated by Gnecchi, of type of Constantine II as Caesar with VOTIS / X / CAESS NN in wreath:—(1) Paris no. 36a, mint-mark MNM. **Pl. XIII, 7.** (2) *Trau Collection Sale Catalogue* 1935, Taf. 46, Nr. 4058, mint-mark MN·B. **Pl. XIII, 8.** The variant illustrated by Gnecchi (G I, tav. 9, no. 9) has mint-mark MNΓ".

[83] E. g. Constantius II, with legend GAVDIVM POPVLI ROMANI / TES and SIC / X / SIC / XX in wreath (Vienna: Kubitschek Taf. 16, Nr. 308 = G I, p. 66, no. 33). **Pl. XIII, 9.** Constans, same legend and mint-mark and SIC / V / SIC / X in wreath (*Evans Collection Sale Catalogue* 1934, pl. 61, no. 1923). **Pl. XIII, 10.** Constans, same, but with mint-mark SIS᠑ (Newell Collection, New York) **Pl. XIII, 11.** Constantius Gallus, XX in wreath, mint-mark SIS (*Trau Collection Sale Catalogue* 1935, Taf. 50, Nr. 4336). **Pl. XIV, 1.** *Ibid.*, with mint-mark LVG (Mazzini Collection, Turin). **Pl. XIV, 2.**

With a few exceptions, the reverse types of medallions of this group depict, in varying ways, the actual processus consularis of the Emperor to the Capitol on New Year's Day. It is well known that under the Empire the pomp and pageantry reserved for triumphs in earlier times were extended to the ceremonies attending the consul's entry upon office.[84] The processus consularis was, in other words, closely assimilated to the processus triumphalis; so that, legends and dates apart, it would often be hard to decide from the processional type itself whether it was as consul or as triumphator that the Emperor was portrayed. For example, the eagle-topped consular ivory sceptre is often combined with other accessories of a definitely triumphal character, while the triumphator's branch occurs as an imperial attribute in processional scenes which are otherwise purely consular. Tribunician dates and emphasis upon the consulship in the legends are the decisive criteria; and from these it emerges that, with two exceptions,[85] all processional scenes on medallions[86] can be safely interpreted as primarily consular, although not a few contain secondary references to victories and triumphs of the previous year.

While the processus triumphalis is by no means uncommon as a coin type from Augustus to Trajan, we have no certain coin representation of the imperial processus consularis earlier than the reign of Antoninus Pius.[87] Aurei of 140 show as reverse type Pius in a quadriga to left, holding the eagle-topped sceptre and accompanied by the two princes Marcus and Verus, with COS III in a prominent position at the top of the design.[88] The Emperor's colleague in the consulship for that year was, indeed, the young Marcus, consul for the first time, and for him Pius issued a "framed" medallion, of which the reverse type shows the Caesar riding in a quadriga to left and holding a branch, while the obverse legend reads AVRELIVS CAESAR AVG PII F COS.[89] For his entry upon his fourth consulship in 145 Pius struck medallions with his own portrait and COS III on the obverse and the consular procession on the reverse—the Emperor in a quadriga to left, holding the eagle-topped sceptre and accompanied by the two princes.[90] The close connection between consular and triumphal processions is well illustrated by a pair of medallions issued by Marcus Aurelius in 167. One of these, with the portrait of Marcus on the obverse, shows Marcus and Verus in a quadriga to right, each holding a branch, while Virtus leads the horses, and a trophy with captives is borne along on a platform by soldiers in the background: the legend in the exergue reads TR P XXI IMP IIII/COS III.[91] Here is an obvious allusion to the Emperors' triumph in the autumn of 166, after the eastern campaigns. But, unlike the sestertii of 166 with MEDIC added to the obverse titles and TR POT XX on the reverse,[92] the medallion does not depict the processus triumphalis. A twin medallion issued for Lucius Verus shows precisely the same reverse

[84] *RM* 1934, SS. 95 ff.; 1935, S. 32.

[85] G II, tavv. 109, no. 8; 123, no. 8. *Vide infra* pp. 86, 88.

[86] This is, of course, exclusive of types in which the pompa circensis is obviously portrayed (e. g. G II, tav. 104, no. 10).

[87] Strack III, S. 65, Anm. 170a.

[88] *Ibid.*, Taf. 1, Nr. 67.

[89] Specimen in a private collection in Rome. Pl. XIV, 3. The piece figured by Gnecchi (III, tav. 150, no. 5) is probably another specimen of the same medallion, but with reverse remade.

[90] G II, tavv. 53, no. 3; 55, nos. 6, 7.

[91] G II, tav. 63, no. 1.

[92] *RIC* III, p. 288, no. 940.

type, but with the procession moving towards the left, In the exergue we read TR P VII IMP IIII/COS III, proving beyond doubt that both pieces were struck for Verus' entry upon his third consulship on January 1, 167.[93] Marcus, although his own consulship was not renewed that year, rides beside Verus in the consular car by virtue of the recent celebration of their joint triumph. A parallel pair of medallions were issued ten years later, this time for Marcus and Commodus. Marcus' piece, dated TR P XXXI, shows Marcus and Commodus, each holding an eagle-topped sceptre, in a quadriga to left, while Virtus leads the horses and Victory floats in the air above: the exergue legend reads IMP VIII COS III / P P.[94] Commodus' medallion shows the same scene, apart from the fact that the Emperors each hold a branch, while the legend in the exergue reads TR POT COS.[95] Both were issued for Commodus' entry upon his first consulship on January 1, 177, with a secondary allusion to the triumph for the Germanic and Sarmatian victories held on December 23, 176, when Commodus shared his father's honors.[96]

Processional types dating from the accession of Commodus to the reign of Elagabalus are purely processional in character. They show simple scenes of the Emperor in his quadriga, holding consular sceptre or branch, without secondary triumphal references in the shape of trophies or figures of Victory. Two were struck for Commodus' entry upon his fifth and sixth consulships, in 186[97] and 190[98] respectively. One was issued for Geta's first consulship in 205, with COS in solitary prominence upon the reverse;[99] while the third consulship of Caracalla in 208[100] and of Elagabalus in 220[101] were similarly commemorated. More complicated designs reappear under Alexander Severus, who struck medallions for each of the three occasions on which he assumed the consulship. A gold piece issued for the first consulship on January 1, 222 shows the Emperor alone in his chariot, holding sceptre and branch.[102] On a bronze medallion of 226, the year of the second consulship, Victory stands in the car behind the Emperor and crowns him.[103] But for January 1, 229, when Alexander assumed his third consulship, with the historian Dio Cassius as his colleague, medallions were struck showing three different variations on the processus consularis theme. In the first case Victory stands in the car with Alexander and crowns him.[104] In the second, the Emperor holds neither sceptre nor branch, but a globe in one hand and a Victory carrying a trophy on the other.[105] In the third case Emperor and Victory stand together in a chariot shown, not from the side, as heretofore, but as practically,[106] or completely,[107] frontal—the first appearance, in fact, of the frontal chariot *motif* in imperial art,[108] while Virtus and Mars lead the two outermost horses of the team. Some of the obverses combined with these reverse types show the bust of the Emperor wearing consular dress and

[93] G II, tavv. 73, no. 2; 74, no. 4.
[94] G II, tav. 60, no. 7.
[95] G II, tavv. 87, nos. 6, 7; 90, no. 1.
[96] *Vita Commodi*, 12, 5.
[97] G II, tavv. 83, no. 10; 84, nos. 1, 2.
[98] G II, tav. 85, nos. 2, 3.
[99] G II, p. 78, no. 5.
[100] G II, tav. 95, no. 5.
[101] G II, tav. 96, no. 4.
[102] *RIC* IV, ii, p. 72, no. 15.
[103] G II, p. 82, no. 21. **Pl. XIV, 4.**
[104] G II, p. 81, no. 12.
[105] G II, tav. 99, no. 2.
[106] G II, tav. 99, no. 4.
[107] G II, tav. 99, no. 7.
[108] *JDAI* 1936, S. 94, Anm 1.

holding the eagle-sceptre, a style of obverse portrait now introduced upon medallions for the first time. The medallion struck for Maximinus' consulship in 236 returns to the profile view of the procession: Victory, Virtus and the soldiers, who accompany it, suggest the victories gained in Germany during the winter of 235.[109]

For the period extending from 239 to 248 we have a complete series of medallions corresponding to each occasion of an imperial consulship; and in every case the consular date is set out prominently, as though to catch the eye, in the exergue of the reverse design. Gordian III inaugurated his first consulship, held in 239, with the simple processional type of the Emperor holding the eagle-sceptre, in a quadriga.[110] This he repeated for his second consulship in 241,[111] but he issued at the same time two new and more elaborate compositions with triumphal elements—Victory, Virtus, Mars and soldiers with palms: in one of these types the frontal chariot reappears.[112] Under Gordian's successor, Philip, consular medallions may be said to reach their peak. No less than ten different types commemorate the three occasions on which he assumed the consul's office—in 245 with Titianus, in 247 and 248 with the younger Philip, as his colleague. The medallions issued for January 1, 245 repeat, with some minor variations, one of the types of Gordian's second consulship.[113] On January 1, 247 Philip II obtained both the rank of Augustus and the office of consul for the first time; and a bronze medallion issued in his name shows the joint processus consularis of father and son in a quadriga to left with Victory and the father's consular date—COS II—in the exergue.[114] A piece with busts of Philip I, Otacilia and Philip II on the obverse shows the procession frontally, with Victory, Virtus and Mars in attendance and COS II in the exergue;[115] and this, too, is the type employed for another medallion with the three obverse busts—our first instance among medallions of a true processus triumphalis, with reverse legend VICTORIAE AVGVSTORVM and no mention of the consulship, commemorating the Germanic victories of 246 to 247.[116] Five medallions were issued for the second joint consulship of Philip I and Philip II in 248. A bronze piece of Philip II, with his father's COS III in the exergue, shows the quadriga to left.[117] A gold piece of Philip I has the frontal chariot, accompanied by Victory, Virtus and Mars;[118] and a bronze medallion of Philip I, Otacilia and Philip II in a private collection in Liège shows the same design, except that Philip II stands in the car to the right, facing his father. By far the most interesting of the 248 medallions is an exceptionally fine piece in Paris, also of Philip I, Otacilia and Philip II.[119] It shows a quadriga to left with Victory in the car, bending down and inviting Philip I and Philip II to mount. Both Emperors are togate and one, at least, holds a short sceptre. Above their heads hovers Mars; and in front of the chariot wheel two captives are seated. The circumference legend reads GERM MAX CARPICI MAX; and

[109] G II, p. 86, no. 3. [110] G II, tav. 105, no. 1. [111] G II, tav. 105, no 4.
[112] G II, tav. 105, nos. 5, 6; III, tav. 153, no. 12.
[113] G II, tav. 107, no. 7 (**Pl. XLV, 3**); III, tav. 153, no. 16. [114] G II, tav. 108, no. 4.
[115] G II, tav. 109, no. 4. *Cf.* G II, p. 95, no. 8 (Philip I) and tav. 108, no. 6 (Philip II).
[116] G II, tav. 109, no. 8. [117] G II, tav. 108, no. 5.
[118] G I, tav. 2, no. 4. [119] G II, tav. 109, no. 1 (**Pl. XLV, 4**).

the stage seems to be set for a triumph scene in honor of Philip's recent victories over the Goths. But the emphatically consular exergue legend—III ET II COS, combined with the Emperors' consular dress and attribute, leaves us in no doubt that the triumphal allusions are secondary and that the type depicts, not the processus triumphalis, but the processus consularis, just due to start. Finally, it seems reasonable to suppose that of the medallions of Otacilia with the busts of her husband and son as reverse type, those at least which bear the exergue legend III ET II COS (and they are far more numerous than those without it), were issued for presentation on January 1, 248.[120]

During the second half of the third century the output of consular medallions, though fairly continuous, is far less abundant, relatively, than at earlier periods. A bronze piece of Trebonianus Gallus and Volusianus, issued for the former's second and for the latter's first, consulship in 252, shows a remarkable composition—a frontal chariot, drawn by six horses, in which the Emperors stand facing, the senior consul holding the triumphator's branch, while Victory hovers between them with wings outspread, crowning both at once. Virtus and Mars, as usual, guide the team, while the legend reads PONTIF MAX TR P II COS II / ET COS.[121] Here the triumphal details are purely conventional, for defeats, not victories, had preceded this particular New Year's Day. For his own fourth, and Gallienus' third, consulship in 257 Valerian struck a bronze medallion showing a frontal quadriga, in which he stands with his two sons and Victory; the legend is FELICITAS TEMPORVM—a New Year wish—with IIII ET III COS conspicuous in the exergue below.[122] The pieces issued for Gallienus' entry upon his fifth (262) and sixth (264) consulships show the simplest version of the processus consularis, with the imperial bust in consular dress on the obverse;[123] while an interesting piece struck for January 1, 268, when Marinianus, the Emperor's third son and destined successor, assumed the consulship, shows Gallienus, crowned by Victory, in the car, carrying the sceptre for the youthful consul, to whom a flying genius offers a wreath (XX COS . . . MARINIANO).[124] Probus issued medallions for his second consulship (278) with frontal chariot (IMP PROBVS CONS II)[125] and for his fourth consulship (281) with profile chariot and palm-bearers in attendance (PROBVS P F AVG / COS IIII).[126] The medallion struck for his fifth consulship (282) is more ambitious, both in legend and in design. The legend reads GLORIA ORBIS / COS V and the Emperor appears in a six-horse frontal chariot, accompanied by Mars, Virtus and four figures with palms.[127] Probus' triumph, celebrated in Rome at the end of 281, has obviously lent color to this processus consularis. Twin medallions, with reverse legend P M TRI P COS P P / S C, were issued by Carinus in 283[128] and by Numerianus in 284[129] respectively, the first with Carinus, consul for the first, and Carus, consul for the second, time in a quadriga to right, the second piece with Numerianus, consul for the first, and

[120] G II, tav. 110, no. 3.
[121] G II, tav. 112, no. 2.
[122] G II, tav. 112, no. 6.
[123] G II, tav. 114, no. 9 (cos v); III, p. 55, no. 67; *ZN* 1930, Taf. 1, Nrr. 4, 5 (cos vi). Pl. XIV, 5, 6.
[124] G II, tav. 113, no. 10.
[125] G III, tav. 156, nos. 20, 21.
[126] G II, tav. 121, no. 5.
[127] G II, tav. 119, no. 8.
[128] G III, tav. 161, no. 10.
[129] G III, tav. 161, no. 9.

Carinus, consul for the second, time. And here we may note, by way of contrast, the second of our two medallic representations of the processus triumphalis on a piece struck for Numerianus in 283 to 284. Carus and Numerianus stand in a profile quadriga, accompanied by Victory and a trophy with captives, carried by soldiers, while two more captives are seated in the exergue. The legend reads TRIVMFV QVADOR: no mention is made of the consulship; and the occasion would appear to be a belated triumph for Carus' defeat of the Quadi in 282.[130]

One bronze medallion of Maximian, struck for his first consulship in 287, shows the by now familiar frontal quadriga with its usual *entourage*.[131] The remaining consular types of the Diocletianic and Constantinian periods, however, break boldly away from the conventional processus consularis tradition. January 1, 287 was, indeed, a notable date in Maximian's career. Not only did it see him consul for the first time, but this was his first New Year's Day since Diocletian had taken him into partnership—a day rendered all the more auspicious by his recent military successes against the Bagaudae in Gaul. On that day, too, Diocletian entered upon his third consulship; and he issued for this occasion, in his own name and in that of his colleague, some remarkable gold medallions, of which two examples, worth ten and five aurei respectively,[132] have come down to us. The obverse of these pieces bears the legend IMPP DIOCLETIANO ET MAXIMIANO AVGG and busts of the two Augusti in rich consular dress. On the reverse we read IMPP DIOCLETIANO ET MAXIMIANO CCSS and the type shows a novel version of the processus consularis theme—a frontal chariot drawn, not by horses, but by four elephants, with palm-bearers in attendance.[133] Thus elephants, associated heretofore with triumphs or consecrations, now have their place in the consular processions as well and may, in actual fact, have drawn the consular car. On the occasion of his sixth consulship in 296 Diocletian struck a 2½-aurei medallion with the legend CONSVL VI P P PROCOS and the imperial consul standing in his official dress, a globe in his right hand and a sceptre in his left.[134] After this we have no other consular issues until 320, when Constantine I, entering upon his sixth consulship, struck a 2½-solidi medallion with a reverse legend similar to that on Diocletian's piece—P M TRIB P COS VI P P PROCOS, accompanying a portrait of himself as consul, seated on a curule chair with globe and sceptre.[135] Six years later, in 326, Constantine was consul again for the seventh time, with his son, Constantius Caesar, consul for the first time, as his colleague. To this occasion we may safely attribute the 2-solidi pieces, issued at the mint of Trier, with the young Caesar as consul on the obverse and on the reverse the legend AETERNA GLORIA SENAT P Q R and a frontal elephant-quadriga, in which father and son, both nimbate, stand side by side.[136] A similar, and almost certainly contem-

[130] G II, tav. 123, no. 8.

[131] G II, p. 130, no. 24. The reverse legend reads P M TRI P / COS P P. Pl. XIV, 7.

[132] The pieces weigh 53.10 and 26.6 grammes respectively and appear to have been struck on the 1/60 of a pound aureus standard, although the date usually assigned to its substitution for the 1/70 of a pound standard is *c.* 290 (*RIC* V, ii, p. 207).

[133] G I, tav. 5, nos. 1, 2. *Cf. supra* pp. 51 f.

[134] G I, tav. 4, no. 9.

[135] G I, p. 19, no. 39. Pl. XV, 1.

[136] G I, tav. 10, nos. 6, 7. *Cf. supra* p. 52.

porary, version of the processus consularis appears upon the 4½-solidi medallion at Stockholm, also issued at the Trier mint, with Constantine's own portrait, as consul, on the obverse and on the reverse a frontal elephant-quadriga, containing the Emperor, crowned by Victory, and accompanied by the legend INNVMERI TRIVMFI AVG N, which is quite general in its significance and cannot be associated with any particular triumph.[137] With a bronze piece of Constans, showing the imperial bust in consular dress on the obverse and the Emperor standing togate, with short sceptre and branch (?), on the reverse, our series of consular medallions ends.[138]

So far we have been dealing with medallions of which the date alone, or the date supported by the content of the legend, or the legend alone, undated, or the date, legend and reverse type all combined, prove conclusively that they were imperial strenae, struck for distribution on New Year's Day. The number of such pieces, which thus admit of no alternative theory of the occasion of their issue, is, as we have seen, considerable; and in view of this we may reasonably attribute to the same occasion other pieces, which, if they are not certainly New Year gifts, bear types at least suggestive of New Year thoughts, hopes and aspirations. At the same time, the Hercules medallions of Commodus' eighteenth tribunician year will remind us that many other pieces, besides those with reverse designs which directly convey such "compliments of the season," may well have been issued for presentation at the New Year.[139]

One recurrent theme which we have noted on exclusively New Year medallions is that of felicitas—annum felicem, feliciter, omnia felicia, temporum felicitas combined with attributes of Felicitas, vota felicia, felicissimus Augustus, felicitas temporum or temporum felicitas combined with a scene of sacrifice and felicia decennalia. It would seem, then, not unnatural to ascribe to New Year's Day the issue of the numerous pieces on which the figure of Felicitas herself occurs, whether alone or in a group with other figures.[140] Again, we may recognize New Year allusions in the FORT FELI medallion of Commodus' fourteenth tribunician year (188 to 189) with Fortuna standing, the caduceus of Felicitas in her hand and her foot set on the prow of a ship—

[137] *ZN* 1928, Taf. 3, no. 3 (**Pl. IV, 3**). *Cf. supra* p. 52. These two Treviran pieces may well have been designed for father and son by the same hand. For "dynastic" consular types of Crispus and Constantine II and of Crispus and Constantius II as Caesars *vide infra* pp. 197 f.

[138] G II, tav. 134, no. 12. Constans was consul in 339, 342 and 346. *Cf.* also the 1½-solidi piece of Constantius II probably struck for his joint consulship with Constans in 339 (*vide infra* p. 179). A bronze medallion of Licinius II, with the bust of the young Caesar in consular dress on the obverse and a scene of imperial sacrifice and the legend EXERC AVGVSTORVM on the reverse, may have been struck for the joint consulship of the two Licinii in 322 (G II, p. 133, no. 1). **Pl. XV, 2.**

[139] Another interesting example is Commodus' Hilaritas and Salus medallion (G II, tav. 84, no. 9). The type obviously commemorates the Emperor's escape at the Hilaria in the spring of 187; but the piece is dated TR P XIII (Dec., 187 to Dec., 188). A retrospective allusion so striking and direct is only explicable as borne by a New Year gift from the Emperor, recording the most important event, from his personal point of view, of the previous year. (*Cf. BMCCRE* IV, p. clxiii and note 2).

[140] E. g. types of Alexander Severus and Julia Mamaea and of Julia Mamaea showing Felicitas grouped with imperial figures (**Pl. XLIV, 6**). N. B. small Æ type of Alexander Severus and Julia Mamaea with legend FELICITAS PERPETVA = Paris no. 7460 (G III, p. 44, no. 15). **Pl. XV, 3.**

a corn ship, it may be, hinting at New Year promises for the annona;[141] and in Julia Domna's piece with the legend FORTVNAE FELICI, showing Fortuna seated, with Spes on a column on the right and on her left a naked boy offering her three corn-ears.[142]

The legend TEMPORVM FELICITAS has also a particular connotation, namely that of the "kindly fruits of the earth" brought forth in due season by Nature's bounty or the toil of man—a context at once suggestive of a New Year wish. Thus, on a medallion of Commodus, we find the legend combined with the seated figure of Pomona (?) holding corn-ears and poppies and surrounded by children gathering grapes.[143] Normally, however, this legend accompanies a group of four young—almost baby—boys bearing attributes of the Seasons—an engaging composition, obviously attractive to Roman taste, for it constantly recurs on medallions of Hadrian,[144] Antoninus Pius, Faustina II, Commodus and Annius Verus, Commodus, of Trebonianus Gallus, Probus, Carus and Carinus, where the legend appears in a different version as SAECVLI FELICITAS,[145] and of Licinius II, where the legend reads FELICIA TEMPORA.[146] This Four Seasons type as first introduced was exclusively medallic: until the time of Commodus it was never shared with the regular coinage.[147] An unusual version of the theme is found on a medallion of Marcus Aurelius as Caesar with the legend TEMPORVM FELICITAS and showing Hercules, complete with club and trophy, drawn along in a chariot by four Centaurs, who carry symbols of the Seasons.[148] Hercules' victory over the Centaurs symbolizes the victory of good over evil in general: the forces of evil are subdued and harnessed to the service of good and good times begin for the world in general and for agriculture in particular.[149]

New year wishes for a fruitful and prosperous New Year are again implied by another popular and specifically medallic type, first issued on a medallion of Antoninus Pius, which portrays the Four Seasons in a more elaborate context.[150] On the left stands a half-draped male figure holding a short sceptre in his left hand and resting his right hand upon the top of an oval frame, from which four young girls, draped and holding attributes of the Seasons, are about to emerge:[151] on the right,

[141] G II, tav. 78, no. 10.

[142] G II, tav. 94, no. 9. *Cf.* variant in Jameson Collection, Paris (*Jameson Collection Catalogue* iv, pl. 25, no. 505). **Pl. XV, 4.**

[143] G II, tav. 87, no. 2.

[144] G III, tav. 146, no. 1.

[145] G II, tavv. 111, no. 6; 121, no. 6; 122, no. 3.

[146] G I, tav. 6, no. 6 (**Pl. XLVIII, 5**). Struck for his quinquennalia in 321? *Vide supra* p. 39, note 129.

[147] For representations of the Four Seasons as boys in imperial-age sculpture see J. M. C. Toynbee, *The Hadrianic School*, p. 218, and pl. 50.

[148] G II, tav. 61, no. 6.

[149] *Cf.* Strack III, SS. 72, 138. For Hercules as patron of agriculture *cf.* also the Hercules and Ceres medallion type of Pius, which shows Ceres handing a cornucopiae to Hercules (G II, tav. 44, no. 2); types of Pius, Marcus Aurelius and Commodus as Caesar, in which Hercules is crowned by a Victory holding a cornucopiae (G II, tavv. 45, no. 2 (**Pl. XLI, 1**); 60, no. 2; 87, no. 8); and a type of Commodus, showing Hercules sacrificing and holding a cornucopiae in his left hand (G II, tav. 79, nos. 5, 6).

[150] G II, tav. 48, no. 9.

[151] For parallel representations of the Horae as girls on the silver patera from Aquileia, on imperial sarcophagi and on terracotta reliefs, gems and vases of Hellenistic and imperial times see J. M. C. Toynbee, *op. cit.*, pls. 32, no. 2; 42, no. 3; pp. 183, 190. *Cf.* also the mosaic from Isola Sacra, near Ostia, showing the Seasons as four girls issuing from an oval frame supported by Hercules (?) (G. Calza, *La necropoli del Porto di Roma nell' Isola Sacra*, p. 184, fig. 92. *Cf. infra* p. 349).

facing this group, stands a naked *putto*, supporting on his shoulders a well-stocked cornucopiae, symbol of Felicitas; he may represent the infant year.[152] That the frame is the zodiac frame, although the twelve signs are not actually visible upon it, is certain. The Parabiago patera at Milan (Brera Gallery) shows an identical half-draped and sceptred figure, standing in this case within, and grasping with his right hand, an oval frame on which the signs are clearly rendered;[153] while the mosaic from Sentinum at Munich shows the same zodiac frame grasped by a similar, but naked and sceptreless, personage standing inside it.[154] This figure, whether he be naked or draped and placed inside or outside the frame, we may interpret as the Genius Anni or Genius Saeculi,[155] presiding over the yearly cycle of the seasons, which are portrayed on the patera as four little boys in a row, closely resembling their medallic counterparts, and in the mosaic as four male children clustering round Tellus in the lower part of the design. Pius' medallion is dated TR POT XXI (December, 157 to December, 158). On February 25, 158, Pius solemnized his vicennalia; and his Genius Saeculi medallion may have been struck for January 1, 158, with this coming celebration in view; or possibly, like the contemporary vota medallions, for the actual anniversary day of the Emperor's accession as inaugurating another series, or saeculum, of "happy New Years." The corresponding medallions of Commodus are dated TR P X[156] and these, too, are contemporary with vota medallions struck for an accession anniversary, Commodus' fifth, on March 17, 185. What is the relation between the Emperor who issued these medallions and the Genius Saeculi portrayed upon them? A reverse type common to three later medallions, struck for Alexander Severus and Julia Mamaea, Gordian III and Tacitus respectively, offers a clue. The type shows the Emperor, togate, in the centre, seated to the front upon a large star-bespangled globe: he holds a short sceptre in his left hand, while his right hand rests upon a zodiac frame with four little draped figures of the Seasons emerging from it. Victory crowns the Emperor, and behind the frame stands a half-draped figure holding a sceptre.[157] In this later type the Genius Saeculi presiding over the cycle of the seasons is indisputably the Emperor himself, enthroned upon the globe as cosmocrator, master, not only of a world-wide Empire, but of the world of Nature herself, including the orbis anni and the stars which are the seasons' signs.[158] As for the figure standing behind the frame, we may interpret him as the purely abstract personification of the saeculum,

[152] *Cf.* A. B. Cook, *Zeus*, II, p. 372.

[153] A. Levi, "La patera d'argento di Parabiago," (*R. Istituto di Archeologia e Storia dell' Arte: opera d' arte*, fasc. v. 1935, tav. 3, no. 2).

[154] J. M. C. Toynbee, *op. cit.*, pl. 33, no. 3.

[155] The latter title is suggested by the legend SAEC AVR which accompanies a half-draped figure holding a phoenix and standing within, and grasping, an oval frame on an early aureus of Hadrian, struck to advertise the new reign as another Golden Age (*RIC* II, pl. 13, no. 239).

[156] G II, tav. 83, nos. 3, 4.

[157] G II, tavv. 101, no. 10; 105, no. 7; III, tav. 156, no. 14 (**Pl. XLVII, 3**).

[158] *Cf.* J. M. C. Toynbee, *op. cit.*, pp. 142 f. For representations of the "cosmic Juppiter" enthroned between Sol, Luna, Gaia and Thalassa within a zodiac frame on imperial coins of Nicaea in Bithynia (Antoninus Pius) and of Perinthus in Thrace (Alexander Severus) see A. B. Cook, *op. cit.*, I, p. 752, figs. 551, 552.

who has, as it were, abdicated in favor of the concrete, earthly ruler.[159] On the medallions of Alexander Severus and Julia Mamaea and of Gordian III this type is accompanied by the familiar New Year wish TEMPORVM FELICITAS, on the medallion of Tacitus by the legend AETERNITAS AVG, suggesting, perhaps, a Happy New Year that is never to end.[160] To return to the earlier type of Pius and Commodus, we may, in the light of these later pieces, see in the central figure both Genius and Emperor, abstract and concrete, as it were, in one; and this conflation of Genius and Emperor would seem to offer the true explanation of a curious medallion type issued by Hadrian without accompanying legend. The three extant specimens are all in poor condition, but the general content of the type is clear. It shows a half-draped male figure seated to the front within a zodiac frame, which he grasps with his raised right hand. Above, below and to right and left of the design, just outside the frame, are four little draped figures, closely akin to those of the Seasons in our medallion type of Pius and Commodus.[161] Gnecchi interprets the seated figure as Juppiter-Trajan;[162] Strack sees in him Hadrian as the New Augustus or as the τρισκαιδέκατος θεός, enthroned in the centre of the twelve "Monatsherrscher."[163] But clearly we should identify the figure as Hadrian-Genius Saeculi and assign the medallion a place in our New Year series. The obverse legend and portrait are those of the 123 to 128 issue; and what New Year's Day occasion could be found more suitable to such a piece than Hadrian's decennalia, celebrated on August 11, 127, of which Strack finds no trace upon the coinage,[164] but to which Mattingly sees an allusion in the globe commonly found in the exergue of denarii of this time?[165] The medallion may have been issued for the accession New Year's Day itself or for one, or both, of the calendar New Year's Days which preceded and followed the August celebrations. Hadrian, then, was responsible for the first type of the Emperor-Genius Saeculi medallion series. The last type of the series appears on gold medallions of Probus, which repeat the type of Pius and Commodus and bear the legend TEMP FELICITAS.[166]

The Four Seasons occur as a medallion *motif* in other New Year contexts besides that of the zodiac. Large bronze medallions of Julia Mamaea and Salonina bear the legend ABVNDANTIA TEMPORVM and show the Empress as Abundantia, seated and pouring out the contents of a cornucopiae in the direction of four small boys, obviously the Seasons, who stand with outstretched hands to receive her bounty. She is attended by Liberalitas (?) and Felicitas (?), while the rudder of Fortuna, on whose smiles the success of each New Year depends, leans against her

[159] Kubitschek S. 12 suggests that this figure is Juppiter—the heavenly cosmocrator watching over his imperial vice-gerent.

[160] *Cf.* RECTOR TOTIVS ORBIS aureus of Constantine I, showing the Emperor seated and crowned by Victory, with his right hand resting on a zodiac frame (C², VII, p. 282, no. 463) and RESTITVTOR LIBERTATIS aureus of Constantine I, showing the same type, but without the Victory (*Trau Collection Sale Catalogue* 1935, Taf. 45, Nr. 3937).

[161] G III, tav. 147, nos. 3, 4.

[162] G III, p. 21, no. 105.

[163] II, S. 107.

[164] II, S. 121.

[165] *BMCCRE* III, pp. cxxxvi f.

[166] G I, tav. 4, no. 2.

throne.[167] Again, the procession of the Seasons round the globe, or orbis anni, is portrayed on the TELLVS STABIL medallions of Hadrian and Commodus.[168] There the Four Seasons appear as girls and the globe of Tellus is spangled with stars. Four of Commodus' pieces are dated TR P XII (186 to 187) and may thus be connected with his vota soluta decennalia,[169] while the obverse of one of the variants, which bears the jugate busts of Commodus and Janus, at least suggests that it was issued for presentation on "Janus' Day" at the calendar New Year. The Seasons appear once more in association with Tellus, shown this time without her globe, on a medallion of Pius; here they figure as little boys again, sporting round Tellus, who reclines in a cave (?) against the back of a cow, a cornucopiae in her hand.[170]

Tellus, too, without the Seasons may well convey the notion of good wishes for a happy and prosperous agricultural New Year. Thus we find her on a medallion of Commodus reclining against a basket, a vine-branch in her hand, while a herdsman with two oxen stands before her.[171] On a medallion of Pius she reclines below and holds up the fold of her himation to receive the seed which Triptolemus, hovering above her in his serpent-drawn car, scatters into her lap.[172] Other medallions of Pius and of Commodus show Tellus again reclining below, with a cornucopiae and a baby at her breast, while Sol, guided by Lucifer, drives his team heavenward above a bank of clouds.[173] Strack sees an allusion here to the Emperor as Sol Invictus.[174] But this seems hardly probable in the second century, nor does the god on the medallions make the "salute" with the right hand characteristic of Sol Invictus.[175] The primary allusion is surely to Sol as disposer of the agricultural year—"anno qui solstitiali circumagitur orbe,"[176] with a secondary reference, it may be to the Emperor, who could take the place of Sol, metaphorically, and mediate his gifts to the world.[177] On medallions earlier than the time of Aurelian Sol, even when dissociated from Tellus, may always have had this New Year significance, as when he is seen driving his quadriga on bronze medallions of Hadrian[178] and Aelius[179] and on a gold piece of Caracalla,[180] or portrayed in the form of a radiate bust on a small bronze medallion of Hadrian.[181]

[167] G II, tavv. 100, no. 7 (Julia Mamaea); 115, no. 8 (Salonina); III, tav. 153, no. 1 (Julia Mamaea).

[168] G III, tav. 145, no. 12; II, tavv. 86, nos. 8–10; 87, no. 1.

[169] *RIC* III, p. 364.

[170] G II, tav. 54, no. 7.

[171] G II, tav. 84, no. 8.

[172] Strack III, Taf. 21, Nr. 599. **Pl. XV, 5, 6.** *Cf.* the same scene on a posthumous medallion of Faustina I, with the addition of Faustina-Ceres (?) with a torch (?), standing on the left (*ibid.*, S. 139, Nr. 701). **Pl. XVI, 1.**

[173] G II, tavv. 50, no. 6; 78, nos. 3, 4. *Cf.* a similar type of Faustina II, showing Sol rising heavenward in his chariot out of the sea, with Oceanus and Tellus reclining below (G II, tav. 68, no. 8).

[174] Strack III, S. 57.

[175] E. g. SOLI INVICTO bronze medallions of Aurelian (G II, tav. 117, nos. 9, 10).

[176] Livy i, 19, 6.

[177] *Cf.* (1) Lucan's address to Nero (*BC* i, 48–50):—"seu te flammigeros Phoebi conscendere currus/telluremque nihil mutato sole timentem/igne vago lustrare iuvet." (2) The relief from Ephesus at Vienna, showing Marcus Aurelius in the chariot of the Sun, with Tellus reclining below (E. Strong, *La scultura romana*, tav. 50).

[178] *ZN* 1927, Taf. 8, Nr. 1; 1930, Taf. 2, Nr. 2 = **Pl. XVI, 2.**

[179] G II, tav. 42, nos. 8, 9.

[180] G I, tav. 1, no. 4.

[181] Strack II, Taf. 16, Nr. 434. **Pl. XVI, 3.**

Triptolemus is equally suggestive of New Year aspirations when associated with Ceres, as on two posthumous medallions of Faustina I, of which one shows Ceres seated and handing corn-ears to Triptolemus, who stands before her beside her serpent-drawn car,[182] while the other shows the goddess kindling an altar, with a small statuary group of Triptolemus in his serpent-drawn car on a pillar to the right.[183] Possibly all medallion types of Ceres, whether they portray her alone, standing (Faustina I, Julia Domna[183a]) or seated (Crispina),[183b] or grouped with Annona (Hadrian), Securitas (Faustina II, Lucilla), Hercules (Antoninus Pius), Neptune (Antoninus Pius,[184] Marcus Aurelius as Caesar) or the Emperor (Aelius Verus,[185] Antoninus Pius),[186] should also be interpreted as New Year types, conveying good wishes for New Year blessings of a more strictly material kind.

Finally, we may add to our list a few types somewhat loosely connected with New Year thoughts—Bonus Eventus (Hadrian, Antoninus Pius, Marcus Aurelius), Providentia, whether depicted as a woman holding agricultural implements (Hadrian)[187] or as a corn ship (Commodus),[188] and Mercury, as the symbol of New Year luck (Trajan, Hadrian, Antoninus Pius, Marcus Aurelius as Caesar). Commodus' Janus types (bust, statue standing under an arch) suggest January 1, 187 (they are dated TR P XII).[189] Marcus Aurelius' Abundantia types, showing her seated and receiving an enormous cornucopiae borne towards her on the shoulders of two boys,[190] or standing and pouring the contents of a cornucopiae into a modius,[191] remind us of the ABVNDANTIA TEMPORVM medallions of Julia Mamaea and Salonina. Faustina II's Isis Pharia medallion[192] is an interesting precursor of the Isis-festival medallion group; while Albinus' seated figure labelled SAECVLO FRVGIFERO and Gallienus' piece with the legend VBERITAS suggest "felicitas" and the whole range of associated ideas.

[182] G II, tav. 57, no. 10.
[183] G II, tav. 58, no. 1.
[183a] **Pl. XLIV, 2.**
[183b] **Pl. XLIII, 4.**
[184] G II, p. 16, no. 65. **Pl. XVI, 4.**
[185] Strack II, Taf. 20, Nr. 896. **Pl. XVI, 5.**
[186] G II, p. 22, no. 114. The interpretation of this type is, however, uncertain. The seated male figure may be, not the Emperor, but Juppiter, and the standing female figure, leaning on a column and presenting him with corn-ears, may be, not Ceres, but Securitas. **Pl. XVI, 6.**
[187] Cf. **Pl. XVII, 1.**
[188] The medallion is dated TR P XII and may thus have been issued for Jan. 1, 187 with reference to the equipping of a new African corn fleet in the previous year (*RIC* III, p. 422, nos. 486, 487 = sestertii dated TR P XI).
[189] These also allude, no doubt, to Commodus' calendar reforms of 186.
[190] G II, tav. 63, no. 6.
[191] G II, tav. 66, no. 1.
[192] G III, tav. 151, no. 4.

CHAPTER II

THE OCCASIONS OF MEDALLION ISSUES (2)

II. Imperial Adoptions, Marriages, Births and Deaths

The TR P XVIII Hercules medallion series of Commodus has proved to us that in one instance at least the medallions of a given year were prepared well ahead of the regular coinage for distribution as imperial strenae on New Year's Day.[1] Similarly, in the case of medallions of other groups with legends and content conveying direct, or almost direct, New Year allusions, the large proportion of types which are exclusively medallic proclaims the same divergence between medallions and coins as regards the actual occasion and moment of their release. New Year celebrations and aspirations are, of course, not infrequently reflected in the ordinary coinage; but this is done in a way which does not necessarily suggest a very close or immediate connection with the New Year's Day itself. In fact it would appear that many New Year coin types could commemorate retrospectively the New Year thoughts and activities inaugurating the year of their issue; whereas medallions were literally "occasional" pieces, struck for the actual day. Again, coin types with vota allusions are sometimes spread out over a wide period, extending over two tribunician years and thus covering issues released at intervals before, and, possibly, after, the final and culminating celebrations to which the vota medallions normally belong. Furthermore, cases of identity of coin with medallion New Year types provide no argument for ascribing the issue of the coins which bear the types in question to New Year's Day. There are cases, such as that of the Four Seasons *motif*, in which the coin type has been simply borrowed from medallions issued at a much earlier date.[2] Conversely, there are instances, such as that of the Hercules ploughing type of Commodus, of the translation of pre-existing coin types into a new medallic setting for New Year purposes.[3] When we pass from the New Year medallions to those concerned with imperial adoptions, marriages, births and deaths, we shall inevitably find, in certain fields, a less intimate association of medallion, as distinct from coin, issues in point of time with the occasions which inspired them. In the case of such pre-arranged affairs as adoptions and marriages, it was obviously possible to prepare medallions beforehand for presentation on the day itself, as on New Year's Day. On the other hand, medallions relating to births and deaths are, of their very essence, retrospective and commemorative, rather than "occasional" in the strictest sense of the term: some interval at least must have elapsed between the event and the distribution of the gifts connected with it. In the case of deaths, this distribution may well have taken place at the time of the official consecration, as the consecration types and legends possibly, although not necessarily, imply. A possible moment for offering presents in honor of a new arrival in the imperial

[1] *Vide supra* pp. 74 ff. [2] *Vide supra* p. 90. [3] *Vide supra* p. 74.

family is suggested by the dies lustricus, the eighth or ninth day after birth, when the child received its name: but the interval may well have been longer. Nor, again, shall we find in these medallions a content as specifically and exclusively medallic as in those of other categories. Such events in the lives of rulers were, under the Roman Empire, as always, matters of wide, popular appeal and lent themselves more readily to striking representation on the current coinage than the ever-recurring thoughts and ceremonies of New Year's Day, which, just because they were, in a sense, common property, demanded that their treatment on the Emperor's New Year gifts should assume ever novel and original forms. Hence the frequent overlapping of coin and medallion consecration types. Hence, too, since Antoninus Pius' dynastic programme involved the focusing of public interest on the numerous confinements of Faustina II, the fact that the births of royal children during his principate are recorded almost more completely and literally on the coinage than on the corresponding medallions: and here also the identity of coin and medallion types is not uncommon.[4] At the same time there remains a not inconsiderable number of types, issued in these contexts, which are peculiar to medallions and record their respective occasions in an outstandingly vivid or personal manner.

ADOPTIONS

The adoption of Aelius Verus by Hadrian is the only occasion of its kind, so far as we know, on which medallions were distributed. Coins of Aelius refer to the event in a general and impersonal way with types of Concordia, Pietas, Spes, Roma greeting the Emperor-to-be, and the like. But a medallion reverse type, combined with obverse portraits of both parties concerned, offers a quasi-realistic scene of the adoption ceremony itself. Hadrian and his adopted heir stand confronted, clasping one another by the hand. The legend reads CONCORDIA; and between the two men stands Concordia herself, facing the spectator, with a hand laid on the shoulder of each.[5]

MARRIAGES

We have no direct medallic allusions to the marriage of Marcus Aurelius and Faustina II, solemnized in the spring, or early summer, of 145. It would be strange, however, if an imperial union of such special dynastic significance had occasioned no issue of medallions for presentation on the auspicious day. Hence the attractiveness of Strack's suggestion that the medallion type of Marcus showing Bacchus riding in a biga drawn by Centaurs and attended by Satyrs and an Amor, depicts in allegory the wedding of the imperial Bacchus and Ariadne.[6] If straight-forward wedding scenes were planned for the regular coinage,[7] this vivid mythological version, although less strictly personal, has its natural place on pieces designed as special gifts for cultured people. The realistic wedding scene appears, however,

[4] *Cf.* Strack III, S. 108 ff.

[5] G II, tavv. 38, no. 3; 42, no. 7.

[6] G II, tav. 65, nos. 8, 9 (**Pl. XLI, 6**); Strack III, S. 110 (*vide infra* p. 139).

[7] E. g. *RIC* III, pls. 3, no. 71; 4, no. 79. It is possible that this type was originally inspired by the Hadrianic adoption medallion.

on a medallion struck for the occasion of Lucilla's marriage with Lucius Verus in 164, with the legend CONCORDIA FELIX and the bridal pair clasping hands.[8] It is also possible that one of Faustina II's medallions was struck for Lucilla's wedding. It shows Juno Lucina (?) enthroned, with sceptre, crowning a small female figure, with skirt uplifted in the attitude of Spes, who receives statuettes of the three Graces from Venus (?).[9] The Graces symbolize conjugal fertility; and the little figure enshrining the hope of royal offspring is at this stage—the obverse bears the later version of the legend, FAVSTINA AVGVSTA—probably not Faustina herself, but her newly-wed daughter, Lucilla. The same *motif* of a girl receiving statuettes of the three Graces at Venus' (?) hands appears on medallions struck both in Faustina's and in Lucilla's name, which may also have been issued as presentation pieces for the latter's wedding-day.[10] On Lucilla's coins references to the wedding are all impersonal—Concordia, sometimes accompanied by Spes, and VOTA PVBLICA ("marriage vows") within a wreath. Similar types—Concordia, clasped hands, a lighted altar (DIS CONIVGALIBVS)—on Crispina's coinage allude to her marriage with Commodus in 177. These may be retrospective, for it is uncertain whether coins were struck for Crispina before her husband's sole reign began.[11] But the bronze medallions with twin busts of bride and bridegroom on the obverse, to which no coin parallel exists, can hardly be other than contemporary pieces, presented by Marcus to wedding guests and other friends on the wedding day itself, which, as Capitolinus tells us, he made the occasion of a congiarium.[12] One of the reverse types is strictly allegorical—Concordia enthroned, with her elbow resting on a statuette of Spes. But the second type shows the quasi-realistic scene of bride and bridegroom joining hands under Concordia's auspices, with the legend VOTA PVBLICA.[13] No less than sixteen extant specimens of this type are recorded: Marcus must have been liberal with his gifts. Twin busts of a youthful bride and bridegroom again appear on a small "framed" medallion of Septimius Severus, the reverse of which shows portraits of Caracalla and Plautilla and the titles borne by Caracalla in 202 (PONT TR P V COS), the year of their marriage.[14] The next medallion in the marriage series is a large bronze of Elagabalus and Aquilia Severa, known from a unique "framed" specimen in Paris. This sacrilegious union of the priest-Emperor with a Vestal Virgin took place in 219 to 220 and is recorded by Concordia coin types.[15] According to Dio, Elagabalus had the impudence to declare, apropos of his conduct, "I did this in order that godlike children might spring from me, the high priest, and her, the high priestess"[16]—words which give special point to our medallion. The obverse shows twin busts of the bridal pair;

[8] G II, tav. 76, no. 1. This medallion is, unfortunately, known only from a single, somewhat suspicious, piece in Paris.

[9] G II, tav. 69, no. 7.

[10] G II, tavv. 68, no. 2 (FAUSTINA AVGVSTA); 76, no. 7 (Pl. XLII, 5). For Pansa's theory that the three figures represent, not Graces, but children see *RIN* 1920, pp. 163 ff.

[11] *RIC* III, p. 356.

[12] *Vita Marci*, 27, 8.

[13] G II, tav. 91, nos. 7, 8, 9.

[14] G III, tav. 152, no. 6.

[15] One piece (*RIC* IV, ii, p. 59, no. 395), showing Elagabalus and his bride united by Concordia, has no S C and may be a small medallion.

[16] Dio 80, 9, 3.

the reverse bears the legend SPES PVBLICA and portrays Spes stepping out jauntily—the personification of that very hope of godlike offspring, which the Emperor thus advertised to the recipients of his wedding-day gifts.[17] In the year 225, in deference to his mother's wish, Alexander Severus took to wife a lady of patrician birth, Sallustia Barbia Orbiana. Bronze medallions of Alexander, of Alexander and Orbiana and of Orbiana show the usual wedding group with CONCORDIA AVGVSTORVM as accompanying legend.[18] Another bronze piece of Alexander and Orbiana shows bride and bridegroom solemnizing their union by a sacrifice.[19] In view of the part played by Julia Mamaea in bringing off the match it would not be unreasonable to attribute to the same occasion a small silver medallion with her own bust on one side and those of her son and daughter-in-law on the other.[20] The last medallic record of an imperial marriage is a bronze piece of Salonina, with legend CONCORDIA AVGVSTORVM and Salonina and Gallienus clasping hands.[21]

BIRTHS

Imperial births are naturally recorded mainly on medallions of Empresses and in association, for the most part, with the female imperial virtues of fecunditas, pietas and pudicitia. It is, indeed, comparatively rare to find births providing occasions for medallion issues; and the earliest and largest group of "birthday" medallions was inspired by special circumstances—Antoninus Pius' preoccupation with the need for securing a dynastic succession to the principate within his own family. The birth of Pius' eldest grandchild, Faustina Parvula, which took place not later than April, 146, has left no trace on either coins or medallions. But the arrival, in the following year, of a male heir to the throne, reflected in the Juno Lucina, Venus Genetrix and Laetitia coin types, is commemorated on a medallion of Faustina II in a strikingly vivid and pleasing reverse design. The imperial baby is seen riding on the back of the peacock of Juno Lucina, who assisted at his birth, while two guardian Curetes, one on either side, execute an armed dance.[22] Unfortunately the little "Zeus" only survived his birth by a few weeks. In 149, however, Faustina presented her husband with twins, a boy, who died soon after birth, and a girl, the future Empress Lucilla. Direct reference to the happy event is, in this case, reserved for the coinage, in the TEMPORVM FELICITAS type showing busts of the new arrivals, as the harbingers of a "Happy New Year," emerging from cornuacopiae.[23] But Strack[24] convincingly ascribes to this occasion three medallions of Marcus Aurelius dated TR P III (149)—Mars-Marcus seated, with Venus-Faustina standing beside him,[25] Bacchus-Marcus and Ariadne-Faustina in a panther-biga, with a Bacchic train in attendance,[26] and the small bronze pieces with an Amor

[17] G II, tav. 97, no. 2.

[18] *RIC* IV, ii, p. 114, no. 551; G II, tavv. 98, no. 4; 102, no. 2; III, tav. 153, no. 9; p. 44, no. 2 (N. B. Berlin piece). **Pl. XVII, 2.** *Cf.* coins with the same type (*RIC* IV, ii, pl. 9, no. 1).

[19] G II, tav. 102, no. 3.

[20] G I, tav. 23, no. 5.

[21] G II, p. 111, no. 7. **Pl. XVII, 3.**

[22] G II, tav. 67, no. 10 (= obverse), no. 7 (= reverse).

[23] *RIC* III, pl. 2, no. 35.

[24] III, S. 114.

[25] G II, tav. 61, no. 7.

[26] G II, tav. 65, no. 7.

riding on a lion.[27] No more births in the imperial family are recorded on medallions until 157, when a third daughter, Domitia Faustina, arrived, only to be carried off by death in early infancy. Bronze medallions of Faustina II, large and small, bear the legend FECVNDITATI AVGVSTAE and the Empress seated with the baby on her lap, while her only two other surviving children, Faustina Parvula and Lucilla, stand on either side.[28] After the death of their little sister, Faustina Parvula and Lucilla were again the sole survivors, and as such they appear on a medallion of Faustina which shows her standing between her two daughters—a type not, this time, occasioned by, but anticipating, another birth, perhaps to advertise to relatives and friends the good news that the imperial lady was once more with child.[29] Indeed, in 159 Faustina was again confined, this time with happier results, for her fourth daughter, Fadilla, contrived to survive her infancy. Two medallions show the Empress as the mother once more of three children. On one piece she stands in the centre with the new baby in her arms, while Lucilla stands on the right and from the left Faustina Parvula staggers along beneath the weight of an enormous cornucopiae.[30] The second piece shows Faustina seated on a chair with arms formed of two cornuacopiae, on which are perched the little Fadilla as Spes—new hope for the Domus Augusta, and Lucilla as Abundantia, handing the Empress two corn ears, while Faustina Parvula stands at her mother's side.[31] The same occasion inspired the PIETATI AVG coin and medallion of Pius (TR P XXIII)—Pietas-Faustina standing, a globe in one hand and Fadilla in the other, between the two elder girls.[32] In the summer of 160 Faustina II gave birth to yet another daughter, Cornificia. This occasioned a medallion of Pius showing the Emperor writing upon a shield, presented to him by Victory, and accompanied by Faustina and her four daughters, the new baby in her arms.[33] Fate dealt somewhat hardly with Pius in this matter of the succession. Twice his hopes of a male heir had been doomed to disappointment; and now it was not until after his death in the summer of 161 that Faustina gave birth to twin sons, one of whom was really destined to succeed his father and grandfather as the Emperor Commodus. But at any rate what Pius had hoped for was at last achieved. The TEMPOR FELIC legend reappears upon the aes coinage, accompanied by a standing type of Faustina with her six children;[34] while a medallion shows the Empress seated with the twins in her arms and their four admiring sisters clustering around.[35] It is perhaps noteworthy that, apart from the two cases in which the medallion types exactly coincide with those of coins,

[27] Strack IV, Taf. 4, Nr. 613. **Pl. XVII, 4.**

[28] G II, tav. 67, no. 2; III, tav. 150, no. 9. *Cf.* aurei of Faustina II with the same type and legend (*RIC* III, p. 269, nos. 681, 682). The Bacchus and Ariadne type struck for Marcus Aurelius in 157 (G II, tav. 62, no. 3) may celebrate this birth.

[29] G II, tav. 69, no. 4.

[30] G II, tav. 69, no. 6.

[31] G II, tav. 69, no. 9.

[32] G II, tav. 46, no. 7; *RIC* III, pls. 2, no. 47; 6, no. 116.

[33] G II, tav. 55, no. 5. The Victory-and-shield *motif* must allude to the crushing of a rebellion in Africa during the early part of the year.

[34] Strack III, Taf. 20, Nr. *.

[35] G II, tav. 69, no. 8. As far as we know, Marcus issued no "birthday" medallions for the children born to him and Faustina after 161.

none of the medallions of this "birthday" series bear explanatory reverse legends. On the coins these were needed to make explicit to the people at large the thoughts suggested by imperial motherhood. But the types themselves, without comment, sufficed for the relatives, personal friends and high-placed officials for whom the medallions were designed. The next "birthday" medallion was struck for Lucilla, who presented her husband with a daughter in 166; it shows her seated, suckling her child, and bears the legend FECVNDITAS AVGVSTAE.[36]

The FECVNDITATI AVG medallions of Julia Domna are frankly retrospective. They show the Empress enthroned and suckling an infant (Geta), while a small boy (Caracalla) stands at her knee.[37] This reverse design is combined with two varieties of obverse legend, IVLIA DOMNA AVGVSTA, assigned to the years 193 to 196, and IVLIA AVGVSTA, assigned to the years 196 to 211. The portraits on both obverses are very similar and we should be inclined to ascribe both medallions to 196, the year in which the change from one legend to another took place and when the striking of both the old and the new obverse type in the same issue might be expected. Moreover it was on May 27 of this very year that Septimius Severus, on his way back to Rome from the East, celebrated the birthday of his younger son in Thrace by holding military games, with dynastic propaganda in view.[38] A liberalitas and public games marked his return to the Capital, while his PROVIDENTIA AVG denarii seem to refer to the designation of Caracalla as the heir.[39] The medallions may well have been struck, also as part of the dynastic programme, for the same occasion, before Severus left Rome for Gaul.[40] We have no direct evidence that the marriage of Alexander Severus and Orbiana was ever blessed with children; but a bronze medallion of Orbiana with the legend FECVNDITAS TEMPORVM shows the Empress enthroned with Felicitas (?) kneeling at her feet and presenting her with a cornucopiae, while a baby is perched on each of her shoulders.[41] Did Orbiana, then, bear twins, whose birth is otherwise unknown to us? As far as we are aware, Otacilia had no other children after giving birth to her son Philip II in 237 to 238. It would seem, therefore, that her TEMPORVM FELICITAS, PVDICITIA AVG and PIETAS AVGVSTAE medallions, which show her grouped with several children, had a general and symbolic significance.[42]

The PIETAS AVGVSTES [*sic*] bronze medallion of Helena, showing the Empress with two children, which was struck for her by Constantine, possibly in 325 for the occasion of his vicennalia, when the title of "Augusta" was conferred upon her, is, of course, a general and retrospective tribute to her imperial motherhood.[43] "Birthday" medallions were also struck for Fausta, two in gold and one in bronze. The first gold type, with the legend PIETAS AVGVSTAE, shows the Empress nimbate and frontal, seated with a baby on her lap and attended by Felicitas, another female

[36] G II, tav. 76, no. 2.
[37] G II, tav. 94, nos. 6, 7.
[38] *Vita Max. du.*, 2; *JRS* 1920, p. 164.
[39] *RIC* IV, i. pl. 5, no. 22.
[40] *Cf.* also the AETERNIT IMPERI medallions of Julia Domna with confronted busts of Septimius Severus and Caracalla and of Septimius Severus and Geta (*vide infra* p. 159, note 154).
[41] G II, tav. 102, no. 1.
[42] G II, tavv. 107, no. 10; 108, nos. 1, 2; III, tav. 153, no. 18.
[43] G II, tav. 128, no. 9.

figure and winged Genii with garlands.[44] The occasion was, presumably, the birth of Fausta's eldest child, Constantius II, in 317. The second gold type shows the legend SPES REIPVBLICAE and Fausta standing with an infant on either arm.[45] As Seeck observes,[46] Nazarius (*Paneg.* 10, 36) speaks of the Caesars Crispus and Constantine II as having "fratres" in 321; and the piece may thus commemorate the birth of another boy in 318 to 319, soon enough, at any rate, after the birth of Constantius II for the pair to be represented in the guise of twins. As we hear nothing more of this second son of Fausta we may conclude that he died in early childhood; and her bronze medallion with the legend PIETAS AVGVSTES [*sic*], the "twin" of Helena's piece and presumably issued at the same time and mint,[47] shows the Empress standing with Constans, born in 323, in her arms and only one other child, Constantius, by then a boy of six, beside her:[48] this piece was, of course, retrospective, if struck in 325.

DEATHS

In view of the abundant output of current coins with consecration types and references, the comparative scarcity of medallions occasioned by deaths in the imperial family need not surprise us. The consecration of an Emperor or Empress was essentially a public event, whereby the seal of official approval was set upon the life and character of the deceased. The distribution of medallions as individual and private gifts was therefore less appropriate to these occasions than to others of a more personal kind. Again, there are few consecration medallions of which the types do not coincide, in all but a few details at the most, with the types of the corresponding coins. If some special pieces were struck for presentation, as has been suggested, on the actual consecration day, their types appeared later, in an identical or modified form, and accompanied by a wide variety of other types, on the coins of the next regular issues of imperial currency. The series of consecration medallions opens,[49] however, with no less than six different types issued for the occasion of Faustina I's death and consecration in 141. Some of these show interesting divergencies from the corresponding coins. The rogus type (CONSECRATIO), with Faustina in a biga crowning the elaborate erection, is shared with the coinage.[50] But the type of the Empress with flying cloak, driving beside Aeternitas in a biga to right (CONSECRATIO), is peculiar to medallions.[51] A third medallion, without reverse legend, shows Faustina, wearing a stephane, in the act of stepping into a biga, the reins of which she holds in her hands, for her last journey.[52] Aurei show the same design; but the figure wears no stephane and has a decidedly more juvenile

[44] G I, tav. 8, no. 10; Maurice I, pl. 23, no. 11. **Pl. XVII, 5.** The first variant shows four Genii, the second only two.

[45] G I, tav. 8, nos. 11, 12.

[46] *ZN* 1898, SS. 40, 41. There seem to be no serious grounds for rejecting Seeck's conclusion (P-W[2] *s. v.* Fausta, Bd. 12, 2085) that Fausta really was the mother of Constantius II and Constans.

[47] *Vide supra* p. 54, note 93.

[48] G II, tav. 133, no. 1.

[49] A bronze medallion of Sabina (CONSECRATIO, spread eagle) was in trade with Cahn in 1936, but it seems to be of doubtful authenticity (cast in B. M.).

[50] G II, tav. 56, no. 7.

[51] G II, tav. 56, no. 8.

[52] G II, tavv. 58, no. 2; 59, no. 3.

appearance than her opposite number on the medallion.[53] Is she, not Faustina starting for heaven, but Aeternitas waiting for the imperial traveller to mount—on the coins an abstraction, on the more personal medallions Faustina herself? Another legend-less medallion portrays the Empress in a galloping biga, holding her flying cloak with both hands.[54] Sestertii show a somewhat similar type, but there the figure suggests Aeternitas, for she holds a long torch.[55] A fifth medallion, to which, again, no coins correspond, shows a dignified, matronly standing figure, leaning on a column and holding a globe surmounted by a nimbate phoenix (AETERNITAS)[56] In spite of the legend we may, perhaps, discern in this stately personage the features and bearing of the Empress herself, with the symbols of Eternity, rather than Eternity personified. Similarly, in Faustina's sixth, also legend-less, reverse type we may possibly see, not Aeternitas, but the immortal Empress in the figure who stands beside a lighted altar and holds a bust of Sol (?) and a zodiac frame.[57] On the other hand, the legend AVGVSTA, which accompanies a somewhat similar figure on the coinage, does not necessarily imply that the person there depicted is the Empress, for it is also combined with a variety of other types.[58] The CONSECRATIO bronze medallion of Antoninus Pius has no counterpart on the regular coinage. It shows an apotheosis scene in which Pius is borne aloft on the back of an eagle, while Campus Martius reclines below.[59] Both of Faustina II's consecration medallions are shared with coins. One shows Diana standing with crescent, quiver and torch (SIDERIBVS RECEPTA);[60] the other shows Faustina-Aeternitas standing and leaning on a column, a sceptre in one hand, in the other a phoenix perched on a globe (AETERNITAS)[61]

After the Antonine period only three more consecration medallions remain to be recorded. A bronze piece of Divus Pertinax (193) has the legend AETERNITAS and a type unknown to his ordinary consecration coinage—an elephant-quadriga carrying a statue of the deceased Emperor beneath a canopy.[62] We know that Septimius Severus, in his capacity as the avenger of Pertinax, celebrated his apotheosis in full style.[63] For Valerian II (died *c.* 255) we have a bronze piece with the legend CONSECRATIO and a rogus topped by the dead prince in a biga.[64] The fine gold medallion struck at Ostia in memory of Maxentius' son Romulus (died 309) has an obverse portrait peculiar to itself, but shares its reverse legend and type—AETERNAE MEMORIAE and circular temple—with the regular coinage.[65]

III. RELIGIOUS CELEBRATIONS

A small series of medallions with sacrificial scenes would appear to have been

[53] Strack III, S. 92, Taf. 6, Nr. 437.
[54] G II, tav. 59, no. 4.
[55] Strack III, Taf. 18, Nr. 1231 a.
[56] G II, tav. 56, no. 5 (Pl. **XLI, 4**).
[57] Strack III, Taf. 4, Nr. 708. **Pl. XVII, 6.**
[58] *RIC* III, pp. 70–72.
[59] G II, tav. 43, no. 5.
[60] G II, tav. 67, no. 4.
[61] G II, tav. 67, no. 1.
[62] G II, tav. 91, no. 10.
[63] *Cf. CAH* xii, p. 5. The large bronze CONSECRATIO medallion of Julia Domna (G II, tav. 96, no. 1) is of very dubious antiquity.
[64] G II, tav. 116, no. 3. *Cf. RIC* V, i, p. 120, no. 35.
[65] G I, p. 14, no. 1 (**Pl. IV, 11**). The original disappeared from Paris in 1831, but a copy is preserved in Berlin.

struck for distribution at the "Birthday of Rome" celebrations on April 21. A unique large bronze piece of Septimius Severus at Zagreb bears the legend RESTITV-TOR VRBIS and shows Roma enthroned and the Emperor sacrificing to her at a tripod: by this act of worship the Emperor renews, as it were, or "restores" the eternal life of Rome.[66] Bronze medallions of Alexander Severus and of Alexander Severus and Julia Mamaea, struck in 228, with the legend P M TR P VII COS II P P or ROMAE AETERNAE, depict the Emperor, accompanied by priests and attendants, sacrificing in front of a temple, in which a statue of Roma is enshrined.[67] J. Gagé identifies the temple with that of Venus and Rome, built by Hadrian, and believes that the year 128 may, after all, prove to have some connection with its beginnings, since the choice of the year 228, exactly a hundred years later, for the issue of these medallions suggests centenary celebrations.[68] Mattingly[69] and Strack[70] favor a later date for the foundation of this temple, 136 to 137, when representations of it first appear on Hadrian's coinage. Possibly the consecration of the site and the foundation ceremony took place in 128, while the building was not completed and dedicated until 136 to 137.[71] We may also ascribe to the Natalis Urbis celebrations two bronze medallions of Constantius Chlorus and Galerius respectively, both with the reverse legend ROMAE AETERNAE and a scene in which the two Augusti, supported by the two Caesars, sacrifice before a temple, presumably that of Venus and Rome.[72]

Similar medallions with sacrificial scenes were occasioned by the "non-canonical," centenary Ludi Saeculares held by Philip I in 248, the thousandth anniversary of the foundation of Rome. The extant pieces bear portraits of Philip I and Philip II, of Philip I, Otacilia and Philip II and of Philip II alone and the reverse legend SAECVLVM NOVVM, with father and son offering sacrifice in front of a temple, again identifiable as that of Venus and Rome.[73] The legend SAECVLVM NOVVM shows, as Gagé has observed,[74] that the celebrations were as much prospective as retrospective, looking forward to the new age of Eternal Rome as well as backwards to her distant origins. Another piece of Philip I, Otacilia and Philip II, struck for the same occasion, refers specifically to the games themselves. It bears the legend SAECVL-ARES / AVGG and shows the interior of the circus, with a palm tree, various small, circular structures and racing chariots.[75]

IV. IMPERIAL COMINGS AND GOINGS

The comings and goings of Emperors to and from Rome and, under the later

[66] Pl. XVII, 7. Not quoted by Cohen and Gnecchi. But *cf. RIC* IV, i, p. 194, no. 757.

[67] G II, tavv. 99, no. 1; 100, nos. 1, 2 (Pl. XLIV, 4); 101, no. 9; III, tav. 153, no. 8.

[68] *Trans. Internat. Num. Congr.* 1936, pp. 182 f.

[69] *BMCCRE* III, p. cxlv.

[70] II SS. 174 ff.

[71] This is suggested by the analogy of the Ara Pacis Augustae and the Ara Fortunae Reducis. The main festival held in connection with each of these altars was on the anniversary of their foundation, not of their dedication (E. Welin, "Die beiden Festtage der Ara Pacis Augustae." ΔΡΑΓΜΑ *Martino P. Nilsson dedicatum*, 1939, pp. 500 ff.).

[72] *Trau Collection Sale Catalogue* 1935, Taf. 42, Nr. 3563 (Pl. IV, 9); Vienna: Nr. 86360 (not quoted by Cohen and Gnecchi).

[73] G II, p. 100, no. 5; tavv. 108, no. 9; 109, no. 6.

[74] *Loc. cit.*, p. 180.

[75] G II, tav. 109, no. 5.

Empire, to and from the great provincial capitals, were obvious occasions for the distribution of imperial gifts. Fortune, the goddess who leads the Emperor out and brings him safe home again, would naturally figure among the medallion types issued in this context; and we may, perhaps, ascribe to Hadrian's final home-coming after the Jewish war his bronze medallion with the obverse legend of 130 to 138 and on its reverse FORTVNAE REDVCI and a scene showing Fortuna seated, while the Emperor stands before her and gratefully clasps her hand.[76] On medallions dating from Commodus' fifth consulship the legends FORTVNAE DVCI and FORTVNAE REDVCI both occur; both accompany the type of the Emperor sacrificing to Fortuna, who stands in the first case and is seated in the second.[77] The Fortuna Redux type likewise appears on a piece with reverse legend P M TR P XIII IMP VIII COS V P P,[78] which fixes the date of the Fortuna group as 187 to 188. Lampridius tells us that Commodus planned a visit to Africa and raised a levy to defray the cost—on false pretences, as the journey never actually took place.[79] Were these medallions presented, by way of acknowledgment, to a circle of selected "subscribers"? Another unaccomplished return suggests the occasion of the FORTVNAE REDVCI / COS II medallion of Albinus, which portrays the goddess seated with a wheel beneath her throne.[80] In the summer of 193 Septimius Severus left Rome for the East, after offering Albinus the position of Caesar in the West. The title was formally conferred upon him by the Senate and coins were struck for the governor of Britain in Rome,[81] where Albinus was popular and a movement was soon on foot to encourage him to march on the Capital and seize the Empire. The appearance of Fortuna Redux on his COS II (194 to 195) coinage indicates that he was willing and ready to return. With Septimius safely away in the East, Albinus' party in Rome could doubtless influence, up to a point, the choice of coin types. As for the bronze medallions, we can imagine that they were struck at Albinus' orders and released in anticipation of the event, as gifts for leading senators and other friendly notables, whose good will it was important to foster against his coming. The FORTUNAE REDVCI medallions of Trebonianus Gallus, of Trebonianus Gallus and Volusianus and of Volusianus display a type unknown to the regular coinage—the two Emperors, accompanied by attendants and soldiers, sacrificing together in front of a temple.[82] The occasion was doubtless the return of Trebonianus and Volusianus in 252 from the Gothic war. We may ascribe to Gallienus' famous entry into Rome, on his return from the East, the bronze piece with the legend FORTVNA REDVX and the type of Fortuna standing.[83] Lastly, an actual imperial home-coming, safely accomplished with Fortuna's aid, is depicted on a small bronze medallion of Probus with the legend

[76] G II, tav. 39, no. 6.

[77] G II, tav. 79, nos. 2, 3, 4. It has been well observed that the difference in posture between Fortuna Dux and Fortuna Redux corresponds to the difference between her "active" and "passive" roles (*BMCCRE* IV, p. clxxxi).

[78] G II, tav. 85, no. 1.

[79] *Vita Commodi*, 9, 1.

[80] G II, tav. 92, nos. 2, 3. Gnecchi's no. 1 is certainly false.

[81] Herodian ii, 15, 5:—ὁ δὲ Σεουῆρος . . . νομίσματά τε αὐτοῦ κοπῆναι ἐπέτρεψε.

[82] G II, tav. 111, nos. 4, 9, 10; Kubitschek Taf. 9, Nr. 140. Pl. XVII, 8.

[83] G II, tav. 113, no. 9.

REDITVS ROMAE and a scene showing Roma seated and offering a Victory to the Emperor, who stands, togate, before her.[84] The piece may have been issued for Probus' triumphal entry into Rome in the winter of 281 to 282. It bears the mint-mark of Siscia, where Probus must have had it struck when passing through Illyricum on his way westward, bringing it with him for distribution in the Capital on his arrival.

Three medallions, two of Hadrian and one of Marcus Aurelius, appear to be gifts of acknowledgment distributed by the Emperor to senators in return for vows offered for his safe home-coming by the Senate and People of Rome. It was in 121, when Hadrian set out from Rome upon his first imperial tour, that such vows were first offered on the imperial traveller's behalf; and contemporary aurei with the legend V S PRO RED show the Genius Senatus and the Genius Populi Romani sacrificing together.[85] A bronze medallion with the same obverse legend and an almost identical scene on the reverse, describes more explicitly the part played by Senate and People on this occasion—SENATVS POPVLVSQVE ROMANVS / VOTA SVSCEPTA.[86] Other pieces of the same date show the right-hand half only of the design—the Genius of the Roman People sacrificing, with the legend GENIO POPVLI ROMANI or GENIVS POPVLI ROMANI.[87] Were these medallions parting presents from the Emperor to senators, presented, perhaps, on the very day on which the vows were made? Marcus Aurelius' medallion shares its obverse legend with coins dated 161 to 163. The reverse, which bears no legend, shows two figures, readily identifiable as the Genius Senatus and the Genius Populi Romani, supporting between them, on a garlanded altar, a shield on which, on a good specimen, VO / TA can be clearly seen.[88] Was the occasion of this piece the profectio of Marcus and Lucius from Rome for Capua in the spring of 162, preparatory to Lucius' departure for the eastern front?

The profectio medallions all fall within the century separating Hadrian from Gordian III. The earliest piece, issued, most probably, on the occasion of Hadrian's departure for the Jewish war in the summer of 134,[89] is based upon the decursio coin types of Nero and Trajan and shows the Emperor cantering, lance in rest, and accompanied by another rider and a foot-soldier.[90] The continuous wars of Marcus Aurelius' principate produced quite a crop of profectio scenes. The first of these, which closely resembles its Hadrianic predecessor, dates from Marcus' sixteenth tribunician year and was obviously struck for Lucius' departure for the East in the spring of 162: the imperial colleagues are seen riding out of the city side by side.[91] The type is repeated on a medallion of Lucius dating from the end of 167 (TR P VIII), when both Emperors left Rome for the northern front—a departure unrecorded on the regular coinage.[92] Late in 169 Marcus made a second profectio for the North, this time alone, for Lucius had died early in the year: the second rider shown on the

[84] G III, tav. 156, no. 19. [85] *BMCCRE* III, pl. 52, no. 14. [86] G III, tav. 145, nos. 8, 9.

[87] G II, tav. 39, nos. 7, 8, 9. *Cf.* the contemporary GEN P R coins (Strack II, Taf. 1, Nr. 67).

[88] G II, tav. 66, no. 4. A particularly fine specimen was in trade with Münzhandlung Basel in Sept., 1938 (cast in B. M.).

[89] Strack II, SS. 133, 137. [90] G II, tav. 42, no. 2.

[91] G II, tav. 66, no. 7. [92] G II, tav. 74, no. 5.

medallion struck for this occasion (TR P XXIV) must therefore be a general, or attendant, as in Hadrian's type.[93] On August 5, 178, Marcus and Commodus set out together for the Expeditio Germanica Secunda. The coins make no reference to this profectio; but a bronze medallion of Marcus, with the title SARMATICVS on its obverse and a repetition of the 169 reverse type, must portray it, the second rider being now identifiable as Commodus.[94] A profectio type of Commodus dated TR P XIII (187 to 188)[95] may have been occasioned by the unfulfilled project of an African trip and, like the Fortuna pieces, distributed for "programme" purposes to distinguished "contributors."[96] A heavy piece of Septimius Severus with the legend P P TR P XVI / S C / PROFECTIO AVG must refer to the Emperor's departure for Britain in 208.[97] Alexander Severus' profectio for the East in 231 occasioned bronze medallions, struck both in his own name and in the joint names of himself and his mother, which introduce a new type—the Emperor on horseback preceded by Victory and followed by one, or more, soldiers.[98] Another "going out" piece of Alexander, with portraits of mother and son on the obverse, was issued for the Emperor's departure on the German expedition towards the end of 234: it shows him, with Victory and four soldiers, crossing the Rhine bridge, while the Rhine god reclines below—a "programme" type, if the medallions were distributed when Alexander left Rome.[99] The new profectio type reappears on a curious "framed" piece of Gordian III, of which the obverse and reverse types were beaten out in thin silver plates applied to a bronze flan.[100] Its occasion was the inauguration of the Persian campaign in the spring of 242. To the same event must be ascribed Gordian's fine series of TRAIECTVS AVG medallions, struck in gold and bronze, which depict the Emperor and his troops crossing the Hellespont in an elaborately decorated trireme.[101] It is possible that these medallions were issued as "programme" pieces at the time of Gordian's profectio for the East; or they may have been prepared beforehand and released when the news reached Rome that the expeditionary force had been safely landed on the Asiatic shore. The same possibilities may apply to medallions depicting the crossing of the Euphrates and the recovery of Mesopotamia in 243: a small bronze piece with legend TRAIECTVS AVG shows the Emperor and his retinue crossing a bridge of boats,[102] while a large piece with legend FIDES EXERCITVS portrays him, crowned by Victory, shaking hands with a soldier in the presence of Euphrates and Tigris reclining below.[103]

Adventus medallions, which become relatively plentiful from the middle of

[93] G II, tav. 61, nos. 4, 5.

[94] G II, p. 31, no. 32.

[95] G II, tav. 79, no. 3.

[96] *Vide supra* p. 104.

[97] Modena. This piece is not a pseudo medallion, since its type is not a mere reproduction of the PROF AVGG sestertii of this year (*RIC* IV, i, p. 197, no. 780). It appears to be genuine, in spite of its exceptional character.

[98] G II, tavv. 99, nos. 9, 10; 101, nos. 7, 8. For the "schema" of this profectio type, and of the corresponding adventus types, *cf.* early third-century reliefs depicting the journey of a knight to the next world (*PBSR* xv, 1939, pp. 27 ff., pls. 1, 2 and fig. 1).

[99] G II, tav. 101, no. 5.

[100] Paris: no. 30; G II, p. 91, no. 37.

[101] G II, tav. 105, no. 8; *Jameson Collection Catalogue* IV, pl. 25, no. 511. **Pl. XVII, 9.**

[102] G III, tav. 153, no. 15.

[103] G II, tav. 104, no. 1.

the third century onwards, were only issued sporadically under the early Empire. During the second century numismatic interest in imperial arrivals seems to have exhausted itself in the great adventus coin series of Hadrian, recording his many solemn entries into Rome and the provinces. During the whole of the Antonine period, from Pius to Commodus, only two coins, both of Commodus, with the adventus legend are known to us.[104] This scarcity of adventus coin types lends a special interest to our small series of second-century adventus medallions. The earliest, issued by Trajan in silver and bronze, bears the legend ADVENTVS AVG / S P Q R OPTIMO PRINCIPI and shows the Emperor on horseback, preceded by Felicitas (?) and followed by soldiers:[105] it was doubtless struck for Trajan's home-coming in 106 from the second Dacian war.[106] After a gap of over sixty-five years the adventus type reappears on two medallions of Marcus Aurelius, dated TR P XXVII and TR P XXVIII respectively, with legend ADVENTVS AVG and the Emperor, attended by soldiers and Victory, marching towards a triumphal arch.[107] The date of issue can be fixed exactly: it was December, 173, when Marcus' twenty-seventh tribunician year ended and his twenty-eighth began. As Macdonald pointed out,[108] these pieces suggest, what we know from no other source, that during the course of the Quadic war Marcus paid at least a flying visit to the Capital in 173, before the opening of the winter campaign.

Adventus coins grow commoner under the Severi; but we have only one Adventus medallion type of this period, and that does not tally, either in date or design, with any known coin. Large bronze pieces of Septimius, with the legend ADVENTVI AVG P M TR P II / COS II P P, show the Emperor on horseback, his hand raised in greeting, with a soldier in attendance.[109] The medallions were struck, as the legend shows, in 194, when Septimius was away in the East. They must, therefore, have been occasioned, not by an actual, but by an anticipated arrival, issued, presumably, under the influence of the Severan party in Rome as "programme" pieces and as a counterblast to the Fortuna Redux medallions prompted by Albinus' supporters.[110] After another interval of nearly half a century adventus medallions reappear under Philip I, on the occasion of his return, with his son Philip II, to Rome from the Danube front at the end of 247. A silver piece with busts of Philip I and Otacilia on the obverse revives the decursio type, with the two Augusti galloping side by side (ADVENTVS AVGG);[111] while a small, but distinctly medallic, bronze piece shows the third-century profectio design of the Emperors riding with Victory and soldiers adapted to an adventus type.[112] The latter type is repeated on the ADVENTVS AVGG medallions of Trebonianus Gallus, of Trebonianus Gallus and Volusianus and of Volusianus issued for the occasion of their return to Rome in 252;[113] another piece with the two busts on the obverse shows the decursio type again.[114]

[104] *RIC* III, pp. 263, no. 604 (Commodus as Caesar); 401, no. 294.
[105] G I, tav. 21, no. 6; II, tav. 38, no. 1.
[106] Strack I, SS. 130 f.
[107] G II, tav. 59, no. 5; p. 27, nos. 2, 3.
[108] *NC* 1906, p. 98.
[109] G II, tav. 92, nos. 7, 8 (Pl. XLIII, 6).
[110] *Vide supra* p. 104.
[111] G I, tav. 24, no. 8.
[112] *Evans Collection Sale Catalogue* 1934, pl. 52, no. 1665. Pl. XVII, 10.
[113] G II, pp. 103, no. 2; 104, no. 1; tav. 111, nos. 1, 2.
[114] G II, tav. 111, no. 8.

During the second half of the third century adventus legends and types become very frequent on the coinage and correspondingly more numerous upon medallions. The imperial riders with Victory and soldiers in attendance is the type adopted for the adventus pieces of Valerian and Gallienus,[115] issued, presumably, at, or soon after, Gallienus' promotion to the rank of Augustus in 253, for an early adventus medallion of Gallienus of about the same date[116] and for later pieces of Gallienus and Salonina[117] and of Gallienus and Valerian II,[118] struck between the latter's promotion to the rank of Caesar in 256 and his death in 258. Other medallions of silver and bronze, ascribable to the years 256 to 258, with the legend ADVENTVS AVGG and the three riders—Gallienus, Valerian II and Saloninus—were struck for Gallienus[119] and for Gallienus and Valerian II;[120] while a later bronze piece, dating from the sole reign of Gallienus, shows the Emperor riding unaccompanied, with his right hand raised in salute.[121] The type of the Emperor accompanied by Victory and soldiers is repeated on bronze medallions of Claudius Gothicus (*c.* 268),[122] Tacitus (*c.* 275)[123] and Probus (281 to 282).[124] A bronze piece with the three obverse busts of Carus, Carinus and Numerianus shows the three Emperors, each with his right hand raised, riding slowly along, attended by Victory, Virtus (?) and several soldiers.[125] Our last bronze adventus medallion, a piece of Maximian, portrayed in consular dress on the obverse, shows the two Augusti in slow procession with Victory and a soldier (ADVENTVS AVGG / S C).[126] It obviously dates from November 20, 303, when Diocletian appeared in Rome with his colleague to celebrate his vicennalia: Maximian was consul in 303 for the seventh time.

All remaining adventus medallions are of gold and all, with one exception, show the same design—the Emperor riding slowly towards the left, unaccompanied, a sceptre in his left hand, his right hand raised in greeting; and, again with one exception, none of their types occur upon the regular gold coinage. This gold series begins with two small pieces, one of Aurelian, issued, perhaps, for his triumphal entry into Rome in 274,[127] and the other of Probus, known from a single specimen at Gotha,[128] which differs from the ordinary adventus aurei not only in weight but also in the fact that its type shows the Emperor unaccompanied by the subsidiary figure which their types include:[129] like Probus' bronze medallions, it was probably struck for his triumphal entry into Rome during the winter of 281 to 282. Most interesting of all adventus medallions is the unique 9-solidi piece of Constantine I in the Beistegui Collection in Paris.[130] The obverse bears the legend INVICTVS CONSTANTINVS MAX AVG and busts, side by side, of Constantine and Sol. The reverse shows the legend FELIX ADVENTVS AVGG NN and Constantine on horse-

[115] G II, tavv. 109, no. 9 (wrongly assigned to Philip I and Philip II); 113, nos. 2, 3; III, tav. 154, no. 9.
[116] G II, tav. 113, no. 7.
[117] G III, tavv. 153, no. 17 (wrongly assigned to Philip I and Otacilia); 155, nos. 9, 11, 12.
[118] G II, tav. 116, no. 2.
[119] G II, tav. 113, no. 8.
[120] G I, tav. 27, no. 10; II, tav. 109, no. 10 (wrongly assigned to Philip I and Philip II).
[121] G III, tav. 154, no. 13.
[122] G II, tav. 117, no. 1.
[123] G II, tav. 118, nos. 2, 3.
[124] G II, tav. 119, nos. 3, 4, 5, 6.
[125] G II, tav. 123, no. 10.
[126] G III, p. 94, no. 62 (**Pl. IV, 7**).
[127] G I, tav. 3, nos. 9, 10, 11.
[128] Not quoted by Cohen and Gnecchi (**Pl. II, 6**).
[129] E. g. *RIC* V, ii, pl. 1, no. 2.
[130] J. Babelon, *op. cit.*, pl. 13, no. 233. **Pl. XVII, 11.**

back, preceded by Victory and followed by Virtus (?)—a "felix adventus" indeed, for the occasion of the piece was Constantine's arrival at Milan in 313 for that conference with Licinius of which the outcome was the "Edict of Milan," granting freedom of worship to the Catholic Church; thus the Emperor's companion, the Unconquered Sun, was conquered by the Sun of Righteousness. All the other medallions of the series are 1½-solidi pieces. They were issued in the name of Constantine I (FELIX ADVENTVS AVG N),[131] Crispus (FELIX ADVENTVS CAESS NN),[132] Constantius II (FELIX ADVENTVS AVG N and GLORIA REIPVBLICAE),[133] Valentinian I (FELIX ADVENTVS AVGGG and FELIX ADVENTVS AVG M[134]—the latter struck for Valentinian's solemn entry into Milan in the autumn of 364), Valens (FELIX ADVENTVS AVG N,[135] FELIX ADVENTVS AVGGG[136] and GLORIA ROMANORVM),[137] Gratian (FELIX ADVENTVS AVG N),[138] Valentinian II (FELIX ADVENTVS AVG N),[139] Honorius (ADVENTVS D N AVG—the Emperor is nimbate)[140] and Marcianus (ADVENTVS S D N AVG—the Emperor is nimbate).[141]

V. ALLOCUTIONS

Adlocutiones or harangues, delivered by the Emperor to the Praetorian Guard or to other units of the imperial armies, had figured on the current coinage for more than a century before they confront us as occasions for medallion issues. The normal adlocutio scene is well known—the Emperor, or Emperors, standing to right or left on a low platform, set to one side of the design, accompanied by one or more officials and addressing a group of soldiers below. The coins struck by Gaius, Nero (ADLOCVT COH), Galba (ADLOCVTIO), Nerva (ADLOCVTIO AVG) and Hadrian (COH PRAETOR) probably refer in a general way to friendly relations between the Emperor and his troops; we need not suppose that they, or their second- and third-century successors, were necessarily issued for distribution when an adlocutio was held. Hadrian's famous exercitus sestertii, depicting harangues to provincial forces, were minted long after the adlocutiones in question, if actual and not merely symbolic, must have taken place. The earliest adlocutio medallion was struck for Lucius Verus in 162 to 163.[142] One specimen is "framed"; and there can be little doubt that these large bronze pieces were struck for presentation to

[131] G I, tav. 6, no. 13. Variant with SIS in exergue (*Vierordt Collection Sale Catalogue* 1923, pl. 59, no. 2641). **Pl. XVIII, 1.** Two other similar pieces of Constantine, stolen from Paris, with the legends ADVENTVS AVG N and ADVENTVS AVGVSTI are quoted by Gnecchi (p. 15, nos. 1, 2).

[132] G I, tav. 8, no. 16.

[133] G I, tavv. 10, no. 10; 11, nos. 2, 4. *Jameson Collection Catalogue* IV, pl. 26, no. 535. **Pl. XVIII, 2.** *Trau Collection Sale Catalogue* 1935, Taf. 47, Nr. 4143. **Pl. XVIII, 3.** *NZ* 1926, Taf. 2, Nr. 1. **Pl. XVIII, 4.**

[134] G I, p. 35, no. 3 (Paris no. 48, mint-mark SMTR); tav. 14, no. 6; Bansa, *op. cit.*, pp. 58–60; B. M. piece, mint-mark MED.

[135] G I, tav. 14, no. 13: Kubitschek Taf. 19, Nr. 353. **Pl. XVIII, 5.** *Jameson Collection Catalogue* IV, pl. 26, no. 537. **Pl. XVIII, 6.**

[136] The Hague. **Pl. XVIII, 7.** G I, p. 36, no. 2.

[137] G I, tav. 14, no. 12. This type and legend also occur on ordinary solidi (C^2 viii, p. 103, no. 14).

[138] A. Evans bequest, Ashmolean Museum, Oxford. **Pl. XVIII, 8.** Not quoted by Cohen and Gnecchi.

[139] G I, p. 38, nos. 1, 2. **Pl. XVIII, 9.**

[140] G I, tav. 19, no. 10.

[141] J. Sabatier, *Monnaies byzantines* I, p. 123, no. 1.

[142] G II, tavv. 70, no. 3; 72, no. 3. *Cf.* the "framed" piece of Marcus (G II, tav. 58, no. 3, 171 to 172).

officers on the actual occasion of the imperial discourse. A later medallion, struck in 166, shows Verus commending a boyish figure—the youthful Commodus (?)—to the troops.[143] Commodus' adlocutio coins and medallions bear a new legend—FIDES EXERCIT: the medallions all belong to his eleventh tribunician year (185–186)[144] and may have been issued for an adlocutio held on New Year's Day, 186, reasserting the loyalty of the Guards to Commodus after the fall of Perennis in the previous year. Septimius Severus' adlocutio medallions, minted in 194 (?) and 195 (TR P II(?) and TR P III) were probably "programme" pieces distributed in Rome during the Emperor's absence and anticipating a harangue to be delivered to the Guards on his return (FIDEI MILIT).[145] Adlocutio medallions of the normal type appear continuously throughout the third century, a splendid group of large bronze pieces of Gordian III, struck between 240 and 244, being specially noteworthy.[146] Under Probus the adlocutio occurs in gold[147] as well as in bronze;[148] and a new variation shows the imperial platform in the centre, with soldiers grouped around.[149] The series closes with this centralized version of the adlocutio scene on Constantine I's small silver piece, struck *c.* 315, with the legend SALVS REIPVBLICAE.[150]

VI. LIBERALITIES

The liberalitates or money distributions by the Emperor to the poor of Rome (and of provincial cities, under the later Empire) were occasions of medallion issues which need not detain us long. Celebrated with considerable frequency upon the regular currency, on coins minted either commemoratively, after the liberalitas had taken place, or possibly as part of the imperial bounty itself, these largesses were essentially popular and proletarian events. It was only incidentally, as it were, that they occasioned the issue of medallions destined primarily, it may be, for those officials who had personally assisted the Emperor on the actual day. The familiar scene shows the imperial philanthropist seated on a platform with Liberalitas and other supporters, distributing cash to the citizens below. The series begins[151] with the bronze pieces, large and small, struck by Alexander Severus; among them are small S C pieces of which the distinctively medallic style justifies their inclusion among medallions.[152] The types continue, with little variation, under Gordian III, Philip I, Valerian and Gallienus.[153] But we may also ascribe to a liberalitas occasion the bronze type of Philip I depicting a great precinct in which the Emperor and his son (?), enthroned and flanked by rows of other seated figures, are distributing

[143] G II, tavv. 74, no. 1 (**Pl. XLII, 4**); 75, no. 10.

[144] G II, Tav. 78, nos. 6–9.

[145] G II, tav. 93, nos. 6–9. The legend suggests hopes for the continued loyalty of the troops.

[146] G II, tav. 103, nos. 1–7 (**Pl. XLV, 2**). N. B. also (1) fine bi-metallic adlocutio type of Alexander Severus (*Trau Collection Sale Catalogue* 1935, Taf. 32, Nr. 2513). **Pl. XVIII, 10.** (2) Small Æ type of Alexander Severus and Julia Mamaea (G III, p. 44, no. 14). **Pl. XVIII, 11.**

[147] G I, tav. 3, no. 16.

[148] N. B. very small, but medallic, piece of Probus in Copenhagen (G III, p. 69, no. 64). **Pl. XVIII, 12.**

[149] G II, tav. 119, no. 1.

[150] G I, tav. 29, no. 3.

[151] The Hadrianic piece quoted by Gnecchi (II, p. 6, no. 36) cannot be verified.

[152] G II, tav. 98, nos. 8, 9; III, tav. di suppl., no. 3.

[153] Pupienus' piece in the B. M. is very doubtful (G II, tav. 102, no. 10).

largess to a crowd.[154] Fourth-century types are comparatively few. Bronze pieces of Constantius II and Magnentius with the legend LARGITIO show the Emperor enthroned to the front, while Roma, on the right, lays her hand on his shoulder and Constantinopolis, on the left, bends down to receive the money which he pours into her hands.[155] The rest are "Fest-aurei," which portray the Emperor erect in a frontal chariot, flinging coins to an imaginary crowd (Constantine I, Constantius II, Constans, Valentinian I, Valentinian II and Eugenius).[156] Finally, we may append to the liberalitas series two bronze medallions labelled "munificence." One, issued by Antoninus Pius on the occasion of the public beast-shows of 149, displays a prowling lion (MVNIFICENTIA);[157] the second piece, struck by Gordian III in 244, depicts the Colosseum where his shows were held (MVNIFICENTIA GORDIANI AVG).[158]

[154] G II, tavv. 107, no. 5; 109, no. 3. *Cf.* also single figure of Liberalitas on small Æ pieces of Alexander Severus and Julia Mamaea (*RIC* IV, ii, p. 123, no. 663). **Pl. XVIII, 13.**

[155] G II, tavv. 136, no. 7; 138, no. 4.

[156] *Vide supra* p. 40. We might also add to this series the processional type of Constantius II, Valens, Arcadius and Honorius with the Emperor, or Emperors, standing in a frontal six-horse chariot, on the strength of the wreaths, laurel-leaves, money-chests etc. in the exergue, which are suggestive of imperial largitiones (G I, tavv. 10, no. 8; 11, no. 1; 15, no. 1; 36, no. 15; *cf.* Delbrück, *op. cit,* Taf. 16, Nr. 3; S. 69, Abb. 25).

[157] G II, tav. 46, no. 5.

[158] G II, tav. 104, nos. 5, 6.

CHAPTER III

MEDALLIONS AND THEIR RECIPIENTS

I. The Character and Status of Recipients

Archaeological discoveries have so far failed to disclose the name of one single recipient of Roman medallions. Any conclusions we may draw as to the status of the donees must be based upon indirect evidence, upon the internal evidence of the medallions themselves and upon the external evidence of find spots. The fact that the great majority of medallions are severally represented by only a comparatively small number of examples, while not a few are known from one specimen alone, indicates that they were minted for distribution to circles of selected individuals. Excellence of technique and often exquisite artistic finish suggest that the minting authorities had persons of taste and culture in view; and the choice of reverse types tells the same story. While it is true to say that medallion types do, up to a point, fit into the general scheme for ventilating news and ideas laid down for the ordinary coin types in any given period, marked differences still remain. On the earlier medallions, at any rate, allusions are often less obvious, the subjects chosen of more specialized interest, than on the contemporary coinage; and in cases where the subjects of medallions and coins coincide, they are often treated on the former with a wealth of detail which only persons with training in art and letters could fully appreciate. For instance, it is noteworthy that Hadrian's "imperial idea," boosted so vigorously on the coins of his famous "province" series, has left little impress upon his medallions. This was a popular appeal, addressed to the world at large. For the *élite* were reserved special types relating to the Emperor's personal life, tastes and qualities or reflecting public affairs through the indirect medium of mythology. Specially instructive from this standpoint are the numismatic preparations made by Antoninus Pius for celebrating in 147 the nine-hundredth anniversary of the "Birthday of Rome." Whereas on the coins of his third consulship the familiar groups of the wolf and twins and of Aeneas fleeing with Anchises and Ascanius from Troy[1] sufficed to stir appropriate sentiments in the hearts of the rank and file, for the chosen few Pius issued a series of splendid medallions on which were depicted, in the most minute detail, scenes from the early history and legends of ancient Rome—some, it would seem, directly inspired by passages of Livy, Vergil and Ovid.[2] With the later Antonines direct allusions to contemporary events become more frequent on medallions; but again the medallion types are specially chosen and strike a more personal and individual note. Under Commodus, indeed, and on into the third century, this distinction in content between medallions and coins is sometimes blurred: medallion types are occasionally but coin *motifs* rendered either with additional detail or simply on a more imposing scale upon large bronze

[1] *RIC* III, pl. 1, no. 19. [2] *Vide infra* pp. 143 f., 193 f. *Cf. CR* 1925, pp. 170 ff.; *AJ* 1943, pp. 43 ff.

flans. But such repetitions are still in the minority; and, in general, apart from exceptional cases which seem to suggest an abnormal extension of the list of donees, the number of extant specimens of any given type is not appreciably larger than in earlier times. In the second half of the third century, when coin designs grow comparatively more monotonous and stereotyped, medallion types, whether in bronze, silver or gold, stand out in contrast for their variety and clearly mirror the distinction and individuality of their recipients. It is only the Tres Monetae medallions from Valerian to Diocletian and Maximian which show any definite symptoms of mass production: and even there the monotonous reverse is combined with an extraordinarily varied repertory of obverse types. The meaning of these pieces will be discussed later on.[3] Here we may note them as an outstanding instance of the occasional extension of medallions to a wider circle. Constantine I's Urbs Roma and Constantinopolis medallions afford a parallel instance at a later date and on a more restricted scale.

There are, indeed, a certain number of medallions of which the content offers a fairly reliable clue as to the exact profession or position of the persons for whom they were designed. Such, to take the most obvious example, are those with legends and types directly alluding to the army. Besides the adlocutio medallions discussed in the last chapter and the numerous pieces with the more familiar military scenes and legends—FIDES EXERCITVS, FIDES MILITVM, GLORIA EXERCITVS, CONCORDIA EXERCITVS, VIRTVS ROMANI EXERCITVS, MATRI CASTRORVM[4] and the like, a special group of unusual types, all issued by Gallienus, calls for comment. COHORS TERTIA PRAETORIA, with the Emperor standing between standards (gold),[5] and [QVARTA (?)] / CHORS (?) / PRAETO / RIAE within a wreath (bronze "strike" from gold medallion dies ?)[6] were clearly destined for officers of the Guards. FIDES / MILI / TVM in a laurel wreath (gold) implies donees of a similar kind.[7] But the most interesting of the group shows the legend GALLIE / NVS OB / FIDEM RE / SERVATAM in a laurel wreath (gold).[8] Gallienus as it were congratulates himself that the allegiance of his army has been "safeguarded" or "maintained"; and the natural recipients of such a souvenir piece were the officers of the troops whose loyalty had stood the test. The medallion is dated from the Emperor's fifth consulship (262 to 263); and J. Babelon refers it to the incident of 261 to 262, when Aureolus, commanding Gallienus' new cavalry corps, allowed the rebel Postumus to slip away without breaking openly with his sovereign.[9]

It is possible that we have in the medallions which present the heir-apparent or, later, the reigning Emperor in the guise of Princeps Iuventutis another instance of legend and type providing a clue to the status of donees; and that such pieces

[3] *Vide infra* pp. 148 f.

[4] E. g. Julia Domna (G II, tav. 94, no. 10); Julia Mamaea (G II, tav. 100, no. 9; III, tav. 153, no. 3).

[5] G I, p. 6, no. 2.

[6] *Trau Collection Sale Catalogue* 1935, S. 81, Nr. 2985. A. Evans bequest, Ashmolean Museum, Oxford. Pl. XIX, 1.

[7] G I, p. 7, no. 8. Pl. XIX, 2.

[8] J. Babelon, *op. cit.*, pl. 12, no. 229 (Pl. III, 12).

[9] *CAH* xii, p. 186. *Cf. Mélanges offerts à M. Nicolas Jorga*, 1933, pp. 109 ff.

were intended primarily for distribution to prominent members of the Iuventus itself, the military "youth movement" for upper class boys—iuvenes nobilissimi. After a few sporadic issues, such as the notorious gold piece of Augustus at Este, struck in honor of Gaius and Lucius Caesar,[10] and the "framed" bronze piece of Geta, showing Septimius Severus, Caracalla and Geta on horseback in full career,[11] type and legend settled down in the third century to a more or less fixed norm—the prince standing in military dress, with his title PRINCIPI IVVENTVTIS in the dedicatory dative case.[12] But it was not until the late third, and early fourth, centuries that the Princeps Iuventutis became to any degree a common medallion type. It now appears exclusively on gold[13] medallions struck on a carefully graduated scale of values, wherein we may see reflected the hardening, as it were, of Roman society into fixed social categories determined by birth. If iuvenes nobilissimi were in fact the recipients of the Princeps Iuventutis pieces, the value of their gifts was now proportioned to that degree of nobilitas into which they had severally been born. The possibility that these pieces were struck less to do honor to the acclamation as Princeps Iuventutis of an imperial person than with a view to their function as presents for the Iuventus is supported by two facts: first, that the figure of the Princeps on the reverse does not always correspond in age and appearance with the imperial portrait on the obverse, and, secondly, that the date of issue does not always tally with the date at which the acclamation of the person portrayed on the obverse actually took place. The 10-aurei piece from the Arras hoard struck in the names of Constantius Chlorus and Galerius on the occasion of their promotion to the rank of Caesar in 293 bears on its reverse the legend PRINCIPVM IVVENTVTIS and the two Caesars offering sacrifice.[14] Here the date of issue and the date of the acclamation of the Caesars as Principes Iuventutis do appear to tally; and, moreover, the bearded Principes of the reverse are obviously the contemporaries of, and identical with, the busts on the obverse. On the other hand, a 2½-aurei piece of Constantius probably of the same date as the Arras medallion, in view of the close resemblance of its obverse portrait to that of the latter, shows on its reverse, not a mature, bearded man, but a mere boy—a quasi-ideal figure, the personification, it may be, of imperial youth.[15] Date of issue and of occasion and obverse portrait and reverse figure all tally again on a 1½-aurei piece of Constantine I as Caesar, struck, presumably, in 306, when Constantine

[10] *AA* 1928, S. 122, Abb. 3; *cf.* S. L. Cesano in *Atti e memorie del Istituto Italiano di Numismatica* 1934, pp. 107 ff., tav. 7, no. 3 and *Numismatica augustea*, 1937, pp. 32 ff, tav. 5, nos. 1, 2. **Pl. XIX, 3.**

[11] G II, tav. 96, no. 3.

[12] E. g. G III, tav. 152, no. 12 (Diadumenianus); II, tav. 108, nos. 7, 8 (Philip II) (**Pl. XLV, 5**); II, tav. 110, no. 9 (Hostilianus); II, tav. 116, no. 5 (Saloninus).

[13] The bronze pieces of Crispus and Constantine II (G II, tav. 133, nos. 6, 9, 10) are either false or highly dubious.

[14] *NNM* 28, 1926, pl. 1 (**Pl. IX, 4**). The very unusual and interesting use of the genitive case on the reverse must denote "[the sacrifice] of the Principes Iuventutis." For parallel uses of the genitive on imperial coins see the "republican" issues of Clodius Macer, the Civil Wars and Galba (*BMCCRE* I, pls. 49, nos. 5, 6, 9, 24; 50, no. 4; 51, no. 24; 55, no. 13).

[15] G I, tav. 5, no. 11.

was accepted as Caesar by Galerius.[16] But his second Princeps Iuventutis medallion, a 2-solidi piece, while showing an obverse portrait and a reverse figure which more or less correspond, was issued at least six years later than the proclamation of Constantine as Princeps. It bears the mint-mark POST; and as the Ostian mint was opened by Maxentius in 309, passed into Constantine's hands after Maxentius' defeat in 312 and was closed in 313, the piece must date from 312 to 313.[17] At this time, it would seem, the reigning Augusti all reaffirmed, as it were, their relation with the Iuventus, for in addition to this medallion PRINCIPI IVVENTVTIS solidi were struck at the Ostian mint for Constantine's colleagues Maximinus Daza and Licinius I.[18] Discrepancy in age between obverse portrait and reverse figure confront us again in a series of 1½-, 2- and 4½-solidi pieces, all struck at Trier, which show elderly portraits of Constantine, radiate or helmeted, on the obverse and the Princeps Iuventutis as a young boy on the reverse.[19] It is possible that this medallion series dates from 324, the year of Constantine's victory over Licinius and of Constantius II's proclamation as Caesar and Princeps Iuventutis, and that the youthful Princeps of the reverse is Constantius II.[20] Princeps Iuventutis medallions with a youthful Princeps on the reverse were also issued by Constantine I in the names of Constantine II and Constantius II at various dates unconnected with their original reception of the title and on occasions appropriate for distributing gifts to members of the Iuventus. A 1½-solidi piece struck at Sirmium for Constantine II shows an exceptionally boyish obverse portrait of the youthful Caesar.[21] The mint at Sirmium was opened in 320 and the piece may have been issued in honor of Constantine II's first consulship, assumed by him in that year at the age of three. The existence of a half-solidus of Constantine I inscribed VOT / XX with the mint-mark THES[22] fixes the date of two parallel pieces of Constantine II and Constantius II, which bear the same version of the Thessalonican mint-mark.[23] This date was July, 325, the occasion of the first celebration of their father's vicennalia during his absence from Rome for the Council of Nicaea. To the same occasion, or possibly to 326, the year of Constantine II's decennalia and of the second celebration of his father's vicennalia, may be ascribed another pair of medallions minted for the two brothers at Constantinople.[24] The year 326 was also the year of Constantius II's first consulship; and a 2-solidi Princeps Iuventutis piece struck in his name at

[16] Berlin. Not quoted by Cohen and Gnecchi. **Pl. XIX, 4.**

[17] **Pl. XIX, 5.** Maurice I, pl. 19, no. 14. On grounds of similarity of obverse portraiture we might ascribe to the same date as the Ostian piece the two PRINCIPI IVVENTVTIS medallions of Constantine from Arras, worth 9 solidi (*Aréthuse*, Jan., 1924, pl. 8, no. 9 (**Pl. IX, 5**)) and 2 solidi (*Jameson Collection Catalogue* IV, pl. 26, no. 531 (**Pl. IX, 6**)) respectively and with obverse portraits and reverse figures which again roughly correspond in age. Constantine's title INVICT on the latter piece recalls the great adventus gold piece of 313 (*vide supra* pp. 108).

[18] Maurice I, p. 288, nos. 10, 11.

[19] G I, tav. 7, nos. 11–14.

[20] *Cf.* S. L. Cesano, *Rassegna Numismatica* 1911, pp. 33–92. G I, tav. 13, no. 7 (Constantius II) may belong to the same series.

[21] G I, tav. 9, no. 3.

[22] *NZ* 1930, S. 44.

[23] *NZ* 1930, Taf. 2, Nrr. 5, 8. **Pl. XIX, 6, 7.**

[24] G I, p. 24, no. 9 (= Constantine II, stolen from Paris, copy in Berlin: *cf. Pisciculi Franz Joseph Dölger dargeboten*, 1939, Taf. II, Nr. 2. **Pl. XIX, 8**); tav. 13, no. 5 (= Constantius II).

Trier shows him on the obverse in consular dress.[25] Constantine II's last group of Princeps Iuventutis medallions can be dated precisely. They show a new type of reverse with the Caesar setting his foot on the knee of a suppliant, who kneels before him with outstretched arms, and the legend PRINCIPIA IVVENTVTIS / SARMATIA.[26] In 332, in answer to the Sarmatians' appeal, Constantine II proceeded to the Danube frontier and inflicted a crushing defeat upon the Goths: our medallions must commemorate this victory. While Constantine II was fighting on the Danube, Constantius II was sent to take his place in Gaul. To the occasion of his arrival in the Gallic capital we may ascribe his 1½-solidi piece minted in Trier, the obverse portrait of which is decidedly more mature and bears a very close resemblance to that on his brother's PRINCIPIA IVVENTVTIS / SARMATIA medallions: the reverse shows the usual Princeps figure.[27] The Princeps Iuventutis series closes with a 3-solidi piece of Decentius, struck at Trier in 352, the year of his consulship, for on the obverse the Caesar wears consular dress. The figure of the Princeps on the reverse is a realistic portrait of Decentius.[28]

The establishment, with Constantine I, of a fixed and carefully graded scale of multiples certainly implies the grading of the recipients of these multiples in a corresponding hierarchy of social values. The preponderance of 1½- and 2-solidi pieces over the higher multiples, in hoards and elsewhere, is but natural. Minor officials drawn from the less exalted ranks of society, were obviously more numerous: those who were high enough up in the social scale to merit the more expensive prizes were comparatively few. Under the early Empire it had been customary for rich persons on the occasion of banquets to distribute gifts in kind (apophoreta) or money (sportulae) to guests and clients graded according to rank. So, in the later third and fourth centuries, distinguished Romans, celebrating births or marriages, or their entry upon a consulship or other office, made presents to their friends according to an ascending scale of values—money gifts, or actual baskets (sportulae) of exact weight with a money significance, to less important persons, ivory diptychs to high officials and the same in gold settings to the Emperor himself. As O. Seeck has pointed out,[29] money medallions of the fourth century were the imperial counterpart of these private gifts. Very rarely the types themselves suggest, as in the case of the Princeps Iuventutis medallions, or actually reveal, the donee's precise status. For instance the SENATVS gold pieces (Emperor standing in senatorial dress), of which we know three examples, two equivalent to 4½ solidi and one to 3,

[25] G I, tav. 13, no. 6.

[26] G I, tav. 9, nos. 1, 2 (with mint-mark TR); *Trau Collection Sale Catalogue* 1935, Taf. 46, Nr. 4079 (without the mint-mark and showing a deeper obverse bust, but doubtless also minted at Trier). Pl. XIX, 9. The use of the word "principia," instead of the usual "principi," on the reverse should be noted. Mattingly (*Roman Coins*, p. 243) interprets it as "the first stage of military training for the career of Emperor." But as a parallel to "princeps" (= "chief of the Iuventus") some notion of "first in rank" or "chief," such as "front line" or "chief's headquarters" or even "chief of staff" would seem to be implied (*cf.* Frontinus, *Strat.* II, v, 30: "tempus elegit, quo missa principia quietem omnibus castrensibus dabant").

[27] *Trau Collection Sale Catalogue* 1935, Taf. 49, Nr. 4263. Pl. XIX, 10.

[28] The Hague. Not quoted by Cohen and Gnecchi. For the obverse see Delbrück, *op. cit.*, Taf. 12, Nr. 1. Pl. XIX, 11.

[29] *ZN* 1898, S. 17 ff.

were obviously designed for senators,[30] while those with the legend EQVIS ROMANVS (Emperor on horseback to right), of which at least sixteen specimens have come down to us, fifteen worth 1½ solidi and one worth 2, were clearly meant for knights.[31] But normally we can only gauge the general degree of a recipient's nobility and importance from the size and weight of the gifts, measured according to a scale which ascends from the "Fest-aurei" of 5+ grammes and the lower multiples, worth 1½, 2, 2½, 3 solidi, and so on up to the giant medallions of Constantius II, Valens and Justinian, worth 30, 36, 48 and even 72 solidi apiece.[32]

The information derived from our knowledge of provenances within the confines of the Empire is of an equally general character. Apart from the Monte della Giüstizia, the proximity of which to the Castra Praetoria makes it not improbable that the numerous medallions found there had been owned by officers of the Guards,[33] no other Roman find spot tells us anything definite of the actual status of the donees. Obviously we should not expect Pompeii to yield more than a few sporadic medallions, since it was destroyed before the issue of the bronze medallion series proper began. But the fact that a site so continuously occupied throughout the imperial period, and so thoroughly explored in modern times, as Ostia has so far yielded the record of but one medallion may be significant, suggesting that men who pursued the more bourgeois avocations of commerce and industry did not as a rule qualify for these awards. In the provinces we have already noted the preponderance among recorded find spots, as far as bronze medallions are concerned, of great military headquarters, frontier stations and important centres of local and imperial administration—cities in which legionary commanders and other higher officers of the army, provincial governors and representatives of the Emperor, higher-grade civil servants and government officials were permanently resident or constantly passing through.[34] Such factors as theft or concealment, in the case both of isolated pieces and of hoards, explain the fortuitous and uninformative character of many of the provenances of gold medallions. Meanwhile, the substantial number of gold find spots known in Pannonia and the northern Balkan provinces may reflect the military and political importance of those regions in the third and fourth centuries; just as finds on the actual boundaries of the Empire reflect the concentration of military effort on frontier defense. Nor is it without interest that the one gold piece recorded from Great Britain should have come to light near Cardiff, where a "Saxon Shore" fort was erected under Diocletian, the very Emperor whose image and superscription this medallion bears.[35]

There can, however, be little doubt as to the status of those who owned the large gold pieces of ex-Dacian, "free" German and southern Scandinavian provenance. Literature has revealed what archaeology has so far denied, the name of one recipient of medallions—Chilperic, the sixth-century Frankish king, whom, as we

[30] G I, tav. 7, no. 17; Grueber, pl. 57, no. 2. Pl. XX, 1.

[31] G I, tav. 6, no. 12; *NZ* 1930, Taf. 2, Nr. 11. Pl. XX, 2.

[32] *Cf.* F. Lenormant, "Le poids des médaillons d'or impérieux" (*RN* 1867, pp. 127 ff.); *La monnaie dans l'antiquité*, I, pp. 13 ff.

[33] *Vide supra* p. 60.

[34] *Vide supra* p. 61.

[35] *NC* 1900, p. 32, pl. 3, no. 1.

saw,[36] the Emperor Tiberius II presented with "aurei" of the largest size, worth 72 solidi each. Chilperic's precursors in such favors may be nameless; but this transaction was not the first of its kind. From what we know of Rome's dealings with the northern tribesmen during the third and fourth centuries it is clear that she had many occasions for bestowing on barbarian princes gifts of a complimentary, remuneratory and even propitiatory character.[37] And when we discover outside the Empire, either singly, as in East Prussia and Denmark or in hoards as at Szilágy-Sómlyó and Boroczzce, gold medallions often of quite spectacular dimensions embellished with ornamental rings or set in the most elaborate frames of non-Roman workmanship,[38] it is obvious for whom they had been designed. The richness of the Germanic settings is proof of how highly the medallions themselves were prized.[39] Again, where the protection afforded by frames was lacking, pieces were not infrequently rubbed almost smooth on one or both sides by constant contact with the persons of their assiduous wearers. Such gifts, we may conclude, were thoroughly acceptable and seldom failed to make their appeal.

II. THE USES OF ROMAN MEDALLIONS

These gold medallions of the later Empire, found beyond the confines of the Imperium Romanum and decked with rings and frames of barbaric technique, afford, of course, striking instances of one of the favorite and most obvious uses to which medallions were put by their recipients, namely their use as personal ornaments and jewellery. The transformation of ordinary gold and silver coins into jewels by this device of adding rings and mounts or by setting them in objects such as precious vessels is a common phenomenon. Among the earliest examples of this process is the Augustan denarius, set in a frame while still in almost mint condition, which came to light in the grave of a British chieftain at Lexden near Colchester.[40] Fine examples of mounted aurei attached to necklaces are to be seen in the Cabinet des Médailles, Paris[41] and in the Kunsthistorisches Museum, Vienna.[42] Single gold coins in elaborate settings are occasionally, and erroneously, classed as medallions—for instance, the DEO AVGVSTO aureus of Gallienus at Padua, mounted in a wide, ornamental frame with a ring,[43] and a mounted solidus of Honorius in Paris;[44] while aurei and solidi equipped with rings and sometimes with simple settings are a not uncommon feature of great coin collections. The gold Dionysiac patera from Rennes in the Cabinet des Médailles, the rim of which is set with sixteen framed

[36] *Vide supra* p. 24; *cf.* E. Babelon, *op. cit.*, part i, p. 536; W. Wroth, *Imperial Byzantine Coins in the British Museum*, I, p. 105.

[37] Presentations of these gifts may have taken place on such occasions as that of Constantine I's tricennalia in 336, when the Emperor received solemn deputations from foreign states (Eusebius, *Vita Constantini* iv, 46, 47, 51).

[38] For a full account of these settings and a discussion of their *motifs* see Alföldi, *NK* 1929–1930, SS. 17–25.

[39] It had been remarked (Alföldi, *op. cit.*, S. 11) that the Szilágy-Sómlyó medallions must represent the collection of at least three generations of Germanic princes.

[40] *Archaeologia* 1926–1927, p. 251, pl. 62, no. 2.

[41] E. g. the "collier" found at Naix (Meuse).

[42] E. g. necklaces from Egypt and from Petrijanec in Croatia in Saal xiv.

[43] G I, tav. 2, no. 9.

[44] Classified in the Cabinet des Médailles as gold medallion no. 56.

aurei of Emperors and Empresses ranging from Hadrian to Septimius Severus and Julia Domna, is an outstanding example of the ornamental application of coins to vessels.[45] Under the later Empire an extensive use as jewels of coins no longer in circulation can be deduced from a sentence of Pomponius: "nomismatum aureorum vel argenteorum veterum, quibus pro gemmis uti solent, usus fructus legari potest."[46] But gold medallions, with their higher intrinsic value, more imposing size and rarer types, pieces essentially decorative in character and issued, moreover, on special or solemn occasions as personal gifts, were almost asking, one might say, to be adapted as jewellery for their owners to display upon their persons or apply to some object of ornament or use. Of the few pre-Gallienic gold medallions which have come down to us two pieces of Caracalla in Paris are set in large octagonal frames of gold filigree work, one equipped with a ring.[47] Of Gallienus' gold medallions a number have rings attached to them;[48] while from Constantine I onwards frames and rings, or traces of rings, either attached to frames or directly to the medallion flans, are increasingly common. In all cases the ring is applied immediately, or almost immediately, above the Emperor's portrait, a proof that it was the obverse of such pieces, when worn as pendants or necklaces, that was meant to show; and this is borne out by the fact that it is the reverse of worn specimens that has generally suffered most.[49] Moreover, when the frames are set with precious stones or engraved with designs, it is to the obverse side that such decorations are normally applied.[50] But far more often, of course, medallions were converted into jewels by the simple expedient of boring a hole through the flan, into which a thread, wire or fine chain could be inserted and the piece suspended round the owner's neck. Such holes, pierced directly, or nearly directly, above the obverse head or bust, are of constant occurrence in gold medallions from the time of the Severi onwards: they are also found in small silver medallions of Constantinian date.[51] Bronze medallions are occasionally found with a hole pierced through above the obverse portrait in such a way as to suggest that they too were used as "jewels" in the sense of being worn as ornaments. Before the beginning of the fourth century instances of this are extremely rare;[52] among medallions of the later Empire, however, they grow considerably commoner.[53] But other pieces show holes which are either not punched right through the flan[54] or are bored through below,[55] to one side of,[56] or even through

[45] Reinach, *Répertoire des reliefs grecs et romains*, ii, 233.

[46] *Digest* vii, 1, 28.

[47] G I, tav. 1, nos. 3, 6.

[48] E. g. G I, tav. 3, nos. 4, 5.

[49] E. g. G I, tavv. 5, no. 4; 6, no. 8; 7, no. 10. A fine gold piece of Constantius II in the Walters Art Gallery, Baltimore, U. S. A., set in an elaborate openwork frame, is equally well preserved on both sides: it has no ring for suspension; but two sets of pendants are attached to the frame. Pl. XXI.

[50] E. g. G I, tavv. 11, no. 8; 12, no. 1; 15, nos. 1, 2; 16, nos. 2, 3; 18, no. 4; 20, nos. 1, 2; Delbrück, *op. cit.*, S. 89, Abb. 27.

[51] E. g. G I, tavv. 28, no. 8; 29, nos. 3, 5, 11, 15.

[52] E. g. G II, tavv. 53, no. 1 (Antoninus Pius); 77, no. 1 (Lucius Verus).

[53] E. g. G II, tavv. 129, no. 10 (Licinius I); 131, no. 10 (Constantinopolis); 133, no. 4 (Crispus), 12 (Constantine II); 140, nos. 3 (Valentinian I), 6 (Procopius), 10 (Theodosius I).

[54] E. g. G II, tavv. 52, no. 1 (Antoninus Pius); 77, no. 2 (Commodus); 115, no. 3 (Gallienus) (Pl. XLVI, 5).

[55] E. g. G II, tavv. 50, no. 1 (Antoninus Pius); 130, no. 8 (Constantine I); 133, no. 3 (Crispus); 139, no. 12 (Jovian); 140, no. 4 (Valens).

[56] E. g. G II, tavv. 121, no. 2 (Probus); 137, no. 6 (Constantius II); 140, no. 8 (Gratian).

the centre of,[57] the Emperor's or Empress's portrait, in positions which suggest that their purpose was not for suspension but for attachment to some object. Other pieces, again, are punched by two or more holes, which definitely rules out their use as pendants.[58] Finally, we should note in this connection the hammering up of the edges of the flan on both sides—occasionally on one side only—which is found so frequently on bronze medallions, especially on those of the later period. The purpose of this must have been to insert the piece securely in some such object as a box or vessel, or in a piece of armor—a scabbard, corselet or the like, although no actual instance of a medallion discovered in such a position has come to the knowledge of the present writer.

One use of medallions for purposes other than those of ornament and decoration has been revealed in a most striking manner by the recent excavations in the Panfilo and Verano Catacombs.[59] On both of these sites excavations in galleries untouched since ancient times have brought to light coins (both Roman and Greek imperial) and medallions affixed to the plaster on the walls surrounding the loculi or the terra-cotta slabs which covered their openings. Other pieces were found in the earth on the floor of the galleries, some with wall-plaster still adhering to one side, a proof that they had fallen from their original positions on the walls. In the Panfilo Catacombs the coins, which are of bronze and silver and number fifty-six in all, range from Trajan to Maxentius, the medallions, of which six are in bronze and one in silver, range from Hadrian to Valerian and Gallienus. The proportion of medallions to coins is high, in view of the formers' comparative rarity; and a similar proportion is to be observed in the pieces of the Verano find, where five medallions, three of bronze and two of silver, ranging from Commodus to Numerianus, have been discovered. As Serafini points out, the object of those who fixed these coins and medallions to the Catacomb walls cannot have been to mark the date of the burials, since pieces of Emperors widely separated from one another in time were found clustered round the same loculus. They must have been set there to serve as guides to relatives and friends of the deceased, enabling them to identify the resting place of particular individuals whose remains they had come to visit or venerate. All the medallions found fixed to the walls had their obverse facing the visitor, with the exception of one bronze of Antoninus Pius in the Panfilo Catacombs, the flan of which had been sliced through down the centre, so that both obverse and reverse could be fixed to the wall and exposed to view.[60] The choice of the obverse, rather than of the reverse, type for exhibition may have been due to the fact that a portrait head or bust was easier to distinguish in the dim light than a more complicated reverse design; or else to Christian aversion to the display of pagan scenes and deities. The exceptional display of Pius' Minerva and Prometheus reverse type may possibly be explained by supposing that the piece in question was a specially valued and famous family possession. It is obvious, indeed,

[57] E. g. G II, tav. 133, no. 1 (Fausta).

[58] E. g. G II, tavv. 92, no. 3 (Albinus); 139, no. 2 (Constantius Gallus). Vienna Nr. 21893 has three holes punched through it.

[59] C. Serafini, *op. cit.* *Vide supra* pp. 59 f.

[60] Serafini, *op. cit.*, tav. 65, no. 5.

that these medallions were regarded as precious heirlooms, handed down in the family from one generation to another and preserved with the greatest care. In fact, two of the Panfilo bronze medallions, one of Lucius Verus[61] and the other of Albinus,[62] were found in a quite remarkably fine state of preservation, cherished from the date of their issue in 164 to 165 and 193 to 197 respectively to be affixed a century later, in something approaching mint condition, to the walls of a Christian tomb. These discoveries are of the first importance, for it is more than likely that the many hundreds of bronze medallions of known or very probable Catacomb provenance,[63] the exact position of which when found no one troubled to record, were fixed in a similar manner to the walls of galleries, revealing this same attitude of respectful care and appreciaticn on the part of medallion owners and their heirs towards these gifts. An interesting parallel to the Catacomb finds came to light at Dunapentele (Intercisa) on the Danube in 1926, where a bronze medallion of Antoninus Pius in splendid condition was found in a late fourth-century grave.[64]

[61] Serafini, *op. cit.*, tav. 65, no. 8. Pl. XX, 3.

[62] Serafini, *op. cit.*, tav. 66, no. 2.

[63] *Vide supra* p. 60.

[64] *NK* 1926, S. 219, Nr. 1, Taf. 8, Nr. 4. Pl. XX, 4.

PART IV

THE HISTORICAL DEVELOPMENT OF ROMAN MEDALLIONS

CHAPTER I

INTRODUCTION

The study of Roman medallions reveals three main phases in their historical development corresponding, roughly, to the second, third and fourth centuries of our era respectively. Standing apart from the regular coinage and unaffected by the practical exigencies of currency supply in all three metals, medallions can claim to interpret in a specially penetrating way the political, cultural, and spiritual background of imperial history in the successive stages of its evolution. Thus the second century, from Trajan to Commodus, the period of the great imperial peace, when the Emperor was still Princeps, when the traditional polytheism of the Roman state was still a reality and when the widespread cultivation of art and letters by a leisured urban society attained its zenith, is, almost exclusively, the period of the bronze medallions proper, classical in style, civilian and "objective" in content and prized primarily for their artistic excellence and for the appeal made by their extensively varied types to a refined and educated taste. Both in quantity and in spectacular quality these bronze medallions reached their peak under Commodus. The imperial crisis of the third century, reckoned from the reign of Septimius Severus to that of Carinus and Numerianus, essentially the transitional phase of Roman imperial history, is represented by medallions correspondingly transitional in character. As Principatus is transformed into Dominatus, as peace, "the tranquillity of order," is exchanged for disorder and an almost unremitting state of war, so the medallions begin to close in, as it were, round the person of the Emperor and to strike an increasingly military note.[1] Again, as the hold of official polytheism succumbs to the growing claims and attractions of the cult of the Emperor or of deities specially honored by imperial devotees, so on third-century medallions the denizens of the Graeco-Roman pantheon, with their wealth of artistic, antiquarian and literary interest, tend to vanish or to figure only in some specially intimate association with the imperial person. Throughout the century bronze medallions of high artistic merit continued to appear. They show that even in these troubled and, generally speaking, less cultured times works of art as such were still acceptable as imperial gifts; though from Gallienus onwards the choice of reverse designs for bronze is largely confined to that of the Tres Monetae type. Meanwhile the more materialistic outlook of the age is reflected in the issue of money medallions in progressively larger quantities, the silver issues beginning under Septimius Severus, the gold under Caracalla and both continuing on relatively modest lines down to the time of Valerian. With Gallienus, however, the output of "silver" or billon multiples grows strikingly more abundant; and although, after his reign, the billon series is merged in that of the bronze, the increased proportion of gold pieces issued by him is well maintained by Aurelian, Probus, Carus, Carinus and Numeri-

[1] *Cf. CAH* xii, pp. 221 f.

anus. In the fourth century the Roman Empire as reorganized by Diocletian and Constantine passes into its final phase as an undisguised and absolute, but necessary, autocracy, entirely dependent for its maintenance and cohesion upon the Augustus and his colleagues, now that the cultural bonds of a widely diffused and prosperous bourgeois civilization were loosened by pressure from without and by social and economic disintegration within. Turning to the medallions, we observe that in a far higher proportion of types than ever before, the Emperor, or some other member of his family, appears in person and in a setting which may be described as ceremonial and hieratic rather than strictly historical. The remaining types—Victoria, Roma, Constantinopolis, imperial vota inscriptions and the like—recur so often and with so little variation that they fail to hold our attention on themselves, but seem to direct it onwards to the august imperial figure who looms behind them. Almost all types are now more or less "subjective" in character. As gifts, medallions were no longer designed to fascinate the cultured connoisseur or to delight the artistic eye. They had to satisfy a taste for outward display and a demand for objects ratable in monetary terms. The intrinsic worth of a piece was now the vital element. With the reign of Diocletian was inaugurated the series of large gold pieces, with that of Constantius II the series of large silver multiples; and it is in these, as contrasted with the dwindling bronze series, that the typical medallions of our third phase are to be sought. Moreover, it is in the types and style of the large gold pieces in particular that we find the concentrated essence of late-antique, as contrasted with earlier classical, art. The Dominus, the permeating spirit of this later art, is their constant theme; and in an age in which relief sculpture, with its greater ceremonial potentialities, had practically ousted sculpture in the round from the field, these medallion reliefs, with their static, centralized and frontal compositions, were peculiarly at home.[2]

This division of medallions into three successive phases obviously cannot be taken as absolute. At the end of our first phase, under Commodus, the tendencies of the second phase are foreshadowed in the content of the medallions and, to a lesser degree, in their style. The central phase shows "throw-backs" to the first and reveals, towards its close, not a little that is characteristic of the third. When the third phase opens with Diocletian, who has been described as "the first to gather together into a completed whole the various experiments and expedients of his predecessors,"[3] we find recorded on his medallions an attempt to revive, on restricted lines, polytheistic religion. The wolf and twins types of Constantine, struck in honor of Old Rome for the foundation of the New, suggest at least some faint reminiscence of the Roman history types of the Antonine age. So, too, such graphic, "objective" scenes as that of Londinium kneeling beside her walls and towers to welcome Constantius Chlorus on the famous Arras medallion of that Emperor, or the view of Trier and the Moselle on Constantine's double solidi, have their counterpart in the pictorial views of public buildings and temples which occur on medallions of Gordian III, Philip and Trebonianus Gallus.

[2] *Ibid.*, pp. 562, ff.

[3] *Ibid.*, p. 407.

CHAPTER II

AUGUSTUS TO COMMODUS

I. General Characteristics

(*a*) *Money Medallions.* The real history of our subject begins with the issue of the first bronze medallions proper under Trajan and Hadrian. But the earliest medallic essays of imperial Rome date from the days of the first Princeps. Some account has already been given of the bronze pseudo medallions struck more or less continuously throughout the first century from the time of Augustus to that of Domitian.[1] Sporadic issues of money medallions, both in gold and silver, are likewise a mark of this experimental period. Two Augustan pieces, each worth four aurei, have come down to us, the hotly disputed Este piece, struck in 2 B. C., with Gaius and Lucius Caesar as Principes Iuventutis on the reverse,[2] and the famous piece from Pompeii at Naples, struck in A. D. 2, with reverse legend IMP XV/SICIL and the type of Diana advancing with bow and quiver. The latter piece commemorates the capitulation of Artagira to Gaius Caesar, which brought the Armenian revolt to a close, and, secondarily, the victory of Naulochus off the Artemision of Mylae in 36 B. C.; while the leftward direction of the head on the obverse, a rare feature in Augustan coinage, marks it out as a special issue.[3] Other events of the principate of an equal, or even greater, importance, may well have inspired the striking of other such multiples which chance has not spared to us. The earliest known post-Augustan money medallions are those of Domitian. They reflect two outstanding features of his reign, his devotion to his patron goddess Minerva and his German campaigns. Of his three Minerva types two, those of Athene Promachos advancing, with or without a supporting prow,[4] repeat types well known to the regular coinage. The three extant pieces, struck in 92, are of silver:[5] a fourth specimen, struck in gold in 88, was lost from Paris in the theft of 1831, but is known from casts.[6] The third Minerva type, struck in 85 and showing the goddess enthroned with Victory, spear and richly ornamented round shield, is not shared with the coins.[7] Lastly, the fine 5-denarii piece in the British Museum, struck in 85, repeats the familiar Germania capta coin type of Germania seated on a shield in an attitude of grief.[8]

[1] *Vide supra* pp. 24 ff.

[2] For arguments against the authenticity of this piece see L. Laffranchi, *Historia* 1933, pp. 600–614. *Cf. supra* p. 114 (**Pl. XIX, 3**).

[3] G I, tav. 1, no. 1.

[4] G I, tav. 21, nos. 3, 4, 5.

[5] British Museum, Rome (Gnecchi Collection), Berlin, worth 5, 4 and 5 denarii respectively.

[6] *BMCCRE* II, pl. 63, no. 8. **Pl. XX, 5.** The original piece was worth 4 or 5 aurei.

[7] G I, tav. 21, no. 2 (B.M.). The bronze piece, also in the B.M., stamped with the same reverse type but with different legends (G III, tav. 143, no. 7) is too puzzling and unconvincing a piece to be cast for the role of the first bronze medallion proper. If genuine, it might be a strike from the dies of a gold or silver medallion.

[8] G I, tav. 21, no. 1.

Trajan and Hadrian, the latter in the early years of his principate, carried on for a time these first-century experiments in money medallions. The extant specimens of this Trajano-Hadrianic group are all of silver and each Emperor has two types to his credit. Trajan's first type appears in 98 to 99, on a 5-denarii piece with the legend PROVIDENTIA SENATVS and confronted figures of the Emperor and the Genius Senatus, the latter handing to the former a globe, the symbol of imperial power.[9] His second type, the adventus type of the 7-denarii piece struck in 106 (?), has already been described.[10] Both of the Hadrianic medallion types date from 119 to 123. One shows Juppiter enthroned with Victory and sceptre,[11] the other Felicitas (or Pax ?) standing with caduceus and cornucopiae.[12] The remainder of the second century is represented by one solitary silver multiple, the 8-denarii piece of Lucius Verus with the type of the seated Salus.[13] Under Commodus the gold multiples appear, foreshadowing the Severan revival of money medallions. The originals, lost from Paris in 1831, were probably worth four aurei apiece: their types are Fortuna standing and Pax seated.[14] But apart from these rare gold and silver multiples and a certain number of bronze pseudo medallions,[15] the whole medallic interest of the period from Trajan to Commodus is centred upon the development of the bronze medallions proper, the structure, die-positions, style and iconography of which we must now review.

(*b*) *Structural Features of the Bronze Medallions.* The structural features soon to be fixed as the norm for large bronze medallions, namely diameter, weight and thickness of flan exceeding those of the sestertii, are by no means always to be found in those Trajanic and Hadrianic pieces which inaugurate the series of bronze medallions proper. Of Trajan, indeed, no large bronze medallions are known, so far, to exist.[16] We have seen that in the first century various groups of common aes coins, indistinguishable from their fellows in weight, size and style, appear to betray some more particularly personal connection with the Emperor by the absence from their reverses of the senatorial formula S C.[17] Such pieces remain coins and nothing more. But in the early decades of the second century we are confronted with a number of bronze pieces without S C, which, for all their structural kinship with the regular aes, satisfy all other medallic criteria—extreme rarity, a stylistic delicacy and finish well above that of the common coinage and a content which testifies to their function as individualized and special gifts.[18] The pieces of sestertius size belonging to this category were, indeed, transitory and experimental in character.[19] Just occasionally a piece was executed in a somewhat more commonplace style,

[9] G I, tav. 21, no. 7. This would appear to be the natural meaning of the scene and legend—the wisdom shown by the Senate in conferring world-sovereignty on the "Optimus Princeps."

[10] *Vide supra* p. 107.

[11] G I, tav. 21 nos. 11, 12. Four examples are known, three worth 8, and one worth 7½, denarii.

[12] G I, tav. 21, nos. 8, 9, 10. Three specimens are worth 8, 7½ and 7 denarii respectively. A fourth specimen, in the Gnecchi Collection, worth 12 denarii is gravely suspect.

[13] G I, tav. 22, no. 1.

[14] G I, p. 3, nos. 1, 2. **Pl. XX, 6, 7.**

[15] *Vide supra* pp. 26 f.

[16] G II, tav. 38, no. 1, is a sestertius-size "framed" piece.

[17] *Vide supra* pp. 28 ff.

[18] *Vide supra* pp. 20 f.

[19] *Vide supra* p. 21.

which leaves its content as its sole, yet decisive, medallic criterion. But, taken as a whole, none of these issues can be adequately described as "imperial bronze": they are true medallions.

On this basis we may reckon as our earliest examples of medallions proper six Trajanic pieces of sestertius size, all distinguishable in style and/or content from the regular sestertii. One of these bears the reverse type of Trajan's silver adventus medallion, but combines it with a different obverse.[20] Most outstanding for their medallic quality are those with the Capitoline Triad and the head of Juppiter Ammon as their respective reverse types.[21] The medallic style of the remaining three pieces, with reverse types of Roma seated,[22] Pax setting fire to a pile of arms[23] and Mercury with purse and caduceus,[24] is less pronounced; but none of these types appear on the ordinary coinage of the reign. Of the sixty-three verifiable bronze medallion types of Hadrian thirty-five appear on large medallion flans; while ten of these are also found on pieces of sestertius, and, occasionally, of smaller, size.[25] Twenty other types occur only on sestertius, and, in four cases, also on smaller, flans; while eight others are found only on flans corresponding roughly in weight and dimensions with those of dupondii and asses. One of the types which appear only on sestertius- and dupondius-size flans, that of Aequitas, occurs on specimens which are differentiated from the corresponding S C coins by their medallic style alone:[26] while the SICILIA sestertius-size medallion, showing as type a gorgoneion in the centre of a triskelis, surrounded by Scylla, a pharos and various other figures,[27] is paralleled by an as-size piece, with S C and without the surrounding figures, so rare and so medallic in style that we may reckon it as a S C medallion.[28] But the great majority of pieces with non-medallic flans—and they form a high proportion of the total number of Hadrianic bronze medallions—are as clearly distinct in style and content from the current coinage as those which are also of medallic structure. The medallions of Sabina and Aelius Verus all have large flans. Of the numerous bronze medallions issued by Antoninus Pius only a small proportion of types occurs on flans of sestertius size—eight struck for Pius himself, two for Faustina I and two for Faustina II. Meanwhile the smaller medallions of dupondius and as weight and dimensions grow more frequent—fifteen struck for Pius himself, three for Faustina I, four for Marcus Aurelius as Caesar and six for Faustina II. But the vast majority of the pieces of this period show the normal structural features of the large medallions. Under Marcus Aurelius only four types appear on sestertius flans, two of Marcus himself and two of Lucius Verus; on smaller flans we have one type of Marcus himself, two of Faustina II, two of Lucius Verus, one of Commodus

[20] G II, tav. 38, no. 1. [21] G III, tav. 143, nos. 10, 11. [22] G III, tav. 143, no. 8.

[23] *BMCCRE* III, p. 157, note †. [24] G III, tav. 143, no. 12.

[25] E. g. sestertius-size piece in Ryan Collection with Aesculapius and Salus reverse type (= G II, tav. 38, no. 5, but with different obverse: *cf.* G III, tav. 147, no. 6). **Pl. XX, 8.**

[26] Of this type there are two variants:—(1) MONETA AVGVSTI: Aequitas with scales and cornucopiae (G III, tav. 145, no. 6: *cf.* *BMCCRE* III, pl. 78, no. 14); (2) COS III: Aequitas with scales and sceptre (G III, tav. 147, no. 7: *cf.* *BMCCRE* III, pl. 81, no. 8).

[27] G III, tav. 145, no. 10.

[28] *BMCCRE* III, pl. 95, no. 16. **Pl. XX, 9.** This is the only example known to the present writer.

and Annius Verus and one of Commodus as Caesar. Finally, Commodus struck one type on a sestertius flan and four types on smaller flans.[29] Meanwhile the flans of the large bronze medallions tend to grow thicker and heavier. Under Commodus medallions frequently turn the scale at over sixty grammes: seventy grammes and over is by no means an uncommon weight, especially for bi-metallic pieces; while eighty grammes and over, almost always in the case of bi-metallic medallions, are occasionally registered and one bi-metallic piece weighs over ninety grammes.[30] Two important structural features of the bronze medallions belonging to the first phase of historical development, "framing" and the bi-metallic process, have already been fully discussed and the chronological distribution of the pieces which display them analyzed.[31]

(c) *Die-positions.* The relative positions of obverse and reverse dies on Roman medallions may either be such that the tops of both designs correspond on their respective sides of the flan, that is to say that the piece, when viewed on the obverse, has only to be turned sideways for the reverse to be seen the right way up ("seitwendig": ↑↑, occasionally ↑ ↖ or ↑ ↗); or they may be such that the top of the obverse corresponds to the bottom of the reverse on the flan, which must be turned over "head to tail" for the reverse to be shown in its right position ("kopfwendig": ↑↓, occasionally ↑ ↘ or ↑ ↙). The normal die-positions of first-century pseudo medallions are, as we have seen,[32] ↑↓. With the exception of the Principes Iuventutis gold piece of Augustus, which shows die-positions ↑ ↖, all the money medallions of Augustus, Domitian, Trajan and Hadrian show die-positions ↑↓.[33] Domitian's solitary bronze piece has die-positions ↑↓; and the same is true of all Trajan's bronze pieces, with three exceptions. Of Hadrian's bronze pieces there are fourteen known to the present writer with die-positions ↑↓, three of them small, five of them sestertius-size, medallions. Six of these pieces date from the years 119 to 123, six from the years 123 to 128 and two from the year 128 to 129; a number of other Hadrianic medallions, however, struck during these years show die-positions ↑↑. But from 129 down to the death of Commodus the normal die-positions of Roman medallions are ↑↑, with a small minority of pieces showing die-positions ↑↓.[34]

The study of die-positions is of some interest as providing us with another general point of differentiation between medallions and the regular coinage during our first phase. In the reign of Hadrian, as Strack was the first to observe,[35] bronze medallion die-positions follow rules which are almost the exact opposite of those

[29] The APOL MONETAE bronze piece figured by Gnecchi (III, tav. 152, no. 1) shows no medallic features and must rank as an as without S C: the type is a common one on the regular coinage.

[30] "Framed" medallions are, of course, not included in the above analysis of weights.

[31] *Vide supra* pp. 17 f.

[32] *Vide supra* p. 26.

[33] The analysis of die-positions which follows in this and in the two succeeding Chapters is based upon the pieces, forming the great majority of known medallions, the die-positions of which the present writer has been able to record by autopsy or by means of information from reliable sources.

[34] Thirty-one pieces in all are known to the present writer.

[35] II, SS. 21 f.; 200 f. *Cf. BMCCRE* III, pp. xx, cxviii, note 1.

followed by the aes coin die-positions. Whereas aes coins before 128 to 129 show die-positions ↑↓, bronze medallions struck before that date show ↑↑ as well as ↑↓ and, again, while the positions ↑↓ and ↑↑ alternate on the aes coinage after 128 to 129, on bronze medallions of Hadrian's last decade the die-positions are invariably ↑↑. So, too, on the coinage of the period extending from Pius' accession to the death of Commodus both sets of positions occur, neither very clearly dominant at any time; whereas on the bronze medallions of the period die-positions ↑↑ are very distinctly dominant over the positions ↑↓.

(*d*) *Style.* In the bronze medallions of the second century, from Trajan to Commodus, the art of die-cutting under the Roman Empire reached the acme of its achievement. Indeed, we may go so far as to say that these medallions can often lay claim to an artistic beauty in its own way unsurpassed in the whole history of ancient numismatics. The artists who designed their types created no new style, in the sense in which the artists of the later Empire, swept forward by new political and spiritual currents, may be termed creative. The Hadrianic age, the true springtime, as it were, of medal-engraving in the ancient world, was essentially an age of synthesis. In art it combined the fresh developments which the first century of imperial history had witnessed with a new sensitiveness to the past, a new awareness of the significance of its archaic, classical and Hellenistic heritage. The invention of medallions proper opened up a fresh field of "minor" art precisely adjusted to the tastes and culture of the time. Here was an accessible and convenient medium in which all styles could be studied and appreciated, one which offered a history in miniature, an epitome or anthology,[36] of ancient art in all its phases. Meanwhile, in our delight at the designs—spontaneous, graceful, vivacious, almost gay—we tend to forget that their types and motives are largely derivative. Again, as special gift pieces, bestowed by the most distinguished giver in the Roman world, medallions attracted the skill and care of the most accomplished artists of the day. For sheer technique nothing can rival them. Nearer, in many respects, to gems than to coins, they show a delicacy of touch and finish which is truly exquisite. The height of relief which they often display, particularly in the obverse portraits, immediately catches the eye as distinguishing medallions from the common coinage; while individual figures and other details of the reverse types show a plasticity, suppleness and generosity in the modelling which become peculiarly striking when a medallion and a coin of the same, or similar, content are set side by side.

In composition, no less than in technique, the reverse designs of this phase reflect the same variety of traditions. Under Hadrian, Pius and Marcus Aurelius the prevailing note is one of spaciousness and simplicity. Now a single, statuesque, "classical" figure of a god or hero stands out boldly against the centre of a plain background, either alone[37] or flanked by minor accessories, such as an altar,[38] or an altar and a cippus.[39] Often a simple group set against a plain background unifies

[36] *Cf.* Fröhner, apropos of Hadrianic medallions, "c'est l'Anthologie après les grands poètes" (*Les médaillons de l'empire romain*, p. 24).

[37] G II, tavv. 40, nos. 5, 6; 43, nos. 3, 8.

[38] G II, tavv. 46, no. 6; 48, no. 7.

[39] G II, tav. 58, no. 1.

in a yet more satisfying manner the circular field—Diana standing in front of her stag,[40] Victory slaying a bull,[41] Victory driving in a biga,[42] Sol mounting his quadriga,[43] Cybele riding on her lion,[44] Diana on her stag,[45] Apollo on his griffin[46] and the Emperor on his horse.[47] At other times a single divine being appears in a setting of scenery, executed in the manner of Hellenistic and early imperial paintings and reliefs, with rocks, trees, temples and ritual objects.[48] But in such settings, kept strictly subordinate, fussiness is avoided and the emphasis upon the central figure is not obscured. Again, in the more complicated mythological and historical scenes, involving two, three, four or even more figures, with accessories, the component elements of the design are clear, distinct and well spaced out, unless, as in the scene of the Sabine women[49] and in scenes of the vota publica,[50] adlocutio[51] or processions, [52] the point of the picture is to give the illusion of a crowd: and there we may note the obvious influence of historical relief sculptures and paintings—Flavian, Trajanic and contemporary Antonine. On many of the finest Hadrianic and Antonine pieces no reverse legend is allowed to appear, distracting the eye or disturbing the design. On others the reverse legend is reduced to a minimum or set in the exergue. Before the time of Marcus long circumference legends, girdling the whole reverse design, are rare. On medallions of Commodus, just as the technique thickens and coarsens, so, as regards composition, certain types tend to grow fussier[53] and heavier;[54] and on some the central figure, no longer fully harmonized with, and adjusted to, the limited field, towers up as though seeking to emancipate itself from its restrictions.[55] Reverse legends too, are longer and larger and definitely detract something from the dignity and unity of the type. Yet in the wide and varied repertory of Commodus' medallions, side by side with the pieces which display these aesthetically less pleasing features, not a few are to be found with types composed and executed according to the principles of the best Hadrianic and early Antonine designs.[56]

(*e*) *Iconography*. Iconography is the one field in respect of which the most adverse critics of imperial art refrain from applying the terms "decline" and "decadence" to the later phases of its development. The rendering of the actual physiognomy of the imperial persons portrayed upon the obverses of Roman medallions is, indeed, as skillful and vital in the third and fourth centuries as in the second—and more so, in fact, as the "classical" idealism of the Hadrianic and Antonine periods yields place to that striking, at times almost startling, realism and individualism

[40] G II, tav. 43, no. 7.
[41] G II, tav. 55, no. 4.
[42] G II, tav. 38, nos. 8, 9 (**Pl. XL, 2**).
[43] G II, tav. 42, nos. 8, 9.
[44] G II, tav. 42, no. 6.
[45] G II, tav. 68, no. 4.
[46] G II, tav. 52, no. 1.
[47] G II, tav. 48, nos. 1, 2.
[48] G II, tavv. 38, no. 6; 41, no. 4; 43, no. 9; 48, no. 5; 50, no. 8; 52, nos. 6, 7, 8; 68, no. 1.
[49] G II, tav. 56, no. 6.
[50] G II, tav. 63, no. 9.
[51] G II, tav. 58, no. 3.
[52] G II, tavv. 63, no. 1; 74, no. 4.
[53] G II, tavv. 80, no. 6 (**Pl. XLIII, 3**); 85, no. 5.
[54] G II, tavv. 85, no. 7; 86, nos. 2, 3.
[55] G II, tavv. 80, nos. 2, 3, 4; 81, no. 4.
[56] G II, tavv. 77, no. 3; 78, no. 2; 83, no. 6; 91, nos. 2, 6.

which attained their zenith in Diocletianic portraiture. Moreover, in the later portrait types we find a whole wealth of new motives in the representation of dress, armor and attributes and in the general treatment of the head or bust, quite unknown on medallions of the second century. Meanwhile there remains a large proportion of third- and fourth-century obverses which are derived from types already in vogue before the death of Commodus.

Many of the more common types of medallion obverses can, of course, be paralleled on the regular coinage, particularly upon the aurei and denarii. In their general scheme such medallion and coin portraits are identical: the distinction between them lies in technique and in small points of detail. For example, in a few rare instances the bust is seen almost directly sideways on, and the back is hardly shown at all;[57] while a few medallions of Commodus show a specially deep type of bust, with cuirass and aegis covering the chest.[58] Again, while rightward facing portraits are, on the whole, commoner on medallions than those which face to the left, a far higher proportion face leftwards than on the regular coinage. There are, however, a number of obverse portrait types quite peculiar to medallions. A deep bust of Hadrian is draped in an ample aegis, fastened on the shoulder and falling down over chest and back, while leaving a generous expanse of fleshy upper arm and breast exposed to view.[59] The type appears again on medallions struck for Marcus Aurelius[60] and Commodus,[61] both as Caesar. The only other piece, known to the present writer, on which this remarkable type occurs is a medallic coin of Trajan, which combines a common sestertius reverse type with this unique obverse portrait, completely strange to the regular coinage and presumably struck from some otherwise unknown medallion die.[62] A rare medallion portrait of the youthful Marcus shows him with the bare upper part of his chest twisted round into an almost frontal position.[63] A fine portrait of Marcus as Emperor, obviously based upon the famous Blacas cameo of Augustus,[64] shows him with his back turned almost completely to the spectator: the right side of the back is naked, but the left side is covered by an aegis held in position by a strap passing over the shoulder; in his right hand he holds a sceptre (or spear?).[65] The same portrait appears again on medallions of Lucius Verus[66] and Commodus.[67] Another obverse portrait of Commodus shows him with his chest almost frontal and naked save for an aegis secured on the shoulder by a strap.[68] A small bronze medallion of Hadrian displays the head of the Emperor in a lion-skin hood, a motive quite unknown to his current coinage.[69] This motive next appears in the magnificent series of portraits of Commodus combined with Herculean reverse types, struck for the New Year, 193.[70] It is true that the lion-skin hood is also found on Commodus' coins of 192.[71] But there the heads face

[57] G III, tav. 149, nos. 5, 7.

[58] G II, tavv. 81, no. 4; 82, no. 3.

[59] G II, tavv. 38, no. 9 (Pl. **XL, 2**); 39, no. 2.

[60] G II, tavv. 65, no. 1; 66, no. 10 (Pl. **XLI, 5**).

[61] G II, tav. 87, nos. 6, 8.

[62] Strack I, Taf. 7, Nr. 403. Pl. **XX, 10.** *Vide supra* p. 32, note 41.

[63] G III, tav. 150, no. 5 (Pl. **XIV, 3**).

[64] *Vide infra* p. 227.

[65] G II, tavv. 59, no. 5; 60, no. 7 (Pl. **XLII, 1**).

[66] G II, tav. 74, no. 9.

[67] G II, tavv. 78, no. 8; 84, no. 1.

[68] G II, tavv. 83, no. 10; 86, no. 8.

[69] G III, tav. 145, no. 12. *Cf.* J. M. C. Toynbee, *op. cit.*, p. 142.

[70] *Vide supra* pp. 74 ff.

[71] *RIC* III, pl. 15, no. 310.

only to the right, instead of to the right or to the left, as on the medallions, where the treatment is, moreover, so infinitely more vivid, vigorous and varied than on the coins that the motive may, in general, be claimed as a peculiarly medallic one. Other rare medallion portraits of Commodus show him wearing the lion-skin knotted round his neck;[72] and in a janiform bust, combined with Janus.[73] Again, we have two jugate obverse portraits, one of Commodus and Minerva, who wears a helmet with down-turned peak,[74] and the other of Commodus and an Amazon, who wears a helmet with up-turned peak, while a pelta is shown below.[75] Finally, a unique and unfortunately much damaged piece in the British Museum bears on its obverse a deep, full-face bust of Commodus.[76]

The portrayal of two imperial persons on the obverse, a rare phenomenon on the Roman imperial coinage of the first and second centuries,[77] is a distinctive feature of medallic iconography. This motive of two portraits *vis-à-vis*, very effective as a composition, makes its first appearance during our first phase upon medallions struck by Marcus Aurelius with his own head or bust and that of his colleague, Lucius Verus, on the obverse[78] and, later, with his own bust and that of the youthful Commodus as obverse type.[79] Marcus, again, issued one medallion with obverse busts of his sons Commodus and Annius Verus as small boys[80] and two with portraits of Commodus and his bride Crispina.[81]

Medallions struck for the Empresses of the second century, for Sabina, Faustina I, Faustina II, Lucilla and Crispina, show no distinctive obverse types unknown to the current coinage, apart from one exceptional portrait of Faustina II, in which the bust is deep and the breasts visible.[82] Among medallic portraits of imperial children, in fact, throughout the whole range of imperial child-iconography, numismatic and otherwise, we might look in vain for anything comparable to the small medallion struck by Marcus Aurelius with busts of his young sons, Commodus and Annius Verus, one on either side.[83] In these delightful portraits of the two little fellows, Commodus aged five years and curly-headed Annius Verus aged three, is enshrined all the charm of those glimpses into the imperial nursery which Fronto's correspondence affords us.

It is, indeed, the obverse portraits which, taken as a whole, represent the high water-mark of second-century medallic technique. For height of relief and for gem-like clarity and precision in the treatment of hair and beards the portraits of

[72] G II, tav. 87, no. 3. [73] G II, tav. 87, no. 1. [74] G II, tavv. 85, nos. 7, 8; 86, no. 2; 87, no. 4.

[75] G II, tavv. 85, nos. 9, 10; 86, no. 3; 87, no. 5. The Amazon doubtless portrays Commodus' concubine, Marcia. [76] Grueber p. 30, no. 45. **Pl. XXII, 1.**

[77] The best known instance is that of the twin busts of Nero and his mother, either *vis-à-vis* (*RIC* I, pl. 9, no. 139) or jugate (*ibid.*, pl. 9, no. 140), on aurei and denarii of 54 to 55. *Cf.* the heads, back to back, of Augustus and Agrippa on colonial aes of Nemausus (*ibid.*, p. 44) and the busts of Claudius and Agrippina, jugate, on "cistophoric medallions" struck at Ephesus (*ibid.*, pl. 6, no. 98).

[78] G II, tavv. 70, no. 2; 71, nos. 2–6.

[79] G II, tav. 71, no. 10; *BMQ* 1934–1935, pl. 16, no. 4. **Pl. XXII, 2.** [80] G II, tav. 72, no. 1.

[81] G II, tav. 91, nos. 7, 8, 9. *Vide supra* p. 97. [82] G II, tav. 67, no. 3

[83] G III, tav. 151, no. 8. **Pl. XLII, 6.** The piece was most probably struck in honor of the boys' elevation to the rank of Caesar in 166.

Aelius Verus, Marcus Aurelius as Caesar and Lucius Verus are outstanding among them; while the obverse busts of the Empresses, and those of Faustina II and of Lucilla in particular, offer some of the finest material available for students of feminine coiffure in early imperial times.

II. THE CHOICE OF REVERSE TYPES

In our chapters on the purpose of Roman medallions we have already considered in detail a number of reverse types of which the content proclaims either the occasions of their issue or the character of the recipients for whom they were designed. In the present chapter, and in the two following, our main concern is with the classification of types as a whole in each of the three successive phases of their historical development; for this will disclose how the distribution of emphasis on different subjects at different times, and, again, on different aspects of these subjects, reflects the varying stages in the political, cultural and spiritual evolution of the Empire. The conclusions to be drawn from this classification will be summarized in our final chapters on the place of medallions in imperial life.

Medallion reverse types can be considered under seven heads:—(a) personal types of the Emperor and his family, (b) public and historical events, (c) deities, (d) mythology and legend, (e) personifications, (f) buildings and (g) animate and inanimate objects.[84]

(a) *Personal Types of the Emperor and his Family.* The majority of these types show the Emperor, or Caesar, in a setting which appears to be of personal, rather than of specifically public or historical, significance. We see him galloping, standard in hand (Marcus Aurelius as Caesar), or mounted on a standing or walking horse, with one hand outstretched in greeting[85] (Antoninus Pius, Marcus Aurelius as Caesar[86] and as Emperor, Lucius Verus, Commodus as Caesar). Sometimes he stands alone, flanked by standards (Hadrian); or two imperial colleagues stand confronted, clasping one another by the hand (CONCORD AVGVSTOR, CONCORDIAE AVGVSTORVM: Marcus Aurelius,[87] Lucius Verus).[88] A favorite type of the Emperor, or Caesar, on horseback, hunting lion or boar, is dedicated VIRTVTI AVGVSTI, to the imperial virtue *par excellence* of courage or prowess in the hunt, whether actually or as an allegory of war (Hadrian, Marcus Aurelius as Caesar, Lucius Verus,[89] Commodus[90]). Finally, we must include among these personal types reverse portraits of the Emperor's heir (Antoninus Pius: Marcus Aurelius, Marcus Aurelius: Commodus) or consort (Antoninus Pius: Faustina I, Marcus Aurelius: Faustina II).[91]

[84] In the sections on reverse types in this chapter, and in Chapters III and IV, references will generally be given only to pieces not illustrated in Gnecchi's plates.

[85] *Vide infra* p. 223.

[86] Strack III, Taf. 21, Nr. 607. **Pl. XXII, 3.**

[87] Budapest, National Museum. **Pl. XXII, 4.**

[88] *Weber Collection Sale Catalogue* 1909, Taf. 23, Nr. 1664 (with S C); Vatican (without S C). Also a coin type. **Pl. XXII, 5, 6.**

[89] Very poor specimen in Vienna (Nr. 40726). Cast in B. M. of very fine specimen of unknown location. **Pl. XXII, 7.**

[90] Also a coin type.

[91] "Framed" piece in Berlin. **Pl. XXIII, 1.** For types alluding to imperial adoptions, marriages, births and deaths and to the Princeps Iuventutis *vide supra* Part III, Chs. II, III.

(*b*) ***Public and Historical Events.*** Under the Hadrianic and Antonine peace, direct medallic allusions to public and historical events are rare. Types of Pius which show the Emperor accompanied by Victory erecting a trophy and by Africa reclining below, struck in 160, commemorate the suppression of the Mauretanian disturbances:[92] one of these types was copied by Commodus' medallist in 190 to 191 to record another defeat of the Mauri by Rome.[93] But the troubled reign of Marcus produced a whole series of historico-military types, struck in his own name and in that of Lucius and commemorative of their northern and eastern wars. A type struck by Marcus in his own name shows Lucius offering a Victory to his colleague in the presence of officials and soldiers.[94] A scene labelled GERMANIA SVBACTA and struck in Marcus' name shows the Emperor with Victory, trophy and captives (172 to 173);[95] another scene portrays him with trophy and captives (177 to 178); in a third, entitled CLEMENTIA AVG, a prisoner kneels in supplication at the Emperor's feet.[96] A piece issued in the joint names of the two colleagues between 161 and 166 shows the Emperors, with soldiers and captives in attendance, supporting a Victory (VICTORIA AVGG). Of Lucius' types the most interesting displays the Emperors each crowned by a Victory, while Euphrates and Tigris recline below (168). Other scenes show Lucius crowned by Victory (163), sacrificing and crowned by Victory (166 to 169) or receiving a wreath from Victory (166). Types directly alluding to the eastern campaigns, with or without the legend ARMENIA, show him standing or on horseback, with Armenia kneeling before him, or galloping along as he strikes down an Armenian with his lance (163 to 165).[97] The comparatively brief and unimportant campaigns waged under Commodus are recorded by a number of general historical types—Commodus crowning a trophy (183), receiving a wreath from Victory (184), holding Victory on a globe and a spear (185) and crowned by Roma (186).[98]

(*c*) *Deities.* Representations of deities form by far the largest class of second-century medallion types. From the Diana of Augustus' gold medallion, struck in A. D. 2, down to the Hercules types of Commodus' eighteenth tribunician year, the Roman medallists' main achievement was the creation of a splendid galaxy of types of gods and goddesses, reflecting, as it were in concentrated form, the great religious and artistic interests of the age. These types are at once an epitome of ancient art and an irrefutable proof of the vitality and influence in the second century of our era of Rome's ancient and official creeds. But these are questions to which we shall

[92] *Vita Pii* 5, 4; Pausanias viii, 43, 3. *Cf. supra* p. 99, note 33. [93] *Vita Commodi* 13, 5.

[94] *BM* 1917, S. 49, Abb. **Pl. XXIII, 2.**

[95] *Cf.* the type of this year (TR P XXVII) with legend VICT GERM and Victory driving in a quadriga towards the left. **Pl. XLI, 7.**

[96] *Cf.* the somewhat similar CLEMENTIA AVG sestertii.

[97] *Cf.* sestertii of 163 to 164 and aurei of 164 to 165. A variant of the second type, on a magnificent piece from the Catacombs (now in the Vatican) shows Lucius involved in a regular *mêlée* (Serafini, *op. cit.*, tav. 64, no. 3 (**Pl. XX, 3**)).

[98] G II, p. 62, no. 91. For public and historical allusions in types of vota publica, processus consularis, state sacrifices and festivals, profectio, reditus (including types of Fortuna Dux and Redux), adventus, adlocutio, liberalitas etc. *vide supra* Part III, Chs. I, II.

return later on.[99] Here we must confine ourselves to a general survey of the deities represented and of the aspects under which they are portrayed.

First of all come the great patrons of the Roman state, the Capitoline Triad shown standing (Trajan,[100] Hadrian, Commodus) or seated (Hadrian, Antoninus Pius, Marcus Aurelius and Lucius Verus): neither type occurs on current coins. On medallions of Hadrian and of Pius the members of the Triad are represented by their attributes—eagle, peacock and owl. Juppiter, both protector and prototype of the divinized Emperor, appears enthroned towards the left on a silver multiple of Hadrian and on a bronze medallion of Pius. On a bronze piece of Lucius Verus he is seated on a rock, receiving back the Victory, of which he was the source, from the Emperor. Medallions of Commodus show him seated and presenting a globe to his imperial *protégé*, or enthroned to the front between the Dioscuri. But in the majority of types Juppiter stands, protecting the Emperor, or Emperors, beneath the shadow of his mantle (IOVI CONSERVATORI: Hadrian, Antoninus Pius, Marcus Aurelius, Lucius Verus, Commodus as Caesar);[101] holding sceptre and fulmen, with or without his eagle (Hadrian (IOVI TONANTI),[102] Antoninus Pius), with tree, altar and eagle (Antoninus Pius), with Atlas and with eagle perched on an altar (Antoninus Pius) or with eagle and altar (Antoninus Pius, Commodus (IOVI IVVENI)); holding sceptre and eagle, with altar (Marcus Aurelius as Caesar); and holding sceptre and patera, with altar (Antoninus Pius). Less than half of these Juppiter types are shared with the regular coinage. Other types of Juppiter, all confined to medallions, show him driving a slow quadriga (Antoninus Pius) or a swift quadriga, hurling his bolt at a snake-legged giant (Antoninus Pius) or at a German warrior (Marcus Aurelius). The head of Juppiter Ammon appears on a small bronze piece of Trajan and on a large bronze medallion of Commodus (I O M). The reverse of a sestertius-size medallion of Hadrian shows the inscription IOVI / OPTIMO / MAXIMO / S P Q R within an oak-wreath—a type struck, it would seem, to "return the compliment" of a senatorial dedication to Juppiter and, by implication, to the Emperor, as Juppiter's vice-gerent. Indeed, from the wide range and variety of Juppiter types stamped upon these imperial personal gifts we may gauge the strength of the Emperor's sense of personal relationship with Juppiter "Best and Greatest", lord and conserver of the Roman world.

Apollo, the peculiar patron of the first Augustus, is, after Juppiter, the most prominent deity on second-century medallions. First, as Apollo Palatinus and Musagetes, he plays the lyre to three Muses (Hadrian), strides along in flowing chiton, lyre and plectrum in hand (Antoninus Pius), leans upon his lyre, plectrum and patera(?) in hand and with a griffin at his side (Antoninus Pius),[103] stands facing the spectator with lyre and patera (Antoninus Pius (APOLLINI AVGVSTO)), is seated to the front with lyre and plectrum (Marcus Aurelius as Caesar and as Emperor) and

[99] *Vide infra* Part V, Chs. II, III. [100] **Pl. XL, 1.**

[101] *Trau Collection Sale Catalogue* 1935, Taf. 25, Nr. 1884. **Pl. XXIII, 3.**

[102] Strack II, Taf. 16, Nr. 497. **Pl. XXIII, 4.**

[103] G II, p. 17, no. 68. Badly worn specimen in National Museum, Sofia.

stands, plectrum in hand, receiving a lyre from Victory (Commodus (APOL PALATINO)). Secondly, as archer, he rides a griffin, holding quiver and bow (Antoninus Pius) and stands to the front, with bow and quiver, between a tripod and a table (Marcus Aurelius as Caesar). Thirdly, as Apollo Salutaris, he stands with bow and branch, a table on one side, a tripod and tree-trunk on the other (Hadrian), holds the serpent-staff of Aesculapius, flanked by tree and thymiaterium (Antoninus Pius),[104] sacrifices over an altar, flanked by tripod and tree (Marcus Aurelius as Caesar) and is grouped with Salus, who feeds the snake entwined about his shoulders (Marcus Aurelius as Caesar). Only two of these Apollo types—those which are accompanied by legends—are shared with coins.[105]

On Hadrianic and Antonine medallions Aesculapius plays a conspicuous part as guardian, proximately, of the Emperor's, or Caesar's, personal health, ultimately, of the public health of the Empire. As a youthful deity, holding, or leaning on, the serpent-staff, he is grouped with Salus and the figure of Apollo Salutaris on a column (Hadrian)[105a] or stands alone (Antoninus Pius). As an elderly, bearded god he stands facing, propped on his serpent-staff (Hadrian,[106] Aelius Verus, Antoninus Pius) or holding the staff and flanked by a couple of rearing snakes (Marcus Aurelius as Caesar), and he is grouped with Salus, either enthroned to the front, with serpent-staff and patera in his hands (Antoninus Pius), or standing, staff in hand (Lucius Verus). All these types are peculiar to medallions.

Hercules, the Emperor's prototype as benefactor and friend of man, is naturally a popular figure on second-century medallions, even before Commodus installed him as his "patron saint." The Hercules types of Commodus' eighteenth tribunician year, his earlier Hercules types and the New Year types of Hercules as patron of agriculture, struck for Antoninus Pius, for Marcus Aurelius as Caesar and as Emperor and for Commodus as Caesar and as Emperor, have been fully described in a previous chapter.[107] Other types, of which the great majority are unknown to the coinage, show him standing to the right, holding lion-skin, club and branch (Hadrian, Antoninus Pius), or the left, between a dolium and a tree (Antoninus Pius), crowning himself, between an apple tree and an altar (Marcus Aurelius and Commodus,[108] Lucius Verus), sacrificing before a temple (Antoninus Pius) and seated to the front, with a selection of his usual attributes (Hadrian,[109] Antoninus Pius, Marcus Aurelius as Caesar).[110]

Mercury figures on medallions of the earlier part of our first phase as another imperial prototype, in his role as divine guardian and overseer of the commerce of the Roman world.[111] He stands with caduceus and purse (Trajan), with caduceus

[104] Strack III, Taf. 4, Nr. 563. **Pl. XXIII, 5.**

[105] For a puzzling Apollo type of Antoninus Pius, in which the god appears in both pastoral and Delphic capacity in the same design, see *NC* 1940, pp. 2 ff., pl. 1, no. 1. **Pl. XXIV, 1.**

[105a] **Pl. XL, 3.**

[106] **Pl. XL, 4.** *Cf.* the somewhat similar figure on Asiatic cistophori of Hadrian (*BMCCRE* III, pl. 72, no. 2).

[107] *Vide supra* pp. 74 ff; 75, note 12; 90 and note 149.

[108] *BMQ* 1934–1935, pl. 16, no. 4 (**Pl. XXII, 2**).

[109] G III, p. 21, no. 112: small bronze medallion type. **Pl. XXIII, 6.**

[110] Badly worn specimen in Hall Collection, Llanymynech.

[111] *Cf. RM* 1935, SS. 225, 231. For a possible connection between Mercury types and the New Year *vide supra* p. 94.

and goat (Hadrian), with caduceus and ram (Antoninus Pius)[112] and with caduceus and purse between a table and a pillar, on which a cock is perched (Marcus Aurelius as Caesar). A curious bearded Mercury type of Hadrian portrays him with pedum, ram and cock, a tree behind him, striding towards an altar and a shrine.[113] Bacchus, armed with thyrsus, is seated in a car, drawn by panther and goat, with Apollo, holding a lyre, at his side (Hadrian, Antoninus Pius);[114] he drives beside Ariadne in a car drawn by panther and Satyr (Antoninus Pius) or by two panthers, in the midst of a Bacchic rout (Marcus Aurelius as Caesar)[115] or alone in a Centaur-biga, attended by Amor and a Bacchic train (Marcus Aurelius as Caesar).[116] He sits with Ariadne on a rock, with revellers around (Antoninus Pius);[117] he is seated in conversation with Ariadne, who stands beside him (Marcus Aurelius as Caesar);[118] and he sleeps upon a rock, while a Maenad approaches stealthily (Antoninus Pius). Bacchus, again, is a prototype of the Emperor in the role of Neos Dionysos.

Neptune stands facing Minerva, an olive tree between them (Hadrian, Marcus Aurelius as Caesar(?),[119] or sits, while Minerva stands confronting him from the opposite side of an olive tree and a table supporting a voting urn, from which Victory draws out the votes (Antoninus Pius, Marcus Aurelius as Caesar).[119a] He is grouped with Ceres (Antoninus Pius, Marcus Aurelius as Caesar)[120] and with the Emperor (Commodus);[121] and he stands alone, with trident and anchor(?), before the walls of Troy (Marcus Aurelius as Caesar). Mars stands facing the spectator beside a trophy (Antoninus Pius) or with olive-branch and spear reversed (Commodus (MART PACAT)); he advances towards the left with trophy and Victory (Marcus Aurelius (MARTI VICTORI)) or towards the right with trophy and spear (Marcus Aurelius and Commodus, Commodus);[122] he stands to the right beside a Victory-topped cippus (Commodus); and he receives a sacrifice from the Emperor, while Victory either crowns the imperial celebrant or advances with wreath and palm (Commodus).[123] Again, we have Mars grouped with Venus—the god seated, while his consort stands beside him (Marcus Aurelius as Caesar), or standing opposite his consort, who either sits and offers him a helmet (Faustina II) or stands, resting her hands on his shoulder (Faustina II) or leaning on a pillar (Commodus). Vulcan is grouped with a statuette of Minerva, standing and working on a pair of greaves (Antoninus Pius), or with the goddess herself, seated and forging, now a helmet (Antoninus Pius),[124] now a fulmen (Marcus Aurelius as Caesar) in her presence. The New Year types of Sol have been discussed above.[125] Pan, young and beard-

[112] **Pl. XL, 6.**

[113] *Cf. NC* 1940, pp. 3 ff., pl. 1, no. 3.

[114] This reverse type, accompanied by a medallic obverse portrait, was copied on a Greek coin of Antoninus Pius struck at Tralles (*BMCGC: Lydia*, pl. 36, no. 7).

[115] *Vide supra* p. 98.

[116] *Vide supra* p. 96. **Pl. XLI, 6.**

[117] Vienna Nr. 37404.

[118] Wrongly interpreted by Gnecchi (II, p. 32, no. 41) as representing Hercules and Omphale. *Vide supra* p. 99, note 28.

[119] Imhoof-Blumer and P. Gardner, *A Numismatic Commentary on Pausanias* p. 131, Pl. Z, no. 15 (reverse only). **Pl. XXIV, 2.** *Vide infra* p. 217.

[119a] Properly speaking, the Greek names Poseidon and Athene should be used in this context.

[120] *Vide supra* p. 94.

[121] *Vide supra* p. 77.

[122] G II, p. 61, no. 84.

[123] G II, p. 60, no. 82. **Pl. XXIV, 3.**

[124] Strack III, Taf. 21, Nr. 544. **Pl. XXIV, 4.**

[125] *Vide supra* p. 93.

less, is seated with his dog beneath a tree, a cippus at his side (Hadrian); he drags a goat towards an altar (Antoninus Pius);[126] and he stands to the front, a pedum and twisted hunting net (?) in hand (Antoninus Pius). An unidentifiable country god, similar to Silvanus in character, holding falx and branch and flanked by dog and altar, appears on a bronze piece of Antoninus Pius;[127] and Silvanus may be the god to whom the Emperor offers sacrifice in a wood in the PROVIDENTIAE DEORVM type of Commodus. Commodus' Janus types have their place among New Year medallions.[128] The Dioscuri appear together on medallions of Antoninus Pius, of Marcus Aurelius and Lucius Verus and of Commodus;[129] one twin is shown alone (Marcus Aurelius as Caesar) or grouped with the Emperor (Commodus). A perplexing male figure with long sceptre (?) and chlamys, seen from behind and conducting a woman with flying veil towards a ship, has been interpreted (not very convincingly) by Strack as Saturn-Kronos, with Aeternitas.[130]

Among goddesses portrayed on second-century medallions Diana, Venus and Minerva are the most prominent. The Diana series starts with Augustus' gold multiple.[131] It was doubtless the part ascribed to Diana in the battle of Naulochus, the reaffirmation thereby of Italian hegemony and the consequent adoption of Diana by the first Princeps as co-patron with Apollo, which made her specially attractive to these Emperors who proposed themselves as "new Augusti" or as admirers in particular of the Augustan attitude to Italy. It was, then, as a "second Augustus" that Hadrian issued two Diana types, one of which depicts her standing with long chiton, bow and arrow,[132] the other as Diana Lucifera, striding to the right, with crescent, long chiton, flying himation and a torch in either hand.[133] But it was Pius' devotion to Diana as goddess of the Italian country-side which produced the largest and most charming series of medallion types. First we see her as huntress, with short chiton, bow and quiver, flanked by hounds (139). Next she stands in long chiton, caressing a favorite stag (140 to 144).[134] As Diana Lucifera she rides a horse, grasping a long torch in both hands (140 to 144), or a horned lion-griffin, torch and bow in hand, her quiver slung behind (145 to 147). Pius' remaining types are all of the years 145 to 147. They show her unrobing beside a woodland spring; speeding swiftly with quiver, bow and arrows, a hound at her side; standing in long chiton, a hunting spear in her left hand and a little stag crouched on her extended right; and standing, again in long chiton, with bow and quiver slung behind, a torch in one hand, with the other feeding a stag. Of the types struck by Pius for

[126] This medallion is not in Paris, as Gnecchi states, and the present writer has been unable to trace its location.

[127] *Cf.* the relief of Antinous-Silvanus (?) by Antonianus of Aphrodisias (E. Strong, *op. cit.*, tav. 43). The god may, perhaps, be Belenus, who is coupled with Antinous in *CIL* xiv, 3535 (Tivoli).

[128] *Vide supra* p. 94.

[129] Grouped with Juppiter.

[130] III, S. 157, Nr. 647 Anm. 475. The ship is certainly suggestive of Neptune, but on the B. M. specimen the attribute looks more like a sceptre than a trident. Of all the medallion types described above, from those of Mercury onwards, only five—three of Mars, one of Sol and one of Janus—are shared with current coins.

[131] *Vide supra* p. 127.

[132] *Cf.* sestertii and denarii.

[133] *Cf.* Asiatic cistophorus.

[134] **Pl. XLI, 2.** Was this type possibly inspired by Vergil's delightful picture of Silvia and her pet stag (*Aen.* vii, 484 ff.)?

Faustina II, one repeats the scene of Diana unrobing, the other shows her riding on a stag, with a long, flaming torch and patera in hand. All the Antonine Diana types so far cited are peculiar to medallions; but later types of Faustina II, Diana standing in long chiton with bow and arrow and her consecration type (SIDERIBVS RECEPTA), are paralleled on sestertii.[135]

Venus, as divine ancestress and protectress of the Julian gens, was another obvious legacy from Augustus to his successors. Thus Venus is portrayed on a medallion of Hadrian (130 to 138) with Victory and a shield adorned with Aeneas' flight from Troy (VENERI GENETRICI).[136] But, once again, it was Pius' special taste for things Roman and Italian which inspired the finest and most varied set of Venus types. We see her first on a small bronze piece of Faustina I with apple and sceptre (VENERI AVGVSTAE). Six Venus types were struck for Faustina II in Pius' life-time. She stands in a walled garden amid a cloud of Cupids and pulls a tree towards her; she stands with apple and sceptre flanked by a Triton and by Cupid bestriding a dolphin (VENVS), with apple and sceptre between doves drinking from a vase and Cupid on a cippus, veiling herself, apple in hand (VENVS),[137] or holding sceptre and dove: only the last type is shared with the coinage. A later type, also shared with coins, shows Venus enthroned with sceptre and Victory (VENVS FELIX).[138] Types of Lucilla show Venus in the garden with Cupids, standing with sceptre and one hand laid on Cupid's shoulder (VENVS), and enthroned with sceptre and Victory, while Cupid stands before her (VENVS FELIX),[139] a type shared with sestertii.[140] A type similar to the last, but without Cupid, was struck for Crispina (VENVS FELIX) and is also found on her sestertii: a second medallion of Crispina shows Venus seated with a sceptre in her left hand and the three Graces on her extended right (VENVS FELIX).[141]

Domitian's silver multiples stamped with types of his patroness Minerva have already been described.[142] A curious type of Hadrian shows Minerva standing with her right hand raised to her face, a prow and her owl on a rock behind her. On pieces struck for Marcus Aurelius as Caesar she rides, armed, on a griffin,[143] drops incense onto a brazier, holds fulmen and cornucopiae[144] and sits feeding a snake coiled round a tree. The last type was repeated by Marcus as Emperor (164 to 165) and a new type was added in the next year—Minerva and Victory standing confronted with an altar between them. All these types are peculiar to medallions. Commodus' devotion to the goddess expressed itself in four medallion types—Minerva plucking an olive-spray as she speeds towards an altar (MINER AVG),

[135] *Vide supra* p. 102.
[136] *Cf.* aurei of 134 to 138 (*BMCCRE* III, pl. 57, no. 12).
[137] *Trau Collection Sale Catalogue* 1935, Taf. 23, Nr. 1778. **Pl. XXIV, 5.**
[138] **Pl. XLII, 2.**
[139] G II, p. 50, no. 6. Autun, Musée Rolin. **Pl. XXIV, 6.**
[140] For marriage types of Faustina II and Lucilla, with Venus (?) presenting statuettes of the three Graces to the bride, *vide supra* p. 97 f.
[141] Known from an unpublished bronze specimen in the Lébioles Collection, Liège.
[142] *Vide supra* p. 127.
[143] The ancient cast at Gotha probably represents a lost original (Strack III, Táf. 4, Abh. II, D. i). **Pl. XXIV, 7.**
[144] *ZN* 1897, Taf. 7, Nr. 1. **Pl. XXV, 1.**

standing and holding a Victory with a trophy shown on the right (MINER VICT),[145] seated with Victory and spear, and seated opposite Fortuna, while the Emperor offers sacrifice.[146] Only the last of these types is not shared with the coinage.

Second-century medallion types of Ceres have been reviewed among the New Year pieces:[147] all but one, that of Aelius Verus, are confined to medallions. Vesta is shown seated with Palladium and sceptre (Hadrian,[148] Faustina I). Other Vesta types of Faustina I, all peculiar to medallions, show the goddess standing with sceptre and patera, an altar and a pillar, topped by the Palladium, on one side (VESTA), and seated with sceptre and Palladium, while a Vestal with a vase on her head, in one case, two Vestals, in another, stand before.[149] Cybele, long established in Rome, occurs on medallions with her usual attributes—towered crown, tympanum, sceptre, pine-branch and tree with cymbals. She drives a car drawn by four lions (Hadrian),[150] rides on a lion (Sabina,[151] Faustina I, Faustina II, Lucilla), is enthroned to the front between lions, with Atys at her side (Faustina I, Faustina II, Lucilla) and, attended by Atys, is grouped with the Emperor and Roma (Antoninus Pius). All but the enthroned, frontal type are unknown to the current coinage. Isis, the last foreign deity, by Hadrian's time, to be officially installed in the Roman pantheon, is seen with lotus, sceptre and sistrum, riding on a dog (Hadrian, Faustina I, Faustina II).[152] Under Marcus Aurelius three new Isis types were struck for Faustina II. The goddess stands with sistrum and corn-ears (?) between lion and peacock;[153] she is enthroned to the front beneath an arch, wearing a long, stiff, diaper-patterned robe; and as Isis Pharia she advances rapidly with flying veil and sistrum in hand, a ship in full sail in front of her and a pharos behind. None of these Isis types are shared with the regular coinage.

(*d*) *Mythology and Legend.* Closely allied to the types of deities are those portraying gods and heroes in more complicated pictorial scenes from Greek and Roman mythology or depicting episodes from the legendary history of Rome. Greek myths include stories of the infancy of Zeus—the goat Amalthea suckling the god (Hadrian (I O M))[154] or carrying him on her back (Antoninus Pius),[155] the divine child seated on a peacock between two dancing Curetes;[156] the story of Athene and Poseidon;[157] of Triptolemos;[158] of Athene and Prometheus (Antoninus Pius); of Athene and the Argo (Marcus Aurelius as Caesar); and of Dionysos and Ariadne.[159]

[145] **Pl. XLIII, 2.**

[146] **Pl. XLIII, 1.**

[147] *Vide supra* p. 134.

[148] G III, p. 20, no. 93. *Cf.* coins of Sabina.

[149] Faustina I's devotion to Vesta is reflected in another medallion type which shows the Empress, accompanied by a priest, or by the Emperor himself, as Pontifex Maximus, driving in an ox-cart to worship at Vesta's shrine (G II, tav. 59, no. 2). Strack (III, S. 83) interprets the type as alluding to Cybele; the veiled lady in the cart is, according to him, the black stone of Pessinus equipped with a head. The idea is ingenious: but the circular temple in the background is unmistakably that of Vesta.

[150] The "framed" piece of Antoninus Pius in Berlin bearing this type is not ancient (G II, tav. 51, no. 2). *Vide infra* p. 231 and note 3.

[151] **Pl. XL, 5.**

[152] Struck under Antoninus Pius.

[153] **Pl. XLII, 3.**

[154] Strack II, Taf. 16, Nr. 444 (**Pl. I, 1**).

[155] Strack III, Taf. 4, Nr. 658a. **Pl. XXV, 2.**

[156] *Vide supra* p. 198.

[157] *Vide supra* p. 139; *vide infra* p. 216 ff.

[158] *Vide supra* p. 194.

[159] *Vide supra* p. 139. The Paris Theseus and Centaurs piece of Antoninus Pius illustrated by Gnecchi (II, tav. 54, no. 4), is not ancient work. *Vide infra* p. 231 and note 4.

Myths from the Herakles cycle include Herakles and Nessus (Antoninus Pius,[160] Marcus Aurelius as Caesar), Herakles and Telephos (Antoninus Pius) and Herakles in the garden of the Hesperides (Hadrian, Antoninus Pius). None of these scenes occur as coin types. Among scenes from Roman legend are the famous sow suckling her piglets beneath a tree (Hadrian) or within a walled enclosure, with Aeneas etc. above (Hadrian),[161] and the still more familiar wolf and twins (Hadrian, shared with aurei). As "second Augustus" Hadrian inherited the first Princeps' role of "new Romulus". Hence his type of Romulus advancing with spear and trophy on sestertius-size medallions (ROMVLO CONDITORI), a type shared with aurei and denarii. A similar type of Romulus, also with coin parallels, appears on a large bronze medallion struck for Commodus as Caesar.

The most interesting series of Roman legendary types was issued by Antoninus Pius between 139 and 147 for "programme" purposes, to prepare the way for the celebration of the nine-hundredth anniversary of the "Birthday of Rome," which fell in the latter year.[162] The earliest of these (139) reproduces Hadrian's type of the sow and piglets within a walled enclosure, with Aeneas etc. above. Six types bear the legend COS III and must therefore be assigned to the years 140 to 144. The first portrays the story of Hercules and Cacus: Hercules stands before the monster's cave, receiving the thanks of the Aventine-dwellers for their deliverance.[163] The second, struck on a pseudo medallion, shows Aeneas' flight from Troy with Anchises, the Di Penates and Ascanius. The third depicts Aeneas and Ascanius disembarking on the coast of Latium: in the foreground is the sow with her litter and in the background are seen the walls and monuments of Lavinium. The fourth type, which bears the legend NAVIVS, portrays the augur Attus Navius, cutting the whetstone in the presence of Tarquinius Priscus.[164] In the fifth type, labelled COCLES, Horatius swims the Tiber, with three Romans, one destroying the Pons Sublicius, on the left bank, and two Etruscans on the right.[165] The sixth type has the legend AESCVLAPIVS and shows the god of healing in the form of a serpent arriving at the Insula Tiberina on a ship, which passes beneath a bridge: on the right is Tiberis, greeting the immigrant. All but the pseudo medallion type are peculiar to medallions. Two later types of the series are dated COS IIII and must therefore belong to the years 145 to 147. One, unknown to the coinage, depicts Hercules seated at table with the Pinarii and Potitii;[166] the other shows the familiar coin type of the wolf and twins in a grotto.[167]

With these nine medallions struck for Pius we must group two types struck for Marcus Aurelius as Caesar and four struck posthumously for Faustina I. Marcus' first type (145 to 146) shows Aeneas, veiled, wearing military dress and accompanied

[160] *Numismatik* Dec., 1933–Jan., 1934, S. 145, Abb. **Pl. XXV, 3.**

[161] *Levis Collection Sale Catalogue* 1925, pl. 21, no. 526. **Pl. XXV, 4.**

[162] J. M. C. Toynbee, "Some 'Programme' Coin Types of Antoninus Pius" (*CR* 1925, pp. 170 ff.) and "An Imperial Institute of Archaeology as revealed by Roman Medallions" (*AJ*, 1942, pp. 33 ff., pl. 4–6).

[163] *Cf.* Vergil, *Aen.* viii, 265–267.

[164] *Cf.* Livy i, 36.

[165] *Cf.* Livy ii, 10.

[166] *Cf.* Vergil, *Aen.* viii, 269–270; Livy i, 7.

[167] G II, p. 12, no. 27.

by Ascanius in Phrygian cap, sacrificing at an altar. Marcus' second type (147) occurs on a "framed" piece in Vienna of doubtful, though possible, antiquity:[168] it portrays Hercules standing before the cave of Cacus. Faustina's types show Mars appearing to Rhea Silvia;[169] the rape of the Sabine women in the circus (SABINAE);[170] the Sabine women intervening in the conflict between their Roman consorts and indignant relatives (SABINAE);[171] and the story of Claudia Quinta[172] dragging Cybele's ship to land. The political and propagandist significance of this series will be considered in a later chapter.[173]

There remain three miscellaneous mythological types of our first phase—a Bacchante seated on a lion (Marcus Aurelius as Caesar), an Amor riding on a lion (Marcus Aurelius as Caesar)[174] and an Amazon, armed with a bipennis, standing in front of her horse (Commodus).[175]

(*e*) *Personifications.* A number of the medallion types of our first phase belonging to this category have been reviewed already in connection with the New Year.[176] Such are Felicitas, Fortuna with the attributes of Felicitas, the Genius Saeculi, Tellus, the Four Seasons, Annona, Pomona (?) Abundantia, Bonus Eventus and Providentia with agricultural implements. The remaining personifications may be classed under the headings of geography, beneficent powers linked with imperial rule, Victory types and miscellaneous abstractions. Unless otherwise stated, the types are peculiar to medallions.

The geographical series opens with Domitian's Germania. Hadrian's SICILIA pieces show the province personified by a gorgoneion set in a triskelis at the junction of the legs. Antoninus Pius' Italia coin type was issued on a fine bronze medallion of his third consulship (ITALIA). Marcus Aurelius' Tiberis coin type was adapted for medallic purposes with the additional *motif* of a bridge, under which the god reclines. Commodus' Britannia medallion portrays the province seated on a rock, with spear, standard and large spiked shield (BRITTANIA). Among the numerous Roma types the most interesting are two struck by Hadrian—Roma seated, sword in hand, while Victory stands behind her with a shield (FELIX ROMA), and Roma seated, presenting the Palladium to the Emperor.[177]

[168] Nr. 32463. It is not in Paris as Gnecchi states (II, p. 35, no. 70).

[169] A similar, but not identical, type occurs on aurei and denarii of Antoninus Pius' third consulship.

[170] *Vjesnik* 1928, pl. no. 2 illustrating B. Horvat's article. **Pl. XXV, 5.** *Cf.* Livy i, 9. *Vide infra* p. 185.

[171] Not AETERNIT, as Cohen and Gnecchi read. *Cf.* Livy 1, 13.

[172] Strack III, Taf. 21, Nr. 691. **Pl. XXV, 6.** *Cf.* Ovid, *Fasti* iv, 305–328.

[173] *Vide infra* pp. 193 f. For Pius' interest in the origins and early history of Rome *cf.* Pausanias viii, 43.

[174] *Vide supra* pp. 98 f.

[175] The piece described and illustrated by Gnecchi as belonging to his own collection (II, p. 71, no. 177, tav. 89, no. 9) could not be traced by the present writer among the Gnecchi medallions in Rome. The type, if genuine, doubtless alludes to the concubine Marcia.

[176] *Vide supra* Part III, Ch. I.

[177] Of the twelve other Roma types all but two, one of Marcus Aurelius (Roma seated between trophy and Victory, *NZ* 1876, Taf. 2, Nr. 1) and one of Lucius Verus (same type, Hall Collection, Llanymynech. **Pl. XXV, 7.**) are illustrated by Gnecchi, and only two, one of Trajan and one of Hadrian, are shared with coins. Roma, although technically a goddess (Dea Roma), is classified in this section, and in the corresponding sections of Chapters III and IV, as a "geographical" figure, since she personifies a locality (as do other city goddesses

Beneficent powers linked with imperial rule include Pax setting fire to arms (Trajan, coin type) or seated with sceptre and olive-branch (Commodus, coin type (PACI AETER));[178] Hilaritas, grouped with Salus (Commodus);[179] Salus, feeding a snake coiled round a tree, shown standing (Hadrian, Antoninus Pius (SALVS inscribed on an altar)) or seated (Hadrian,[180] Antoninus Pius, Faustina II, Lucius Verus (SALVS), all coin types), sometimes on an elaborate throne, with a flat, rectangular object at her feet[181] (Faustina II (SALVS), Commodus (SALVS)[182]);[183] and Securitas, sometimes seated on a throne with cornuacopiae for its arms, with a snake in her lap (Hadrian, coin type,[184] Faustina I (SECVRITAS)).[185]

The most beautiful of the many Victory types show Victory driving a swift biga towards the right (Hadrian,[186] Antoninus Pius) and Nike Tauroctonos (Antoninus Pius).[187] Noteworthy, too, are the types which depict her flying with palm and Palladium (Antoninus Pius), hovering with a trophy in either hand (Marcus Aurelius as Caesar) and leaning, palm and wreath in hand, against a pillar (Commodus as Caesar). One type of Marcus Aurelius shows two Victories hovering in mid-air and supporting between them a shield inscribed S P Q R / VIC / PARTH: it must commemorate some gift offered by Senate to Emperor after victories in the East.[188]

The miscellaneous types include the Genius Populi Romani (Hadrian, coin type (GENIO POPVLI ROMANI));[189] Fortuna enthroned, with Spes on a column behind her and before her a nude child offering corn-ears (Faustina II);[190] and Virtus seated, alone (Marcus Aurelius, coin type,[191] Commodus (VIRTVTI AVG)) or grouped with Victory (Commodus (VIRTVS AVG)). Pietas stands with children (Antoninus Pius, coin type (PIETATI AVG));[192] she officiates at an altar, raising her right hand and holding an incense-box in her left (Antoninus Pius, Lucilla, coin types (PIETAS)), or throwing on incense (Antoninus Pius),[193] or grouped with a naked youth (Marcus

(Antioch, Constantinopolis, Londinium), Respublica (the Empire), Italia, the provinces Gallia, Germania, Britannia, the territories Francia and Alamannia and the river gods Tiberis and Rhenus) as well as the divine power of the Roman state. The sections on deities are reserved for gods and goddesses of the Graeco-Roman pantheon, and for foreign divinities such as Cybele, Atys, Isis, Serapis and Sol Invictus, who are never thought of as allegorical figures representing countries or cities.

[178] **Pl. XLII, 8.**

[179] *Vide supra* p. 89, note 139.

[180] Strack II, Taf. 16, Nr. 437a. **Pl. XXVI, 1.**

[181] *Vide infra* p. 222.

[182] *Vierordt Collection Sale Catalogue* 1923, pl. 41, no. 1749. **Pl. XXVI, 2.**

[183] For the pictorial scene of an offering to Salus (Antoninus Pius, Marcus Aurelius as Caesar and as Emperor, Commodus as Caesar) *vide infra* pp. 222 f. **Pl. XXVI, 3.**

[184] Without snake.

[185] G III, p. 234 = Securitas seated to left, variant in Rome. **Pl. XXVI, 4.** A piece formerly in the Vierordt Collection with the reverse type of Securitas seated to right shows Faustina veiled on the obverse (*Vierordt Collection Sale Catalogue* 1923, pl. 34, no. 1565). **Pl. XXVI, 5.**

[186] **Pl. XL, 2.**

[187] **Pl. XL, 7.**

[188] Of the eleven other Victory types all but one, of Antoninus Pius (*Walters and Webb Collections Sale Catalogue* 1932, Taf. 29, Nr. 852. **Pl. XXVI, 6.**), are illustrated by Gnecchi, and only one, of Commodus, is shared with coins.

[189] *Vide supra* p. 105.

[190] *Bulletin d'archéologie et d'histoire dalmate* 1928–1929 (1932), pl. 18. **Pl. XXVII, 1.** The Capitoline piece with this type, figured by Gnecchi, was worked over in ancient times (*vide supra* p. 57). For types of Fortuna Dux and Redux *vide supra* p. 104.

[191] G II, p. 34, no. 59. **Pl. XXVI, 7.**

[192] *Vide supra* p. 99.

[193] *Walters and Webb Collections Sale Catalogue* 1932, Taf. 9, Nr. 853. **Pl. XXVI, 8.**

Aurelius as Caesar); and she is seated, sceptre in hand, with a naked child standing before her (Commodus, coin type). Aequitas stands with scales and sceptre (Hadrian, coin type), Moneta with scales and cornucopiae (Hadrian, coin type (MONETA AVGVSTI)); while the famous Tres Monetae type makes its *début* on a medallion of Lucius Verus, reappearing on bronze pieces of Commodus (coin type (MON AVG)).[194]

(*f*) *Buildings.* Buildings form the main *motif* of four second-century medallion types. Two, struck by Hadrian, show the temple of Diva Matidia (DIVAE MATIDIAE SOCRVI S C)[195] and a seven-arched bridge[196] respectively. A bronze piece of Antoninus Pius shows a circular temple of Bacchus, with conical roof, high podium and lateral porticoes: within are visible a lamp (?), or large tassel (?), hanging from the ceiling, and the cult-statue, surrounded by worshippers. Lastly, a fine type of Lucilla and Crispina depicts the circular temple of Vesta, with conical roof and cult-statue visible within through the open door; six Vestals stand at the entrance, offering sacrifice.

(*g*) *Animate and Inanimate Objects.* Among these miscellaneous animate types are two gladiators (?) in combat (Antoninus Pius),[197] a prowling lion (Antoninus Pius (MVNIFICENTIA))[198] and a peacock standing to front with tail spread, symbol of Juno Lucina (?) (Faustina II). Inanimate objects include a pile of arms (Hadrian);[199] an elaborate tensa, the front of which is adorned with a figure of Roma and the legend ROM—an allusion to the celebration of Rome's nine-hundredth "birthday" (Antoninus Pius);[200] a ship in full sail (Lucius Verus (FELIC AVG), Commodus, coin type (PROVID AVG));[201] and sacrificial instruments (Commodus as Caesar (PONTIF)).[202] Commodus' types with attributes of Hercules and a caduceus between two crossed cornuacopiae belong to the New Year series.[203]

[194] *Vide infra* pp. 148 f.

[195] *Cf.* H. Dressel, *Corolla Numismatica*, pp. 16–28.

[196] The bridge has been identified with the Pons Aelius over the Tyne. Of the five examples of this type inspected by the present writer all are open to suspicion and it is possible that the type itself is not antique. *Vide infra* p. 232.

[197] If, as has been suggested (*BMCCRE* IV, p. xcv), these warriors are Turnus and Aeneas the type would belong to the Roman history series of 140 to 144.

[198] *Vide supra* p. 111.

[199] Strack II, Taf. 16, Nr. 443. **Pl. XXVI, 9.**

[200] **Pl. XLI, 3.**

[201] *Vide supra* p. 94.

[202] **Pl. XLII, 7.**

[203] *Vide supra* pp. 75, 77.

CHAPTER III

SEPTIMIUS SEVERUS TO CARINUS AND NUMERIANUS

I. General Characteristics

(*a*) *Money Medallions.* During the eighty-three years which elapsed between the opening of Hadrian's principate and the close of the second century only one silver medallion, that of Lucius Verus, is known to have been issued;[1] while the single gold multiple of Domitian[2] is separated from Commodus' gold pair[3] by a hundred years. But throughout the second phase of Roman medallic history, that of the third century, there flows a continuous stream of issues in the precious metals; slender at first, but gathering volume as the century proceeds, until the relatively abundant, and often striking, gold pieces of Gallienus and his successors prepare the way for the great gold series of our third and latest phase.

The extant gold medallions issued by the Severan Emperors during the first two decades of the third century are all of modest proportions. None are worth more than two aurei. Of these biniones one was struck for Julia Domna, five by Caracalla and one by Elagabalus.[4] Of Alexander Severus we have two "biniones": but his reign also inaugurates the issue of larger multiples—two 4-aurei pieces[5] and one, the famous Tarsus medallion in Paris, an 8-aurei piece. The three extant gold multiples of Gordian III are worth 1½, 2 and 5 aurei respectively; while for Philip I we have one gold piece worth 5, or possibly 6, aurei. Under Gallienus gold medallions not only became far more numerous,[6] but also display a much wider variety of weights, ranging from 2-, 2½-, 4- and 6-aurei pieces to multiples worth 8[7] and 9½ aurei. Froehner figures a large gold medallion of Tetricus I, set in an ornamental frame, now vanished and of unrecorded weight.[8] The large gold piece of Claudius Gothicus in Vienna is the equivalent of 5 aurei. Aurelian issued at least four, Probus no less than fourteen, quite small medallions, worth about 1½ aurei apiece. Under Carus and his sons the larger multiples reappear—a 5-aurei piece struck for Carus and Carinus, a 5-aurei piece for Carinus (in addition to a binio with Magnia Urbica's bust as reverse type) and a 5-aurei piece for Carinus and Numerianus. These form a natural transition to the large gold medallions of Diocletian and his colleagues.

The silver medallions present a more complicated problem, owing to the steady deterioration of silver in general during the third century. For the first half of the

[1] *Vide supra* p. 128. [2] *Vide supra* p. 127. [3] *Vide supra* p. 128.

[4] The small gold pieces quoted by Gnecchi (I, p. 4, nos. 2, 3, 4) are not medallions.

[5] One of these, formerly in Paris, is known from a cast in Berlin. **Pl. XXVII, 2.**

[6] Nineteen gold medallions, including several varieties of obverse portrait combined with the same reverse type, are known to the present writer.

[7] This would appear to have been the weight of the lost gold piece, measuring 37 mm. in diameter, reproduced from Tanini by Alföldi (*NK* 1927–1928, S. 27, Abb. 2).

[8] *Cf. RM* 1935, S. 37, Abb. 4. The reverse type is unknown.

century we can, indeed, with some degree of confidence, describe these multiples as silver. Analysis of the weights reveals a fairly regularly graduated scale of multiples ranging in weight from between three and five grammes (= *c.* 2 denarii) to between thirty-two and thirty-three grammes (= *c.* 11 denarii) and even, occasionally, to thirty-six grammes (= *c.* 12 denarii), the commonest multiples weighing between twenty and twenty-three grammes (= *c.* 7 denarii), between twenty-three and twenty-six grammes (= *c.* 8 denarii), between twenty-six and twenty-nine grammes (= *c.* 9 denarii) and between twenty-nine and thirty-two grammes (= *c.* 10 denarii). A 10-denarii piece of Septimius Severus bears the reverse legend IOVI VICTORI and the type of Juppiter in a quadriga hurling his bolt at two giants[9] and an exceptionally fine 10-denarii piece of Julia Domna shows the legend VESTA MATER and six Vestals sacrificing before Vesta's shrine.[10] A small 2-denarii piece of Caracalla has Victory in a quadriga,[11] a 4-denarii piece of Alexander Severus the bust of Julia Mamaea[12] and a 2-denarii piece of Julia Mamaea confronted busts of Alexander Severus and Orbiana.[13] Apart from these, all silver medallions down to the reign of Maximinus bear the Tres Monetae reverse type. From Gordian III to Valerian the range of types other than that of the Tres Monetae on silver pieces is slightly wider than during the preceding reigns. We have small multiples worth *c.* 2 antoniniani of Trajan Decius with busts of Herennius and Hostilianus[14] and of Etruscilla, Herennius and Hostilianus[15] as reverse types, and a *c.* 2-antoniniani piece of Herennius shows a tetrastyle temple.[16] Volusianus issued a *c.* 3-antoniniani piece with Felicitas[17] and Valerian a *c.* 2-antoniniani piece with the bust of Roma.[18] Larger multiples with non-Tres Monetae types were struck for Gordian III (VIRTVS AVGVSTI, worth *c.* 10 antoniniani),[19] for Philip I and Otacilia (ADVENTVS AVGG, worth *c.* 10 antoniniani),[20] for Philip II (CONCORDIA AVGVSTORVM, confronted busts of Philip I and Otacilia, worth *c.* 8 antoniniani),[21] for Trebonianus Gallus (IVNONI MARTIALI, circular temple, worth *c.* 7 antoniniani),[22] for Valerian I (ADLOCVTIO. worth *c.* 8 antoniniani)[23] and for Valerian I and Valerian II (CONCORDIA AVGVSTORVM, confronted busts of Gallienus and Salonina, worth *c.* 9 antoniniani).[24] But in spite of these varieties, the Tres Monetae still dominate the field; and the constant occurrence of this type on silver medallions in particular is highly significant. The more the value of the precious metal declines, the louder become the protests of the government that all is really well. The three figures, traditionally symbolic of the three metals, gold, silver and bronze, with their accompanying legends AEQUITAS AVGVSTI, AEQVITAS PVBLICA and MONETA AVGVSTI, are a reassurance that the Emperor is giving due measure, especially in the matter of the silver coinage, and that the mint and its

[9] G I, tav. 22, no. 2. [10] G I, tav. 22, no. 4 (**Pl. XLIV, 1**). [11] Vienna, Nr. 15372.
[12] G I, tav. 23, no. 3. [13] G I, tav. 23, no. 5.
[14] G I, tav. 24, no. 10. [15] G I, tav. 24, no. 11.
[16] G I, tav. 24, no. 12. For the striking, however, of very heavy antoniniani *c.* 250, *vide supra* p. 37.
[17] G I, tav. 25, no. 7. [18] G I, tav. 26, no. 4.
[19] G I, tav. 24, no. 3. [20] G I, tav. 24, no. 8.
[21] Kubitschek Taf. 8, Nr. 131. **Pl. XXVII, 3.** [22] G I, tav. 25, no. 1.
[23] G I, tav. 25, no. 9. [24] G I, tav. 26, no. 6.

products receive his personal care. The state of the currency being so obviously a matter of general concern, the Tres Monetae pieces were extended to a wider circle of recipients than that for which medallions were normally designed. Indeed, the comparative abundance of these pieces suggests that they had first-class propaganda value. Possibly they were presented as mementos to any persons visiting the mint.[25]

"Silver" medallions of the time of Gallienus are for the most part struck in silver-washed base alloy or billon. Frequently it is hard to decide whether a given piece should be described as billon or as bronze. Pieces described as bronze are often no heavier than the so-called silver pieces; and many Tres Monetae medallions of the reign, now classified as bronze, show traces of silvering. It is, indeed, not unlikely that all the bronze pieces with this type, and possibly some, at least, of those with other types, were silver-coated originally.[26] Many of Gallienus' Tres Monetae medallions, both "silver" and bronze, also show traces of gilding—an additional embellishment pandering to a taste for the superficial and "showy" in the less select *milieu* in which these pieces were distributed; occasionally, however, "silver" and bronze Gallienic medallions with other types and legends are similarly adorned.[27] Under Gallienus' successors down to Carinus and Numerianus the issue of medallions in any sense describable as "silver" or billon ceased. But the practice of silvering and gilding bronze medallions still continued; traces of both processes are found very commonly on pieces with the Tres Monetae type, occasionally on pieces with other types and legends.[28] To return to the types of Gallienus' "silver" pieces, twenty-six out of the thirty-five varieties of Tres Monetae medallions are represented by pieces to which the term "silver" or billon, as opposed to silvered bronze, may possibly be applied. Small billon pieces of Gallienus show the types of Libertas,[29]

[25] Pl. XLVI, 6, 7; Pl. XLVII, 1, 4–6, 8; Pl. XLVIII, 3. In *BMCCRE* IV, p. clxxvi, note, 1, it is suggested that these medallions represented the standard metal, fixed from time to time, for the mint. Moneta was, of course, originally the epithet of a goddess, Juno Moneta, in whose temple on the Capitol the mint was established. When used alone, the name Moneta denotes the divine patroness, or personification, of the mint and of the money coined therein, these being the two meanings covered by the common substantive moneta. The present writer is in full agreement with Mattingly's criticism (*BMCCRE* III, pp. xxxvi f.) of Strack's theory (I, S. 154 ff., where a full account of the literature of the subject is to be found) that there is no personification Moneta, the figure with scales and cornucopiae being always Aequitas, sometimes associated, by the accompanying legend MONETA AVGVSTI, with the mint as her sphere of activity. Mattingly's arguments for the existence of a separate personification Moneta seem to be conclusive. But is he happy in describing the personification of the mint or money as a "virtue"? Aequitas is a "virtue," or quality, of the Emperor, but Moneta personifies the establishment for which he is responsible and the cash which he supplies; just as Annona is not a "virtue," or quality, of the Emperor, but personifies the "Ministry of Food" and the actual food supplied. (See further note at end of chapter.)

[26] Two instances of non-Tres Monetae Gallienic bronze medallions with traces of silvering are known to the present writer:—a VICTORIA AVGVSTORVM piece of Gallienus and Valerian II in Vienna (Nr. 32271) and a PRINCIPI IVVENTVTIS piece of Saloninus in the *B. M.*

[27] E. g. VOTIS / DECENNA / LIBVS / S C (Gallienus, bronze); ADLOCVTIO AVGG (Gallienius, bronze); IVNO REGINA (Salonina, "silver"); PIETAS AVGG (Salonina, "silver"). Traces of gilding are also visible on a pre-Gallienic silver medallion, the VIRTVS AVGVSTI piece of Gordian III in the B. M., and on a pre-Gallienic bronze medallion of Philip I, Otacilia and Philip II in the Lébioles Collection, Liège.

[28] E. g. IMP PROBVS CONS II (Probus, gilded); VIRTVS AVGVSTI (Probus, silvered); TRIVMF QVADOR (Numerianus, gilded); ADLOCVTIO AVGG (Numerianus, gilded.)

[29] G I, tav. 27, nos. 4, 5.

Salus,[30] Victoria[31] and a bust of Salonina;[32] while larger medallions bear the legends ADLOCVTIO,[33] FIDES EXERCITVS,[34] VIRTVS AVGVSTORVM,[35] VIRTVS GALLIENI AVG,[36] PAX AVG[37] and VBERITAS AVG,[38] with corresponding types. Vienna has a billon version of the PIETAS FALERI gold medallion of Gallienus and Salonina.[39] For Gallienus and Valerian II we have a "silver" ADVENTVS AVGG piece,[40] for Salonina "silver" pieces with the legends IVNO REGINA,[41] PVDICITIA AVGVSTAE[42] and PVDICITIA AVG;[43] and the third-century "silver" series closes with a somewhat dubious piece of Postumus with the legend SALVS PROVINCIARVM.[44]

(*b*) *Structural Features of the Bronze Medallions.* From the structural point of view, the large bronze medallions proper struck during the first half of the third century, from the reign of Septimius Severus to that of Valerian, adhere closely to Commodus' traditions. While the majority of such medallions show weights ranging from forty to sixty grammes, a high proportion, especially of those issued under Septimius Severus, Gordian III and Philip I, weigh between sixty and seventy grammes, not a few over seventy. One exceptional piece of Septimius Severus at Modena weighs as much as 106.6 grammes; a piece of Julia Domna in the Jameson Collection, Paris, weighs 82.36. The proportion of "framed" bronze medallions is far lower during this period than during the first phase of medallic history.[45] The number of bi-metallic medallions, on the other hand, is markedly higher: in fact, apart from the reign of Commodus, under whom at least one hundred and forty-one bi-metallic pieces were struck, the bi-metallic process was never more popular as a device for enhancing medallic character than under the Severi, Gordian III and Philip I.[46] The majority of the early third-century bi-metallic medallions weigh between sixty and seventy-five grammes; one piece of Gordian III turns the scale at 88.85 grammes, one of Philip I, Otacilia and Philip II at ninety. Lighter medallions, weighing from thirty to forty grammes, are fairly plentiful under Alexander Severus; under the early Severi and under Alexander's successors, down to Valerian, they are comparatively rare. Smaller bronze medallions of sestertius size and weight, weighing between twenty (or just under) and thirty grammes, so plentiful under Hadrian, but growing progressively rarer during the latter half of the second century, were struck but sparingly during the first half of the third. For Gordian III seven such pieces are on record: five were struck for Otacilia; while the other Emperors and Empresses of the time are represented by one or two pieces each. But the really characteristic small bronze medallions of the period are the neat, sometimes quite exquisite, little pieces, roughly of as size, executed in true medallic style, often with obverse portraits in high relief. Fairly uniform in size, they vary very considerably in weight, according to the thick-

[30] G I, tav. 27, no. 3.
[31] G I, p. 54, no. 29. **Pl. XXVII, 4.**
[32] G I, tav. 27, no. 9.
[33] G I, tav. 26, no. 7 (**Pl. XLVI, 4**).
[34] G I, tav. 26, no. 8.
[35] G I, tav. 27, no. 7.
[36] G III, tav. di suppl., no. 6.
[37] G II, tav. 114, nos. 6, 7, 8.
[38] G I, tav. 27, no. 6.
[39] G I, tavv. 3, no. 7; 27, no. 8.
[40] G I, tav. 27, no. 10.
[41] G I, tav. 28, no. 2.
[42] G I, tav. 28, no. 3.
[43] Grueber pl. 50, no. 3. *Cf.* G III, tav. 155, no. 15.
[44] G III, tav. di suppl., no. 9.
[45] *Vide supra* p. 17.
[46] *Vide supra* p. 18.

ness of the flan. Weights normally range from nine to thirteen grammes, though exceptional pieces weigh as little as five, or as much as over twenty, grammes. These small medallions enjoyed a quite special vogue under Alexander Severus, seventy pieces struck in his own name and in the names of his mother and wife being known to the present writer. The amount of care and skill lavished upon these tiny presents is out of all proportion to their low intrinsic worth. They are interesting as evidence that art for its own sake could still have an appeal even in a less cultured and more mercenary-minded age.[47]

The numerous bronze pieces of Gordian III and of his immediate successors, so impressive for their size, weight and thickness of flan, represent the last flowering of the second-century medallic tradition. With Gallienus we observe the beginnings of a marked decline in the structural qualities of bronze medallions proper. Pieces weighing from forty to sixty grammes are, indeed, not uncommon under Gallienus and Probus: a few pieces weighing over sixty grammes are known; and at the very end of our third phase we have PVDICITIA AVG medallions of Magnia Urbica weighing over sixty. So, too, with Probus notably large, spreading flans are again in fashion. But the large quantities of bronze pieces bearing the Tres Monetae reverse type, which form the main bulk of the bronze medallions of the time, show weights which range from fourteen to forty-two grammes, only exceptional pieces weighing over fifty. Gallienus and Probus also issued a number of sestertius-size pieces weighing from fifteen to twenty grammes. A few quite small pieces of true medallic style, weighing from six to thirteen grammes, were struck by Gallienus, Tacitus and Probus[48] in the tradition of Alexander Severus' series. Among these two pieces of Tacitus, with fine medallic obverses and the reverse legends AETERNITAS AVG[49] and VOTIS X ET XX, are specially noteworthy.

(*c*) ***Die-positions.*** The "Seitwendig" die-positions ↑↑, adopted as the normal ones for second-century bronze medallions, were, on the whole, retained as such during the first part of the transitional phase of medallic development. For the whole period extending from Septimius Severus down to Valerian no more than *c.* forty-four bronze pieces with the die-positions ↑↓ have been noted by the present writer. Of the money medallions with the die-positions ↑↓ there are two small gold pieces (Caracalla) and ten silver multiples (Alexander Severus, Trajan Decius, Philip I and Otacilia, Trebonianus Gallus, Volusianus, Valerian). Under Gallienus a break was made with second-century tradition. Die-positions ↑↓ are no longer exceptional, but appear commonly, on pieces of all three metals, as alternatives to die-positions ↑↑. Occasionally the examples of a given type with the former die-positions even outnumber those with the latter, as, for example, in the case of small gold medallions of Gallienus and Aurelian. But taking the medallions of the late third century as a whole, we find that pieces with the die-positions ↑↓, though now far from rare, are still outnumbered by those with the positions ↑↑. This can be

[47] *Vide supra* p. 21.
[48] One piece of Probus with adlocutio scene, in Copenhagen, weighs only 3.64 grammes.
[49] G III, tav 156 nos. 14 (Pl. XLVII, 3), 15.

seen most clearly in the case of the billon and bronze Tres Monetae pieces, where the proportion of die-positions ↑↑ to ↑↓ is well over 2 : 1.

(*d*) *Style.* The coarser and heavier technique which we observed on some of the large bronze medallions of Commodus, as contrasted with those of his predecessors,[50] is much in evidence on the large and structurally imposing bronze pieces issued for Septimius Severus, Albinus, Julia Domna, Caracalla and Geta. Certain types of this time consist of single figures, or pairs of figures, which present a curiously "lumpish" and "overgrown" appearance.[51] But against these we must set other types, or similar types struck from superior dies, well-proportioned, lighter in treatment and designed on a scale more in harmony with the size of their field.[52] The slightly smaller flan introduced under Alexander Severus remains the standard for large bronze medallions down to Valerian; and in the reverse designs of this period the figures, correspondingly reduced in size, are, almost without exception, well-proportioned in themselves and skilfully adjusted to the field which they occupy. The technique, too, is finer and more delicate, especially on pieces issued by Alexander Severus, Gordian III and Philip I;[53] and while we miss, on the reverses of the large bronze medallions of this time, the exquisite, gem-like quality which marks the medallions of Hadrian and the early Antonines, we meet it again on not a few of the small bronze pieces of Alexander's series. High relief, particularly in the case of the obverse portraits, is a characteristic of early third-century medallions, whether of gold, silver or bronze. Noteworthy for this among pieces struck in the precious metals are the large gold piece of Alexander Severus from Tarsus[54] and an outstandingly fine VESTA MATER silver multiple of Julia Domna.[55] Conspicuous among the bronze are such obverses as the view of Septimius Severus seen from behind, where the naked back is modelled with a naturalism and sensitiveness unrivalled in the whole history of Roman medallions;[56] the exquisite and, in this case, truly gem-like girlish bust of Julia Domna, with waved hair and no diadem;[57] and the trio of portraits of Philip I, Otacilia and Philip II.[58] More rarely reverses show a similarly high relief—on bronze pieces of Septimius Severus,[59] for example, of Gordian III[60] and of Trebonianus Gallus.[61] From Gallienus onwards the technique of reverse designs grows undeniably poorer and less interesting in quality. Delicacy of touch, *finesse* and high relief are rare, with a few exceptions, such as the small gold medallions of Gallienus with Hercules types,[62] the still smaller gold pieces of Aurelian and Probus[63] the large gold multiples of Carus, Numerianus and Carus and Carinus[64] and some large bronze medallions of Postumus,[65] Tacitus[66] and

[50] *Vide supra* p. 132.
[51] E. g. G II, tavv. 92, nos. 3, 9; 93, no. 2; 94, nos. 2, 3.
[52] E. g. G II, tavv. 92, no. 1; 93, no. 10; 94, nos. 4, 9.
[53] E. g. G II, tavv. 100, no. 7; 101, nos. 2, 10; 105, nos. 5, 8; 107, no. 7 (**Pl. XLV, 3**); 109, nos. 1, 4.
[54] G I, tav. 1, no. 9 (**Pl. XLIV, 5**).
[55] G I, tav. 22, no. 4 (**Pl. XLIV, 1**).
[56] G II, tavv. 92, no. 9; 93, nos. 9, 10 (**Pl. XXVIII, 4**).
[57] G II, tav. 94, no. 5.
[58] G II, tav. 109, nos. 1 (**Pl. XLV, 4**), 5.
[59] G II, tav. 93, no. 5.
[60] G II, tav. 104, no. 5.
[61] G II, tav. 111, no. 6.
[62] G I, tav. 3, nos. 3–6.
[63] G I, tavv. 3, nos. 9–11, 16; 4, nos. 2, 3.
[64] G I, tav. 4, nos. 5, 7, 8 (**Pl. XLVII, 7**).
[65] G II, tav. 116, nos. 6–8.
[66] G II, tav. 118, no. 2.

Probus.[67] An exceptionally flat style of relief, more pictorial than plastic, appears on the large gold and silver PIETAS FALERI pieces of Gallienus and Salonina.[68] In obverse portraits of the second half of the third century height of relief is fairly well maintained on medallions of all three metals, particularly on medallions of Probus,[69] but, on the whole, less conspicuously so than during the preceding period. Occasionally, too, the obverse busts exhibit a delicacy of technique in the rendering of dress and armor which no other age can surpass.[70]

The simple compositions specially characteristic of second-century medallions, with one, or two, statuesque figures standing out against a plain background,[71] confront us at the beginning of the third century on the large bronze pieces of Septimius Severus,[72] Albinus[73] and Julia Domna;[74] and in the second half of the century this tradition again reasserts itself with Gallienus' "classical renaissance."[75] But the great majority of third-century reverse types are scenes involving many, sometimes a veritable crowd of, figures—scenes of liberalitas, adlocutio, adventus or profectio, battle scenes, scenes of imperial sacrifice before a temple, consular and triumphal processions, scenes enacted in the circus[76] or in some great religious precinct,[77] or historico-allegorical scenes with the Emperor standing or seated in the presence of deities or personifications.[78] The actual content of a number of these scenes can, of course, be paralleled on second-century medallions, notably on those of Commodus. In the third century, however, the tendency is for such compositions to grow more detailed and more complicated. Figures are multiplied, and an impression of depth in several receding planes is produced by the use of perspective. Clarity and distinctness of outline may, indeed, sometimes be sacrificed; but the pictorial and decorative effects achieved are admirable. The great spreading wings of Victory in an adventus or profectio, the long, waving palms held by soldiers and officials in processions; minute architectural features attentively reproduced in scenes of worship, ritual or public displays—such details give the large bronze medallions of our third phase a variety and richness which render them, from the standpoint of pure design, no less excellent in their own way than the more "classical" compositions of earlier times. Two compositional features of third-century reverse types are of special interest as foreshadowing what were destined to become the outstanding characteristics of fourth-century medallion designs—first, a movement towards frontality and, secondly, a taste for heraldic schemes. A striking illustration of the first feature is the frontal chariot *motif* in processional scenes, which makes its first appearance in imperial art on bronze medallions of Alexander Severus;[79] another instance is a version of Probus of the

[67] G II, tav. 121, no. 6.
[68] G I, tavv. 3, no. 7; 27, no. 8.
[69] E. g. *RIC* V, ii, pl. 9, no. 3.
[70] G I, tav. 3, nos. 9, 10; II, tavv. 119, no. 10; 120, nos. 5, 9.
[71] *Vide supra* p. 131 f.
[72] E. g. G II, tavv. 92, nos. 9, 10; 93, nos. 2–5, 10.
[73] E. g. G II, tav. 92, no. 4.
[74] E. g. G II, tav. 94, no. 5.
[75] E. g. G II, tavv. 113, no. 9; 114, nos. 6–8; I, tav. 3, nos. 3–6.
[76] E. g. G II, tav. 104, no. 10.
[77] E. g. G II, tavv. 107, nos. 5, 6; 109, nos. 2, 3, 5.
[78] E. g. G II, tavv. 98, no. 10; 101, no. 2; 104, no. 1; 106, nos. 8, 9; 118, no. 11; 121, no. 9.
[79] *Vide supra* p. 85.

adlocutio scene, which shows the imperial platform set well in the centre, instead of to one side, of the design.[80] As regards the second feature, the rare Antonine *motif* of two symmetrical Victories upholding a shield between them[81] displays, in the latter part of the third century,[82] signs of the prominence in store for it in Constantinian and later times; and a large gold multiple of Numerianus shows a remarkable battle scene heraldically composed.[83]

(*e*) *Iconography.* The most usual obverse types of second-century medallions were heads or, more commonly, draped busts, terminating just below the shoulders and showing the Emperor in cuirass and paludamentum or in cuirass alone. These are "objective" portraits, shared with the regular coinage.[84] The Emperor's dress gives the minimum required for representing him as commander-in-chief of the imperial armies. But the military element is not specially stressed and he carries no arms. Nor, again, is the Emperor given divine attributes, apart from the small fold of aegis sometimes visible against the side of the neck when the head, without the bust, is shown.[85] At the same time we noted, from the reign of Hadrian onwards, a number of portrait types peculiar to medallions[86] in which the prominence of divine *motifs*, such as full-dress aegis, lion-skin hood and deep semi-nude bust, reflects a more "subjective" aspect of the imperial person—an aspect familiar enough on first- and second-century cameos and sculptured portraits, whether in relief or in the round, but rare on the current coinage.[87] Such types as emphasized or elaborated in the third-century medalists' repertory, together with new types of a similar character and, in particular, with the appearance there for the first time of consular or triumphal robes as a ceremonial, quasi-liturgical dress, remind us that the Emperor is now officially no longer Princeps, or even the plain "dominus" of Pliny's address to Trajan, but god and lord by divine right, "deus et dominus natus." Again, as the part played by the army in imperial politics develops during the third century, so in medallion portraits the Emperor's arms and armor receive more elaborate, detailed and emphatic treatment; and to give scope for this deep busts now appear as a normal feature of medallic portraiture.

Occasionally the new emphasis is expressed by simple variations on common types of our first phase. A spear held over one shoulder appears with a cuirassed bust of Septimius Severus[88] and a bust of Geta wearing paludamentum and cuirass.[89]

[80] G II, tav. 119, no. 1.

[81] G II, tavv. 62, no. 9; 63, no. 5; 64, no. 1.

[82] E. g. G I, tav. 4, nos. 3, 8 (**Pl. XLVII, 7**); III, tav. 157, no. 3.

[83] G I, tav. 4, no. 7.

[84] *Vide supra* p. 133 f.

[85] E. g. G II, tavv. 44, no. 3; 45, nos. 2 (**Pl. XLI, 1**), 4, 5; 47, no. 3. For this *motif* on the regular coinage see obverse portraits of Nero (*BMCCRE* I, pls. 41, no. 3; 47, no. 4), Galba (*ibid.*, I, pl. 59, no. 2), Domitian (*ibid.*, II, pls. 70–77), Nerva (*ibid.*, III, pl. 24, no. 12), Trajan (*ibid.*, III, p. 594), Hadrian (*ibid.*, III, pp. 581–582), Antoninus Pius (*ibid.*, IV, pp. 868–869), Marcus Aurelius (*ibid.*, IV, pp. 884–885), Lucius Verus (*ibid.*, p. 883) and Commodus (*ibid.*, IV, pp. 872–873).

[86] *Vide supra* pp. 196 ff.

[87] For these *motifs* on current coins see obverse portraits of Nero, with full-dress aegis (*BMCCRE* I, pl. 41, no. 1), of Galba, with full-dress aegis (*BMCCRE* I, pl. 52, no. 6), of Commodus, with lion-skin hood (*supra* p. 133) and of Trajan, with deep semi-nude bust (*supra* pp. 32, note 41, 133 = medallic coin (**Pl. XX, 10**)).

[88] G II, tav. 94, no. 1.

[89] G II, tav. 95, nos. 9, 10.

An ordinary cuirassed bust of Gordian III shows a large fold of aegis on the left shoulder;[90] cuirassed busts of Septimius Severus and Trebonianus Gallus show both prominent aegis-fold and sword.[91] But other types are more elaborate. One, of Gordian III, shows the Emperor wearing an ornate cuirass adorned with figures in relief and holding a spear over his shoulder;[92] again, a cuirass with balteus passing across it or adorned with a simple gorgoneion is combined with a spear held over the shoulder and a round shield, decorated with a figure scene or a gorgoneion, held on the other arm.[93] A Gallienic type shows a deep bust, in paludamentum and cuirass, combined with spear and shield;[94] and a unique portrait of Numerianus depicts the Emperor in chain-mail cuirass, with spear and globe, the symbol of world dominion.[95] A favorite type portrays the Emperor from behind, wearing paludamentum and cuirass and holding a spear in rest and a richly decorated shield.[96] But the type on the whole most favored shows a deep cuirassed bust with aegis prominently displayed across the chest. This type had first appeared under Commodus;[97] but in the third century it is combined with various accessories—with a sword, with a spear, with shield and spear, or with Victory standing directly on the hand or on a globe.[98]

Helmeted busts first appear on medallions of Gallienus[99] and of Probus:[100] one helmeted portrait of Probus shows two javelins held in the left hand. The radiate crown, unknown on medallions of the second century apart from the small dupondius-size pieces of Hadrian[101] and the large pieces of Commodus with jugate busts of the Emperor and Marcia,[101a] is fairly common on third-century medallions—on gold pieces of Caracalla, Elagabalus, Alexander Severus, Gordian III, Tetricus I,[102] Aurelian and Probus, on silver of Trajan Decius and Gallienus and on bronze of Trajan Decius, Trebonianus Gallus, Volusianus, Gallienus[103] and Probus. One radiate type of Probus shows a new *motif*—a horse led by the bridle,[104] which appears once more during our third phase on a fine gold piece of Numerianus.[105] The plain diadem appears for the first time on a silver multiple of Gallienus,[106] whose head is

[90] G II, tav. 103, no. 2 (**Pl. XLV, 2**).

[91] G I, tavv. 22, no. 2; 25, no. 6. With the eagle-headed sword-hilt as a common imperial attribute in third-century medallion obverse busts *cf.* the Windsor cameo of Claudius (*JRS* 1939, pl. 16).

[92] G I, tavv. 23, no. 10; 24, no. 3; II, tavv. 103, no. 10; 104, no. 10.

[93] G II, tavv. 104, nos. 7, 8; 106, nos. 1, 9 (Gordian III); 115, nos. 2, 5, 6; I, tavv. 26, no. 11; 27, no. 7 (Gallienus).

[94] G II, tav. 114, no. 10.

[95] G II, tav. 123, no. 8.

[96] G II, tavv. 103, no. 4; 104, nos. 1, 5 (Gordian III); I, tavv. 26, no. 8; 27, nos. 3, 5; II, tavv. 113, no. 10 (Gallienus); 120, no. 5 (Probus); 122, no. 7 (Carinus).

[97] *Vide supra* p. 133.

[98] E. g. G I, tavv. 1, no. 9 (**Pl. XLIV, 5**); 3, no. 16; 25, no. 10; II, tavv. 95, 98–100, 102–106, 113, 118–123 (**Pl. XLVI, 3; Pl. XLVII, 5**).

[99] G I, tavv. 2, no. 11; 3, nos. 5, 6.

[100] G II, tavv. 119, nos. 5, 9; 120, nos. 2, 3; III, tav. 157, nos. 2, 3, 4, 6.

[101] *Vide supra* p. 129.

[101a] *Vide supra* p. 134.

[102] If we reckon as gold the obvious bronze "strike" in Paris (No. 78616).

[103] I. e. on the INT VRB etc. border-line pieces (*vide supra* p. 36).

[104] G III, tavv. 156, no. 21; 157, no. 11.

[105] G I, tav. 4, no. 7.

[106] G I, tav. 26, no. 7 (**Pl. XLVI, 4**).

shown crowned with reeds (or corn-blades?) on a small bronze "strike" from gold medallion dies and on a large bronze piece.[107]

If third-century medallists did not invent the type of deep semi-nude bust, they eagerly copied it, with variations of their own, from their second-century predecessors, as one of the most arresting representations known to them of imperial godhead. A bronze Tres Monetae piece of Gallienus shows a deep bust with aegis covering chest and back while leaving a large expanse of breast and upper arm exposed to view.[108] Something of the same impression is conveyed by another obverse, on which Gallienus wears only a paludamentum, which leaves the upper arm bare.[109] Most striking of all is a third Gallienic variant on this theme—a deep bust almost completely naked, but for the folds of a himation visible on the left shoulder, over which the Emperor holds, not a spear or sceptre, but Mercury's caduceus.[110] The view of the nude back with aegis secured on the left shoulder, a type first seen on medallions of Marcus Aurelius, reappears upon a unique silver Tres Monetae piece of Gordian III at Cologne.[111] We meet it next on two small bronze pieces of Tacitus;[112] and it finally emerges as one of the most favored types of obverse portrait on the large bronze medallions of Probus.[113] A very effective variant is that struck for Septimius Severus and Caracalla, showing a completely nude back with balteus passing across it and a shield covering part of one shoulder.[114] Fine, but less imposing, is another portrait of Septimius with bare chest viewed from the front and an aegis folded against the neck.[115] The lion-skin hood completes the list of divine attributes. Introduced, in an isolated instance, by Hadrian and adopted by Commodus as the outstanding feature of his latest medallion portraits, it reappears on a small bronze piece of Septimius Severus;[116] Gallienus[117] favored it again and bequeathed it to Probus.[118]

The third-century medallists' most original iconographic achievement was the type of the Emperor as consul, holding eagle-topped sceptre and arrayed in ceremonial robes. In the type as it first confronts us on bronze pieces of Alexander Severus[119] the robes are plain, without trace of embroidery, as is also the case with the consular portraits of Gordian III,[120] Volusianus,[121] Valerian,[122] Gallienus[123] and Tacitus.[124] But a bronze piece of Trebonianus Gallus shows the toga picta, richly adorned with elaborate stitching;[125] and the same can be seen in Probus' consular

[107] G I, tav. 3, no. 2; II, tav. 114, no. 4 (**Pl. XLVI, 6**).

[108] *Trau Collection Sale Catalogue* 1935, Taf. 37, Nr. 2987. **Pl. XXVII, 5.**

[109] G II, tav. 114, no. 3.

[110] G II, tav. 115, no. 3 (**Pl. XLVI, 5**).

[111] Niessen Collection (Wallraf-Richartz Museum).

[112] G III, tav. 156, nos. 14 (**Pl. XLVII, 3**), 15.

[113] G II, tavv. 119, no. 4; 120, nos. 8, 9 (**Pl. XLVII, 6**); 121, no. 10.

[114] G II, tavv. 92, no. 9; 93, nos. 9, 10 (**Pl. XXVIII, 4**); 95, no. 2, (**Pl. XLIV, 3**). *Vide supra* p. 152.

[115] G II, tav. 93, no. 2.

[116] G III, tav. 152, no. 6.

[117] G II, tavv. 113, no. 9; 114, no. 5; III, tav. 161, no. 8.

[118] G II, tav. 118, no. 25; p. 121, no. 4.

[119] G II, tav. 99, no. 7.

[120] G II, tav. 105, no. 5.

[121] G II, tav. 112, no. 3.

[122] *Trau Collection Sale Catalogue* 1935, Taf. 37, Nr. 2919: A. Evans bequest, Ashmolean Museum, Oxford. **Pl. XXVII, 6.**

[123] G I, tav. 27, no. 4; II, tav. 114, no. 9.

[124] G II, tav. 118, no. 3.

[125] G II, tav. 111, no. 6.

portraits, both in gold and bronze.[126] On the lost gold medallion of Tetricus as consul the Emperor holds eagle-topped sceptre in one hand and in the other a laurel branch, symbol of the pacator orbis.[127] A gold obverse of Probus shows the Emperor in embroidered robe with sceptre and laurel-branch;[128] while Numerianus appears on bronze with toga picta, sceptre and Victory-on-globe.[129] These gaudily decorated consular garments on third-century pieces are only a degree less splendid than the dazzling gala costumes which adorn imperial persons on medallions of our next phase.

Jugate obverse busts, first introduced on medallions under Commodus, reappear in the third century under Postumus and Probus. The large bronze pieces showing Postumus coupled with Hercules are among our finest examples of third-century iconography.[130] Probus' companion is Sol, radiate, on gold[131] and on bronze.[132]

The portrayal of more than one imperial personage on the obverse is a far commoner feature of third-, than of second-,[133] century medallic portraiture. We have double portraits, confronted, of Elagabalus and Aquilia Severa, of Alexander Severus and Julia Mamaea, of Alexander Severus and Orbiana, of Maximinus and Maximus, of Philip I and Philip II, of Philip I and Otacilia, of Trajan Decius and Etruscilla, of Trebonianus Gallus and Volusianus, of Valerian I and Gallienus, of Valerian I and Valerian II,[133a] of Gallienus and Salonina,[134] of Gallienus and Valerian II (or Saloninus?), of Carus and Carinus and of Carus and Numerianus. Two instances of triple portraits have come down to us—those of Philip I, Otacilia and Philip II[135] and of Carus, Carinus and Numerianus.[136] The prominent part played by royal ladies of the Severan House may well explain the frequency with which the portrait of a reigning Emperor's wife or mother is promoted to share the obverse with that of her husband or son on Severan medallions. Aquilia Severa, Julia Mamaea and Orbiana set the precedent in this respect for Otacilia, Etruscilla and Salonina.[137] For the elevation of the heir or colleague to the Emperor's side there was second-century medallic precedent.[138] On the regular coinage double obverse portraits are almost as rare in the third century[139] as in the first and second centuries of our era; and thus in our second phase, as in our first, plurality of obverse portraits may be reckoned as a specifically medallic feature.

[126] G II, tav. 120, no. 10. [127] *RM* 1935, S. 37, Abb. 4. [128] G I, tav. 4, no. 1.

[129] G II, tav. 123, nos. 2, 3 (**Pl. XLVII, 8**).

[130] G II, tav. 116, nos. 6, 7, 8 (**Pl. XLVI, 8**).

[131] *Jameson Collection Catalogue* III, pl. 22, no. 467: the accompanying legend reads SOL COMIS PROBI AVG.

[132] G II, tavv. 119, no. 7; 121, nos. 1, 2, 3; III, tav. 156, no. 20.

[133] *Vide supra* p. 134. [133a] **Pl. XLVI, 2.**

[134] N. B. fine Æ Tres Monetae piece at Boston. **Pl. XXVIII, 1.**

[135] G II, tavv. 108, no. 10; 109, nos. 1–8. [136] G II, tav. 123, no. 10.

[137] The medallions struck by Marcus Aurelius with confronted busts of Commodus and Crispina were a special wedding issue (*vide supra* p. 97). For the possibility that the medallions with twin portraits of Elagabalus and Aquilia Severa and of Alexander Severus and Orbiana were also marriage pieces *vide supra* p. 97.

[138] *Vide supra* p. 134.

[139] N. B. denarii of Valerian I and Gallienus and aurei and denarii of Gallienus and Salonina with confronted portraits (*RIC* V, i, pp. 61, no. 3; 191, nos. 1–3, 6; pl. 4, no. 56). Jugate busts occur on aurei and antoniniani of Carus and Carinus struck at Lugdunum and on some very rare aurei and denarii of Carinus and Numerianus issued in Rome (*ibid.*, V, ii, pp. 152, 153, nos. 135, 138–143; pl. 6, no. 2; p. 180, nos. 330–332; pl. 10, no. 12).

From among obverse portraits of third-century Empresses we may single out two as specially worthy of note. The first appears on silver and bronze medallions of Julia Domna: it shows a deep bust of the Empress, diademed, holding a cornucopiae in her left hand and on her extended right a statuette of Concordia, with cornucopiae and patera.[140] Even more remarkable is the second portrait, showing a deep bust of Julia Mamaea as Dea Panthea, in bronze. The Empress has the lotus of Isis, the wings of Victoria, the crescent of Diana, the cornucopiae of Abundantia, the caduceus of Felicitas and the torch of Ceres—a veritable epitome of the syncretistic tendencies of third-century religion.[141]

The legends accompanying the obverse portraits on third-century medallions present us with a few novelties unknown to the first phase of medallic history, during which the Emperor's name and titles in the nominative case are the normal formula. On small billon and bronze pieces of Gallienus we find the formulae GALLIENVM AVG SENATVS and GALLIENVM AVG P R. In the case of the billon pieces the corresponding reverse legends read OB CONSERVATIONEM SALVTIS, OB LIBERTATEM RECEPTAM and OB REDDIT LIBERT; and it is very likely that the two sets of legend should be read together as denoting that the Senate, or people of Rome, honors Gallienus for preserving the public health of the state and for giving back, or restoring, liberty.[142] Again, on the bronze pieces, the reverses of which show the processus consularis and the imperial titles P M TR P XII COS VI P P, we should read the legends together as signifying "the Senate congratulates Gallienus, now in his twelfth tribunician year, on the occasion of his entrance upon his sixth consulship."[143] A small bronze "strike" from gold medallion dies is dedicated to Gallienus as CONSERVATORI ORBIS without mention of his name;[144] similarly, on a small bronze piece of Saloninus, now lost, the obverse portrait was accompanied by the simple legend SPES PVBLICA.[145] The title "dominus," now introduced into the obverse legends of small gold medallions of Aurelian,[146] is, of course, a normal feature of his current coinage.[147] Common, too, on the regular coins are the epithet "invictus" and the abstract formula VIRTVS PROBI AVG in place of the concrete name, which now appear on Probus' medallions.[148] On third-century medallions with two, or three, obverse portraits such legends as CONCORDIA AVGVSTORVM and PIETAS AVGVSTORVM are often substituted for the actual names: and to this, too, there are a few parallels on current coins. On the bronze medallions with twin busts of Carus and Carinus and of Carinus and Numerianus, and on the bronze piece with busts of Carus, Carinus and Numerianus, the names are in the dedicatory dative case: for this again we have a parallel on Carus' Siscian aurei etc. with obverse legend DEO ET DOMINO CARO AVG and a bust of Carus alone or confronted busts of Carus and Sol.[149] Finally, on the

[140] G I, tav. 22, no. 4 (**Pl. XLIV, 1**); II, tavv. 94, no. 9; 95, no. 1.

[141] G II, tav. 100, no. 8 (**Pl. XLIV, 6**).

[142] G I, tav. 27, nos. 3, 4, 5.

[143] *ZN* 1930, Taf. 1, Nrr. 4, 5 (**Pl. XIV, 5, 6**). For current coins with the GALLIENVM AVG etc. formulae see *RIC* V, i, pp. 135, 153, 157.

[144] G I, tav. 3, no. 2.

[145] G III, tav. 155, no. 17.

[146] G I, p. 9, nos. 1–3.

[147] *RIC* V, i, pp. 263–264.

[148] G II, p. 16, no. 12 etc. *Cf. RIC* V, ii, pp. 18, 19.

[149] *RIC* V, ii, pp. 133, 145, 146, pl. 6, nos. 11, 13.

bronze medallion of Carus and Carinus Carinus is described as N CAES—the first instance on a medallion of the epithet "nobilissimus" accompanying the title "Caesar."[150]

II. THE CHOICE OF REVERSE TYPES.

(*a*) *Personal Types of the Emperor and his Family.* The growing concentration of interest, in the third century, upon the imperial person as the sole master of the world and supreme symbol of Rome is reflected in the marked increase in the number and variety of personal types during our second phase of medallic history. The Emperor appears alone, in military dress, holding globe and spear (Alexander Severus, coin type) or flanked by standards (Geta (CONCORDIA MILITVM), coin type) or in pontifical dress, sacrificing at a tripod (Gordian III, coin type; Gallienus; Tetricus I, coin type). He advances towards the right, accompanied by soldiers and crowned by Victory (Alexander Severus (VIRTVS AVGVSTI)) or towards the left, alone, holding a vexillum in both hands (Gallienus (VIRTVS GALLIENI AVGVSTI)).[151] He stands, accompanied by three or four soldiers (Philip I), or sacrifices at a tripod, with attendants at his side, while a soldier crowns him (Volusianus (VIRTVS AVGVSTORVM)).[152] He stands beside a trophy, sometimes with Victory crowning him (Gallienus (VIRTVS AVG)); or he is seated on a cuirass, receiving a branch from Virtus and crowned by Victory (Gallienus (VIRTVS AVGVSTORVM)). A favorite *motif* is that of the Emperor on horseback, in battle, lance in rest, and accompanied by Victory and a soldier (Alexander Severus, coin type) or in the act of riding down his foes, occasionally with Victory in attendance (Gallienus (VIRTVS GALLIENI AVG); Probus (VIRTVS AVGVSTI)). He rides towards the right, attended by Victory and Virtus (Gallienus)[153] or he is shown on horseback with a captive walking on either side (Probus (VIRTVS AVGVT [*sic*] NOSTRI)). On a bronze piece of Caracalla the imperial brothers, Caracalla and Geta, offer sacrifice together, each crowned by a Victory. A far larger proportion of personal types of our second, than of our first, phase consists of reverse portraits of members of the imperial family.[154]

(*b*) *Public and Historical Events.* The military character of so many of the personal types of Emperor just described makes it difficult, in some cases, to differ-

[150] G II, tav. 122, no. 3.
[151] *NK* 1927–1928, S. 27, Abb. 2.
[152] **Pl. XLVI, 1.**
[153] G I, p. 7, no. 11 (formerly in Paris: cast in Berlin). **Pl. XXVIII, 3.**
[154] Such are medallions of Septimius Severus (Caracalla and Plautilla: *vide supra* p. 97); of Julia Domna (Septimius Severus and Geta (AETERNIT IMPERI): the medallion of Julia Domna with reverse portraits of Septimius Severus and Caracalla (G II, tav. 90. no. 3) is of doubtful authenticity); of Macrinus (Diadumenianus); of Alexander Severus (Julia Mamaea); of Julia Mamaea (Alexander Severus and Orbiana: *vide supra* p. 98); of Maximinus (Maximus); of Philip I (Philip II and Otacilia (PIETAS AVGVSTORVM): *Trau Collection Sale Catalogue* 1935, Taf. 34, Nr. 2732. **Pl. XXVIII, 2.**); of Otacilia (Philip I and Philip II (PIETAS AVGVSTORVM), coin type); of Philip II (Philip I and Otacilia (PIETAS AVGVSTORVM, CONCORDIA AVGVSTORVM)); of Trajan Decius (Herennius and Hostilianus, Etruscilla); of Trajan Decius and Etruscilla (Herennius and Hostilianus (PIETAS AVGVSTORVM)); of Valerian I (Gallienus and Valerian II (CONCORDIA AVGVSTORVM): *Trau Collection Sale Catalogue* 1935, Taf. 37, Nr. 2919: A. Evans bequest, Ashmolean Museum, Oxford (**Pl. XXVII, 6**)); of Valerian I and Valerian II (Gallienus and Salonina (CONCORDIA AVGVSTORVM)); of Gallienus (Salonina); and of Carinus (Magnia Urbica, coin type). For types alluding to imperial adoptions, marriages, births and deaths and to the Princeps Iuventutis *vide supra* Part III, Chs. II, III.

entiate between them and the types struck to commemorate particular military events. A type of Gordian III, issued in 239 and again in 243, which shows the Emperor on horseback, attended by Victory and soldiers (VICTORIA AVGVSTI), alludes, presumably, to Gordian's victorious accession in the first instance and, in the second, to successes in the East. The eastern victories would also appear to have occasioned the type of Gordian seated, with Victory and soldiers standing by (VIRTVS AVGVSTI, VICTORIA AVG). More explicit in its reference is the type of Caracalla, depicting a bridge over which a number of persons are passing, while boats are seen below (TRAIECTVS): this type was struck in 208 to 9 and records the bridging of the Forth during the British campaign.[155] A bronze type of Alexander Severus with the Emperor crowned by Victory, while a river god reclines at his feet, was issued in 233 and must record his victories on the eastern front. Types of Maximinus and of Maximinus and Maximus with the Emperor riding down two foes (VICTORIA GERMANICA)[156] and of Maximinus and Maximus with the two Emperors holding up a Victory between them (VICTORIA AVGVSTORVM) refer to the German campaigns of 236 to 238. A type of Philip I showing the Emperor and his son holding a globe between them (VICTORIAE AVGVSTORVM) alludes to victories over the Germans in 246 or over the Carpi in 247. Valerian's type with Valerian and Gallienus supporting a Victory on a globe between them (VICTORIA AVGVSTORVM) may possibly commemorate victories over the Persians in 259. Gallienus' German successes are recorded in the type of the Emperor, crowned by Victory, with a captive at his side (VICTORIA GERMANICA) and in the type of Gallienus and Valerian II upholding between them a Victory on a globe (VICTORIA AVGVSTORVM). Finally, Carus' victories over the Quadi in 282 are the theme of two types of Numerianus—Carus and Numerianus, in a quadriga to the left (TRIVMFV QVADOR) and Carus and Numerianus, each crowned by a flying Victory, riding towards one another over the prostrate bodies of six Germanic foes (VIRTVS AVGVSTORVM).[157]

(*c*) *Deities.* As regards the reverse types of deities, our second phase of historical development falls into two distinct parts. During the earlier and shorter of the two periods, from the accession of Septimius Severus to the death of Elagabalus, the second-century tradition is carried on in a fine series of representations of the gods, mainly statuesque in character. In these the divine figure dominates the whole field; he, or she, is still depicted primarily for his, or her, own sake, as it were: the god's or goddess's, secondary significance, in relation to the Emperor or to public events, is kept subordinate. Juppiter stands, holding Victory and sceptre, his eagle at his feet (Septimius Severus, coin type), or is seated, with the same attributes (Caracalla), or he drives in a quadriga and hurls his bolt at a giant (Septimius Severus (IOVI VICTORI), coin type). Aesculapius, so much favored on second-century medallions, has completely vanished from the scene. Apollo appears once

[155] *NC* 1931, p. 137 ff.

[156] Pl. XLIV, 7.

[157] For public and historical allusions in types of vota publica, processus consularis, state sacrifices and festivals, profectio, reditus (including types of Fortuna Redux), adventus, adlocutio, liberalitas etc., and in types and legends suggestive of military recipients, *vide supra* Part III, Chs. I, II, III.

only, robed in a long chiton and holding lyre and patera (Septimius Severus (APOLLINI PALATINO), coin type). Two types of Mars, both struck by Septimius Severus, show him standing, with spear and shield, his cuirass beside him;[158] and advancing, with spear and trophy (MARS PATER, coin type). Bacchus, with thyrsus, oenochoe and panther, and Hercules, with lion-skin and club, stand side by side on a bronze medallion of Septimius (coin type): the legend DIS AVSPICIBVS reveals them as the African Bacchus and Hercules, personal patrons of the African Emperor.[159] Sol drives in a quadriga (Caracalla, coin type). Serapis stands with polos, sceptre and right hand raised (Caracalla).[160] Elagabalus' patron, the Baal of Emesa, is drawn along in a quadriga under the form of a conical stone surmounted by an eagle: the legend CONSERVATOR AVGVSTI suggests that here thoughts of the imperial *protégé* are well to the fore (coin type). Venus is seated with sceptre and patera (Julia Domna (VENVS GENETRIX), coin type) or she stands, holding Victory and spear and leaning on a shield (Caracalla (VENVS VICTRIX), coin type). Minerva stands with spear and shield (Septimius Severus, coin type)[161] or with shield, spear and olive branch (Albinus (MINER PACIF), coin type);[162] or she is seated with owl (or Victory?), spear and shield (Geta, coin type). Ceres stands, veiled, holding torch and corn-ears, beside a garlanded altar (Julia Domna (CERES), coin type). Lastly, Diana-Luna drives a bull-biga, with crescent on her brow and flying veil (Caracalla, coin type).

Under Alexander Severus we observe a change. With a few exceptions, the gods no longer appear alone, as single figures on the grand scale, but as part of complicated scenes composed of small figures, involving the Emperor and his retinue. They are depicted, not for themselves, but in their role as patrons or protectors of the imperial person. Juppiter stands between standards, while the Emperor, accompanied by soldiers, offers sacrifice (Alexander Severus, Alexander Severus and Julia Mamaea (FIDES MILITVM, IOVI CONSERVATORI)). Standing or seated, he hands a globe to the Emperor (Alexander Severus (FELICITATI POPVL ROM, PERPETVITAS IMP AVG), Philip I (VIRTVS AVGVSTI)). Maximinus and Maximus sacrifice together at an altar, each with his divine patron, Hercules and Apollo respectively, at his side. Sol, as representative of the Orient, scene of imperial victories, appears in a frontal chariot on the left, with Euphrates and Tigris reclining below, while the Emperor makes sacrifice (Gordian III (PAX AETERNA)); or he stands and presents the Emperor with a globe (Gordian III (VIRTVS AVGVSTI)).[163] On the other hand Apollo is shown seated alone, with lyre and laurel branch, on a small gold piece of Gordian III (coin type); similarly, the ARNAZI Apollo type of Trebonianus Gallus and of Volusianus shows a fine statuesque figure of the god, "classically" conceived, standing on a mountain top with lustral branch and snake.[164] Gallienus' "classical renaissance" produced another series of single divine figures:

[158] Pl. XLIII, 7.
[159] *CAH* xii, p. 413.
[160] *RIC* IV, i, p. 250, no. 263a.
[161] Paris, No. 352a. Pl. XXVIII, 4.
[162] Pl. XLIII, 5.
[163] Pl. XLV, 1.
[164] For the derivation of Arnazi from Arna, signifying healing spring, see *JDAI* 1937, S. 104 f.

but, as the accompanying legends prove, these deities have no *raison d'être* apart from their imperial counterparts or *protégés*. The gold Hercules medallions bear the legends VIRT GALLIENI AVG and VIRTVS AVG. Serapis, standing with sceptre and raised hand, is labelled SERAPIDI COMITI AVG.[165] Postumus' fine type of the Emperor sacrificing to Hercules bears the legend HERCVLI COMITI AVG.[166] The legend of Tetricus II's Sol in quadriga reads AETERNITAS AVGG; and the Sol types of Probus depicting the god in his quadriga, with Nox fleeing before him, and a radiate bust of the god (coin type) have the legends SOLI INVIC COMITI AVG and SOLI INVICTO COMITI AVG respectively. VIRTVS AVG accompanies an Aurelianic type of Mars advancing with spear and trophy; while Mars stands with Roma (?) as spectator in Florian's RESTITVTOR SAECVLI / VOT X scene.[167] Tacitus' Hercules stands alone, labelled VIRTVS AVGVSTI. The gold multiple of Carinus showing Carus and Carinus, with a Victory supported between them, crowned by Sol and Hercules respectively again has the legend VIRTVS AVGVSTOR. Similarly, Gallienus' Diana, speeding along with bow and quiver (coin type) is described as DIANA FELIX, bringer of imperial good luck; and Victorinus' type of the bust of Diana is labelled ADIVTRIX AVGVSTI, the Emperor's helper.[168] A few types of deities make no explicit reference to the Emperor in their legends. Such are Gallienus' Mars advancing with spear, shield and branch;[169] Salonina's Juno standing with sceptre and patera (IVNO REGINA, coin type); the Hercules type of Probus with the legend HERCVLI HERIMANTHIO; and the types of Sol in leftward or frontal quadriga, with the legend SOLI INVICTO, on bronze medallions of Aurelian, Tacitus and Probus.[170]

(*d*) *Mythology and Legend.* Preoccupied as they were with wars and political upheavals, or with appeals to the gods to preserve the Roman state and bless their own efforts to maintain it, the Emperors of the third century had little leisure for literary and archaeological pursuits. Indeed, the contrast between the second century of imperial peace and the third century of imperial crisis is nowhere more vividly revealed than in our study of medallion reverse types with scenes from mythology and legend. For as against the splendid and varied series of such types designed by the Hadrianic and Antonine medallists, a mere couple of types, both of the Gallienic age, is all that our second phase of medallic history can produce. The most interesting of these, struck on gold and "silver" medallions of Gallienus and Salonina, shows the legend PIETAS FALERI and the she-goat Amalthea suckling the infant Zeus beneath a tree: another child (=Veiovis?) is seated between the foster-mother's forelegs, an eagle stands on the right and a fulmen adorns the exergue. The giant Falerius, or Valerius, was claimed as ancestor by Gallienus; and the type has

[165] G III, p. 53, no. 52.

[166] **Pl. XLVI, 8.**

[167] *Vide supra* p. 81.

[168] G III, p. 63, no. 2. **Pl. XXVIII, 5.**

[169] A cast of this medallion, which was offered to Messrs. Spink and Son, was seen by the present writer in Sept., 1938. The reverse legend reads P M TR P XI COS V P P and the obverse shows Gallienus in consular dress. The piece is not known to Cohen and Gnecchi. **Pl. XXVIII, 6.**

[170] Copenhagen has a SOLI INVICTO piece of Probus (Ramus Cat. no. 258) and an obverse different from that figured by Gnecchi. **Pl. XXVIII, 7.** Claudius Gothicus' medallion with Hercules standing (P M TR P II COS P P) is a very doubtful piece.

been explained as an allusion to Salonina's charity in rescuing children abandoned during the plague of 262.[171] The second type, issued on a bronze medallion of Saloninus, once in the Vatican Collection and now lost, bears the reverse legend SALVS VRBIS accompanying the familiar group of the wolf and twins.[172]

(*e*) *Personifications*. The great bulk of the personifications depicted on third-century medallions consists of the silver, bronze and billon series of Tres Monetae types, issued almost continuously from the time of Septimius Severus to that of Carinus and Numerianus. Accompanied by the legends AEQVITAS PVBLICA or AEQVITATI PVBLICAE and AEQVITAS AVGVSTI or AEQVITATI AVGVSTI in the earlier part of the century, by the legends MONETA AVG or AVGG from the reign of Trajan Decius onwards,[173] these types reveal a certain number of minor variations which need not detain us here. The New Year types—Four Seasons, Genius Saeculi, Felicitas, Abundantia, Uberitas, Saeculum Frugiferum etc.—have been described elsewhere.[174] The remaining types may be classified under the headings of geography, beneficent powers linked with imperial rule, imperial virtues and Victory types.

Roma is shown alone, standing or seated, in long or short chiton, with Victory, spear, sword and shield as her attributes (Septimius Severus, coin type; Elagabalus,[175] coin type; Probus (ROMAE AETERNAE), coin type), or, with long chiton and spear or cornucopiae, presenting a globe to the Emperor, with soldiers, or with Felicitas and Victory, in attendance (Gordian III, Tacitus (TEMPORVM FELICITAS);[176] Probus (TEMPORVM FELICITAS)). A small silver piece of Valerian I, with the legend ROMAE AETERNE [*sic*], shows her helmeted bust. Postumus' billon SALVS PROVINCIARVM piece shows the Rhine god reclining. Victorinus' RESTITVTORI GALLIARVM type portrays the Emperor raising up the kneeling turreted figure of Gallia; while a somewhat similar type of Tacitus, with the legend RESTITVT REIPVBLICAE, shows the Emperor raising up from her knees the turreted figure of the Roman state.

Among beneficent powers linked with imperial rule we have Salus, seated and feeding her snake in the Emperor's presence (Alexander Severus (SALVTI AVGVSTAE)); and standing, with her snake in her arms (Gallienus (OB CONSERVATIONEM SALVTIS), coin type).[177] Pax stands or sits with sceptre and olive branch (Alexander Severus (PAX AETERNA AVG), coin type;[178] Gallienus (PAX AVG), coin type). Spes offers Victory to the Emperor (Alexander Severus (SPES PVBLICA)). Concordia stands, veiled, with patera and cornucopiae (Gallienus (CONCORDIA AVG), coin type); she is

[171] E. Babelon, *Mélanges numismatiques* III, pp. 179 ff. *Cf. supra* p. 153. Gallienus claimed membership of the gens Valeria of which Valerius was the mythical founder. The gens Valeria had instituted the Ludi Saeculares, celebrated by Gallienus in 262; for that occasion, presumably, he struck the antoninianus with the reverse legend PIET SAECVLI and the type of Amalthea suckling the infant Zeus (*RIC* V, i, p. 99, no. 394).

[172] *Cf. supra* p. 158.

[173] The formula AEQVITAS PVBLICA occurs occasionally on medallions of Gallienus, of Gallienus and Salonina and of Salonina.

[174] *Vide supra* Part III, Ch. I.

[175] In a private collection in Rome. **Pl. XXVIII, 8.**

[176] Vienna, Nr. 32280.

[177] Elagabalus' offering-to-Salus type is obviously modelled on that of the Antonine age (*vide supra* p. 145 note 183 and *infra* pp. 222 f.).

[178] Munich. **Pl. XXIX, 1.**

seated with patera and double cornucopiae (Aurelian (CONCORDIA AVG)); or she stands flanked by standards (Claudius Gothicus (CONCORDIA EXERCITVS)). Libertas holds a cap of liberty and a transverse sceptre (Gallienus (OB REDDIT LIBERT etc.), coin type). Fides offers Probus a globe (FIDES MAXIMA).[179] Securitas is enthroned with sceptre (Probus (SECVRITAS SAECVLI), coin type).[180]

Two imperial virtues appear on medallions of third-century Empresses—Pietas and Pudicitia. Pietas stands with both hands extended in the presence of Julia Mamaea (PIETAS AVGVSTAE)[181] or with right hand extended and incense box in her left in Julia Mamaea's MATER AVGVSTI ET CASTRORVM type. On bronze and billon pieces of Salonina she is seated with patera and sceptre and accompanied by three small boys (PIETAS AVGG, coin type). Pudicitia is seated, veiling her face, alone (Salonina (PVDICITIA AVG), coin type), or in the presence of Felicitas and Venus (Julia Mamaea (PVDICITIA AVGVSTAE)), or grouped with Felicitas and Salus (Etruscilla (PVDICITIA AVGVSTAE); Salonina (PVDICITIA AVGVSTAE)), or with Felicitas and two children (Otacilia (PVDICITIA AVG);[182] Magnia Urbica (PVDICITIA AVG)[183]).

Of the Victory types the most unusual are those which show her standing to the right, surrounded by Cupids (Caracalla); standing towards the front with a long garland held in both hands and S C in the field (Gallienus (VICTORIA AVGG), coin type);[184] and in the form of a bust, a wreath in her right hand, side by side with Felicitas on a small gold medallion of Postumus (coin type).[185]

(*f*) *Buildings.* A fine series of types depicting public buildings is, perhaps, the most notable contribution made by medallions of our second phase to the store of reverse designs. At times when danger threatened the Empire's circumference, it was well to advertise the imposing grandeur and stability of the Empire's heart, and to strengthen loyalty at home by stressing imperial solicitude for the recreational and spiritual needs of the Roman populace. The series opens with a large bronze type of Septimius Severus, which shows an elaborate, single-arched, arcaded bridge, spanning a river, with five persons standing on it and a boat in the water below: this bridge is flanked by two towers, each topped by five statues (?). Bronze and silver pieces of Julia Domna repeat Lucilla's and Crispina's type of the temple of Vesta, with Vestals sacrificing before it (coin type).[186] A small bronze piece of Elagabalus shows a great precinct, at the back of which is a tetrastyle temple,[187]

[179] This medallion is doubtful.

[180] *Cf.* Securitas (?) leaning on a pillar in Julia Mamaea's MATER CASTRORVM type.

[181] In a private collection in Rome. **Pl. XXIX, 2.**

[182] **Pl. XLV, 6.**

[183] **Pl. XLVII, 9.**

[184] *Trans. Internat. Num. Congr.* 1936, pl. 16, no. 10 (**Pl. III, 13**).

[185] G I, p. 8, no. 1 (formerly in Paris: cast in Berlin; *cf.* bronze "strike" in Vienna). **Pl. XXIX, 3, 4.** Of the ten other Victory types all but two, one of Caracalla (Victory in quadriga to left, silver "strike" from gold dies (?): Vienna, Nr. 15372) and one of Gallienus (Victory standing with wreath and palm and captive beside her: Ashmolean Museum, Oxford, A. Evans bequest (**Pl. XXVII, 4**)), are illustrated by Gnecchi and four, one of Septimius Severus and three of Gallienus, are shared with coins.

[186] **Pl. XLIV, 1.**

[187] Identified as the temple of Sol Invictus by D. F. Brown in "Temples of Rome as Coin Types" (*NNM* 90, 1940).

with the Emperor performing a sacrifice. Bronze pieces, large and small, of Alexander Severus and of Alexander Severus and Julia Mamaea portray large thermae (coin type);[188] the temple of Juppiter Ultor, hexastyle, with a courtyard enclosed by a portico in front of it (IOVI VLTORI) appears on small bronze medallions of Alexander; while another of Alexander's small bronze pieces depicts the Colosseum (coin type).[189] A bronze medallion of Maximinus shows a circular temple before which the Emperor offers sacrifice.[190] Magnificent large bronze pieces of Gordian III display an interior view of the circus, within which the Emperor stands in a frontal six-horse chariot, watching chariot races, gladiatorial combats and boxing and wrestling matches in progress around him; and an exterior view of the Colosseum, flanked by the Meta Sudans and an arch (MVNIFICENTIA GORDIANI AVG).[191] One type of Gordian seems to depict a non-Roman building—a round Doric temple with dome and tetrastyle portico, surmounted by pediment and frieze, on which ΝϵΙΚΗ ΟΠΛΟΦΟΡΟϹ is inscribed: within is a standing cult-statue and in front the Emperor and his retinue perform a sacrifice.[192] Medallions of Philip I and of Philip I, Otacilia and Philip II show father and son sacrificing before a temple with a lateral portico surmounted by eight gables; and a vast precinct, in the centre of which Philip I and his son (?) preside over a "liberalitas" (medallion of Philip I only).[193] Another medallion with the three obverse portraits depicts a round, domed, colonnaded temple standing on a lofty podium and approached by a flight of steps, with the seated cult-statue visible within (EX ORACVLO APOLLINIS). A small silver piece of Herennius bears the reverse legend SPES PVBLICA and shows a tetrastyle temple with cult-statue. Lastly, there are the IVNONI MARTIALI silver and bronze pieces of Trebonianus Gallus and of Trebonianus Gallus and Volusianus.[194] These show an elaborate circular temple, with Corinthian columns and ribbed, domed roof; within are seen two garlands depending from the roof, with a tassel-like object hanging between them, and the cult-statue of Juno, flanked, on some specimens, by two curious objects resembling large urns, with a peacock at her side and two corn-ears (?) in her right hand.[195]

(g) *Animate and Inanimate Objects.* Animate objects include Pegasus flying towards the right (Gallienus (ALACRITATI))[196] and a peacock with spread tail (Salonina (IVNONI REGINAE)).[197] Among inanimate objects are a galley (Septimius

[188] Alexander Severus: The Hague (G III, p. 42, no. 40). **Pl. XXIX, 5.** Alexander Severus and Julia Mamaea (*Vierordt Collection Sale Catalogue* 1923, pl. 49, no. 2066). **Pl. XXIX, 6.**

[189] Grueber pl. 38, no. 4. **Pl. XXIX, 7.**

[190] Vienna, Nr. 32201.

[191] *Vide supra* p. 111.

[192] It has been suggested that this temple was erected in a Greek city of the East to commemorate victories scored over the Persians in 242, when Gordian took command in person of the Roman troops (*NNM* 17, 1923, pp. 30 ff.

[193] *Vide supra* p. 110.

[194] For the theory that the new goddess Juno Martialis represents a deification of Mater Castrorum and refers to Gallus' wife Baebiana see *CAH* xii, p. 167, note 5.

[195] **Pl. XLV, 7.** For buildings depicted in types struck for "Birthday of Rome" and Ludi Saeculares celebrations *vide supra* pp. 102 f.

[196] R. Mowat, *op. cit.*, pl. 17, no. 3 (**Pl. II, 1**). An allusion to Gallienus' famous cavalry corps?

[197] Florence. **Pl. XXIX, 8.**

Severus),[198] instruments of sacrifice (Caracalla, coin type) and a trophy, with a captive seated on the ground on either side (Gallienus (GERMANICVS MAXIMVS),[199] coin type; Probus (VICTORIA AVG), coin type).

[198] *Trau Collection Sale Catalogue* 1935, S. 55, Nr. 2082.
[199] Examples in Berlin and Copenhagen (**Pl. II, 2**).

ADDITIONAL NOTE

(*Vide supra* p. 149, note 25.)

The present writer remains unconvinced by W. Giesecke's theory (*FM* 1933, SS. 99 f.) that bronze Tres Monetae pieces dating from the reign of Florian to that of Constantine I are not medallions, but represent a revival of the old sestertius. These pieces stand completely apart from the contemporary bronze coins, unlike the Tres Monetae S C sestertii of Septimius Severus, for example (*RIC* IV, i, pl. 9, no. 19), which, while sharing their reverse type with silver money medallions of the period, are themselves non-medallic in style and form part of the normal coinage.

CHAPTER IV

DIOCLETIAN TO JUSTINIAN

I. General Characteristics

(*a*) *Money Medallions.* Our third phase of medallic history, upon which we enter with the reign of Diocletian, is essentially the age of gold money medallions. From Diocletian to Constantius II the bronze medallic tradition of the second and third centuries partially, at least, survived. Constantine I initiated a new series of silver multiples, which were issued more or less continuously down to the reign of Honorius and spasmodically down to that of Justinian. But it is the gold multiples which now form the great bulk of our material and it is in them that the main interest, whether of style or content, centres. After Diocletian had stabilized, *c.* 290, the weight of the aureus at 1/60 of a pound (*c.* 5.46 grammes) and Constantine had introduced, *c.* 310, his solidus of 1/72 of a pound (*c.* 4.55 grammes), all gold medallions were struck as definite, standardized multiples of these two units. The distinction between gold coin and gold medallion is now clearly and, as it were, automatically, fixed; while the "Fest-aurei" occasionally struck by Constantine and his successors on the Diocletianic standard, now no longer current, are, in virtue of this very fact, endowed with a decisively medallic character, in spite of their small size and low intrinsic value.[1] In this ascending scale of multiples are now reflected the whole hierarchical structure of fourth-century society and the whole system of imperial festivals with their accompanying largitiones, at which each man received the gift appropriate to his station. Viewed from this aspect alone, as a mirror of the social order of the day, the gold medallions can claim to rank as the most important and typical numismatic product of their age—a claim strongly supported, indeed, by their subject matter and artistic style.

For the period extending from Diocletian's accession down to the introduction of the Constantinian solidus we have multiples ranging from 1½-aurei pieces (*c.* 7 to 8 grammes) to pieces worth 10 aurei (*c.* 53 grammes). Three pieces worth 1½, four worth 2 (*c.* 10 to 11 grammes), eight worth 2½ (*c.* 13 to 14 grammes), six worth 4 (*c.* 21 grammes), eighteen worth 5 (*c.* 26 grammes), one worth 6 (*c.* 31 grammes), one worth 8 and nine worth 10 aurei are known to the present writer; while the existence during this period of gold multiples considerably larger than any of our extant specimens is attested both by the great lead "proof" in Paris and by reports of what was discovered in the Arras hoard.[2] With a very few exceptions, each of the types of Diocletianic multiples is known by one specimen only. Turning to the known examples of multiples of the Constantinian solidus, we have for the reign of Constantine I himself ninety-five 1½-solidi pieces, sixty-four worth 2,

[1] For a discussion and analysis of "Fest-aurei" *vide supra* pp. 40 f.

[2] *Vide supra* p. 67.

eight worth 3, nineteen worth 4½, twelve worth 9, and one worth 30 solidi.[3] In the case of the smaller multiples we occasionally find a considerable number of specimens all bearing the same, or very similar, reverse types. For instance, we know of at least sixteen 1½-solidi pieces of Constantine I with the EQVIS ROMANVS legend and type, twelve, either of Constantine or of his sons, with the various Princeps Iuventutis types, eighteen covering Constantine's various types with the legend GLORIA CONSTANTINI AVG and showing the Emperor with trophy and two captives, and ten covering his type of Virtus and two captives with the legend GLORIA CONSTANTINI AVG. Of the 2-solidi pieces there are ten of Fausta showing the Empress, seated or standing, with two babies, and seven of Constantine II as Caesar with reverse legend CONSTANTINI CAES and VOTIS/X in a laurel-wreath. It is clear that some definite connection existed between certain types and multiples of a certain size. Of the extant specimens of gold multiples struck between the death of Constantine I in 337 and that of Jovian in 364, we know of thirty-four pieces worth 1½ solidi, twenty-four worth 2, three worth 3, twenty-one worth 4½ and six worth 9 solidi. Fifteen of the twenty-one 4½-solidi pieces show Constantius II's type of Constantinopolis enthroned towards the left. For the period running from Valentinian I's accession onwards, down to Justinian, we have twenty pieces worth 1½-solidi, eight of them with the type of Valens on horseback, twenty-four worth 2 solidi, of which nineteen show the type of Roma and Constantinopolis seated side by side, five worth 3 solidi, nineteen worth 4½ solidi, of which five show Constantinopolis seated towards the left and fourteen Roma enthroned towards the front, five worth 5, or 5½, solidi,[4] eight worth 9, three worth 10, one worth 12, three, including a Germanic imitation of Valens, worth 36 and two other Germanic imitations, of Valentinian I and Valens and of Valens, respectively, worth 48 and 72 solidi apiece.

When Constantine introduced his new silver coinage, the siliqua (*c.* 2.59 grammes) and miliarense (*c.* 3.89 grammes) *c.* 310 and a heavier miliarense (*c.* 4.53 grammes) *c.* 330, he inaugurated a new series of silver multiples—the first silver medallions to be struck since the days of Gallienus. Less regular, on the whole, in weight than the gold medallions, these silver pieces are often only approximate multiples of the standard units. Constantine I struck for himself, Licinius I, Crispus and Constantine II a number of small medallions, the weights of which range from 4 + to 6 + grammes, the equivalent, that is to say, of about 2, or 2½, siliquae and possibly struck as multiples of that unit.[5] Another silver issue, with Constantinopolis seated as reverse type, probably commemorating the solemn consecration of the new Capital in 330, consists of multiples which range in weight from 14 + to 16 + grammes and seem to represent from 5½- to 6½-siliquae pieces.[6]

[3] In addition, we have four pieces of the Licinii struck on the aureus standard, two worth 1½, and two worth 4, aurei.

[4] The pieces of this size being all framed, or, in one case, known only from a lost Paris specimen their original weight cannot be precisely determined.

[5] *Vide supra* pp. 38 ff.

[6] G I, tav. 28, nos. 11–13 (**Pl. XXXVII, 9**). *Vide infra* p. 196.

After Constantine's death his sons and their successors, down to Justinian, issued a fairly continuous series of multiples with large, thin flans, weighing from 10+ to 13+ grammes and corresponding roughly to 4½, 5 and 5½ siliquae or the 2, 2½ and 3 miliariensia of the heavier standard. In contrast to the rich variety of fourth-century gold medallion types, the silver multiples are confined to a comparatively narrow repertory of designs—vota inscription in wreaths and variations on the theme of the Emperor standing in military dress with the legend TRIVMFATOR GENTIVM BARBARARVM around him. The CAESAR-in-wreath types of Constantine II,[7] the fine FELICITAS PERPETVA type of Constans, with the three Emperors enthroned to the front,[8] and the SECVRITAS REIPVBLICAE of Magnentius[9] alone enliven the monotony. The most lavish strikers of silver multiples were Constantius II and Constans: nineteen pieces bearing the name of the former, twenty-eight that of the latter, are known to the present writer. Silver medallions of the Valentinian House are scarce: but the output was revived to some extent under Arcadius and Honorius, of whom five and nine pieces respectively have come down to us. We must exclude from the silver series proper pieces which have every appearance of being "strikes" in silver from gold medallion dies. Such, for example, are the unpublished RESTITVTOR REIPVBLICAE piece of Gratian in Paris, set in an elaborate frame, the copy of a lost gold medallion needed to complete a series in which Valens, Valentinian II and Theodosius are already represented by large gold *c.* 9-solidi multiples stamped with the same legend and type;[10] the GLORIA ROMANORVM piece of Honorius in Vienna,[11] obviously a copy of a lost gold companion piece to Arcadius' gold medallion with the six-horse chariot type;[12] and, very probably, the heavy INVICTA ROMA AETERNA pieces of Attalus,[13] which so closely resemble the large gold Roma types of Valens, Gratian and Honorius with the legend GLORIA ROMANORVM.[14]

(*b*) *Structural Features of the Bronze Medallions.* There is no very clear distinction, from the structural point of view, between the bronze medallions of the latter half of the third century and those of the earlier part of our third phase, as reckoned from Diocletian's accession in 284 to the death of Constantius II in 361. As under Gallienus and his successors, so in the later period, pieces weighing over 40 grammes are rare. Only twenty-four pieces in all weighing between 40 and 50 grammes are known to the present writer: one piece of Diocletian and one of Maximian weigh between 50 and 60 grammes: three pieces of Diocletian and one of Constantine I weigh between 60 and 70 grammes; and one piece of Maximian turns the scale at 74 grammes. Down to the death of Constantine I 20 to 30 grammes is by far the commonest range of weights: the range of 30 to 40 grammes covers the next largest number of pieces; while the 10 to 20 grammes

[7] G I, tav. 31, nos. 5, 6, 8. [8] G I, tav. 30, no. 2. [9] G I, tav. 33, no. 10.

[10] This gold type, the existence of which is postulated for Gratian by Ulrich-Bansa (*op. cit.*, pp. 66, 67) was identified by the present writer on the reverse of Paris No. 53a. *Cf. NC* 1940, p. 12, note 11. **Pl. XXIX, 9.**

[11] G I, tav. 36, no. 15.

[12] Delbrück, *op. cit.*, Taf. 16, Nr. 3. The original was lost in the Paris theft. **Pl. XXX, 1.**

[13] G I, tav. 37, nos. 6, 7.

[14] G I, tavv. 14, nos. 14, 15; 18, no. 4; 19, no. 11; 20, no. 1.

range comes but a short way behind. After Constantine's death bronze medallions definitely tend to grow lighter. The 10 to 20 grammes range now covers a considerably larger number of pieces than the 20 to 30 grammes range, and pieces weighing between 30 and 40 grammes are relatively scarce. From Julian onwards bronze medallions weighing as much as 20 grammes are practically unknown; many weigh less than 10.

The series of small bronze medallions proper, so attractive a feature of second- and third-century medallic history, closes with a little Diocletianic group of seven extant pieces. Three were issued in Diocletian's name (Emperor, Juppiter and Victory: 9.38 grammes;[15] Serapis and Isis: 9.38 grammes;[16] Neptune and Isis: 9.2 grammes),[17] two in that of Maximian (Hercules seated: 5.91 grammes;[18] Serapis and Isis: 8.81 grammes),[19] one in that of Constantius Chlorus (Neptune and Isis: 6.58 grammes)[20] and one in that of Galerius (Neptune and Isis: 6.3 grammes).[21] All show comparatively high relief and fine medallic workmanship.

With the death of Constantius II the long and brillant history of the bronze medallions proper comes to an end. The day of their fascination for men of cultured taste was over. The thin, light and, for the most part, unimpressive pieces issued from the reign of Julian to that of Theodosius I are border-line cases, often indistinguishable from large bronze coins.[22]

(*c*) *Die-positions.* In our study of late third-century medallions, from Gallienus to Carinus and Numerianus, we noted a marked increase in the number of pieces with die-positions ↑↓, as contrasted with the positions ↑↑, hitherto the normal and traditional medallic die-positions for bronze. Pieces with the positions ↑↑ still, however, preponderated. In the Diocletianic age, while the proportion of gold medallions with positions ↑↑ to those with positions ↑↓ is roughly 3 : 1, bronze pieces with positions ↑↓ slightly outnumber those with positions ↑↑. The bronze medallions of Constantine I show a fair preponderance of pieces with positions ↑↑ over those with positions ↑↓; but in the case of the gold and silver, pieces with positions ↑↓ are twice as numerous as those with positions ↑↑. For the period extending from 337 to 361 the number of bronze pieces with positions ↑↑ is not much less than double that of those with positions ↑↓; whereas, in the case of the money medallions, the proportions are reversed, the ratio of pieces with positions ↑↓ to those with positions ↑↑ being 2 : 1 for the gold and 3 : 1 for the silver. Finally, we find the same preponderance of pieces with the positions ↑↓ over those with the positions ↑↑ among money medallions issued between 361 and the reign of Justinian, the ratio being 2 : 1 for gold and silver alike. It seems clear that during the fourth century the choice of one set of die-positions as against the other was a question, not of principle, but of practice.

[15] G III, tav. 158, no. 8.
[16] Alföldi, *A Festival of Isis at Rome*, pl. 1, no. 1 (**Pl. XII, 6**).
[17] G III, tav. 158, no. 11.
[18] G III, tav. 158, no. 20.
[19] Alföldi, *op. cit.*, pl. 1, no. 2 (**Pl. XII, 7**).
[20] G III, tav. 158, no. 30.
[21] G III, tav. 158, no. 24: the piece is wrongly ascribed by Gnecchi to Maximian.
[22] *Vide supra* p. 37.

(*d*) *Style.* Among the gold and bronze medallions of Gallienus and his successors, many of which are less skilful and interesting as works of art than those of their predecessors, we noted not a few outstanding examples of high relief, plastic modelling and delicacy in the rendering of detail. These qualities of style confront us still more conspicuously at the beginning of our third phase on the medallions of Diocletian and his imperial colleagues, as is obvious from a study of Gnecchi's plates[23] and of the Diocletianic pieces in the Beistegui Collection and in the Arras hoard. The most striking instances of high relief and plastic modelling in obverse portraits are on the 10-aurei pieces and bronze pieces of Diocletian showing a head of the Emperor, without laurel-wreath or diadem, designed on an exceptionally ample scale;[24] the 5-aurei pieces and large bronze pieces of Maximian hooded in Hercules' lion-skin;[25] the 2½-aurei pieces of Diocletian and of Constantius Chlorus with radiate busts;[26] the short laureate busts of Maximinus Daza;[27] the famous London and Britannia medallions of Constantius Chlorus from Arras, which show the Caesar either laureate or wearing the lion-skin hood;[28] and a specially fine large bronze piece of Constantius in the British Museum with the Tres Monetae reverse type.[29] In the case of most of the medallions just cited the height of relief and the plasticity of treatment on the reverse is as great, or nearly so, as in the obverse portrait; two gold pieces of Diocletian and Maximian show a reverse design—the processus consularis with elephant-quadriga—executed in relief even higher than that in which the confronted busts of the two Emperors are portrayed upon the obverse.[30]

Side by side with this plastic style, another style of a very different character, flat, linear and pictorial, more closely akin to engraving than to modelling, makes its appearance on Diocletianic medallions. With this style is often associated a quite astonishing *finesse* shown in the rendering both of dress and attributes in the obverse portraits and of details in the reverse designs. Occasionally the bronze displays the new technique;[31] but it is seen to best advantage in the gold. The flat, linear elements are most arrestingly illustrated by the 4-aurei piece of Maximian in Budapest, with the two imperial colleagues sacrificing on the reverse,[32] and by the 4-aurei piece of Constantius Chlorus in Berlin, which so vividly portrays the scene of Maximian's abdication.[33] Of minute and delicate workmanship in obverse portraits in particular and of pictorial treatment of reverse designs, especially of those showing scenes of imperial sacrifice, the Arras medallions afford an unrivalled series of examples.[34]

[23] G I, tavv. 4, nos. 9–15; 5; 6, nos. 2, 3, 5; II, tavv. 124–129.
[24] G I, tav. 4, nos. 10, 12, 13; II, tav. 124, nos. 2, 6.
[25] G I, tav. 5, nos. 5, 7, 8; II, tavv. 126, no. 7; 127, nos. 1, 9.
[26] G I, tavv. 4, nos. 14, 15; 5, no. 11.
[27] G I, tav. 6, no. 5; J. Babelon, *op. cit.*, Pl. 12, no. 231 (**Pl. IV, 10**).
[28] *Aréthuse*, Jan., 1924, pls. 7; 8, nos. 5, 6 (**Pl. VIII, 4, 5, 6**).
[29] G II, tav. 128, no. 3.
[30] G I, tav. 5, nos. 1, 2.
[31] G II, tavv. 125, nos. 3, 4, 6; 126, nos. 5, 10; 127, nos. 5, 6.
[32] G I, tav. 5, no. 3: mint of Ticinum (**Pl. XLVIII, 2**).
[33] G I, tav. 5, no. 9: mint of Siscia.
[34] *Aréthuse*, Jan., 1924, pl. 8, nos. 2, 7, 8; J. Babelon, *op. cit.*, pl. 12, no. 230 (**Pl. VIII, 2**); *NNM* 28, 1926, pls. 1, 3, 4 (**Pls. VI, 8; VIII; IX**).

The medallions struck under Constantine I reveal the gradual abandonment of the plastic, in favor of what we might call the "engraving," medallic technique. A few obverse portraits dating from the earlier part of the reign show well-rounded forms and fairly high relief. We can observe this on the large gold Princeps Iuventutis medallion from Arras (312 to 313 ?),[35] for example; on the Constantinopolis silver multiples (330 ?);[36] and, most notably, on a large bronze piece of Licinius II (322 ?),[37] on a large gold piece of the same Caesar (321 ?)[38] and on a small silver piece of Crispus (321 ?).[39] The gold medallion of Licinius II is also remarkable for the plastic treatment of its reverse design; and for this parallels are to be found among "Fest-aurei" of Constantine I, showing the Emperor in a frontal quadriga,[40] on the large framed gold medallion of Constantius II from Szilágy-Sómlyó[41] and, among the bronze, on a fine VIRTVS AVG piece of Constantine I in Vienna,[42] on his GLORIA SAECVLI VIRTVS CAESS pieces[43] and on the RESTITVTOR REIP medallions with Constantinopolis on the obverse.[44] But these are exceptional. Low, flat relief is the normal feature of both gold and bronze. The standard of technique attained by Constantine I's bronze medallions varies considerably. Reverse designs can often be coarse and ungainly; but the level of skill maintained by the obverse portraits is relatively high. The bust of Constantinopolis on the Berlin RESTITVTOR REIP piece is, in fact, little short of exquisite. Meanwhile the gold medallions, taken as a whole, display an elegant, delicate finish and delight in minute detail which are extraordinarily attractive. The 3-solidi SENATVS piece of Constantine I in the British Museum,[45] his 4½-solidi INNVMERI TRIVMFI AVG N in Stockholm,[46] the 2-solidi pieces of Fausta,[47] the VOTIS DECENN D N CONSTANTINI CAES 3-solidi pieces of Constantine II as Caesar[48] and the AETERNA GLORIA SENAT P Q R 2-solidi pieces of Constantius II as Caesar[49] are veritable triumphs of the fourth-century die-cutter's skill. Indeed, they are as admirable an illustration of the most typical characteristics of contemporary art as are the bronze masterpieces of the Hadrianic and Antonine medallists.

The principles thus established under Constantine I govern the whole subsequent history of Roman medallic style. The bronze pieces issued in the names of Constantine II, Constantius II and Constans as Emperors, after their father's death, of the usurper Magnentius and of the Caesars Decentius and Constantius Gallus show the same somewhat clumsy technique on the reverse and superior workmanship on the obverse[50] which characterize the bronze issues of Constantine I.

[35] *Aréthuse*, Jan., 1924, pl. 8, no. 9 (**Pl. IX, 5**).

[36] G I, tav. 28, nos. 11–13 (**Pl. XXXVII, 9**).

[37] G II, p. 133, no. 1 (**Pl. XV, 2**). The consular dress worn by Licinius and the reverse legend EXERC AVGVSTORVM suggest that the piece may date from 322, when Licinius was consul for the second time, as his father's colleague.

[38] G I, tav. 6, no. 6 (**Pl. XLVIII, 5**).

[39] G I, tav. 29, no. 11.

[40] G I, tav. 8, no. 9.

[41] G I, tav. 12, no. 1.

[42] Delbrück, *op. cit.*, S. 75, Abb. 26. **Pl. XXX, 2.**

[43] G II, tav. 130, no. 2.

[44] G II, tav. 131, no. 7.

[45] Grueber pl. 57, no. 2 (**Pl. XX, 1**).

[46] *ZN* 1928, Taf. 3, Nr. 3 (**Pl. IV, 3**).

[47] G I, tav. 8, nos. 10–12 (**Pl. XVII, 5**).

[48] G I, tav. 9, nos. 7, 8.

[49] G I, tav. 10, nos. 6, 7.

[50] E. g. G II, tavv. 133, no. 8; 134, no. 11; 136, no. 3; 138, nos. 5, 6, 11, 12.

The obverse portraits are almost invariably done in low relief. Among the reverses we find sporadic instances of higher relief and more plastic treatment, as in the SABINAE type of Constantius II[51] and in the largitio types of Constantius II and Magnentius.[52] On the large silver multiples the relief is uniformly low; the technique is extremely refined and elegant, down to the death of Constantius II,[53] but grows coarser and heavier from Valentinian I onwards. It is the gold pieces struck after 337 which display the style of the time to perfection. Occasionally, on the very large gold multiples of the latter part of the fourth century and later, we are confronted with high relief, as on the 36-solidi piece of Valens from Hungary,[54] on the 12-solidi piece of Libius Severus,[55] and on the 36-solidi medallion of Justinian.[56] Apart from these rarities the flat, minute "engraving" style is universal. From Valentinian I onwards a slight coarsening of technique is perceptible, much less so, however, than on the silver multiples. But such superb pieces as those of Constantius II showing the frontal six-horse chariot[57] and the seated Constantinopolis combined with the helmeted full-face obverse bust,[58] or those of Constans with the three seated Emperors,[59] with the seated Constantinopolis[60] and with the armed and helmeted Emperor between two captives,[61] rival, if they do not surpass, the most successful of their Constantinian predecessors.

Diocletian's conservative tendencies, his concern to revive devotion to the old protectors of the Roman state, had their effect upon the composition of medallion designs. Back come the great statuesque figures of the gods, occupying the whole field—Juppiter, Diocletian's own patron, seated to the left[62] or standing;[63] Hercules, patron of Maximian, standing[64] or seated to the front;[65] Mars advancing towards the right,[66] Apollo-sol;[67] and Venus.[68] The same simple, single-figure schemes of composition persist under Constantine I and his successors, although the pagan gods have retired in favor of imperial personages or of allegorical figures personifying their achievements and virtues. Now the imperial figure stands in magnificent isolation in the centre of the field;[69] now he is flanked by a trophy[70] or by standards;[71] now cap-

[51] G II, tav. 136, no. 9.

[52] G II, tavv. 136, no. 7; 138, no. 4.

[53] The two FELICITAS PERPETVA (three Emperors seated) pieces of Constans (Paris and Berlin: G I, tav. 30' no. 2) are specially noteworthy for fineness of style.

[54] G I, tav. 18, no. 1. The large medallions of Valentinian I and Valens, cast and of Germanic workmanship (*vide supra* p. 66), cannot, of course, be used as evidence for Roman technique.

[55] *NC* 1940, pl. 4, no. 3. **Pl. XXX, 3.**

[56] G I, tav. 20, no. 4.

[57] G I, tavv. 10, no. 8; 11, no. 1 (**Pl. XXI**).

[58] G I, tav. 13, no. 2 (**Pl. XLVIII, 7**).

[59] G, I, tav. 9, no. 11.

[60] G I, tav. 9, no. 13.

[61] G I, tav. 10, no. 3.

[62] G I, tav. 4, nos. 10, 12; II, tavv. 124, no. 2; 128, no. 10 (*cf.* **Pl. XXXI, 5**). *Cf.* G I, tav. 21, nos. 11, 12 (Hadrian).

[63] G I, tavv. 4, no. 13 (**Pl. XLVIII, 1**); 5, no. 6; 6, no. 5; II, tavv. 129, no. 10. *Cf.* G II, tavv. 43, nos. 6, 9; 45, no. 1 (Antoninus Pius).

[64] G I, tav. 5, no. 10; *Aréthuse*, Jan., 1924, pl. 8, no. 4 (**Pl. VIII, 3**). *Cf.* G II, tav. 83, nos. 5, 6 (Commodus).

[65] G II, tav. 126, no. 4; III, tav. 158, no. 20. *Cf.* G II, tav. 45, no. 4 (Antoninus Pius); III, tav. 159, no. 5 (Hadrian).

[66] *NNM* 28, 1926, pl. 2 (**Pl. IX, 3**). *Cf.* G II, tav. 71, no. 10 (Marcus Aurelius and Commodus).

[67] J. Babelon, *op. cit.*, pl. 12, no. 231, **Pl. IV, 10.**

[68] G I, tav. 6, no. 3.

[69] G I, tav. 7, no. 17; II, tavv. 134, no. 12; 138, no. 9 (**Pls. II, 5; IX, 5, 6; XIX, 5, 10, 11; XX, 1; XXX, 5; XXXI, 10; XXXII, 2–9**). *Cf.* G I, tav. 4, no. 9 (Diocletian).

[70] G I, tav. 9, no. 4; II, tav. 137, no. 12 (**Pls. XXXII, 1; XXXIII, 4**).

[71] G I, tav. 13, no. 5 (**Pl. XIX, 4, 6–8**).

tives crouch at his feet.[72] Again, in place of the Emperor, we have statuesque figures of his Virtus, flanked by captives,[73] of the Securitas which he bestows,[74] of his Victory, standing[75] or seated,[76] or of the great imperial Capitals, Rome[77] and Constantinople,[78] where he resides. Other single-figure compositions show the Emperor advancing on foot, accompanied by one[79] or two[80] captives, or on horseback;[81] or Victory advancing, with[82] or without[83] captives at her feet. More complicated, but still essentially single-figure, designs show Hercules coping with hydra[84] or stag;[85] or, later, the Emperor riding down one[86] or two[87] foes or a serpent, symbol of the enemy's wiles.[88] The crowded compositions of earlier times are now replaced by simple, spaced groups of two, three or, at the most, four figures—the Emperor crowned[89] or led by Victory,[90] Constantinopolis crowned by Victory[91] two Emperors sacrificing,[92] Maximian abdicating in Constantius' favor,[93] Constantius "restoring" Britain,[94] Constantine I receiving a captive presented by a soldier[95] or "restoring" Constantinople.[96] Again, we have Constantine II (?), accompanied by a deferential panther, offering a phoenix on a globe to his father,[97] Jovian seated in the presence of Victory, with a captive at his feet[98] and Neptune grouped with Victory.[99] Of really crowded scenes two instances only are known to the present writer, the adlocutio of Constantine I's small silver medallion[100] and the incident of the Sabine women depicted on bronze pieces of Constantius II.[101] Pictorial compositions with architectural features are comparatively scarce; and all date from the earlier part of our third phase. Of these the most striking are the TEMPORVM FELICITAS scenes on gold medallions of Constantius Chlorus, which show the imperial colleagues sacrificing before a temple façade,[102] Constantius' entry into London,[103] the view of Trier and the Moselle on 2-solidi pieces of Constantine I[104] and Constantine's bronze type of the Danube bridge (DANVVIVS).[105] "Adventus" processions seen from the

[72] G I, tav. 7, no. 5; II, tav. 137, nos. 6–9, 11 (**Pls. III, 10; XIX, 9; XXXIII, 1–3, 6–9**).

[73] G I, tav. 7, no. 6.

[74] G II, tav. 130, no. 7; I, tav. 33, no. 10 (**Pls. XXXIV, 8; XLVIII, 4**).

[75] G I, tav. 8, no. 3; II, tav. 134, no. 11; 139, no. 2 (**Pls. III, 6; XIII, 6; XXXVII, 13; XXXVIII, 9**). *Cf.* G I, tav. 4, no. 15 (Diocletian).

[76] G II, tav. 130, no. 9 (**Pl. XIII, 5**).

[77] G II, tav. 135, no. 1 (**Pls. V, 3; VI, 6; VII; XXXV, 3–9; XXXVII, 1, 2; XLIX, 2**).

[78] G I, tav. 9, no. 13 (**Pls. XXXVII, 9, 11, 12; XXXVIII, 1–4; XLVIII, 7**).

[79] G II, tav. 134, no. 6; I, tavv. 8, no. 6; 14, no. 2 (**Pls. XXX, 6; XXXIV, 3**).

[80] G I, tavv. 7, no. 4; 10, no. 3 (**Pls. VI, 3, 4; XXXIV, 1, 2; XLVIII, 8**).

[81] G I, tav. 11, no. 2 (**Pls. XVIII, 1–9; XX, 2**).

[82] G II, tavv. 138, nos. 7, 10; 139, no. 4 (**Pl. XXXVIII, 6, 7**).

[83] G II, tav. 138, no. 8 (**Pls. III, 8, 9; XXXVIII, 8**).

[84] G II, tav. 126, no. 5.

[85] *Aréthuse*, Jan., 1924, pl. 8, no. 8 (**Pl. IX, 2**).

[86] G II, tav. 131, no. 3 (**Pls. XXX, 2**).

[87] G II, tav. 133, no. 8 (**Pls. III, 14; XXXIV, 5**).

[88] G I, tav. 10, no. 9.

[89] G II, tavv. 5, nos. 5, 8; 9, no. 12; II, tav. 138, nos. 5, 6 (**Pls. XXXI, 4; XXXIII, 5**).

[90] G II, tav. 137, no. 5.

[91] G II, tav. 131, no. 10 (**Pl. XXXVII, 10**).

[92] *Aréthuse*, Jan., 1924, pl. 8, no. 2; G I, tav. 5, no. 3; *NNM* 28, 1926, pl. 1 (**Pl. VI, 8; IX, 4**).

[93] G I, tav. 5, no. 9.

[94] *Aréthuse*, Jan., 1924, pl. 8, nos. 5, 6 (**Pl. VIII, 5, 6**).

[95] G I, tav. 6, no. 10.

[96] G I, tav. 7, nos 9, 10 (**Pl. VI, 2**).

[97] G II, tav. 130, no. 2. *Cf. RN* 1934, pp. xxxii–xxxvi.

[98] Delbrück, *op. cit.*, S. 89, Abb. 27 (**Pl. XI**).

[99] G I, tav. 4, no. 14.

[100] *Vide supra* pp. 39, 110.

[101] G II, tav. 136, no. 9. *Vide infra* p. 284.

[102] *Vide supra* pp. 81 f. (**Pls. VIII, 7, 8; IX, 1**).

[103] *Aréthuse*, Jan., 1924, pl. 7 (**Pl. VIII, 4**).

[104] G I, tav. 7, nos. 2, 3.

[105] G II, tav. 130, no. 6.

side are rare. Processional scenes now normally display frontal chariots drawn by horses or elephants. The passion for frontality in composition is, of course, a well-known and conspicuous feature of late third- and fourth-century monuments, not least of medallions, when they bring us into the presence of imperial personages, standing or enthroned. Thus we see Diocletian and Maximian, each crowned by their divine patrons, enthroned to the front,[106] Constantine I standing or enthroned between his sons,[107] Fausta enthroned with her baby,[108] Constantius II and Magnentius enthroned in the largitio scene,[109] the three Emperors standing or seated in a row on Constans' and Valens' gold and silver multiples[110] and Galla Placidia enthroned.[111] So, too, Roma enthroned to the front encounters us for the first time on Valens' gold medallions.[112] No less characteristic of the art of these later times is the love of symmetrical, heraldic compositions—two Victories[113] or two Genii[114] upholding a shield between them, two Genii with garlands,[115] Roma balanced by Constantinopolis,[116] Libertas and Victoria confronted.[117] Nor must we overlook the fine decorative qualities displayed by the simple, yet highly effective, compositions showing vota numbers,[118] or the legend CAESAR,[119] in a wreath.

(*e*) *Iconography.* Medallion portraits executed between the accession of Diocletian and the death of Constantine I have a quite unparalleled interest from the physiognomic point of view. Diocletian the low born Dalmatian, Maximian the Pannonian peasant, Constantius Chlorus the Illyrian, Galerius the Dacian shepherd's son and the Menapian Carausius are all portrayed with an unflinching, almost startling, realism. There is no attempt to disguise or idealize their coarse and homely features, which offer so lively a contrast to their gorgeously embroidered robes of state.[120] A special *motif* of medallic iconography of this period is the large, bare head, filling the entire obverse field, on gold and bronze pieces of Diocletian, Maximian and Galerius;[121] a similar large-scale head, combined with a low, cuirassed bust, occurs on a bronze piece of Maximian.[122] The large head, with or without legend, is combined, on medallions of Constantine I, Constantius II as Caesar and Constantius II as Caesar, with the diadem and upward gaze borrowed from Alexander the Great to symbolize the heavenward aspirations of Rome's first Christian Emperor.[123] In

[106] G I, tav. 5, no. 7.

[107] *RN* 1906, pl. 7, nos. 1–4; G II, tav. 130, no. 5 (**Pls. V, 4–7; VI, 1, 5; XXXIX, 1–3**).

[108] G I, tav. 8, no. 10 (**Pl. XVII, 5**).

[109] G II, tavv. 136, no. 7; 138, no. 4.

[110] G I, tavv. 9, nos. 11, 14; 30, no. 2; 16, no. 3 (*Cf.* **Pls. III, 7; XXXIX, 4**). *Cf.* two 1½-solidi pieces of Constantius II and Constans respectively (**Pl. XXXI, 1, 9**) (*vide infra* p. 179).

[111] G I, tav. 20, no. 2 (**Pl. XLIX, 1**).

[112] G I, tav. 14, nos. 14, 15 (**Pl. XXXVII, 2**).

[113] G I, tav. 10, nos. 4, 5 (**Pl. XIII, 1–4**).

[114] G I, tav. 11, no. 3 (**Pl. XII, 11**).

[115] G I, tav. 6, no. 14 (**Pl. XLVIII, 6**).

[116] G I, tav. 11, nos. 5, 7 (**Pl. XXXVII, 3–8**).

[117] G I, tav. 14, no. 4 (**Pl. VI, 7**).

[118] G I, tavv. 8, nos. 20, 21; 30, no. 3; III, tav. di suppl., no. 11 (**Pls. III, 4, 5; XIII, 7–11; XIV, 1, 2**).

[119] G I, tav. 31, nos. 5, 6, 8.

[120] G II, tavv. 125, nos. 3, 4 (Diocletian); 126, no. 10 (Maximian); 129, no. 4 (Galerius). *Cf.* Arras medallions of Constantius Chlorus and an unpublished bronze "strike" from the dies of a gold medallion of Carausius. **Pl. XXX, 4.**

[121] G I, tav. 4, nos. 10, 12, 13 (**Pl. XLVIII, 1**); II, tav. 124, nos. 2, 6 (Diocletian); I, tav. 5, no. 4 (Maximian); II, tav. 128, no. 10 (Galerius).

[122] G II, tav. 126, no. 5.

[123] G I, tav. 7, nos. 5, 17; *NZ* 1930, Taf. 2, Nr. 7; *NNM* 6, 1921, pl. 1 (Constantine I); G I, tav. 8, no. 8 (Constantine II); *Jameson Collection Catalogue* IV, pl. 26, no. 534 (Constantius II) (**Pls. II, 15; VI, 3; XX, 2; XXXIV, 1, 2; XXXV, 3**). **Pl. XXX, 5–7.**

these Constantinian heads the physiognomic interest resides, of course, not in their realism, but in their idealism; and from Constantine onwards realistic portraits are rare. Only the bare-headed busts of Magnentius[124] and Decentius[125] and, to a lesser degree, the heads of Constantius Gallus on his silver multiples[126] are in any way comparable with the portraits of Diocletian and his colleagues; while the great gold piece of Justinian, on the other hand, rivals anything yet achieved in the field of realistic portraiture during the whole history of Roman medallions.[127]

The most characteristic series of late third-century and fourth-century portrait types are those which depict the Emperor or Caesar in consular dress, in toga picta and tunica palmata, lavishly adorned with rich embroidery. It is obvious that such types reflect the development of court ceremonial and the hieratic and mystical significance with which the imperial person was now invested. These imperial consuls are equipped with a variety of attributes—eagle-topped sceptre, globe, plain or surmounted by a Victory, laurel-branch, mappa or money bag: sometimes the right hand is raised in greeting. The patterns stitched upon toga picta and tunica palmata display widely varying degrees of richness. Some portraits show a large laurel-wreath embroidered on the breast of the tunic.

Quite a number of new varieties of busts, displaying novel *motifs* in attributes, dress and gesture, make their appearance among the obverse types of our third phase. Bronze medallions of Diocletian show a deep bust of the Emperor in the guise of Juppiter, sceptred and nude save for a himation folded round the shoulders.[128] A large bronze piece of Maximian[129] and small bronze pieces of Constantius Chlorus and of Galerius[130] shows a similar deep bust, but arrayed in paludamentum and cuirass, or in cuirass with aegis, and armed with shield and spear: Galerius holds two javelins in his hand. A unique bronze piece of Maximinus Daza, unfortunately retouched, displays a bust with cuirass and aegis and a club held over the shoulder.[131] A specially deep bust with paludamentum and cuirass, transverse spear and globe surmounted by Victory occurs on a gold piece of Licinius II, on a small silver piece of Crispus and on large bronze pieces of Decentius.[132] A fine gold medallion of Constantine II as Caesar from the Borča hoard shows a deep bust with very elaborate cuirass and gloved hand.[133] The *motif*, already noted among the consular types, of the hand raised in greeting to people or troops is a favorite one from Constantinian times onwards.

Of portrait types specially popular on third-century medallions, that of the Emperor seen from behind, with paludamentum, spear and richly ornamented shield,[134] appears now on four occasions only—on bronze pieces of Diocletian, of

[124] G I, tavv. 14, nos. 1–3; 33, no. 10; II, tav. 138, nos. 4–9.

[125] G I, tav. 14, no. 4; II, tav. 138, nos. 10–12.

[126] G I, tav. 33, nos. 15, 16.

[127] G I, tav. 20, no. 4 (**Pl. XLIX, 3**).

[128] G II, tav. 124, no. 1; III, tav. 158, no. 11.

[129] G II, tav. 127, no. 5.

[130] G III, tav. 158, nos. 30 (Constantius Chlorus), 24 (Galerius, wrongly ascribed by Gnecchi to Maximian). *Cf.* similar busts with cuirass, balteus, shield and transverse spear, of Constantius II (G I, tav. 11, no. 3) and Constans (unpublished 1½-solidi piece at Gotha). **Pl. XXXI, 1.**

[131] G II, tav. 129, no. 6.

[132] G I, tavv. 6, no. 6 (**Pl. XLVIII, 5**); 29, no. 11; II, tav. 138, nos. 11, 12.

[133] *NZ* 1930, Taf. 2, Nr. 5.

[134] *Vide supra* p. 155.

Maximian and of Crispus[135] and on the large gold framed piece of Constantius II from Szilágy-Sómlyó.[136] A variant of this type, showing scale cuirass without paludamentum, occurs on gold medallions of Valentinian I and of Valens.[137] A bronze piece of Galerius revives the *motif* of deep bust with aegis covering chest and back and large portions of the naked breast and upper arm exposed to view.[138] The lion-skin hood, common, for obvious reasons, on gold and bronze pieces of Maximian,[139] is also found on two medallions of Constantius Chlorus from the Arras hoard;[140] with the conversion of Constantine it naturally disappeared from imperial iconography. The type of the Emperor leading a horse by the bridle, first seen on medallions of Probus and Numerianus,[141] occurs twice again on medallions of our third phase, on bronze pieces of Maximian[142] and on a small silver piece of Constantine I, where the Emperor is shown full-face and wears a crested helmet with the Christian monogram.[143] The regular crested helmet is found on small gold pieces of Constantine I,[144] on small silver pieces of Constantine I and Licinius I[145] and on a bronze piece of Crispus.[146] A 4½-solidi piece of Constantine I in the Beistegui Collection shows a laurel-wreath encircling the helmet;[147] while on a unique bronze medallion of the same Emperor at Trier the helmet is topped by a tall, narrow crest springing from the back of the crown.[148] A fine 4½-solidi piece of Constantius II in the British Museum shows a deep, frontal bust with diademed helmet;[149] and a gorgeous helmet with elaborate crest and triple pearl diadem, adorns the nimbate full-face bust of Justinian.[150] Fourth-century medallion portraits naturally display that ever increasing tendency towards frontality which stamps the whole art of the time. Other instances, besides those already quoted, of the frontal obverse portrait are the large gold piece of Valentinian from Poland[151] (bust frontal, face profile) and the gold medallion of Theoderic in Rome.[152]

Nimbi, combined, of course, with frontal busts, occur thrice only on medallions of our third phase, on a "Fest-aureus" of Constantine I, where the Emperor is shown with globe and right hand raised,[153] on the Beistegui piece with portraits of

[135] G II, tavv. 125, no. 5; 127, no. 2; 133, no. 3.

[136] G I, tav. 12, no. 1.

[137] G I, tavv. 14, no. 11; 18, no. 3.

[138] G II, p. 132, no. 5.

[139] **Pl. XLVIII, 3.**

[140] *Aréthuse*, Jan., 1924, pl. 8, no. 6; *NNM* 28, 1926, pl. 2 (**Pls. VIII, 5; IX, 3**).

[141] *Vide supra* p. 155.

[142] G II, tav. 127, nos. 6, 10.

[143] G I, tav. 29, no. 3.

[144] G I, tav. 7, nos. 11, 14; *Jameson Collection Catalogue* IV, pl. 26, no. 531 (**Pl. IX, 6**).

[145] G I, tavv. 28, no. 8; 29, no. 5.

[146] G II, tav. 133, no. 4.

[147] J. Babelon, *op. cit.*, pl. 13, no. 235. **Pl. XXXI, 2.** *Cf.* 2-solidi piece in British Museum (G I, p. 20, no. 58). **Pl. XXXI, 3.**

[148] *Acta Archaeologica* 1934, p. 100, fig. 1 (**Pl. V, 1**).

[149] G I, tav. 13, no. 2 (**Pl. XLVIII, 7**).

[150] G I, tav. 20, no. 4 (**Pl. XLIX, 3**).

[151] *NK* 1929–1930, Taf. 3, a, 10: in the Newell Collection, New York City. **Pl. XXXI, 4.**

[152] G I, tav. 20, no. 3. On medallions of Constantine I the laurel-wreath is worn with busts turned three-quarters towards the spectator (e. g. G I, tav. 6, no. 12; II, tav. 130, no. 3), whereas the royal diadem is combined with almost frontal busts (e. g. G I, tav. 6, no. 14; II, tav. 130, no. 2). Diadems on fourth-century medallions are composed of leaves alternating with squares (e. g. G I, tav. 28, nos. 11–13) and rosettes (e. g. G II, tav. 130, no. 8), of a continuous band, plain (e. g. G I, tav. 8, no. 9) or ornamented (e. g. G I, tav. 7, nos. 4, 5, 17), or of pearls arranged in two (e. g. G I, tav. 11, nos. 4, 9) or three (e. g. G I, tav. 7, no. 8) rows.

[153] G I, tav. 8, no. 2.

Licinius I and Licinius II[154] and on Justinian's great gold piece.[155] Bearded portraits are known of Procopius,[156] Eugenius[157] and Justinian.[158] Portraits of two imperial persons on the obverse are far rarer than during the previous phase and are mainly confined to the Diocletianic and Constantinian periods.[159] Only one instance of jugate busts is known, the adventus piece of Constantine I in the Beistegui Collection with Sol Invictus and his *protégé* side by side.[160]

Medallion obverse portraits of four Empresses of our third phase have come down to us. On gold pieces of Helena, of Galeria Valeria and of Fausta and on a bronze piece of Fausta the Empress is diademed and wears her hair fastened up on the top of her head in a loop or plait.[161] Another portrait of Helena, on bronze, shows the hair confined by a wide stephane;[162] while 2-solidi pieces of Fausta show the head bare and the hair "permanently waved" and gathered into a knot behind.[163] The obverse portrait on Galla Placidia's gold medallions depicts her in rich robes, with the Christian monogram embroidered on the shoulder, a heavy double necklace and a pearl diadem confining her elaborately coiffured hair.[164] Constantine I's Constantinopolis and Urbs Roma bronze pieces, the obverses of which contain, not imperial portraits, but busts of the cities personified, are without parallels in the whole history of Roman medallions.[165]

With Constantine I was introduced the legendless obverse, on gold and silver multiples showing head without bust. The substitution, after Constantine's conversion, of the title VICT(or) for INVICTVS, epithet of the Unconquered Sun, is reflected on bronze medallions of Constantine II.[166] Large silver multiples of Constantine II bear the simple legend AVGVSTVS,[167] those of Constantius Gallus the single word CAESAR.[168] On gold pieces of Constantius II and Constans, PERP(etuus) appears for the first time on medallion obverses as an imperial epithet.[169] Decentius is described as FORT CAES.[170] Theoderic is REX THEODERICVS PIVS PRINC I(nvictus) S(emper).[171]

[154] J. Babelon, *op. cit.*, pl. 12, no. 232. **Pl. XXXI, 5.**

[155] **Pl. XLIX, 3.**

[156] G II, tav. 140, no. 6.

[157] G I, tav. 19, no. 9.

[158] *NZ* 1927, p. 21.

[159] Diocletian and Maximian (G I, tav. 5, nos. 1, 2; II, tav. 126, nos. 1, 2; *Numismatika* 1933, Pl. 1, no. 3 (**Pl. IV, 4**)); Diocletian and Galerius (*NNM* 28, 1926, pl. 4 (**Pl. VIII, 2**)); Constantius Chlorus and Galerius (*ibid.*, pl. 1 (**Pl. IX, 4**)); Crispus and Constantine II (G I, tav. 9, no. 10); Licinius I and Licinius II (J. Babelon, *op cit.*, pl. 12, no. 232 (**Pl. XXX, 5**)). The Germanic piece from Poland with confronted busts of Valentinian I and Valens (*vide supra* p. 68 (**Pl. X**)) may well be based on a genuine Roman original.

[160] J. Babelon, *op. cit.*, pl. 13, no. 233 (**Pl. XVII, 11**).

[161] G I, tav. 6, no. 1 (Helena); I, tav. 6, no. 3 (Galeria Valeria); II, tav. 133, no. 1 (Fausta).

[162] G II, tav. 128, no. 9.

[163] G I, tav. 8, nos. 10–12.

[164] G I, tav. 20, no. 2.

[165] G II, tavv. 131, 132.

[166] G II, tavv. 133, no. 8; 134, nos. 1, 4.

[167] G I, tav. 31, nos. 5, 6, 8.

[168] G I, tav. 33, nos. 15, 16.

[169] G I, tavv. 9, no. 13; 10, nos. 9, 10.

[170] G I, tav. 14, no. 4.

[171] G I, tav. 20, no. 3. *Cf.* the legend RESIS ROMANORVM on the obverse of the Germanic gold piece of Valentinian I and Valens (*vide supra* p. 68 (**Pl. X**)).

II. THE CHOICE OF REVERSE TYPES

(*a*) *Personal Types of the Emperor and his Family.*[172] The all-pervasiveness of the imperial figure in every department of fourth-century life is amply illustrated by the choice of reverse types in our third phase of medallic development. Setting aside those types in which the Emperor plays the leading part in some specific historical scene or is grouped, himself still the centre of interest, with deities or with allegorical figures other than his "shadow," the ubiquitous Victory, the largest and most varied class of types consists of designs wholly dominated by the imperial presence. Many of these types were doubtless inspired by specific events. But in such cases the "particular" is absorbed in the "universal": the individual achievements of Roman arms are merged in the general capacity for prowess (virtus) and glory, for victory, conquest and triumph inherent in the Emperor as such; while moments of prosperity, peace and security, of hope, restoration and joy need no specification, since all are continuously present, as it were, in him.

A few personal types are heads or busts of the Emperor's kinsfolk—of Constantius Chlorus[173] (Diocletian), of Galerius (Diocletian;[174] Maximian), of Maximian and Constantius Chlorus (Diocletian and Galerius),[175] of Crispus and Constantine II (Constantine I),[176] of Crispus and Constantius II (Constantine I), of Constantine II and Constantius II (Constantine I) and of Crispus and Constantius II (Constantius II as Caesar).[177] A gold piece of Crispus shows Fausta standing to the front, a hand resting on the shoulder of each of two imperial princes (FELIX PROGENIES CONSTANTINI AVG).[178] A remarkable series of dynastic types, showing the Emperor, seated or standing, grouped with his sons, was struck on large gold multiples under Constantine I: these, together with other large gold pieces continuing the family group *motif* by Constantine's sons after his death and large gold medallions of Valens with the same *motif*, will be discussed in our next Chapter.[179] Two 1½-solidi pieces of Constantius II and Constans respectively show the two brothers side by side, frontal and nimbate. Constantius' piece, struck at Antioch with the Emperor as consul on the obverse, portrays them standing, in consular dress: it was doubtless issued in honor of their joint consulship in 339.[180] Constans' piece, struck at Siscia with the Emperor in military dress on the obverse, shows them in liturgical dress, enthroned on a dais on which vota numbers (?) are inscribed, between two togate figures.[181]

[172] For personal types alluding to imperial births, deaths, consulships and to the Princeps Iuventutis *vide supra* Part III, chs. I, II, III.

[173] Not, as Gnecchi states (II, p. 127, no. 3), of Maximian.

[174] Paris No. 121 (billon ?): C 2, VI, p. 483, no. 1.

[175] *NNM* 28, 1926, pl. 4.

[176] For pieces additional to those illustrated by Gnecchi: see *Trau Collection Sale Catalogue* 1935, Taf. 46, Nrr. 3969, 3970, and *NZ* 1930, Taf. 2, Nr. 6. **Pl. XXXI, 6, 7.** For these and the following, reverse types with portraits of Constantine's sons *vide infra* p. 197.

[177] Delbrück, *op. cit.*, Taf. 7, Nr. 2 (enlarged). Not in the B. M., as Delbrück states (S. 80): its present location cannot be traced.

[178] Delbrück, op. cit., Taf. 5, Nr. 4. *Vide infra* pp. 197 f. **Pl. XXXI, 8.**

[179] *Vide infra* pp. 198.

[180] British Museum, acquired 1930, unpublished. **Pl. XXXI, 9.** Constans' first consulship was in 339.

[181] Gotha, unpublished, *cf.* G I, p. 27, no. 6 (**Pl. XXXI, 1**).

The great majority of personal types, however, depict a single imperial figure, that of the Emperor, Empress or Caesar whose portrait the obverse bears. The Emperor stands alone, in military dress, with labarum (Constantius II: TRVMFATOR GENTIVM BARBARARVM; Constans: same legend[182]), with spear or sceptre and labarum (Constantine I: GLORIA SECVLI [*sic*];[183] Constantius II: TRIVMFATOR GENTIVM BARBARARVM; Constans: same legend); with spear, erecting a trophy (Constantine I: SECVRITAS PERPETVAE[184] (coin type); Constantius II as Caesar: same legend); with trophy and shield (Constantine II: GLORIA EXERCITVS; Constantius II: same legend; Constans: same legend[185]); with spear and sword (Constantius II: VIRTVS AVGVSTORVM;[186] Magnentius: same legend); with spear and laurel-branch (Constantius II: VIRTVS AVG NOSTRI;[187] Magnentius: VIRTVS AVGVSTORVM[188]); with globe and spear (Constantius II: VIRTVS AVG N; Constans: VIRTVS AVGG NN; Decentius: VIRTVS AVGG,[189] Valens: same legend); with vexillum or labarum and Victory-on-globe (Valentinian I: GLORIA REIPVBLICAE; Gratian: RESTITVTOR REIPVBLICAE (coin type[190]); Arcadius: SECVRITAS REIPVBLICAE[191]); and with vexillum or labarum and shield (Constantius II: TRIVMFATOR GENTIVM BARBARARVM;[192] Constans: same legend; Valentinian I: VIRTVS ROMANI EXERCITVS (*cf.* similar coin type); Theodosius I: VIRTVS AVGVSTORVM, RESTITVTOR REIPVBLICE [*sic*][193]); or he stands togate, with sceptre and branch (Constans: GLORIA ROMANORVM). Other types show the Emperor standing and accompanied by subsidiary figures. He holds spear and globe, sceptre and globe, trophy and spear, trophy and shield or labarum and spear and is flanked by two seated captives (Constantine I: VBIQVE VICTORES (coin type);[194] Roma: VIRTVS AVGG; Constantius II as Caesar: VIRTVS CAES, VIRTVS CONSTANTI CAES (coin type);[195] Constantine II: VIRTVS CONSTANTINI AVG;[196] Constantius II: VIRTVS EXERCITVM,[197] VIRTVS AVG,[198] VIRTVS AVG N; Constans: VIRTVS EXERCITVM,[199] VIRTVS CONSTANTIS AVG;[200] Constantius Gallus: VIRTVS AVG; Julian: VIRTVS CAESARIS); he stands, holding a spear, beside a trophy, at the foot of which a captive is seated (Constantine II as Caesar: VIRTVS CAESS, VIRTVS CAESARVM; Constantius II as Caesar: same legends; Constans: VIRTVS CAESARVM[201]); he stands with spear and globe, spear and labarum, spear and Victory-on-globe, spear and branch or vexillum

[182] *Trau Collection Sale Catalogue* 1935, Taf. 47, Nr. 4136. **Pl. XXXI, 10.**

[183] *NZ* 1930, Taf. 2, Nr. 7 (**Pl. XXX, 5**).

[184] Variant in Rome (SMN) = G I, p. 20, no. 49 = *Caruso Collection Sale Catalogue* 1923, tav. 16, no. 558. **Pl. XXXII, 1.**

[185] *NC* 1939, pp. 143 ff., figs. 1–3. **Pl. XXXII, 2, 3.**

[186] *Vierordt Collection Sale Catalogue* 1923, pl. 61, no. 2743. **Pl. XXXII, 4.**

[187] G II, p. 151, no. 53. **Pl. XXXII, 5.**

[188] G II, p. 154, no. 9.

[189] G II, p. 155, no. 5.

[190] G II, p. 158, no. 1. **Pl. XXXII, 6.**

[191] *NC* 1940, pl. 3, no. 3. **Pl. XXXII, 7.**

[192] Kubitschek Taf. 17, Nr. 314. **Pl. XXXII, 8.**

[193] Paris no. 217. **Pl. XXXII, 9.**

[194] G I, p. 20, no. 55. Coats Collection, Glasgow University. **Pl. XXXIII, 1.**

[195] *RN* 1906, pl. 9, no. 16 (**Pl. VI, 4**).

[196] G I, p. 25, no. 18.

[197] G I, p. 33, no. 51.

[198] *Evans Collection Sale Catalogue* 1934, pl. 62, no. 1942. **Pl. XXXIII, 2.**

[199] G I, p. 28, no. 21; example in Florence. **Pl. XXXIII, 3.**

[200] G I, p. 28, no. 20.

[201] *RN* 1906, pl. 3, no. 7. **Pl. XXXIII, 4.**

and branch, while one captive is seated on the ground beside him (Constantine II as Caesar: VBIQVE VICTORES;[202] Constantius II: VIRTVS CONSTANTI AVG, VIRTVS AVG, VIRTVS AVG N; Constans: VIRTVS AVG; Constantius Gallus: same legend;[203] Julian: VIRTVS AVG N); he stands, crowned by Victory, holding spear and globe or labarum and globe, with one captive seated on the ground (Maximian: VICTORIA AVGG;[204] Valentinian I: VICTORIA D N AVGVSTI),[205] or holding spear and sword, his foot set on a captive's back (Constantius II: VIRTVS AVGVSTI[206]); or, again, Victory crowns him as he stands, unaccompanied by captive or captives, holding spear and Victory-on-globe or labarum and sceptre (Constantius II: VICTORIA AVG; Constans: GAVDIVM POPVLI ROMANI; Magnentius: VICTORIA AVGG), or holding the labarum and resting one foot on a prow (Constans: TRIVMFATOR GENTIVM BARBARARVM).[207] He stands to receive a prisoner presented to him by Virtus (?) (Constantine I: DEBELLATORI GENTIVM BARBARARVM); he holds the labarum and rests one hand on the head of a captive at his side (Magnentius: VIRTVS AVGVSTI NOSTRI); he holds globe and labarum, while a captive kneels before him (Valentinian I: TRIVMFATOR GENT BARB (coin type);[208] Valens: same legend;[209] Valentinian II: same legend; Theodosius I: same legend;[210] Arcadius: same legend;[211] Honorius: same legend).

Walking types of the Emperor show him advancing with spear and trophy, a captive seated on the ground before him (Constantine I: VIRTVS AVG ET CAES NN); or kicking the captive (Constantine I VIRTVS D N CONSTANTINI AVG);[212] or with two captives seated, one on either side (Constantine I: GLORIA CONSTANTINI AVG);[213] or he carries a trophy, kicks one captive and drags another captive along by the hair (Constantine I: same legend). He advances, trophy in hand, and glances back towards a captive whom he drags by the hair after him (Constantine II as Caesar: VIRTVS CAESS; Constantius II as Caesar: VIRTVS CAES,[214]); or he carries shield and spear and drags a captive by the hair behind him (Magnentius: VIRTVS AVGVSTI NOSTRI). Helmeted and armed with spear and shield, he drags a captive by the hair, while a female prisoner kneels on the right (Constans: VICTORIA AVGVSTI NOSTRI).[215] He moves off towards the right, with spear and branch, while Victory, walking in the opposite direction, lays her hand upon his shoulder, as though to recall him to yet further conquests (Constantius II: VICTORIA AVGVSTORVM; Decentius: same legend).

A few types portray the Emperor seated on arms, receiving a globe from Victory (Constantine I: GLORIA ROMANORVM)[216] or a phoenix on a globe from an

[202] G I, p. 25, no. 16.
[203] An unpublished piece in the Gnecchi Collection, Rome.
[204] *NZ* 1920, Taf. 11 (first piece on left in fourth row).
[205] *NK* 1929–1930, Taf. 3, a, 10 (**Pl. XXXI, 4**).
[206] Kubitschek S. 35, Nr. 324, Abb. **Pl. XXXIII, 5.**
[207] G I, p. 27, no. 11.
[208] *NZ* 1895, Taf. 4, Nr. 5. **Pl. XXXIII, 6.**
[209] Grueber, pl. 65, no. 1. **Pl. XXXIII, 7.**
[210] Kubitschek S. 41, Nr. 372, Abb. **Pl. XXXIII, 8.**
[211] Kubitschek S. 42, Nr. 377, Abb. **Pl. XXXIII, 9.**
[212] *NNM* 6, 1921, pl. 1 (**Pl. XXX, 6**).
[213] In addition to the walking type with mint-mark SMTS illustrated by Gnecchi there is a similar type with mint-mark SMN on a B. M. piece. **Pl. XXXIV, 1.** For the quasi-running version of this type *vide supra* p. 62, n. 36 (Helleville piece): *cf.* variant in the Hague Collection. **Pl. XXXIV, 2.**
[214] G II, p. 152, no. 62 (wrong legend). **Pl. XXXIV, 3.**
[215] **Pl. XLVIII, 8.**
[216] Kubitschek S. 25, Nr. 239, Abb. **Pl. XXXIV, 4.**

imperial prince, beside whom crouches a panther with head humbly bowed (Constantine I: GLORIA SAECVLI, VIRTVS CAESS); or holding sceptre and Victory-on-globe, while two captives are seated on the ground, one on either side (Constantine I: EXVPERATOR OMNIVM GENTIVM); or on a high-backed throne, in festive dress, with shield and sceptre, extending his hand towards a kneeling captive woman, while Victory looks on (Jovian: GAVDIVM ROMANORVM).[217] Finally, Galla Placidia is enthroned towards the front, with nimbus, richly embroidered robes and her feet on a footstool.[218]

A series of mounted types depicts the Emperor galloping over the bodies of one, or two, falling or prostrate foes (Constantine I: VIRTVS AVG N, GLORIA ROMANORVM,[219] VIRTVS AVGVSTORVM NN;[220] Constantine II as Caesar; VIRTVS CAESS; Constantine II: DEBELLATORI GENTT BARBARR, VICTORI GENTIVM BARBARR; Constantius II: DEBELLATORI GENTT BARBARR, VIRTVS AVG N; Constans: same legends and VICTORI GENTIVM BARBARR; Decentius: VIRTVS AVGG). One variant shows Victory flying above the Emperor and crowning him (Constantine I: VIRTVS AVG);[221] on another, not human foes, but a serpent is seen beneath the horse's legs (Constantius II: DEBELLATORI HOSTIVM).

The last-quoted type and legend perhaps provide a key to the solution of an apparent paradox. In the fourth century the Empire was officially Christian; yet, as our survey of personal types has shown, the Christian Emperors figure on their medallions in the guise of pitiless conquerors, kicking their captives, dragging them by the hair, riding them down or, at the best, standing fully armed and triumphant over their crouching or kneeling forms. But these captives, viewed with the eyes, not of modern sentiment, but of contemporary Rome, personify, not weak and defenseless "natives," but ruthless, barbaric hordes who threatened to destroy all that the ancient world held dear—city life and culture, commerce, agriculture and industry, art and religion. A serpent, the traditional emblem of the powers of darkness, is the appropriate symbol of such "hostes." In the fourth century it might well be a Christian Emperor's duty to check their onslaught with all the forces at his command, "parcere subiectis," but "debellare superbos."[222]

(*b*) *Public and Historical Events.* Apart from the types depicting vota and "Birthday of Rome" celebrations, consular processions etc. and scenes of imperial adventus, adlocutio and largitio,[223] the reverse designs of our third phase which can be definitely connected with specific events are relatively few. The defeat of Allectus and the overthrow of Carausius' abortive "British Empire" by Constantius Chlorus in 296 are recorded on that Caesar's London medallion from

[217] Delbrück, *op. cit.*, S. 89, Abb. 27. Warsaw (**Pl. XI**).
[218] **Pl. XLIX, 1.**
[219] G II, p. 134, no. 2.
[220] G I, p. 21, no. 63. **Pl. XXXIV, 5.**
[221] Delbrück, *op. cit.*, S. 75, Abb. 26 (**Pl. XXX, 2**).
[222] Ulrich-Bansa, however, (*op. cit.*, p. 56), connects this piece, which bears the mint-mark of Milan, with Constantius' sojourn in that city in November, 352, when, having driven Magnentius from Italy, he repealed the latter's laws and celebrated his own victory. In that case "hostes" would denote the yet more deadly foes who seek to disrupt the Empire's unity from within its fold.
[223] *Vide supra* Part III, chs. I, II.

Arras, which portrays him riding along the Thames bank beside a troop ship, to restore the city, who kneels as a suppliant outside her gates, to Rome's eternal light (REDDITOR LVCIS AETERNAE).[224] The same event inspired a type struck on gold medallions in the names of Diocletian, Constantius Chlorus and Galerius, which shows Constantius, crowned by Victory, "restoring" Britannia to the Empire in the name of imperial compassion (PIETAS AVGG).[225] The defeat of the Persians in the same year is celebrated on a bronze piece of Galerius, on which he gallops over the bodies of four Persians, while Victory, hovering in the air, crowns him (VICTORIA PERSICA). The abdication of Maximian in Constantius' favor on May 1, 305, is depicted of the latter's CONCORDIA AVGG ET CAESS / XX gold multiple.[226] Constantine I's victory over Licinius at Chrysopolis on September 18, 324, and the inauguration, in the November of that year, of the process of transforming Byzantium into Constantinople, are commemorated on his PIETAS AVGVSTI N 2-solidi medallions, and Constantine, crowned by Victory, standing and raising up from her knees the towered Constantinopolis, rescued from the enemy and "restored" through the Emperor's compassion, and on the larger PIETAS AVGVSTI NOSTRI multiples, struck in his own name and in that of Constantius II, showing the same type with the addition of Roma, or Virtus, presenting the kneeling city (coin type).[227] The reverse design of Justinian's great gold piece, depicting the Emperor, nimbate and helmeted, on horseback, preceded by Victory with trophy and spear (SALVS ET GLORIA ROMANORVM), must allude to Belisarius' defeat of the Vandals in 534.[228]

(*c*) *Deities.* To Diocletian's campaign in the cause of Graeco-Roman polytheism we owe a remarkable series of medallion types of deities, the swan-song, as it were, of the old religion before its final abdication, as far as official imperial art is concerned, in favor of the new. The dominant figures are, of course, Juppiter and Hercules, the respective patrons of the two senior Augusti. Juppiter is seated to the left, with fulmen, sceptre and eagle (Diocletian: IOVI CONSERVATORI (coin type), CONSERVAT AVGG V ET IIII COS; Galerius: IOVI CONSERVATORI), or with sceptre and Victory (Diocletian: IOVI VICTORI AVGG;[229] Maximian: same legend);[230] or he is seated to the front, with sceptre, eagle and Victory-on-globe (Licinius I and Licinius II: IOVI CONSERVATORI LICINIORVM AVG ET CAES),[231] or to the front, with sceptre and fulmen, within a hexastyle temple (Diocletian: IOVI CONSERVATORI AVG), before which a sacrifice is sometimes offered (Diocletian: same legend). He stands to the left, with sceptre, Victory-on-globe and eagle (Diocletian: IOVI CONSERVATORI (coin type)),[232] sometimes without the eagle (Galerius: same legend), or with sceptre,

[224] *Aréthuse*, Jan., 1924, pl. 7 (**Pl. VIII, 4**).

[225] Diocletian: in private hands? (*NC* 1933, p. 274); Constantius Chlorus: British Museum (*Aréthuse*, Jan. 1924, pl. 8, nos. 5, 6 (**Pl. VIII, 5, 6**)); Galerius: in private hands, but as yet unpublished (*NC* 1933, p. 274). We may assume that this type was also struck for the fourth member of the Tetrarchy, Maximian. All our extant examples are from the Arras hoard.

[226] *Vide supra* p. 82.

[227] For these types and for the copy of them on a remarkable 12-solidi piece of Libius Severus see *NC* 1940, pp. 17 ff., pls. 4, nos. 2–7; 5, nos. 1–5 (**Pls. VI, 2; XXX, 3**).

[228] **Pl. XLIX, 3.**

[229] *NC* 1930, p. 242.

[230] *Loc. cit.*

[231] J. Babelon, *op. cit.*, pl. 12, no. 232 (**Pl. XXXI, 5**).

[232] **Pl. XLVIII, 1.**

fulmen and eagle (Galerius: IOVIS CONSERVATOR AVGG,[233] IOVI CONSERVATORI AVGG; Maximinus Daza: IOVI CONS CAES (coin type); Licinius I: IOVI CONSERVATORI (coin type)), sometimes without the eagle (Maximian: IOVI CONSERVAT AVGG);[234] or he stands to the left, with sceptre, fulmen and eagle, within a hexastyle temple (Diocletian: IOVI CONSERVATORI AVG;[235] Maximian: same legend) or within an octostyle temple (Diocletian: IOVI CONSERVATORI).[236] Juppiter is grouped with Diocletian, offering sacrifice and crowned by Victory (Diocletian: IOVI CONSERVAT); or stands with his foot on a captive, while Victory advances and proffers a globe (Diocletian: PERPETVA FELICITAS AVGG). Diocletian and Maximian sacrifice together at a tripod, with frontal statuettes of Juppiter and Hercules standing on a garlanded altar above (Diocletian and Maximian): the legend reads IOVIO ET HERCVLIO—"in honor of Juppiter's and Hercules' *protégés*."[237] The two Augusti are enthroned to the front, side by side, each crowned by his divine patron (Maximian: PERPETVA CONCORDIA AVGG). Licinius II is crowned by Juppiter (IOVI CONSERVATORI). Moneta stands in the centre, flanked by Juppiter and Hercules: the legend MONETA IOVI ET HERCVLI AVGG suggests the dedication of the imperial mint to the Emperors' heavenly patrons, who bless financial administration and reforms (Diocletian, Diocletian and Maximian, Maximian).

Hercules is seated to the front, on a throne by Maximian's side, with lion-skin, club, quiver and bow (Diocletian: HERCVLIO MAXIMIANO AVG), or alone, on a rock, with the same attributes (Maximian: HERCVLI VICTORI, HERCVLI CONSERVATORI (coin types)). He stands to the right with lion-skin, apples and club (Maximian: HERCVLI CONSERVATORI AVGG ET CAESS NN (coin type)),[238] or to the right with club, lion-skin, quiver and bow (Maximian: same legend (coin type)),[239] or to the front with club, lion-skin and apples (Constantius Chlorus: HERCVLI CONS CAES (coin type)), or to the left in an octastyle temple, with club and lion-skin (Maximian: HERCVLI VICTORI / VOT X).[240] His bust is shown, with lion-skin and club (Maximian: HERCVLI CONSERVATORI AVGG (from Szilágy-Sómlyó)). He wrestles with the Lernaean hydra (Maximian: HERCVLI DEBELLATORI (coin type)) and kneels on the back of the Ceryneian stag (Constantius Chlorus: VIRTVS AVGG) (coin type)).[241] Such labors of Hercules are prototypes of the imperial labors against the forces of evil and barbarism.

Mars advances rapidly, with spear and trophy, helmeted and nude, save for a cloak flying out behind (Constantius Chlorus: MARTI VICTORI).[242] Apollo-Sol stands, radiate, in long-sleeved, belted chiton and himation, "saluting" with his right hand and holding on his left a bust of Serapis (Maximinus Daza: SOLE INVICTO (coin type)).[243] Venus stands to the left, an apple in one hand and a fold of her drapery

[233] *Trau Collection Sale Catalogue* 1935, Taf. 42, Nr. 3636. **Pl. XXXIV, 6.**

[234] *NZ* 1931, Taf. 1, Nr. 7 (**Pl. IV, 5, 6**).

[235] *Aréthuse*, Jan., 1924, pl. 8, no. 3 (**Pl. VIII, 1**).

[236] Turin, Medagliere del Re, D C. 14181. *Cf.* G II, p. 124, no. 4.

[237] *NZ* 1931, Taf. 1, Nr. 2 (**Pl. III, 15, 16**).

[238] *Aréthuse*, Jan., 1924, pl. 8, no. 4; *NC* 1933, p. 274 (**Pl. VIII, 3**).

[239] *NC* 1933, p. 274.

[240] *Vide supra* p. 81, note 71 (**Pl. XII, 10**).

[241] *Aréthuse*, Jan., 1924, pl. 8, no. 8 (**Pl. IX, 3**).

[242] *NNM* 28, 1926, pl. 2 (**Pl. IX, 3**).

[243] J. Babelon, *op. cit.*, pl. 12, no. 231 (**Pl. IV, 10**).

in the other (Galeria Valeria: VENERI VICTRICI (coin type)). The Unconquered Sun, the last pagan deity to figure on Roman medallions, stands with globe and raised hand (Severus II: SOLI INVICTO CONSERVAT AVGG ET CAESS NN), or with globe, whip and raised hand, while a captive is seated on the ground beside him (Constantine I: SOLI INVICTO COMITI); or he crowns the emperor (Constantine I: same legend (coin type)),[244] sometimes whip in hand (Constantine II as Caesar: same legend).[245]

(*d*) *Mythology and Legend.* Types of Roma, designed to honor Old Rome, while Constantine founded the New, depict Aeneas fleeing from Troy and the wolf and twins in a cave, sometimes flanked by two shepherds, while twin stars illumine the sky. Constantius II borrowed the scene of the rape of the Sabine women (SABINAE) from Antoninus Pius' famous series.[246]

(*e*) *Personifications.*[247] After the personal types of the Emperor and his family, personifications form the largest class of reverse types of our third phase. If the range of subjects treated is less extensive than in the earlier phases, interest is well maintained by the numerous variations played upon individual themes. It was, indeed, in the realm of abstraction and allegory that the ancient classical tradition flourished most vigorously in fourth-century medal designing, as in other departments of late antique art.

The Tres Monetae type, so prominent a feature of third-century medallions, falls out of favor in later times. Common on medallions of Diocletian, of Diocletian and Maximian, of Maximian, of Constantius Chlorus, of Galerius, of Maximinus Daza and of Maxentius, where it doubtless bears testimony to Diocletian's famous reform, it is relatively rare in the Constantinian age. A few pieces with the type struck in Constantine I's name have come down to us. It occurs on a small silver piece of Crispus, and on bronze pieces of Crispus and of Constantine II as Caesar, accompanied by new legends—MONETA CAESARVM, MONETA AVG ET CAESS NN, MONETA VRBIS VESTRAE, SACRA MONETA VRBIS. Constantius II alone among Emperors of the Constantinian House issued Tres Monetae medallions in any

[244] *NZ* 1930, Taf. 2, Nr. 2. **Pl. XXXIV, 7.** For Sol Invictus as Constantine's "dynastic patron" see *CAH* xi, pp. 349, 680.

[245] For types of Serapis and Isis and of Neptune and Isis on vota publica medallions of Diocletian, Maximian, Constantius Chlorus and Galerius *vide supra* p. 78.

[246] It is possible, indeed, that this SABINAE type as first struck by Antoninus Pius had more than a merely historical interest. Was it also inspired by some actual show, dramatizing the story, held annually in the circus, perhaps at the Consualia, which are mentioned by Tertullian in his *De Spectaculis* (5), written at the end of the second century; and did this show survive into the middle of the fourth century of our era? If so, it would be an interesting example of the survival of pagan customs in the capital of a now officially Christian Empire. How deeply Constantius II himself was impressed by the monuments of pagan Rome, when he visited the city for the first time in 357, we know from Ammianus Marcellinus (xvi, 10, 13 ff.). The historian tells us that the Emperor actually gave orders for the erection of an obelisk in the circus (xvi, 10, 17; xvii, 4); and the commemorative verses inscribed on that obelisk have come down to us (*ILS* 736). Was our medallion struck for that occasion? Obviously, the vitality and fascination of the old tradition were enormous. For contorniates with this scene and legend see J. Sabatier, *Description générale des médaillons contorniates*, XV, 5; Bernhart, *Handbuch zur Münzkunde der römischen Kaiserzeit*, Taf. 48, Nr. 7 (*vide infra* pp. 234 ff.).

[247] For types of the Four Seasons and for vota medallions with types of Genii, Victory or Victories, Roma and Constantinopolis *vide supra* Part III, Ch. I.

quantity. After his time the type appears sporadically on small bronze borderline pieces of Julian, Jovian, Valentinian I, Valens, Gratian[248] and Valentinian II.[249]

The main series of fourth-century personifications may be classified under the headings of beneficent powers linked with imperial rule, imperial virtues, geography and Victory types.

Beneficent powers linked with imperial rule are Libertas, Pax and Securitas. On a "Fest-aureus" of Magnentius[250] and on a 1½-solidi piece of Decentius, Libertas, sceptre and trophy in hand, confronts Victory, to whom she owes her preservation (VICTORIA AVG LIB ROMANOR (coin type)). Pax leans, with legs crossed, upon a column, holding sceptre and olive-branch (Constantine I: PAX AETERNA).[251] Securitas, the power whose presence the fourth-century world so sorely needed, appears six times. She stands to the front, leaning on a column, her right hand raised to her head, while captives sometimes crouch at her feet (Constantine I: SECVRITAS AVGVSTI N; Crispus: SECVRITAS REIPVBLICAE;[252] Magnentius: same legend); or she stands to the left, with transverse spear, handing Victory-on-globe to Respublica (Constantine I: same legend),[253] or veiled and holding a branch (Helena: SECVRITAS REIPVBLICE [*sic*]),[254] or with sceptre and a captive on the ground at her side (Constans: SECVRITAS AVG). We might also include among beneficent powers, as symbols of general prosperity, two winged Genii holding up a garland between them (Constantine I: GAVDIVM AVGVSTI NOSTRI).[255]

The only imperial virtue depicted on fourth-century medallions is Virtus, the imperial quality of prowess in war.[255a] On numerous 1½-solidi pieces of Constantine I she stands in Amazonian dress, with spear and Victory-on-globe, while two captives, on the back of one of whom she sets her foot, are seated beside her (GLORIA CONSTANTINI AVG); and on gold multiples of Crispus and of Constantine II as Caesar she advances, holding spear and trophy, with one, or two, captives seated on the ground (Crispus: VIRTVS AVG ET CAESS NN; Constantine II as Caesar: VIRTVS AVG ET CAESS NN, VIRTVS CONSTANTINI CAES).[256]

The geographical types are by far the most interesting of the series. Constantius Chlorus' Londinium and Britannia have been described above.[257] Francia and Alamannia each appear as a female figure, seated on the ground at the foot of a

[248] The Hague, No. 12521.

[249] The Hague, No. 12590. For Moneta grouped with Roma (?) or Virtus (?) and Felicitas (?) or Abundantia (?) *vide supra* p. 82, note 75a.

[250] *Münzhandlung Basel Sale Catalogue* Nr. 6, 1936, Taf. 26, Nr. 2041 (**Pl. VI, 7**).

[251] A cast of a piece (said to be gold) with this type was seen by the present writer in Vienna in Feb., 1938. The original is, so far, untraceable.

[252] *Hirsch Sale Catalogue* Nr. 29, 1910 Taf. 31, Nr. 1406. **Pl. XXXIV, 8.**

[253] *Jameson Collection Catalogue* II. pl. 16, no. 348. **Pl. XXXIV, 9.**

[254] **Pl. XLVIII, 4.**

[255] *Cf.* similar Genii on vota medallions. This type may have been struck for the solemn consecration of Constantinople on May 11, 330 (*RN* 1906, p. 170). The two pieces on which it occurs show the long-haired obverse portrait of the period. One bears the mint-mark of Constantinople, the other that of Nicomedia. The mint of the latter city, officially closed from 327 to 333 or 335 (Maurice III, p. 72), could have been specially opened to mark the great occasion (*vide supra* p. 83, note 81).

[255a] For Pietas "birthday" types *vide supra* pp. 100 f.

[256] G I, p. 26, nos. 19, 20.

[257] *Vide supra* pp. 182 f.

trophy, wearing Phrygian cap and bracae and resting her head on her hand (Crispus: GAVDIVM ROMANORVM / FRANCIA,[258] GAVDIVM ROMANORVM / ALAMANNIA (coin types)). The turreted woman, with flaming torch, who genuflects before the Emperor on Valens' Germanic GLORIA ROMANORVM gold pieces, may be Antioch since the mint-mark is of that city; Tellus reclines in the exergue, with cornucopiae and fruits in the fold of her garment. Respublica, or the Empire in general, shown as a turreted female figure, hands a Victory-on-globe to Constantine I (SALVS ET SPES REIPVBLICAE)[259] or kneels to be "restored" by him, in the presence of a captive (Constantinopolis: RESTITVTOR REIP); holding a cornucopiae, she genuflects before Magnentius, who advances towards her, nimbate, on horseback (LIBERATOR REIPVBLICAE),[260] and before Valens, Gratian,[261] Valentinian II[262] and Theodosius I,[263] who raise her from her knees (RESTITVTOR REIPVBLICAE).[264]

The favorite geographical types are, naturally, those of the senior capitals, old and new, Rome and Constantinople. Roma is seated to the left on throne or arms, wearing long or short chiton, with globe, or Victory, or Victory-on-globe, on one hand and spear or sceptre in the other, and a shield at her side (Constantine I: GLORIA ROMANORVM (coin type);[265] Roma: VRBS ROMA; Constantine II as Caesar: GLORIA ROMANORVM (miliarense type);[266] Constantius II as Caesar: GLORIA ROMANORVM, VRBS ROMA; Constantius II: GLORIA ROMANORVM, VRBS ROMA, ROMA BEATA, VRBS ROMA BEATA;[267] Constans: same legends;[268] Magnentius: GLORIA ROMANORVM;[269] Decentius: same legend;[270] Constantius Gallus: VRBS ROMA;[271] Jovian: same legend; Valentinian I: same legend (coin type);[272] Valens: same legend (coin type);[273] Gratian: same legend (coin type); Valentinian II: same legend (coin type)[274]). She is seated to the front on a high-backed throne, with short, slipped chiton, sceptre or spear and globe (Valens: GLORIA ROMANORVM;[275] Gratian: same legend; Honorius:

[258] *Jameson Collection Catalogue* II, pl. 16, no. 359. **Pl. XXXIV, 10.**

[259] Variant with CONS in exergue (*Trau Collection Sale Catalogue* 1935, Taf. 44, Nr. 3883). **Pl. XXXIV, 11.**

[260] *NK* 1929–1930, S. 28, Abb. **Pl. XXXIV, 12.** This was a propaganda piece, struck by Magnentius between 350 and 352 at Aquileia, where he had his headquarters while preparing for war against Constantius II.

[261] *Vide supra* p. 169.

[262] Variants in Paris (TROBT: Bansa, *op. cit.*, tav. 6, no. 39) and formerly in Paris (TROBS: Berlin cast). **Pl. XXXV, 1, 2.**

[263] Variant in Freer Collection, Washington, U. S. A. (COMOB: W. Dennison, *Studies in East Christian and Roman Art*, 1918, pls. 10, 11). **Pl. XXXVI.**

[264] For Respublica grouped with Securitas *vide supra* p. 186.

[265] Variants in British Museum (SMN: obverse, head with diadem, Paris (CONS) and Münzhandlung Basel, 1939 (TR). **Pl. XXXV, 3–5.**

[266] C [2] VII, p. 379, fig.

[267] Unpublished bronze piece at Naples.

[268] For VRBS ROMA type see G II, p. 146, no. 31. **Pl. XXXV, 6.** Type GLORIA ROMANORVM known from 2-solidi piece at Sofia.

[269] *Münzhandlung Basel Sale Catalogue* Nr. 6, 1936, Taf. 25, Nr. 2040 (**Pl. VI, 6**).

[270] G I, p. 34, no. 1.

[271] Grueber, pl. 64, no. 2. **Pl. XXXV, 7.**

[272] *Trau Collection Sale Catalogue* 1935, Taf. 50, Nr. 4409 **Pl. XXXV, 8.**

[273] Bronze piece at Dresden. **Pl. XXXV, 9.**

[274] *Weber Collection Sale Catalogue* 1909, Taf. 51, Nr. 2769. **Pl. XXXVII, 1.**

[275] Variant in Rome, formerly in Caruso Collection, with mint-mark TROBT (*Caruso Collection Sale Catalogue* 1923, tav. 18, no. 598). **Pl. XXXVII, 2.**

same legend; Attalus: INVICTA ROMA AETERNA).[276] She is seated to the right in long chiton, with spear and shield, receiving a wreath from Victory, who presents a prisoner (Constantine I: VICTORIA GOTHICA).[277] She is carried towards the front, sceptre in hand, between two women, each attended by a boy (Roma: SECVRITAS ROMAE). Seated to the left, with long chiton, spear and Victory-on-globe, she is crowned by Victory (Roma: VICTORIA AVG N), or, seated on arms, she receives a branch from Virtus, while Victory stands by (Licinius I: VIRTVS AVGG NN).[278] A common gold type shows Roma and Constantinopolis enthroned side by side, Roma helmeted, on the left, with sceptre and Victory-on-globe, Constantinopolis turreted, on the right, with Victory-on-globe and sceptre or cornucopiae, her foot on a prow (Constantius II as Caesar;[279] Constantius II;[280] Constantius Gallus;[281] Julian;[282] Valentinian I;[283] Gratian; Valentinian II; Eugenius (all with legend GLORIA ROMANORVM)); one variant shows Constantinopolis helmeted (Valentinian II: same legend).[284]

Constantinopolis[285] is seated to the right on a high-backed throne, turreted, cornucopiae in hand, her foot on a prow (Constantine I: D N CONSTANTINVS / MAX TRIVMF AVG),[286] or to the left on a stool, with branch and cornucopiae, with or without a prow at her feet, sometimes crowned by Victory (Constantinopolis: VICTORIA AVGG NN, VICTORIA AVG N, VICTORIA AVGVSTI, VICTORIAE AVGVSTI;[287] Roma: VICTORIA AVGVSTI;[288] Constantine II: same legend; Constantius II: same legend;[289] Constans: same legend);[290] or on a high-backed throne, with sceptre and Victory-on-globe, her feet on a prow, helmeted (Valentinian I: GLORIA ROMANORVM; Theodosius I: same legend;[291] Arcadius: same legend)[292] or wearing stephane (or coif ?) (Constantius II: GLORIA ROMANORVM;[293] Constans: same legend; Valens: same legend). As Victoria-Constantinopolis she is seated to the left on a stool, winged and turreted, with branch and cornucopiae (Constantine I: VICTORIA AVGVSTI; Constantinopolis: VICTORIA AVG, VICTORIA AVGG NN,[294] CONSTANTINOPOLIS; Constantine II as Caesar: CONSTANTINOPOLIS).[295] She stands, turreted, with vexillum and branch, a prow at her feet (Constantinopolis: FEL TEMP REPARATIO).

[276] **Pl. XLIX, 2.**

[277] A. D. 332.

[278] G I, p. 14, no. 1.

[279] G I, p. 31, no. 21.

[280] N. B. (1) variant of Antioch mint (not quoted by Gnecchi) in A. Evans bequest, Ashmolean Museum, Oxford; (2) G I, p. 30, nos. 19, 20, mint-mark = 'TES'. **Pl. XXXVII, 3, 4.**

[281] G I, p. 34, no. 1.

[282] Variant formerly in Paris: cast in Berlin = G I, p. 34, no. 1. **Pl. XXXVII, 5.**

[283] N. B. variants (1) formerly in Paris: cast in Berlin. **Pl. XXXVII, 7.** (2) in B. M. = G I, p. 35, no. 7. **Pl. XXXVII, 6.**

[284] G I, p. 38, no. 5 (formerly in Paris: cast in Berlin). **Pl. XXXVII, 8.**

[285] For Constantinopolis kneeling in the "restoration" types of Constantine I etc., *vide supra* p. 183.

[286] Variant in Berlin with M CONS Z in exergue. **Pl. XXXVII, 9.**

[287] G II, p. 137, no. 14. **Pl. XXXVII, 10.**

[288] *Riechmann Sale Catalogue* Nr. 20, 1922, Taf. 31, Nr. 1363. **Pl. XXXVII, 11.**

[289] G II, p. 149, no. 32.

[290] G II, p. 144, no. 21. **Pl. XXXVII, 12.**

[291] *NC* 1940, pl. 3, no. 1. **Pl. XXXVIII, 1.**

[292] *Ibid.*, pl. 3, no. 2. **Pl. XXXVIII, 2.**

[293] **Pl. XLVIII, 7.** N. B. variants (1) formerly in Paris, mint-mark RM; (2) formerly in Trau Collection, mint-mark ·SMANTB· *Trau Collection Sale Catalogue* 1935, Taf. 48, Nr. 4171. **Pl. XXXVIII, 3, 4.**

[294] Kubitschek S. 27, Nr. 258, Abb. **Pl. XXXVIII, 5.**

[295] G II, p. 140, no. 1.

The commonest types of Victory show her advancing to the left, holding wreath and palm, with a captive seated on either side (Constantine I: VICTORIA AVG ET CAESS NN; Crispus: same legend),[296] or with one captive kneeling (Roma: VICTORIA ROMANORVM;[297] Constantius Gallus: same legend), sometimes kicking the captive (Magnentius: VICTORIA AVGG; Decentius: same legend), or unaccompanied by captive or captives (Constantius II: VICTORIA AVGVSTI (miliarense type); Magnentius: VICTORIA AVGVSTORVM; Constantius Gallus: GLORIA ROMANORVM; Jovian: VICTORIA AVGVST N;[298] Valens: VICTORIA AVGGG (coin type); Gratian: VICTORIA AVGVSTORVM (coin type);[299] Valentinian II: VICTORIA AVGGG (coin type));[300] or advancing to the right, with wreath and palm, a captive at her feet (Constantius Gallus: GLORIA ROMANORVM),[301] or to right or left, with a wreath in either hand, flanked by two seated captives (Constantius II: VICTORIA AVG N, VICTORIA AVGVSTI; Constantius Gallus: VICTORIA ROMANORVM). Other types portray her walking towards the left and holding a wreath, while she drags a captive along by the arm (Constantius II: VICTORIA AVGVST N), or towards the right and holding a trophy, while she drags her victim by the hair (Valentinian I: VICTORIA AVGVSTORVM (miliarense type)),[302] or standing with trophy and wreath (Constantius II: GLORIA ROMANORVM),[303] or standing, nimbate, with vexillum and branch, her foot on a captive (Constans: GLORIA ROMANORVM; Magnentius: same legend).[304] A bronze "strike," recently come to light, from a lost gold medallion of Carausius shows Victory driving a swift biga (VICTORIA CARAVSI AVG).[305] The two finest Victory types respectively date from the beginning and end of our third phase. The first, struck in gold by Diocletian, shows Victory poised on a globe, facing the spectator, a trophy held erect with both hands (VICTORIA AVGG). The second type, struck by Theoderic, also in gold, depicts her standing on a globe towards the right, with wreath and palm (REX THEODERICVS VICTOR GENTIVM). The barbarian, now in his turn victorious, has assumed the role of King of Italy and the end of the ancient world is at hand.

(*f*) *Buildings*. The gold consecration medallion of Romulus shows a round temple with cupola and half-open door (coin type).[306] A bronze piece of Constantine I depicts a three-arched bridge, over which Victory and the Emperor advance towards a kneeling captive, while Danuvius reclines below (SALVS REIP / DANVBIVS). The gates, walls and public buildings of Trier were reconstructed under Constantine I's supervision between 310 and 316; and the view of the city struck at the local mint on his 2-solidi medallions with the legend GLORIA AVGG is by far the most picturesque and attractive type of its class. We are shown seven towers, part of the walls and one of the gates, the Incluta Porta, crowned by the Emperor's statue, while the Moselle, spanned by a bridge, flows below.[307]

[296] *Jameson Collection Catalogue* II, pl. 16, no. 357. **Pl. XXXVII, 13.**

[297] *FM* 1931, Taf. 5, Nr. 5. **Pl. XXXVIII, 6.**

[298] G II, p. 157, no. 4.

[299] Ulrich-Bansa Collection, Padua.

[300] G II, p. 159, no. 1.

[301] G II, p. 155, no. 3.

[302] Grueber p. 92, no. 2. **Pl. XXXVIII, 7.**

[303] *BM* 1919, Taf. 85, Nr. 9. **Pl. XXXVIII, 8.**

[304] Kubitschek Taf. 18, Nr. 330. **Pl. XXXVIII, 9.**

[305] *Vide supra* p. 61 (**Pl. XXX, 4**).

[306] *Vide supra* p. 102 (**Pl. IV, 11**).

[307] *NNM* 6, 1921, pp. 37, ff.

(g) *Inanimate objects.* A small collection of miscellaneous types completes our survey. These include a trophy flanked by two captives (Constantine I: VIRTVS AVGVSTI);[308] a galley with five rowers and the Emperor seated at the stern, while either Victory or two standards are seen at the prow (Constantinopolis: VICTORIA AVG; Constantine II as Caesar: same legend); three vexilla in a row (Constantine II as Caesar: FIDIS [*sic*] MILITVM); and the legend CAESAR within a wreath (Constantine II).[309]

[308] G II, p. 136, no. 21. **Pl. XXXVIII, 10.**

[309] For vota inscriptions with or without encircling wreaths *vide supra* p. 83.

PART V

MEDALLIONS AND IMPERIAL LIFE

CHAPTER I

MEDALLIONS AND POLITICS

The significance of the role assigned to Roman medallions in political life should be already apparent from our chapters on the occasions of their issue, the character of their recipients and the successive phases of their historical development. In this chapter we shall consider their specific function as vehicles of political propaganda and review the objects to which they were, as such, directed. This propaganda was of two main kinds. Some types were strictly topical; they were meant to drive home a special point or to ventilate the issuing authority's version of a particular situation. But the large majority of types were designed to emphasize and reiterate certain general and permanent aspects of imperial rule. They were a continual restatement, varying from age to age, of the bases upon which the imperial system rested and of the aims which it set itself to fulfil. Even in the days of its greatest security and stability in the second century, and still more so during the crises of the third, the Roman Empire could never escape the urge to self-advertisement. "Totalitarian," omni-competent, an end in itself, the imperial state lacked the serenity and assurance which spring from a government's acceptance of a Supreme Being utterly "other" than itself, transcending it, maintaining it and claiming its complete allegiance. In a truly Christian state propaganda—apart from the "propagatio Fidei"—is superfluous. But in the officially Christian Rome of the fourth and fifth centuries the pagan tradition of imperial propaganda was still so strong that the Christian Emperors could not break away from it. If they have "put off" the gods of the old religion, they have not, apart from their display of certain Christian symbols—labarum,[1] cross and monogram, as yet "put on" the God of the new, so far, at least, as numismatics are concerned. It is still their own power, their own prowess, their own achievements which their types advertise, and that in the name, not of God, but of Eternal Rome. Thus as instruments of propaganda Roman medallions present throughout their history one continuous stream of tradition; and among the select circles of their cultured, highly-placed on high-born recipients they accomplished, on more intensive and specialized lines, much the same work as that performed among the masses by the regular coinage and by public monuments. It is this specialized aspect of their work for the imperial department of propaganda which gives medallions their distinctive interest.

By far the most striking instance of imperial propaganda through the medium of medallions is that of Antoninus Pius' series of Roman history types, struck in connection with the nine-hundredth anniversary of the foundation of Rome. The actual scenes there portrayed have been described in detail in an earlier chapter.[2]

[1] For the Constantinian labarum adorned with discs representing precious stones and symbolizing the sky see Rostovtzeff, *JRS* 1942, p. 104.

[2] *Vide supra* pp. 143 ff.

Our concern here is with the political significance of the issue and the dates of their "release." It is, of course, a commonplace that Pius did not wholly share the philhellenic and cosmopolitan tastes of his predecessor Hadrian and that his interests lay mainly in Rome and Italy and in his efforts to arouse enthusiasm for the "national" religion and for ancient Roman and Italian legend and history.[3] His zeal for such things found a natural outlet in the splendor of his "Birthday of Rome" celebrations in 147.[4] The bronze medallions, with their wealth of mythological, historical and artistic interest, not only cast a vivid light upon the strength of Pius' own antiquarian tastes and on his determination to kindle similar tastes among official circles, but they also yield independent evidence as to the extent of his preparations for the great occasion and as to his method of underlining its importance as a "national" event. The campaign was launched in the first year of the reign, in 139, with the issue of a medallion reproducing a Hadrianic reverse type (sow and young etc.). Six types combined with Pius' own portrait on the obverse are dated COS III, i. e. 140 to 144, and a seventh, struck for Marcus Aurelius as Caesar, bears the date of the latter's second consulship, i. e. 145 to 146. All were, therefore, "programme" pieces, anticipating the event, in the majority of cases, by several years, heralding an occasion which did not inspire the medallists, but which the medallists, in a sense, themselves inspired. There is nothing against the supposition that the four types issued posthumously for Faustina I also appeared soon after her death, between the years 141 and 144. Again, the two COS IIII medallions with Pius' portrait, struck between 145 and 147, may, like Marcus' 145 to 146 piece, have anticipated the actual celebrations by at least a year. A second piece of Marcus, dated TR P, may have been struck for his reception of the tribunician power early in 147. Thus, during the eight years which elapsed between Pius' accession and the anniversary, the imperial propagandist released at intervals a series of magnificent presentation pieces, designed to excite the imagination of those who received them and to stir their pride in the glorious past of Rome. It has been suggested[5] that the two SABINAE types of Faustina I had a special *Tendenz* of their own: the type of the rape of the Sabine women was part of a "drive" to revive the ancient custom by which young Romans "raped" their *fiancées* from the arms of their mothers on the eve of the marriage;[6] while the scene of their intervention in the battle was to be an exhortation to conjugal love. Finally we must include among the "Birthday of Rome" propaganda pieces two more medallions of Pius' third consulship with the types of Tiberis,[7] the "deus Tiberinus senior" of the *Aeneid*,[8] and of Italia, enthroned, with mural crown, sceptre and cornucopiae, upon a great star-bespangled globe as the sovereign province.[9]

Among the numerous medallion types commemorating success in war, there

[3] It should, however, be noted that the wide range and variety of Pius' Greek mythology medallion types (*vide supra* pp. 142 f. and *infra* pp. 215–218) reveal a capacity for combining "national" predilections with a genuinely Hadrianic philhellenism.

[4] Sexti Aurelii Victoris, *Liber de Caesaribus* 15, 4:—"celebrato magnifice urbis nongentesimo."

[5] *Vjesnik* 1928.

[6] Plutarch, *Vita Romuli* 15.

[7] G III, tav. 160, no. 2.

[8] viii, 31.

[9] G II, tav. 45, no. 10.

are some which suggest propagandist implications of a special character. It would seem, for example, that the imposing bronze medallions of Antoninus Pius and of Commodus with types of Africa reclining at the foot of a trophy, which Victory erects in the Emperor's presence[10] were designed with a view to making the most of the somewhat insignificant operations in Mauretania in reigns undistinguished by warlike achievements of the first rank.[11] Similarly, Commodus' fine Britannia medallion[12] was struck to enhance the import of the British rising and of the punitive expedition under Marcellus Ulpius which suppressed it.[13] The issue of a Germania capta type by Domitian on silver medallions of 85[14] hints at an effort to convince sceptical aristocratic circles in Rome of the permanent results to be expected from the German campaigns.[15] Again, Marcus Aurelius' bronze medallion, struck in 172 to 173, with the type of Juppiter in his chariot hurling his bolt at a German foe presents the northern wars as a veritable "crusade" of the forces of religion and civilization against the powers of evil and barbarism.[16] Gordian III's types of the Emperor, crowned by Victory, offering sacrifice to Sol (PAX AETERNA)[17] and, crowned by Virtus, receiving a globe from Sol (VIRTVS AVGVSTI)[18] suggest the submission of the entire Orient to Rome as a result of the victories of 243. Victorinus' successful usurpation in Gaul in 267 to 268 appears in the light, not of rebellion against Rome, but of the restoration of the Gallic provinces from the danger of barbarian incursions (RESTITVTORI GALLIARVM);[19] while the overthrow of Allectus and of Carausius' "British Empire" by Constantius Chlorus in 296 is shown on the famous Arras medallion as the restoration of Britain, through the Emperors' compassion (PIETAS AVGG), to the Empire and to Rome's "eternal light" (REDDITOR LVCIS AETERNAE).[20] Again, Constans' grandiose VICTORIA AVGVSTI NOSTRI medallion, if struck for the Sarmatian victories of 338, may well have been issued with the ulterior motive of impressing his fraternal mentor, Constantine II.[21]

Fortuna Redux types of a blatantly propagandist kind were struck for Commodus and Albinus for the occasion of imperial "home-comings," well in advance of these auspicious events, which never actually took place.[22] The suppression by medallic propaganda of part, at least, of the truth may be illustrated by Gallienus' GALLIENVS AVG OB FIDEM RESERVATAM gold multiple, possibly struck in 262 to 263. Gallienus' new cavalry corps commanded by Aureolus had in that year been within an ace of mutiny when it refused to give chase to Postumus, while refraining from an open breach with imperial authority. Yet, if that be indeed the occasion of this

[10] G II, tavv. 45, no. 7; 47, nos. 1, 2; 78, no. 5.

[11] *Vita Pii* 5, 4; Pausanias viii, 43, 3; *Vita Commodi* 13, 5.

[12] G II, tav. 78, no. 2.

[13] Dio 73, 8. *Cf. Vita Commodi* 8, 4:—"appellatus est Commodus etiam Britannicus ab adulatoribus."

[14] G I, tav. 21, no. 1.

[15] *Cf.* J. M. C. Toynbee, *The Hadrianic School*, pp. 88 ff.

[16] G II, tav. 60, no. 1. *Cf. supra* p. 182.

[17] G II, tav. 104, nos. 7, 8.

[18] G I, tav. 24, no. 3; II, tav. 106, nos. 8, 9 (**Pl. XLV, 1**).

[19] G II, tav. 116, no. 9. For the view that this version of the Gallic Empire was really the true one see A. N. Sherwin White, *The Roman Citizenship*, pp. 277 ff.

[20] *Aréthuse*, Jan., 1924, pls. 7; 8, nos. 5, 6 (**Pl. VIII, 4, 5, 6**). *Cf.* Sherwin White, *op. cit.*, p. 280.

[21] *ZN* 1898, S. 57 f (**Pl. XLVIII, 8**).

[22] *Vide supra* p. 104.

medallion, the Emperor congratulates himself on the retention of their loyalty without a hint as to how near he came to losing it altogether.[23]

The momentous change effected by the foundation of the New Rome at Byzantium was an obvious occasion for medallic propaganda. The PIETAS AVGVSTI N and PIETAS AVGVST NOSTRI gold multiples, struck by Constantine I in his own name and in that of Constantius II, commemorate the essential preliminaries to the whole enterprise, namely the defeat of Licinius at Chrysopolis in September, 324, which left Constantine supreme in the East. The city is rescued from the enemy and "restored" through the Emperor's compassion, so that she may begin her new life as Constantinople.[24] Constantine's silver multiples with the city enthroned in state on the reverse show his later, long-haired portrait on the obverse and must date from the solemn consecration of Constantinople on May 11, 330.[25] Propagandist, too, in character are the parallel series of Roma and Constantinopolis types struck by Constantine I in the first instance and continued by his successors.[26] The Emperors are at pains to assure Old Rome that the appearance of a partner in the East will detract nothing from her past glory or diminish her present prestige. Constantine's bronze series with busts of the cities as obverse types show Constantinopolis assimilated to Roma by her helmet and distinguished from her by her sceptre alone. Roma's reverse types show her time-honored symbol, the wolf and twins; those of Constantinopolis, with victory as their dominant note, suggest insistence on the victory at Chrysopolis, preceding her foundation, which united East with West. In the gold type of the cities seated side by side Roma is frontal, while Constantinopolis turns deferentially towards her sister. The fine gold pieces with Constantinopolis seated towards the left are balanced by the equally splendid pieces with Roma enthroned to the front. Nor is it without significance that the last Roma type of our whole series, that of Attalus, the puppet Emperor installed by the Goths on the throne of the West, bears the exultant legend INVICTA ROMA AETERNA.

Dynastic problems, the perpetual preoccupation of successive Emperors, were among the most constant objects of imperial propaganda; and in this medallions in particular took their full share. We have already noted the elaborate types in which Antoninus Pius, son of an Emperor and father of an Emperor by adoption, and Marcus Aurelius, Pius' adopted son, anxiously recorded Faustina II's numerous confinements, eager to reverse the principle to which they owed their succession to the Empire in favor of the hereditary principle which saddled the world with Commodus;[27] and as heir Commodus is presented to the troops on medallions of Lucius Verus.[28] Similarly, the design struck for Faustina II and Lucilla, in which Venus presents Lucilla-Spes with statuettes of the three Graces, symbols of conjugal fertility, is a propaganda type announcing in more general terms the prospect of heirs of the Emperor's own blood.[29] Propagandist, too, in a special sense are the retro-

[23] *Vide supra* p. 113.
[24] *Vide supra* p. 183.
[25] G II, tavv. 74, no. 1; 75, no. 10 (**Pl. XLII, 4**).
[26] G I, tav. 28, nos. 11, 12, 13 (**Pl. XXXVII, 9**).
[27] *Vide supra* pp. 98 ff.
[28] *Vide supra* pp. 187 f.
[29] *Vide supra* p. 97.

spective FECVNDITATI AVG medallions of Julia Domna, issued as part of Septimius Severus' dynastic programme in 196.[30] Nor did Constantine I fail to exploit medallions for the furtherance of his dynastic schemes when he founded an imperial House and arranged for the Empire's apportionment, after his death, among his children. Not only did "birthday" medallions advertise the arrival of the children (Constantius II and Constans) born to him by Fausta,[31] but two notable series of gold pieces, one running from 317 (?) to the spring of 326, the other from 326 to 335, honored the Emperor's sons at significant moments in his and their careers. The earlier series consists mainly of small multiples with confronted busts of two of the youthful Caesars on the reverse: with two exceptions all bear Constantine's own portrait on the obverse. One type, struck at Siscia, shows Crispus and Constantine II in military dress (CRISPVS ET CONSTANTINVS IVN NOBB CAESS):[32] it might be assigned to 317, when both boys received the title of Caesar. A second type of the same Caesars, again in military dress (NOBB CAESS), must be later than November, 324, as it bears the mint-mark CONS.[33] A third type of these Caesars, struck at Nicomedia, depicts them in consular dress (CRISPVS ET CONSTANTINVS NOBB CAESS):[34] it may date from 320, when Constantine II held his first consulship, Crispus having already been consul in 318. The fourth type, struck at Antioch and Sirmium, can be dated exactly to New Year's Day, 321, for its legend reads CRISPVS ET CONSTANTINVS NOBB CAESS COSS II:[35] both Caesars are shown in consular dress, as also on a contemporary 1½-solidi piece, struck at Sirmium, with their busts on the obverse (CRISPVS ET CONSTANTINVS NOBB CAESS COSS II) and VOT/V on a shield upheld by two Victories on the reverse.[36] A Nicomedian 2-solidi piece of Constantine I shows Crispus and Constantius II, the former in consular, the latter in military, costume (CRISPVS ET CONSTANTIVS NOBB CAESS):[37] we may date it to November 8, 324, when Constantius was made Caesar, Crispus being consul for the third time that year. A type struck at Antioch with Constantine II and Constantius II both in consular dress dates from 326, when Constantius held his first consulship (CONSTANTINVS ET CONSTANTIVS NOBB CAESS):[38] its contemporary, a bronze "strike" with the mint-mark of Nicomedia, has the bust of Constantius in consular dress on the obverse and on the reverse (CRISPVS ET CONSTANTIVS NOBB CAESS) Crispus, the larger bust on the left, as consul and Constantius, the smaller bust on the right, arrayed, somewhat oddly not in consular, but in military, costume.[39] The most interesting type of this series shows Crispus in consular robes on the obverse and on the reverse Fausta, facing the spectator, with her arms round the shoulders of two boys in liturgical dress, who stand clasping hands (FELIX PROGENIES

[30] *Vide supra* p. 100.
[31] *Vide supra* pp. 101 f.
[32] G I, tav. 8, no. 14.
[33] G I, tav. 29, no. 10 = silvered bronze "strike" from gold medallion dies. For a variant of this type with uncertain mint-mark, also on a bronze "strike," see *Trau Collection Sale Catalogue* 1935, Taf. 46, Nr. 3969 (Pl. V, 2).
[34] G III, tav. di suppl., no. 12.
[35] *NZ* 1930, Taf. 2, Nr. 6 = 2-solidi piece with mint-mark SMAN; *Trau Collection Sale Catalogue* 1935, Taf. 46, Nr. 3970 = 4½-solidi piece with mint-mark SIRM (Pl. XXXI, 6).
[36] G I, tav. 9, no. 10.
[37] G I, tav. 8, no. 13.
[38] G I, tav. 8, no. 15.
[39] *Vide supra* p. 179, note 177.

CONSTANTINI AVG).[40] The boys on the reverse must be Constantine II and Constantius II, united in fraternal harmony with each other and with their brother of the obverse, since all three alike are the Emperor's "happy offspring." The piece was presumably struck for Constantius' elevation to the rank of Caesar in 324, the year of Crispus' third consulship. It bears the mint-mark of Trier and must, as Lederer has pointed out, be the work of the same medallist who designed Constantine I's INNVMERI TRIVMFI Treviran gold medallion.[41]

The importance attached by Constantine to his "felix progenies," his insistence upon the fact that on their peaceful and unchallenged succession to imperial power the whole future of the Empire depends—its felicitas, salus and spes, its gaudium and securitas, is still more vividly illustrated by the family group types of the second dynastic series, struck on large gold medallions, some in his own name, others in that of his sons. Types belonging to the period of two Caesars only, from Crispus' death to 333, show Constantine, nimbate and wearing liturgical dress, enthroned to the front, while Constantine II and Constantius II stand in military dress on either side of him. The pieces (all worth 9 solidi) displaying the earlier Constantinian portrait, with short hair on the nape of the neck, may be assigned to the culminating vicennalia celebrations of July 25, 326 (Constantine I: FELICITAS PERPETVA AVG ET CAESS NN, mint-mark SMN,[42] SALVS ET SPES REIPVBLICAE, mint-mark CONS;[43] Constantine II: FELICITAS PERPETVA AVG ET CAESS NN, mint-marks SMN,[44] CONS).[45] The pieces (all worth 9 solidi) depicting the later portrait, with long hair on the neck, may have been issued for the solemn consecration of Constantinople on May 11, 330 (Constantine I: SALVS ET SPES REIPVBLICAE, mint-mark CONS;[46] Constantine II: same legend and mint-mark;[47] Constantius II: same legend and mint-mark).[48] On December 25, 333 Constans attained the rank of Caesar. To this date we may ascribe the 9-solidi piece struck for Constans, with the type of Constantine I, standing, grouped with Constantine II, Constantius II and the new Caesar on the reverse (SECVRITAS PERPETVA, mint-mark CONS),[49] and the great 30-solidi medallion from Szilágy-Sómlyó struck for Constantius II, with reverse type showing Constantine standing between Constantine II, crowned by Victory, and the little Constans, crowned by Virtus (GAVDIVM ROMANORVM, mint-mark M CONS).[50] Finally, for Delmatius' promotion to the rank of Caesar on September 18, 335 were presumably issued the two 9-solidi pieces with the type of Constantine enthroned with his four sons grouped around him, one struck in the

[40] Delbrück, *op. cit.*, Taf. 5, Nr. 4 (**Pl. XXXI, 8**).

[41] *ZN* 1928, S. 67; Taf. 3, Nr. 3 (**Pl. IV, 3**).

[42] *RN* 1906, pl. 7, nos. 1 (= obv.), 2 (= rev.). Lost from Paris (**Pl. V, 5**).

[43] *Ibid.*, p. 490, fig. 1. In The Hague (**Pl. V, 6**). The bronze piece in Paris with this type and legend, but with different obverse (laurel-wreath, consular dress, but the same short hair) and the mint-mark PR (G II, tav. 130, no. 5) may be a "strike" from a lost gold piece.

[44] *RN* 1906, pl. 7, no. 3. Lost from Paris (**Pl. V, 7**).

[45] Cast in Berlin. Lost from Paris. **Pl. XXXIX, 1.**

[46] *RN* 1906, pl. 7, nos. 2 (= obv.) 1 (= rev.). Lost from Paris (**Pl. V, 4**).

[47] Cast in Berlin. Lost from Paris. **Pl. XXXIX, 2.**

[48] *RN* 1906, pl. 8, no. 4. Lost from Paris (**Pl. VI, 1**).

[49] G I, tav. 10, no. 2.

[50] G I, tav. 12, no. 1.

Emperor's own name (SALVS ET SPES REIPVBLICAE, mint-mark TSE),[51] the other in that of Constantius II (SECVRITAS PERPETVA, mint-mark CONS).[52]

The dynastic tradition inherent in these family group *motifs* was continued by Constantine's sons after his death. The three brothers, Constantine II, Constantius II and Constans, stand in a row to the front, Constantine II in the centre, each in military dress (Constantius II: SALVS ET SPES REIPVBLICAE, mint-mark TES;[53] Constans: same legend and mint-mark).[54] Two seated types of the three Augusti are interesting examples of propaganda and counter-propaganda within the family circle. Both bear the legend FELICITAS PERPETVA / VOT V and are combined with Constans' portrait on the obverse. The earlier of the two, struck in silver at Siscia, shows the three all wearing liturgical dress. Constantine II is enthroned in the centre, nimbate and frontal, on a dais, his right hand raised to give the imperial "benediction," while his two brothers, seated on either side at a lower level, have no nimbi and gaze, not to the front, at the spectator, but inwards at their senior.[55] The scene vividly reflects the predominant position which Constantine II had acquired over his brothers at the time of the congress at Viminacium held in the summer of 338. It was for this congress, no doubt, that our piece was issued, with a secondary reference to Constans' coming quinquennalia celebrations. In the second type, struck in gold at Thessalonica, all three are seated at the same level on a long, high-backed seat and all gaze straight out before them.[56] Constantine II has no nimbus and gives no "benediction"; and whereas he wears liturgical dress, Constantius II and Constans appear in consular costume. The type may be assigned to December 25, 338, when Constans, celebrating his quinquennalia, was already beginning to free himself from the fraternal leading-strings: the consular dress worn by him and by Constantius points to their impending entry upon their joint consulship on January 1, 339. The dynastic *motif* appears once more as propaganda for the House of Valentinian on two gold pieces struck for Valens. One shows Valentinian I and Valens, each nimbate and robed in liturgical dress, seated side by side on a high-backed throne with their feet on footstools (GLORIA ROMANORVM, mint-mark R M).[57] The other depicts Valentinian I standing nimbate and frontal in the centre, while Valens and Gratian stand, turning towards him, on either side: all three wear military dress (PIETAS DDD NNN AVGVSTORVM, mint-mark TESOB).[58]

So far we have considered medallion types which served as media for specific objects of imperial propaganda. We must now turn to types of a more general kind whereby the government sought to advertise the principles on which it claimed to rule and the amenities which it promised to the peoples living under its aegis.

[51] In Leningrad See *Comptes rendus de l'Académie des Sciences de l'URSS* 1929. **Pl. XXXIX, 3.**

[52] In Königsberg. *BM* 1923, Taf. 264, Nr. 13 (**Pl. VI, 5**).

[53] *ZN* 1898, Taf. 3, Nr. 7. Lost from Paris. **Pl. XXXIX, 4.**

[54] G I, tav. 9, no. 14.

[55] G I, tav. 30, no. 2. *Cf.* "Fest-aureus" in Jameson Collection, Paris (*vide supra* p. 40 and note 142) (**Pl. III, 7**).

[56] G I, tav. 9, no. 11.

[57] G I, tav. 18, no. 1 (364 to 367).

[58] G I, tavv. 16, no. 3; 18, no. 2 (367 to 375).

These may be described as imperial virtues on the one hand and imperial blessings on the other.

First in the list of "imperial virtues" comes virtus, "virtue" itself, the Emperor's own capacity for prowess and bravery in war. The earliest medallic advertisements of this imperial quality are the types depicting the Emperor as hunting lion or boar (Hadrian, Marcus Aurelius as Caesar, Lucius Verus, Commodus); later the symbolic beast is exchanged for an actual human enemy; or the VIRTVS legend accompanies the figure of the Emperor, either alone or grouped with other persons, portrayed in military dress and with military attributes and *entourage* (third- and fourth-century types *passim*). Volusianus is shown sacrificing in honor of the virtus shared by himself with his colleague, Trebonianus Gallus (VIRTVS AVGVSTORVM). Other types show Virtus herself personified (Marcus Aurelius, Constantine I, Constantius II as Caesar). Concordia in the sense of imperial unity (as distinguished from conjugal unity) is advertised by an allegorical figure personifying the virtue (Gallienus, Claudius Gothicus, Aurelian), by a scene in which imperial colleagues clasp one another by the hand (Marcus Aurelius and Lucius Verus) or by twin or triple busts of members of the reigning House (Philip I etc., Valerian, Gallienus etc.). Pietas, embracing alike the loving service of the gods and family affection, its earthly counterpart, appears in the guise of an allegorical figure (Antoninus Pius, Marcus Aurelius as Caesar, Commodus, Julia Mamaea, Salonina) or of two or three family portraits on obverse or reverse (Philip I etc., Trajan Decius etc., Valerian etc.) or of a mythological scene (Gallienus and Salonina). Empresses set an example of pudicitia to the women of the Empire (Julia Mamaea, Etruscilla, Salonina, Magnia Urbica). Clementia is enjoined on a bronze piece of Marcus Aurelius, portrayed as pardoning a suppliant foe. Liberalitas and munificentia as imperial qualities are advertised not only by scenes of largess, but also by objects symbolic of public games and shows—lion, gladiators (?), tensa (Antoninus Pius), or by places of public recreation and entertainment erected at the imperial expense—thermae, Colosseum, circus (Alexander Severus etc., Gordian III).

The "Happy New Year" medallions discussed at length in an earlier chapter[19] present a whole galaxy of imperial blessings—felicitas, abundantia, uberitas, agricultural prosperity as a result of the Emperor's providentia, plentiful food supplies symbolized by types of Ceres grouped with Annona, Securitas or the Emperor or by a corn ship making for port. Among other blessings none was more earnestly desired by the Roman world than securitas and none was more persistently promised in medallic propaganda, where this blessing appears, now personified (Hadrian, Faustina I, Commodus, Probus, Helena, Constantine I, Crispus, Constans, Magnentius), now incarnate in the person of the Emperor or Caesar (Constantine I, Constantine II as Caesar, Constantius II as Caesar, Arcadius). Pax, so common a figure on the current coinage is, perhaps for this very reason, promised but rarely on medallions (Trajan, Alexander Severus, Gordian III, Gallienus, Constantine II). Spes (apart from "hope of offspring") is offered by Alexander Severus and Heren-

[19] *Vide supra*, Part III, Ch. I.

nius; libertas by Gallienus, Magnentius and Decentius; gaudium by Constans and Jovian; hilaritas, coupled with salus, by Commodus. Salus, the Roman counterpart of Hygieia, is a complicated conception. In the second and early third centuries she seems to symbolize the personal health of the Emperor, or of members of his family, on which the health of the state in a sense depends; one type shows a devotee making offerings at her shrine. Later she appears to stand more directly for public health (e. g. Saloninus, SALVS VRBIS); while in the fourth century "salus reipublicae" is a general term for the Empire's well-being secured by military success or by the provision of heirs to the imperial throne or embodied in an imperial personage (e. g. Galla Placidia). Victory, glory and triumph are themes too common to require illustration. Financial stability and abundant supplies of currency are promised, often vainly, by the Tres Monetae pieces of the third and early fourth centuries. Lastly, a general restoration of the Empire is advertised by the type of the Emperor raising up the kneeling figure of Respublica, accompanied by the slogan RESTITVTOR REIPVBLICAE, on medallions of Tacitus, Valens, Gratian, Valentinian II and Theodosius.

CHAPTER II

MEDALLIONS AND RELIGION

The study of Roman religion has probably suffered more than any other branch of Roman studies from the presuppositions and prejudices of modern critics. In their unquestioning acceptance of the dogmas of agnosticism and unbelief, many of these critics are unable to envisage an educated and practical mind unreservedly convinced of the existence and operation of supernatural powers.[1] Thus their approach to the Graeco-Roman pantheon of the Empire starts from the assumption that its denizens must be anything but what the ancient sources declare them to be, namely divine personalities belief in whom could genuinely affect the thought and actions of intelligent men. To the majority, perhaps, the gods are popular superstitions devoid of any reality or true religious significance for the upper strata of Roman society, skilfully manipulated by imperial authority for purposes of propaganda among the ignorant masses. To others they are survivals from an age of primitive agricultural economy, long since outmoded and obsolete in late republican and imperial times, but artificially conserved by the governing, land-monopolizing classes, with all their paraphernalia of cult and ritual, as "dope" for the proletariate.[2] At the best the gods could be interpreted away philosophically as metaphors or allegories for the benefit of enlightened sceptics, who could then be expected to lend unqualified support to the political exploitation of traditional beliefs. The theory of philosophic interpretation has, however, recently been exposed by Altheim as lacking foundation.[3] Again, the "opium of the people" theory (of transparent origin) is unsubstantiated by the ancient evidence;[4] while it ignores the obvious fact that the urban communities of later days were no less really dependent upon the rural, food-producing areas (and their gods) throughout the Empire than were the early Italic village communities upon their neighboring countryside. It might be argued that the strong religious element in "popular" official art, in coin types and public monuments, could reflect piety among the masses coexisting with scepticism among the cultured classes. But the permeation by religion of literature and works of art written and executed in the first instance expressly for these cultured classes,

[1] *Cf. BMCCRE* IV, pp. xxv, xxvii.

[2] E. g. B. Farrington, *Science and Politics in the Ancient World* (1939), p. 160 on the "police function of religion."

[3] *A History of Roman Religion*, pp. 372 ff.

[4] In his chapter on Lucretius, Farrington (*op. cit.*, pp. 172 ff.) makes an unconvincing attempt to distinguish between "the superstition of the little people" which was not the object of the poet's attack, and "the organized religion of the great," which was. But Lucretius himself draws no such class-distinctions. His polemic is directed against the tales of popular mythology and what he regarded as superstitious practices wherever and by whomever they were believed and practiced; and while he himself labels all "religio" as "superstitio," he nowhere states that the governing classes deliberately "labelled *superstitio* as *religio* for the consumption of the masses."

for persons of education and of high position, is a fact fatal to the theory which would draw a line of division between the sceptical upper, and credulous lower, sections of the population. It is here that Roman medallions, works of art designed as personal gifts for selected individuals, can make an important contribution to our understanding of the religious situation under the Empire. If the Graeco-Roman pantheon inspired no real religious sentiments in such persons, it is hard to see why the gods and their cults figure so prominently in medallic reverse types of all periods prior to 313. It is true that these types have often an artistic interest additional to, and, in a sense, detachable from, their devotional content. But we cannot suppose that all the recipients of pieces with religious types were specialists in Greek sculpture and painting or professional connoisseurs. Moreover the religious element is, in general, too closely linked with the person of the Emperor or with matters of imperial import for a purely antiquarian interpretation of these types to carry conviction. In Augustus' religious observances as described by Suetonius there is expressed, so Altheim maintains,[5] "a genuine *religio*," a belief, that is to say, in ties binding man to the gods and the gods to man. "There is not a word," he continues, "to suggest that any kind of speculative interpretation was applied to the Palatine Apollo or to his sister or to the deities of the Capitol"; they are "divine powers, figures of the religious domain and of no other."[6] If their domain is not that of philosophy, neither is it that of disingenuous and cynical propaganda. The gods are not Augustus' political puppets, but his prototypes and patrons, and acknowledged as such. And it is to a real belief in divine protection and patronage that the religious medallion types issued by the "new Augusti" from Trajan to Constantine bear witness. What gave the Romans their "drive and irresistible power" was the "consciousness of being the forerunners of *fatum* and thus the builders of an order and an Empire, the erection of which had been willed by the gods themselves."[7] For this idea as worked out in successive reigns there is evidence in plenty on Roman medallions. Each Emperor is at pains to declare himself the faithful minister of *fatum*, "the word of the gods." But this implies a living faith in the gods and in Rome's divine mission in the hearts of those for whom these types were designed.

The unreservedly religious atmosphere in which the great public celebrations of imperial Rome were conducted pervades the medallions issued as gifts to be distributed on such occasions. New Year ceremonies, whether calendar or regnal, are commemorated by depicting the actual vota themselves, scenes of imperial sacrifice, with or without a temple façade as background. Senatorial vota offered for the Emperor's "intention" are chosen as types for pieces presented on the occasion of his departure from Rome. And, again, it is the solemn moment of sacrifice

[5] Altheim, *op. cit.*, p. 375.

[6] Farrington (*op. cit.*, p. 224) joins issue with Altheim for his "habit of assuming the objective truth of ancient religious beliefs," so that "critics have suspected him . . . of literally accepting the existence of the pagan deities of Greece and Rome." Such criticism is, of course, absurd. Altheim's point is, not that he himself accepts the existence of the gods, but that Augustus, Vergil, Horace and other educated Romans literally did.

[7] Altheim, *op. cit.*, p. 428.

to the gods which is most often chosen for portrayal on medallions issued for "Birthday of Rome" and Ludi Saeculares festivities. Victories, too, are not seldom recorded by scenes of imperial sacrifice offered in thanksgiving. Of medallion types struck for Empresses one of the finest is that which shows a group of Vestals sacrificing before the circular temple of Vesta, symbol *par excellence* of the religious basis of the Roman state. Of other types the main *motif* is the temple itself—of Diva Matidia (Hadrian), of Bacchus (Antoninus Pius), of Juppiter Victor (Alexander Severus), of Victoria Augusta (Gordian III), of Apollo (Philip I etc.), of Spes Publica (Herennius), of Juno Martialis (Trebonianus Gallus etc.) and of Divus Romulus (Romulus)—or a series of sacrificial implements and symbols—knife, apex, simpulum, lituus, patera, jug, bucranium and sprinkler.

But it is the great series of types of the gods themselves which make the chief medallic contribution to the study of religion in imperial times. All the known types of deities, male and female, have been briefly described in our chapters on historical development. Their artistic aspect will be studied in our last chapter. In the present chapter we propose to review the medallic evidence for the Emperors' attitude towards, and relations with, the divine powers under whose patronage they placed themselves through tradition, circumstances or personal choice.

Preëminent among these heavenly patrons is Juppiter Optimus Maximus of the Capitol. It is no accident that the earliest numismatic representation of the Capitoline Triad in imperial times[8] should appear upon a medallion of Trajan, who adopted Juppiter's own cognomen "Optimus" and on whose arch at Beneventum Juppiter, accompanied by Juno, Minerva and other Italian deities, delegates his fulmen, the symbol of his divine authority, to the Emperor, his vicar or vice-gerent on earth.[9] This appeal to the protection of Rome's time-honored Triad recurs on one medallion of every reign from Hadrian to Commodus. As vicar of Juppiter the Emperor was entitled to display the god's own attributes, aegis and sceptre, in his obverse portraits; while the very number of Juppiter types—sixty in all—depicted on reverses down to Constantine's conversion in itself bears witness to the closeness of the tie which linked the Father of Gods and Men with his earthly counterpart, the imperial Pater Patriae. Some of these types deserve special comment in our present context. The belief in a special protection exercised by Juppiter over the imperial person is vividly expressed in the design, first struck under Hadrian, showing the god standing with fulmen and mantle extended over the Emperor's head, while the legend IOVI CONSERVATORI sometimes accompanies the scene. The same legend appears on a bronze piece of Alexander Severus and Julia Mamaea, with the type of the Emperor sacrificing to his preserver. During the troubled times of the Empire's great crises in the third century, from Maximinus to Carinus and Numerianus, faith in Juppiter's patronage seems to have waned; for he vanishes almost completely from medallic reverse designs, though his attributes still figure in the obverse portraits. But the many and varied Juppiter types of Diocletian's revival hail the god once more as preserver of the Emperor—IOVI CONSERVATORI,

[8] *Cf.* Strack I, S. 197.

[9] E. Strong, *op. cit.*, p. 193, fig. 110. *Cf.* Pliny, *Paneg.* 80.

IOVI CONSERVATORI AVGG; the Emperors themselves are described as "Juppiter's and Hercules' own"—IOVIO ET HERCVLIO; and Moneta acknowledges her debt to the gods who, as it were, personally belong to the imperial reconstructors—MONETA IOVI ET HERCVLI AVGG. Similarly, the legends accompanying Juppiter types of Galerius, Maximinus Daza and the Licinii proclaim him as IOVI CONSERVATORI AVGG, IOVI CONS CAES and IOVI CONSERVATORI LICINIORVM AVG ET CAES. In their foreign wars, in their "crusade" against the forces of destruction and barbarism, the Emperors recognize in Juppiter their heavenly prototype and very present ally. From a quadriga Juppiter hurls his bolt at giant (Antoninus Pius) or German (Marcus Aurelius). He hands a Victory to Lucius Verus. He stands as the type of the young imperial warrior—IOVI IVVENI—beside an altar adorned with the scene of his giant-slaying (Commodus). He keeps the imperial armies faithful to their Emperor—FIDES EXERCITVS (Alexander Severus etc.). He is victor on the Emperors' behalf—IOVI VICTORI AVGG (Diocletian, Maximian). Again, he delegates to the Emperor world dominion, symbolized by a globe (Commodus)—world dominion which is to bring happiness to the Roman people—FELICITATI POPVL ROM (Alexander Severus)[10]—and which implies the perpetuity of imperial rule—PERPETVITAS IMP AVG (Alexander Severus). Conversely, the "perpetual happiness of the Emperors" (Diocletian and Maximian, PERPETVA FELICITAS AVGG) is sealed by Juppiter's acceptance of the world dominion, which their victories have secured, as willed by him (Juppiter receives a globe from the hands of Victory). When the first Tetrarchy was formed in 293 Juppiter and Hercules crown their *protégés*, each seated, globe in hand, in token of the fact that world empire is shared between them in unbroken harmony—PERPETVA CONCORDIA AVGG. The strongly personal character of the relationship between the divine and the earthly ruler is emphasized by Hadrian's piece with the legend IOVI OPTIMO MAXIMO S P Q R in an oak wreath—a type which can only mean that the Senate's and people's dedication to Juppiter was directed through the god to his imperial representative. So, too, it is possible that the horned head of Trajan's own particular Juppiter, the Phoenicio-Carthaginian Juppiter Ammon worshipped in his Spanish home, is portrayed on a small bronze medallion as an intermediary, so to speak, between the Emperor and Rome's highest god;[11] while a large bronze piece of Commodus shows the fusion of the two Juppiters completed—the horned Juppiter accompanied by the legend I O M. Lastly, in the scenes from Juppiter's childhood—Amalthea suckling the infant god (Hadrian) or carrying him on her back (Antoninus Pius)—we may see the Emperor, or his heir, in the guise of Juppiter Crescens, inaugurating a new Golden Age.[12]

Juppiter's consort, Juno, the second member of the Triad, is seen but rarely as a medallion type. On medallions of Salonina she appears as Juno Regina, the

[10] This legend is, however, not quite certain: it depends on a single specimen which has been much retouched.

[11] Strack I, S. 198.

[12] Strack, II, S. 108; III, S. 161. It has been suggested (*BMCCRE* IV, p. clxxx) that Commodus' medallion type of Juppiter enthroned between the Dioscuri refers to some eastern cult in which the sky-god was associated with the morning and evening stars.

Empress's patroness, in her own person or represented by her peacock. As Juno Martialis she is seated within a circular shrine on bronze and silver pieces of Trebonianus Gallus etc., perhaps as protectress of Gallus' Empress, Baebiana, in her capacity as Mater Castrorum.[13]

When Minerva, the third member of the Triad, appears without her colleagues as an independent type, it is not so much the Roman goddess of the Capitol as the Greek Athene who confronts us as imperial patroness. We see her first as the Emperor's patroness and ally in war, seated, fully armed, or advancing into battle and brandishing her spear, in the manner of Athene Promachos, on silver medallions of Domitian, her ardent devotee. So, too, in her role of warrior she rides armed upon a griffin (Marcus Aurelius as Caesar); she stands in full panoply, throwing grains of incense on a brazier in thanksgiving for victory (Marcus Aurelius as Caesar); she stands with Victory at an altar, on which her snake is coiled (Marcus Aurelius). As Athene Nikephoros she is seated alone (Commodus) or in a scene of imperial sacrifice (Commodus) or she stands beside a trophy, with the title MINER VICT (Commodus). As dispenser of peace after victory she plucks an olive-branch, hailed as "the Emperor's own"—MINER AVG (Commodus); or she is entitled "the peace-bringer"—MINER PACIF (Albinus). She is armed, again, when she makes her last appearance on medallions, standing or seated, on bronze pieces of Septimius Severus and Geta. More Roman, perhaps, in character are two types struck for Marcus Aurelius as Caesar. The first portrays her standing with the fulmen of her father in one hand and in the other a cornucopiae, symbol of the material blessings which the Emperor wins for his people by her aid. In the second type she is seated with Athene's helmet and shield; but the back of her throne, on which her elbow rests, is formed by a cornucopiae and she feeds a snake twined around a tree; here again, as imperial benefactress, she bestows on the world three notable blessings—abundantia, salus and securitas. The mythological types of Minerva, struck for Hadrian, Antoninus Pius, Faustina I and Marcus Aurelius as Caesar, are frankly Greek in character. Two types which show Vulcan-Hephaistos forging arms in her presence may allude to war. But the other types cannot be definitely connected with contemporary events. Two of these illustrate the myth of Athene's contest with Poseidon on the Acropolis and were doubtless inspired in the first instance by Hadrian's visits to Athens;[14] while in another pair of types—Athene watching Prometheus at work and Athene superintending the building of the Argo—we may just possibly, perhaps, see allegories of the provident Emperor, toiling for his people under the aegis of his heavenly patroness.

As special protectors of the first Princeps, Apollo and Diana rank only second to the Capitoline Triad as patrons of his successors. Diana of Sicily, source of the victory at Naulochus, figures, indeed, on a gold piece struck for Augustus himself; it may be that he also issued a pendant multiple of Apollo Actius, which awaits discovery. Translated to the Palatine, the Augustan Apollo became the prototype of the Emperor as patron of culture and the arts: so he plays the lyre to a group of

[13] *CAH* xii, 167, note 5.

[14] *Vide infra* pp. 216 ff.

Muses (Hadrian) and advances, stands or sits, lyre in hand, as Apollo Citharoedus (Antoninus Pius, Marcus Aurelius, Commodus, Septimius Severus, Gordian III). Another important role played by the god as imperial patron is that of Apollo Salutaris, dispeller of plagues and purifier. Thus he stands with bow and branch (Hadrian), rides with bow and quiver upon a griffin (Antoninus Pius), leans upon Aesculapius' serpent-staff, flanked by laurel tree and thymiaterium (Antoninus Pius), stands with bow and quiver beside a table, or with patera beside an altar, flanked in both cases by a tree and a tripod, on which the dead Python, symbol of pestilence is deployed (Marcus Aurelius as Caesar). And, again, it is as god of healing that he is depicted on bronze pieces of Trebonianus Gallus and Volusianus, standing on a mountain-top with lustral branch and snake (ARNAZI). Diana appears on medallions of Hadrian as huntress, patroness of the Italian countryside, and as Diana Lucifera-Luna, with crescent and lighted torch. To Pius' special devotion to the gods of Italy we owe the charming series of rural Diana types, struck in his own name and in that of Faustina II, which portray her, not as huntress only, but in her ancient role as protectress of wild things. After the Antonine period there is little medallic evidence for personal devotion in imperial circles to the Augustan twins. Diana figures as rarely as her brother in third-century medallion types. As Diana-Luna she drives a bull-biga, with flying veil and crescent on brow (Caracalla); while Gallienus and Victorinus appeal to her, in her familiar role of huntress, as "felix" and "adiutrix," to bring them good luck and aid in troubled times.[15]

Venus, divine mother of the imperial race, ranks high as patroness of Emperors and Empresses alike; and it is as Venus Genetrix that she first confronts us on medallions of Hadrian (VENERI GENETRICI), where she is portrayed with the arms and Victory of Aeneas, precursor of Augustus and of all "new Augusti" after him. Similar armed types of Venus as bringer of luck or prosperity (VENVS FELIX) were struck for Faustina II, Lucilla, Crispina and Caracalla. As "Augustan Venus" (VENERI AVGVSTAE) she is shown with apple and sceptre, after the manner of Arkesilaos' famous statue (Faustina I). Grouped with Mars she stands for conjugal love in the Emperor's own family (Marcus Aurelius as Caesar, Faustina II, Commodus); while the numerous types of Faustina II and Lucilla, which show her alone, or with Cupid, or Cupids, or with Lucilla-Spes, the "hope of offspring," and the three Graces, symbols of fertility, mark her out as a model for Empresses in discharging the duties of motherhood. So, too, Julia Domna's "civilian" type of Venus Genetrix, seated unarmed, with sceptre and patera, points less to the mother of Aeneas than to Julia's own child-bearing. But when, a century later, Venus appears once more, and for the last time, as a medallion type, on a gold multiple of Galeria Valeria, she recalls the "Augustan Venus" by her apple and by her title, VENVS VICTRIX, the armed mother of Aeneas' victorious race.

Among other deities specially linked with Rome's early beginnings is Vesta,

[15] Constantine I's and Licinius' appeal to Apollo and Diana in the sculptured "medallions" of the Arch of Constantine is not reflected in their medallion types.

who appears but rarely on medallions as an object of personal cult. Her types are, in fact, confined to pieces struck for Faustina I, where she is shown as guardian of the Palladium and patroness of piety and chastity, no doubt as part of Pius' programme of preparation for the nine-hundredth anniversary of the "Birthday of Rome." Meanwhile the public sacrifices before her temple are recorded in medallion types of later Empresses. As "second founders" of Rome Hadrian and Commodus identify themselves with Romulus (ROMVLO CONDITORI); while Pius struck for Marcus Aurelius a type of Neptune standing before the walls and gates of Troy, prototype of the "new founder" of the "New Troy," Rome.[16]

Hercules, son of Juppiter by a mortal woman, the traveller and adventurer, the fellow-sufferer, benefactor and friend of man, was, perhaps, the best qualified of all deities for the role of a Roman Emperor's heavenly patron. To the generous appreciation of this fact by the Emperors themselves medallions bear striking witness. Hadrian was the first to issue an obverse portrait of himself with lion-skin hood; and a wide range of types of Hercules and his exploits adorn the reverses of medallions of Hadrian, Pius, Marcus Aurelius, Lucius Verus and Commodus. Commodus' series reached its climax in the great "New Year" group of the Emperor's eighteenth tribunician year, with their magnificent obverse portraits of Commodus in lion-skin hood, their rich variety of reverse designs and their legends—HERCVLI ROMANO, HERCVLI ROMANO AVGVSTO, HERCVLI ROMANO CONDITORI, which reveal the final stage in the evolution from Hercules as an independent deity (types of 184 to 185 and 186 to 189), through Hercules "Commodus' own" (HERC COMMODIANO, types of 190 to 191), to "the Roman Hercules" (types of 192 to 193), the complete identification of the Emperor with his god. Commodus' self-deification as Hercules profoundly shocked Roman religious sentiment. Though Septimius Severus paid honor to his African Hercules, it was more than half a century before a Roman Emperor ventured again to proclaim Hercules as his personal patron on medallions. When the god reappears as a medallion type under Gallienus and Postumus he is hailed as the source of imperial prowess—VIRTVS AVG, VIRTVS GALLIENI AVG—and as Postumus' divine companion—HERCVLI COMITI AVG, who deigns to appear on the obverse beside his devotee. Again, his labors are commemorated as prototypes of the Emperor's own toils—HERCVLI HERIMANTHIO (Probus). In a few of their obverse portraits both Gallienus and Probus wear the lion-skin hood. But this did not in itself involve actual identification with Hercules. In Hercules' last great epiphany on medallions of the Tetrarchy as protector of Maximian and Constantius Chlorus, as "opposite number" of Diocletian's and Galerius' Juppiter, the two Herculean Emperors naturally wear the lion-skin as his *protégés*. Yet god and human ruler are still kept clearly distinct. The god gives his name to the man, not the man to the god; and "Herculius" as applied to Maximian no more denotes identification with Hercules than "Iovius" denotes identification with Juppiter in

[16] *Cf.* the scene of Neptune and Apollo contemplating the walls of Troy on the Augustan patera from Fins d'Annecy (Butae), now at Geneva (M. Rostovtzeff, *Augustus*, pl. 3). But the authenticity of this patera, of which the present writer has not seen the original, is far from certain.

Diocletian's case.* Hercules is VICTOR and CONSERVATOR AVGG, cause of the Emperors' victories and their preserver. As he wrestled with the hydra long ago, so now he strikes down their foes (Maximian, HERCVLI DEBELLATORI); his slaying of the stag foreshadowed their prowess (Constantius Chlorus, VIRTVS AVGG).

Such were the great protectors on whom the Emperor relied for aid in his mighty task as "director general" of the Roman world, for the preservation of the Empire and for the perpetual renewal of the life of Rome as the Empire's centre and symbol. Further, there were the divine "experts," patrons of the special departments of imperial responsibility, whose cooperation is also acknowledged on medallions, particularly on those of our first phase. Foremost among his undertakings was that of ensuring the Empire's food supply. Each New Year's Day he renewed his promises for the year's annona, under Janus' auspices and with Ceres' aid, while Neptune guaranteed "omnia felicia" for the imperial corn ships. Mercury appears as patron of the Empire's trade and commerce; in one obverse portrait (Gallienus) the Emperor himself shoulders the god's caduceus. To Sol the Emperors of the second century turned for aid in bringing forth the fruits of the earth; and in their work for farming, agriculture and forestry they had recourse to the gods of the fields and woods—to Pan, to Silvanus and his kindred deities, to Hermes-Mercurius (?) as patron of flocks and herds and to the pastoral Apollo-Nomios (?).

"Fortunatus et ille deos qui novit agrestes,
Panaque Silvanumque senem Nymphasque sorores."[17]

Aesculapius safeguards public health (salus), for which the state of the Emperor's personal health is, in a sense, an omen for good or ill. The patrons of the imperial war department are obvious—Mars and Vulcan. The Dioscuri possibly figure as patrons of the Equites. Finally, the series of elaborate Bacchus types has been ingeniously referred to imperial interest in public recreation. The Emperor as Neos Dionysos is protector of the Dionysiac τεχνῖται who organized musical and gymnastic entertainments throughout the Empire.[18]

The company of oriental deities honored on Roman medallions is small by comparison with the great concourse of gods of the Graeco-Roman pantheon. Cybele and Isis, long since established, with temples and organized priesthoods, in Rome and Italy in response to popular pressure from below, are, indeed, fairly prominent as imperial patrons in second-century types (Cybele:—Hadrian, Sabina, Antoninus Pius,[19] Faustina I, Faustina II, Lucilla; Isis:—Hadrian, Faustina I, Faustina II). It is noteworthy that Cybele had already gained a place on medal-

* (See note at end of Chapter.)

[17] Vergil, *Georg.* ii, 493, 494. From the lines immediately preceding this couplet:—"Felix qui potuit rerum cognoscere causas,/atque metus omnes et inexorabile fatum/subiecit pedibus strepitumque Acherontis avari."—it is clear that Vergil did not consider knowledge of natural processes and the banishment of blind, unreasoning terror from religion to be incompatible with the worship of the traditional gods. The phraseology of the passage is in part Lucretian: not so the theology.

[18] Strack III, S. 32 ff.

[19] Pius' type of Roma greeting the Emperor in the company of Cybele and Atys certainly suggests the grant of some new privilege to worshippers of Cybele in Rome (*BMCCRE* IV, p. xcvii).

lions some time before she was first admitted to the Roman coinage.[20] Isis gives her attributes to Alexandria and stands with Serapis to welcome Hadrian and Sabina to the Egyptian capital in Hadrian's "province" coin series;[21] but as a type in her own right she appears on medallions alone.[22] Serapis and Isis have their place on medallions of the vota publica;[23] and Serapis occurs as Gallienus' comrade—SERAPIDI COMITI AVG. Septimius Severus honors the Bacchus and Hercules of his African home under the title of DIS AVSPICIBVS.[24] The Baal of Emesa was imported by Elagabalus. To Aurelian's introduction of the cult of Sol Invictus from the East as imperial comrade we owe the third-century series of Sol types; while Maximinus Daza imported on one occasion the eastern Apollo-Sol-Serapis (SOLE INVICTO) as propaganda for his anti-Christian campaign.[25]

The history of the imperial cult as reflected on medallions can best be studied in the development of the obverse portraits and in the personal types of the Emperor and his family among reverse designs. The progressive elaboration of divine attributes (some of them already prominently paraded at an early stage in medallic history) and of the imperial robes and regalia and the innovations in the formulae of obverse legends vividly mirror the process whereby the citizen Princeps was gradually transformed into the monarch by divine right. So, too, a survey of reverse types discloses an increasing concentration of interest upon the Emperor's person as the gods' elect, the divinely appointed centre upon whom all eyes throughout the Empire are fixed. The details of this medallic evidence need not be recapitulated here. Summarized, it reveals a relationship between the Emperors and their protecting deities growing ever closer and more intimate up till the eve of Constantine's conversion, without involving the complete and formal identification of the human ruler with the god. Commodus' brief experiment in this type of godhead was an abortive enterprise.

The "conversion" of Roman medallions to Christianity was, in the main, an external conversion only.[26] The Emperor holds in his hand the labarum, the Christian standard; the Christian monogram adorns his breast[27] or helmet[28] or it

[20] Cybele's first appearance on a Roman coin is on the MATRI DEVM SALVTARI sestertius of Diva Faustina I (*ibid.*, p. lxxxiii).

[21] J. M. C. Toynbee, *op. cit.*, pl. 2, nos. 17–21. *Cf. ibid.*, pl. 11, nos. 2, 3 (Commodus).

[22] There is no confirmation of the S C varieties of the type of Isis riding on a dog recorded by Cohen for Hadrian and Faustina I (*BMCCRE* III, p. 485; IV, p. 255). Here we may note the strongly conservative official attitude of the Roman government towards the mystery cults. They were fully recognized and approved as authorized cults (religiones licitae), but never regarded as an essential or integral part of the religion of the imperial state. Their festivals find no place at all in the *Feriale Duranum* (Alexander Severus; see *Yale Classical Studies* vii). Mithras, for all his popularity in the second and third centuries A. D., never appears at all upon a Roman coin or medallion. The admission of the foreign cults of Cybele and Isis to medallions earlier than to coins throws an interesting side-light on the more personal and unofficial character of medallions as gifts for special individuals in contrast to the mass of the regular currency.

[23] *Vide supra* p. 78.

[24] *CAH* xii, p. 413. We should probably connect with this cult, rather than with that of the imperial Hercules, the medallion obverse portrait of Septimius with lion-skin hood (*vide supra* p. 156).

[25] *Trans. Internat. Num. Congr.* 1936, pp. 151 ff.

[26] *Vide supra* p. 193.

[27] *Vide supra* p. 179, note 181.

[28] *Vide supra* p. 177.

serves as a "filling" in the field of the design; and the ancient gods have gone. But the spirit and interest of fourth-century types are still within the tradition of pagan Rome. One remarkable obverse portrait of Constantine I foreshadows, indeed, the conquest of pagan by Christian Rome which was to come. Constantine carries a round shield on which the Lupa Romana, the most venerable symbol of Roma Aeterna, is depicted in relief. But immediately above the shield appears the Emperor's sceptre topped by a Cross surmounting a globe, symbol of the world-wide diffusion and dominion of the Catholic Faith.[29]

[29] G I, tav. 29, no. 3. *Cf.* the eighth-century "Cross of Rambona" showing the Crucifixion above the Lupercal with wolf and twins (E. Strong, *Art in Ancient Rome*, II, p. 207, fig. 584).

ADDITIONAL NOTE

(*Vide supra* p. 209, l. 1*)

The unique obverse legend IOVI DIOCLETIANO AVG on the small vota publica medallion of Diocletian (*vide supra* p. 78) must, in the present writer's opinion, be taken as equivalent to "Iovi *et* Diocletiano Aug" and as containing a joint dedication to the god and his imperial *protégé*. The alternative interpretation, which could only mean "to Juppiter who is the Emperor Diocletian," is hardly credible in the light of what we know of Diocletian's religious conservatism.

CHAPTER III

MEDALLIONS AND ART

Of the three spheres of politics, religion and art, it was undoubtedly in the sphere of art that Roman medallions made their most original and valuable contribution to imperial life. Their political function was that of a specialized department of imperial propaganda. They were concerned with selected persons and concentrated, in the main, upon particular aspects of the events and aspirations of the day. Moreover, the impression made by personal gifts upon their recipients would inevitably be a more profound and permanent one than that produced by current cash upon the public mind. But the general political background of coins and medallions of any given period was the same. The difference between the two departments in the political sphere was, indeed, a real one; but it was a difference of scope, rather than of kind. Similarly, the religious faith and cult fostered by the medallion types were essentially the same as those which the coins reflected. The medallions cover a wider range: sometimes they take the initiative in introducing deities to the Roman numismatic field; they give far more detail and they depict the relationship between men and gods in a more intimate and personal way. But they do not propagate peculiar devotions or introduce new creeds. On the other hand, the invention of the bronze medallions proper in the early years of the second century signified the emergence of a completely new field of "minor" imperial art. The Roman medallists inherited from coinage in general the aesthetic amenities of the circular field and the practical advantages of a compact and handy format. They were heirs to the whole artistic tradition of classical and Hellenistic Greek coin-designing and to the notable iconographic achievements of first-century Roman imperial coins. But untrammelled by the inevitable exigencies attending the mass-production of objects which were, for all their secondary qualities, primarily media of exchange, the medallists, unlike the coin-designers, were free to develop a branch of numismatics in which art took precedence over everything else, the very *raison d'être* of which was its aesthetic appeal. With more time and leisure at their disposal, and with the new possibilities afforded by the more extensive fields of the large bronze medallions and by the thicker flans of the smaller pieces, they could surpass the finest effects of Neronian obverse portraits and perfect in their reverse designs a technique unattempted on the bronze coinage. The difference in technical excellence between the money medallions and coins struck in the precious metals (particularly those in gold) was obviously less marked than the difference between the bronze medallions and the ordinary aes. But here again the larger flans and wider range of subject-matter afforded opportunities for aesthetic achievement beyond the reach of coin designers. We have already surveyed the stylistic features of obverse portraits during the three successive phases of medallic history[1] and, for the period extending from Gallienus to the universal adoption of mint-marks for gold and silver, the various peculiarities, or mannerisms, in portrait types which characterize the work of individual mints, Roman and provincial.[2] Again, in our historical chapters we have traced the development of technique and composition in reverse designs.[3] In our present chapter our primary concern will be, not with the style, but with the artistic content, of Roman medallions.[4]

The novelty of their contribution lay in the fact that they provided for cultured circles throughout the Empire what might be described as a portable Museum of Fine Art, consisting of a series of miniature bas-reliefs, more closely related in technique and composition to the works of the painter, relief-sculptor and gem-engraver than to those of the coin die-sinker, and inspired by monuments of all periods and of all kinds—masterpieces of classical and Hellenistic sculpture in the round and in relief, small reliefs with religious, mythological and legendary subjects, paintings both earlier and contemporary, portraits, mosaics, sarcophagi, metal work, cameos and Greek coins. Here the expert and the art-collector would recognize reproductions of the old masters, others would make their acquaintance with them by this means for the first time; while contemporary works could be studied and pondered upon at leisure in this handy and readily accessible form. Medallions must, in fact, have played a very considerable part in spreading knowledge of art and in arousing interest in *Kunstgeschichte* among the educated and intelligent persons who owned them through gift or inheritance. In order to illustrate these points we shall review a selection of the medallion designs most artistically interesting from this point of view, grouped under heads corresponding to the classes of monuments which served as their prototypes or were of kindred content.

Statues of Deities. Foremost among medallion reverse types based on famous statues of deities is the Hadrianic type reflecting the Olympian Zeus of Pheidias, struck on silver multiples of 119 to 120.[5] Of the main features of the Olympian Zeus, as we know him from Pausanias' description and from the Greek Hadrianic bronze pieces struck at Elis with the bust of Hadrian on the obverse and Pheidias' masterpiece on the reverse,[6] the Zeus of the Roman medallion displays the following: he holds a Nike on his extended right hand, he grasps a sceptre in his left hand and the himation in which he is draped covers the left upper arm and hangs down the back. On the other hand, his Nike faces away from him, instead of being turned

[1] *Vide supra* Part IV, Chs. II, III, IV.

[2] *Vide supra* pp. 48 ff.

[3] *Vide supra* Part IV, Chs. II, III, IV.

[4] Exigencies of space have made it impossible to attempt, in what only purports to be a general survey of Roman medallions, the assignment of groups of individual pieces to different artists. The fascinating task of detecting and characterizing the various hands at work in this department of the imperial mint demands the most minute examination of stylistic details and the arrangement of the material, as far as possible, according to identities, or close similarities, of dies. The present writer has already in hand separate studies of the medallions of each reign on these lines. Such work will obviously be an essential feature of a new corpus of medallion types.

[5] G I, tav. 21, nos. 11, 12.

[6] A. B. Cook, *Zeus*, III, pl. 69.

towards him, his throne has no high back and his left arm, with the sceptre, is bent behind his head instead of projecting in front of him. The silver medallion type is thus not a direct copy of the Pheidian Zeus, but a reflection of it, retaining its chief characteristics, but reproducing a definite variant on the original theme. This variant had already appeared in the work of the imperial mint on denarii of Vitellius (IVPPITER, no footstool),[7] on Domitianic sestertii (IOVI VICTORI, throne high-backed or backless, with or without footstool)[8] and on aurei of Trajan.[9] A sestertius of Hadrian, contemporary with the medallion, bears the same type, but without the footstool.[10] Was this Zeus type struck on coins and medallions of 119 to 120 as a "programme" type, with Hadrian's projected visit to Greece in mind? Had he already planned to complete the Olympieion at Athens and to consecrate therein a gold and ivory statue of the Olympian Zeus?[11] At Athens, presumably as a record of this plan's accomplishment, Hadrian issued a bronze coin with this very reverse type, but showing a high-backed throne and no footstool.[12]

A type of Juppiter standing to the front with sceptre and fulmen and himation draped on the left shoulder, labelled IOVI TONANTI, appears on small bronze medallions of Hadrian and Antoninus Pius.[13] This may possibly be a reminiscence of the statue of Juppiter Tonans by Leochares, which stood, so Pliny tells us, on the Capitol.[14] Second-century medallion types of Aesculapius have their statuary counterparts. The type of the elderly god, half-draped, leaning on his serpent-staff, with his left hand resting on his hip,[15] is, of course, very common in sculpture.[16] The type of the young, beardless Aesculapius, naked or with himation hanging down behind, with serpent-staff and hand resting on the hip,[17] recalls the half-draped statue of the youthful god in the Vatican.[18] The medallion type of Apollo standing to the front with long chiton, patera and lyre (Antoninus Pius, Septimius Severus)[19] reflects another well-known statuary type.[20] The Lysippic Herakles, best known from the "Farnese Hercules" at Naples, signed by Glaukon of Athens,[21] is the prototype of several Hercules medallion types of Commodus.[22] The Hercules of Gallienus' small gold multiples, standing to the right with club, lion-skin and bow (VIRTVS AVG)[23] recalls a marble statuette at Boston of a type attributed to Alkamenes.[24] The Hercules kneeling on the back of the stag on Constantius Chlorus' Arras medallion (VIRTVS AVGG)[25] must be modelled on the same sculptured original as the bronze at Palermo.[26]

[7] *BMCCRE* I, pl. 60, nos. 20, 27.

[8] *Ibid.*, II, pls. 72, no. 10; 75, no. 2; 77, no. 3; 79, no. 5.

[9] *Ibid.*, III, pl. 14, no. 2.

[10] *Ibid.*, III, pl. 77, no. 6.

[11] Pausanias i, 18, 6.

[12] *BMCGC*: *Attica*, pl. 18, no. 4.

[13] Strack II, Taf. 16, Nr. 497; G III, tav. 149, no. 2 (**Pl. XXIII, 4**).

[14] Pliny, *NH* xxxiv, 79.

[15] G II, tavv. 40, no. 6; 41, no. 2; 42, no. 10; 44, no. 1 (**Pl. XL, 4**).

[16] E. g. Neugebauer, *Asklepios*, Taff. 2, Nrr. 1, 2; 3, Nrr. 1–3.

[17] G II, tav. 65, no. 6; III, tav. 149, no. 3.

[18] Neugebauer, *op. cit.*, Taf. 2, Nr. 3.

[19] G II, tav. 43, no. 3; 92, no. 9.

[20] Overbeck, *Kunstmythologie*, Atlas, Taf. 21, Nr. 30 (Munich), 31 (Vatican).

[21] F. P. Johnson, *Lysippus*, pl. 37.

[22] *FM* 1931, Taf. 5, Nr. 4 (**Pl. XII, 1**); G II, tavv. 80, nos. 2, 3; 85, nos. 8, 9.

[23] G I, tav. 3, nos. 5, 6.

[24] Walston, *Alcamenes*, p. 216, pl. 21.

[25] *Aréthuse*, Jan., 1924, pl. 8, no. 8 (**Pl. IX, 2**).

[26] A. Maviglia, *L'attività artistica di Lisippo*, fig. 18.

Among medallion types of goddesses the most obvious instance of a copy of a well-known statue is the Athene Promachos of Domitian's silver multiples.[27] Augustus' Diana[28] follows an archaising type similar to, though not identical with, that of the Naples Diana from Pompeii.[29] Two charming Antonine Diana types, Diana caressing a stag and Diana riding on a stag, may well be modelled on bronze groups;[30] while Pius' graceful Diana in a long chiton, with spear and little stag on her extended hand, also suggests a bronze original.[31] Faustina II's Venus, lifting her veil with her right hand and holding an apple in her left,[32] is of the type of Arkesilaos' cult statue of Venus Genetrix;[33] and we may also detect the copy of a cult statue in Hadrian's VENERI GENETRICI medallion type.[34] Lastly, the gold medallion Victory types of Diocletian and Theoderic, showing the goddess poised on a globe,[35] indicate bronze originals such as the bronze Victory from Calvatone in Berlin, dated 161 to 165.[36]

Statuary Groups of Deities. Two medallion types of Aesculapius and Salus, struck for Hadrian and Antoninus Pius respectively, suggest that their ultimate prototypes were classical statuary groups of Asklepios and Hygieia. Hadrian's type shows the young, beardless god standing on the right, with serpent-staff and hand on hip, while Salus, standing on the left, feeds the snake twined round Aesculapius' staff and rests her hand on his shoulder.[37] This pair may well be descended from the group of the beardless Asklepios and Hygieia made by Skopas for Gortys in Arcadia.[38] Pius' type, showing the bearded Aesculapius seated on the right, with Salus standing on the left,[39] recalls the Vatican group.[40]

Medallion types depicting the Dioscuri[41] were clearly derived from some such statuary group as that of the two colossal figures on the balustrade bounding the northern approach to the Capitol.[42] In both sets of monuments, medallic and sculptural, each twin wears a pileus, is naked, apart from his chlamys, and holds a horse by the bridle. Similarly, medallion types showing one twin alone[43] must be based on one or other member of such a statuary pair.

Statuary groups of Mars and Venus, showing a figure of Mars derived from the Ares Borghese type and of Venus based on the type of the Melian Aphrodite, are reproduced on a medallion reverse of Faustina II.[44] Mars stands on the right, with

[27] G I, tav. 21, nos. 2–5.

[28] G I, tav. 1, no. 1.

[29] Ruesch, *Guida illustrata del Museo Nazionale di Napoli*, p. 32, fig. 8.

[30] G II, tavv. 43, no. 7 (**Pl. XLI, 2**); 68, no. 4.

[31] G II, tavv. 49, no. 3; 50, no. 9; III, tav. 148, no. 14.

[32] *Trau Collection Sale Catalogue* 1935, Taf. 23, Nr. 1778 (**Pl. XXIV, 5**).

[33] E. Gardner, *Handbook of Greek Sculpture*, p. 506, fig. 127 (Louvre).

[34] G III, tav. 146, no. 2. Strack (II, S. 179) suggests that this is the type of Venus Genetrix Populi Romani, as distinct from the Venus Genetrix Caesaris.

[35] G I, tavv. 4, no. 15; 20, no. 3.

[36] P. Ducati, *L'arte in Roma*, tav. 156, no. 2.

[37] G II, tav. 38, no. 5; III, tav. 147, no. 6 (**Pls. XX, 8; XL, 3**).

[38] Pausanias viii, 28, 1.

[39] G II, tav. 52, no. 9.

[40] Amelung, *Sculpturen des vatikanischen Museums* Bd. II (Tafeln), Taf. 51, Nr. 399.

[41] G II, tavv. 54, no. 6; 71, no. 5; 83, no. 2.

[42] Clarac, *Musée de Sculpture*, V, pl. 812, nos. 2044, 2045.

[43] G II, tavv. 62, no. 2; 84, nos. 6, 7.

[44] G II, tav. 67, no. 8.

helmet, chlamys, shield and spear, facing Venus, who stands on the left and places both hands on her consort's shoulder. Just such a group is to be seen in the Capitoline Museum.[45] The heads in this group are portraits; and the woman's hair is arranged after a fashion not far removed from that of the Empress on the medallion obverse.

Sculptures adorning Architectural Features of Temples and Monumental Altars. It is highly probable that the famous groups of the Parthenon pediments were among those temple sculptures of the classical period which inspired the Roman medallists. The seated type of Zeus, with sceptre, fulmen and eagle, "canonised" by the masterpiece of the eastern pediment, gave birth to a vast progeny of copies and adaptations in the form of marble and bronze statuettes, paintings, gem-engravings and coin types dating from imperial times.[46] The oldest medallic member of this family is the bronze piece of Antoninus Pius, showing Zeus enthroned towards the left with his eagle at his side.[47] Our sole surviving specimen of this type is, unfortunately, so badly worn that the god's other attributes have practically vanished. But his general pose closely resembles that of the Parthenon type, with the direction reversed; and the position of the right arm is certainly more suggestive of a sceptre as its original attribute than of the Victory which Gnecchi[48] and Strack[49] would discern. The object held in the left hand may well have been a fulmen. The same type, but with the position of sceptre and fulmen reversed, reappears on gold multiples of Diocletian[50] and on bronze medallions of Diocletian and Galerius.[51] Another type possibly reminiscent of the eastern pediment is Commodus' running Minerva (MINER AVG).[52] The goddess, fully armed with helmet, spear and shield, hastens towards the right, while glancing back over her shoulder in the pose of Athene in the birth-scene on the Madrid puteal.[53] On the other hand, the olive-spray which she has plucked from the tree on the right suggests that we have here a free adaptation, in reverse position, of the Athene of the western pediment, starting away from her rival Poseidon, after the manner of the Kertsch vase.[54] Again, it is at least credible that the fine types of Hadrian and Aelius Verus showing Sol in his quadriga mounting towards the right[55] were derived from the Helios in the left-hand angle of the eastern pediment.

The group in the western pediment of the Parthenon was not the only representation on the Acropolis of the ἔρις of Athene and Poseidon. "A group," says Pausanias,[56] "representing Procne and Itys, at the time when Procne had taken her resolution against the boy, was dedicated by Alkamenes; and Athene is represented exhibiting the olive-plant and Poseidon exhibiting the wave"; and an account follows of statues of Zeus by Leochares and of Zeus Polieus. The mention of

[45] Ed. Stuart Jones, *Sculptures of the Museo Capitolino*, pl. 73, no. 34.
[46] A. B. Cook, *op. cit.*, II, pp. 753–757, figs. 693–699; cf. pls. 33, 34.
[47] G II, tav. 48, no. 8.
[48] G II, p. 15, no. 53.
[49] Strack III, S. 63.
[50] G I, tav. 4, nos. 10, 11.
[51] G II, tavv. 124, no. 2; 128, no. 10.
[52] G II, tav. 81, no. 6.
[53] Baumeister, *Denkmäler des klassischen Altertums*, I, S. 219, Abb. 172.
[54] *JIAN* 1912, p. 214, fig. 7.
[55] *ZN* 1927, Taf. 8, Nr. 1; 1930, Taf. 2, Nr. 5 (Pl. XVI, 2); G II, tav. 42, nos. 8, 9.
[56] i, 24, 3.

representations of olive-plant and wave in this ἔρις scene suggests relief work or figures in the round against a background of accessories in high relief; while the word "exhibiting" (ἀναφαίνων) seems to hint at some dignified, well-ordered competition, as contrasted with the violent conflict portrayed in the Parthenon version of the myth. A peaceful ἔρις scene, originally executed in relief, or in the round against a relief background, is precisely what two bronze medallion types, struck for Hadrian[57] and for Marcus Aurelius (as Caesar ?)[58] respectively, depict. On the left stands Poseidon, facing towards the right, his left foot on a rock (from which water gushes?), his himation draped over his left knee, on which his left elbow rests, and a trident in his right hand. Behind him is a rock, with a long-necked bird perched on it. In the centre is an olive-tree; and to the right of the tree Athene stands towards the left, her left hand on her hip, while she touches with her right hand the stem of the tree, against which she has leant her spear. Behind Athene is her shield, with a serpent rearing against it, and a second serpent is seen at the foot of the tree. Poseidon extends his left hand towards the goddess, as though engaging her in conversation, while Athene, serene and dignified, gazes quietly down. The rivals have shown their tokens and calmly await the issue, which the votes of the twelve gods,[59] or of the people,[60] will decide. According to Hesychius,[61] Athene promised Zeus that, if he gave his vote for her, a victim should be sacrificed on an altar to him under the title of Zeus Polieus—a story which gives special point to the proximity of the statue of Zeus Polieus to the ἔρις representation. The same scene is depicted on the well-known Paris cameo.[62] Another bronze medallion type, struck for Antoninus Pius[63] and for Marcus Aurelius as Caesar,[64] brings out the peaceful aspect of this version of the myth still more clearly. Athene stands on the left, facing towards the right, her spear in her left hand, her right hand on her hip, and her shield and snake behind her. On the right is Poseidon, seated at his ease, facing Athene and grasping his trident. Between the two are an olive-tree and a table supporting a voting urn, from which Nike, standing to the front behind the table, draws out the votes. The correctness of this interpretation, as against Strack's theory of an agonistic table with a prize vase,[65] is proved by a marble relief found at Aphrodisias in Caria and now at Smyrna.[66] This shows Poseidon and Athene, each with an olive-tree behind them, standing on either side of a table, behind which Nike stands and extracts the votes from an urn. A snake is twined round the table legs and an anchor and dolphin are seen below. Svoronos suggests[67] that these variants of the peaceful ἔρις scene represent Alkamenes' version of the theme, originally submitted, in competition, for the western pediment of the Parthenon, rejected by the judges

[57] G III, tav. 146, nos. 8, 9.

[58] Imhoof-Blumer and P. Gardner, *A Numismatic Commentary on Pausanias*, p. 131, pl. Z, no. 15 (**Pl. XXIV, 2**). This piece is said to be at Bonn; but the present writer was informed in 1938 that the Rheinisches Landes-Museum possessed no bronze medallions. The type must have been struck for Marcus as Caesar by Pius (*cf. infra*, note 64).

[59] Apollodorus iii, 14, 1.

[60] Varro, quoted by St. Augustine, *De Civitate Dei*, xviii, 9.

[61] *S. v.* Διὸς θᾶκοι καὶ πεσσοί.

[62] E. Babelon, *Camées de la Bibliothèque Nationale*, p. 18, pl. 5, no. 27.

[63] G II, tavv. 51, no. 1; 52, no. 5.

[64] G II, tav. 65, no. 1.

[65] Strack III, S. 109.

[66] *AM* 1882, SS. 48–58, Taf. 1. *Cf.* A. B. Cook, *op. cit.* III, pp. 757, 758.

[67] *JIAN* 1912, p. 293 ff.

in favor of the more violent version, but accorded a place of honor on the Acropolis. The fact that Pausanias mentions this representation of the conflict in juxtaposition to a group by Alkamenes may, perhaps, afford a clue to the authorship of the former work. Did it catch Hadrian's fancy, when he visited the Acropolis, as an interesting antiquarian discovery to be imitated on medallions? Hadrian's suite during the Greek tours may well have included court artists, who made sketches or models of Greek masterpieces for reproduction in the work of the medallic department of the imperial mint.

A fragment from the relief sculpture of one famous monumental altar of the Hellenistic age is reflected in a medallion type of Antoninus Pius. This shows Herakles standing and contemplating the infant Telephos, who is being suckled, according to the traditional version of the myth, by a hind.[68] The general scheme of this design may well be ultimately derived from the corresponding scene in the Telephos frieze of the Pergamene altar.[69] But in details the medallion and the marble slab differ considerably, notably in the fact that, on the altar, the foster mother is not a hind but a lioness.

Turning to temple sculptures of imperial times, the group of the Capitoline Triad in the pediment of the Capitolium doubtless inspired the types of the three deities shown seated on medallions of Hadrian,[70] of Antoninus Pius[71] and of Marcus Aurelius and Lucius Verus.[72] Juppiter is enthroned in the centre, with sceptre and fulmen, Minerva on the right, with a spear, and Juno on the left, with sceptre and patera. This pedimental group is, indeed, portrayed in a representation of the Capitoline temple on an Aurelian relief in the Palazzo dei Conservatori;[73] but there the relative positions of Juno and Minerva are reversed. On medallions and relief alike Minerva's right hand is raised to her head and Juppiter holds sceptre and fulmen, while a fold of his himation is visible on his left shoulder; on the medallions, but not on the relief, Juppiter's high-backed throne is shown. Hadrian's type differs from the two other medallions and from the relief in showing a Victory placing a wreath on Juppiter's head—a feature which also appears on an engraved chalcedony of imperial date in Berlin, with an almost identical figure of the god.[74] In this Juppiter type with himation on the shoulder and high-backed throne we may see, in fact, the imperial-classical type of the cult statue of Juppiter Capitolinus set up in the Vespasianic temple, as contrasted with the republican-Hellenistic type of the cult statue of Catulus' temple, with nude torso and backless seat.[75]

One relief from the most famous monumental altar of imperial times, the Ara Pacis Augustae, is copied on the reverse of a bronze medallion struck for Marcus Aurelius as Caesar.[76] The type shows the sacrifice of Aeneas to the Penates and

[68] G II, tav. 53, no. 2.
[69] *Altertümer von Pergamon*, III, 2, Taf. 31, Nr. 6.
[70] G III, tav. 146, nos. 5, 6.
[71] G II, tav. 50, no. 5.
[72] G II, tav. 71, no. 6.
[73] Ed. Stuart Jones, *Sculptures of the Palazzo dei Conservatori*, pl. 12 (Scala II, 4); cf. Baumeister, *op. cit.*, I, S. 765 Abb. 820.
[74] A. B. Cook, *op. cit.*, I, p. 42, fig. 12.
[75] *JRS* 1938, p. 50 ff., pls. 2–5.
[76] G II, tav. 66, no. 6.

follows the corresponding slab from the Ara[77] closely, with two notable exceptions. In the place of the actual Aeneas, draped, in heroic guise, in a long mantle veiling the head and reaching to the feet, is the "new pius Aeneas," Antoninus himself, wearing cuirass and paludamentum, the latter garment being drawn over his head to betoken his sacerdotal act.[78] The type belongs to the "Birthday of Rome" legendary series; but here the reigning Emperor, whose armed might keeps peace secure, links the past with the present, symbolizing the unbroken continuity of the life of Eternal Rome. Again, in place of the adult Achates (?) on the right of Aeneas on the Ara Pacis slab, the medallion shows the little Ascanius, with pedum and Phrygian cap, typifying, no doubt, the youthful heir to the imperial throne, whose portrait appears on the obverse of the piece.

Imperial Reliefs with Historical Scenes. Nothing is more natural than that we should find in medallion types, designed as official imperial gifts, echoes of the great imperial reliefs with historical scenes which adorned the public monuments of Rome and of provincial cities in Italy and abroad. The eight Hadrianic *tondi* on the Arch of Constantine portray the Emperor as embodying the imperial virtues of virtus, prowess in the hunting field, and pietas, dutifulness towards the gods. They are doubtless representative of a whole series of similar reliefs, both contemporary and of later date, commemorating historical occasions on which imperial virtues were displayed. Such occasions were Hadrian's bear-hunt at Hadrianutherai in 123 and his boar-hunt in Asia Minor in 129. It is hard to believe that the *tondi* recording these events[79]—and others, it may be, of the same series, now lost to us, composed as they are within a circular "medallic" field, did not directly inspire the designers of the later series of Hadrian's boar-hunt and lion-hunt (VIRTVTI AVGVSTI) medallion types,[80] which may, in their turn, have served as models for the similar hunting types of Marcus Aurelius, Lucius Verus and Commodus. Again, some such relief as the sacrifice-to-Silvanus *tondo*[81] may be behind Commodus' medallion type with a scene of imperial sacrifice in a woodland setting (PROVIDENTIAE DEORVM).[82]

The CONSECRATIO medallion struck for Divus Antoninus, which shows Pius borne aloft on the back of an eagle, while Campus Martius reclines below,[83] has its obvious counterpart in two imperial reliefs—the Apotheosis of Plotina (?) in the Palazzo dei Conservatori and the Apotheosis of Antoninus and Faustina on the base

[77] E. Strong, *La scultura romana*, tav. 7.

[78] The figure on the medallion wears a short tunic, reaching only to the knees, and the lappets of the cuirass are clearly visible on the left arm. He cannot, therefore, be described as "Aeneas in heroischer Nacktheit" (Strack III, S. 70).

[79] *JDAI* 1919, S. 144 ff., Abb. 1, Nrr. 3, 6.

[80] G III, tavv. 144, no. 12; 146, nos. 3, 4, 7 (*Cf.* **Pls. XXII, 7; XLI, 5**). Two of the four lion-hunt types bear the obverse legend of *c.* 129. But the other two lion-hunt types, and all three boar-hunt types, have the obverse legends of 130 to 138. The *tondi* can be exactly dated, some to 137, others to between Feb. 25, 138 and July, 138, by the portraits of Aelius Verus and of Antoninus Pius which they respectively bear. The later medallion series may thus commemorate the erection of the monument for which the *tondi* were originally carved.

[81] *JDAI* 1929, S. 144 ff., Abb. 1, Nr. 2.

[82] G II, tav. 86, nos. 5, 6.

[83] G II, tav. 43, no. 5.

of the Antonine Column in the Vatican. The passage-way reliefs of the Arch of Titus, the Flavian Vatican fragment, showing Roma (or Virtus ?) leading the way in an imperial triumph, the Hadrianic adventus and adlocutio reliefs in the Palazzo dei Conservatori, the eleven Aurelian panels—eight on the Arch of Constantine and three in the Palazzo dei Conservatori, the Severan relief in the Palazzo Sacchetti and the Diocletianic basis in the Roman Forum (to mention the most obvious and familiar extant imperial reliefs) suffice to indicate the probable source of a whole array of second- and third-century medallion types—the processus consularis, processus triumphalis, adventus, profectio, adlocutio, liberalitas and scenes of vota, "Birthday of Rome," saeculum novum and other imperial sacrifices.

Reliefs from great imperial monuments may, perhaps, have afforded models for the Africa reverse designs of Antoninus Pius and Commodus.[84] The type of Lucius Verus, showing the imperial colleagues standing between the Euphrates and the Tigris,[85] and that of Gordian III, with the Emperor and Roma (?) standing between the same rivers,[86] recall the Mesopotamia panel of the Beneventum Arch. The other attic panels of the Arch depicting the Emperor in divine company suggest that similar imperial reliefs may have been the prototypes of the numerous medallions which portray the Emperor grouped with the great gods of the Roman state. Types such as that of Alexander Severus crossing the Rhine,[87] of Gordian crossing the Hellespont,[88] and Euphrates[89] (TRAIECTVS AVG), of Galerius riding down four Persians (VICTORIA PERSICA)[90] and of Constantine I crossing the Danube (DANVBIVS)[91] may reflect excerpts from continuous series of historical scenes on such imperial monuments as the Columns and the Arch of Septimius Severus in the Roman Forum. Lastly, imperial reliefs (or, possibly, paintings) displayed to the public in honor of special events and solemn occasions, may have suggested the landscape types with views of city-walls and rivers, that of Constantius Chlorus' London medallion, for example, and of Constantine I's Trier.

Reliefs and Paintings of Deities. A number of medallion designs with types of deities display the main figure with an architectural or landscape background or accessories suggesting that the picture as a whole had been inspired by some bas-relief or painting now lost to us. Outstanding examples of such designs are Hadrian's Apollo seated on a rock, playing the lyre to a group of Muses,[92] Hercules crowning himself between a large apple tree and an altar (Marcus Aurelius and Commodus, Lucius Verus, Commodus),[93] offering sacrifice at an altar beneath a large, spreading tree (Commodus)[94] and standing, seen from behind, between large rocks, on which his attributes are deployed (Commodus).[95] Similarly, the Hermes-

[84] G II, tavv. 45, no. 7; 47, nos. 1, 2; 78, no. 5.
[85] G II, tavv. 74, no. 8; 75, no. 6.
[86] G II, tav. 104, no. 1.
[87] G II, tav. 101, no. 5.
[88] G II, tav. 105, no. 8; III, tav. 153, no. 13.
[89] G III, tav. 153, no. 15.
[90] G II, tav. 129, no. 4.
[91] G II, tav. 130, no. 6.
[92] G II, tav. 40, no. 7. *Cf.* Reinach, *Répertoire de peintures grecques et romaines*, p. 28, no. 6.
[93] G II, tavv. 75, no. 1; 77, no. 1; 83, nos. 5, 6; *BMQ* 1934–1935, pl. 16, no. 4 (**Pl. XXII, 2**).
[94] G II, tav. 79, nos. 5, 6.
[95] G II, tav. 80, nos. 5, 6 (**Pl. XLIII, 3**).

Mercurius type of Hadrian,[96] Hadrian's seated Pan,[97] Pius' Silvanus (?)[98] and the types of Pius and of Commodus with Sol mounting heavenward in his chariot above a bank of clouds, beneath which Tellus reclines,[99] clearly indicate painting or bas-reliefs as their models. In Marcus Aurelius' type of Neptune standing before the walls of Troy[100] the figure of the god is based upon the Lysippic Poseidon; but the prominent and carefully rendered architectural background of city-walls and gate is treated precisely after the manner of architectural *motifs* in Hellenistic and imperial reliefs. The Antonine types of Vulcan in his workshop[101] again suggest pictorial originals; while the types of Cybele enthroned to the front between lions, with Atys and, in some[102] cases, a tree adorned with cymbals (Faustina I, Faustina II, Lucilla),[102] recall *motifs* from the Isola Sacra reliefs of a priest of Cybele officiating[103] and from the Scipio Orfitus altar in the Villa Albani.[104] Most picturesque of all are a Diana type of Antoninus Pius and of Faustina II[105] and a Venus type struck for Faustina II and Lucilla.[106] The first shows Diana unrobing and preparing to bathe in a spring, which gushes from a grotto. On the ground, at the goddess's feet, are her bow and quiver and a dog drinking from the stream. On the rock, above the spring, are a tree and the head and antlers of a deer; while a deer-skin hangs on a second rock on the other side of the design. The closest parallel to this type is to be found in one of the sculptured panels on the back of the Melfi sarcophagus; but there the landscape setting is reduced to rocks and three animal heads suspended in mid air.[107] The Venus type shows the goddess standing to the front in a walled garden and pulling a tree towards herself, while a bevy of Cupids flutter and tumble around her—an attractive and intriguing design, so far without known parallel in ancient art. The nearest approach to it is made by two paintings, one found in Rome, the other at Pompeii. The Roman painting[108] depicts the birth of Adonis in the presence of Venus, who stands to the front and grasps a tree with her left hand. In the Pompeian painting[109] Venus is seated at the foot of a tree with a Cupid perched on her shoulder, while another Cupid is led along by a nymph, apparently for chastisement at Venus' hands. But while they recall certain *motifs* in our medallion type, these paintings afford no clue as to the source of the whole design.[110]

Reliefs and Paintings with Scenes from Mythology and Legend. The myth of Athene and the Argo depicted on a bronze medallion of Marcus Aurelius as Caesar[111]

[96] G II, tavv. 39, nos. 1–3; 41, no. 4.

[97] G III, tav. 146, no. 10.

[98] G II, tav. 52, no. 8.

[99] G II, tavv. 50, no. 6; 78, nos. 3, 4.

[100] G II, tav. 62, no. 6.

[101] G II, tavv. 51, no. 3; 52, nos. 4, 7; 59, no. 1; 65, no. 2; Strack III, Taf. 21, Nr. 544 (Pl. XXIV, 4).

[102] G II, tavv. 57, no. 4; 68, no. 7; 76, no. 5.

[103] G. Calza, *La Necropoli del Porto di Roma nell' Isola Sacra*, figg. 110, 111.

[104] Reinach, *Répertoire des reliefs grecs et romains*, III, 134, 2.

[105] G II, tavv. 50, no. 8; 68, no. 5.

[106] G II, tavv. 68, no. 1; 76, no. 8.

[107] E. Strong, *op. cit.*, tav. 35.

[108] Reinach, *Répertoire de peintures grecques et romaines*, p. 64, no. 3.

[109] *Ibid.*, p. 78, no. 2.

[110] Pansa (*RIN* 1920 p. 164 ff.) suggests that the scene represents some Eleusinian rite.

[111] G II, tav. 65, no. 10.

is also treated on somewhat similar lines in a Roman terra-cotta mural relief.[112] The types of Herakles in the garden of the Hesperides (Hadrian, Antoninus Pius)[113] and other types drawn from the Herakles cycles—Herakles and Nessos (Antoninus Pius, Marcus Aurelius as Caesar),[114] Herakles and the Nemean lion (Commodus),[115] Hercules and Cacus (Antoninus Pius,[116] Marcus Aurelius as Caesar)[117] and Hercules dining with the Pinarii and Potitii (Antoninus Pius)[118]—all hint at originals in painting or sculpture. The existence of a small marble relief in the British Museum showing Aeneas and Ascanius arriving in Latium, with Lanuvium and the sow and her young on the left[119]—a composition practically identical with the corresponding Antonine medallion type[120]—suggests, indeed, the possibility that a set of reliefs lay behind the whole series of Pius' "Birthday of Rome" reverse types with scenes from legend and history. With his AESCVLAPIVS types,[121] for example, we may compare the version of the same subject on the Palazzo Rondanini relief.[122]

Reliefs and Paintings with Miscellaneous Subjects. An elaborate medallion type (SALVS) struck for Faustina II[123] and for Commodus[124] shows Salus seated to the left on a marble seat with a back, on which her left elbow rests, while a crouching sphinx is carved on its side. With her right hand she feeds from a patera a snake rearing up above a curious rectangular slab-like object at her feet. On the left is a tall cippus surmounted by a small female figure, wearing a short chiton and holding a spear or long sceptre; and to the left of the cippus is a tall, branching tree. This design is closely paralleled by a marble relief found on the site of a villa of Herodes Atticus at Loukon in Thera and now in the National Museum at Athens.[125] It shows a female figure precisely similar to the Salus of our medallions, seated in the same pose on a similar marble seat, by the side of which is a crouching sphinx. From the patera in her right hand a snake (most of which is broken away) is feeding. In front of her is a statuette of Euthenia, standing with a fruit basket on a basis carved with her name: behind the statuette is a tall cippus topped by a small female figure in a short chiton and with left hand raised; and behind the cippus is a branching tree. Only the mysterious slab-like object of the medallion is missing from the relief where its place is occupied by the statuette. The seated woman's name—ΕΠΙΚΤΗCΙC—is carved on the back of her seat; and the word ΤΕΛΕΤΗ inscribed on the background suggests that Epictesis is represented as heroized under the guise of Hygieia.

The offering-to-Salus medallion type, issued for Antoninus Pius, Marcus Aurelius and Commodus,[126] shows a devotee standing with legs crossed beneath a

[112] *Catalogue of Terra-cottas in the British Museum*, pl. 43.
[113] G II, tavv. 42, no. 1; 52, no. 10; 54, no. 1.
[114] G II, tav. 65, no. 5.
[115] G II, tav. 80, no. 4.
[116] G II, tav. 53, no. 1.
[117] G II, tav. 64, no. 2.
[118] G II, tav. 54, no. 3.
[119] *BMQ* 1928, pl. 52.
[120] G II, tav. 54, no. 9.
[121] G II, tav. 43, nos. 1, 2.
[122] E. Strong, *op. cit.*, p. 243, fig. 148.
[123] G II, tav. 67, no. 3.
[124] *Vierordt Collection Sale Catalogue* 1923, pl. 41, no. 1749 (Pl. XXVI, 2).
[125] J. Svoronos, *Das athener Nationalmuseum*, II, S. 336 ff., Nr. 1390, Taf. 55.
[126] G III, tav. 149, no. 7; II, tavv. 60, no. 10; 63, no. 3; 80, no. 10 (Pl. XXVI, 3).

tree and feeding a snake twined round a statuette of Salus, which stands on a table beside a vase and flower-garland, while a bird perches on a cross-bar between the table's legs. This design vividly recalls a small *rosso antico* relief in the Capitoline Museum:[127] the only important point in which the relief differs from the medallion is that in the former the devotee is offering Salus fruit, while the snake helps itself from a patera held in Salus' hand.

Among other examples of medallion types specially suggestive of reliefs or paintings are those of Pomona (?) seated to the right on a high-backed throne in a vineyard, accompanied by three children plucking and treading grapes (Commodus);[128] and of Victory standing to the right with a vota shield supported on her knee, while a troupe of Cupids, waving palms, throngs around her (Caracalla).[129] The Nike Tauroctonos type of Antoninus Pius[130] recalls the identical *motif* in minor reliefs from imperial monuments, in the frieze between the upper and lower pylon panels of the Beneventum Arch,[131] for example, and in the frieze from the Basilica Ulpia, now at Munich.[132] Again, the types of Commodus and of Caracalla with sacrificial implements[133] were possibly copied from architectural friezes adorned with such *motifs*—those of the temple of Vespasian in Rome, for instance, and of the Porta Argentariorum.

Equestrian Statues. Equestrian statues such as the famous bronze of Marcus Aurelius on the Capitol may well have inspired the types of the Emperor, or Caesar, seated on horseback to right or left, with his right hand extended in greeting.[134] Possibly the erection of an equestrian statue of the imperial person portrayed on the obverse was the occasion for which such a type was struck. So, too, the gold type of Constantine I with the legend EQVIS ROMANVS and the types struck in gold for Aurelian, Probus, Constantine I and later Emperors with the legend ADVENTVS AVG, FELIX ADVENTVS AVG may be associated with statues of this class.[135]

Sculptured Portraits. The debt of the Roman medallists to imperial cuirass-statues, both for obverse busts of the Emperor wearing paludamentum and cuirass, or cuirass alone, and for full-length figures of the Emperor in military dress in reverse types, is too obvious to require further comment. The upper parts of full-length statues of the imperial figure in quasi-divine guise would seem to be behind the series of specially fine and plastically modelled deep busts of Hadrian, Marcus Aurelius as Caesar, Commodus as Caesar and Gallienus, which portray the Emperor, or Caesar, with naked upper arm and a large expanse of naked breast exposed to view and draped in an aegis falling over chest and back.[136] Busts of Trajan, Hadrian

[127] Ed. Stuart Jones, *Catalogue of Sculptures in the Museo Capitolino*, p. 266, no. 111, pl. 61.

[128] G II, tav. 87, no. 2.

[129] G II, tav. 95, no. 4.

[130] G II, tav. 55, no. 4.

[131] E. Strong, *op. cit.*, p. 195, figg. 111, 112.

[132] *JDAI* 1936, Taf. 1.

[133] G III, tav. 152, no. 4 (**Pl. XLII, 7**); II, tav. 95, nos. 6, 7.

[134] G II, tav. 48, nos. 1, 2 (Antoninus Pius); Strack III, Taf. 21, Nr. 607 (Marcus Aurelius as Caesar) (**Pl. XXII, 3**); G II, tavv. 60, no. 8; 66, no. 8 (Marcus Aurelius); G II, tav. 75, no. 7 (Lucius Verus); G II, tav. 87, no. 9 (Commodus as Caesar).

[135] *Vide supra* pp. 109, 117.

[136] G II, tavv. 38, no. 9 (**Pl. XL, 2**); 39, no. 2; 65, no. 1; 66, no. 10 (**Pl. XLI, 5**); 87, nos. 6, 8; 115, no. 3 (**Pl. XLVI, 5**); *Trau Collection Sale Catalogue* 1935, Taf. 37, Nr. 2987 (**Pl. XXVII, 5**).

and Marcus Aurelius as Caesar, either completely nude or with a tiny fold of drapery on one shoulder,[137] are obviously reproductions of marble portrait busts; while works such as the famous Commodus-Hercules bust in the Palazzo dei Conservatori[138] must have furnished models for the magnificent heads of the Emperor in lion-skin hood on obverses of Commodus, Gallienus, Probus, Maximian and Constantius Chlorus.

Painted Portraits. The rare instances of frontal portraits on medallion obverses suggest that paintings, rather than sculptured busts, inspired the medallists. The single full-face portraits of Commodus,[139] Constantius II[140] and Justinian[141] are, indeed, decidedly pictorial in quality. The obverse of the gold multiple of the two Licinii in the Beistegui Collection, showing nimbate busts of father and son,[142] reminds us of such family group paintings as those of Septimius Severus with his wife and sons, executed on a circular wooden panel found in Egypt and now in the Berlin Antiquarium,[143] and of a mother with her son and daughter, executed by the potter Bounneri in gold leaf on a glass medallion, now in the Museo Cristiano Civico at Brescia.[144] Again, obverse portraits of third- and fourth-century Emperors in consular robes, with rich and delicate embroidery rendered in minute detail, are strongly suggestive of painted models and recall the painted portraits of Constantius II and Constantius Gallus in the Calendar of 354.[145]

Mosaics. Of the subjects common to mosaics and medallions one of the most interesting is that of the Genius Saeculi with the zodiac frame, accompanied by Tellus and/or the Four Seasons.[146] In the Sentinum mosaic at Munich[147] the Genius Saeculi stands within the zodiac frame which he upholds, and recalls the medallion designs with the Emperor seated within, or, more commonly, standing or seated outside, the frame which he is supporting. In this mosaic the Four Seasons appear as children grouped round the reclining figure of Tellus—a group suggestive of the reclining Tellus and Seasons types of Hadrian, Antoninus Pius and Commodus. For the Genius Saeculi medallion types in which the Four Seasons, in the guise of maidens, come tripping through the zodiac frame, and particularly for those types which show the Genius Saeculi as seated, we have an interesting parallel in a mosaic recently discovered in Tomb 101 in the Necropolis of Isola Sacra, near Ostia.[148] It shows a half-naked male figure on the right, seated on a rock and holding with his right hand a zodiac frame, through which the Four Seasons are passing in procession, on the left, while Tellus reclines above. The Genius Saeculi here portrayed can hardly be Helios, as Calza thinks, for he has no rays and the skin of a beast (the paws are clearly visible) is deployed across the rock on which

[137] G I, tav. 21, nos. 6, 11, 12; III, tavv. 143, nos. 8, 10; 145, no. 8; 150, no. 5 (**Pl. XIV, 3**).

[138] E. Strong, *op. cit.*, p. 387, fig. 233.

[139] Grueber, p. 30, no. 45 (**Pl. XXII, 1**).

[140] G I, tav. 13, no. 2 (**Pl. XLVIII, 7**).

[141] G I, tav. 20, no. 4 (**Pl. XLIX, 3**).

[142] J. Babelon, *op. cit.*, pl. 12, no. 232 (**Pl. XXXI, 5**).

[143] *Die Antike* 1936, Taff. 10, 11.

[144] *Ibid.*, S. 171, Abb. 12.

[145] Delbrück, *Die Consular-Diptychen*, S. 50, Abb. 19, 20.

[146] *Vide supra* Part III, Ch. I.

[147] J. M. C. Toynbee, *op. cit.*, pl. 33, no. 3.

[148] G. Calza, *op. cit.*, p. 184, fig. 92.

he sits. Is he not Hercules with his lion-skin? The bronze medallion struck for Marcus Aurelius as Caesar, with the legend TEMPORVM FELICITAS and a design showing Hercules with club and trophy drawn along in a chariot by four Centaurs, who bear emblems of the Seasons,[149] supports the suggestion.

Sarcophagi. The series of Antonine sarcophagi depicting scenes from the life of an Emperor or general[150] furnish parallels for medallion types of imperial virtues struck for Hadrian, Antoninus Pius, Marcus Aurelius, Lucius Verus and Commodus. These sarcophagi portray, either singly or in combination, the four Roman cardinal virtues: of virtus, courage on hunting- or battle-field; clementia, generosity to conquered or submissive foes; pietas, dutifulness towards the gods, shown in the offering of sacrifice; and concordia, domestic harmony, symbolized by the dextrarum iunctio. Virtus alone is often represented on hunt-, or battle-, sarcophagi adorned with elaborate scenes, of which medallion types of the Emperor hunting or riding down prostrate foes are simplified versions. On other sarcophagi all four virtues appear together in a series of successive scenes; or clementia, pietas and concordia are shown in full, virtus being represented by the single figure of Virtus or of Victory, standing behind the compassionate victor. In the clementia scenes the victor stands upon a low platform, while the captives—men, women and children—kneel or genuflect before him: they recall the CLEMENTIA AVG medallion type of Marcus Aurelius[151] and certain ARMENIA types of Lucius Verus.[152] The pietas scenes of sacrifice suggest the vota types of the pious Emperor sacrificing to the gods on New Year's Day. Lastly, the concordia scenes showing husband and wife clasping hands, while Concordia stands between them, may have inspired such types as the VOTA PVBLICA design struck for Commodus and Crispina on their wedding day.[153]

The Bacchic medallion types issued for Hadrian, Antoninus Pius and Marcus Aurelius,[154] may be compared with the numerous Bacchic sarcophagi of Antonine date, depicting Bacchus, alone or accompanied by Ariadne, drawn along in a chariot amid a revel rout. Other mythological medallion types may also have had their source, direct or indirect, in sarcophagus designs. For example, the Prometheus and Athene type of Antoninus Pius[155] closely resembles the central group on the front of a small sarcophagus in the Capitoline Museum,[156] though this actual piece would appear to be of early third-century date. Similarly, types depicting the labors of Hercules are paralleled in the series of scenes on the large columned sarcophagus in the Villa Umberto I.[157]

We may also see reflections of later third-century Amorini-and-garlands—

[149] *Vide supra* p. 90 and note 151.

[150] *Cf.* Rodenwaldt, *Über den Stilwandel in der antoninischen Kunst.*

[151] G II, tav. 59, no. 6.

[152] G II, tav. 72, nos. 4, 6.

[153] G II, tav. 91, nos. 8, 9. But *cf.* also the CONCORDIA adoption medallion type of Hadrian and Aelius Verus (G II, tavv. 38, no. 3; 42, no. 7).

[154] *Vide supra* pp. 96, 139, 142.

[155] G II, tav. 54, no. 8.

[156] Ed. Stuart Jones, *Sculptures of the Museo Capitolino*, pl. 34, no. 13.

[157] P. Ducati, *op. cit.*, tav. 161, no. 1.

sarcophagi, with Genii supporting swags of fruit and flowers,[158] in the GAVDIVM AVGVSTI NOSTRI type of Constantine I and the VOTIS DECENN D N CONSTANTINI CAES type of Constantine II, both of which show two Genii holding a long flower-garland between them.[159]

Metal Work: Paterae and Missoria. The most striking example known to the present writer of correspondence between a medallion type and a patera design is that between a Mercury type of Antoninus Pius and the emblema of a silver patera from the Berthouville (Bernay) hoard, now in the Bibliothèque Nationale. The medallion shows Mercury standing towards the left. His gaze is directed upwards, he is naked, save for a chlamys draped over his left shoulder, and he holds a caduceus in his left hand and a ram by the horns in his right. On the right of the design is a tree, on the left, a cippus, surmounted by a tortoise.[160] The emblema bears an almost identical figure of Mercury, but with purse, instead of a ram's horns, grasped in his right hand. The subsidiary objects which complete the picture are also strikingly similar, though their relative positions are reversed: on the left is a tree and a cippus, surmounted by a cock; on the right is a second cippus, surmounted by a tortoise, in front of which a ram is seen with forelegs resting on a rock.[161] Such patera emblemata offered ideal models for medallion designs; and Pius' reverse type may well have been copied from a work of the same school as that which produced the Berthouville piece.

In the all too rare examples of silver missoria of the later Empire which have come down to us we may recognize the type of monument from which a number of fourth-century gold and silver medallion designs were derived. The missorium of Madrid, showing Theodosius I enthroned between Valentinian II and Arcadius,[162] immediately recalls the great family group series of the Constantinian and Valentinianic Houses.[163] Similarly, the PIETAS AVGVSTAE type of Fausta, showing the Empress enthroned to the front with an infant on her lap,[164] suggests derivation from a missorium of like content. The type of Valentinian I, in which the Emperor stands to the front with vexillum and Victory-on-globe,[165] looks like an extract from such a work as the Geneva missorium.[166] The silver missorium in the Hermitage, showing Constantius II, nimbate and armed with a spear, riding towards the right, while Victory goes before him and a soldier follows behind,[167] suggests the kind of work which might have inspired the designers of such types as that of Magnentius riding, nimbate, to the right towards Respublica,[168] that of Valens riding, nimbate, towards Antioch[169] and that of Justinian riding, nimbate, to the

[158] E. g. J. M. C. Toynbee, *op. cit.*, pl. 48, no. 2.

[159] G I, tavv. 6, no. 14; 7, no. 1; 9, no. 7, 8 (**Pl. XLVIII, 6**).

[160] G II, tav. 52, no. 6.

[161] *JHS* 1882, pp. 96 ff., pl. 22. For the type of Mercury *cf.* the Skopaic figure of Hermes with caduceus on the sculptured drum from Ephesus (E. Gardner, *op. cit.*, p. 420, fig. 102).

[162] Delbrück, *op. cit.*, S. 235 ff., Taf. 62.

[163] *Vide supra* pp. 198 f.

[164] G I, tav. 8, no. 10 (**Pl. XVII, 5**).

[165] G I, tav. 14, no. 8.

[166] Delbrück, *Spätantike Kaiserporträts*, Taf. 79.

[167] Delbrück, *Die Consular-Diptychen*, S. 71, Abb. 26.

[168] *NK* 1929–1930, S. 28, Abb. (**Pl. XXXIV, 12**).

[169] G I, tavv. 16, no. 1; 17, no. 1.

right, preceded by Victory.[170] Again, the types of the Emperor (or Emperors) in a frontal six-horse chariot,[171] those of "Fest-aurei" in which the Emperor scatters coins from a frontal quadriga[172] and the largitio types of Constantius II and Magnentius[173] can, on the score both of their subject-matter and the essentially "circular" character of their composition, readily be imagined as derived from missoria designs.

Cameos. Two medallion reverse types find their nearest parallel among extant monuments of ancient art in a cameo design. The well-known Hellenistic sardonyx cameo at Naples, signed by Ἀθηνίων, shows Zeus driving a car drawn by four rearing horses towards the right over the bodies of two snake-legged giants, at whom he hurls his bolt.[174] A "framed" bronze medallion of Antoninus Pius shows the same *motif*, though Juppiter drives towards the left and only one giant appears beneath the horses' hoofs.[175] A bronze piece of Marcus Aurelius follows the cameo design even more closely, for Juppiter is driving towards the right and stands in his chariot in precisely the same pose as that of Zeus on the cameo; but a single German warrior has taken the place of the two giants.[176] On the other hand, quite a number of medallion obverse portraits display an elaboration of design and a style of modelling suggestive of cameo prototypes. Such, for instance, are the busts of Septimius Severus and Caracalla seen from behind and showing a naked back, with shield and balteus;[177] the deep busts, including the breasts, of Faustina II,[178] of Julia Domna, wearing a stephane and holding cornucopiae and statuette,[179] and of Julia Mamaea as Dea Panthea[180] (*cf.* the cameo of Salonina);[181] third-and fourth-century busts of the Emperors shown helmeted, carrying an elaborate shield or leading a horse by the bridle; jugate busts; busts or heads of two or three imperial persons confronted; and frontal portrait busts (*cf.* the Paris cameo of "Honorius and Maria").[182] Again, the pictorial type, introduced on medallions of Marcus Aurelius and copied on those of Lucius Verus, Commodus, Gordian III, Tacitus, and Probus which shows the Emperor seen from behind with bare back, aegis on the left shoulder, balteus and spear,[183] immediately recalls the famous Blacas Cameo of Augustus in the British Museum.[184]

Greek Coins. The fine type of Victory driving a biga of prancing horses towards the right, struck on large bronze medallions of Hadrian[185] and of Antoninus

[170] G I, tav. 20, no. 4 (Pl. XLIX, 3).
[171] *Vide supra* p. 111, note 156.
[172] *Vide supra* p. 111.
[173] G II, tavv. 136, no. 7; 138, no. 4.
[174] Furtwängler, *Antike Gemmen*, I, Taf. 57, Nr. 2; II, S. 259.
[175] G II, tav. 49, no. 1.
[176] G II, tav. 60, no. 1.
[177] G II, tavv. 92, no. 9; 93, nos. 9, 10 (Pl. XXVIII, 4); 95, no. 2 (Pl. XLIV, 3).
[178] G II, tav. 67, no. 3.
[179] G II, tavv. 94, no. 9; 95, no. 1 (Pl. XLIV, 1).
[180] G I, tav. 22, no. 4 (Pl. XLIV, 6).
[181] E. Strong, *Art in Ancient Rome*, II, p. 162, fig. 510.
[182] P. Ducati, *op. cit.*, tav. 281. The cameo probably dates from the time of the Tetrarchy.
[183] *Vide supra* pp. 133, 156.
[184] *Catalogue of Engraved Gems and Cameos in the British Museum*, pl. 38, no. 3577.
[185] G II, tavv. 38, nos. 8, 9; 41, no. 3 (Pl. XL, 2).

Pius,[186] may have been inspired by Hellenistic coin types of Syracuse. Such types are found on gold of Hiketas (287 to 278),[187] on silver and copper of Hiero II (275 to 216)[188] and on gold and silver of Hiero's queen, Philistis.[189]

[186] G II, tav. 46, no. 8.

[187] *BMCGC: Sicily*, p. 200, no. 430.

[188] *Ibid.*, pp. 210, no. 527; 216, no. 578.

[189] *Ibid.*, p. 214, no. 559; G. F. Hill, *Coins of Ancient Sicily*, pl. 13, no. 6.

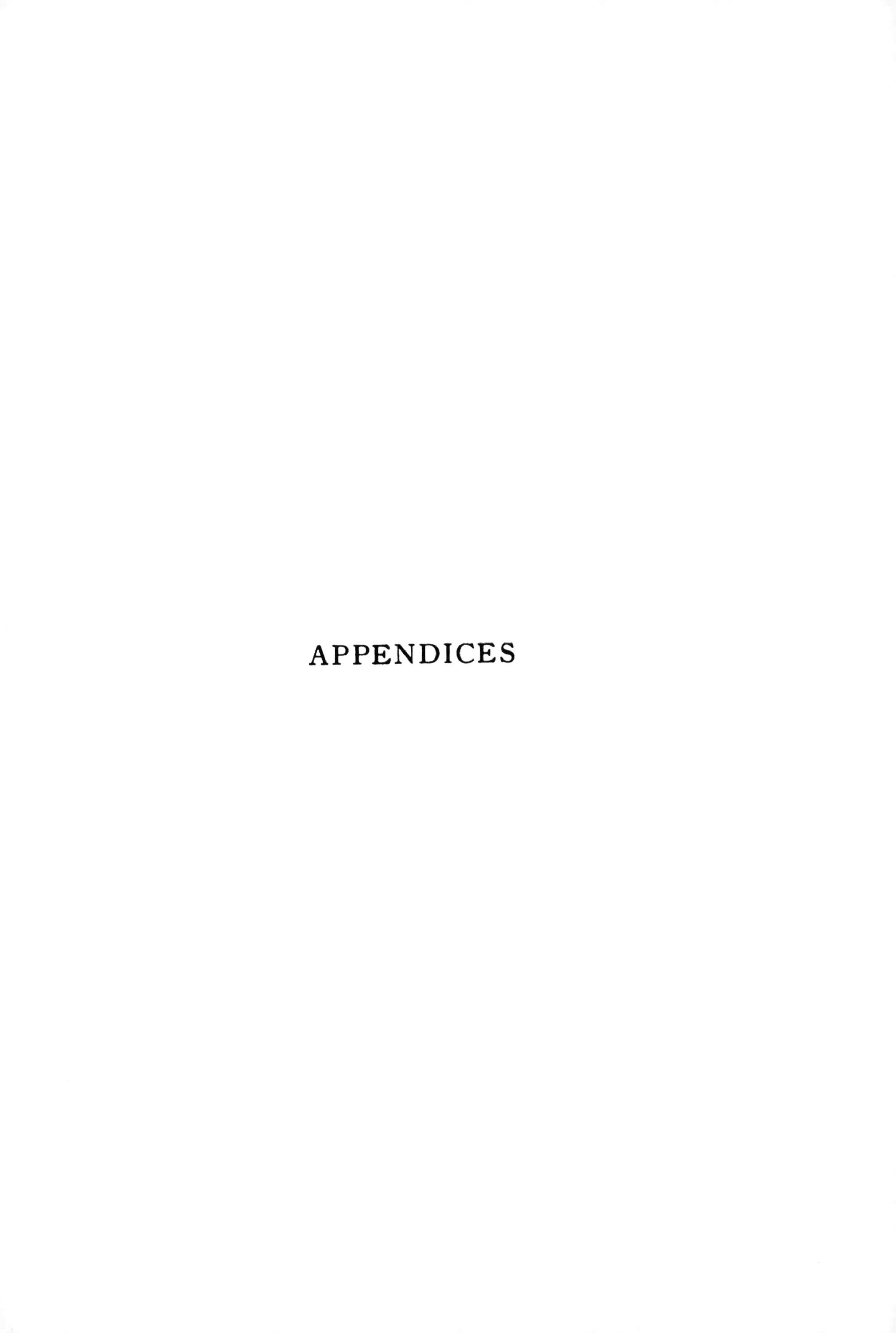

APPENDICES

I

FORGERIES. CASTS. LEAD MEDALLIONS

Forgeries are notoriously the most formidable obstacle with which the student of Roman medallions has to contend. Few monuments of ancient art have offered a more tempting field to the enterprising counterfeiter and "restorer." At one extreme are the "Paduans," which have a distinctive and easily recognizable style of their own; at the other, are modern pieces made with such skill and feeling for the spirit of the antique that they are often extremely hard to detect. It is not so much the style of these pieces which betrays them as details of metal and fabric and the historical probabilities of the types themselves. Such, for example, are the points adduced by Laffranchi against the Augustan gold multiple from Este,[1] the genuineness of which has been vigorously defended by other numismatists.[2] The existence of clever modern forgeries constitutes a double snare; for, besides the danger of mistaking the false for the true, there is also that of mistaking the true for the false. For instance, quite a number of genuine pieces in the Vienna cabinet have had to be rescued from the limbo of the "falsi," to which excessive suspicion had consigned them, and rehabilitated. Between these two extremes—the obvious "Paduans" on the one hand and the elusive modern forgeries on the other—are a number of pieces, still exuding the odor of authenticity in well-known public collections, of which the style and general atmosphere are almost undoubtedly those, not of antiquity, but of the Renaissance or of the eighteenth century. Such, for example, are the Berlin "framed" piece of Antoninus Pius, with Cybele driving a lion-quadriga as reverse type;[3] the Paris piece of Antoninus Pius with Theseus and the Lapiths and Centaurs;[4] the Paris "framed" piece of Faustina I with Diana dancing towards the right and holding a torch;[5] the Paris piece of Faustina I with Vestals sacrificing before the temple of Vesta;[6] and the consecration piece of Julia Domna in Vienna,[7] of which Kubitschek had serious doubts.[8] Other pieces described and illustrated as genuine by Gnecchi, in spite of doubts expressed by him in certain cases, have since been relegated to their true place among the "falsi."[9]

[1] *Historia* 1933, pp. 600–614.

[2] E. g. L. Rizzoli, *Atti e memorie della R. Accademia di Padova*, 1926; M. von Bahrfeldt, *BFM* 1931, SS. 243–244, Abb.; S. L. Cesano, *Atti e memorie del Istituto Italiano di Numismatica*, 1934, p. 107; *Numismatica Augustea*, 1937, p. 32 (Pl. XIX, 3).

[3] G II, tav. 51, no. 2. N. B. especially the style of the obverse portrait and of the lions on the reverse.

[4] G II, tav. 54, no. 4. N. B. the style of the modelling and the complexity of the design, which are non-classical. The central group seems to have been copied from the Herakles and Nessos type of Antoninus Pius and of Marcus Aurelius as Caesar (G II, tav. 63, no. 5; *Numismatik* Dec., 1933–Jan., 1934, S. 145, Abb. (Pl. XXV, 3)).

[5] G II, p. 25, no. 12. N. B. the dancing step and swing of the drapery, which are non-classical.

[6] G II, p. 26, no. 25.

[7] G II, tav. 96, no. 1.

[8] Kubitschek S. 9, Nr. 77.

[9] E. g. G II, tav. 110, no. 8 (Paris); I, tav. 28, no. 6 (Vienna); II, tav. 128, no. 2 (Vienna); II, tav. 129, no. 9 (Vienna); I, tav. 6, no. 9 (not in Vienna, as stated by Gnecchi, but patently false); II, tav. 133, no. 10 (Berlin); III, tav. di suppl., no. 15 (Milan). The patently false piece of Trajan Decius figured by Gnecchi (III, tav. di suppl. no. 8) is said to have been found in Rome in 1910; its present location is unknown.

But by far the most difficult problems are presented by pieces which, although apparently genuine, have been all too lavishly touched up and worked over in ancient or more recent times. We have already noted a remarkable instance of retouching in antiquity.[10] The majority, however, must have undergone the process of "restoration" at the hands of retouchers between the Renaissance period, when the vogue for medallion collecting first set in, and the comparatively recent days of their scientific study. It is, indeed, often frankly impossible to decide absolutely whether a given piece is a genuine antique, retouched, or a piece of later workmanship, copied or adapted from an ancient model. Such pieces must be noted as possibly, though not certainly, ancient, in the hope that new discoveries may one day furnish evidence for reaching a sure conclusion.

Casts of Roman medallions may be either ancient[11] or of later date. Here, again, it is often impossible to attain absolute certainty in distinguishing between the two. Sometimes the general impression conveyed by the style of a bronze cast offers a fairly reliable clue as to the date of its manufacture. For instance, we may attribute to Renaissance workmanship the four casts known to the present writer of Trebonianus Gallus' large ARNAZI medallion, of which the only extant antique specimen is that at Bologna.[12] On the other hand, the small bronze cast at Gotha, with the head of Marcus Aurelius as Caesar on the obverse and Minerva riding, armed, on a griffin on the reverse, may well be ancient and of great value as our sole surviving evidence for a lost original.[13] Again, it is possible that none of the examples extant in public and private collections of Hadrian's Pons Aelius type are genuine medallions.[14] Some are clear forgeries: others are highly suspicious; while a few may be ancient casts representing a lost original piece. Similarly, the SALVS REIP / DANVBIVS type of Constantine I[15] is represented by two specimens, both of which give the appearance of having been cast in antiquity from an authentic medallion. These examples should suffice to illustrate the importance of keeping careful records of all existing bronze casts, particularly of those types of which no certainly genuine specimens exist; while judgment as to the authenticity of the types themselves must in such cases be reserved, pending the discovery of fresh evidence.

Lead medallions appear to be ancient "proofs" from bronze medallion dies. They, too, must be taken into account as possibly affording evidence of lost originals. Six such pieces are reported to have come to light in excavations, two of them in Rome, in 1908,[16] and 1911[17] respectively, one at Reims[18] and three at Narni.[19]

[10] *Vide supra* p. 57.

[11] In the Munich cabinet there is a cast of a medallion of Antoninus Pius (G II, tavv. 44, no. 3; 45, nos. 5, 6) found during excavations in Bavaria.

[12] G II, tav. 111, no. 3. The casts are those in Paris, Vienna, the former Trau Collection and the Lawrence Collection in London.

[13] Strack III, Taf. 4, Anh. II, D, i (Pl. XXIV, 7). *Cf.* the large "framed" piece of Antoninus Pius in Vienna (Nr. 37404), with Bacchus, Ariadne and a Bacchic train on the reverse, which appears to be an ancient cast from a lost medallion.

[14] G II, tav. 42, no. 4.

[15] G II, tav. 130, no. 6.

[16] G II, p. 34, no. 58.

[17] G II, p. 45, no. 6 (not bronze, as Gnecchi states).

[18] G II, p. 34, no. 58.

[19] G II, pp. 63, no. 106; 80, no. 10.

The Narni pieces are said to have been found together with lead replicas of sixteen sestertii; such "proofs" may possibly have been collected in ancient times by persons interested in coins and medallions from the artistic or historical point of view. One of the lead medallions from Narni, of Commodus, shows a well-known reverse design (the Emperor driving a slow quadriga towards the right and crowned by Victory) combined with a type of obverse portrait other than any of those depicted on the extant bronze specimens; it may represent a lost variant, and in the British Museum there is, in fact, a plaster cast of a bronze medallion with precisely this combination of obverse and reverse types, labelled "Franz Maly, Vienna." Again, the British Museum possesses a lead medallion the reverse of which bears the Italia type and legend of Antoninus Pius' bronze medallion at Milan.[20] But whereas the Milan piece shows a laureate bust of the Emperor to right on its obverse, the lead "proof" shows a laureate head, also to right. If the latter represents a genuine original it would add a thirtieth example to the twenty-nine instances noted by the present writer of a familiar feature of medallions of Pius' principate, the combination, that is to say, of the same reverse type with two, occasionally three, different obverse types.[21]

[20] G II, tav. 45, no. 10.

[21] *Cf. NC* 1940, p. 2.

II

CONTORNIATES

Inasmuch as they are coin-like pieces not issued to circulate as currency, the Roman contorniates may be associated with the study of Roman medallions. But whereas medallions were essentially works of art of a high order, executed by the best artists Rome could produce, with selected individuals, highly placed and highly cultured, as recipients in mind, the contorniates were obviously mass-produced by inferior, somewhat illiterate, designers for persons themselves devoid, for the most part, of higher education and cultured tastes. Whether cast or struck, all lack sharpness and delicacy of technique. The draughtsmanship is, in the great majority of cases, rough and slipshod. In the reverse legends spelling mistakes are of frequent occurrence, especially in the Latin transliteration of Greek names, while the same legend occasionally shows a mixture of the two tongues. Mythological scenes sometimes appear with incongruous legends, as though the craftsman were ignorant of the true meaning of the type which he had portrayed. The obverse legends, too, betray misspellings of Greek and Roman names, to say nothing of monstrosities in the forms of imperial titles. The various explanations of the purpose of the contorniates discussed or proffered by Robert,[22] Gnecchi[23] and Pick[24] need not detain us here. But the most recent theory of their meaning and origin, adumbrated by Alföldi in his *Festival of Isis in Rome* (1937) and in an article in *Klio* xxxi (1938), is of special interest to students of medallions. Alföldi believes that the contorniates, which began in the fourth century and continued into the fifth and were issued only in Rome,[25] were pagan propaganda pieces, originating in a *milieu* of aristocratic families obstinately devoted to Rome's ancient faith and way of life and pledged to a systematic anti-Christian campaign, and that they were distributed as strenae to the plebs urbana on the third of January by the nobles who presided at the New Year games.[26] If this theory could be established, the contorniates would afford a parallel to the propagandist function of Roman medallions, though in that case the propaganda would have been of a private, as opposed to an official, kind.[27] But the chief objection to the theory that the con-

[22] *Étude sur les médaillons contorniates* (1882).

[23] *RIN* 1895, pp. 31 ff.; 277 ff.; *Roman Coins*, ed. 2 (1903), pp. 186–190.

[24] P-W², Bd. 7, SS. 1153–1160.

[25] It is noteworthy that after the division of the Empire only western Emperors are portrayed on contorniates.

[26] *Festival of Isis in Rome*, p. 39, note 59; p. 41 and note 79; *Klio* 1938, S. 253.

[27] Alföldi's theory, of course, implies that the contorniates were made, not in the official officinae of the Roman mint, but in workshops owned or controlled by noble families.

torniates were New Year gifts lies in the fact that in their types and legends New Year references are conspicuously scanty. Two pieces bear on the obverse a helmeted bust of Roma with the legend "invicta Roma felix senatus", and on the reverse the legend "reparatio muneris feliciter," accompanying a bestiarius combating a bear in the one case, a vanquished gladiator lying at the feet of a retiarius in the other.[28] "Felix" and "feliciter" have, of course, a New Year ring; while a rare piece, bearing the obverse portrait of Valentinian III, the reverse legend "Petronius Maxsumus v(ir) c(larissimus) cons(ul)" and the type of Petronius seated to the front holding sceptre and mappa (?), with two bags of money (for largess ?) in the exergue below, must commemorate the entry of Valentinian's favorite upon his first consulship.[29] Otherwise New Year allusions are all to seek. Nor have we any real evidence that the contorniates represent deliberate anti-Christian propaganda. In view of what we know of the pagan atmosphere and of the vitality of pagan culture in the Christian Empire of the fourth century[30] it is not surprising to find depicted here the whole panorama of pagan life in the old style—with it gods and heroes, its mythology, legends and history and, above all, with its dazzling spectacles and entertainments, so dear to the people's heart, its horse- and chariot-races, gladiatorial shows, beast-fights, trials of strength and bodily skill, mock battles and naumachies, its processions and pageants, to say nothing of the lectures and antics of its popular "philosophers" (Pythagoras, Apollonius of Tyana) and, for a higher stratum of the people, its musical competitions, theatrical performances and literary recitations (Homer, Euripides, Demosthenes, Accius, Terence, Sallust, Horace, Apuleius).[31] Nero and Trajan, the Emperors most commonly portrayed, were noted as patrons of the games and shows, Caracalla was noted as devotee-in-chief of Alexander the Great, whose portrait, as that of the greatest hero and wonder-worker of the ancient world, is among the most commonly repeated obverse types. The turned-up edges and incised circular grooves certainly suggest that the practical use of contorniates was that of game-counters. But if they were, in the first instance, distributed as gifts, their constant allusions to games, shows and competitions, taken in conjunction with Constantius II's interest in the circus and his circus medallion type (SABINAE), seem to indicate that the occasions of their distribution were exhibitions in the circus and public entertainments of other kinds, not necessarily connected with the New Year. The subsidiary symbols—palms, crowns, leaves, helmets, arms, animals, cups, tripods etc. and the much-disputed P, plain or barred, which most probably stands for "palma"[32]—may represent the prizes awarded at the games to successful competitors, the darlings of the populace, or even largess distributed to the populace itself.[33]

The prevailingly pagan and secular content of the Roman contorniates is in itself sufficient explanation of the fact that they are never found in Christian

[28] J. Sabatier, *Description générale des médaillons contorniates*, pls. x, 1; xix, 13.

[29] *Ibid.*, pl. xvi, 4.

[30] *Vide supra* p. 185, note 246.

[31] For a list of contorniate types reproducing well-known works of art see K. A. McDowall (Mrs. Esdaile), "Contorniates and Tabulae Lusoriae" (*NC* 1906, pp. 232 ff.).

[32] *Cf. NC* 1909, p. 40.

[33] *Cf. supra* p. 111, note 156.

Catacombs. Unlike the medallions, they could have no attraction for educated Christians as works of art or heirlooms.[34]

A new corpus and study of the contorniates has been promised by Alföldi.[35] Pending its appearance the student is referred to the well-known catalogues of Sabatier[36] and Cohen.[37]

[34] Serafini, *op. cit.*, p. 437. The only trace of Christianity on a normal contorniate known to the present writer is the sceptre surmounted by globe and cross held by the Emperor Marjorian in his obverse portrait (Sabatier, *op. cit.*, pl. xix, 5). A unique contorniate in the Vatican Collection shows a bust of Alexander the Great in lion-skin hood on the obverse and on the reverse an incised design consisting of the Christian monogram within a double circle. **Pl. XXXIX, 5.**

[35] *Klio* 1938, S. 253, Anm.:—"eine neue Bearbeitung der ganzen Gattung bereitet Unterzeichneter vor." (See Bibliography.)

[36] *Op. cit.* (1860).

[37] Ed. 2, vol. viii, pp. 273–323.

LIST OF PUBLIC AND PRIVATE COLLECTIONS OF ROMAN MEDALLIONS

(As existing in 1937–1939)

Collections personally examined by the author marked *.
Collections the contents of which are known to the author from casts or written information marked †

GREAT BRITAIN

London. * British Museum
* L. A. Lawrence Collection
* J. W. E. Pearce Collection
* V. J. E. Ryan Collection

Oxford. * Ashmolean Museum (University and A. Evans Collections)
Llanymynech (Montgomeryshire). * H. P. Hall Collection (Pentreheylin Hall)
Glasgow. * Hunterian Museum, The University (Hunterian and Coats Collections)

FRANCE

Paris. * Cabinet des Médailles, Bibliothèque Nationale
* M. Carlos de Beistegui Collection (deposited in Cabinet des Médailles)
* R. Jameson Collection

Arras. Musée Municipal
Autun. * Musée Rolin
Avallon. * Musée Municipal
Grenoble. † Bibliothèque Municipale
Marseilles. † Bibliothèque Municipale

ITALY

Rome. * Museo Nazionale Romano
* Museo Capitolino (Palazzo dei Conservatori)
* Biblioteca Apostolica Vaticana (Gabinetto Numismatico)
* Don Fabrizio Massimo Collection
* Prof. Bettolo Collection
* Cav. Ugo Simonetti Collection

Ancona. R. Museo delle Marche
Aquileia. R. Museo Archeologico
Bologna. * Museo Civico (City and University Collections)
Brescia. * Pinacoteca Tosio Martinengo
Este. * Museo Nazionale Atestino
Florence. * R. Museo Archeologico
Forli. Museo Civico (Piancastelli Collection) [inaccessible in 1938]
Leghorn. Museo Civico
Milan. * Castello Sforzesco (Medagliere Milanese) (State (Brera) and City Collections)
Società Numismatica Italiana Collection [inaccessible in summer of 1938]
* L. Laffranchi Collection (Via Carlo Ravizza 19)

Modena. * Museo Civico (Galleria Estense)

MONACO. Collection of S. M. il Principe
NAPLES. * Museo Nazionale
PADUA. * Museo Civico
* Colonnello nobile Ulrich-Bansa Collection
PARMA. * R. Museo di Antichità
REGGIO EMILIA. * Dr. A. Villani Collection
SYRACUSE. * R. Museo Archeologico
TRENT. † Museo Nazionale
TURIN. * R. Museo di Antichità
* Biblioteca di S. M. il Re (Medagliere di S. M.)
† G. Mazzini Collection
VENICE. * Museo Civico Correr
* R. Museo Archeologico
VERONA. * Museo Civico Castelvecchio

GERMANY

BERLIN. * Kaiser-Friedrich Museum
BONN. * Rheinisches Landes-Museum
COLOGNE. * Wallraf-Richartz Museum
DRESDEN. † Staatliches Münzkabinett
FRANKFURT-AM-MAIN. * Stadtgeschichtliches Museum
GOTHA. * Schloss (Münzkabinett)
HANOVER. * Kestner Museum
KARLSRUHE. * Badisches Landes-Museum
MAINZ. * Römisch-Germanisches Zentral-Museum
MUNICH. * Alte Akademie
STUTTGART. * Altes Schloss
TRIER. † Rheinisches Landes-Museum
WIESBADEN. * Nassauisches Landes-Museum

AUSTRIA

VIENNA. * Kunsthistorisches Museum
* Theresianum Collection
* Hauptmann-Hollschek Collection
PETRONELL. * Graf von Traun Collection
STIFT S. FLORIAN (OBERDONAU).

HUNGARY

BUDAPEST. * Hungarian Historical Museum
* Altdorffer Collection

RUMANIA

BUCHAREST. † Museum of Antiquities [medallions in deposit in Moscow]

BULGARIA

SOFIA. † National Museum

YUGOSLAVIA

BELGRADE. National Museum
The University (Weifert Collection)
PANČEVO. Elmer Collection
KNIN. † Croatian Museum

ZAGREB.	* Archaeological Museum
	* B. Horvat Collection

POLAND

WARSAW.	† State Archaeological Museum

RUSSIA

LENINGRAD.	The Hermitage

SPAIN

MADRID.	Museo Arqueológico Nacional

BELGIUM

BRUSSELS.	* Bibliothèque Royale de Belgique
LIÈGE.	* M. D. de Lébioles Collection

HOLLAND

THE HAGUE.	* Gemeente Museum (Kon. Kabinet van Munten, Penningen en Gesneden Steenen)
NIJMEGEN.	* Kam Museum

DENMARK

COPENHAGEN.	* Nationalmuseet

SWEDEN

STOCKHOLM.	† Statens Historiska Museum och Kungl. Myntkabinettet

EGYPT

ALEXANDRIA.	V. A. Adda Collection

ALGERIA

CONSTANTINE.	Musée Scientifique et Archéologique

U. S. A.

NEW YORK.	† American Numismatic Society Collection
	† Newell Collection
	† Pierpont Morgan Collection
	Dr. de Yoanna Collection (Brooklyn)
	† T. O. Mabbott Collection
BALTIMORE (MD.).	† Walters Art Gallery
	† J. W. Garrett Collection
BOSTON (MASS.).	† Museum of Fine Arts
WASHINGTON.	† Freer Collection
NEW HAVEN (CONN.).	† Yale University Collection

SELECT BIBLIOGRAPHY

(A key to abbreviations used in this bibliography appears on p. 11)

I. General Works on Medallions

Froehner, W. Les médaillons de l'empire romain depuis le régne d'Auguste jusqu' à Priscus Attale (Paris, 1878)

Gnecchi, F. I medaglioni romani (Milano, 1912)

Kenner, F. Der römische Medaillon (*NZ* 1887, SS. 1–173)

Regling, K. P-W[2] *s. v.* Medaillon (Bd. 29, 18–25)

II. General Works Covering Medallions

Babelon, E. Traité de monnaies grecques et romaines, I, pp. 652–670 (Paris, 1901)

Bernhart, M. Handbuch zur Münzkunde der römischen Kaiserzeit (Halle, 1926)

Cohen, H. Description historique des monnaies frappées sous l'empire romain communément appelées médailles impériales. Deuxième édition (Paris, 1880–1892)

Mattingly, H. and Sydenham, E. A. The Roman Imperial Coinage (London, 1923–1933)

III. Catalogues

Babelon, J. La collection de monnaies et médailles de M. Carlos de Beistegui (Paris, 1934)

Grueber, H. A., ed. by Poole, R. S. Roman Medallions in the British Museum (London, 1874)

Kenner, F. Römische Medaillons (*Jahrbuch der Kunsthistorischen Sammlungen des allerhöchsten Kaiserhauses*, Wien, Bdd. I (1883), S. 61 ff.; II (1884), S. 54 ff.; III (1885), S. 11 ff.; V (1887), S. 12 ff.; IX (1889), S. 139 ff.; XI (1890), S. 53 ff.)

Kubitschek, J. W. Ausgewählte römische Medaillons der Kaiserlichen Münzensammlung in Wien, aus dem Illustrationsmaterial der Bände I–XI des Jahrbuches der Kunstsammlungen des A. H. Kaiserhauses neu herausgegaben (Wien, 1909)

Macdonald, G. Roman Medallions in the Hunterian Collection (*NC* 1906, pp. 93–126; 1909, pp. 53–55)

Quilling, F. Ausgewählte römische Münzen und Medaillons der städtischen Münzsammlung in Frankfurt-am-Main (*ZN* 1897, SS. 201–218)

Ružička, L. Römische Medaillons im Bukarester Museum (*BFM* 1914, Nr. 4)

IV. Hoards and Finds. (a) Arras

Babelon, J. and Duquenoy, A. Médaillons d'or du trésor d'Arras. L'Entrée de Constance Chlore à Londres en 296 après J.-C. (*Aréthuse* Jan., 1924, pp. 45–52)

Baldwin, A. (Mrs. Brett). Four Medallions from the Arras Hoard (*NNM*, No. 28, 1926)

——— The Aurei and Solidi of the Arras Hoard (*NC* 1933, pp. 268–348)

Evans, A. Some Notes on the Arras Hoard (*NC* 1930, pp. 221–274)

Kubitschek, J. W. Der Schatzfund von Arras (*NZ* 1924, SS. 81–89)

Pink, K. The Minting of Gold in the Period of Diocletian and the Arras Find (*NC* 1934, pp. 106–113)

(b) Bregetio

Hampel, J. Ein Münzfund aus Bregetio (*NZ* 1891, SS. 85–88)

Kenner, F. Nachtrag zu dem Münzfunde aus Bregetio (*NZ* 1891, SS. 89–94)

——— Zweiter Nachtrag zu dem Münzfunde aus Bregetio (*NZ* 1894, SS. 1–4)

(c) Borča

Elmer, G. Ein Fund römischer Goldmünzen aus Borča (*NZ* 1930, SS. 39–46)

(d) EGYPT

DENISON, W. A Gold Treasure of the Late Roman Period from Egypt (*Studies in East Christian and Roman Art, University of Michigan Studies, Humanistic Series* xii, 1918)

(e) HELLEVILLE

BABELON, E. La trouvaille de Helleville (Manche) en 1780 (*RN* 1906, pp. 160–189, 490–492)

(f) LONDON

SMITH, C. R. On the Roman Coins discovered in the Bed of the Thames, near London Bridge, from 1834–1841 (*NC* 1841, pp. 147–168)

(g) PLANCHE (AIN)

PONCET, E. Le trésor de Planche (*RN* 1889, pp. 514–538)

(h) POITOU

ROBERT, C. Trouvaille de monnaies d'or du Bas-Empire (*RN* 1866, pp. 111–119)

(i) SZILÁGY-SÓMLYÓ

STEINBÜCHEL, A. VON. Notice sur les médaillons en or du musée impérial et royal de Vienne trouvés en Hongrie dans les années MDCCXCVII et MDCCCV (Vienne, 1826)

(j) VELP

KERKWIJK, A. O. VAN. Les médaillons romains en or de la trouvaille de Velp en 1715 (*Mémoires du Congrès international de Numismatique*, Bruxelles, 1910, pp. 29–38)

(k) VOLHYNIA

GASIOROWSKI, ST. J. Un trésor de l'époque de la migration des peuples découvert en Volhynie (*Bulletin international de l'Académie Polonaise des Sciences et Lettres*, 1929, pp. 27–31)

V. AUGUSTUS TO COMMODUS

CESANO, S. L. Numismatica augustea (*Quaderni Augustea* III, Istituto di Studi Romani, 1937)

DODD, C. H. Chronology of the Eastern Campaigns of the Emperor Lucius Verus (*NC* 1911, pp. 209–267)

——— On the coinage of Commodus during the Reign of Marcus (*NC* 1914, pp. 34–59)

DRESSEL, H. Der Matidiatempel auf einem Medallion des Hadrianus (*Corolla Numismatica* 1906, pp. 16–28)

ELMER, G. Zwei neue Schaumünzen des Antoninus Pius (*Numismatik* Dec., 1933–Jan., 1934, SS. 145–147)

HORVAT, B. Médaillon inconnu de l'impératrice Faustine Mère (*Vjesnik* 1928)

KENNER, F. Bronzemedaillon der Kaiserin Faustina (*NZ* 1879, SS. 227–229)

LEDERER, P. Neues Medaillon des Hadrianus (*ZN* 1927, SS. 184–191; 1930, SS. 60–63)

MATTINGLY, H. Coins of the Roman Empire in the British Museum Vol. IV (London, 1940)

RUŽIČKA, L. Ein Medaillon des M. Aurelius (*BM* 1917, SS. 49–53)

STRACK, P. L. Untersuchungen zur römischen Reichsprägung des zweiten Jahrhunderts (Stuttgart, 1931, 1933, 1938)

TOYNBEE, J. M. C. Some "Programme" Coin Types of Antoninus Pius (*CR* 1925, pp. 170–173)

——— A New Bronze Medallion of Antoninus Pius (*NC* 1940, pp. 1–8)

VI. SEPTIMIUS SEVERUS TO CARINUS AND NUMERIANUS

ALFÖLDI, A. Siscia: die Prägungen des Gallienus (*NK* 1927–1928, SS. 14–48)

——— Zur Kenntnis der Zeit der römischen Soldaten-Kaiser (*ZN* 1927, SS. 197–212; 1928, SS. 156–203; 1930, SS. 1–15)

BABELON, E. Médaillon d'or de Gallien et de Salonine (*RN* 1896, pp. 397–424 = *Mélanges numismatiques* III, pp. 179–206.)

——— Contributions à la numismatique de Gallien (*Recueil de Mémoires publiés par la Société Nationale des Antiquaires de France a l'occasion de son centenaire* 1804–1904, pp. 315–331.)

BABELON, J. Sur un médaillon d'or inédit de Gallien (*Mélanges offerts à M. Nicolas Jorga* 1933, pp. 109–120)

PINK, K. The Bronze Medallions of Gordianus III (*NC* 1931, pp. 249–260)

——— and ELMER, G. Apollo Arnazi (*JDAI* 1937, SS. 104–110.)

RIZZOLI, L. Un nuovo medaglione con doppio cerchio dell' imperatore Settimio Severo e i medaglioni romani del Museo Bottacin di Padova (*Bollettino del Museo Civico di Padova* 1910–1911, pp. 123–132)

VII. DIOCLETIAN TO JUSTINIAN

ALFÖLDI, A. Die Donaubrücke Konstantins des Grossen und verwandte historische Darstellungen auf spätrömischen Münzen (*ZN* 1926, SS. 161–174)

——— Ein spätrömische Helmform (*Acta Archaeologica* 1934, pp. 99–144)

——— A Festival of Isis in Rome under the Christian Emperors of the Fourth Century (London, 1937)

BABELON, E. Un nouveau médaillon en or de Constantin le Grand (*Mélanges Boissier* 1903, pp. 49–55 = *Mélanges numismatiques* IV, p. 128–137)

BABELON, J. A Gold Medallion of Maximinus Daza (*Trans. Internat. Congr. Num.* 1936, London, 1938, pp. 151–159)

BALDWIN, A. (Mrs. BRETT) Five Roman Gold Medallions or Multiple Solidi of the Late Empire (*NNM* No. 6, 1921)

BANSA, O. ULRICH- Note sulla zecca di Aquileia romana (Udine, 1936)

CESANO, S. L. Di un nuovo medaglione aureo di Costantino I e del princeps iuventutis (*Rassegna numismatica* 1911, pp. 33–92)

CHABOUILLET, A. Observations sur deux médaillons d'or de Honorius et de Placide (*RN* 1883, pp. 70–91)

DELBRÜCK, R. Spätantike Kaiserportraits von Constantinus Magnus bis zum Ende des Westreichs (Berlin, 1933)

HORVAT, B. Ein unbekannter Bronzemedaillon des Kaiser Diokletian (*Numismatika* 1933, pp. 19–22)

KENNER, F. Römische Goldmünzen der Sammlung Weifert in Belgrad (*NZ* 1889, SS. 369–384)

——— Silbermedaillon der Sammlung Weifert in Belgrad (*NZ* 1896, SS. 107–108)

——— Die aufwärtssehenden Bildnisse Constantin des Grossen und seiner Söhne (*NZ* 1880, SS. 74–107)

LEDERER, P. Unbekanntes Trierer Goldmedaillon des Constantinus I (*ZN* 1928, SS. 59–68; 314; 1930, SS. 63–67)

MAURICE, J. Numismatique constantinienne (Paris, 1908–1912)

——— L'iconographie par les médailles des empereurs romains de la fin du IIIme et IVe siècles (*RN* 1904, pp. 64–104, 473–504; 1905, pp. 177–217, 470–495)

PINK, K. Gold- und Silberprägung der Diocletianischen Tetrarchie (*NZ* 1930, SS. 9–38; 1931, SS. 1–59)

SEECK, O. Zu den Festmünzen Constantins und seiner Familie (*ZN* 1898, SS. 17–65, 323–324)

TOYNBEE, J. M. C. A New Gold Medallion of Constantius II (*NC* 1939, pp. 143–148)

——— Two New Gold Medallions of the Later Roman Empire (*NC* 1940, pp. 9–23)

VIII. MISCELLANEOUS MEDALLIONS

ALFÖLDI, A. Die Ausgestaltung der monarchischen Zeremoniells am römischen Kaiserhofe (*RM* 1934, SS. 1–118)

——— Insignien und Tracht der römischen Kaiser (*RM* 1935, SS. 1–171)

BALDWIN, A. (Mrs. BRETT) Six Roman Bronze Medallions (*NNM* No. 17, 1923)

BROWN, D. F. Temples of Rome as Coin Types (*NNM* No. 90, 1940)

SERAFINI, C. Saggio intorno alle monete e medaglioni antichi ritrovati nelle catacombe di Panfilo sulla Via Salaria Vetus in Roma (*Scritti in onore di Bartolomeo Nogara raccolti in occasione del suo lxx anno*, 1937, pp. 421–443)

SVORONOS, J. N. ΦΩΣ ΕΠΙ ΤΟΥ ΠΑΡΘΕΝΩΝΟΣ (*JIAN* 1912, pp. 193–339)

TOYNBEE, J. M. C. An Imperial Institute of Archaeology as revealed by Roman Medallions (*Archaeological Journal* 1942, pp. 33–47)

IX. CONTORNIATES

ALFÖLDI, A. Die Kontorniaten: ein verkanntes Propagandamittel der stadtrömischen heidnischen Aristokratie in ihrem Kampfe gegen das christliche Kaisertum (Budapest, 1943). (This work reached the author too late for her to make use of it in the text.)

BABELON, E. Traité des monnaies grecques et romaines, I, pp. 689–696 (Paris, 1901)

COHEN, H. *Op. cit.*, VIII, pp. 273–322

MACDONALD, G. Roman Contorniates in the Hunterian Collection (*NC* 1909, pp. 19–55)

McDOWALL, K. A. (Mrs. ESDAILE) Contorniates and Tabulae Lusoriae (*NC* 1906, pp. 232–266)

PICK, B. P-W[2] *s. v.* Contorniaten (Bd. 7, 1153–1160)

ROBERT, C. Étude sur les médaillons contorniates (Bruxelles, 1882)

SABATIER, J. Description générale des médaillons contorniates (Paris, 1860)

INDEX

TABLE OF PLATES

I

Classification: Medallions Proper. Pseudo Medallions. Medallic Coins. Border-line Pieces

			Page Reference
1. Hadrian	Æ	British Museum	21, n. 12. 142, n. 154.
2. Geta	Æ	British Museum	27, n. 46.
3. Trebonianus Gallus	Æ	Berlin	27, n. 48.
4. Hadrian	Æ	Formerly Trau Collection	32, n. 43.
5. Antoninus Pius	Æ	Berlin	32, n. 45.
6. Lucius Verus	Æ	Formerly Vierordt Collection	32, n. 47.
7. Aurelian	Æ	Vienna	33, n. 51.
8. Hadrian	Æ	Paris	33, n. 56. 76, n. 17.
9. Antoninus Pius	Æ	Formerly Evans Collection	34, n. 59.

II

Border-line Pieces

1. Gallienus	Æ	Vienna	35, n. 70. 165, n. 196.
2. Gallienus	Æ	Berlin	35, n. 73. 166, n. 199.
3. Tetricus I	Æ	Paris	35, n. 74.
4. Gallienus	Æ	British Museum	36, n. 84.
5. Jovian	Æ	Budapest	37, n. 88. 173, n. 69.
6. Probus	AV	Gotha	38, n. 109. 51, n. 44. 108, n. 128.
7. Probus	AV	Paris (Jameson Collection)	38, n. 111. 51, n. 45.
8. Probus	AV	British Museum	38, n. 111 51, n. 46
9. Probus	AV	Formerly Paris	38, n. 113.
10. Probus	AV	Vienna	38, n. 114. 50, n. 43.
11. Probus	AV	Copenhagen	38, n. 118.
12. Constantine II	AR	Budapest	38, n. 121.
13. Crispus	AR	Padua (Bansa Collection)	38, n. 123.
14. Constantine I	AR	Berlin	39, n. 124.
15. Constantine I	AV	Vienna	40, n. 132. 175, n. 123.
16. Constantine I	AV	Vienna	40, n. 132.
17. Constantius II	AV	Paris	40, n. 133.

III

BORDER-LINE PIECES. MINTS

				PAGE REFERENCE
1.	CONSTANS	AV	Paris	40, n. 134.
2.	VALENTINIAN I	AV	British Museum	40, n. 135.
3.	VALENTINIAN II	AV	Formerly Trau Collection	40, n. 136.
4.	CONSTANTINE I	AV	Formerly Trau Collection	40, n. 139. 175, n. 118.
5.	CONSTANTINE II	AV	Vienna	40, n. 139. 175, n. 118.
6.	CONSTANS	AV	Paris (Beistegui Collection)	40, n. 140. 174, n. 75.
7.	CONSTANS	AV	Paris (Jameson Collection)	40, n. 142. 175, n. 110. 198, n. 55.
8.	GRATIAN	AV	Vienna	41, n. 144.
9.	ARCADIUS	AV	————	41, n. 145.
10.	VALENS	AV	Gotha	41, n. 149. 174, n. 72.
11.	GALLIENUS	AV	Monaco	49, n. 23. 81, n. 65.
12.	GALLIENUS	AV	Paris (Beistegui Collection)	49, n. 24.
13.	GALLIENUS	Æ	Bologna	49, n. 27. 164, n. 184.
14.	DIOCLETIAN	Æ	Formerly Evans Collection	51, n. 53. 174, n. 87.
15.	DIOCLETIAN AND MAXIMIAN	AV	Trier	51, n. 60. 184, n. 237.
16.	DIOCLETIAN AND MAXIMIAN	AV	Formerly Paris	51, n. 60. 184, n. 237.

IV

MINTS

1.	DIOCLETIAN AND MAXIMIAN	AV	Formerly Paris	51, n. 61.
2.	DIOCLETIAN AND MAXIMIAN	Æ	British Museum	51, n. 61.
3.	CONSTANTINE I	AV	Stockholm	52, n. 63. 89, n. 137. 172, n. 46. 198, n. 41.
4.	DIOCLETIAN AND MAXIMIAN	Æ	Zagreb	52, n. 64. 87, n. 71. 178, n. 159.
5.	MAXIMIAN	AV	Stuttgart	52, n. 68. 184, n. 234.
6.	MAXIMIAN	AV	Formerly Paris	52, n. 68. 184, n. 234.
7.	MAXIMIAN	Æ	British Museum	52, n. 70. 108, n. 126.

			Page Reference
8. MAXIMIAN	Æ	Vienna	52, n. 71.
9. CONSTANTIUS CHLORUS	Æ	Vienna	53, n. 77. 103, n. 72.
10. MAXIMINUS DAZA	AV	Paris (Beistegui Collection)	53, n. 87. 171, n. 27. 173, n. 67. 184, n. 243.
11. ROMULUS	AV	Formerly Paris	53, n. 90. 102, n. 65. 189, n. 306.

V

MINTS. PROVENANCES: VELP, HELLEVILLE

1. CONSTANTINE I	Æ	Trier	54, n. 92. 177, n. 148.
2. CONSTANTINE I	Æ	Vienna	54, n. 92. 197, n. 33.
3. HONORIUS	AV	Formerly Paris	62, n. 35. 174, n. 77.
4. CONSTANTINE I	AV	Formerly Paris	62, n. 36. 175, n. 107. 198, n. 46.
5. CONSTANTINE I	AV	Formerly Paris	62, n. 36. 175, n. 107. 198, n. 42.
6. CONSTANTINE I	AV	The Hague	62, n. 36. 175, n. 107. 198, n. 43.
7. CONSTANTINE II	AV	Formerly Paris	62, n. 36. 175, n. 107. 198, n. 44.

VI

PROVENANCES: HELLEVILLE, HAMMERSDORF, MORENHOVEN, ARRAS

1. CONSTANTIUS II	AV	Formerly Paris	62, n. 36. 175, n. 107. 198, n. 48.
2. CONSTANTINE I	AV	Formerly Paris	62, n. 36. 174, n. 96. 183, n. 227.
3. CONSTANTINE I	AV	Formerly Paris	62, n. 36. 174, n. 80. 175, n. 123.
4. CONSTANTIUS II	AV	Formerly Paris	62, n. 36. 174, n. 80. 180, n. 195.
5. CONSTANTIUS II	AV	Königsberg	65, n. 54. 175, n. 107. 199, n. 52.

			Page Reference
6. Magnentius	AV	————	65, n. 60. 174, n. 77. 187, n. 269.
7. Magnentius	AV	————	41, n. 148. 65, n. 60. 175, n. 117. 186, n. 250.
8. Diocletian	AV	Paris (Jameson Collection)	67, n. 68. 81, n. 72. 171, n. 34. 174, n. 92.

VII

Provenances: Egypt

Honorius	AV	Berlin	64, n. 41. 174, n. 77.

VIII

Provenances: Arras

1. Diocletian	AV	Arras?	51, n. 49. 67, n. 68. 171, n. 34. 184, n. 235.
2. Diocletian and Galerius	AV	New York (Newell Collection)	52, n. 65. 67, n. 68. 171, n. 34. 178, n. 159. 179, n. 175.
3. Maximian	AV	Arras?	52, n. 76. 67, n. 68. 171, n. 34. 173, n. 64. 184, n. 238.
4. Constantius Chlorus	AV	Arras	67, n. 68. 171, ns. 28, 34. 174, n. 103. 183, n. 224. 195, n. 20.
5. Constantius Chlorus	AV	British Museum	67, n. 68. 171, ns. 28, 34. 174, n. 94. 177, n. 140. 183, n. 225. 195, n. 20.
6. Constantius Chlorus	AV	British Museum	67, n. 68. 171, ns. 28, 34. 174, n. 94. 183, n. 225. 195, n. 20.

XI

PROVENANCES: POLAND

				Page Reference
	Jovian	AV	Warsaw	68, n. 76. 174, n. 98. 182, n. 217.

XII

OCCASIONS: THE NEW YEAR

1.	Commodus	Æ	————	75, n. 12. 214, n. 22.
2.	Commodus	Æ	Paris	75, n. 16.
3.	Hadrian	Æ	Vienna	76, n. 22.
4.	Antoninus Pius	Æ	Gotha	77, n. 26.
5.	Faustina II	Æ	Vienna	77, n. 30.
6.	Diocletian	Æ	Copenhagen	78, n. 42. 170, n. 16.
7.	Maximian	Æ	Paris	78, n. 42. 170, n. 19.
8.	Antoninus Pius	Æ	Paris	79, n. 46.
9.	Alexander Severus and Julia Mamaea	Æ	Turin	81, n. 62.
10.	Maximian	Æ	Padua	81, n. 71.
11.	Constans	AV	Formerly Paris	82, n. 77. 175, n. 114.

XIII

OCCASIONS: THE NEW YEAR

1.	Constantius II	AV	Formerly Trau Collection	82, n. 78. 175, n. 113.
2.	Constantius II	AV	British Museum	82, n. 78. 175, n. 113.
3.	Constans	AV	Milan	82, n. 78. 175, n. 113.
4.	Constans	AV	Gotha	82, n. 78. 175, n. 113.
5.	Constantine I	AV	Formerly Trau Collection	82, n. 79. 174, n. 76.
6.	Constantine I	AV	Formerly Trau Collection	83, n. 80. 174, n. 75.
7.	Constantine II	AV	Paris	83, n. 82. 175, n. 118.
8.	Constantine II	AV	Formerly Trau Collection	83, n. 82. 175, n. 118.
9.	Constantius II	AR	Vienna	83, n. 83. 175, n. 118.
10.	Constans	AR	Formerly Evans Collection	83, n. 83. 175, n. 118.
11.	Constans	AR	New York (Newell Collection)	83, n. 83. 175, n. 118.

XIV

OCCASIONS: THE NEW YEAR

			Page Reference
1. CONSTANTIUS GALLUS	AR	Formerly Trau Collection	83, n. 83. 175, n. 118.
2. CONSTANTIUS GALLUS	AR	Turin (Mazzini Collection)	83, n. 83. 175, n. 118.
3. MARCUS AURELIUS	Æ	Rome (Don Fabrizio Massimo Collection)	84, n. 89. 133, n. 63. 224, n. 137.
4. ALEXANDER SEVERUS	Æ	New York (Newell Collection)	85, n. 103.
5. GALLIENUS	Æ	Berlin	34, n. 64. 87, n. 123. 158, n. 143.
6. GALLIENUS	Æ	Vatican	34, n. 64. 87, n. 123. 158, n. 143.
7. MAXIMIAN	Æ	Vienna	88, n. 131.

XV

OCCASIONS: THE NEW YEAR

1. CONSTANTINE I	AV	Florence	88, n. 135.
2. LICINIUS II	Æ	Paris	89, n. 138. 172, n. 37.
3. ALEXANDER SEVERUS AND JULIA MAMAEA	Æ	Paris	89, n. 140.
4. JULIA DOMNA	Æ	Paris (Jameson Collection)	90, n. 142.
5. ANTONINUS PIUS	Æ	Trier	93, n. 172.
6. ANTONINUS PIUS	Æ	Vienna (Theresianum)	93, n. 172.

XVI

OCCASIONS: THE NEW YEAR

1. FAUSTINA I	Æ	British Museum	93, n. 172.
2. HADRIAN	Æ	Vienna	93, n. 178. 216, n. 55.
3. HADRIAN	Æ	Rome	93, n. 181.
4. ANTONINUS PIUS	Æ	Paris	94, n. 184.
5. AELIUS VERUS	Æ	Paris	94, n. 185.
6. ANTONINUS PIUS	Æ	Rome	94, n. 186.

XVII

OCCASIONS: THE NEW YEAR, MARRIAGES, BIRTHS, DEATHS, RELIGIOUS CELEBRATIONS, ADVENTUS

1. HADRIAN	Æ	Copenhagen	94, n. 187.
2. ORBIANA	Æ	Berlin	98, n. 18.
3. SALONINA	Æ	Zagreb	98, n. 21.
4. MARCUS AURELIUS	Æ	Paris	99, n. 27.

				Page Reference
5.	Fausta	AV	Vienna	101, n. 44. 172, n. 47. 175, n. 108. 226, n. 164.
6.	Faustina I	Æ	Paris	102, n. 57.
7.	Septimius Severus	Æ	Zagreb	103, n. 66.
8.	Volusianus	Æ	Vienna	104, n. 82.
9.	Gordian III	AV	Paris (Jameson Collection)	106, n. 101.
10.	Philip I and Philip II	Æ	Formerly Evans Collection	107, n. 112.
11.	Constantine I	AV	Paris (Beistegui Collection)	64, n. 52. 108, n. 130. 178, n. 160.

XVIII

Occasions: Adventus, Adlocutiones, Liberalitates

1.	Constantine I	AV	Formerly Vierordt Collection	109, n. 131. 174, n. 81.
2.	Constantius II	AV	Paris (Jameson Collection)	109, n. 133. 174, n. 81.
3.	Constantius II	AV	Formerly Trau Collection	109, n. 133. 174, n. 81.
4.	Constantius II	AV	Leningrad	109, n. 133. 174, n. 81.
5.	Valens	AV	Vienna	109, n. 135. 174, n. 81.
6.	Valens	AV	Paris (Jameson Collection)	109, n. 135. 174, n. 81.
7.	Valens	AV	The Hague	109, n. 136. 174, n. 81.
8.	Gratian	AV	Oxford	109, n. 138. 174, n. 81.
9.	Valentinian II	AV	Formerly Paris	109, n. 139. 174, n. 81.
10.	Alexander Severus	Æ	Formerly Trau Collection	110, n. 146.
11	Alexander Severus and Julia Mamaea	Æ	Paris	110, n. 146.
12.	Probus	Æ	Copenhagen	110, n. 148.
13.	Alexander Severus and Julia Mamaea	Æ	Vatican	111, n. 154.

XIX

Recipients

1.	Gallienus	Æ	Oxford	113, n. 6.
2.	Gallienus	AV	British Museum	50, n. 35. 113, n. 7.
3.	Augustus	AV	Este	114, n. 10. 127, n. 2. 231, n. 2.

				Page Reference
3.	Marcus Aurelius	Æ	British Museum	135, n. 86. 223, n. 134.
4.	Marcus Aurelius	Æ	Budapest	135, n. 87.
5.	Lucius Verus	Æ	Vatican	135, n. 88.
6.	Lucius Verus	Æ	Formerly Weber Collection	135, n. 88.
7.	Lucius Verus	Æ	————	135, n. 89. 219, n. 80.

XXIII

Historical Development I: Augustus—Commodus

1.	Marcus Aurelius	Æ	Berlin	135, n. 91.
2.	Marcus Aurelius	Æ	Vienna (Ružička Collection)	136, n. 94.
3.	Commodus	Æ	Formerly Trau Collection	137, n. 101.
4.	Hadrian	Æ	Vatican	137, n. 102. 214, n. 13.
5.	Antoninus Pius	Æ	Liège (Lébioles Collection)	138, n. 104.
6.	Hadrian	Æ	Paris	138, n. 109.

XXIV

Historical Development I: Augustus—Commodus

1.	Antonius Pius	Æ	————	138, n. 105.
2.	Marcus Aurelius	Æ	Bonn?	139, n. 119. 217, n. 58.
3.	Commodus	Æ	British Museum	139, n. 123.
4.	Antoninus Pius	Æ	Paris	139, n. 124. 221, n. 101.
5.	Faustina II	Æ	Formerly Trau Collection	141, n. 137. 215, n. 32.
6.	Lucilla	Æ	Autun	141, n. 139.
7.	Marcus Aurelius	Æ	Gotha	141, n. 143. 232, n. 13.

XXV

Historical Development I: Augustus—Commodus

1.	Marcus Aurelius	Æ	Frankfurt-am-Main	141, n. 144.
2.	Antoninus Pius	Æ	Paris	142, n. 155.
3.	Antoninus Pius	Æ	Pančevo (Elmer Collection)	143, n. 160. 231, n. 4.
4.	Hadrian	Æ	Formerly Levis Collection	143, n. 161.
5.	Faustina I	Æ	Zagreb	144, n. 170.
6.	Faustina I	Æ	Paris	144, n. 172.
7.	Lucius Verus	Æ	Llanymynech (Hall Collection)	144, n. 177.

XXVI

Historical Development I: Augustus—Commodus

1.	Hadrian	Æ	Vatican	145, n. 180.
2.	Commodus	Æ	Formerly Vierordt Collection	145, n. 182. 222, n. 124.
3.	Marcus Aurelius	Æ	Vienna	145, n. 183. 222, n. 126.

			Page Reference
4. Faustina I	Æ	Rome	145, n. 185.
5. Faustina I	Æ	Formerly Vierordt Collection	145, n. 185.
6. Antoninus Pius	Æ	Formerly Walters Collection	145, n. 188.
7. Marcus Aurelius	Æ	Venice	145, n. 191.
8. Antoninus Pius	Æ	Reggio Emilia (Villani Collection)	145, n. 193.
9. Hadrian	Æ	Formerly Trau Collection	146, n. 199.

XXVII

Historical Development I: Augustus—Commodus. Historical Development II: Septimius Severus—Carinus and Numerianus

1. Faustina II	Æ	Knin	145, n. 190.
2. Alexander Severus and Julia Mamaea	AV	Formerly Paris	24, n. 24. 147, n. 5.
3. Philip II	AR	Vienna	148, n. 21.
4. Gallienus	AR	Oxford	150, n. 31. 164, n. 185.
5. Gallienus	Æ	Formerly Trau Collection	156, n. 108. 223, n. 136.
6. Valerian I	Æ	Oxford	156, n. 122. 159, n. 154.

XXVIII

Historical Development II: Septimius Severus—Carinus and Numerianus

1. Gallienus and Salonina	AR	Boston	157, n. 134.
2. Philip I	Æ	Formerly Trau Collection	159, n. 154.
3. Gallienus	AV	Formerly Paris	159, n. 153.
4. Septimius Severus	Æ	Paris	152, n. 56. 156, n. 114. 161, n. 161. 227, n. 177.
5. Victorinus	Æ	Trier	162, n. 168.
6. Gallienus	Æ	———	162, n. 169.
7. Probus	Æ	Copenhagen	162, n. 170.
8. Elagabalus	Æ	Rome (Don Fabrizio Massimo Collection)	163, n. 175.

XXIX

Historical Development II: Septimius Severus—Carinus and Numerianus
Historical Development III: Diocletian—Justinian

1. Alexander Severus	AV	Munich	24, n. 22. 163, n. 178.
2. Julia Mamaea	Æ	Rome (Bettolo Collection)	164, n. 181.
3. Postumus	AV	Formerly Paris	164, n. 185.
4. Postumus	Æ	Vienna	164, n. 185.
5. Alexander Severus	Æ	The Hague	165, n. 188.
6. Alexander Severus and Julia Mamaea	Æ	Formerly Vierordt Collection	165, n. 188.

			Page Reference
7. Alexander Severus	Æ	British Museum	165, n. 189.
8. Salonina	Æ	Florence	165, n. 197.
9. Gratian	AR	Paris	169, n. 10.

XXX

Historical Development III: Diocletian—Justinian

1. Arcadius	AV	Formerly Paris	169, n. 12.
2. Constantine I	Æ	Vienna	172, n. 42. 174, n. 86. 182, n. 221.
3. Libius Severus	AV	Turin (Mazzini Collection)	173, n. 55. 183, n. 227.
4. Carausius	Æ	British Museum	175, n. 120. 189, n. 305.
5. Constantine I	AV	Belgrade (Weifert Collection)	173, n. 69. 175, n. 123. 180, n. 183.
6. Constantine I	AV	New York (Pierpont Morgan Collection)	174, n. 79. 175, n. 123. 181, n. 212.
7. Constantius II	AV	Paris (Jameson Collection)	175, n. 123.

XXXI

Historical Development III: Diocletian—Justinian

1. Constans	AV	Gotha	175, n. 110. 176, n. 130. 179, n. 181.
2. Constantine I	AV	Paris (Beistegui Collection)	177, n. 147.
3. Constantine I	AV	British Museum	177, n. 147.
4. Valentinian I	AV	New York (Newell Collection)	174, n. 89. 177, n. 151. 181, n. 205.
5. Licinius I and Licinius II	AV	Paris (Beistegui Collection)	173, n. 62. 178, ns. 154, 159. 183, n. 231. 224, n. 142.
6. Constantine I	AV	Vienna	179, n. 176. 197, n. 35.
7. Constantine I	AV	Belgrade (Weifert Collection)	179, n. 176.
8. Crispus	AV	British Museum	179, n. 178. 198, n. 40.
9. Constantius II	AV	British Museum	175, n. 110. 179, n. 180.
10. Constans	AR	Formerly Trau Collection	173, n. 69. 180, n. 182.

XXXII

Historical Development III: Diocletian—Justinian

1. Constantine I	AV	Rome	173, n. 70. 180, n. 184.
2. Constantius II	AV	Bonn.	64, n. 43. 173, n. 69. 180, n. 185.

			Page Reference
3. Constans	AV	Berlin	173, n. 69. 180, n. 185.
4. Constantius II	Æ	Formerly Vierordt Collection	173, n. 69. 180, n. 186.
5. Constantius II	Æ	Turin (Mazzini Collection)	173, n. 69. 180, n. 187.
6. Gratian	Æ	Vatican	37, n. 98. 173, n. 69. 180, n. 190.
7. Arcadius	AV	Berlin	173, n. 69. 180, n. 191.
8. Constantius II	AR	Vienna	173, n. 69. 180, n. 192.
9. Theodosius I	AR	Paris	173, n. 69. 180, n. 193.

XXXIII

Historical Development III: Diocletian—Justinian

1. Constantine I	AV	Glasgow	174, n. 72. 180, n. 194.
2. Constantius II	Æ	Formerly Vierordt Collection	174, n. 72. 180, n. 198.
3. Constans	AV	Florence	174, n. 72. 180, n. 199.
4. Constans	Æ	Paris	173, n. 70. 180, n. 201.
5. Constantius II	Æ	Vienna	174, n. 89. 181, n. 206.
6. Valentinian I	AR	Belgrade (Weifert Collection)	174, n. 72. 181, n. 208.
7. Valens	AR	British Museum	174, n. 72. 181, n. 209.
8. Theodosius I	AR	Vienna	174, n. 72. 181, n. 210.
9. Arcadius	AR	Vienna	174, n. 72. 181, n. 211.

XXXIV

Historical Development III: Diocletian—Justinian

1. Constantine I	AV	British Museum	174, n. 80. 175, n. 123. 181, n. 213.
2. Constantine I	AV	The Hague	174, n. 80. 175, n. 123. 181, n. 213.
3. Constantius II	Æ	Vienna	174, n. 79. 181, n. 214.
4. Constantine I	AV	Vienna	181, n. 216.
5. Constantine I	AV	Vienna	182, n. 220.
6. Galerius	AV	Formerly Trau Collection	184, n. 233.
7. Constantine I	AV	Belgrade (Weifert Collection)	185, n. 244.

			Page Reference
8. Crispus	AV	———	174, n. 74. 186, n. 252.
9. Constantine I	AV	Paris (Jameson Collection)	186, n. 253.
10. Crispus	AV	Paris (Jameson Collection)	187, n. 258.
11. Constantine I	AV	Formerly Trau Collection	187, n. 259.
12. Magnentius	AV	Formerly Paris	187, n. 260. 226, n. 168.

XXXV

Historical Development III: Diocletian—Justinian

1. Valentinian II	AV	Paris	174, n. 77. 187, n. 262.
2. Valentinian II	AV	Formerly Paris	174, n. 77. 187, n. 262.
3. Constantine I	AV	British Museum	174, n. 77. 175, n. 123. 187, n. 265.
4. Constantine I	AV	Paris	174, n. 77. 187, n. 265.
5. Constantine I	AV	———	174, n. 77. 187, n. 265.
6. Constans	Æ	———	174, n. 77. 187, n. 268.
7. Constantius Gallus	Æ	British Museum	174, n. 77. 187, n. 271.
8. Valentinian I	Æ	Formerly Trau Collection	174, n. 77. 187, n. 272.
9. Valens	Æ	Dresden	39, n. 96. 174, n. 77. 187, n. 273.

XXXVI

Historical Development III: Diocletian—Justinian

Theodosius I	AV	Washington (Freer Collection)	187, n. 263.

XXXVII

Historical Development III: Diocletian—Justinian

1. Valentinian II	Æ	Formerly Weber Collection	174, n. 77. 187, n. 274.
2. Valens	AV	Rome	174, n. 77. 175, n. 112. 187, n. 275.
3. Constantius II	AV	Oxford	175, n. 116. 188, n. 280.
4. Constantius II	AV	Berlin	175, n. 116. 188, n. 280.
5. Julian	AV	Formerly Paris	175, n. 116. 188, n. 282.
6. Valentinian I	AV	British Museum	175, n. 116. 188, n. 283.

			Page Reference
7. Valentinian I	AV	Formerly Paris	175, n. 116. 188, n. 283.
8. Valentinian II	AV	Formerly Paris	175, n. 116. 188, n. 284.
9. Constantine I	AR	Berlin	168, n. 6. 172, n. 36. 174, n. 78. 188, n. 286. 196, n. 25.
10. Constantinopolis	Æ	Paris	174, n. 91. 188, n. 287.
11. Roma	Æ	————	174, n. 78. 188, n. 288.
12. Constans	Æ	Florence	174, n. 78. 188, n. 290.
13. Crispus	AV	Paris (Jameson Collection)	174, n. 75. 189, n. 296.

XXXVIII

Historical Development III: Diocletian—Justinian

1. Theodosius I	AV	Turin (Mazzini Collection)	174, n. 78. 188, n. 291.
2. Arcadius	AV	Paris (Beistegui Collection)	174, n. 78. 188, n. 292.
3. Constantius II	AV	Formerly Paris	174, n. 78. 188, n. 293.
4. Constantius II	AV	Formerly Trau Collection	174, n. 78. 188, n. 293.
5. Constantinopolis	Æ	Vienna	188, n. 294.
6. Roma	Æ		174, n. 82. 189, n. 297.
7. Valentinian I	Æ	British Museum	174, n. 82. 189, n. 302.
8. Constantius II	Æ		174, n. 83. 189, n. 303.
9. Magnentius	Æ	Vienna	174, n. 75. 189, n. 304.
10. Constantine I	Æ	Rome (Museo Capitolino)	190, n. 308.

XXXIX

Medallions and Politics. Contorniates

1. Constantine II	AV	Formerly Paris	175, n. 107. 198, n. 45.
2. Constantine II	AV	Formerly Paris	175, n. 107. 198, n. 47.
3. Constantine I	AV	Leningrad	175, n. 107. 199, n. 51.
4. Constantius II	AV	Formerly Paris	175, n. 110. 199, n. 53.
5. Alexander the Great	Æ	Vatican	236, n. 34.

XL

TRAJAN, HADRIAN, SABINA, ANTONINUS PIUS

			PAGE REFERENCE
1. TRAJAN	Æ	Berlin	137, n. 100.
2. HADRIAN	Æ	Paris	132, n. 42. 133, n. 59. 145, n. 186. 223, n. 136. 227, n. 185.
3. HADRIAN	Æ	British Museum	138, n. 105a. 215, n. 37.
4. HADRIAN	Æ	British Museum	138, n. 106. 214, n. 15.
5. SABINA	Æ	Vienna	142, n. 151.
6. ANTONINUS PIUS	Æ	Vienna	139, n. 112.
7. ANTONINUS PIUS	Æ	British Museum	145, n. 187.

XLI

ANTONINUS PIUS, FAUSTINA I, MARCUS AURELIUS

1. ANTONINUS PIUS	Æ	British Museum	90, n. 149. 154, n. 85.
2. ANTONINUS PIUS	Æ	Berlin	140, n. 134. 215, n. 30.
3. ANTONINUS PIUS	Æ	Berlin	146, n. 200.
4. FAUSTINA I	Æ	Brussels	102, n. 56.
5. MARCUS AURELIUS	Æ	Milan	133, n. 60. 219, n. 80. 223, n. 136.
6. MARCUS AURELIUS	Æ	Berlin	96, n. 6. 139, n. 116.
7. MARCUS AURELIUS	Æ	Paris	136, n. 95.

XLII

MARCUS AURELIUS, FAUSTINA II, LUCIUS VERUS, LUCILLA, COMMODUS

1. MARCUS AURELIUS	Æ	Milan	133, n. 65.
2. FAUSTINA II	Æ	Paris	141, n. 138.
3. FAUSTINA II	Æ	British Museum	142, n. 153.
4. LUCIUS VERUS	Æ	New York (Pierpont Morgan Collection)	110, n. 143. 196, n. 28.
5. LUCILLA	Æ	New York (Pierpont Morgan Collection)	97, n. 10.
6. COMMODUS AND ANNIUS VERUS	Æ	Paris	134, n. 83.
7. COMMODUS	Æ	Paris	146, n. 202. 223, n. 133.
8. COMMODUS	Æ	Vatican	145, n. 178.

XLIII

COMMODUS, CRISPINA, ALBINUS, SEPTIMIUS SEVERUS

1. COMMODUS	Æ	British Museum	142, n. 146.
2. COMMODUS	Æ	British Museum	142, n. 145.

			Page Reference
3. Commodus	Æ	British Museum	74, n. 9. 132, n. 53. 220, n. 95.
4. Crispina	Æ	Paris	94, n. 183b.
5. Albinus	Æ	Milan	161, n. 162.
6. Septimius Severus	Æ	Rome	107, n. 109.
7. Septimius Severus	Æ	Vienna	161, n. 158.

XLIV

Julia Domna, Caracalla, Alexander Severus, Julia Mamaea, Maximinus

1. Julia Domna	AR	Berlin	148, n. 10. 152, n. 55. 158, n. 140. 164, n. 186. 227, n. 179.
2. Julia Domna	Æ	Paris	94, n. 183a.
3. Caracalla	Æ	Rome	156, n. 114. 227, n. 177.
4. Alexander Severus	Æ	British Museum	103, n. 67.
5. Alexander Severus	AV	Paris	24, n. 23. 81, n. 62. 152, n. 54. 155, n. 98.
6. Julia Mamaea	Æ	British Museum	89, n. 140. 158, n. 141. 227, n. 180.
7. Maximinus	Æ	Rome	160, n. 156.

XLV

Gordian III, Philip I, Philip II, Otacilia, Trebonianus Gallus

1. Gordian III	Æ	British Museum	161, n. 163. 195, n. 18.
2. Gordian III	Æ	Formerly Waldeck Collection	110, n. 146. 155, n. 90.
3. Philip I	Æ	Rome	86, n. 113. 152, n. 58.
4. Philip I, Philip II, Otacilia	Æ	Paris	86, n. 119.
5. Philip II	Æ	Milan	114, n. 12.
6. Otacilia	Æ	British Museum	164, n. 182.
7. Trebonianus Gallus	Æ	British Museum	165, n. 195.

XLVI

Volusianus, Valerian I, Valerian II, Gallienus, Salonina, Postumus

1. Volusianus	Æ	Rome	159, n. 152.
2. Valerian I and Valerian II	AR	British Museum	157, n. 133a.
3. Gallienus	Æ	Paris	155, n. 98.

			Page Reference
4. Gallienus	Æ	Milan	49, n. 25. 150, n. 33. 155, n. 106.
5. Gallienus	Æ	Rome	119, n. 54. 156, n. 110. 223, n. 136.
6. Gallienus	Æ	Rome	149, n. 25. 156, n. 107.
7. Salonina	Æ	Boston	149, n. 25.
8. Postumus	Æ	Berlin	157, n. 130. 162, n. 166.

XLVII

Claudius Gothicus, Aurelian, Tacitus, Florian, Probus, Carus, Carinus, Numerianus, Magnia Urbica

1. Claudius Gothicus	Æ	Glasgow	149, n. 25.
2. Aurelian	AV	British Museum	38, n. 117.
3. Tacitus	Æ	Rome	91, n. 157. 151, n. 49. 156, n. 112.
4. Florian	Æ	British Museum	149, n. 25.
5. Probus	Æ	Turin (Mazzini Collection)	149, n. 25. 155, n. 98.
6. Probus	Æ	Paris	149, n. 25. 156, n. 113.
7. Carus and Carinus	AV	Vienna	51, n. 47. 81, n. 70. 152, n. 64. 154, n. 82.
8. Numerianus	Æ	Vatican	149, n. 25. 157, n. 129.
9. Magnia Urbica	Æ	Vienna	164, n. 183.

XLVIII

Diocletian, Maximian, Helena, Licinius II, Constantine II, Constantius II, Constans

1. Diocletian	AV	British Museum	51, n. 48. 173, n. 63. 175, n. 121. 183, n. 232.
2. Maximian	AV	Budapest	52, n. 67. 81, n. 71. 171, n. 32.
3. Maximian	Æ	British Museum	149, n. 25. 177, n. 139.
4. Helena	AV	Paris	174, n. 74. 186, n. 254.
5. Licinius II	AV	Paris	39, n. 129. 90, n. 146. 172, n. 38. 176, n. 132.

			PAGE REFERENCE
6. CONSTANTINE II	AV	New York (Pierpont Morgan Collection)	82, n. 76. 175, n. 115. 226, n. 159.
7. CONSTANTIUS II	AV	British Museum	73, n. 58. 174, n. 78. 177, n. 149. 188, n. 293. 224, n. 140.
8. CONSTANS	AV	Berlin	173, n. 61. 174, n. 80. 181, n. 215. 195, n. 21.

XLIX

GALLA PLACIDIA, ATTALUS, JUSTINIAN

1. GALLA PLACIDIA	AV	Paris	175, n. 111. 182, n. 218.
2. ATTALUS	AR	British Museum	174, n. 77. 188, n. 276.
3. JUSTINIAN	AV	Formerly Paris	173, n. 56. 176, n. 127. 177, n. 150. 178, n. 155. 183, n. 228. 224, n. 141. 227, n. 170.

ERRATA ON PLATES

Plate I. At bottom, in first line of caption: For MEDALIONS read MEDALLIONS

Plate XII, no. 11: For Æ, read AV.

Plate XVIII. At bottom, in caption: For LIBERALITES read LIBERALITATES

Plate XXVII. At bottom, in second line of caption: For SEPTIMUS read SEPTIMIUS

Plate XXXV, no. 6: For AV read Æ.

Plate XL. At bottom, in caption: For ANTONIUS read ANTONINUS

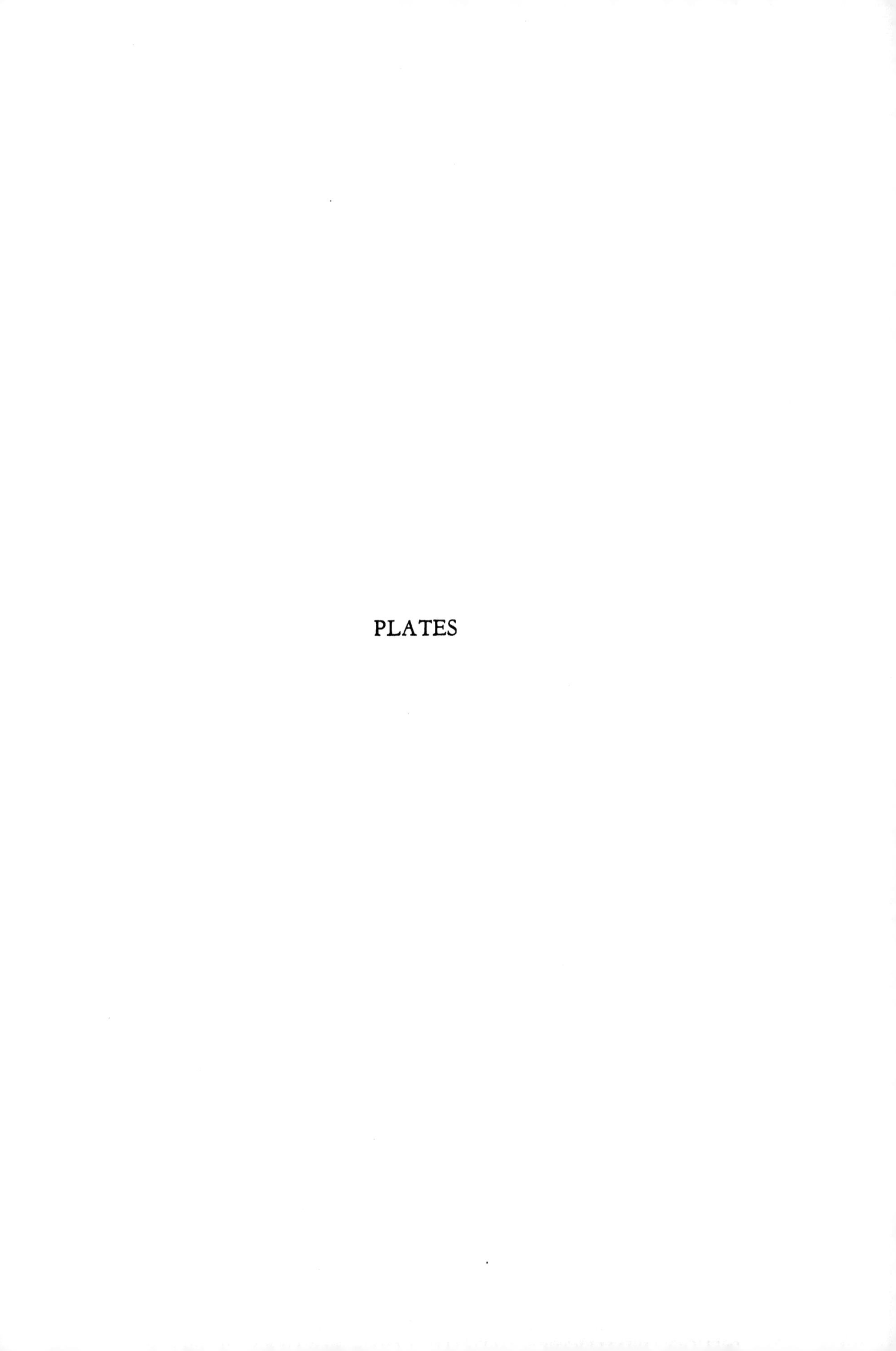

PLATES

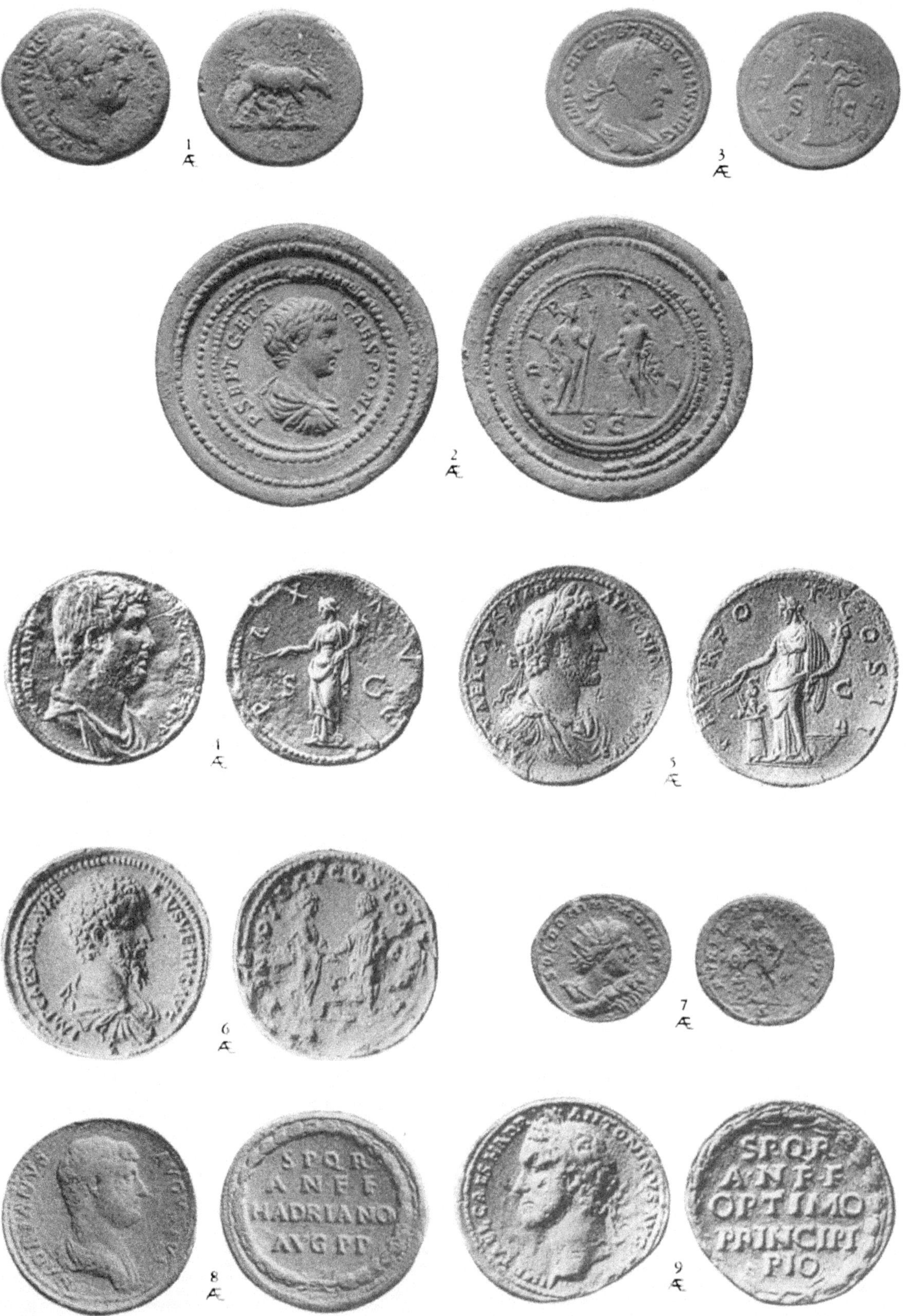

CLASSIFICATION: MEDALIONS PROPER.
PSEUDO MEDALLIONS — MEDALLIC COINS, BORDER LINE PIECES

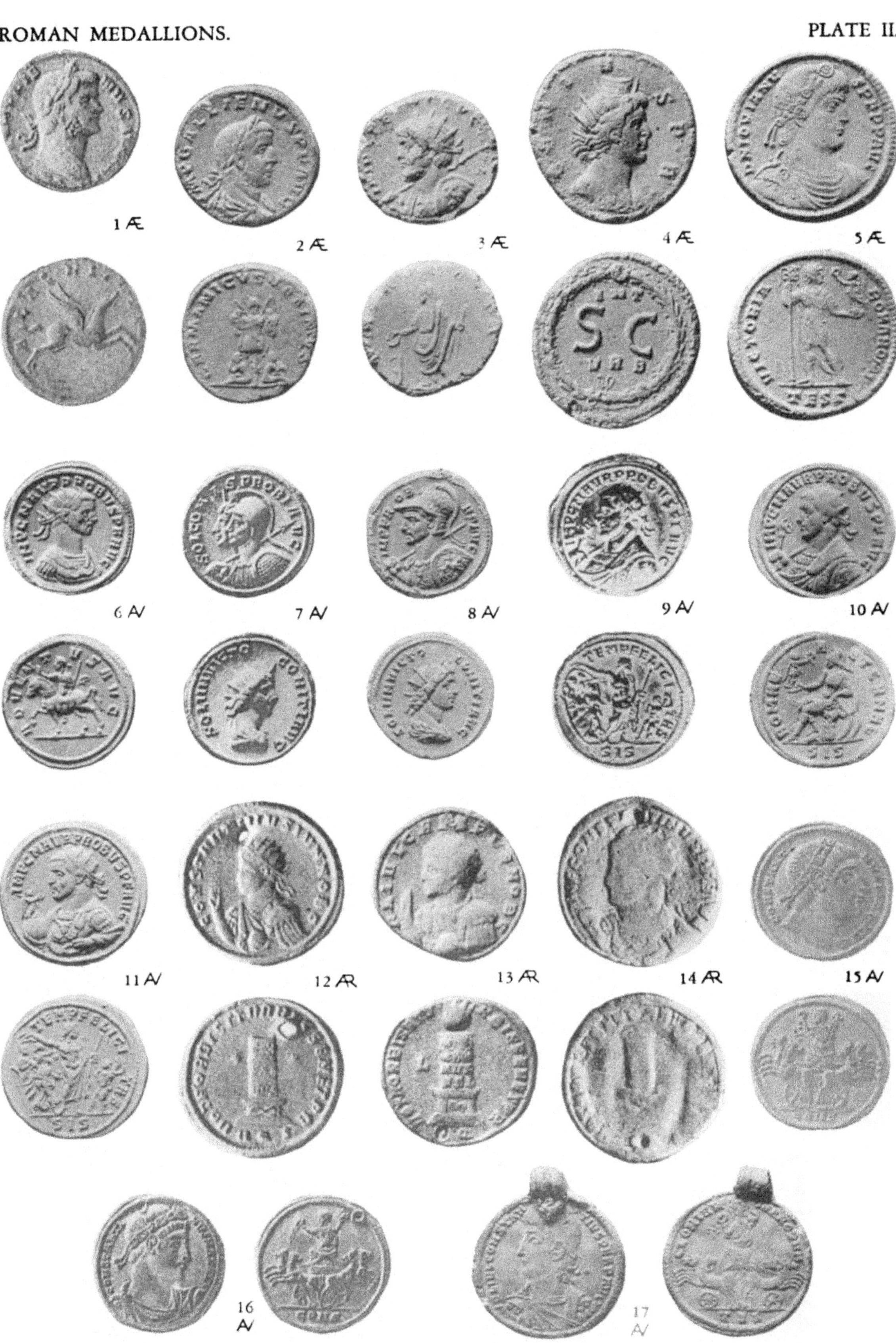

1 Æ 2 Æ 3 Æ 4 Æ 5 Æ

6 AV 7 AV 8 AV 9 AV 10 AV

11 AV 12 AR 13 AR 14 AR 15 AV

16 AV 17 AV

BORDER-LINE PIECES.

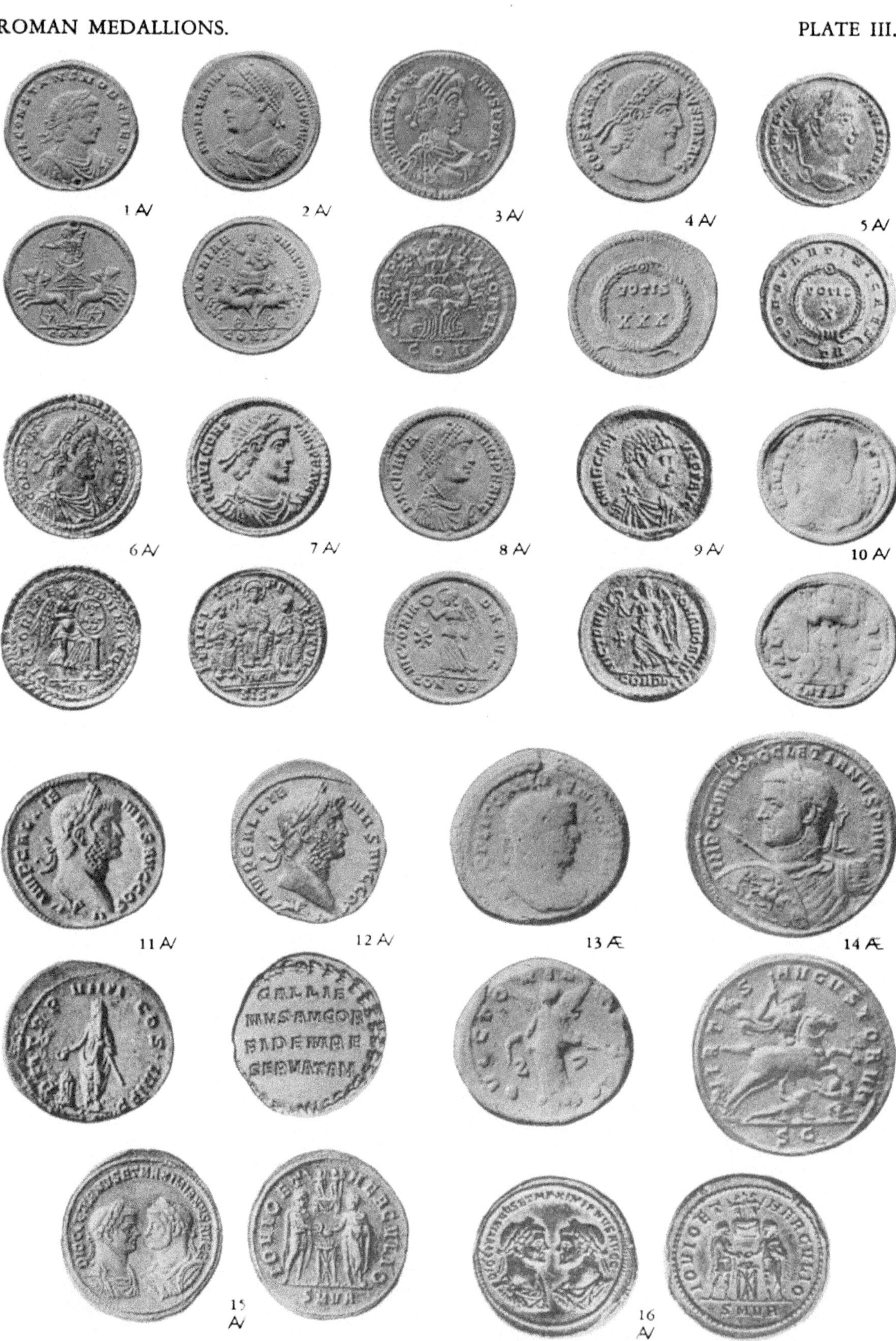

BORDER-LINE PIECES. MINTS.

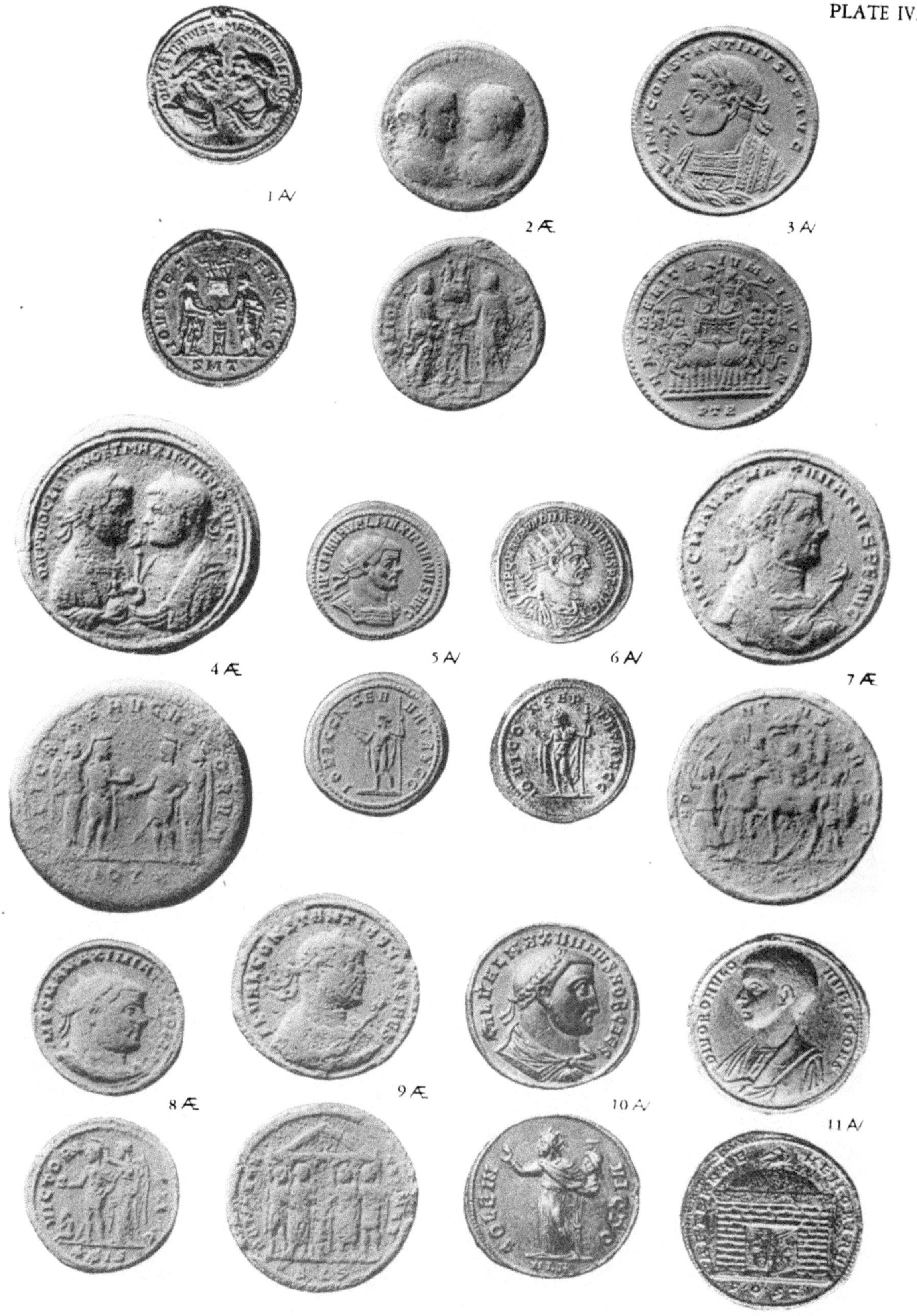

1 AV

2 Æ

3 AV

4 Æ

5 AV

6 AV

7 Æ

8 Æ

9 Æ

10 AV

11 AV

MINTS.

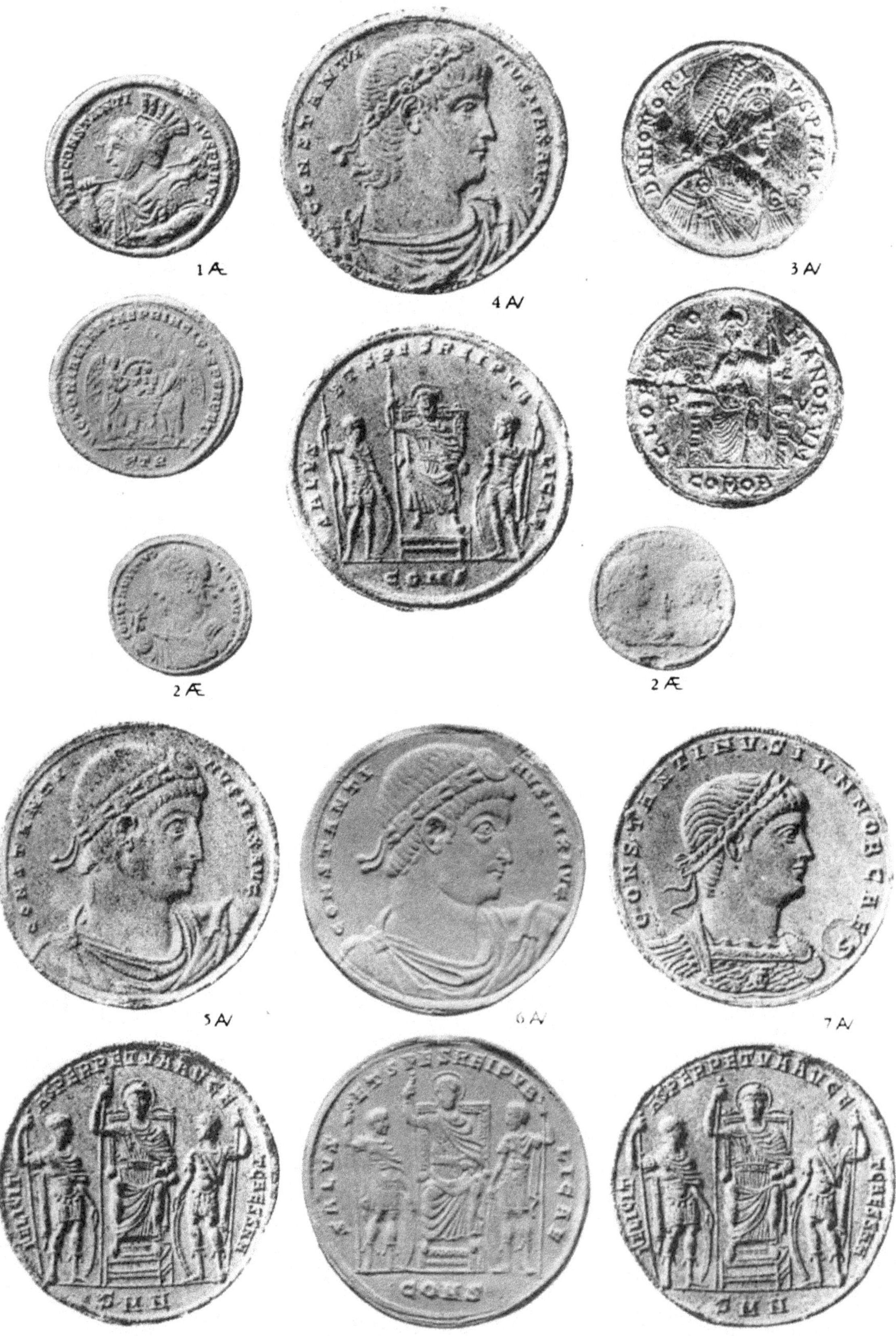

MINTS. PROVENANCES: VELP, HELLEVILLE.

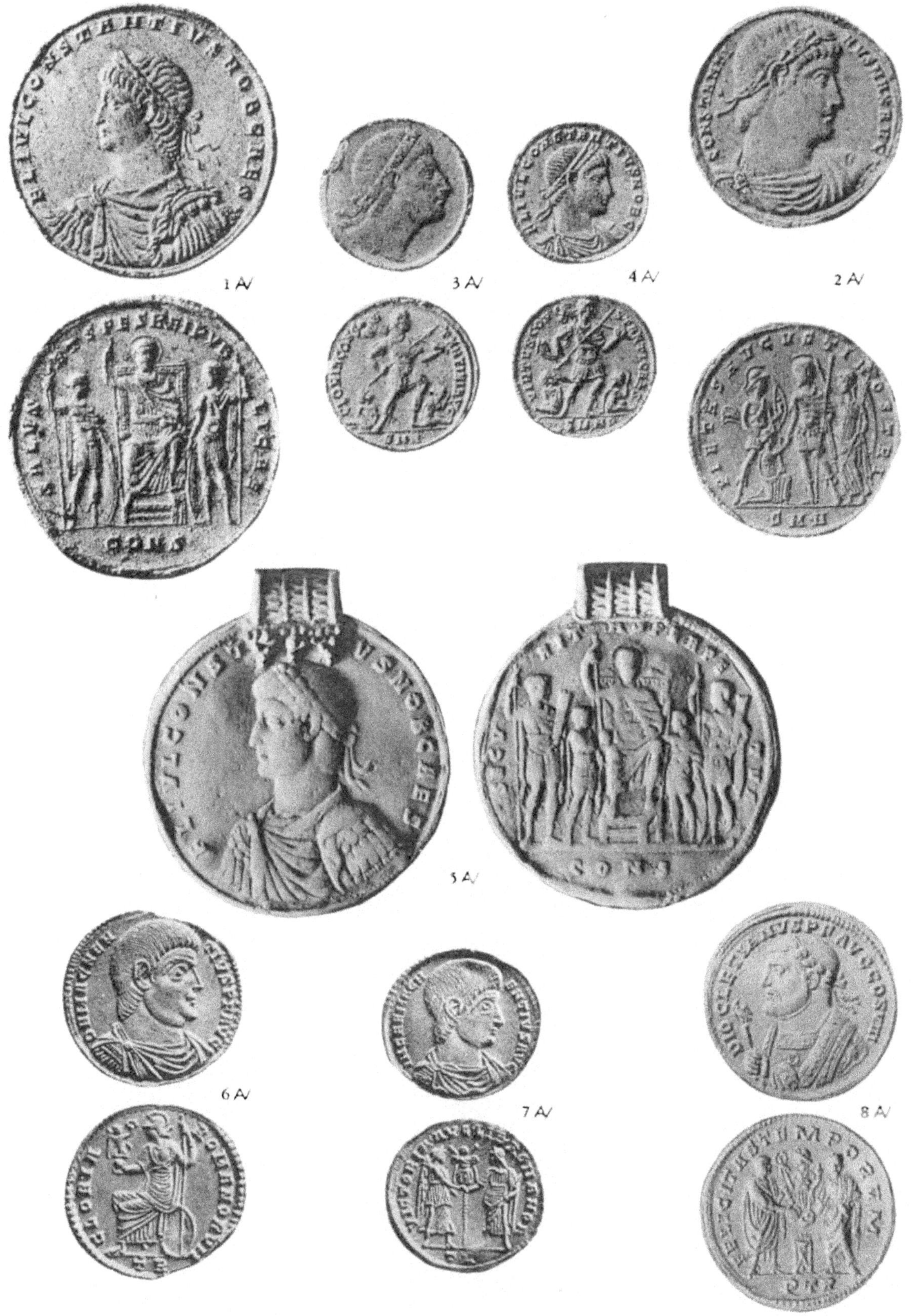

1 AV 3 AV 4 AV 2 AV

5 AV

6 AV 7 AV 8 AV

PROVENANCES: HELLEVILLE, HAMMERSDORF,

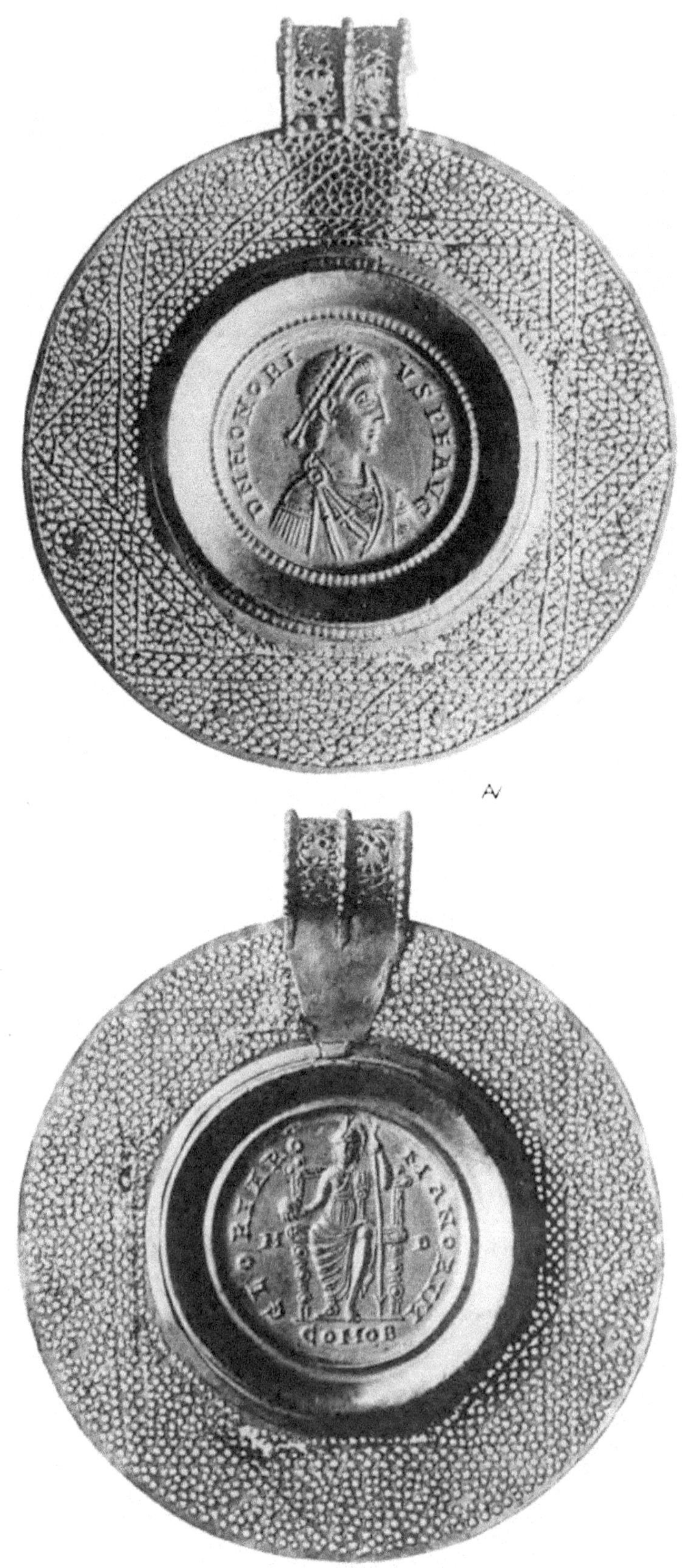

PROVENANCES: EGYPT.

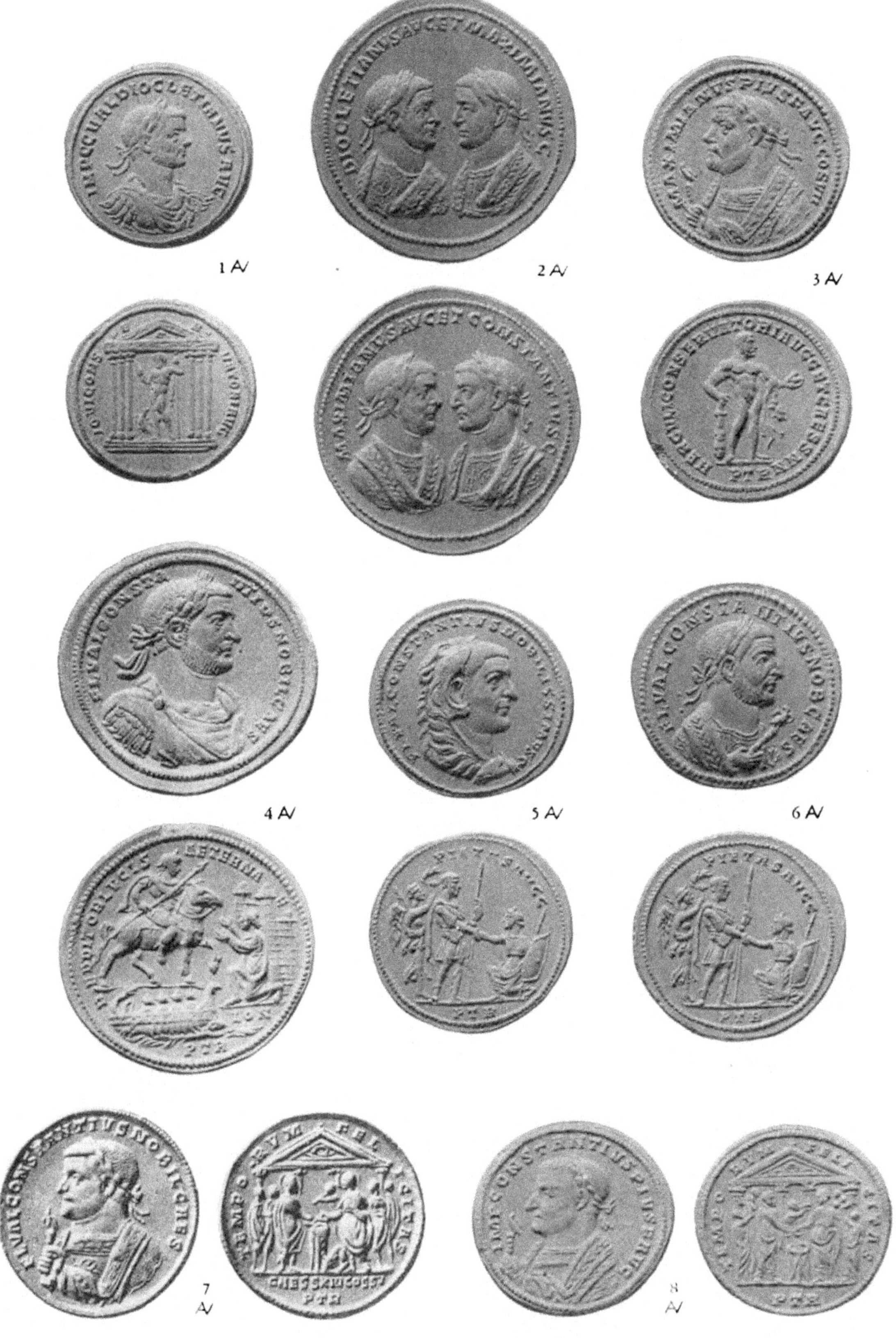

PROVENANCES: ARRAS.

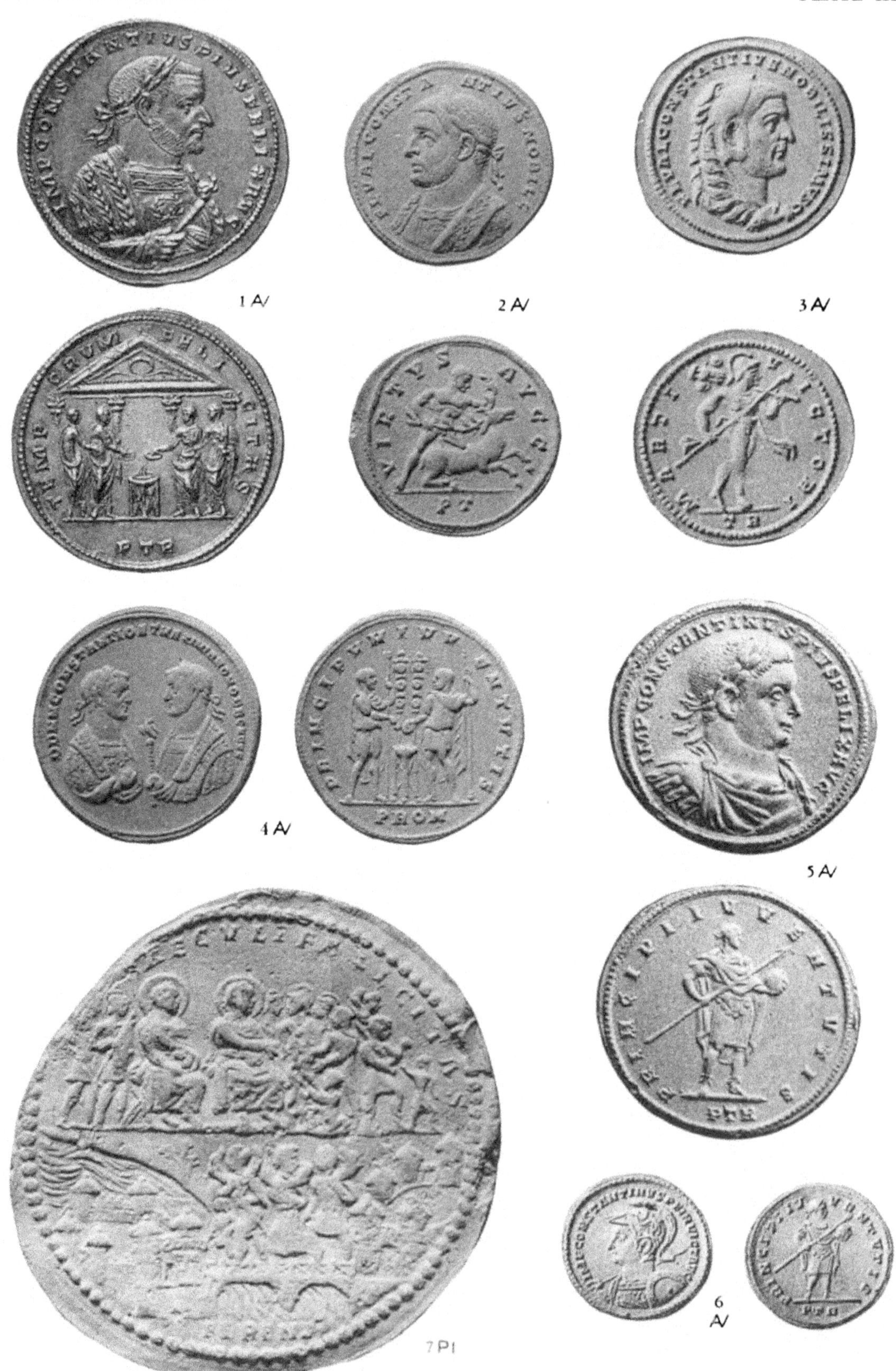

PROVENANCES: ARRAS.

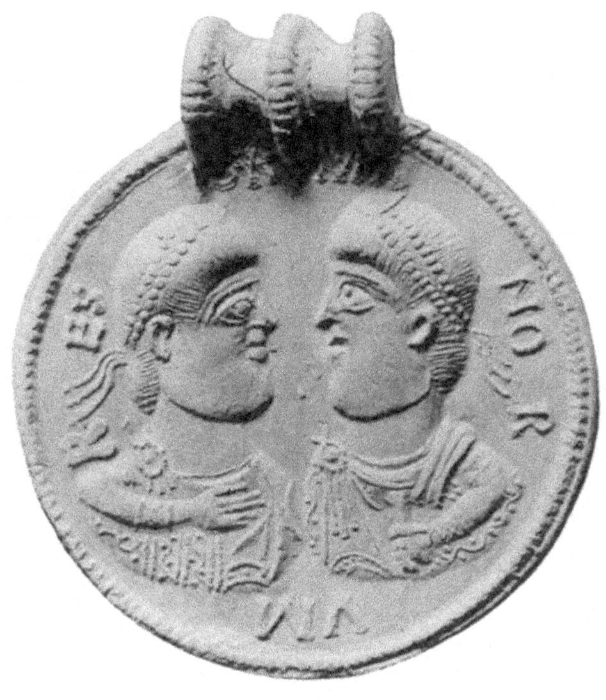

AV

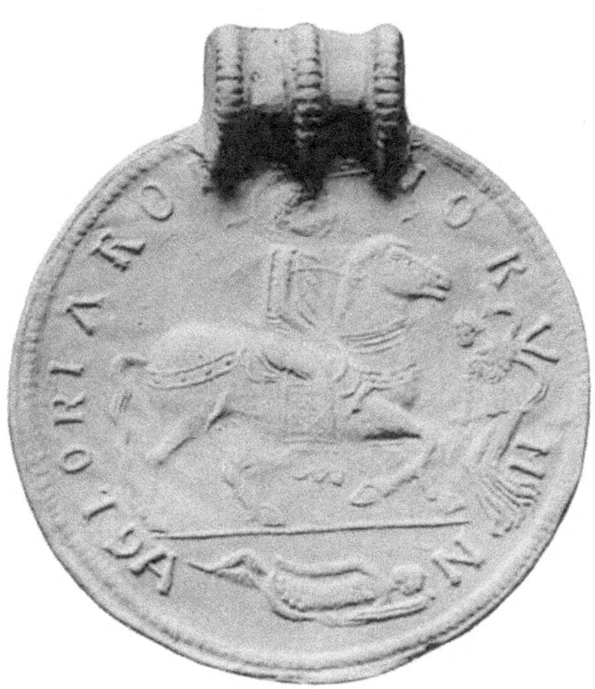

PROVENANCES: GERMANY.

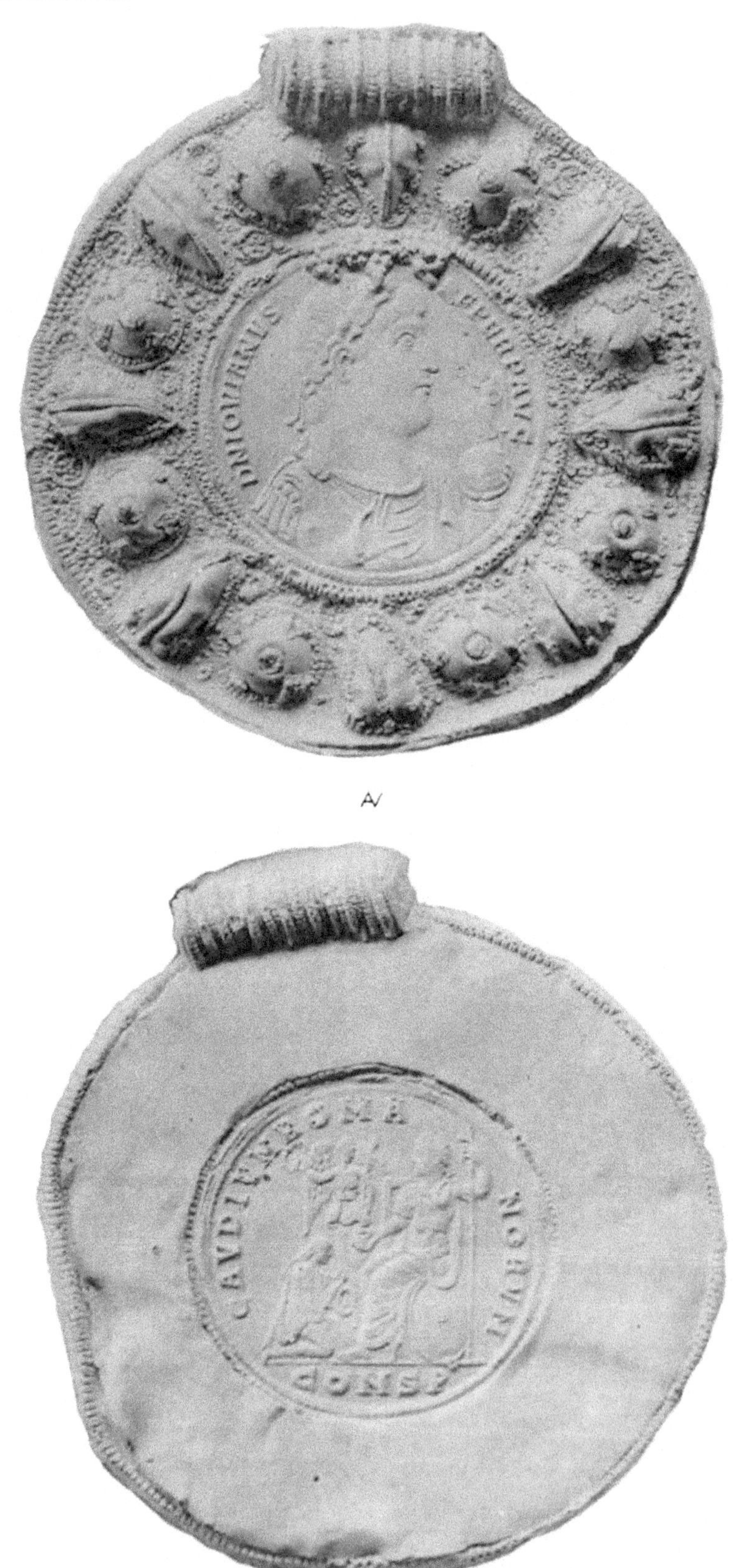

PROVENANCES: POLAND.

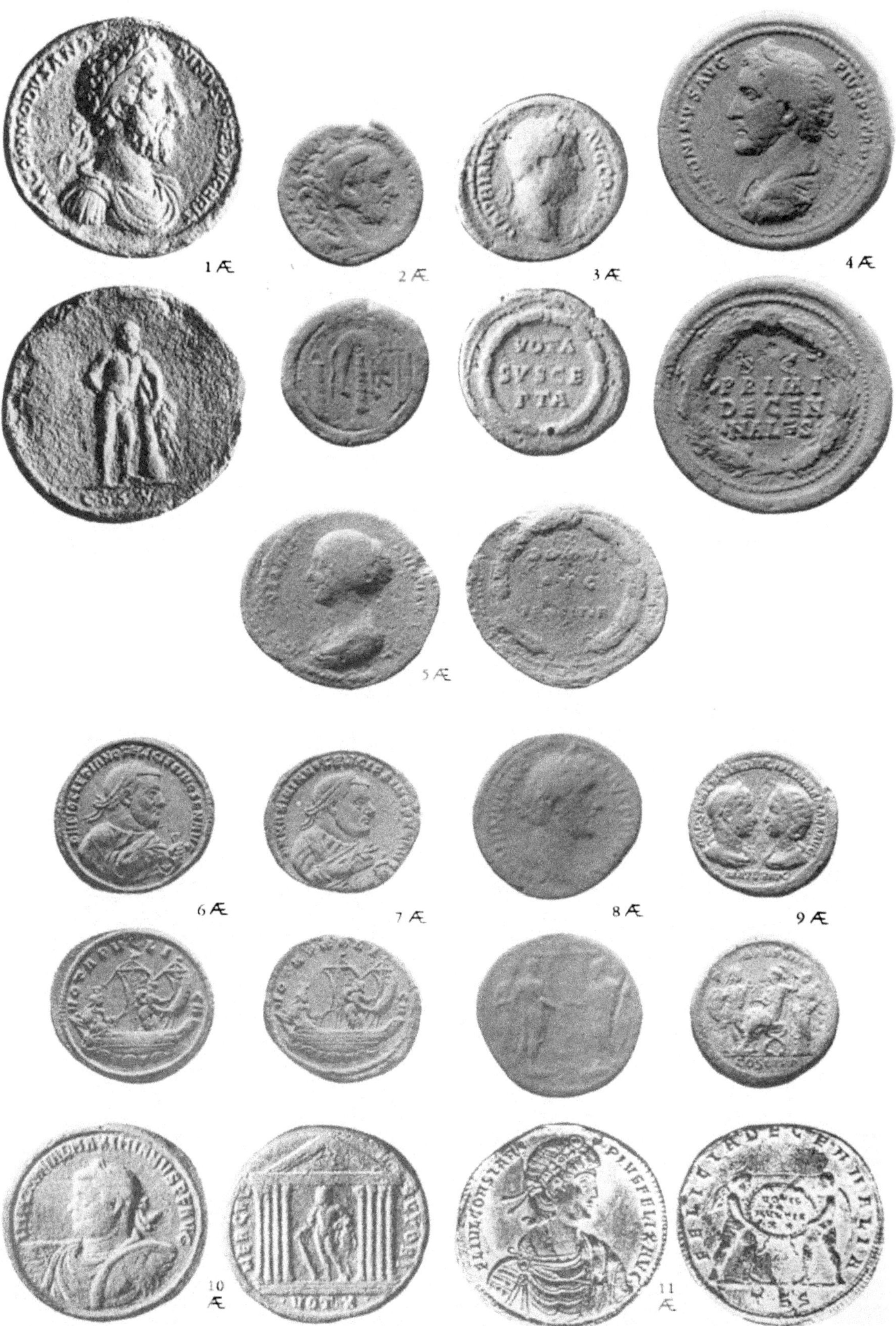
1 Æ
2 Æ
3 Æ
4 Æ
VOTA
SVSCE
PTA
PRIMI
DECEN
NALES
5 Æ
6 Æ
7 Æ
8 Æ
9 Æ
10
Æ
11
Æ

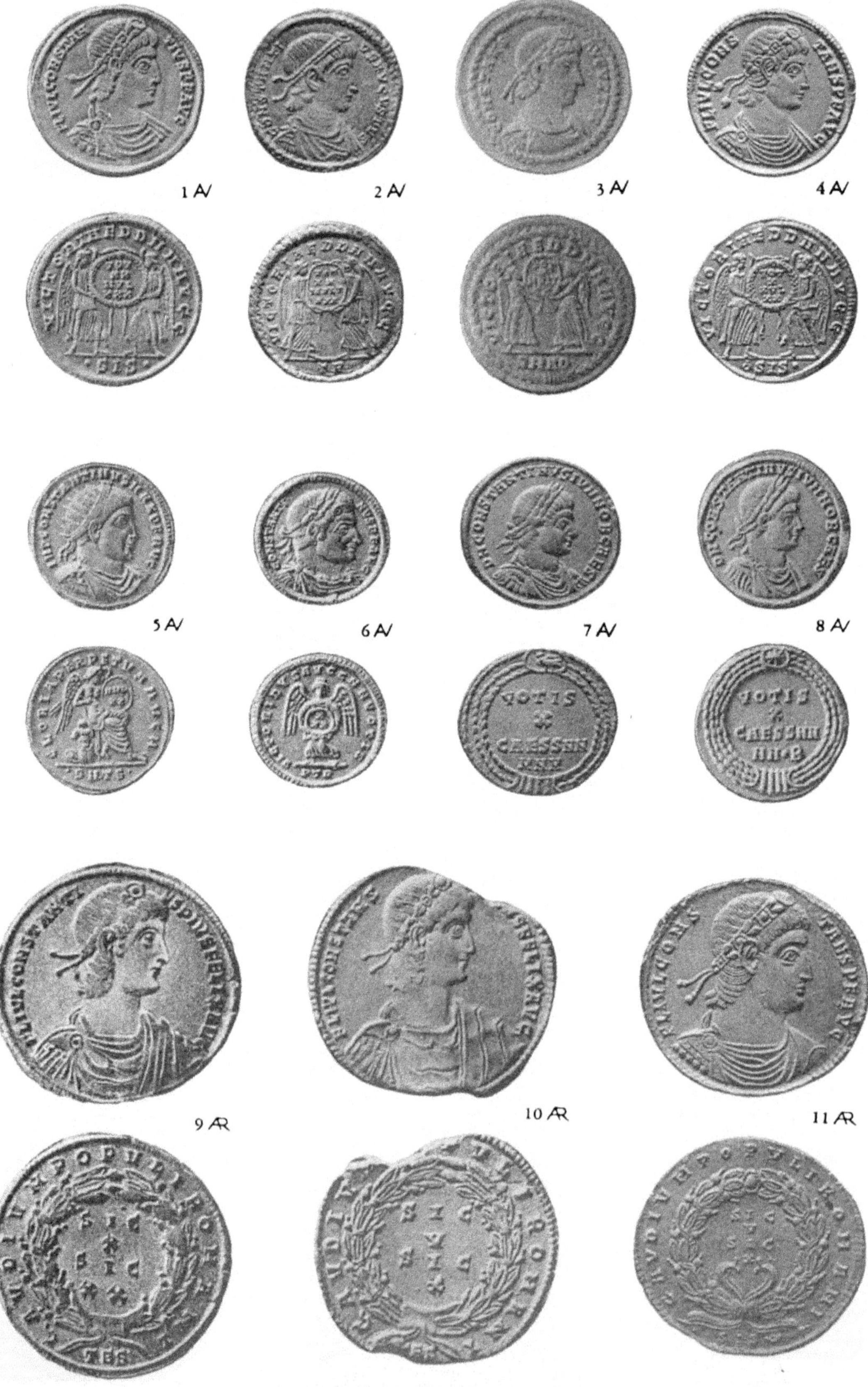

OCCASIONS: THE NEW YEAR

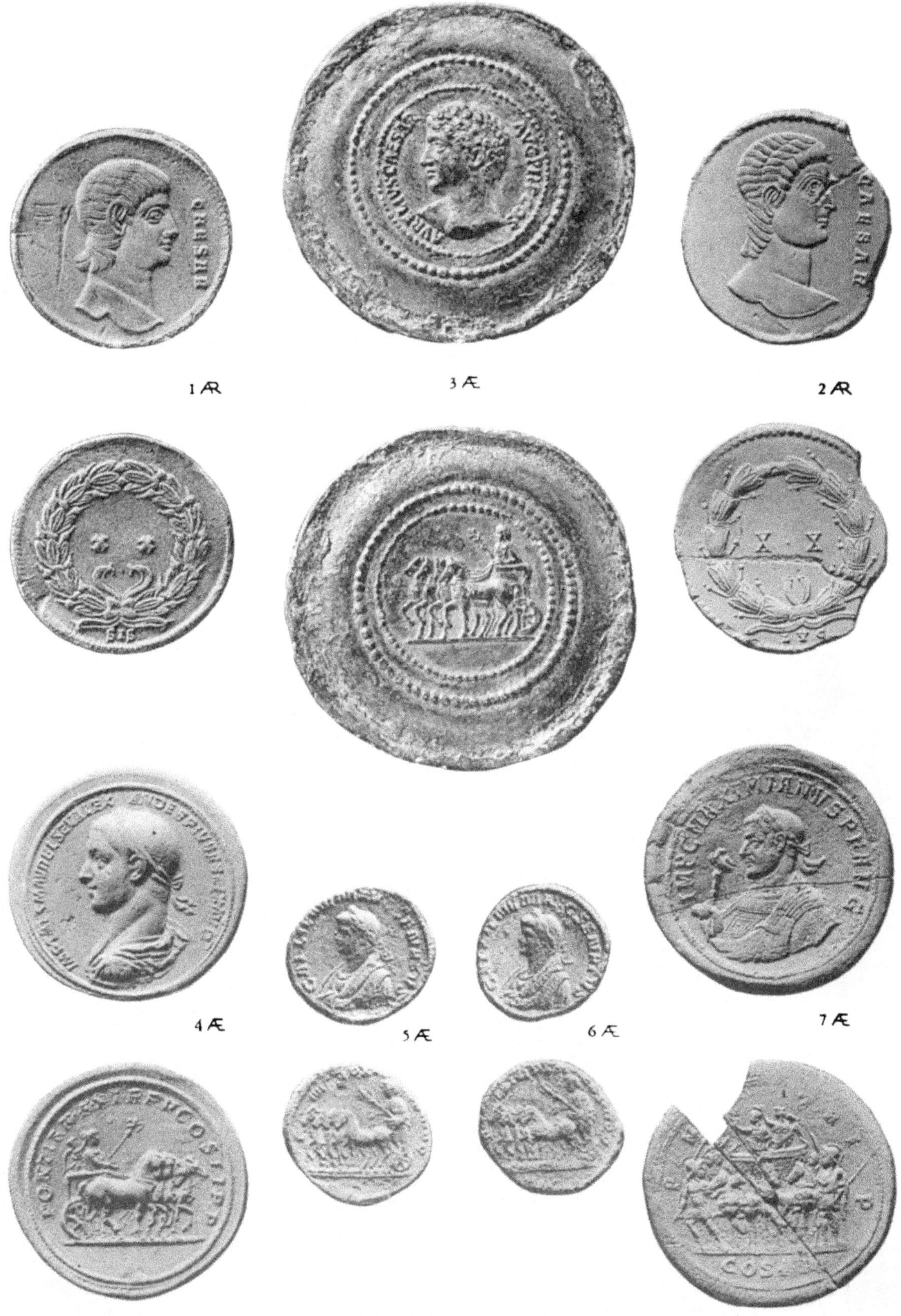

1 AR

3 Æ

2 AR

4 Æ

5 Æ

6 Æ

7 Æ

OCCASIONS: THE NEW YEAR

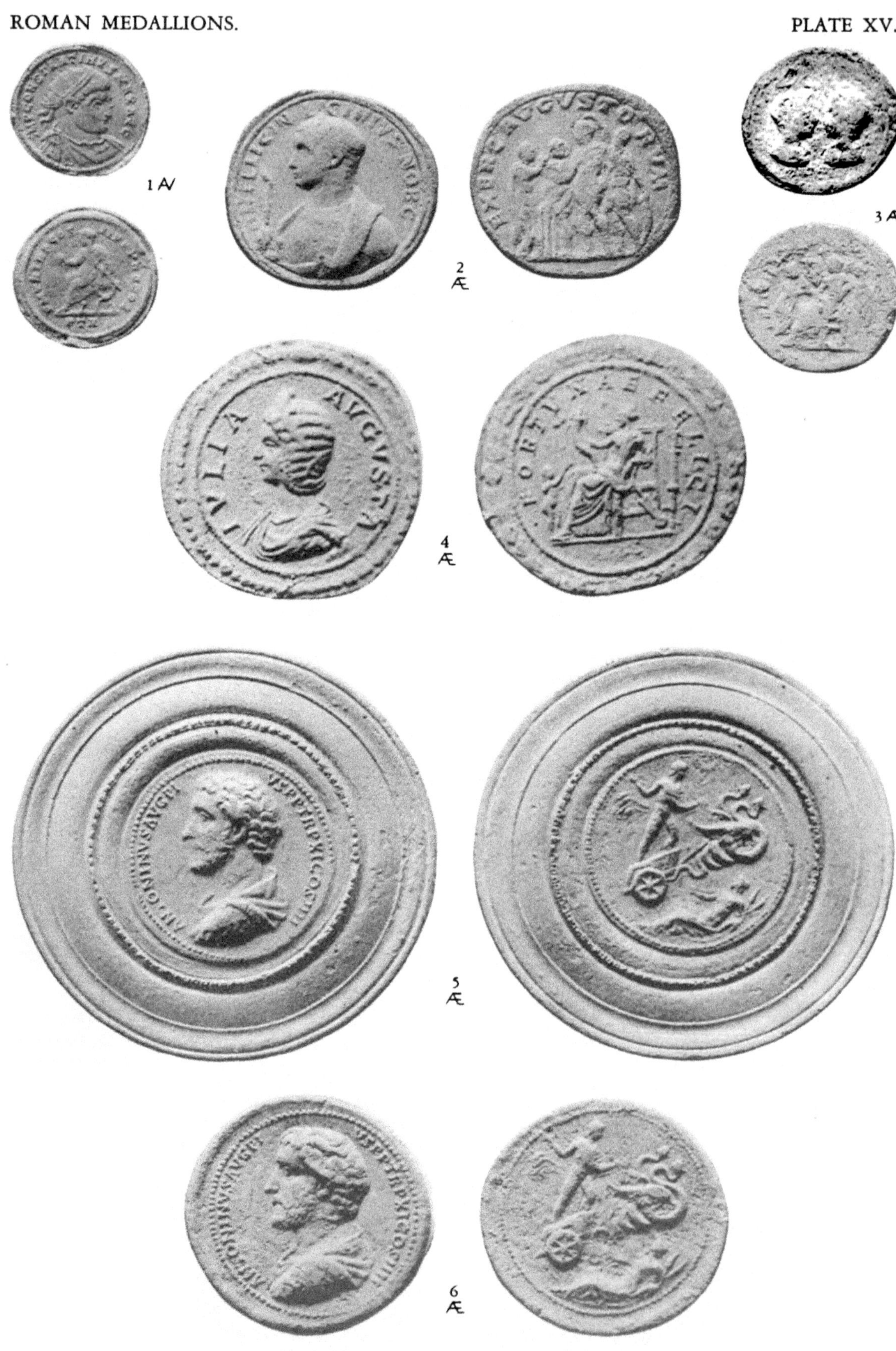

1 AV

2 Æ

3 Æ

4 Æ

5 Æ

6 Æ

1 Æ

2 Æ

3 Æ

4 Æ

5 Æ

6 Æ

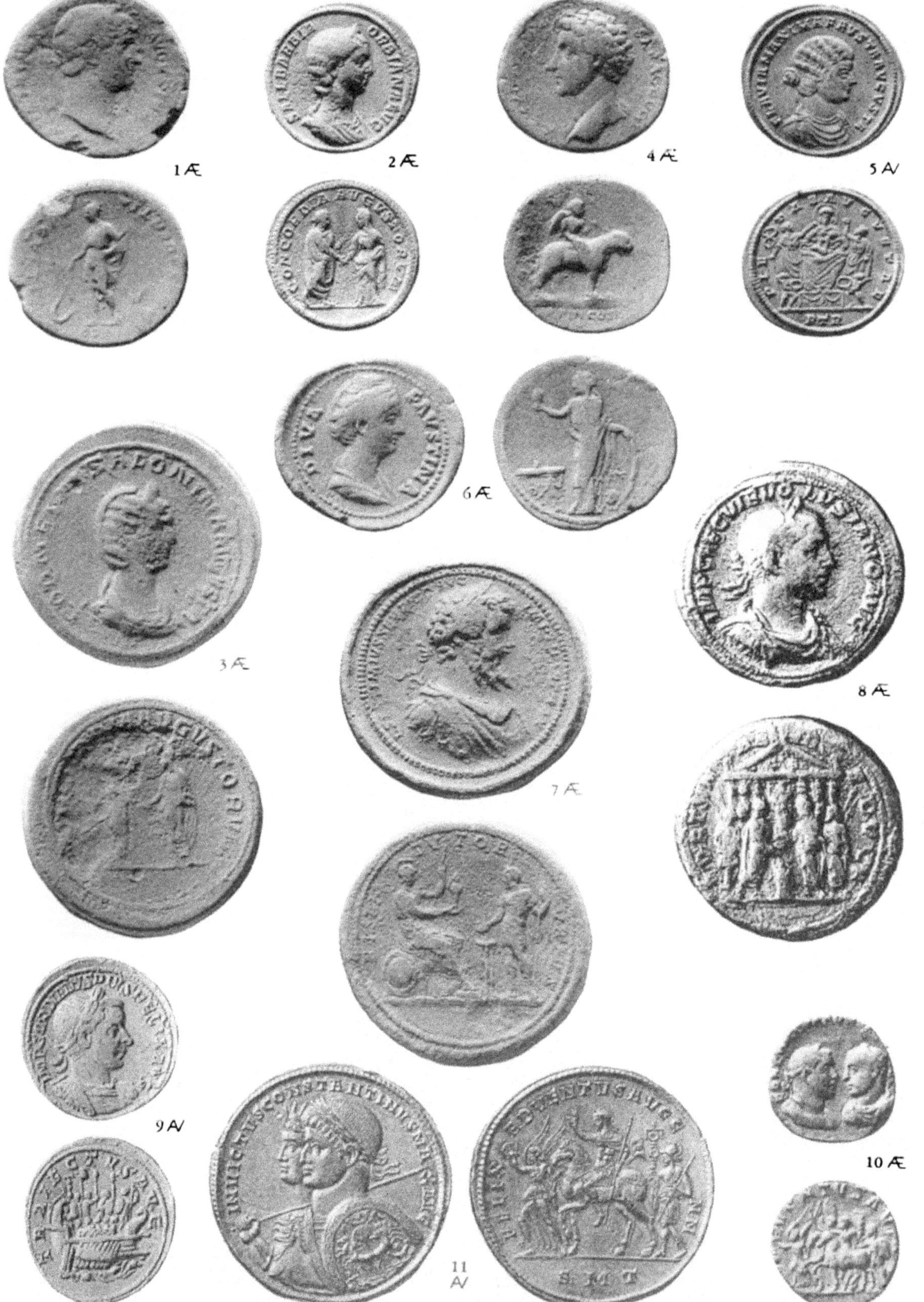
1 Æ 2 Æ 4 Æ 5 AV 6 Æ 3 Æ 8 Æ 7 Æ 9 AV 10 Æ 11 AV

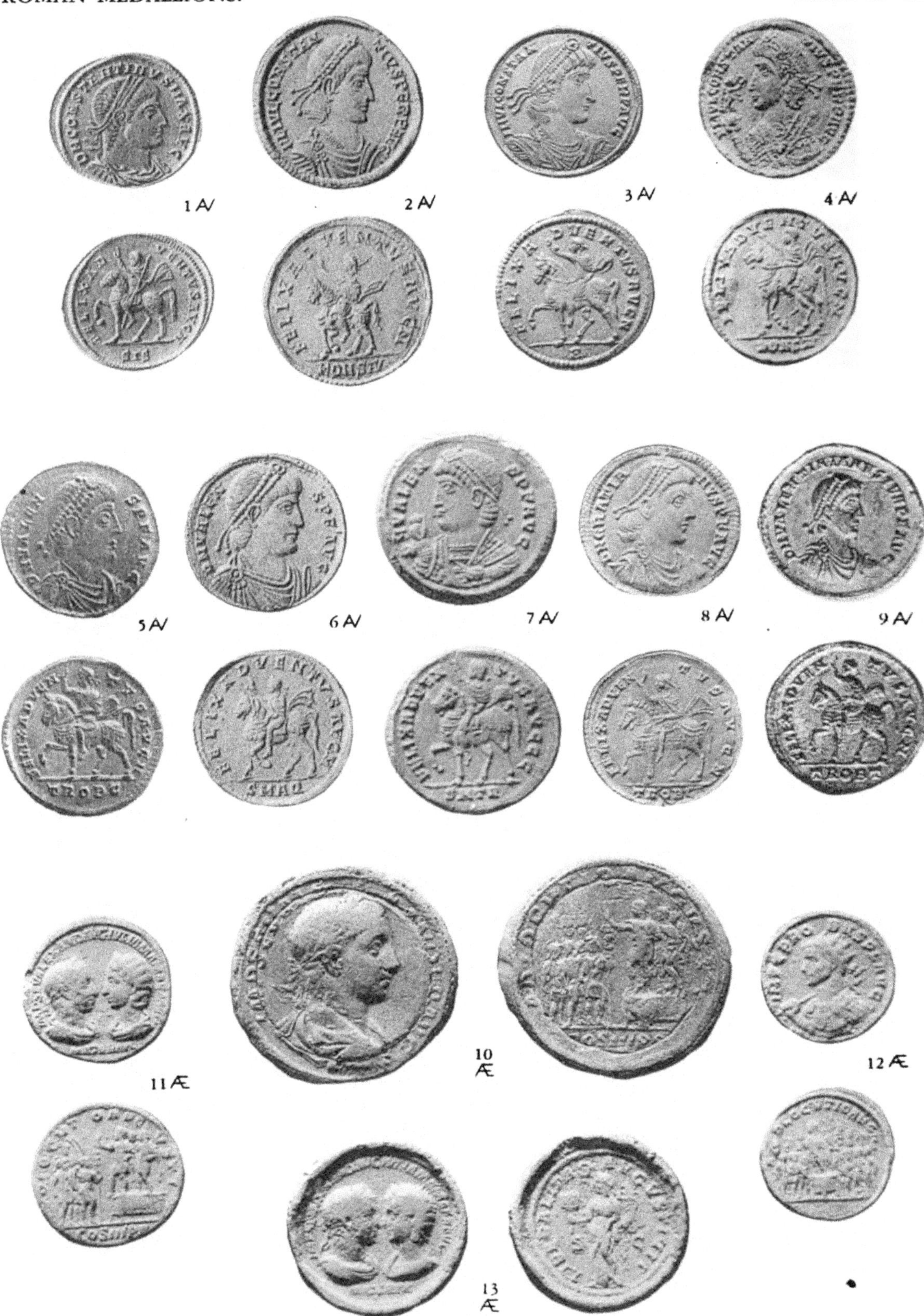

OCCASIONS: ADVENTUS, ADLOCUTIONES, LIBERALITES.

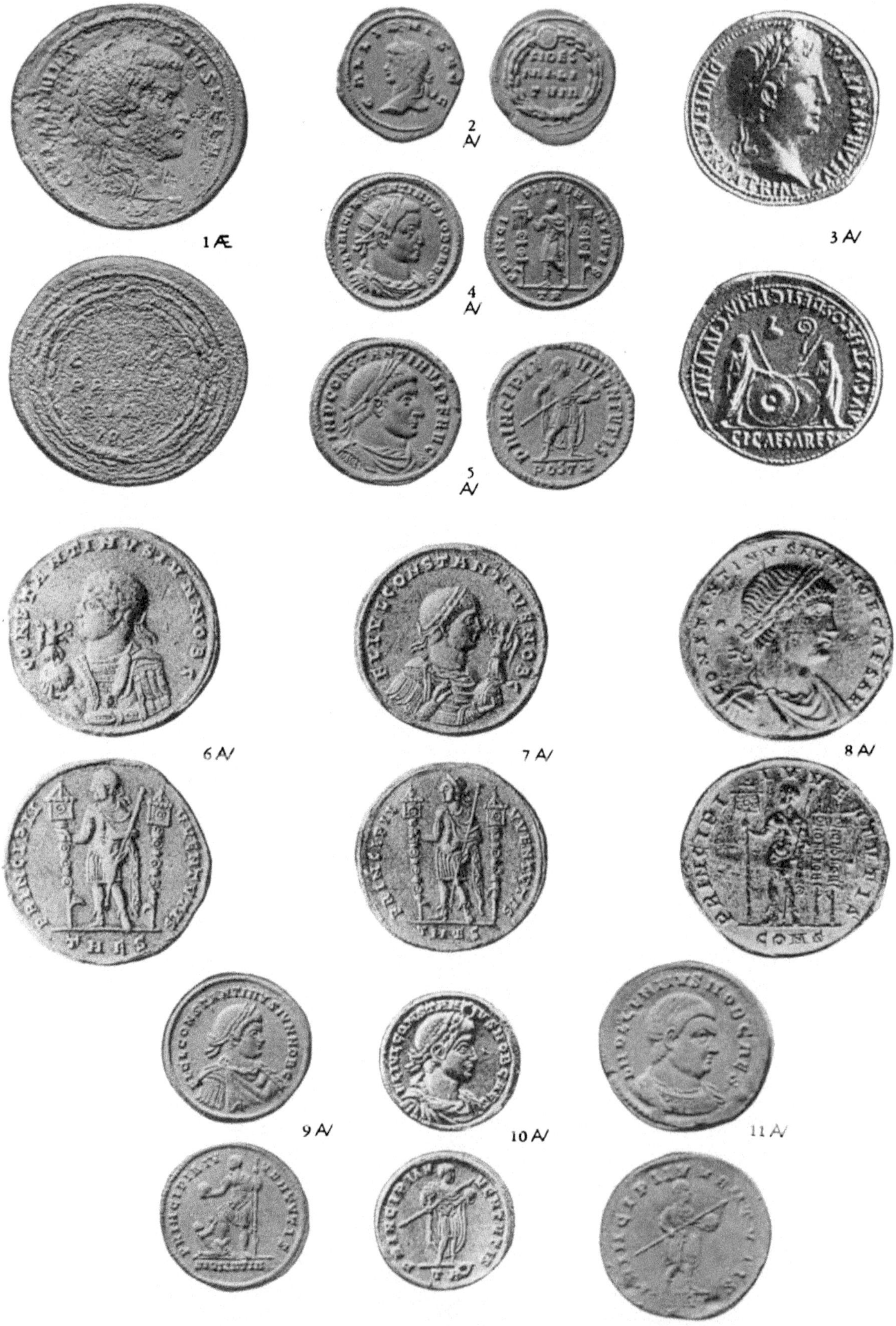

1 Æ

2 AV

3 AV

4 AV

5 AV

6 AV

7 AV

8 AV

9 AV

10 AV

11 AV

RECIPIENTS

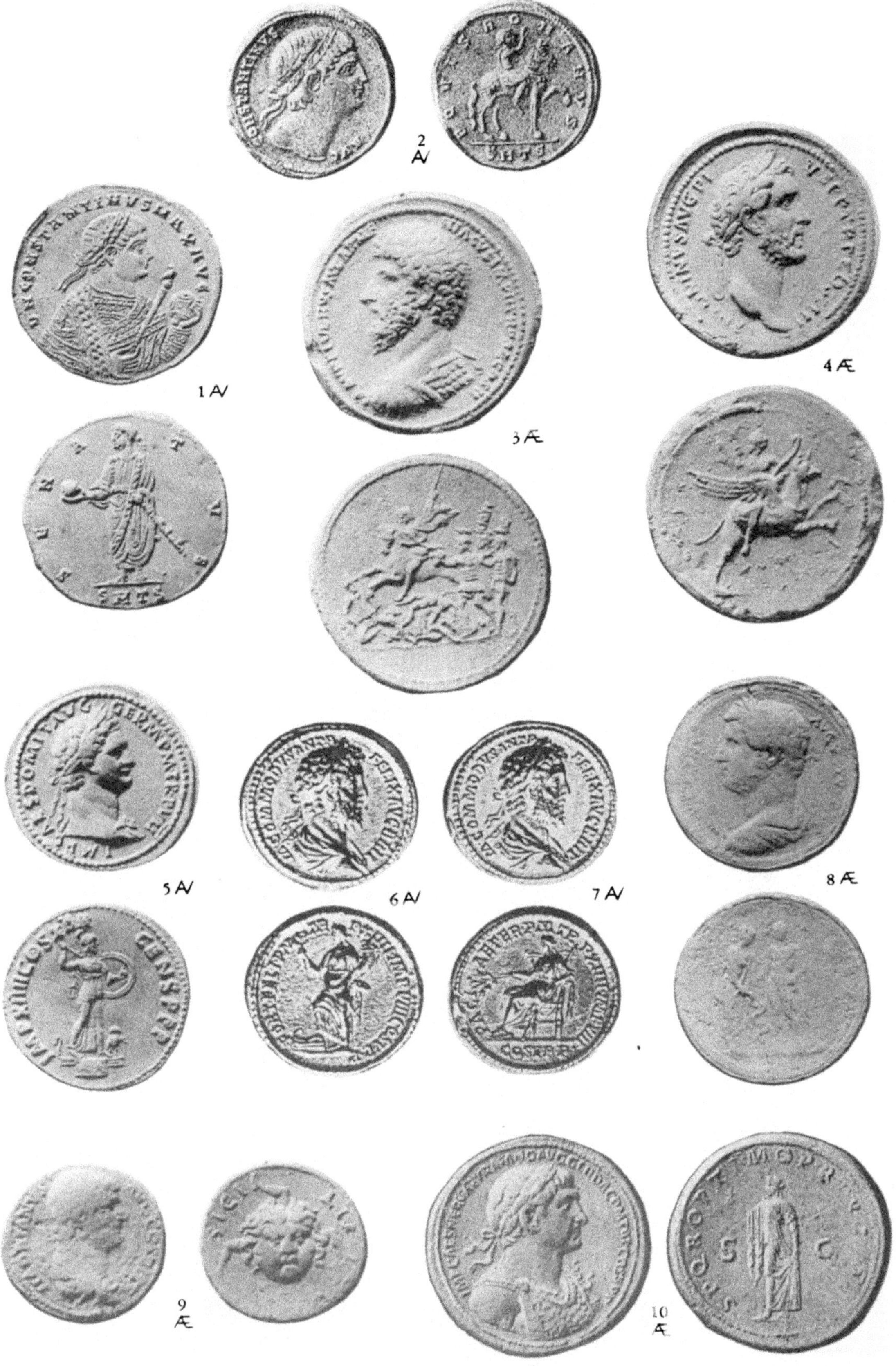

RECIPIENTS

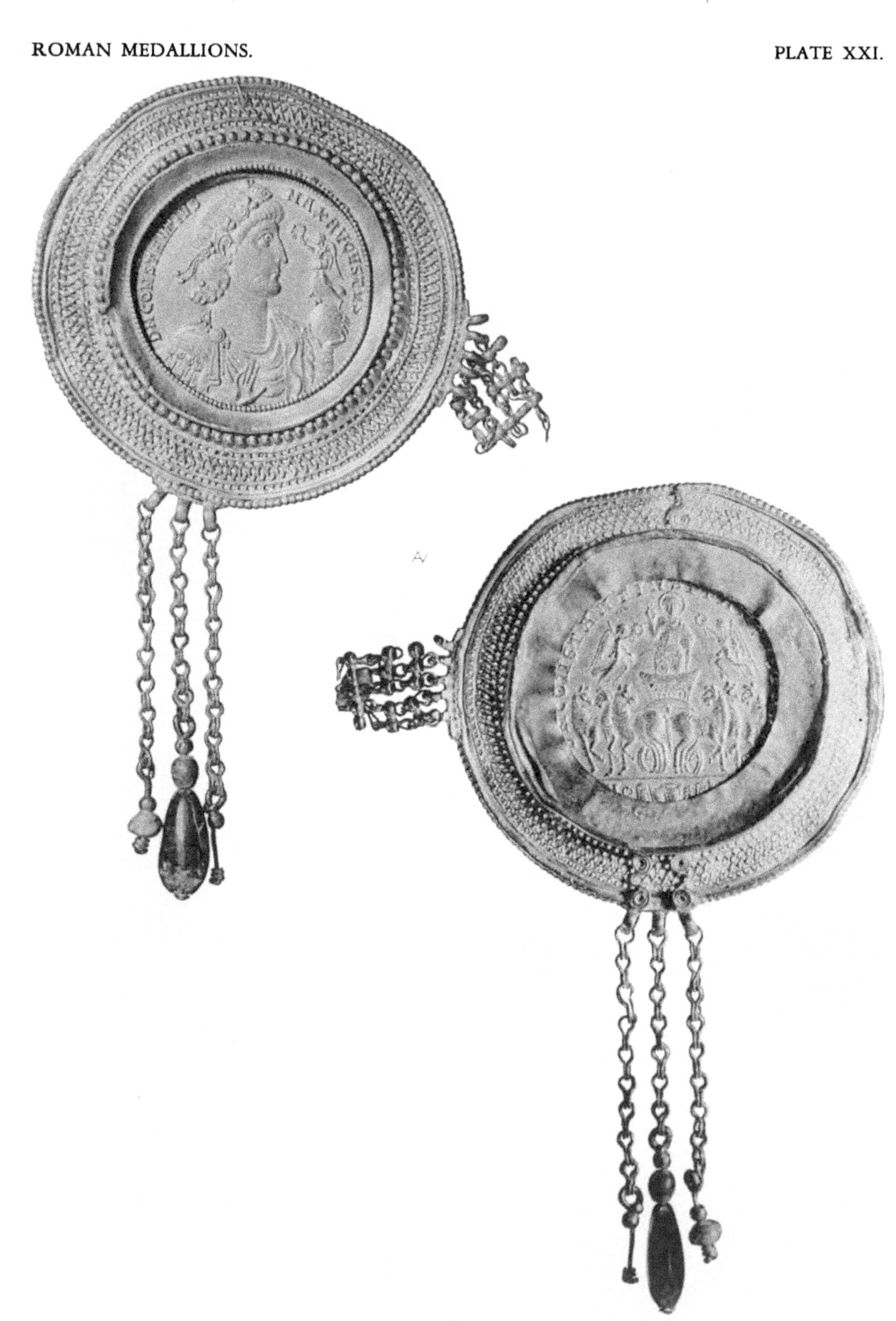

RECIPIENTS.

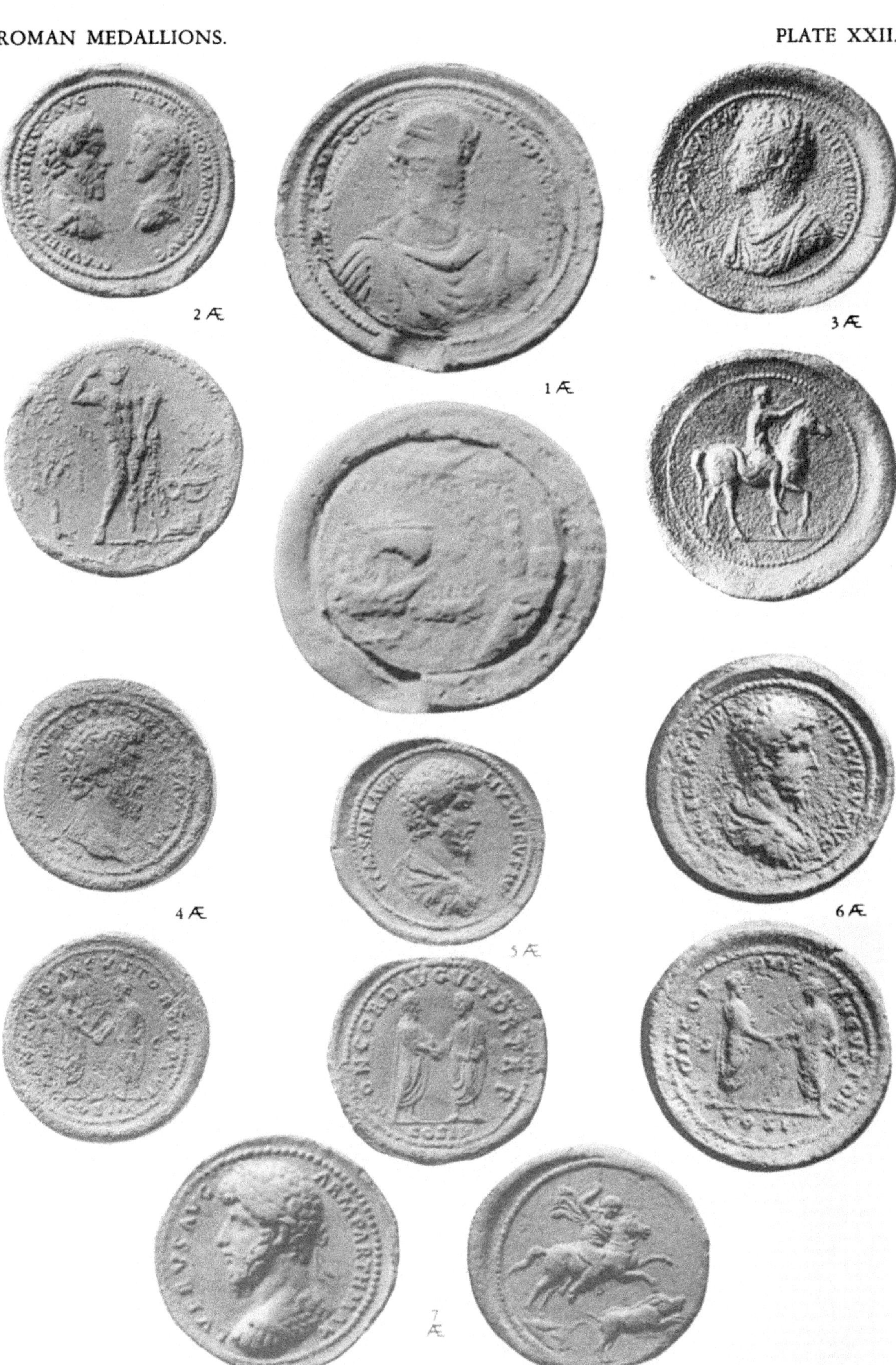

HISTORICAL DEVELOPMENT I: AUGUSTUS—COMMODUS

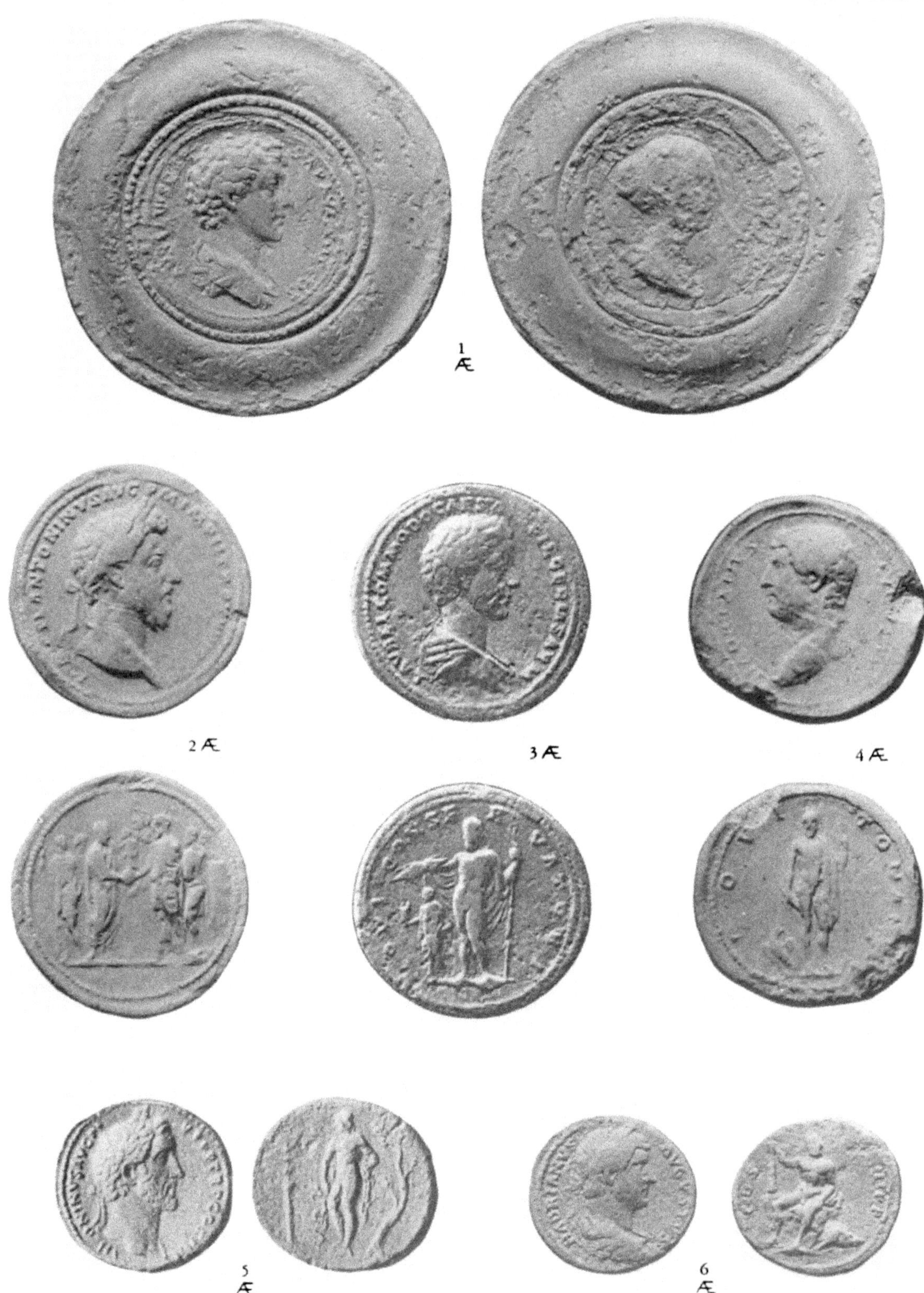

1 Æ

2 Æ

3 Æ

4 Æ

5 Æ

6 Æ

HISTORICAL DEVELOPMENT I: AUGUSTUS—COMMODUS.

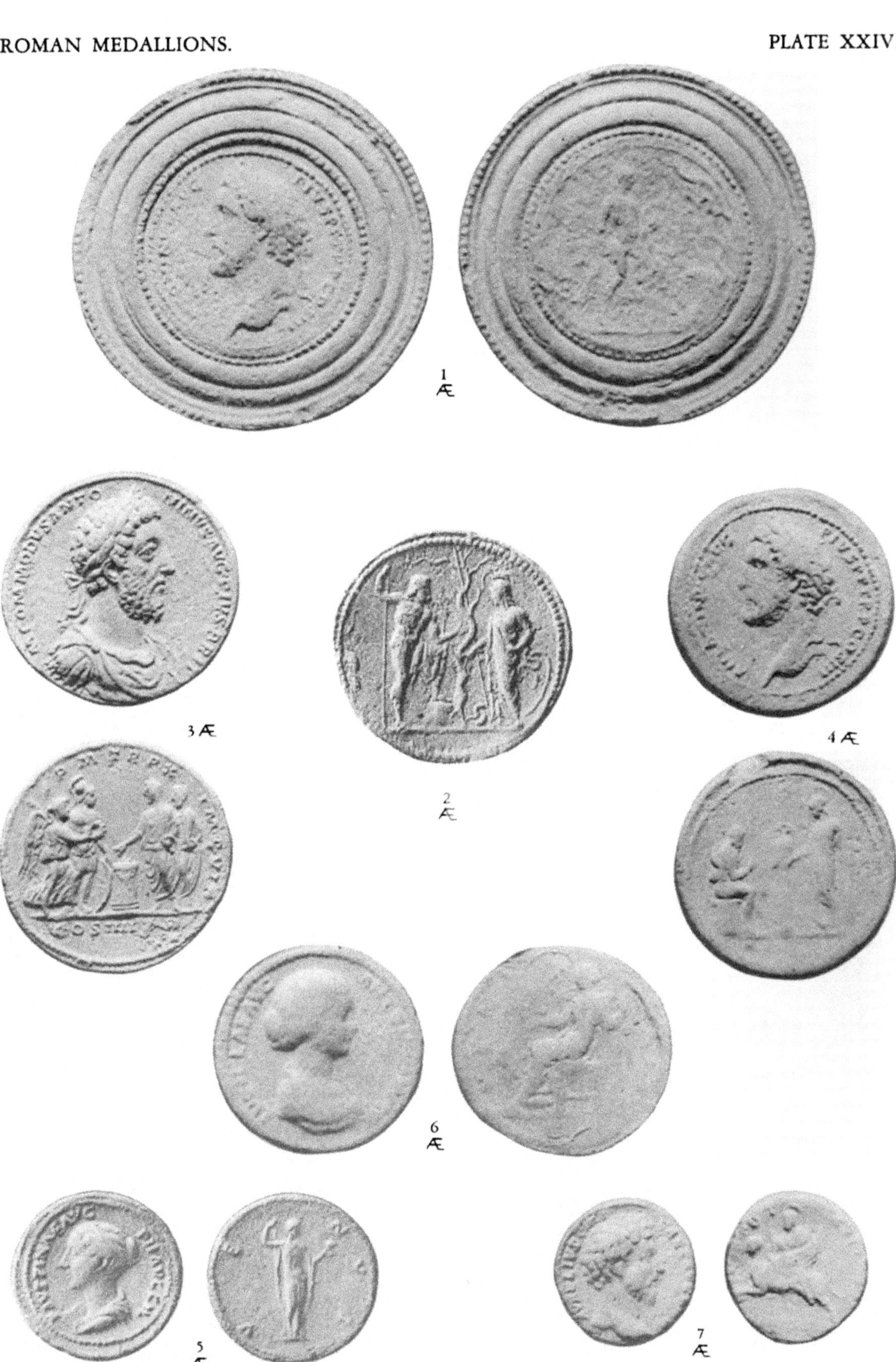

HISTORICAL DEVELOPMENT I: AUGUSTUS—COMMODUS.

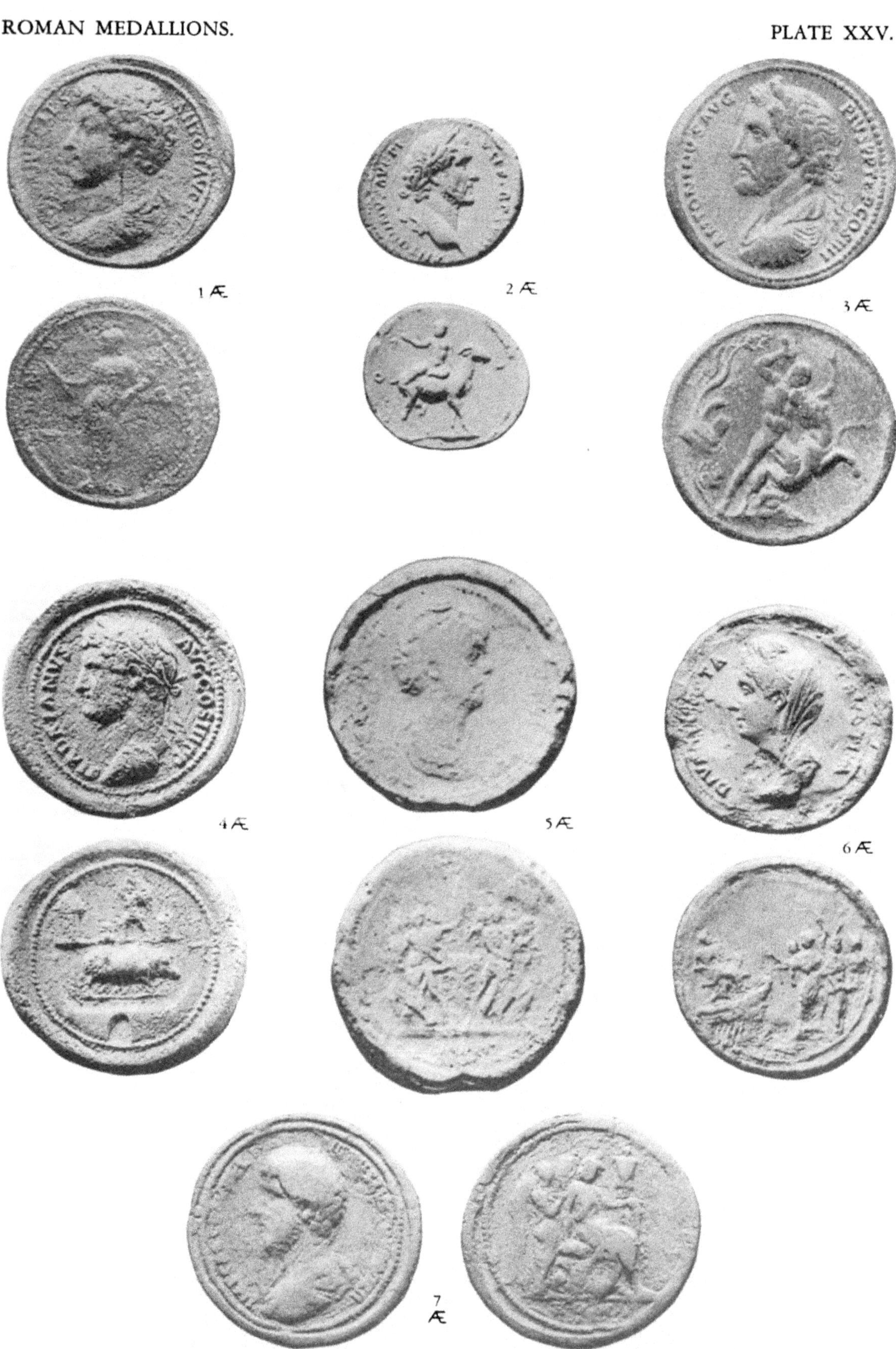
1 Æ 2 Æ 3 Æ 4 Æ 5 Æ 6 Æ 7 Æ

HISTORICAL DEVELOPMENT I: AUGUSTUS—COMMODUS.

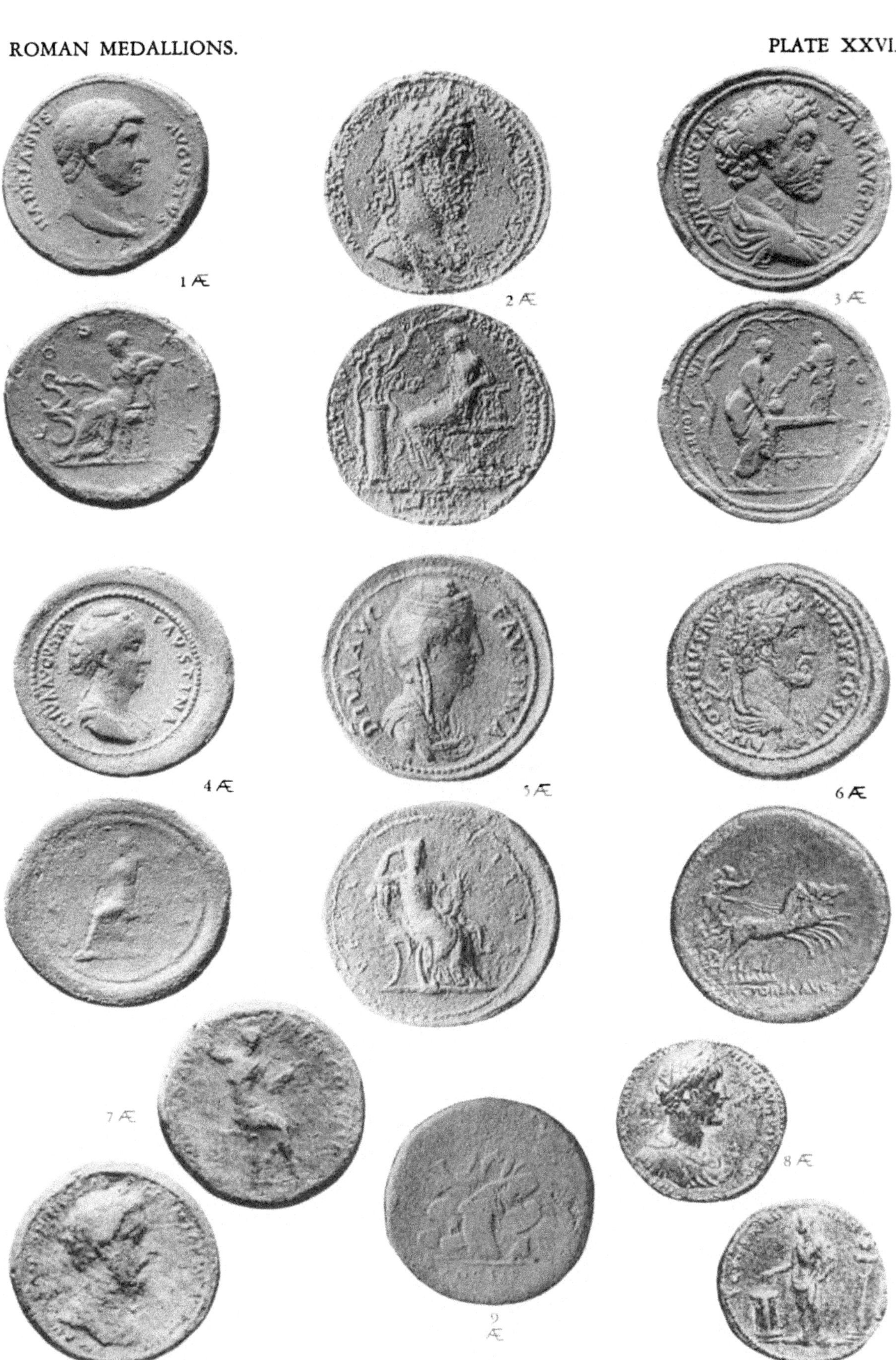

HISTORICAL DEVELOPMENT I. AUGUSTUS–COMMODUS

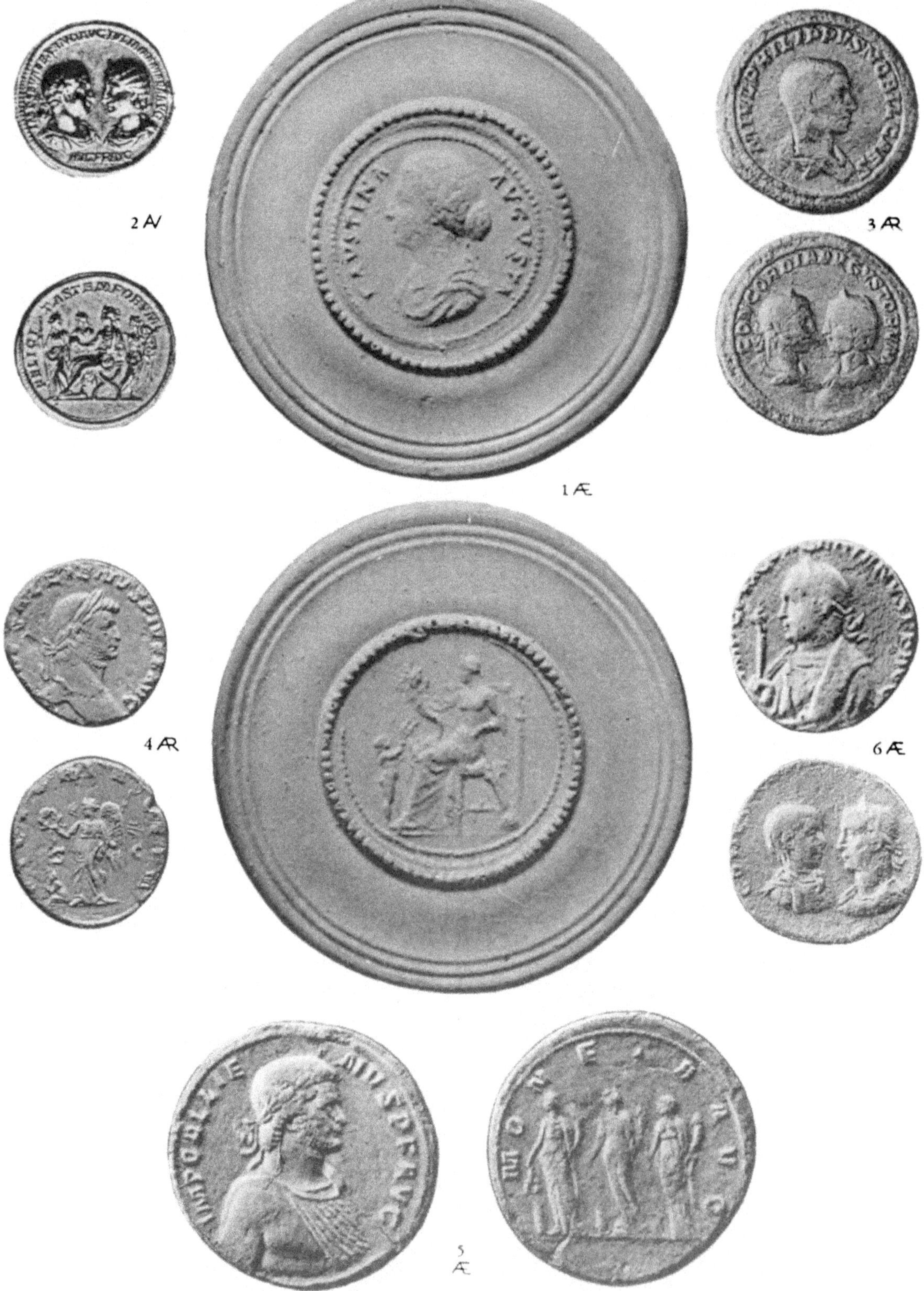

2 AV

3 AR

1 Æ

4 AR

6 Æ

5 Æ

HISTORICAL DEVELOPMENT I: AUGUSTUS—COMMODUS.
II. SEPTIMUS SEVERUS—CARINUS AND NUMERIANUS.

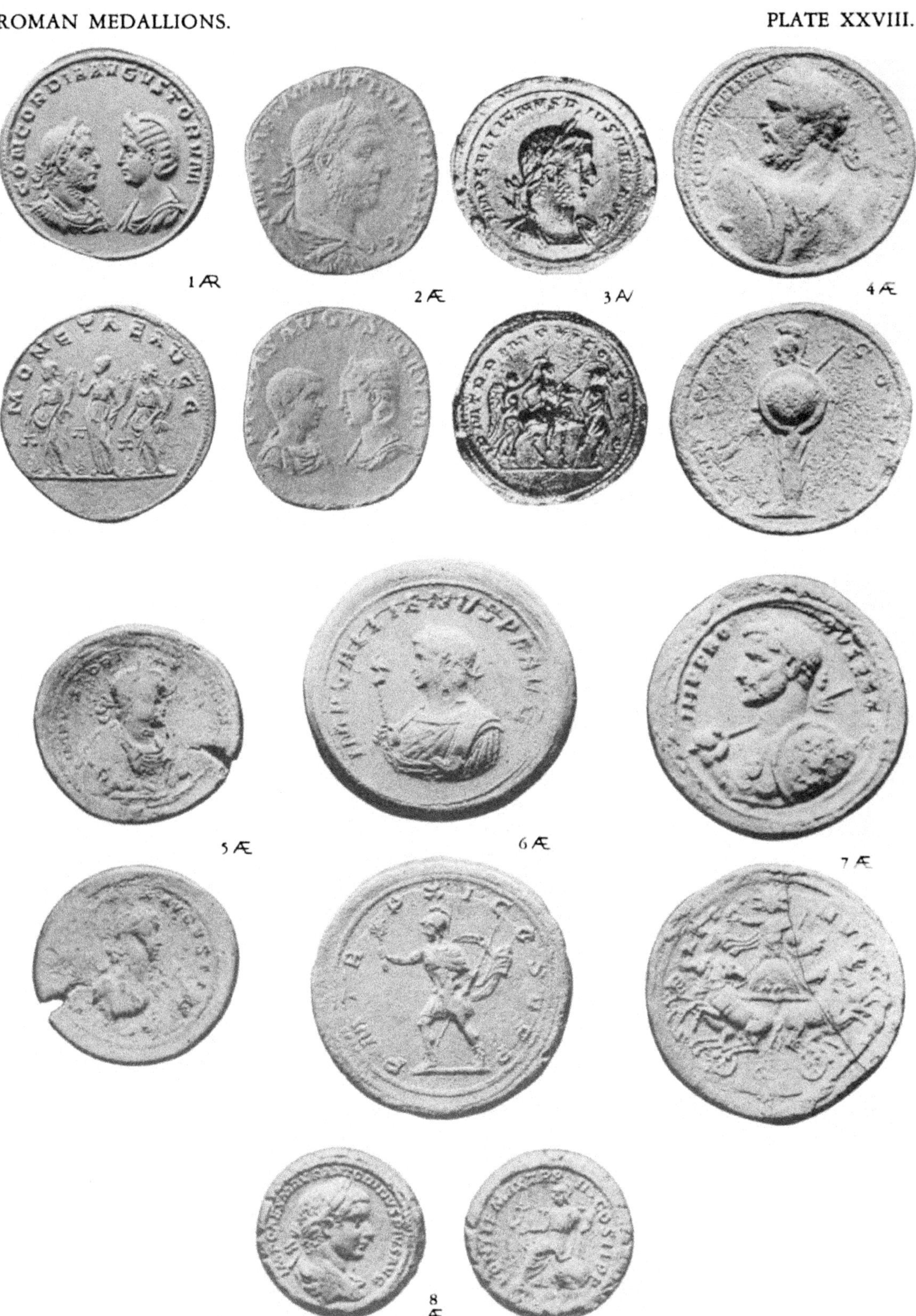

1 AR 2 Æ 3 AV 4 Æ 5 Æ 6 Æ 7 Æ 8 Æ

HISTORICAL DEVELOPMENT II: SEPTIMIUS SEVERUS—CARINUS AND NUMERIANUS.

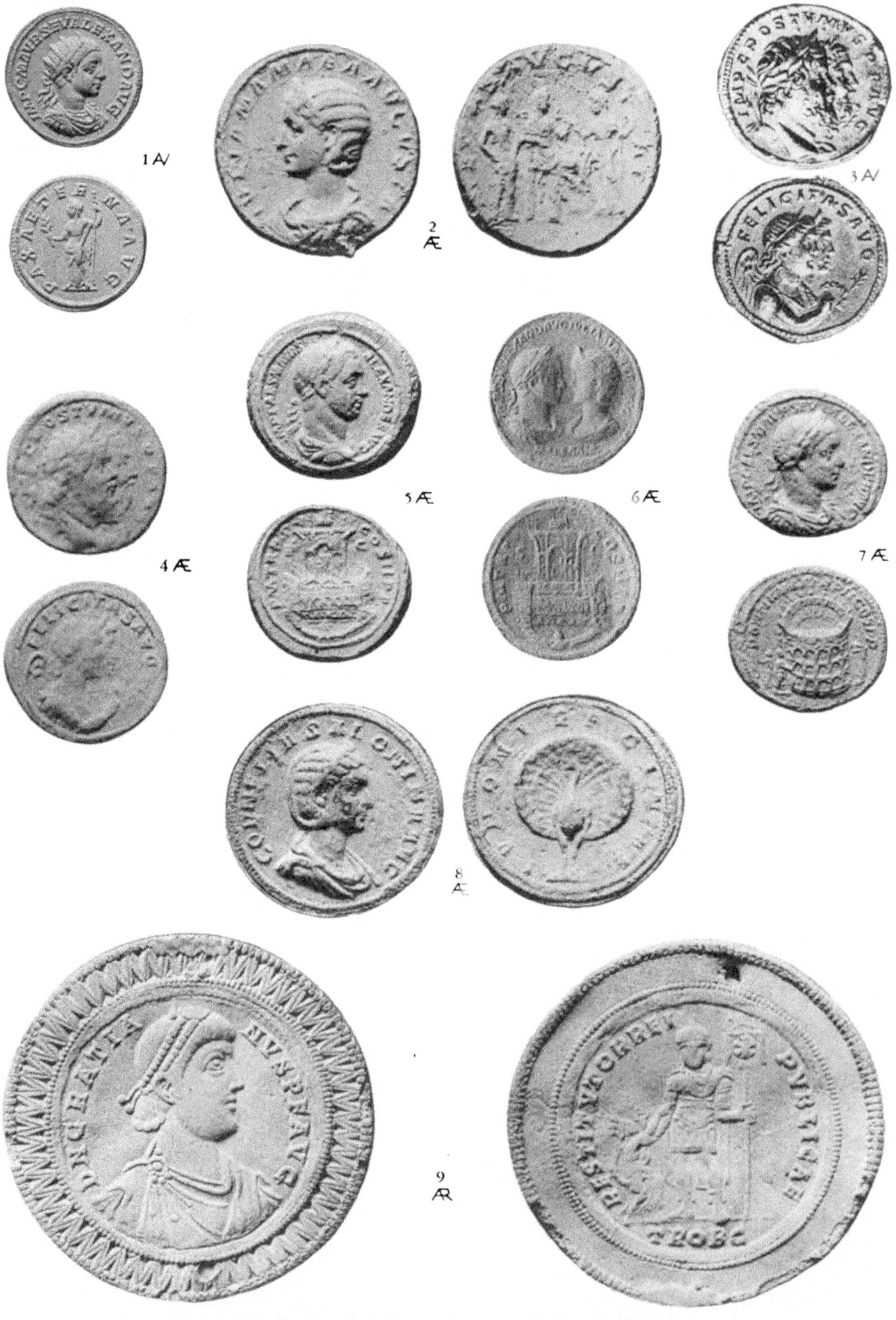

1 AV

2 Æ

3 AV

4 Æ

5 Æ

6 Æ

7 Æ

8 Æ

9 AR

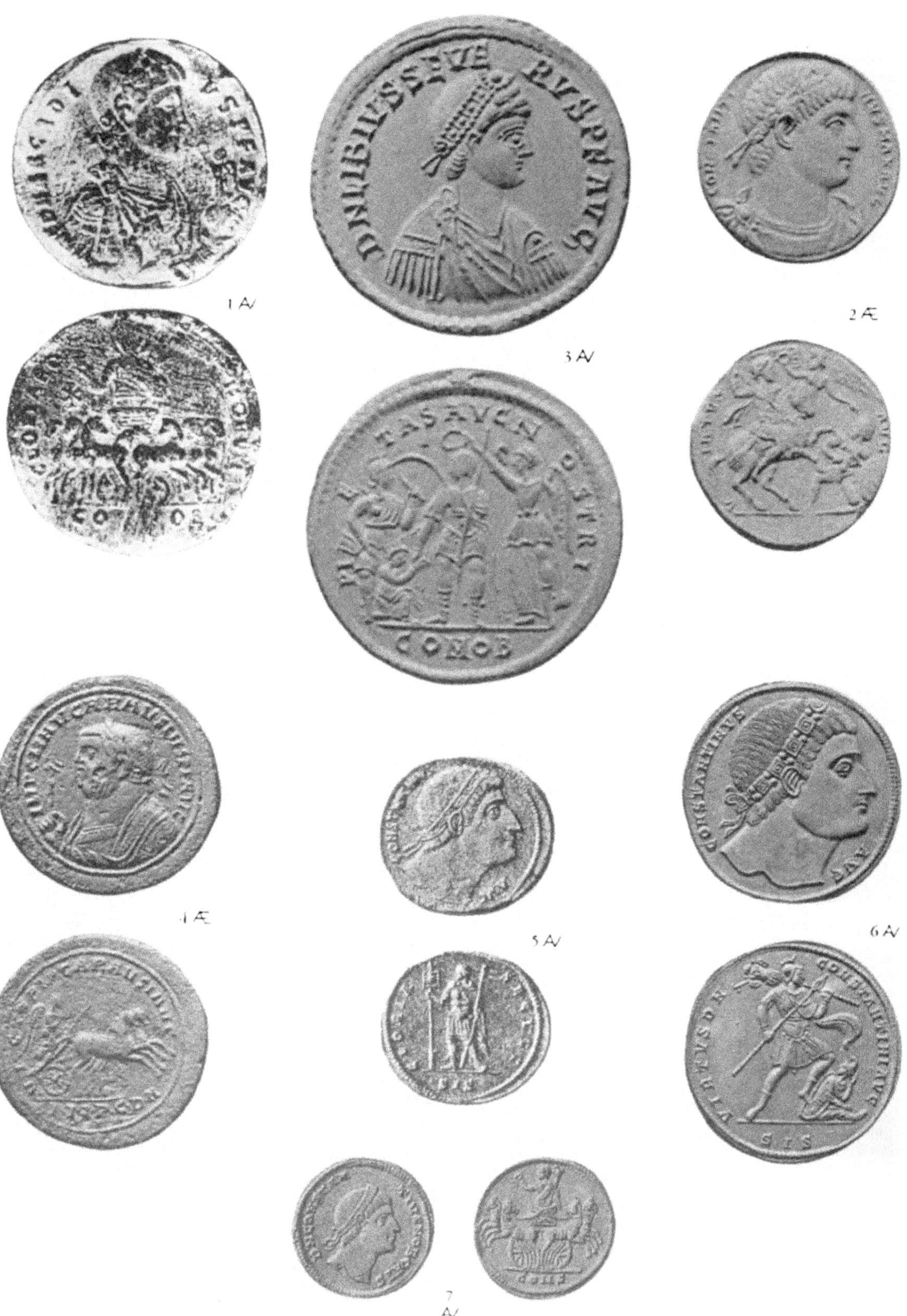

HISTORICAL DEVELOPMENT III: DIOCLETIAN—JUSTINIAN.

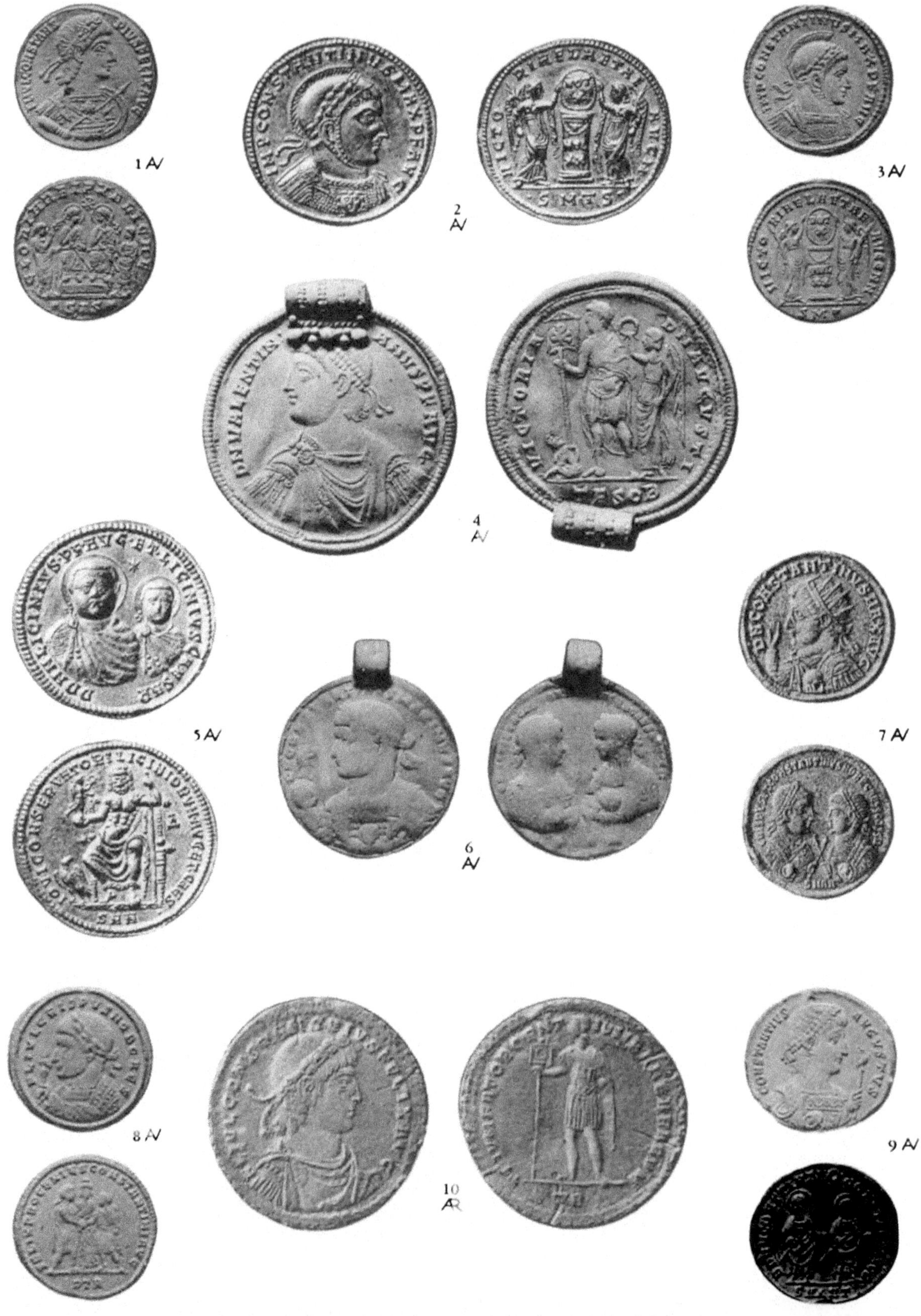

1 AV

2 AV

3 AV

4 AV

5 AV

6 AV

7 AV

8 AV

9 AV

10 AR

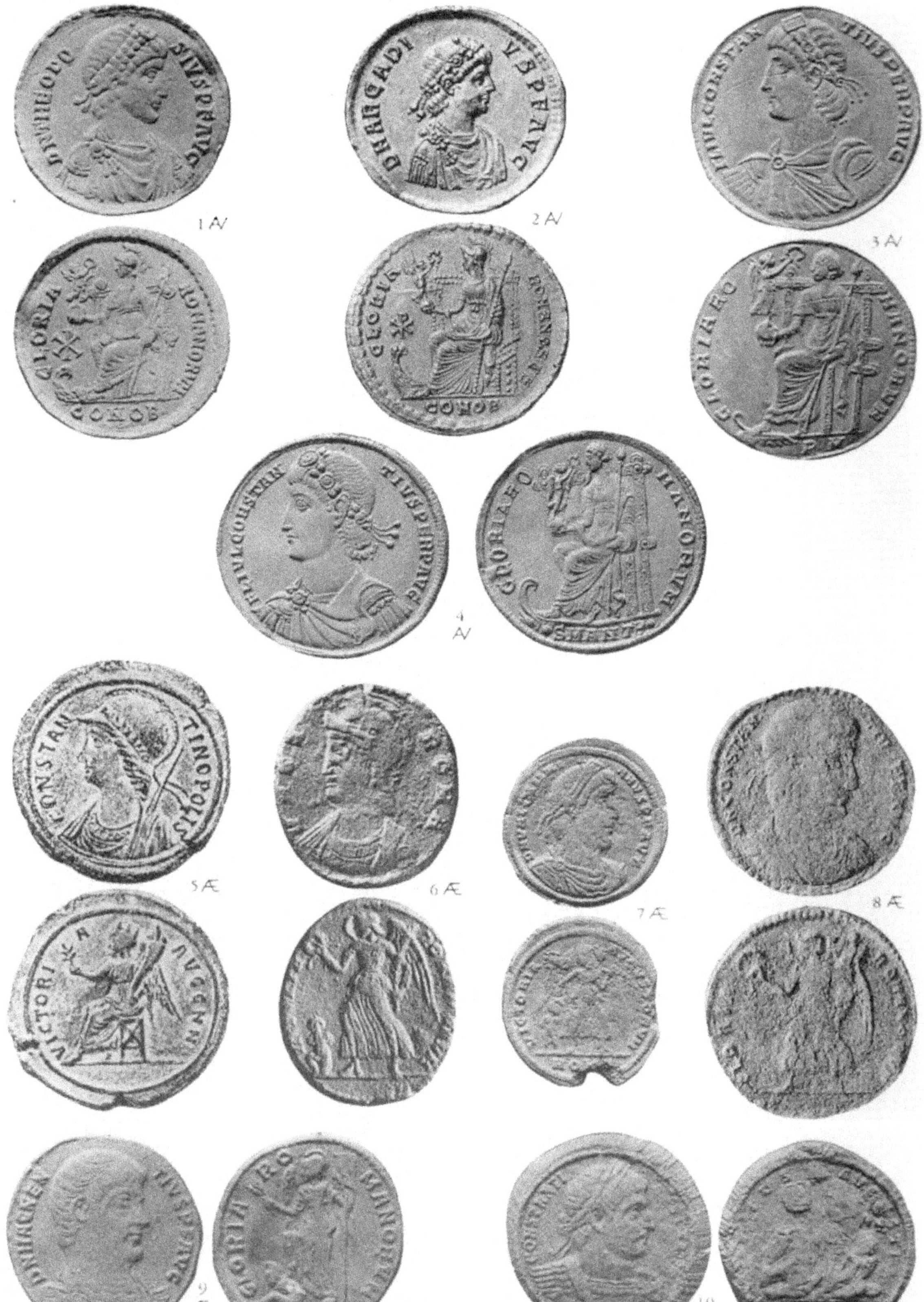

HISTORICAL DEVELOPMENT III: DIOCLETIAN—JUSTINIAN.

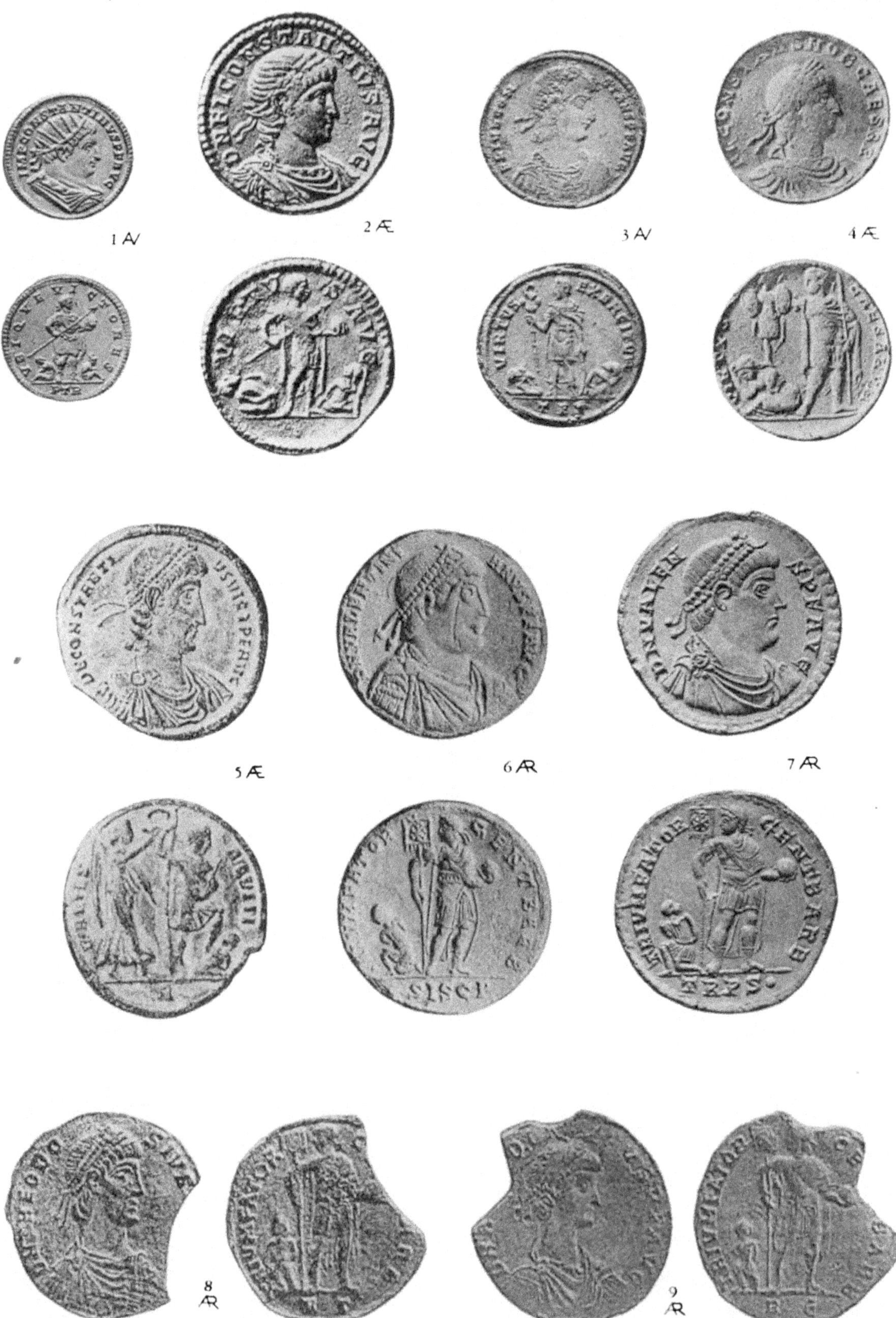

HISTORICAL DEVELOPMENT III: DIOCLETIAN—JUSTINIAN

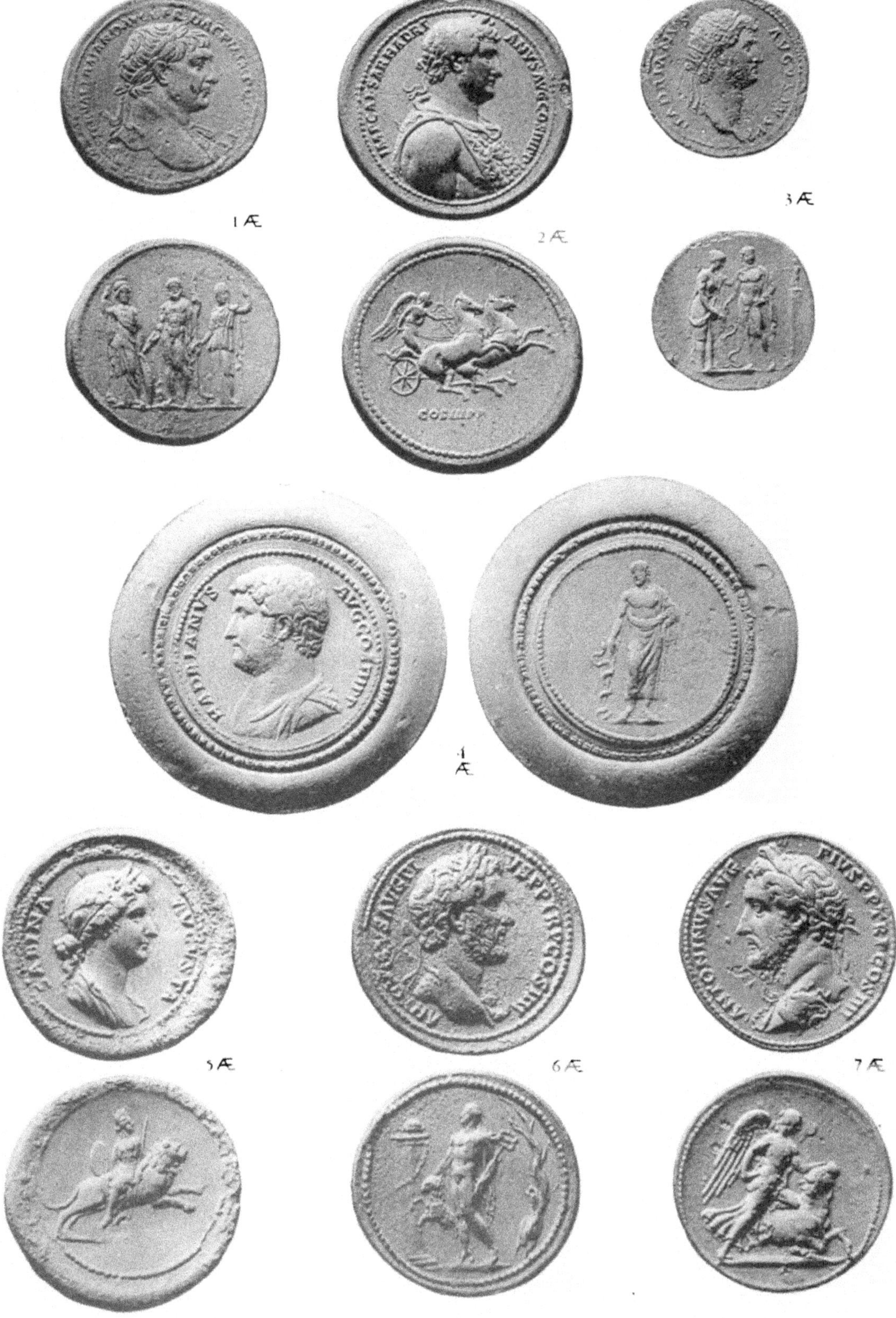

TRAJAN (1), HADRIAN (2-4), SABINA (5), ANTONIUS PIUS (6, 7).

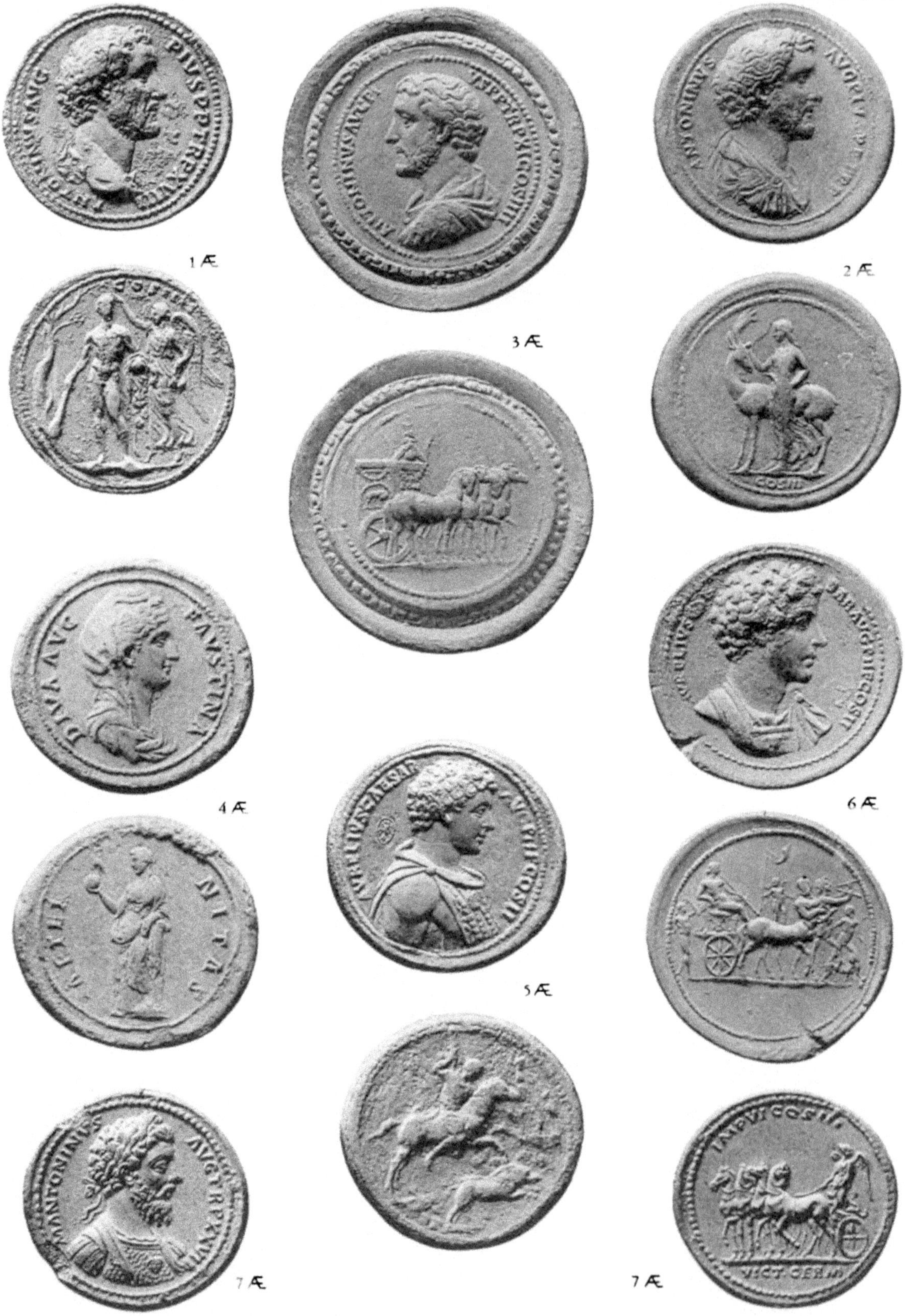

1 Æ

2 Æ

3 Æ

4 Æ

6 Æ

5 Æ

7 Æ

7 Æ

ANTONINUS PIUS (1-3), FAUSTINA I (4), MARCUS AURELIUS (5-7).

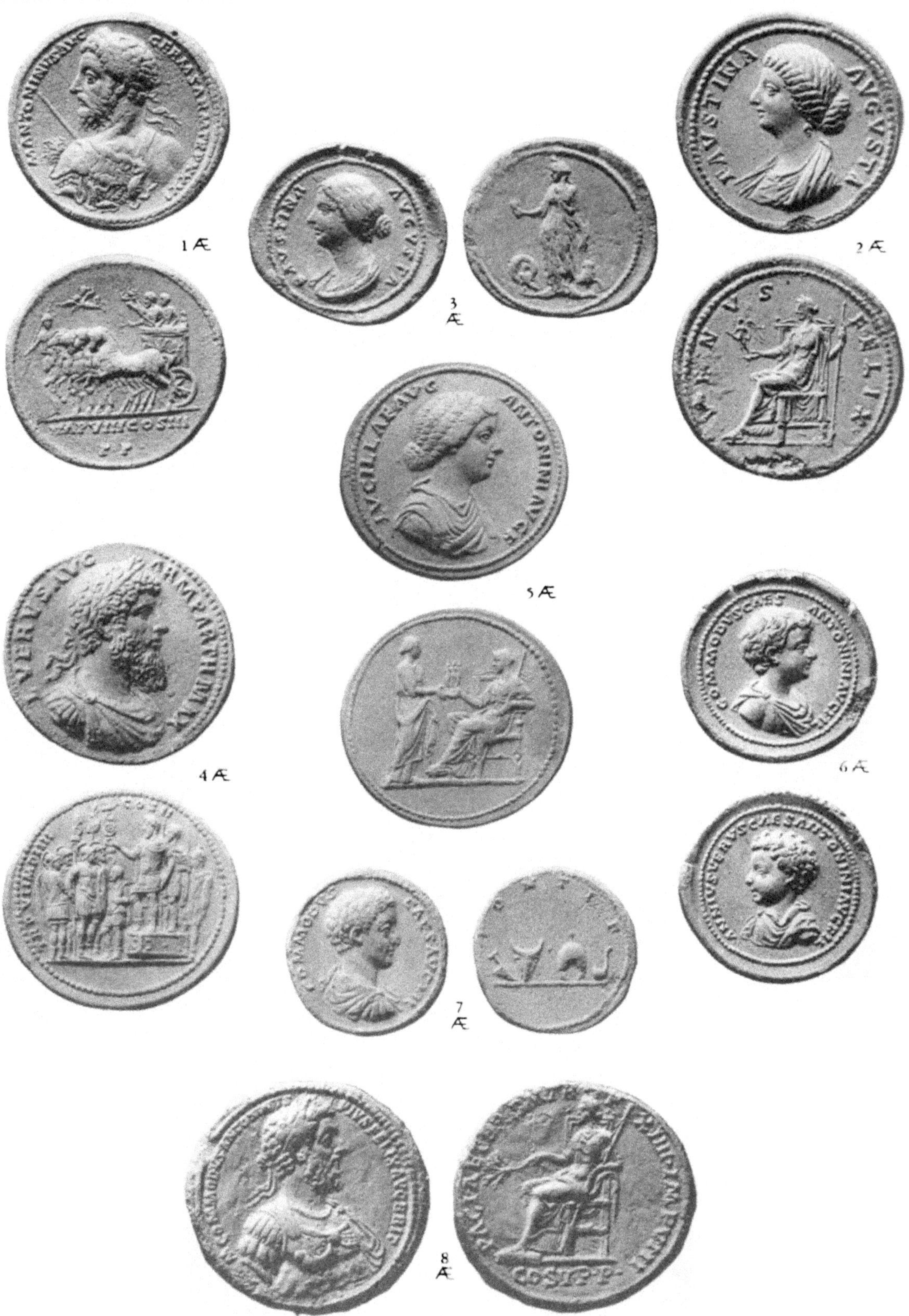

MARCUS AURELIUS (1), FAUSTINA II (2, 3), LUCIUS VERUS (4), LUCILLA (5), COMMODUS (6-8).

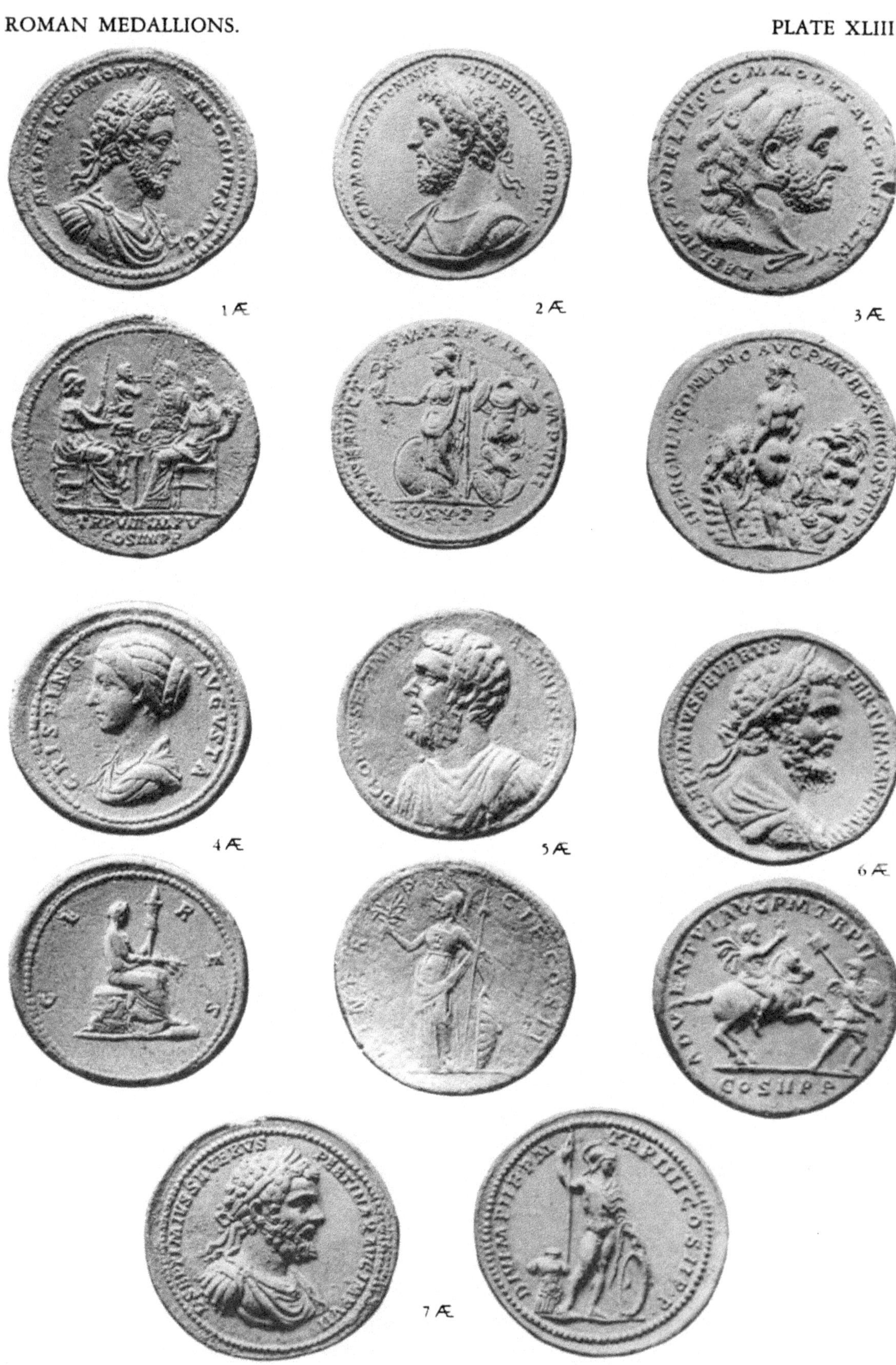

COMMODUS (1-3), CRISPINA (4), ALBINUS (5), SEPTIMIUS SEVERUS (6-7)

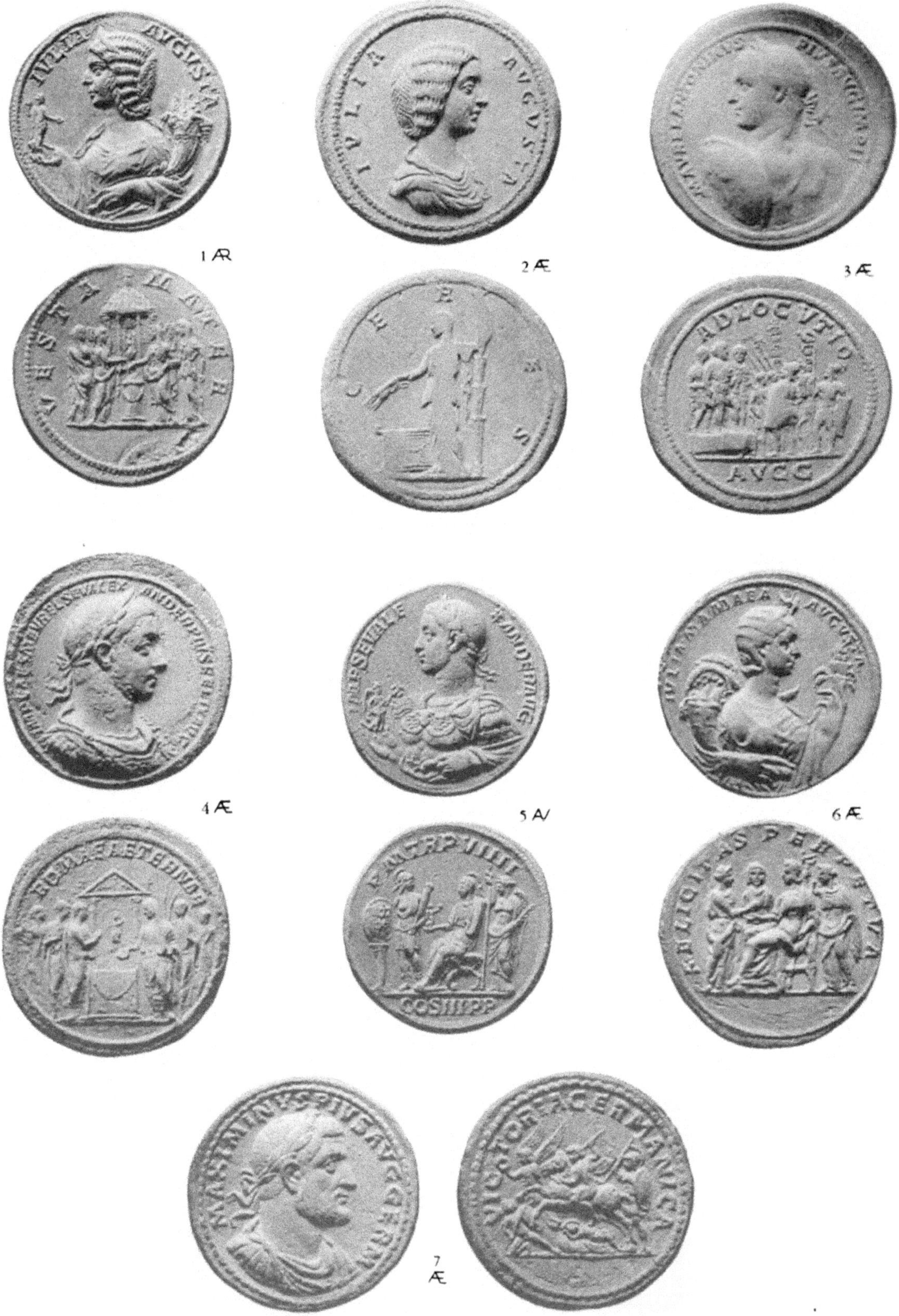

1 AR

2 Æ

3 Æ

4 Æ

5 AV

6 Æ

7 Æ

JULIA DOMNA (1, 2), CARACALLA (3), ALEXANDER SEVERUS (4, 5), JULIA MAMAEA (6), MAXIMINUS (7).

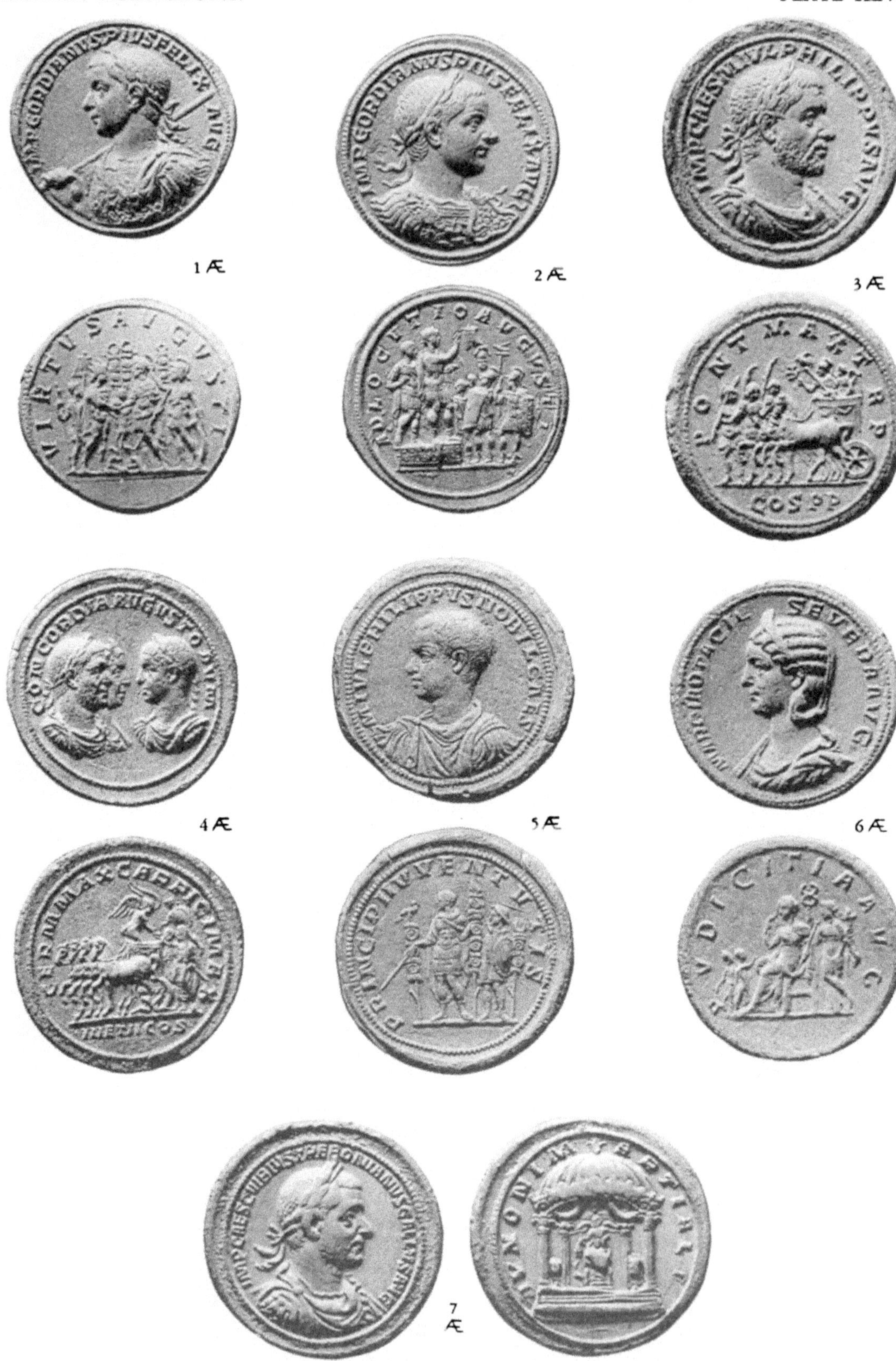

GORDIAN III (1, 2), PHILIP I (3, 4), PHILIP II (5), OTACILIA (6), TREBONIANUS GALLUS (7).

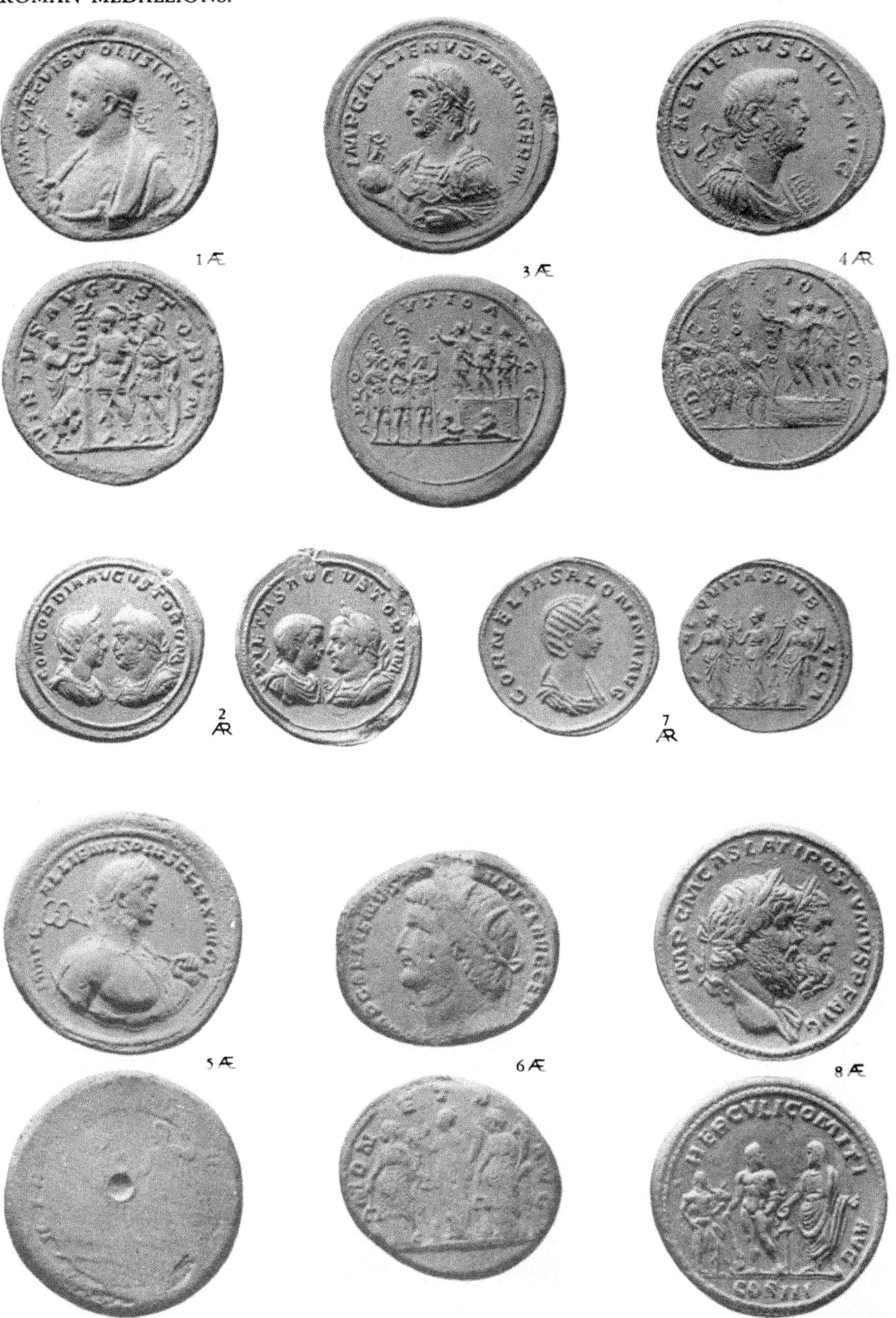

VOLUSIANUS (1), VALERIAN I (2), GALLIENUS (3-6),

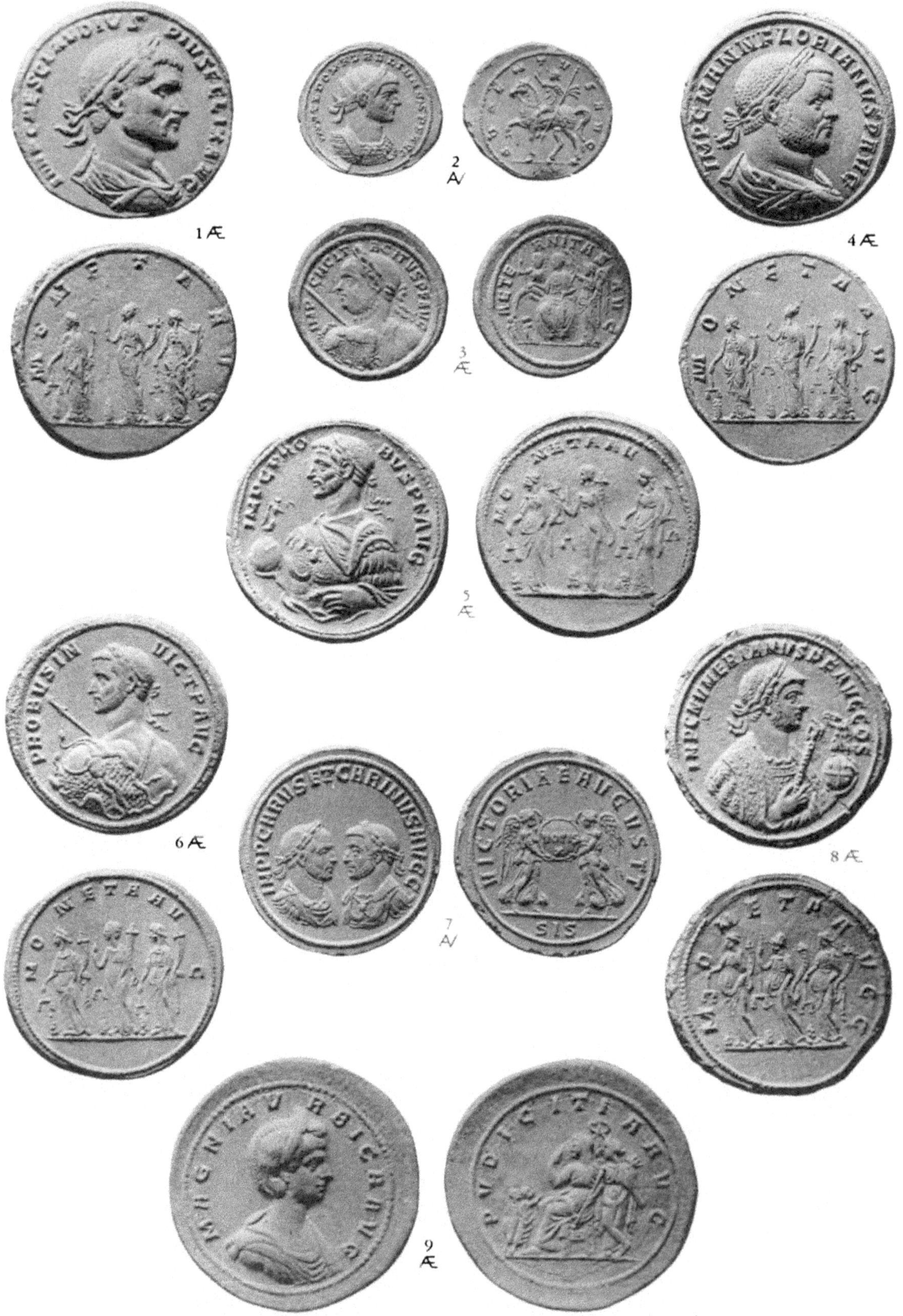

1 Æ

2 AV

4 Æ

3 Æ

5 Æ

6 Æ

8 Æ

7 AV

9 Æ

CLAUDIUS GOTHICUS (1), AURELIAN (2), TACITUS (3), FLORIAN (4)

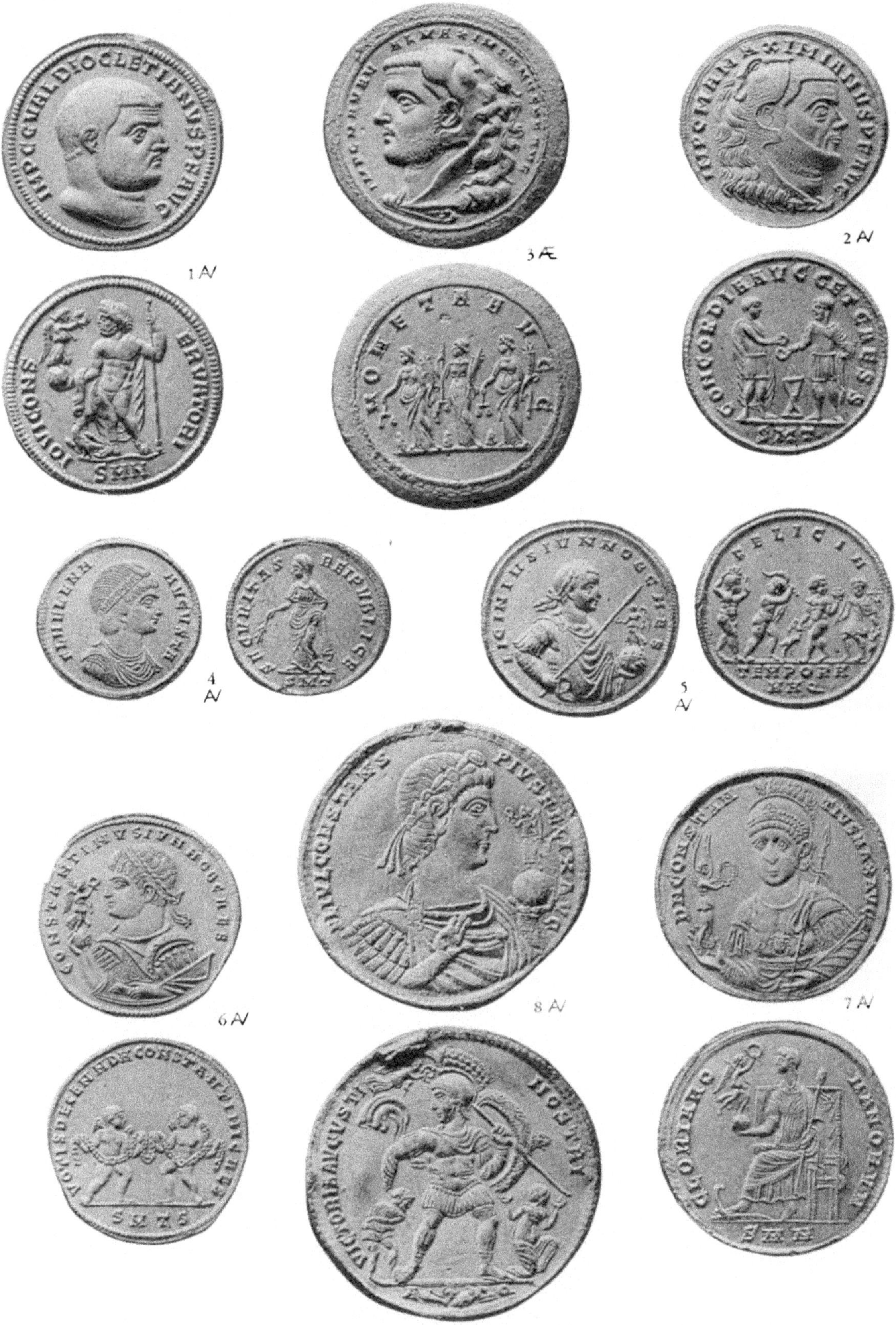

DIOCLETIAN (1), MAXIMIAN (2, 3), HELENA (4), LICINIUS II (5)

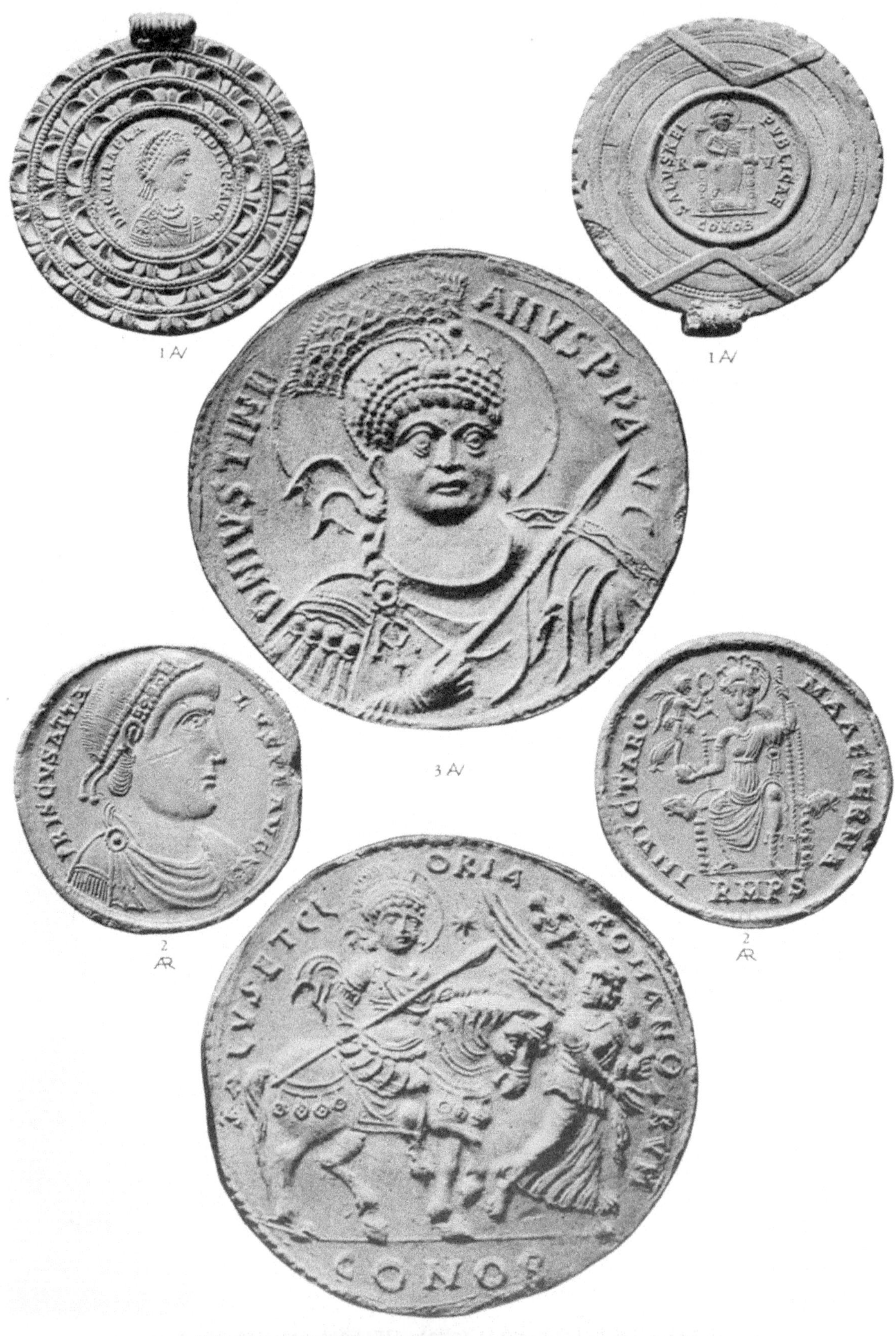

1 AV 1 AV

3 AV

2 AR 2 AR

www.ingramcontent.com/pod-product-compliance
Ingram Content Group UK Ltd.
Pitfield, Milton Keynes, MK11 3LW, UK
UKHW051206260726
13967UKWH00011B/3137